HEALTH CARE ADMINISTRATION

Planning, Implementing, and Managing Organized Delivery Systems

Third Edition

Edited by
Lawrence F. Wolper, MBA
President
L. Wolper, Inc.
Great Neck, New York

AN ASPEN PUBLICATION®
Aspen Publishers, Inc.
Gaithersburg, Maryland
1999

CPT five-digit codes, nomenclature, and other data are © 1997 American Medical Association. All rights reserved. No fee schedules, basic unit, relative values, or related listings are included in CPT. The AMA assumes no liability for the data contained herein.

Camelot quote on dedication page is from *CAMELOT*, by Alan Jay Lerner and Frederick Loewe.
© 1960 (Renewed) Alan Jay Lerner and Frederick Loewe.
Chappell & Co., Inc., Publisher and Owner of allied rights throughout the world.
All rights reserved. Used by permission.
WARNER BROS. PUBLICATIONS U.S., INC., Miami, FL 33014

Library of Congress Cataloging-in-Publication Data

Health care administration: planning, implementing, and managing organized delivery systems/
edited by Lawrence F. Wolper.—3rd ed.
p.   cm.
Includes bibliographical references and index.
ISBN 0-8342-1066-5
1. Hospitals—Administration. 2. Health services administration. I. Wolper, Lawrence F.
RA971.H384   1999
362.1′068—dc21
98-45196
CIP

Copyright © 1999 by Aspen Publishers, Inc.
All rights reserved.

Aspen Publishers, Inc., grants permission for photocopying for limited personal or internal use. This consent does not extend to other kinds of copying, such as copying for general distribution, for advertising or promotional purposes, for creating new collective works, or for resale. For information, address Aspen Publishers, Inc., Permissions Department, 200 Orchard Ridge Drive, Suite 200, Gaithersburg, Maryland 20878

Orders: (800) 638-8437
Customer Service: (800) 234-1660

Editorial Services: Jane Colilla
Library of Congress Catalog Card Number: 98-45196
ISBN: 0-8342-1066-5

Printed in the United States of America

2   3   4   5

The rain may never fall till after sundown.
By eight the morning fog must disappear.
In short, there's simply not
A more congenial spot
For happ'ly-ever-aftering than here
In Camelot.

Table of Contents

About the Author/Editor

Lawrence F. Wolper, MBA, is President of L. Wolper, Inc., in Great Neck, New York. The firm is a full-service consulting organization specializing in strategic planning and marketing, managed care, the implementation of provider and integrated networks, and all aspects of physician group practice management. The firm has implemented multi-county provider networks and physician organizations. In addition, L. Wolper, Inc., has extensive experience in contract-managing large physician group practices and ambulatory surgery centers, as well as practice turnarounds.

Mr. Wolper has over 20 years of consulting experience and represents major group practices, individual practice associations, management services organizations, integrated networks, national health care companies, and hospitals. Prior to founding his firm in 1987, he was a partner in KPMG Peat Marwick, with New York area and national responsibility for physician practice matters and ambulatory care. At that time, he was involved in the development of large group practices and provider networks. Before his partnership in Peat Marwick, he was a consulting partner with Ingram, Weitzman, Mertens & Co., a large regional health care accounting and consulting firm.

Mr. Wolper is one of a number of consultants and health care attorneys to be accepted into the American Medical Association's Consultant's Link™, a consortium of professionals with demonstrated expertise in practice management and managed care. He has published texts and articles frequently. His book *Health Care Administration: Principles, Practices, Structure, and Delivery*, 2nd Edition, won a prestigious national award as one of the top 250 texts in the health sciences industry. He has published articles on a variety of topics, including managed care, operational auditing, planning, cost containment, and practice management, in journals such as *Administrative Ophthalmology*, the *Journal of the Medical Group Management Association*, the *Journal of the Hospital Financial Management Association*, *Hospital Progress*, *Hospitals* (the journal of the American Hospital Association), and *Topics in Health Care Financing*.

Mr. Wolper received an MBA in Health Care Administration from Bernard Baruch College–Mount Sinai School of Medicine and a BA in Advertising/Marketing from Hofstra University. He was a Robert Wood Johnson Foundation Fellow in HMO Management at the Wharton School, University of Pennsylvania and an Association of University Programs in Hospital Administration Fellow studying the British national health system at the Kings Fund College of Hospital Management in London, England. He is an adjunct Associate Professor in the Graduate Program in Public Health at Columbia University, teaching a course on managed care and organized delivery systems.

Contributors

Kevin W. Barr, MBA
Executive Vice President
Bon Secours–Virginia HealthSource, Inc.
Bon Secours Richmond Health System
Richmond, Virginia

Karl Bartscht, MSE, FAAHC
President
Management Consultant Division
Chi Systems, Inc.
Ann Arbor, Michigan

Marjorie Beyers, RN, PhD, FAAN
Executive Director
The American Organization of Nurse Executives
Chicago, Illinois

John D. Blair, PhD
Trinity Company Professor in Management and
　　Health Care Strategy
Coordinator, Area of Management
Director, Center for Health Care Strategy
Texas Tech University
Lubbock, Texas

Greg E. Bloom, CPA, JD
Member, Board of Directors
Garfunkel, Wild & Travis, PC
Great Neck, New York

Charles L. Breindel, PhD
Former Professor
Medical College of Virginia
Virginia Commonwealth University
Richmond, Virginia

Paul J. Brzozowski, MT(ASCP), MPA
Partner
Applied Management Systems, Inc.
Burlington, Massachusetts

Roberta N. Clarke, DBA
Associate Professor
Health Care Management Program
Boston University
Boston, Massachusetts

Mary Reich Cooper, MD, JD
Vice President
Patient Care Evaluation
The New York and Presbyterian Hospital
New York, New York

Michael J. Dalton
Consulting Partner
Health Care and Life Sciences
KPMG Peat Marwick
White Plains, New York

Leslie G. Eldenburg, CPA, PhD
Assistant Professor
Department of Accounting
University of Arizona
Tucson, Arizona

Myron D. Fottler, PhD
Professor and Director
PhD Program in Administration–Health Services
Department of Health Services Administration
University of Alabama at Birmingham
Birmingham, Alabama

Barbara B. Friedman, MA, MPA, FASHMM, CPHM
Director
Material Management
Kingsbrook Jewish Medical Center
Brooklyn, New York

Mark L. Hoelscher, MBA
Doctoral Student
Texas Tech University
Lubbock, Texas

James E. Hosking, MBA, FAAHC
Vice President
TriBrook/AM&G LLC
Westmont, Illinois

Michael J. Kelley, MBA, CMPE
Executive Director
Retina Consultants of Southwest Florida
Fort Myers, Florida

Peter R. Kongstvedt, MD, FACP
Partner
Ernst & Young LLP
Washington, DC

Donna Malvey, PhD
Assistant Professor
Department of Health Policy and Management
University of South Florida
Tampa, Florida

Norman Metzger, MEd
Edmund A. Guggenheim Professor Emeritus
Mount Sinai School of Medicine
New York, New York

Ellen A. Moloney, MT(ASCP), MBA
Director
Laboratory and Imaging Services
Newton-Wellesley Hospital
Newton, Massachusetts

G. Tyge Payne, MBA, RPh
Project Coordinator
Center for Health Care Strategy
Texas Tech University
Lubbock, Texas

Jesus J. Peña, MPA, JD
Former Senior Vice President
Saint Michael's Medical Center
Newark, New Jersey

Loreen A. Peritz, JD
Counsel
The Guardian Life Insurance Company of America
New York, New York

Robert H. Rosenfield, LLB, LLM
Partner
McDermott, Will & Emery
Los Angeles, California

Timothy M. Rotarius, PhD
Assistant Professor
Health Services Administration
University of Central Florida
Orlando, Florida

Grant T. Savage, PhD
Associate Professor
Management and Health Organization Management
Director
MBA and PhD Programs in Health Organization
    Management
Texas Tech University
Lubbock, Texas

Eldon L. Schafer, CPA, PhD
Professor Emeritus
Pacific Lutheran University
Tacoma, Washington
Adjunct Professor
University of Arizona
Tucson, Arizona

William L. Scheyer, CPHM
City Administrator
City of Erlanger
Erlanger, Kentucky

Debra J. Schnebel, MBA, JD
Partner
Gardner, Carton & Douglas
Chicago, Illinois

Geoffrey B. Shields, JD
Partner
Gardner, Carton & Douglas
Chicago, Illinois

I. Donald Snook, Jr., PhD
Senior Lecturer
Penn State Great Valley School of Graduate Professional Studies
Malvern, Pennsylvania

Joseph K. H. Tan, PhD
Associate Professor
Department of Health Care and Epidemiology
Faculty of Medicine
University of British Columbia
Vancouver, British Columbia

Norton L. Travis, JD
Managing Director
Garfunkel, Wild & Travis, PC
Great Neck, New York

Elizabeth W. Walker, RN, MBA
Doctoral Student
Texas Tech University
Lubbock, Texas

Carlton J. Whitehead, MBA, PhD
Professor of Management
Associate Dean
College of Business Administration
Texas Tech University
Lubbock, Texas

E. Gordon Whyte, MHA, PhD
Vice Chairman
Director of Master Programs
Department of Health Systems Management
School of Public Health and Tropical Medicine
Tulane University Medical Center
New Orleans, Louisiana

Andrew L. Wilson, PharmD, FASHP
Associate Professor
Associate Dean for Institutional Program Development
School of Pharmacy
Virginia Commonwealth University
Director of Pharmacy Services
Medical College of Virginia Hospitals
Richmond, Virginia

John Woerly, RRA, MSA, AAM
Director
Patient Registration/Telecommunications
Methodist Medical Center of Illinois
Peoria, Illinois

Lawrence F. Wolper, MBA
President
L. Wolper, Inc.
Great Neck, New York

Hayden S. Wool, JD
Member
Board of Directors
Garfunkel, Wild & Travis, PC
Great Neck, New York

Dwight J. Zulauf, PhD
Professor and Dean Emeritus
School of Business Administration
Pacific Lutheran University
Tacoma, Washington

Preface

The idea for the first edition of this book occurred many years ago when I was completing my master's degree in business and health care administration. I came across a text titled *Hospital Organization and Management* by Dr. Malcolm Thomas MacEachern. A well-respected text, found on every administrator's bookshelf, it was at that time already out of touch with changes that had occurred in the industry since its first printing in 1935 and the editions that occurred thereafter. At that time I decided that I would like to produce a book that would encompass nearly all the topics relevant to the health care industry.

When the first edition of this book was published, the focus was principally the hospital, and it was organized to include sections on departmental operations, as well as one encompassing the functional/technical areas pertaining to hospitals and the industry in general. It included sections on information systems, management engineering, and marketing, among others.

I was pleased when Aspen Publishers asked if I would be interested in doing a second edition of the text. By that time, as a result of major regulatory, delivery system, and technological changes, a number of chapters required updating. In addition, health care reform necessitated the inclusion of several entirely new chapters on topics such as managed care, ambulatory care, physician practice, and international health care systems. In light of the fact that many graduate programs in health care administration use the book, the revisions in that edition added more technical detail to give the student a complete understanding of information systems, inpatient and outpatient Medicare reimbursement, physician practice, ambulatory care, and other topics. The second edition recognized the emergence of organized delivery systems and the changing role of the hospital. Ambulatory care, increased care in doctors' offices, decreasing hospital reimbursement, managed care and utilization review, and other factors were reducing the long-standing role of the hospital as the major locus of care.

Although the second edition *recognized* the emergence of organized delivery systems, the theme of this third edition *is* the organized delivery system. There no longer are three parts, but two. The first and dominant part of the book, Planning, Implementing, and Managing Organized Delivery Systems, broadly begins with international health care. Other chapters in Part I cover a range of detailed functional, technical, and organizational matters that pertain to organized delivery systems from the system and corporate (i.e., not the hospital) perspective.

Part II of the book, The Hospital in an Organized Delivery System, is devoted to matters that relate to the hospital or functions that occur at the hospital level, particularly those in an organized delivery system.

Since MacEachern's first book, there have been many changes in the financing, delivery, and other aspects of health care, but none that compare to what the industry is, and will be, experiencing in years to come. As stated in the first edition of this text, the success of health care reform in the long term will continue to be a function of expert and creative management. Exemplary of this will be a willingness to abandon old paradigms, a drive to be creative even when some goals do not materialize, and an ability to understand and manage the broader range of stakeholders in an integrating industry. By the mid-1990s, the industry already had experienced failures in some of the first attempts at consolidation, and many major failures continue as we enter the next century.

As noted in Chapter 2 and others, the slow growth and failures of many contemporary organized or organizing systems mirror those of similar attempts in the late 1970s and 1980s. Merely merging, acquiring, or networking provider entities for the sake of scale or dominating a marketplace does not necessarily create economies of scale, meet the needs of the community, or result in financial success or better medical care. These structural, financial, and legal changes frequently do not meld clinical operations, practice and management styles, operations, and the other factors that are necessary to successfully operate an organized delivery system. Identified among the most difficult of these issues are consolidating medical staffs, functional consolidations, and managing multiple and new stakeholders. These appear to be critical factors for success, but they generally have not been effectively carried out by most organizing systems since the 1970s.

Further, other segments in the shifting health care industry such as health maintenance organizations (HMOs), physician hospital organizations (PHOs), and practice management companies also are undergoing significant and perhaps unexpected difficulties. HMOs now are under pressure from consumers and government to conform more to the public's needs for access, privacy of medical data, and high quality. They also are becoming less immune to certain lawsuits, and increasingly have to contend with regulations with which indemnity insurers have had to deal for decades. As their subscriber populations have become more heterogeneous, many have not realized the cost-reducing experience and premium stability that they enjoyed in the 1970s and 1980s when large numbers of their subscribers were young individuals with low medical risk profiles. PHOs generally have not fused hospital and physician interests on an equitable or equal basis, often resulting in quiescent organizations. Wall Street is more wary of physician practice management companies, because many are having financial difficulty or have gone bankrupt and have not delivered economies of scale, centralized information systems, and managed care contracts to their providers. Lastly, we also are reminded of a large for-profit hospital chain or two that have been, or are in the process of, divesting as a result of allegations of fraudulent accounting and reporting, as well as of poor operating results. All of these factors contribute to the changing terrain within which the emerging organized delivery system must evolve.

New models are beginning to emerge, many of which are discussed in this third edition (e.g., Chapter 3). The goals of an organizing system may not be achievable in the next few years and may require a decade or more to realize benefits fully. Perhaps the consolidations and creation of new organizations in the late 1990s occurred for some of the wrong reasons. In the future, greater numbers of planners and managers will manage stakeholders and the marketplace more effectively.

In spite of the failures, there have been many successes. It is hoped that in our drive to reduce health care expenditures and restructure a vibrant industry, we do not move so far and fast that the high quality of care always associated with our system will be subordinated to rationing and an overzealous pursuit of the largest market share and the lowest cost. As many of the chapters in this book discuss, this does not always result in profit or success. I speculate that the continued rise of consumer activism and the emergence of large physician organizations will balance these corporate interests more than ever before.

—Lawrence F. Wolper, MBA

Acknowledgments

There are 26 chapters in the third edition of this book, all written by authors with outstanding reputations in each of their respective topical areas. I thank each of the authors who have published in previous editions of this book for their unhesitating willingness to, once again, go through this process. Among these authors, all of whom are more busy than usual as a result of rapid changes in the industry, are: Kevin W. Barr, Karl Bartscht, John D. Blair, Paul J. Brzozowski, Roberta N. Clarke, Michael J. Dalton, Myron D. Fottler, James E. Hosking, Michael J. Kelley, Peter R. Kongstvedt, Grant T. Savage, Geoffrey B. Shields, I. Donald Snook, Jr., Norton L. Travis, E. Gordon Whyte, John Woerly, and all of their co-authors. To Professor Norman Metzger, my long-time mentor and friend, you did it again! While you were certainly doing me a favor by revising your chapter given your very exhausting schedule, you also did one for the thousands of students and professionals who will benefit because the chapter exemplifies the extraordinary wisdom and knowledge that you have acquired in your many years of contributions to this industry.

This book also contains a number of new authors, all of whom wrote chapters that began as concepts and were wonderfully transformed into excellently written and informative contributions. Among these authors to whom I extend my thanks are: Marjorie Beyers, Mary Reich Cooper, Leslie G. Eldenburg, Barbara B. Friedman, Eldon L. Schafer, Joseph K.H. Tan, Andrew L. Wilson, and Dwight J. Zulauf. I am proud to have had the opportunity to work with each of these committed professionals.

I thank Kalen Conerly, my developmental editor at Aspen Publishers, for her insight into planning the book, coordinating with the authors, and making the vast resources at Aspen available. In addition, Jane Colilla, one of Aspen's finest editors, was invaluable throughout the editing of the book. These individuals and their staffs were critical to the production of this book.

My wife, Maxine, has been supportive of this endeavor from its onset many years ago. She has been insightful in her reviews of, as well as a skilled editor for, many chapters in this book. Her understanding of the industry and her perspective on the manner in which medicine is practiced and health care is administered were invaluable. Most of all, I appreciate her patience through the planning and development process of this book, which always seems to coincide with the most beautiful seasons of the year.

In an era of managed care and concerns about deteriorating medical quality and accessibility, my sincere thanks and love are extended to my father-in-law, Moritz Wilchfort, MD. During his many decades as a general practitioner and among the first Board Certified Family Practitioners, he was the doctors' doctor. He consistently received accolades from his colleagues and from medical associations for his medical acumen, achievements, and devotion to medicine. This continued until he retired at the age of 74. During his decades in medical practice he referred to specialists when it was in the best interests of his patients, without the intrusion of government and insurers. This came naturally to him and many of his colleagues of that generation, as it was just considered good medicine. To this day he remains most remembered by his patients for taking care of their medical needs, caring about the other aspects of their lives, and for his warmth and humor. The type of doctor in the famous Rockwell painting "At the Doctor's Office," he was always there for all his patients, both young and old, and was forever a gentleman. The value that he received was the love of most of his patients and the satisfaction that he practiced medicine at a time in which the patients, their families, and all of their needs came first. By his example, he is a model against which I compare all physicians today, and against which they all should be compared, regardless of the excellent quality of their training, area of specialization, or reputation. For this I thank him.

To the youngest generation among those to whom I express my thanks, I am grateful to my daughters Emily and Lisa because they have provided me with a great deal of the energy and enthusiasm required to conceive of, plan, and produce a comprehensive text. As young adults, they and their generation hopefully will benefit from the industry changes that will occur in the coming years. The opinions about the industry that they offered during the development of the book provided me with a different level of understanding as to where our health care system has done well and when it has performed poorly. That input did affect the content of the book.

It is my hope that in some way this book will have a positive effect on the scope of change in the industry and on the provision of health care services in the future. I suspect that with the magnitude of health care reform that is, and will be, occurring in the coming years, corrections to the system will be necessary. It now appears that a major impetus to these changes will be the strong voice of the consumer. Therefore, the challenge for the future that I make to my daughters and their contemporaries is to be vigilant in scrutinizing all aspects of the health care industry, and life in general, and to be tenacious in seeking change when required.

Part I

Planning, Implementing, and Managing Organized Delivery Systems

This Part begins with a chapter on international health care and continues with detailed chapters that cover a range of functional, technical, and organizational matters that pertain to organized delivery systems from the system and corporate (i.e., not the hospital) perspective.

Chapter 1

International Health Care: A Comparison of the United States, Canada, and Western Europe

Grant T. Savage, Mark L. Hoelscher, and Elizabeth W. Walker

The 1990s have been a turbulent time for health care in the United States. While President Bill Clinton's proposed government reforms of the U.S. health care system were stymied during his first term, market-driven changes transformed the financing and organization of health care. Managed care, with its emphasis on prospective payments, has replaced the fee-for-service system, and the growth of integrated—organized—delivery networks and systems is challenging the market segmentation of physician, hospital, and other health care services.[1-4]

These market reforms address concerns about the high portion of the U.S. gross domestic product (GDP)—13.6 percent—devoted to health care[5,6] and the dissatisfaction of the public,[7] small businesses,[8] and legislatures[9] with health care costs and perceived benefits. These reforms have not dealt with a continuing concern about the increasing number—estimated at 35 to 60 million—of uninsured Americans, however.[10,11] The concerns about both cost and financial access reflect well established trends that U.S. and international researchers and policy analysts have tracked during the past 20 years.[12]

Market-driven reforms in the United States clearly contained the growth in the costs of health care from 1993 to 1996.[13] This cost containment has come, in part, because of the relatively rapid adoption of managed care by employers, especially small employers, between 1988 and 1996. By 1996 in the United States, 71 percent of small firms and 75 percent of large firms offered some form of managed care plan.[14] Two clear downsides of this trend for employees have been both a decrease in their choices of health plans and an increase in their share of out-of-pocket expenses for health care.

Less obviously, many employers, especially those that are small firms, as well as larger firms in service-related industries, have been reducing health care benefits to their part-time employees while increasing their reliance on such employees.[15] This trend, along with the adoption of managed care by businesses, marks a change in the way that costs for the uninsured are absorbed. During the 1970s and early 1980s, purchasers of private health care insurance subsidized the indirect and much of the direct costs of the uninsured by paying higher rates than those insured through government programs such as Medicare and Medicaid. In contrast, during the late 1980s and the 1990s, managed care arrangements within the private sector have transformed this cost shifting so that government programs, especially Medicaid, are now covering the costs of the uninsured more fully.

State legislatures throughout the United States have responded to the problems raised by managed care by enacting various forms of so-called anti–managed care legislation.[16,17] They have approved initiatives to curb actual or perceived deficiencies in managed care in three broad areas of concern: (1) access to appropriate care, (2) availability of information, and (3) freedom of choice.[18] This trend toward state government regulation also reflects a shift in the values that are envisioned for a reformed U.S. health care system.[19] Equality of access to, and cost-effective coverage for, health care are perhaps driving most ethical and political arguments for changing the U.S. health care system.

Because of the U.S. system's shortcomings, researchers since the early 1990s have been looking toward the health care systems in Canada[20–23] and in Western Europe[24–27] for new ways to provide health care in hospitals, in outpatient clinics, and in other ambulatory settings. Like the United States, these industrialized countries have been reforming their health care delivery systems. The key issues of access, cost, and quality are driving these reforms. As shown in Table 1–1, these national health care systems can be characterized and evaluated in terms of who may be treated, for how much money, and with what expected outcome.

Every system of health care must deal with the trade-off among these issues. For example, an emphasis on limiting costs influences both patient access and the quality of care. Underlying the trade-offs among these issues are three factors: the organization, financing, and outcomes from the provision of health care.

THE ORGANIZATION AND FINANCING OF HEALTH CARE

National health care systems vary from highly centralized to highly decentralized in their organization and financing of health care (Table 1–2). Canada's public health insurance plan and the United Kingdom's National Health Service (NHS) anchor the centralized end, while the U.S. mixture of fee-for-service care, managed care, Medicare/Medicaid, Veterans Hospital Administration, and charity care anchors the decentralized end. Following Abel-Smith's distinctions, Table 1–2 breaks out two aspects of this continuum, the direct versus indirect provision of health care services by various national governments.[28] Financing of health care services is direct if the main health care insurer or government—whether national, regional, or local—owns health care facilities and employs health care professionals. Financing is indirect if the main insurer or government contracts for the provision of various health care services. Because Medicare/Medicaid is funded by public health insurance in the United States, it is included under the indirect provision of health care services. Many of the health care services provided in the United States are funded via private insurance or direct payments by patients and are not captured in Table 1–2, however.

Significantly, the organization and financing of national health care systems may have a large effect on access, cost, and quality. The decentralized nature of the U.S. system, as well as its mixture of social insurance and voluntary insurance, effectively limits access to preventive and primary forms of health care to anywhere from 35 to 60 million U.S.

Table 1–1 Selected Western European and North American Health Care Systems: Access, Cost, and Quality in 1996

	Access Degree and Form of Coverage	*Cost Percentage of GDP*	*Quality Life Expectancy at Birth*	
			Male	*Female*
Canada	Universal access via a centralized, single-payer system	9.2% .6 Δavg	75.3 years 1.3 Δavg	81.3 years 1.3 Δavg
Denmark	Universal rights via a decentralized, single-payer system	6.4 −2.2 Δavg	72.5 −1.5 Δavg	77.8 −2.2 Δavg
Finland	Universal rights via a decentralized, single-payer system	7.5 −1.1 Δavg	72.8 −1.2 Δavg	80.2 0.2 Δavg
Germany	Universal access within a two-tier system of compulsory insurance (90%) and private insurance	10.5 1.9 Δavg	73.0 −1.0 Δavg	79.5 −0.5 Δavg
Netherlands	Universal access within a two-tier system of compulsory insurance (60%) and private insurance	8.6 0.0 Δavg	74.6 0.6 Δavg	80.4 0.4 Δavg
Norway	Universal rights via a decentralized, single-payer system, with minimal fee-for-service care	7.9 −0.7 Δavg	74.8 −0.8 Δavg	80.8 0.8 Δavg
Sweden	Universal rights via a decentralized, single-payer system, with private insurance permitted	7.2 −1.4 Δavg	76.2 2.2 Δavg	81.5 1.5 Δavg
United Kingdom	Universal rights within a two-tier system of National Health Service and private insurance	6.9 −1.7 Δavg	74.3 −0.3 Δavg	79.7 −0.3 Δavg
United States	Variable access within a multipayer system of private insurance (70%) and Medicare/Medicaid	13.6 5.0 Δavg	72.5 −1.5 Δavg	79.2 −0.8 Δavg
		8.6% Average % of GDP	74.0 Average Life Expectancy	80.0

Source: Data from G.F. Anderson, In Search of Value, *Health Affairs*, Vol. 16, No. 2, pp. 164 and 170, © 1997, Project Hope; and K.R. Levit et al., National Health Spending Trends in 1996, *Health Affairs*, Vol. 17, No. 1, p. 38, © 1998, Project Hope.

Table 1–2 Organization of Selected Western European and North American Health Care Systems, 1991

	Degree of Centralization	Provision of Services		
		Direct	vs.	Indirect
Canada	High	Community services and municipal/county (29%) and provincial (14%) hospitals		All other health services; voluntary (46%) and religious hospitals (11%)
Denmark	Medium-High	Hospitals		GPs, specialists outside hospital, pharmacies, most dentists, and physiothera-pists
Finland	Medium-High	Primary health centers, hospitals, physicians, and nurses		
Germany	Medium-Low	—		All health services
Netherlands	Medium-Low	—		All health services
Norway	Medium-High	Public hospitals, specialists, public health nurses		Private hospitals
Sweden	Medium-High	Public hospitals, health centers, clinics, and nursing homes; physicians and dentists		Private hospitals and some physicians
United Kingdom	High	Hospitals and community services		GPs, pharmacies, most dentists and opticians
United States	Low	Veterans Hospital Adminis-tration and some public health clinics		Medicare/Medicaid accepting hospitals (low-income and elderly patients only)

Source: Reprinted with permission from B. Abel-Smith, Cost Containment and New Priorities in European Community, *Milbank Quarterly*, Vol. 70, No. 3, pp. 393–416, © 1992, Milbank Memorial Fund.

citizens at any given time.[29–31] Moreover, this restricted access raises the cost of health care, because people without health insurance must be very ill before they can obtain treatment and often require more extensive and expensive interventions than would have been necessary had they received preventive or timely primary care. Understandably, with increased morbidity comes the problem of poorer outcomes; hence, the United States fares poorly on several measures of the quality of health care, especially infant mortality.[32]

In contrast, centralized health care systems such as the NHS in the United Kingdom provide preventive and primary health care to every citizen. Nonetheless, this access does not come without rationing and limiting the public's access to secondary and tertiary health care. As noted earlier, the current U.S.

system of health care does provide the underfunded and indigent with access to secondary and tertiary care if they face life-threatening emergencies. Starfield argued that these limitations on access are a function of the way the United States and other nations finance the delivery of health care.[33] Specifically, she argued that financial access, at least to primary care, is the greatest in countries with national health services (e.g., the United Kingdom), is moderately high in countries having compulsory national insurance (e.g., Canada), is moderate in countries with mixtures of compulsory national and private insurance (e.g., Germany), and is low in countries relying primarily on voluntary insurance (e.g., the United States).

OUTCOMES ASSOCIATED WITH VARIOUS HEALTH CARE SYSTEMS

Across the different national health care systems, there is a substantial amount of variance in terms of the outcomes from and the money spent on health care. Figure 1–1 shows both the level of GDP and the per capita amount of money devoted to health

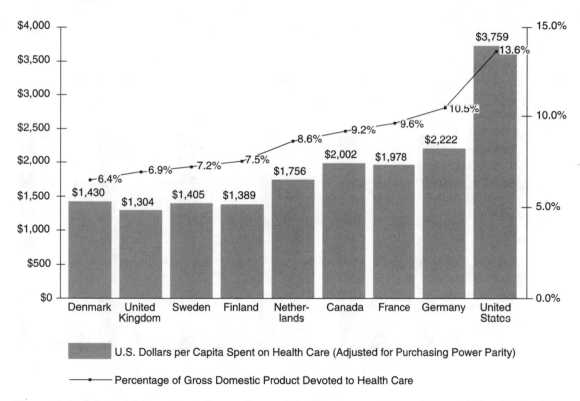

Figure 1–1 Selected International Comparisons of the Percentage of Gross Domestic Product and Per Capita Spending on Health Care in 1996. *Source:* Adapted with permission from G.F. Anderson, In Search of Value, *Health Affairs*, Vol. 16, No. 2, p. 164, Copyright © 1997, The People-to-People Health Foundation, Inc., all rights reserved; and K.R. Levit et al., National Health Spending Trends in 1996, *Health Affairs*, Vol. 17, No. 1, p. 38, Copyright © 1998, The People-to-People Health Foundation, Inc., all rights reserved.

care by the United States, Canada, and seven European countries during 1996. As can be seen, the United States spends much more than any other country on health care. Indeed, Schieber, Poullier, and Greenwald noted that even when taking the influence of per capita GDP on health expenditures (i.e., wealthy nations typically spend more on health than do poor nations), the United States spends far more than other nations of comparable wealth.[34]

Although the total cost of health care in the United States and other industrialized countries is certainly a focus of many reform efforts here and abroad, much of the emphasis in the United States is on obtaining greater value for the money spent. While it would be ideal to compare national health care systems on the basis of clinical outcomes and quality of life, and to use some form of cost–benefit analysis to rank the systems on these outcomes, national data for such comparisons are simply not available. Gross demographic statistics allow some limited inferences about the outcomes from different health care systems, however. Figure 1–2 shows how the United States fares on three well-known health care outcomes—infant mortality, male life expectancy at birth, and female life expectancy at birth—in comparison with five other industrialized countries. The United States has the highest rate of infant mortality per 1,000 births (8.0 versus a low of 4.1 in Sweden), is last for male life expectancy at birth (72.5 years versus a high of 76.2 in Sweden), and ranks last in female life expectancy

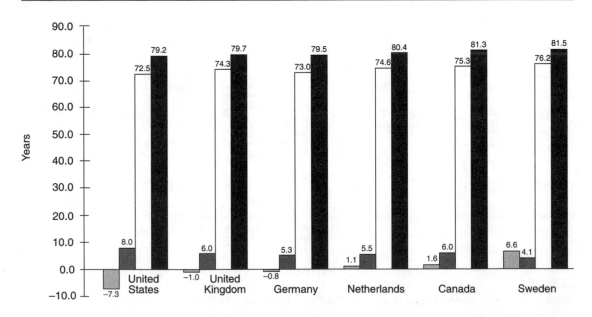

■ Outcome Index   ■ Infant Mortality per 1,000   □ Male Life Expectancy at Birth   ■ Female Life Expectancy at Birth

Figure 1–2 Selected International Comparisons on Three Health Care Outcome Measures in 1995. *Source:* Reprinted with permission from G.F. Anderson, In Search of Value: An International Comparison of Cost, Access, and Outcomes, *Health Affairs*, Vol. 16, No. 6, p. 170, Copyright © 1997, The People-to-People Health Foundation, Inc., all rights reserved.

at birth (79.2 years versus a high of 81.5 in Sweden).

The outcome index in Figure 1–2 is a weighted sum of the standardized scores for the three outcomes previously discussed. Arguably, placing weights on the importance of each of the three outcomes is difficult to justify on a predictive basis, but putting a weight of 2.5 on infant mortality and of 1.0 on life expectancy at birth reflects the general judgment of various experts such as Starfield. Specifically, the algorithm for the outcome index sums the weighted, standardized scores for life expectancy and then subtracts from this subtotal the weighted, standardized score for infant mortality. Based on this index, the United States ranks last. Clearly, the United States should be able to obtain far better value for the amount of money it spends on health care. Given that countries such as Sweden and Canada, ranked first and second on the outcome index, spend much less than the United States, but obtain much better health care outcomes, the United States should be able to learn some lessons from examining their health care systems, as well as those of the United Kingdom and Germany that appear to obtain better cost:benefit ratios than the United States.

COMMON PROBLEMS

The United States and other industrialized countries face some common problems, including populations that have and will continue to have increasing proportions of elderly people who suffer from chronic diseases. Western medicine and science have developed technologies for extending life that are unprecedented in human history. This technical ability, however, is a double-edged sword. Medical technologies are costly, and even in very wealthy nations, some form of rationing is necessary. Lastly, with the pass-

ing of the Cold War, the economies of the West, especially within Europe and North America, have had to make difficult realignments, both in terms of domestic industries and in terms of regional trade alliances. As a result, many of these countries have been or are facing severe budgetary difficulties in sustaining the growth in health care expenditures that their elderly populations have come to expect. Interestingly, many of the countries we will examine have resorted to one or more of four common solutions: cost containment, managed competition, decentralization, and vertical integration.

In the sections that follow, the health care systems in five countries are examined, including Canada, Germany, the Netherlands, Sweden, and the United Kingdom. The discussion of each country's health care system provides background information about how the present system evolved, analyzes the system's structure and financing, and examines the particular problems confronting the system and the steps being taken to address those problems. In addition, because each of the national health care systems is very complex, only two major aspects of any health care system are addressed: the management of hospitals and physicians.

HEALTH CARE IN CANADA

Canadian public health insurance always has resembled a quilt more than a uniform blanket covering the nation. However, the stitching is showing signs of unraveling.[35] Beginning as far back as 1909 when the province of Saskatchewan enacted the Rural Municipalities Act that led to the creation of local medical care insurance schemes, providing medical care to its citizens has been a major concern for Canada.[36,37] Although some of the provinces instituted various initiatives to provide medical care, it was not until 1943 that the Canadian House of Commons considered proposals to provide federal subsidies to provincially administered health insurance programs.[38] Despite much discussion and endorsement, the provinces were unable to reach agreement on a specific proposal, and several provinces proceeded with universal hospital insurance on their own.[39]

By the 1950s, provinces that provided insurance were being compared to provinces without such plans, as well as to early regionally organized capitation plans in the United States. Only the three provinces that had developed state-supported plans were judged to be adequately supplying medical care to their residents, and they were doing so at costs comparable to or less than those provinces without such systems.[40] Moreover, during the 1950s, Canadian leaders and physicians began to support actively the premise that all Canadians, independent of their financial means, should have reasonable access to quality health care. By 1959, a fully universal government-operated hospital insurance system, providing 50 percent federal funding for provincial expenditures on medically necessary hospital care, was in place.[41,42]

When Saskatchewan implemented government-run insurance for physicians' services in 1962, however, physicians were strongly opposed. A bitter and unsuccessful 23-day strike by physicians ensued. As their worst fears failed to materialize and as they quickly became the highest paid physicians in the country, their professional opposition to the program decreased. By 1971, all provinces and territories operated physician insurance programs.[43,44]

As Canada moved into the highly inflationary 1970s, problems began to develop with the health care program. The provinces were unable to control their individual health care services priorities, and because the law required it to match whatever the provinces spent, the federal government lost control of its health budget.[45] During 1977, the matching formulas were abandoned, and the basis for the federal contribution was changed to an indexed per capita block grant. Additionally, the Extended Health Care Services Program was initiated to entice the provinces to develop less expensive support services, such as home and ambulatory health care.

The Canadian Health Act was passed in 1984 to consolidate all the earlier laws that authorized federal subsidies to the various insurance plans. There is now a single, government-operated provincial health plan that is the sole payer for hospital and physician care in each of the 12 provinces/territories. The 1984 Health Act also eliminated (1) all user charges for physician and hospital services, (2) any extra billing by physicians, and (3) private insurance for covering services available under the provincial health plans. Moreover, the Health Act made all residents eligible, regardless of their employment status.[46–48]

System Structure and Financing

All of the 12 provinces and territories have separate plans, and there are major differences among them in the fee schedules used for physician payment and the additional services covered. As a result, Canada's total health care expenditures in the private sector had risen to almost 28 percent by 1991.[49] It has not been determined how much private spending is insured and how much is paid out of pocket.[50] The money for the federal and provincial portions of health care expenditures comes from taxes on personal and corporate incomes at both levels, as well as payroll taxes, nonfederal sales and property taxes, and federal customs and excise taxes, which include a 13 percent national sales tax on (primarily) manufactured goods.[51]

Because of severe cutbacks in Canada's federal allocations for health care (a $7 billion reduction in 1995), provinces and territories have been scrambling to define cost containment measures.[52] All are critically reviewing the services provided and removing those deemed nonessential from coverage through a process referred to as "delisting." Thus private supplemental insurance providers (or patients themselves) must carry an ever-increasing share of the health care cost burden, which contributes to the "creeping privatization" of the Canadian health care system. Furthermore, the cost of extended health care in Canada is increasing dramatically as the government shifts the cost of services that were originally paid through Medicare directly to the public.[53] User charges and co-payments (allowed for some types of added benefits) also are increasing. For example, Quebec has introduced a $2 user fee for its drug plan users, which amounted to a cost shift of $34 million in 1993–1994. In delisting dental care for those aged 10 to 16, Quebec transferred a cost of about $28 million directly to other payers.

During the late 1980s, hospitals accounted for a little more than 39 percent of total health care expenditures, and virtually all hospitals participated in the public insurance program.[54] Not surprisingly, Canada's hospitals are undergoing major restructuring in several areas, including board memberships, mergers, alliances, and closures. Most regionalization models divide the province into a series of geographic sectors, and regional boards replace existing hospital and community boards (with their emotional ties to particular facilities or programs). Regional boards can make tough unbiased choices, as well as gain economies of scale. To date, regionalization has occurred in all provinces except Ontario. In Saskatchewan, 30 district health boards have replaced more than 400 boards, each of which had been dealing with only one type of service.[55]

A commission established in Ontario to review hospital capacity and needs has recommended the closure of 20 to 30 of the current 220 Ontario hospitals by 1999.[56] It is estimated that by the year 2000, the Canadian hospital sector will have decreased from 900 independent hospitals to 150 or 200 integrated, regional health care delivery organizations.[57] This cost containment effort is not without its pitfalls, however. Downsizing has led to the layoffs of an estimated 10,000 nurses and 20,000 other hospital workers.[58] Additionally, a recent study has shown that patients almost everywhere in Canada wait longer for radiotherapy than they do almost anywhere in the United States.[59] Although there are other causal factors, this is in some measure due to the reduced carrying capacity of hospitals.

Another approach receiving attention in Canada as a possible way to gain efficiency is to shift more health care dollars to the community setting, first to care and treatment, then to health promotion and disease prevention.[60,61] There also is an effort currently under way in the Ontario program to shift care from long-term care facilities to the community. The unproved assumption that community care is universally better and less expensive bolsters this initiative.

A later development in the effort to increase efficiency is the change in the legal status of various health care professions and facilities, such as the licensing of midwives, the development of "birthing centers," and the introduction of a formal nurse-practitioner training program.[62] Hospitals also have begun contracting for their nonclinical functions, such as housekeeping, food service, and laundry in the private sector in an effort to increase efficiency. Canada currently has no freestanding ambulatory care centers. To date, all such centers are either located in the hospital or in the home rather than in facilities built specifically for that purpose.

Until recently, participating hospitals negotiated annually with the provincial health ministry to determine a total operating budget (global budget), taking into account such factors as government-determined bed:population and staff:patient ratios.[63,64] The ministry made periodic lump sum payments, and hospital administrators could be relatively flexible in deciding how to allocate resources. Provincial authorities were relatively generous in covering hospital deficits during the 1970s, but since the late 1980s, they have been refusing to finance budget overruns.[65] Now, Canada has started to move hospital financing toward a case-mix approach, following the U.S. trend. In effect, Canada has moved from paying hospitals for being there, to paying them for what they are actually doing.[66] The authority to approve capital expansions and major renovations or acquisitions also rests with the provincial authorities, even if the institution raises the necessary capital. As a result, health care technology does not proliferate as extensively or as rapidly as it does in countries like the United States.[67–69]

With two exceptions, patients have the freedom to select their own physicians, and physicians are paid a fee for service according to fee schedules negotiated periodically between provincial authorities and medical associations. First, a few medical group practices are paid by capitation. Second, some physicians do not participate in the insurance system at all. Patients may pay privately for treatment from these physicians if they wish, but physicians (and hospitals) are prohibited from treating both patients whose care is paid for under provincial plans *and* patients who pay out-of-pocket for their care.[70,71] Nonparticipating physicians account for less than one percent of physicians nationwide.[72]

Community health centers and health service organizations are present in large numbers only in Ontario and Quebec, but such alternative arrangements are expected to increase in number as provinces try to deal effectively with escalating health costs. Community health centers are locally initiated and administered by a board of directors drawn from the communities they serve. Not only do they provide health care access for groups of people who have been identified as underserved, but also they may provide preventive and social services such as nutritional counseling, day care, and literacy programs. In contrast, health service organizations are run by groups of physicians who have agreed to capitated arrangements with the provincial health plan. Like health maintenance organizations in the United States, health service organizations provide only medical care and receive a monthly capitation payment for each patient who has signed with the organization, regardless of whether care has been necessary. Patients are under no obligation to use only those physicians belonging to the health service organization; however, should they seek care elsewhere, the organization loses the payment for that month.[73]

Physicians have an influential voice in health care policy making, there is little questioning of their clinical judgment, and they have the highest incomes among professional groups in Canada.[74] Some provinces have experimented with systems to reduce physician fees in subsequent years if utilization is excessive in the monitored year, but only Quebec has gone so far as to set a yearly maximum amount payable for individual general practitioners (the majority of Canadian physicians are family or general practitioners).[75–77]

Present Problems and Reform Efforts

Although the Canadian health care system has received attention from countries interested in health care reform—most notably the United States[78-81]—the system is not without its problems. Most of the current problems stem from a basic policy conflict inherent in the system.[82-86] That is, while the federal and provincial governments remain adamant in their commitment to (1) public and universal funding of health care, (2) professional autonomy for physicians, (3) first-dollar coverage (i.e., no deductibles) and physician choice for citizens, and (4) budgetary control by provinces, effort to achieve any one of these objectives affects the others. For example, public funding requires public administration, which necessitates some loss of autonomy for physicians; at the same time, budgetary controls may require some modifications to both universal funding and first-dollar coverage for citizens. This latter point has taken on increasing urgency since the federal government has decreased its support of the provincial health plans to try and cope with a large national budget deficit. Indeed, further exacerbating this problem, Ontario and Quebec were still operating with major deficits into the mid-1990s.[87] Even during an economic recession, however, both patients and health care practitioners are demanding better access to new medical technologies and remain generally opposed to raising taxes to meet those demands. Finally, the supply of physicians has increased faster than the population for every year since 1965, yet there is no definitive policy to control and direct this supply at either the federal or provincial level.[88-90]

Because the onus is on the provinces to control their budgets and because national funding to support those budgets is diminishing, the provinces themselves have taken the lead in designing and implementing various experiments in cost containment. Several of these initiatives already have been mentioned: caps on physician salaries and re-

duced fee payments following overutilization; community health centers, health service organizations, and home health care. Other innovations include the following:

- increasing use of alternative providers, such as physician's assistants, nurse-practitioners, and nurse-midwives both to service those areas underserved by physicians (e.g., rural and low-income urban areas) and to aid and supplement physicians in health service organizations and in home births
- closing hospital beds temporarily
- contracting with hospitals in some U.S. cities to provide patient care for certain conditions (mainly coronary bypass surgery and lithotripsy)
- promoting programs that emphasize prevention of disease and injury
- monitoring more strictly physician resource allocations, focusing mainly on patients receiving unnecessary treatments and procedures
- creating blue-ribbon working groups to seek solutions to identified problems
- subsidizing 2 years of intensive training for aspiring dental nurses who provide complete dental care to schoolchildren, countering the shortage of dentists
- providing incentives for using generic drugs.[91-96]

In spite of its present difficulties, the Canadian system remains one of the most admired health care systems both at home—provincial health insurance plans are recognized as the country's most popular institutions—and in the world.[97-101] Undoubtedly, the Canadian system will continue to evolve as medical knowledge and technology advance and as the world's and Canada's economy changes. Whether Canada will choose to turn, as other socialized health care schemes have, to a pluralistic system with multiple-source funding remains unclear.[102,103] While there are proponents of private investment, especially among Canada's medical associations, both the provincial and federal governments seem content, for the moment at least, with developing innovative ways to constrain medical expenditures within the framework of the present system.

HEALTH CARE IN SWEDEN

In 1975, faced with growing concerns about rising costs, fragmented yet ever-increasing demands for care, and an inflexible, centralized system, the Swedish cabinet appointed a Commission of Inquiry to develop new legislation for medical care.[104] The commission was to specify overall goals and criteria for all aspects of health and sickness care under the guiding principle that everyone living in Sweden has an equal right to such care. The Parliament reviewed the commission's recommendations in 1981 and enacted legislation that took effect in 1982. This legislation set general guidelines and parameters for the organization of medical care following four basic tenets:

1. Equality of care and the promotion of good health would be priorities.
2. Counties would have *total* responsibility and accountability for medical care.
3. Physicians would direct all medical activity and delegate responsibility to others as much as possible.
4. The national government would be responsible for setting regulations to protect individuals and stating conditions for employment in medical care settings.

In accord with Swedish culture, details concerning planning and implementation were left to the county councils and local authorities.[105]

System Structure and Financing

Health care services in Sweden almost exclusively are financed and provided within the public sector. At the moment, approximately 80 percent of health care financing is linked to each county council's right to levy taxes. Except for a relatively insignificant fraction from patient fees (about 1 percent), the rest of the financing comes from government contributions allocated to the county councils, generally according to a per capita formula. This taxation power gives the Swedish county councils a stronger and more independent position toward central government than seems to be the case in other countries.[106] In 1991, the government imposed a complete freeze on local government taxes, but this freeze was formally lifted in 1994 with the addition of government incentives to stem tax increases. Employers pay general social insurance taxes for each employee, and part of this money goes to social health insurance funds that finance ambulatory care, both medical and dental, and prescriptions, and also reimburse patients for lost income due to illness (65 percent of social health insurance). In 1987, total social insurance, including pensions, amounted to about 46 percent of an employee's salary.[107,108]

The majority of physicians in Sweden are public employees who work in primary care or hospital settings and are paid on a 100 percent salary basis.[109] The small number who are privately employed or who are in private or group practice (11 percent in 1985) are paid according to their specific contracts with private or public sector purchasers of care. About 20 percent of Sweden's physicians are general practitioners.[110] Public sector physicians have been allowed to treat private (usually fee-for-service) patients in their off-duty time, mainly at the private institutions mentioned earlier.[111]

Patients pay nominal personal charges in connection with publicly provided health care services and the purchase of certain health-related items, such as eyeglasses. These out-of-pocket costs have increased, especially those for pharmaceutical products, but a wide range of indirect subsidies (e.g., pensions, allowances for housing and children, unemployment insurance) permit nearly all Swedes to afford modest personal expenditures for health care. Several private insurance companies offer health care insurance in Sweden, but since tax deductions for private health care insurance premiums were disallowed in 1988, the demand for private medical insurance has been in a steady state of decline and has basically evaporated since 1994.[112]

Present Problems and Reform Efforts

Sweden continues to have one of the industrialized world's healthiest populations, with an infant mortality rate of 3.8 per 1,000 live births and average life spans for males of 76.1 years and for females of 81.4 years in 1996.[113] The changes in medical care delivery under the 1982 law, as well as demographic and economic changes, are creating a crisis at the service delivery level, however. Some of the most pressing problems include the following:

- a rapidly aging population, with the largest percentage of elderly (over 65 years of age) in the world—18 percent
- a need to reduce tax levels (among the highest in Europe) to remain industrially competitive
- demands from a population that, as it has become more affluent, has also become less willing to wait for procedures or to accept a health care system that is not responsive to patient influence

- pressures to keep abreast of new technology
- shortages of new professional personnel because of low salaries and a tight labor market.[114,115]

Proposed solutions to these problems have been many and varied, but most involve some degree of competition and the inclusion of private sector providers and/or insurers. Since 1992, Sweden has embarked on a series of changes to health care policy that are heavily influenced by the British NHS reforms. As a result, most of Sweden's counties have introduced various innovations in service delivery. For example, home addresses of the Swedish citizens determined the hospitals, primary health care centers, and the physicians from which they could seek health care services in the past. During the 1990s, patient choice has been emphasized through the separation of purchasers and providers, the establishment of an internal market regulated by contracts, competitive tendering, and the encouragement of the private sector.[116] The most extensive reform efforts took place in Stockholm County.

In its experiment, Stockholm County established nine semiautonomous health authorities that by 1992 had become purchasers of medical care with responsibilities also for public health and health promotion. One private and nine public hospitals became designated providers with contracts determining the services that they would provide. (Research and education funding, however, was guaranteed.) These providers were reimbursed according to a performance-related system based on diagnosis-related groups (DRGs). Public providers were also required to buy services from other providers and to rent facilities on a cost basis, putting them on an even footing with private providers. In January 1994, private providers were further encouraged and allowed to set up practices on a fee-for-service basis.

The indications from Sweden are that there has been a major re-thinking of the reforms in Stockholm County. Because the productivity of hospitals increased in 1992, the purchasers cut back on DRG rates in 1993 and 1994. Increased fees for private specialists led both to a concentration of these providers in affluent neighborhoods and to concerns about higher costs. As a result, the establishment of new private physician practices is no longer permissible, and the county has set up a hospital board to oversee the provision of services in all county hospitals. The board, in turn, reports to a central political board for health care that coordinates the purchases of acute care hospital services and engages in long-term planning for the county's health care infrastructure.

Other European countries that have similar systems and are facing similar difficulties of increasing demographic and fiscal pressures have been closely watching these attempts to introduce market-style mechanisms into a public system. The re-thinking of managed competition is now apparent in several other countries, including the United Kingdom and the Netherlands.

HEALTH CARE IN GERMANY

With the reunification in 1990, the Federal Republic of Germany (encompassing the former West and East Germany) consists of 16 states and city states with a population of 80.3 million.[117] The health care system in Germany has its roots in cooperative organizations, called sickness funds, that were originally sponsored by guilds during medieval times. These sickness funds provided financial security to guild members and their families in the event of illnesses or injuries, usually by levying fixed fees two or three times a year on all guild members. Unlike the U.S. system of indemnity insurance, which attempts to spread risk across individuals and exclude those with exceptionally high-risk potential, the sickness funds operated on the basis of maximizing social solidarity (group cohesion) rather than on the basis of minimizing individual losses. As the German states became more mercantile between the sixteenth and mid-nineteenth centuries, the sickness funds were extended by various communities to include not only craftsmen, but also miners, foundry workers, and other artisans.

The rapid industrialization of the newly unified Germany in the late nineteenth century created a large urban population of factory workers who were no longer adequately covered by the community-based and craft-centered sickness funds. By 1878, worker dissatisfaction with the monarchy and organized opposition from communists and labor unions so threatened the government that several laws were passed outlawing socialism, trade unions, and the Social Democratic Party. Such legislation did little to obviate the causes of unrest, however. Under the urging of Chancellor Otto von Bismarck, the Parliament (*Reichstag*) in 1883 enacted compulsory national health care insurance for all hourly laborers in order to secure social stability. The Health Insurance Act of 1883 and other acts to extend accident insurance for factory workers (1884) and agricultural workers (1886), as well as old age and disability pensions (1899), established Europe's first social welfare state.[118]

These acts did not create the centrally administered, government-financed health care service that Bismarck originally envisioned. Rather, opposition to his concept from business, agricultural, and other political and religious interests resulted in a health care system in which the national government set policy, but the sickness funds retained their central role of financing and delivering health care. The 1883 Act retained two types of sickness funds—guild- or craft-based funds called *Innungkassen* and miners' funds called *Kappschftskassen*—and established two other types of funds—local sickness funds called *Allgemeine Ortskrankensassen* (AOK) and company sickness funds called *Betriebskrankenkassen*. Although not provided for within the act, substitute funds called *Erstzkassen* that are run as mutual aid societies for salaried employees also prospered.[119]

During the ensuing years 1883–1975, statutory health care insurance was expanded to include not only blue-collar workers, but transport and commercial workers (1901), agriculture and forestry workers and domestic servants (1911), civil service employees (1914), unemployed people (1918), seamen (1927), dependents of fund members (1930), voluntary participants earning wages above the statutory limits (1941), pensioners (1941), farm workers and salesmen (1966), self-employed agriculture workers and dependents (1972), and students and disabled persons (1975).[120] The results of this expansion included an exponential growth in sickness fund enrollment, steady consolidation of the sickness funds,[121] and a large increase in the number of physicians.[122]

During the first three decades of this expansion, the sickness funds exercised a great deal of power. Each fund was free to hire anyone to provide health care, often negotiating extremely low fees from doctors who had not passed their board examinations—and typically restricted fund members from seeing physicians who did not have a contract with a fund. In the first decade of the twentieth century, however, physicians both within and outside the sickness funds began to form unions and to use the strike as a bargaining tool with the funds. In 1911 and in 1913, largely because of the pressure from two large physician groups, the *Hartmannbund* (representing office-based physicians) and the *Deutsche Ärztevereinsbund (DÄV*, the national umbrella group of medical associations), the government had to address the strife caused by the power imbalance. The Imperial Insurance Decree or *Reichsversicherungsordnung (RVO)* of 1911 required sickness funds to (1) give members a choice between at least two physicians, (2) pay physicians on a fee-for-service basis, and (3) pay only physicians with full certification. The decree also expanded the population covered by statutory insurance to include almost 30 percent of all Germans, while permitting sickness funds to reimburse patients for medical services. After the *DÄV* threatened a nationwide strike of physicians, the government intervened, creating the Berlin Treaty of 1913, enabling physicians and sickness funds to negotiate differences and set standards on issues such as the physician:patient ratio.

During the hyperinflationary period following World War I, cost pressures and physician dissatisfaction with the worker-dominated sickness funds caused businesses and physicians to join together in calls for health care reform. The balance of power began to swing more to the physicians' side as the Weimar Republic issued a series of decrees to meet the demands of this stakeholder coalition, culminating in the Weimar Settlement of 1931. This decree increased the ratio of physicians to fund members, recognized medicine as a profession, and created sickness fund physician associations (*kassenärztliche Vereinigungen* [*KVs*]). Significantly, each physician was now legally bound to join a *KV* in order to receive payments from a sickness fund. Most important, each *KV* established a bargaining monopoly for local physicians vis-à-vis the numerous sickness funds with which physicians previously had to arrange separate contracts. From this point forward, the *KV*s have served as the primary mechanism through which physician charges flow to sickness funds and fund payments flow to physicians.

On the one hand, the power of the *KV*s increased under the Nazi regime's policy of purging Jews and socialists from positions of power. This action undermined both the representative governance of the union-dominated sickness funds and their calls for further health care reform, particularly since the funds were placed under the dictatorial rule of Aryan managers. On the other hand, the exclusion of Jewish physicians from the sickness funds weakened the delivery of health care, especially in the large urban areas where they were concentrated.[123]

The fall of the Third Reich divided Germany, creating two distinct health care systems. The Federal Republic of Germany, initially under Allied occupation, continued with the decentralized, sickness fund–based system begun under Bismarck; the German Democratic Republic, under Soviet oversight, developed a centralized, state-directed health care system similar to the U.S.S.R.'s command-and-control model. These separate health care systems were conjoined after the 1990 reunification, with major reforms occurring in East Germany in order to make its system similar to the West German system.

In West Germany, the period after the occupation through the 1960s was one of growth driven by the increasing prosperity of the newly reconstructed Germany. During the 1970s, however, the growth of health care expenditures began to exceed the growth in the GDP to such a degree that a series of reforms were instituted to contain costs.[124] These various cost containment acts are summarized in Exhibit 1–1. One of the most notable elements of these acts was the establishment in 1987 of the Council for Concerted Action in Health Care, a panel of 70 representatives from the interested parties in health care, to set a ceiling on the rate of growth for ambulatory and dental care and pharmaceutical and other medical supplies.[125] Since that time, there have been three more notable attempts at reform: the 1992 Health Care Structure Act, the 1996 Hospital Expenditure Stabilizing Act, and the second Statutory Health Insurance Restructuring Act of 1997.

System Structure and Financing

In 1990, 99.8 percent of Germany's population was covered by some form of health care insurance. The greatest number of people were covered by statutory insurance (86.2 percent), with private insurance (11 percent), and other coverage (2.6 percent)—including social welfare, private charity, and the self-paying wealthy—accounting for the rest of the population.[126] Eight types of sickness funds are included within the statutory insurance category, with the six *RVO* (State Insurance Regulation) fund types encompassing about 60 percent of the population and the two substitute fund types accounting for another 28 percent.[127] While types of sickness funds have changed somewhat by mid-1998, the proportion of the population covered by some form of health care insurance has remained fairly stable.

A highly formalized system of ambulatory care physicians and a large array of individual hospitals dominate the German health care system. Three types of hospitals provide most of the inpatient care: (1) public hospitals, (2) private voluntary hospitals, and (3) private proprietary hospitals. Public hospitals may be the property of federal, state, or local governments, and they account for more than 50 percent of the country's hospital beds. Religious institutions often own the private voluntary hospitals, which have about 35 percent

Exhibit 1–1 The Cost Containment Acts of the Federal Republic of Germany: 1977–1989

Cost Containment Act of 1977

- The principle of an income-oriented expenditure policy is introduced.
- Council of Concerted Action for Health Affairs is created.
- "Lump sum" prospective budgets for payments by sickness funds to physicians' associations are reintroduced.
- Utilization review of physicians is strengthened.
- Co-insurance of prescriptions: Payment of 20 percent of cost (maximum of 2.50 DM) is replaced by a co-payment of 1 DM for each drug.
- Reimbursement for dentures is limited to 80 percent of cost.
- Sickness funds are permitted to introduce co-insurance on orthodontics.
- Nursing care at home is obligatory under certain circumstances to reduce inpatient care.
- Costs for home help given by near relatives are no longer reimbursed.
- Family members with income above a certain level are no longer insured free of charge.
- Retired persons are accepted as members of sickness funds only if they were members during their working years (i.e., risk sharing introduced).

Hospital Cost Containment Acts of 1981 and 1982

- Reduction of number of beds is to be accelerated by subsidies.
- Sickness funds must cooperate with the associations of hospitals in the hospital planning of the states.
- Sickness funds may bargain with hospitals over the level of reimbursement for daily health care rates.
- Regulation of hospital care is included in Concerted Action for Health Affairs.

Supplementary Cost Containment Acts of 1981 and 1982

- Fees for technical dental services are reduced for 1 year by 5 percent.
- Reimbursement for dentures is changed: Insurance pays 100 percent for dentists' services and up to 80 percent of material and laboratory costs.
- Co-payments for medical aids and appliances are introduced.
- New eyeglasses are reimbursable only once every 3 years if visual acuity does not change.
- Rehabilitation cures are granted only once every 3 years; a co-payment of 10 DM per day is required.
- Handicapped persons can become voluntary members of the sickness funds if they or their relatives have been members for at least 3 of the preceding 5 years.
- Length of stay after inpatient admission for childbirth is regularly limited to 6 (formerly 10) days.
- A co-payment of 5 DM is introduced for transportation costs.

Amended Budget Act of 1983

- Insured persons must pay 5 DM per day (for a maximum of 14 days) for inpatient care.
- The co-payment on drugs is raised to 2 DM per item.
- Expenses for home health care may be reimbursable if necessary to minimize inpatient care.
- Medicines for minor ailments are no longer covered after April 1, 1983.

continues

Exhibit 1–1 continued

Amended Budget Act of 1984

- Contributions to sickness funds must be applied on special wages, such as bonuses, tips, etc.
- Patients with sick benefits have to pay contributions to the social old age and unemployment insurance; contributions are split between patients and sickness funds.

Hospitals Financing Act of 1985

- The present mixed financing of construction by the federal government and the states is shifted to the states.
- Sickness funds and hospitals may finance certain kinds of investments by per diem rates.

Federal Hospital Payment Regulation of 1986

- Prospective global budgets are introduced; these are to be negotiated by sickness funds and hospitals, based on inclusive costs and anticipated occupancy rates.
- Average per diem rates are to be set based on anticipated costs, with comparisons to similar efficient hospitals.
- Payments are to be based on 75 percent of the agreed daily rate for shortfalls in actual days compared with expected days; only 25 percent of the agreed rate will be paid for surpluses in actual days compared with expected days.
- Hospitals are able to carry over surpluses into subsequent years.
- If the funds and hospitals do not agree on a budget, a neutral (nonstate) arbitration board decides.
- It is possible to arrange special daily rates for hospital departments and special payments for expensive types of care (e.g., heart operations).
- Patients receive detailed information about the care they receive; hospitals begin keeping statistics on the diagnosis, specialty, age, and length of stay of patients.

Need Planning Law of 1986

- Physicians' associations and sickness funds may lock out certain physician specialists in areas with more than a 50 percent excess of physicians in those specialties.
- Sickness funds and physicians' associations may provide incentives for early retirement of physicians.

Health Care Reform Act of 1989

- Blue-collar workers with incomes above the assessment ceiling may choose among insurance types, making legislation for these workers equal to that already applicable to white-collar workers.
- Sickness fund coverage for students is restricted.
- Compulsory insurance is extended to young adults in secondary educational programs.
- Compulsory insurance for certain categories of self-employed people is abolished.
- Requirements concerning prior insurance periods for retired persons are tightened.
- Qualifying conditions for voluntary membership in sickness funds are made stricter.

continues

Exhibit 1–1 continued

- Provisions are repealed under which retired persons, civil servants, and self-employed persons previously could join a health plan.
- The minimum contribution payable by voluntarily insured persons is doubled; also doubled are contributions for children insured in the public system by privately insured parents.
- The employer's share of contributions is set at 50 percent as a general rule.
- Compulsory and optional contribution-sharing arrangements are introduced.
- The system of revenue sharing of the sickness insurance for retired persons is reduced, with contributions set to the average for workers.
- Coverage for preventive care (e.g., preventive dental care and health checkups) is expanded.
- Concept of "patient pays first, then is reimbursed" is introduced; co-insurance for dentures is increased; bonuses are payable if teeth are regularly attended to.
- Fixed reimbursement levels for pharmaceutical products and appliances are introduced; generic drugs are to be dispensed by pharmacists, following physician prescriptions.
- Family assistance is established as an autonomous insurance right.
- Provision of home care is expanded for long-term illnesses.
- Special services that require continuous attendance are made available.
- Certain provisions concerning death benefits are repealed, and certain transitional provisions are made.
- Severe restrictions are placed on reimbursement for travel or transportation costs.
- In all sickness fund and private insurance contracts, the principle of stability of contribution rates is to be prerequisite.
- Individual sickness funds are authorized to introduce new services temporarily on an experimental basis (for up to 5 years) and to test them scientifically under pilot conditions.
- Tighter procedures are introduced for monitoring the prescribing practices of sickness fund physicians.
- Hospitals must publish price lists; ambulatory physicians must consider the cost-effectiveness of their referrals.
- Utilization review of medical services (both ambulatory and hospital-based) is to be conducted on a sample basis, pending negotiations among sickness funds, hospitals, and physicians' associations.
- General monitoring is to be done of costs and quality in hospitals, especially the coordination of inpatient and outpatient care; similarly, needs for major medical technologies are to be coordinated among sickness funds, hospitals, and physicians' associations; unresolved matters are to be referred to arbitration.
- Sickness funds may terminate contracts with inefficient hospitals.
- Conditions for physicians to be admitted to practice with sickness funds are tightened.
- Medical examiner service is transformed into an independent medical advisory service for the sickness funds.
- State governments are to restrict, through indirect means, the intake to medical schools.
- State governments are to use financial incentives to reduce surplus hospital beds.

Source: Data from J.W. Hurst, Reform of Health Care in Germany, *Health Care Financing Review*, Vol. 12, No. 3, pp. 79–81, 1991; and M. Schneider, Health Care Cost Containment in the Federal Republic of Germany, *Health Care Financing Review*, Vol. 12, No. 3, pp. 90–91, 1991.

of the beds, while physicians own most of the proprietary hospitals with about 14 percent of the beds.[128] Although operating costs for these hospitals come from the sickness funds and private insurers, the state governments provide almost all of the funds for capital investments, even for private hospitals. Both the public and the voluntary hospitals usually have salaried physicians; the per diem rates that the hospitals negotiate, as noted previously, include the physicians' remuneration. In contrast, proprietary hospitals' per diem does not include the charges made by the physicians, who as in the United States, are paid a separate fee. Hospital-based physicians in Germany seldom provide outpatient services, however, and ambulatory care physicians rarely have admitting privileges to hospitals.[129]

As indicated previously, the physicians' associations (*KV*s) and the sickness funds negotiate annually to establish a prospective lump sum for the services of ambulatory care physicians typically adhering to the ceiling set forth by the Council for Concerted Action in Health Care. The *KV* then distributes these monies to individual physicians based on their workload and fee schedule. At the same time, the *KV* monitors each physician's quality of care and volume of patients, disciplining those physicians whose practice patterns endanger patients or are too expensive. This "bilateral monopoly" between the *KV*s and the sickness funds does not extend to control over patient volume. In other words, ambulatory care physicians face the problem of the "commons" since any individual physician's increases in patient volume will depress the overall price for services rendered. Ambulatory physicians utilize a nationally negotiated fee schedule for about 2,500 types of service, based on a relative value scale that generates various points. These points, however, are reimbursable at different rates by private insur-

ers (double that for *RVO*), substitute funds (often slightly higher than *RVO*), and *RVO* funds.[130]

During 1989, almost half (46 percent) of the funding for German health care came from statutory sickness funds, with premiums paid 50/50 by employees and employers. Employers picked up an additional 17 percent of the total cost of health care, primarily in the form of sick pay during the first 6 weeks of employees' illnesses. Public social welfare and health programs accounted for another 14 percent of the total health care cost. Pensioners' insurance—jointly paid, at that time, by pensioners, pension funds, and sickness funds—and out-of-pocket payments by consumers each accounted for 7 percent, while private insurance paid for 6 percent of the health care costs. The remaining 3 percent of the health care costs were paid from statutory accident insurance funds.[131]

Present Problems and Reform Efforts

One of the greatest problems that faced the newly reunited Germany was integrating and financing the provision of health care in the former East Germany, with its aged health care infrastructure, weak economy, and emphasis on preventive and primary health care. Health reforms begun there in 1991 are modeled after the decentralized health care system in West Germany, with most of the population (about 60 percent) obtaining compulsory insurance and served by local sickness funds (*AOK*s).[132] The other problems facing Germany's health care system are well known, and they include the following:

- The aging of the population is straining, and will continue to strain, the existing way of financing social security and health care on a pay-as-you-go basis.[133]
- Because of the demarcation between am-

bulatory care and hospital-based care, the fee-for-service tradition, and the fairly unfettered market for physician services, Germany spends more than most nations on medical technology and on secondary and tertiary care.[134] This overproduction is similar to that in the United States.

- Like the United States, Germany has placed little emphasis on preventive care and psychiatric care.[135] In addition, it also faces a growing problem providing adequate long-term care either in nursing homes or via home health care.[136]
- The average length of stay in hospitals is quite high in Germany. Hurst, among others, has attributed this problem to the "role accorded per diem payments, from the sharp separation between ambulatory and hospital care, and from the dual hospital financing system, which means the State governments, which are responsible for planning and investment in capacity, are not responsible for running costs."[137]
- The projected growth in the number of physicians—50 percent by the year 2000 —is a two-sided blade. On one edge, it will place competitive pressure on the physicians' associations, lowering the cost of providing services. On the other edge, without any change in the fee-for-service system for ambulatory care physicians, it is likely to generate supplier-induced increases in both services and procedures.[138]
- There is an inequity between the sickness fund costs and premiums available to white-collar employees and those available to blue-collar employees, especially for those who have compulsory insurance and for the sickness funds that cover them. Given demographic and lifestyle trends, the risk profiles of these two

groups of employees will continue to diverge, with the poorer blue-collar employee contributing more proportionately for health care services than the white-collar employee who can opt to join a fund with more affluent and lower risk members.[139] Such discrepancies created deficits in the statutory sickness fund system, estimated at 11 billion DM ($5.3 billion) in 1992.[140]

In answer to these concerns, the Health Care Structural Reform Act was implemented in 1992. Until this time, cost containment legislation had been directed at reforming health care services.[141] The 1992 Act became the first major law to affect cost containment in the hospital sector. Its passage was possible only because the Social Democratic Party, the ruling party in most German states, had agreed to cooperate with the federal government to enact reform. The legislation dismantled some key elements of the hospital financing system of the previous two decades. For example, it abolished the "full-cost cover" principle for hospital running costs and required the Federal Ministry of Health to calculate fixed budgets for each hospital for the period 1993–1995. Each hospital's 1992 budget served as its base, with increases in the budget limited to the growth rate in the contributory income to the sickness funds.

There were some exceptions to this rule, particularly in the area of nurse staffing. It was estimated that the introduction of "nursing time standards" in which the care required by each patient could be placed into one of nine nursing time categories would demonstrate a need for 13,000 new nursing positions nationwide and that the cost of these additional positions would be included in individual hospital budgets. This fixed budgeting system was considered an interim measure, to be followed by the implementation of a prospective payment system in 1996. The Hospital Expenditure Stabilizing Act that was passed in 1996, however, provided for the extension of fixed hospital budgets, suspended the use of the nursing time standards, and tied any budget increases to real growth in wages in public service.

In 1997, the Second Statutory Health Insurance Restructuring Act was passed, abolishing the nursing times standard. (These standards had led to more than 20,000 new nursing positions when only 13,000 had been anticipated.) The 1997 Act also raised the level of negotiations about growth rates for hospital expenditures between sickness funds and hospital associations from the state to the national level. This legislation also makes case fees and procedure fees negotiable at the national level from 1999 onward, and it limits the profits gained from servicing higher than negotiated numbers of cases to 25 percent of extra income (currently 50 percent) while increasing the allowable deficit as a result of smaller than negotiated numbers of cases to 50 percent of lost income (currently 25 percent).[142]

One additional effect of the 1992 Health Care Structure Act is the placing of a limit on overall drug costs. The act states that if physicians' national prescribing of drugs exceeds 24.1 DM billion, they are held liable for the first 280 million DM (134 million through the sickness fund physicians associations, with the remainder taken out of future fee reimbursements). The purpose of this portion of the law is to impose a financial penalty on physicians who do not prescribe cost-effective drug treatments, thus giving them the incentive to provide clinically oriented, less emotionally supportive care. The result has been significant feelings of insecurity within both the patient and the physician sectors.[143]

Germany clearly is struggling to contain its health care costs. The oversupply of physi-

cians has kept acute hospital care costs low, as the hospitals benefit by hiring physicians in training for short 3- to 4-year contracts. The ambulatory care side has dealt with this oversupply by limiting the licenses of such physicians. Ambulatory care physicians continue to provide excessive amounts of services, however, largely because of the incentives of a fee-for-service environment, albeit one with a global cap on its budget. It remains to be seen what changes will help to remedy this situation.

HEALTH CARE IN THE UNITED KINGDOM

Although formally implemented in 1948, the NHS has its roots both in the laws for aiding the poor established in the 1600s and in the mutual aid societies that flourished in Great Britain during the 1840s. Well-to-do employers lent support to these societies in order to help sick, but low-paid employees. Although such measures, in combination with the Poor Law system, reduced the drain on general tax revenues, public outrage over the poor condition of recruits for the Boer War (nearly one-half of whom were considered unfit for service) led to the passage of the School Medical Service Act of 1907 and to an investigation by the Royal Commission on the Poor Laws and Relief of Distress. This commission issued two reports—a majority report, advocating better charity care, and a minority report, advocating a unified medical service—in 1909 that laid out the issues involved in establishing a national system of health care.[144]

Based on the Royal Commission's reports, the National Health Insurance Act of 1911, introduced to Parliament by David Lloyd George and virtually unopposed except by physicians, established statutory insurance for all manual workers earning less than £160 (about $780) per year. (Most physicians supported a mixture of voluntary health care insurance and government-funded medical services for the poor, thus advocating a system similar to that in the United States today.) Contributions from both employees and employers were mandatory, with the government funding the administration of the insurance and covering the contributions of exceptionally low-income and indigent persons. Benefits covered visits to physicians who were general practitioners and any prescribed medications. Although there was no coverage for dental and other special services, the free outpatient services of a physician specialist associated with a public hospital were available through referral by the patient's general practitioner. Local government support and charity contributions funded hospitalization in public and some large voluntary hospitals, if necessary; hence, the national insurance act did not include coverage.[145]

In some ways, national insurance in the United Kingdom paralleled the organization and structure of the sickness funds in Germany during the same time. Governmentally approved mutual aid societies received the contributions of employers and employees, but county/borough-based insurance committees—made up of representatives of the insured workers, local physicians, local government, and the Ministry of Health—controlled the payments for visits to a general practitioner and for pharmaceutical supplies. The societies enrolled employees and paid cash disability benefits. They also could fund supplemental benefits, such as part of hospitalization costs, if they accumulated surplus funds. Moreover, approved societies, which typically were nonprofit subsidiaries of commercial insurance companies, could sell insurance for other benefits, including dental care and medical care for those not covered

under the law (e.g., dependents or workers earning high incomes). For those making voluntary payments, these societies often offered expanded medical coverage, including fees for specialists at major hospitals and for general practitioners in private, nursing/obstetric hospitals.[146]

Legally, the physicians on each insurance committee could decide how they were to receive payment for their services, whether on a fee-for-service basis, a capitated basis, or some mixture. As Roemer underscored, by 1927, practically all these general practitioner representatives voluntarily had chosen to receive capitated payments, largely as a way to avoid bureaucratic hassles and to preclude competition among general practitioners in each insurance area. The National Health Service Act of 1946 eventually mandated this voluntary pattern of capitated payment.[147] Here, of course, the British physicians diverged from the fee-for-service model that their German counterparts were striving to preserve and strengthen during this time.

The period from World War I through 1938 established many of the values and the concepts on which the NHS would be based. Several significant documents emerged during this time, including the 1920 Dawson Report on health care policy, which advocated a hospital-centered integrated system of care; the 1920 Cave Report on saving voluntary hospitals; the 1926 Report of the Royal Commission on National Health Insurance; and the 1930 and 1938 Reports of the British Medical Association on national medical care policy. Additionally, under the Labour party government in 1938, the Ministry of Health initiated planning discussions for a national health care program.[148]

By the late 1930s, the number of people covered under mandatory (and voluntary) health care insurance had steadily increased, especially as income thresholds for mandatory insurability were raised. Nonetheless, during the Depression, dissatisfaction with the national health care insurance's "means-tested" coverage and limited benefits reached a level that demanded major reforms.[149] Under Winston Churchill's Conservative Party government and the chairmanship of William Beveridge, an Inter-Departmental Committee on Social Insurance and Allied Services surveyed the existing national policies of social insurance, including health care insurance. The Beveridge Report, issued in 1942, made sweeping recommendations to expand all branches of social insurance, from old age pensions to disability benefits. In particular, it set the stage for the NHS by recommending the establishment of a national health care service to provide medical and rehabilitation treatment for all citizens. While sidestepping the issue of how to organize and administer a national service, the report did set a broad goal for the future:

> A comprehensive national health service will ensure that for every citizen there is available whatever medical treatment he requires, in whatever form he requires it, domiciliary or institutional, general, specialist, or consultant, and will ensure also the provision of dental, ophthalmic and surgical appliances, nursing and midwifery and rehabilitation after accidents.[150]

After World War II, the Labour Party won control of the government and sponsored the National Health Services Act of 1946. This draft legislation for creating a national health service was the target of fiery debates between the British Medical Association and the Minister of Health, Aneurin Bevan, a Welshman and former coal miner. Bevan advocated paying general practitioners a salary with a capitation supplement, requiring private pay patients to use private hospitals, and establishing a network of health centers for both preventive and primary care. The British Medical Association advocated an extension of the national health care insurance to cover a higher level of income, the use of government grants to support voluntary hospitals' outreach to the poor and indigent, and the retention of a private health care market for those with high incomes.[151] An April 1948 plebiscite indicated that continued opposition to the act within the British Medical Association came from specialists rather than general practitioners:

> The plebiscite result, reported on 5 May 1948, still showed an overall majority of the profession against accepting service without further safeguards, but the number of opposing general practitioners had not reached the previously agreed majority. Thus did the NHS come into being on the duly appointed day.[152]

The final legislation for the NHS, enacted in July 1948, contained a number of compromises: (1) universal coverage was financed primarily by general revenues, with social insurance contributions limited to a small percentage of the total; (2) general practitioners were paid via capitation; (3) nearly all public and voluntary hospitals were placed under the control of the national government; (4) public hospitals were permitted to maintain up to 5 percent of beds for the private patients of their consultants (i.e., senior hospital physician specialists); and (5) health care centers were limited to a few experimental facilities.[153]

The basic structure of the NHS, as Roemer noted, was balanced across the four primary stakeholders providing health care: the general practitioners, the community hospitals and their staffs of specialists, the medical school–affiliated teaching hospitals, and the local public health authorities. Under the NHS, the insurance committees that had been overseeing the remuneration of general practitioners became executive councils.[154] These councils took up the task of administering not only primary medical care, but also dental care, optical services, and drug prescriptions, in their designated communities.

To manage the community hospitals, the NHS set up a network of regional hospital boards, modeled on the emergency committees that had coordinated hospital services during World War II. Because each regional hospital board oversaw hospital services for 2 to 3 million people and about 30,000 beds, appointed hospital management teams took care of the day-to-day operations of particular institutions, operating between 1,000 and 2,000 beds. Both capital and operating funds were centrally controlled, however, with each board receiving a budget from the national government. The regional hospital board, in turn, controlled the budgets for each management committee. Unlike the general practitioners who received remuneration through capitation, physician specialists and consultants were likely to be full-time salaried employees (60 percent); even those specialists who retained a private practice (40 percent) often had salaried contracts requiring 70 to 80 percent of their activity to be hospital-based. As in the United States, physician specialists had and continue to have the most prestigious and often the highest paying positions in the medical community. This prestige is accentuated in the United Kingdom, however, since specialists must compete for appointments to NHS hospitals, and local general practitioners seldom have such appointments.[155]

The teaching hospitals for medical schools in England and Wales, arguing that inclusion in the regional hospital boards would undermine their special missions and their long tradition of highly qualified medical staffs, were able to maintain a separate status within the NHS until the 1974 reforms. Prior to that time, the board of governors for the 36 teaching hospitals (26 within London) reported to the Minister of Health and obtained funding directly from the national government.[156]

Local public health authorities, of course, pre-dated the National Health Services Act. Although the local health authorities were no longer responsible for public hospitals under the NHS, they remained responsible for preventive care, and their roles were expanded to include ambulance transport, visiting nurse services, and home-based and institutional services for the chronically ill and the aged. The local health authorities continued to provide preventive health care to children through child welfare stations, as well as maternal health care to pregnant women through health department clinics.[157]

The fourfold structure within the NHS was maintained until 1974, even though problems of coordinating care across the four branches and the increasing dominance of specialized hospital care led to calls for reform during the 1960s.[158] Throughout this period, there were ongoing clashes with both general practitioners and specialists over their remuneration from the NHS. During the mid-1960s, dissatisfaction among general practitioners led to significant changes in their remuneration; by 1970, almost half of their incomes were derived from special fees and grants.[159] In 1962, the British Medical Association's Porritt Committee advocated local coordination of all branches, and in 1968, the Labour Party government issued a green paper exploring the possibility of creating area health authorities for this same purpose. By 1971, the Conservative Party government issued a second green paper, with a white paper following in the next year, and legislation to reform the NHS passed in 1973.[160]

To enhance local control, the NHS was reorganized in April 1974 to include 90 area health authorities (AHAs) and 14 regional health authorities (RHAs). The RHAs not only took over the planning responsibilities of the former regional hospital boards and the functions of the former hospital management committees, but also assumed planning oversight for preventive and ambulatory care. Similarly, each AHA became responsible for preventive, ambulatory, and hospital services, including those at the teaching hospitals. To match the enlarged scope of the AHAs' mission, the representation on their governing boards was broadened to include nonmedical members who had significant managerial experience and community medicine specialists who could serve an important advisory capacity. Family practitioner committees replaced the former executive councils, representing the interests of general practitioners and advising the AHAs, while community health councils represented consumers' interests at the health district level. These councils provided advice to the district management team (i.e., the community medicine specialist, chief administrator, district nurse, a peer-elected general practitioner, and specialist physician).[161]

By the late 1970s, the usefulness of the AHAs for coordinating and responding to local needs had come into question. Rather than adding a fourth level of bureaucracy to the NHS, it was decided to form district health authorities (DHAs) that would serve populations of about 250,000 and would take over the responsibilities of the former AHAs.[162]

During the 1980s, the Conservative Party government led by Margaret Thatcher tried to control rising health care costs by cutting back on the global budgets to the RHAs and expanding the private medical sector. Not only were physicians encouraged to devote part of their practice to private patients, but also both employers and employees were allowed tax deductions for the costs of private insurance. Hence, the private market for health care expanded rapidly, from less than 2 percent of the population being covered by voluntary insurance in 1969[163] to about 6.3 percent in 1980[164] and to more than 10 percent in 1990.[165] Even though only 6 percent of the total health care expenditures during 1987 occurred in the private sector, both the public and the medical professions had become increasingly disenchanted with the NHS.[166] Indeed, the period 1987–1988 was a time of crisis for the NHS, with hospitals closing down thousands of beds to meet budget constraints, long queues forming for all types of care, delays and cancellations for critical surgery, and DHAs running out of money.[167] In response to this turmoil, the Conservative Party government considered radical changes to the NHS, resulting in a white paper in 1989 that set out the reforms implemented between 1990 and 1991.

System Structure and Financing

The NHS offers the entire population of the United Kingdom comprehensive health care largely through general taxation. Approximately 16 percent of the cost during 1989 was derived from national insurance contributions by employers, their employees, and the self-employed.[168] Although this basic formula has not changed, 1990 legislation that provided tax relief to people 60 years of age or older paying voluntary health care premiums expanded the role of the private sector. During the 1990s, three major structural changes have occurred in the NHS integrated system of public hospitals, ambulatory care practices staffed by general practitioners, and health clinics: (1) purchasers (i.e., district and local health authorities) have been distinguished from providers (i.e., public and private hospitals, general practitioners, and home care providers); (2) providers are allowed to compete for contracts with purchasers; and (3) providers are accountable for the efficient and effective practice of medicine.

Public Hospitals

From 1948 through 1991, NHS hospitals were organized under a public integrated model, similar to the U.S. Department of Veterans Affairs hospitals, with global budgets and salaried physicians.[169] Thus, the NHS allocated a global budget to the RHAs, who used a weighted population formula to allocate the budget to DHAs, who served as both purchasers and providers of health care. There was a great deal of physician autonomy under this system, because the RHAs held the contracts with physicians, making it very difficult for the DHAs and/or hospital managers to discipline or dismiss physicians.

Since April 1991, public hospitals have been subject to an internal market reform.[170] One of the primary purposes of these reforms is to counteract the perverse economic incentives that, under the public integrated model, rewarded hospitals for inefficiency and penalized them for efficiency.[171,172] There are four major reforms for public hospitals:

1. DHAs serve solely as purchasers of health care services and administer physician contracts for the RHAs.
2. NHS public hospitals are transformed into NHS trust hospitals with their own board of directors and, thus, operate as freestanding nonprofit hospitals, enabling them, like DHAs, to administer physician contracts and to have managerial discretion over capital, and operational, allocations.
3. NHS trust hospitals, general practitioner fundholders, and private hospitals compete for contracts from DHAs.
4. Clinical managers administer, with the help of a management team that includes a senior nurse and business manager, an operational budget for hospital departments.[173–176] Because of this resource management initiative, consultants (senior physicians) typically are now managing entire departments, not just serving as heads of a medical staff.[177]

General Practitioners

The reform most directly affecting general practitioners is that a group practice with at least 11,000 patients can now become a fundholder; there are about 1,000 groups of this or greater size. General practitioner fundholders, which may soon encompass one-fifth of government health care expenditures,[178] receive a budget for their patients. The services that they provide include outpatient consultations, associated diagnostic and ancillary services and treatments, and inpatient procedures—although limited to such operations as hip or cataract surgery. General practitioner fundholders are allowed to use their budgets on operating and administrative costs as well. As one of a diverse set of providers in the new NHS internal market, general practitioner fundholders may negotiate with public or private hospitals for the services that their patients need. Even though fundholders may recoup up to a 5 percent budget overrun in their next fiscal year, however, they are subject to revocation of their budgets if they overspend 2 years in a row.[179–182]

In April 1993, the fundholders' latitude was extended to include purchasing responsibility for community health services, such as district nursing, health visiting, chiropody, nutrition, all community and outpatient mental health care services, health services for people with a learning disability, and referrals made by health visitors, district nurses, and community mental handicap nurses. Fundholding practices, therefore, have even more latitude in choosing how to spend their allocated budgets.[183]

The Family Health Service Authorities created by the 1990 NHS and Community Act took over the role of the family practitioner committees (which was largely concerned with pay and rations). For a short time, the Family Health Service Authorities maintained this role and contracted with general practitioners, as well as self-employed professionals, to deliver medical services for the population. Eventually, most Family Health Service Authorities also provided professional advice and support for general practitioners and nurse practitioners. In addition, they were charged with facilitating team building in general practice and involving general practitioners in the commissioning and purchasing process. By April 1996, however, they merged with DHAs and other health authorities to form health commissions.[184,185]

Since 1991, an NHS research and development strategy has been in place to generate and disseminate information on the effectiveness and cost-effectiveness of health care interventions. This increased activity in NHS research and development is the result of a commitment to increase spending over 5 years (1997–2001) toward a target of 1.5 percent of the NHS budget.[186] Two specific outputs of the research and development effort are particularly relevant. First, several Effective Health Care Bulletins have been produced. Second, the NHS Centre for Reviews and Dissemination has recently developed a database of economic evaluations that is available through direct on-line access.[187]

Present Problems and Reform Efforts

The United Kingdom is unusual in providing universal free health care in which general practitioner physicians with 24-hour responsibility largely control access to specialists throughout the year, for a defined list of patients of all ages. It generally is believed that this gatekeeper function has contributed significantly to the relatively low cost of the NHS; by the late 1980s, the NHS was spending less than half as much per capita on health care as the United States and only two-thirds as much as Sweden.[188] Approximately 97 percent of the population in the United Kingdom is registered with a general practitioner, and only a small proportion change practices unless they move to another location. The United Kingdom spends 5.9 percent of its GDP on the NHS and a further 1 percent on private health care. This amounts to £43 billion per year. As comparatively small as this is, the two main political parties, the Labour Party and the Conservative Party, have promised to increase the health care budget by only 0.3 percent between 1997 and 2000, while the average annual increase in spending since 1979 has been more than 3 percent. Clearly, something must give.[189] As Filinson stated, "After half a century of socialized benefits, British citizens are being weaned from services they have come to expect, and being told to seek private solutions."[190]

As a whole, the reforms implemented during the early 1990s represent a major trend to decentralize authority within the NHS, to encourage efficiency in operations, and to a lesser degree, to increase responsiveness to patients. The reforms are not without their critics, however, and their effectiveness has been mixed. For example, Pollock argued that the reforms threaten the outlook for equity, comprehensiveness, and equality of access in the NHS. She pointed to two problems facing managers of NHS trust hospitals: (1) chronic underfunding and (2) tight government controls without a clear strategy. The latter leads to conflicts at the local level over preventive versus tertiary care. Additionally, and perhaps more significantly, the growth of the private health care sector means that the NHS has created a multitiered system "with different standards of care available to patient groups depending on their access to private care and ability to pay."[191]

Ham, in contrast, took a more balanced view, noting that the reforms have placed a renewed emphasis on primary care and that more collaborative endeavors involving general practitioners and specialists should upgrade the quality of medical practice. He noted that the balance of power is swinging from hospitals to an alliance between health authorities and general practitioners. Nonetheless, he warned that the underfunding of the NHS may have dire consequences:

> Yet as constraints on funding begin to bite, a new dynamic is becoming apparent. This involves combined action by hospital providers, who have fulfilled their contracts with a quarter of the year remaining, and general practitioners, who as a consequence are unable to obtain hospital treatment for their patients, to put pressure on health authorities to increase the resources available to acute services. . . . [E]quity is sacrificed as purchasing power rather than clinically diagnosed need determines which patients should be treated.[192]

The NHS workforce also has seen change resulting from the 1990 reforms. Paramount among these is the supply of nurses. The overall number of whole time equivalent qualified nurses (registered nurses and enrolled nurses in the NHS who work 37.5 hours per week) has remained relatively static at around 180,000, but there has been a marked decline in the employment of en-rolled nurses. In contrast, there had been a growth of the nursing workforce of approximately 4 percent per year in previous years. Inflow and outflow of nurses to and from non–United Kingdom countries have declined markedly as well since the late 1980s. Neither flow is of significance at the aggregate level.[193] Imbalances between supply and demand for nurses in terms of skill shortages are beginning to present themselves within the United Kingdom, and hospitals are implementing changes to deal with them. These changes include increased use of 12-hour shifts, internal rotations, and annualized hours/flex time. Other management trends involve the use of temporary contracts and short-term fixed contracts for NHS nursing. These recent developments have markedly reduced nurses' perceptions of job security.[194]

Under a new Labour Party government, the NHS is now facing some of the same rethinking about managed competition as has occurred in Sweden. Prime Minister Tony Blair issued a white paper in December 1997 that lays out several new ideas. First, the NHS plans to develop an evidence-based National Service Framework and a new National Institute for Clinical Excellence to help ensure quality of care and cost-effectiveness. Management cost caps are planned. Funding for all hospital and community services, prescriptions, and general practice infrastructure will be brought together into a single stream at the DHA and Primary Care Group level. The government plans to develop a national schedule of reference costs that will itemize the costs of individual treatments across the NHS. Clear incentives to improve performance, clear sanctions for failing to perform, and efficiency standards are also planned. Efficiency and high quality of health care delivery are priorities. The timeline is short for these changes, with full plan implementation projected to be in the year 1999.[195]

HEALTH CARE IN THE NETHERLANDS

Prior to World War II, health care in the Netherlands was provided largely through private enterprise and charity, with the government's role limited to monitoring the quality of care and ensuring the provision of preventive care. During the postwar years, however, the government took an increasingly more central role in the financing and regulation of primary through tertiary care, creating a complex mixture of private enterprise and government oversight.[196,197] Hence, the following acts of legislation were essential in establishing the modern Dutch health care system:

- The Sickness Funds Decree of 1941 and 1948 mandated that sickness funds must contract with all physicians in their region, simultaneously guaranteeing free choice of doctor by patients and eliminating competition among physicians.[198] The Decree of 1948 also created guidelines for social insurance to ensure financial access to health care among the poor while the Netherlands underwent a decade-long period of tightly planned reconstruction.[199]
- The Sickness Funds Insurance Act (*ZFW*) of 1964, which replaced the Decree of 1948, specified the level of income under which social insurance was compulsory for acute and short-term illnesses.[200] It also established the eligible population for sickness funds and the territories set aside for them, and it continued to obligate sickness funds to contract with all providers in their regions. Premiums were paid into a central regulatory body, the Sickness Fund Council, which then reimbursed the funds for the medical expenses of its members.[201] The pre-

miums for social health insurance were based on a percentage of income that varied for the employed, pensioners, and social security recipients. In 1987, the income threshold for *ZFW* was Dfl 49,150 (about $25,000); employees and employers each contributed 5.05 percent of gross wage income; pensioners contributed 3.05 percent; employers contributed 3.0 percent; and social security recipients contributed 5.05 percent.[202]

- The General Special Sickness Expenses Act (*AWBZ*) of 1967 provides universal insurance for catastrophic and long-term illnesses, including physical and mental handicaps.[203] During 1987, *AWBZ* was funded through fixed percentage contributions (4.55 percent) from each employee (paid by employers) and the self-employed.[204]
- The Hospital Facilities Act (*WZV*) of 1971 and 1979 established central government licensing for the construction and for the size of hospitals. Its original goal was to lower the number of beds in acute care hospitals. (More comprehensive legislation, the Health Care Facilities Act of 1982, with implementation planned for 1984, was designed to regulate all institutional and ambulatory care facilities, but this act has been abandoned in light of the reforms.)[205] Under the *WZV*, a "new general hospital [must] have a minimum size of 175 beds, in order to guarantee the availability of two full-time medical specialists of each of the six so-called 'core specialties.'"[206]
- The Health Care Tariffs Act (*WTG*) of 1980, implemented in 1982, created "a specially appointed autonomous body, the Central Office on Health Care Tariffs (COTG) [which] sets out guidelines for the composition and calculation of tariffs," including both fee-for-service and

capitation payments to physicians and hospitals.[207] Rather than directly setting prices, the COTG sets the parameters for a bargaining process between providers (i.e., hospitals, physicians, and other medical professionals) and buyers, including both sickness funds and private insurers, for determining tariffs. The COTG then reviews these tariffs to ensure that they are within the guidelines.[208] This legislation has strengthened the power of the associations both for providers (especially general practitioners and specialists) and for insurers by institutionalizing a bilateral monopoly.[209]

- The Health Insurance Access Act (*WTZ*) of 1986 requires private insurers to provide "specified risk groups a comprehensive benefits package for a legally determined maximum premium."[210] The purpose of this legislation was to counteract the premium differentiation and market segmentation that since the 1970s had eroded universal coverage for the elderly and other high-risk groups. In 1989, these benefits were extended to all people over 65; in 1991, they were mandated for all people who are privately insured who pay more than the maximum standard premium.

Compulsory social health insurance (*AWBZ*) covers the entire Dutch population for chronic care and about 70 percent of the population for acute care (*ZFW*). The remaining population purchases voluntary insurance for acute care.[211] In 1987, health care was financed from five sources in four categories: (1) social insurance—*AWBZ* and *ZFW* (65.8 percent); (2) private insurance (20.2 percent); (3) out-of-pocket payments (7.5 percent); and (4) general taxation (6.6 percent).[212] In 1981, the percentage of gross family income spent on health care insurance varied from less than

4 percent to more than 15 percent.[213] As in Germany, the mixture of public (*ZFW*) and private insurance for acute care has resulted in a regressive form of funding, with the poorest generally paying a greater percentage of their income for health care than the richest.[214]

Significantly, the Dutch system maintains a strict division between health care financing and health care delivery. Sickness funds are "legally forbidden to employ providers or to run health care institutions" and private insurers are not willing to interfere with medical practices.[215] As in the United Kingdom and Germany, general practitioners provide primary care, acting as gatekeepers for *ZFW* and many privately insured patients, and referring them to specialist physicians who provide secondary and tertiary care in hospitals. For these patients, general practitioners often receive a capitation fee.[216] For most privately insured patients, however, both general practitioners and specialists receive fees for service.[217] To control physician supply, the government since 1986 has regulated the location of general practices, setting both upper and lower limits on the size of a practice. Moreover, it has restricted entry into medical schools and, in cooperation with the medical professions that control medical training, has supported the reduction of resident training capacity.[218]

Since 1984, Dutch hospitals, whether owned by local communities or, most typically, by private boards of trustees, have operated with prospective, global budgets that are negotiated annually with third-party payers (i.e., public sickness funds [*ZFW*] and private insurers).[219,220] Prior to that time, hospitals were reimbursed on a price per patient day, which encouraged providers to admit patients for lengthy hospital stays.[221] In contrast to those in the United States, hospitals in the Netherlands are in highly concentrated markets, with more than 70 percent of the 25 regional markets in 1988 exceeding an Herfindahl–Hirschman Index of 1,800. Moreover, Dutch hospitals during the 1980s underwent a wave of government-supported consolidation; as a result, the market share of the two largest hospitals in each region increased an average of 10 percent from 1984 to 1988, while the total number of hospitals decreased from 169 in 1984 to 148 in 1988.[222]

Reflecting even greater market concentration than hospitals, 46 sickness funds (*ZFW*) offered compulsory coverage to residents in the 25 health care regions during 1987. In contrast, during 1986, the top 10 of the more than 60 private insurers held a cumulative market share of 59.7 percent for all private premiums, and their Herfindahl–Hirschman Index measure of market concentration was a relatively low 545.[223] The sickness funds, unlike the private insurers, were retrospectively reimbursed by the Sickness Fund Council up through 1990 for the medical expenses of their enrollees. Private insurers, however, were much more at risk, because the regulation imposed in 1986 (*WTZ*) meant that they incurred losses—35 percent of their total claims in 1991—on those high-risk groups that they were legally mandated to cover at set premiums.[224]

Calls for major reforms of the Dutch system of health care were made during the 1970s and again in the 1980s. In 1974, the "Secretary of Health and Environmental Protection published a comprehensive study on the Dutch health care system, calling for more government controls on prices of medical care, decentralized governmental planning agencies for all health care facilities, and incorporation of the various health insurance Acts into an integrated social security system."[225] Although price controls and government restrictions on hospital capacity and physician supply certainly had an impact dur-

ing the 1980s, their total effect was disappointing.[226] Neither sickness funds nor physicians had any incentives to improve efficiency, while sickness funds and private insurers were unable to direct patients to the most cost-effective providers. At the same time, the growing market segmentation and premium differentiation by private insurers were threatening universal access to acute care. Within this context, the Dutch government set up an Advisory Committee on the Structure and Financing of Health Care, chaired by W. Dekker. The Dekker Report proposed major changes in the health care system that were subsequently endorsed by two coalition cabinets in 1988 and 1990.[227,228]

System Structure and Financing

Since 1990, the Netherlands gradually has been introducing several reforms.[229] The intent of these reforms is twofold: (1) to ensure universal coverage for acute care by gradually eliminating the distinction between sickness funds and private insurance, and (2) to introduce efficiency and greater patient choice into a highly regulated market for third-party payers, hospitals, and physicians by creating managed competition.[230] The following brief description of the reforms and their planned effect on these three stakeholders draws upon the work of Enthoven,[231] Hurst,[232] Kirkman-Liff and van de Ven,[233] Schut,[234] and van der Gaag, Rutten, and van de Ven.[235]

Third-Party Payers

In January 1992, an amendment to the *ZFW* removed both the regional boundary restrictions on the funds' subscriber pools and their obligation to contract with all the health care providers within their region. Hence, two important preconditions have been met for allowing sickness funds and private insurers (1) to compete for subscribers and (2) to contract selectively with health care providers, negotiating both the payments and the types of services to be supplied. Moreover, since 1990, sickness funds have been receiving prospective global budgets from the Sickness Fund Council rather than retrospective reimbursement for enrollees' medical costs.

So that consumers could choose the best benefit-for-value insurer and insurers could choose the most cost-efficient and quality-effective providers, the government proposed setting up a central fund for compulsory national health care insurance with an income-dependent, nominal premium. Insured individuals would choose their insurer and, to some extent, their benefits package and premium.[236] The central fund was to receive income-related contributions from the Dutch population and then pay out risk-related premiums to sickness funds and private insurers, based on the overall risk profile of each insurer's group of subscribers. Because the premiums to be received by third-party payers would cover only about 82 percent of the cost of the basic benefit package, the insurers would charge subscribers a flat premium (but no more than 18 percent of the government's risk-related premium) to make up this difference. The premium would vary among insurers based on their ability to contain costs, allowing insurers to compete for subscribers. In short, the planned reform assumed that if there were sufficient competition within the markets for insurers and for health care providers, then consumer choices should compel third-party payers to contract with cost-effective providers. These proposed reforms met stiff opposition from both insurers and providers, however, and became bogged down in political discussions.

Major players in this discussion have been the Christian Democratic Party, the Liberal Party, and the Labor Party. The Christian Democratic Party, formed as a merger of several parties, tended to retain a belief in the importance of personal responsibility tempered by a communitarian ethic.[237] The Liberal Party, the junior coalition partner of the Christian Democratic Party, represented primarily the interests of private enterprise. Liberals advocated large income differentials and reduced public spending as economically salutary, while taking a tough line on welfare benefits.[238] Finally, as the third major player, the Labor Party was concerned that the flat premium and the gap in public coverage would place a burden on people at the bottom of the wage scale. At stake in this political conflict were the same fundamental issues that confronted the United Kingdom and Sweden. Would all, or only high-income individuals, be entitled to receive high-quality care when they wanted it? Compromise ruled the day, and the Dutch steered a middle course: social democratic welfare generously tempered by conservative cost consciousness.

Even after this intense period of negotiation, Dutch political institutions continued to erect roadblocks to easy reform. The plan's complexity necessitated breaking it down into separate pieces to be adopted individually, which increased the opportunities of its enemies to gain access to the political process. There were committee reports, upper chamber votes, and lower chamber votes. When the balance of votes in the chamber finally tilted against this legislation, health care financing reform was dealt a final blow. The consolidation of the sickness funds with private insurers with payments from a central fund was blocked, and the fixed basis for health care insurance was limited to 10 percent rather than the proposed 18 percent.[239]

Presently, therefore, there are two major types of health care insurance in the Netherlands. Those with an annual income below

Dfl 56,000 (approximately 62 percent of the population) have compulsory health care insurance. Their entitlements are specified by law. The execution organizations are local sick funds and premiums are, to a large extent, income-dependent. Insureds in this category have little freedom for them to choose between different levels of coverage, and only very recently was the possibility created to choose among different levels of personal risk. Those with an annual income above Dfl 56,000 (approximately 38 percent of the population) are free to decide whether they wish to purchase private health care insurance. Most of them choose private insurance.[240]

Hospitals

The 1990 era reforms deregulate the hospital industry in two ways: (1) they limit the application of the *WZV* to the planning of large facilities, and (2) they gradually relax the *WTG*'s detailed guidelines governing the negotiation of prices between hospitals and insurers. Limitations on the impact of *WZV* regulations should enable hospitals to establish freestanding outpatient clinics for secondary and tertiary health care. Given the U.S. experience with outpatient and managed care during the past decade, ambulatory care clinics should provide a robust substitute for many health care services provided by hospitals. Furthermore, relaxation of the *WTG* guidelines should in the short term encourage hospitals to contain costs and to differentiate their services in order to compete for contracts with insurers.

Physicians

Three aspects of the reforms that have been implemented should encourage competition among physicians: (1) as indicated previously, sickness funds are no longer obligated under *ZFW* to contract with all physicians in

their respective regions; (2) *WTG* regulations on negotiating fees for service and capitation rates are gradually being relaxed; and (3) as of 1992, practice locations for general practitioners are no longer regulated. Two assumptions, nonetheless, must be fulfilled if competition within the physician market is to occur as anticipated. First, physicians must be willing to contract with insurers as individuals or groups rather than as a professional collective. Second and perhaps most important, there must be a sufficient supply of physicians to ensure that demand does not outstrip the availability of medical care.

Present Problems and Reform Efforts

Total cost for health care in the Netherlands is about 8.6 percent of its GDP.[241] According to Organization for Economic Cooperation and Development data, this figure is about the average for western European countries. With respect to health status, the Dutch population has on the average a very high standard of health. Life expectancy for men is 74.6 years; for women, 80.4 years. Infant mortality is 5.5 per 1,000 live births, which is among the lowest in the world.[242] Moreover, a recent international comparison of health care systems has shown that differences in delivery of health care between population groups are less pronounced in the Netherlands than in most other countries.[243]

Both the reforms that were proposed and those that have been implemented have had a noticeable impact on the actions of third-party payers and physicians. For example, sickness funds underwent a wave of mergers, reducing their number from 46 in 1988 to 26 in 1991. A dramatic increase in market concentration occurred in the private sector. The average Herfindahl–Hirschman Index for private insurers increased from 545 in 1986 to 1,252 in 1992, with the top 10 insurers accounting for 91.8 percent of the market.[244] In some cases, sickness funds and private insurance companies have merged into large corporations with a broad range of business activities, including health insurance.[245]

In part because the Netherlands lacks antitrust laws, the reforms have induced some hospitals to merge.[246] Thus, not only has the number of hospitals considerably declined, but also those remaining have become larger. By 1995, only nine general hospitals had fewer than 200 beds. Between 1981 and 1995, the total number of acute care hospital beds dropped by 15.9 percent.[247] Similarly, the associations of medical professionals have tried to limit the supply of physicians by reducing the resident training capacity for both specialists and general practitioners.[248]

The plan to establish a national comprehensive health care insurance that incorporates both sickness funds and private insurers has not been implemented. Both employers and employees resisted paying higher premiums than they now do under risk-based private insurance. Equally resistant to this change were physicians; the Royal Dutch Medical Association argued that managed care would lower the quality of medical care by requiring physicians to base treatment decisions on economics. Sickness funds, which insure the poorest and the highest risk groups, were fearful that they would not receive their fair share of the health care budget.[249]

Currently, although clinical care remains regulated in the Netherlands, several pilot sites are experimenting with hospital management by negotiating with health insurance agencies on their number of hospital beds and medical specialist units. It is also possible that hospitals will seek vertical integration with specialists and health care providers in order to increase their bargaining leverage, further consolidating not only the hospital industry, but also all aspects of health care delivery.

SHARED CONCERNS AND LEARNING OPPORTUNITIES

At meetings of medical staffs and other health care providers, it often is claimed that comparisons of the United States with other countries are unfair because other countries do not face the social, demographic, and logistical problems faced by the United States. Although such an argument has some merit, there are countries that have many similarities with the United States. Many of the countries with differences may have even greater problems than those faced by the United States.

As Table 1–3 illustrates, the major demographic characteristic of the United States is its large population, which ranges in size from 32 times the population of Sweden to 3 times the population of Germany. Nonetheless, the United States is blessed both with a lower population density and a younger population than in Western Europe. Moreover, while the populations of the European nations are growing more slowly than the population in the United States, Canada's population is actually growing faster.

Significantly, as displayed in Table 1–3, the United States is not alone in the social problem of assimilating foreign nationals, with both Germany and Canada in 1990 having larger percentages of their population from foreign lands than the United States. Historically both Canada and the United States—despite their national wealth (see Figure 1–1)—have faced daunting social problems because of the level of poverty among these foreign citizens (defined as 50 percent below the median national income) during any single year. Nonetheless, except for Sweden, other European countries have experienced similar problems in helping people escape from poverty (defined as earning 50 percent more income within a year's

Table 1–3 Sociodemographic Comparisons of Selected Western European and North American Countries

	Canada	Germany	Netherlands	Sweden	United Kingdom	United States
Land Area in Square Kilometers	9,976,139	357,410	40,844	449,964	244,100	9,372,614
1995 Population (thousands)	29,606	79,500	15,451	8,831	58,258	263,034
1995 Population (per square kilometer)	3	229	378	20	239	28
1995 Population Growth Rates (%)	Urban 1.2 Rural 1.0	Urban 0.8 Rural –1.1	Urban 0.8 Rural 0.2	Urban 0.5 Rural 0.5	Urban 0.2 Rural –0.1	Urban 1.2 Rural 0.3
1995 Urban Population (%)	77	86	89	83	89	76
1997 Population 60 or older (%)*	15	18	16	19	18	14
2025 Population 65 or older (1990 estimate in %)	20.7	24.4	23.7	23.7	21.5	18.7
Mid-1980s Single-year Poverty Rate (%)	17.0	8.0	3.0	3.0	n.a.	20.0
Mid-1980s Poverty Escape Rate (%)	23.0	24.0	23.0	45.0	n.a.	22.0
1995 Unemployment Rates for Labor Force (%)	9.5	11	7.1	8.7	8.5	5.6
1990 Foreign or Foreign Born Population (%)	14.7	8.2	4.6	5.6	3.3	7.9
1990 Largest Cultural or Language Minority Groups	Caribbean Vietnamese Yugoslav	Turk Yugoslav	Moroccan Turk	Iranian Turk	Caribbean Guyanan Indian	Cuban Mexican

Source: Data from *International Health Statistics: What the Numbers Mean for the United States,* 1993, Office of Technology Assessment; *Statistical Year Book, 42nd Issue,* 1995, United Nations; and *Statistical Abstract of the United States: 1997, 113th Edition,* 1998, United States Bureau of the Census. *Data from <http://www.un.org/Depts/unsd/social/youth.htm> 1998, United Nations.

time). In contrast, the United States has a lower percentage of unemployment than the five other countries.

Although none of the five countries discussed is identical to the United States, they are not so dissimilar that useful comparisons cannot be made, especially with regard to health care policy changes. Each of the systems reviewed has attempted to maintain universal financial and physical access to health care, with each achieving differential success in terms of the quality and cost. Arguably, of the five, the German and Dutch health care systems are the most comparable to the U.S. system.[250–252] Lessons can be drawn from the other national health care systems, however, albeit with careful attention to the fundamental differences with the U.S. system.

Toward U.S. Convergence with European Health Care Systems?

During the early 1990s, the changes not only in Germany and the Netherlands, but also in the United Kingdom and Sweden created a mixture of regulation and market competition that seemed to converge with the government-driven reforms that President Clinton was proposing in the United States.[253,254] That is, the vision of a U.S. health care system of managed competition with a budgetary cap on total spending was similar to that which already existed in several European countries, including the Netherlands, Sweden, and the United Kingdom.[255] Broadly speaking, these two approaches to financing and delivering health care rely on a public contract model, similar to the Medicare payments of health maintenance organizations in the United States.[256] Although Hurst and others have espoused the economic efficiency and effectiveness of managed competition (i.e., the public contract model) in achieving health care policy objectives,[257–260] researchers have just begun to explore its impact on the organizational structures and management of hospitals and medical practices.[261–263] Nonetheless, the combination of budgetary caps and managed competition seems to be effective both in containing the costs and in maintaining adequate access to health care in Western European nations.[264]

With regard to financing health care, Canada, Sweden, and the United Kingdom rely primarily on the income tax and other taxes to fund health care; a single payer, the government, disburses these funds. In contrast, Germany and the Netherlands rely largely on payroll taxes for funding health care, disbursing these funds via a multipayer mixture of public and private insurance (Table 1–4). The problem facing each country, as Ham noted, is that it must determine "how to combine the control of expenditures at the macro level with real incentives for efficiency at the micro level. The country that is able to solve this puzzle will indeed be the envy of the world."[265] Within this context, it is significant that Germany, the Netherlands, Sweden, and the United Kingdom have been implementing various elements of managed competition in order to address the problem that Ham has underscored. Each of these countries has viewed managed competition as a way to increase providers' efficiency when delivering health care, thus balancing the macromanagement of financing health care with a quasi-market mechanism for micromanaging expenditures.[266] Moreover, even Canada has been experimenting with cost containment measures during the 1990s.

As illustrated in Table 1–4, each country has implemented managed competition reforms somewhat differently. On the one hand, the Netherlands has been slowly implementing a complex set of managed competition reforms via demonstration projects and intensive negotiations with the key stakeholders in its health care system. On the other

Table 1–4 Pre-Reform, Proposed Reform, and Actual Reform for Health Care Systems in the United Kingdom, Sweden, The Netherlands, Germany, and Canada

Pre-Reform Health Care System

Characteristic	United Kingdom	Sweden	The Netherlands	Germany	Canada
Finance Method	Taxation and national insurance contributions	County Council income taxes and state transfers out of general taxation	Income-related premiums to a sickness fund paid by two-thirds of population; risk-related premiums to private insurers paid by one-third of population Income-related premiums for exceptional medical expenses paid by everyone	86% of population covered by sickness funds; premiums based on income funded through employer/employee contributions 11% covered by private insurance 3% self-insured	Income and other government-related taxation
Distribution of Resources to Providers	To regions based on size, demographic composition, and standardized mortality ratios of populations To hospitals based on historical costs, adjusted for changes in services To GPs by capitation, fee for service, and practice expenses	To hospitals and primary care centers according to historical costs, adjusted for changing workloads	Providers paid directly or patients reimbursed by insurers Institutions independent but budgeted centrally Specialists paid by fee for service; fees negotiated centrally GPs independent and paid by capitation or fee for service	Ambulatory care physicians paid indexed fee for service; fees negotiated	Separate health care plans in provinces Provincial plans financed through federal contributions as indexed per capita block grants
Provision of Care	Choice of GP No choice of specialist	No choice of provider	Free choice within region	Free choice of ambulatory care physician	Free choice within province

continues

Table 1–4 continued

Proposed Health Care System Reform

Area of Reform	United Kingdom	Sweden	The Netherlands	Germany	Canada
Finance Method	No change	No change	All patients brought under basic insurance 82% of premiums income-related, set by government; 18% f at rate, set by each insurer Distinction between sickness funds and insurers abolished; both bear risk and compete for patients	No change	No change
Distribution of Resources to Providers	Purchaser-provider split: DHAs contract with semi-autonomous trusts, directly managed units, or private providers; mostly block contracts DP "fundholders" purchase some specialist services for their patients	Purchaser-provider split; purchasing agencies contract with providers Production-based payment	Insurers contract selectively with providers	Physicians' association to negotiate annually to establish lump sum for ambulatory care physicians services; monies distributed to physicians based on their workload. Hospital operating costs are derived from sickness funds	A single, government-operated provincial health plan that is the sole payer for hospital and physician care in each of 12 provinces/territories
Provision of Care	Possible reduction of patient choice	Introduction of virtually free patient choice	Possible reduction of patient choice	Reduction of patient choice and services	Possible reduction of services

continues

Table 1–4 continued

Actual Health Care System Reform

Characteristic	United Kingdom	Sweden	The Netherlands	Germany	Canada
Finance Method	Unaffected	No change	90% premiums, income-related, set by government; 10% set by each insurer	No change	Government shifting cost of some Medicare services directly to public (out-of-pocket)
Distribution of Resources to Providers	Reforms carried out intact	Maintained fee for service, but recentralized payments on hospital side	Sickness funds and insurers still separate Insurers contract selectively, only with general practitioners and pharmacists	Fixed budgets calculated for each hospital by Federal Ministry of Health (full-cost cover principle gone) Case fees and procedure fees negotiable at the federal level from 1999 on Limits placed on overall drug costs	Reforms currently restricted to finding innovative ways to constrain medical expenses within the framework of the present system
Provision of Care	Reduced patient choice	Increased patient choice	Reduced patient choice	Reduced patient services	Reduced patient services

Source: Adapted with permission from A. Jacobs, Seeing the Difference, Market Health Reform in Europe, Journal of Health Politics, Policy and Law, Vol. 23, No. 1, pp. 6–7, © 1992, Duke University Press.

hand, the United Kingdom's NHS has been rapidly implementing managed competition reforms while Sweden has implemented somewhat less radical reforms involving both managed competition and the privatization of care. Lastly, while its East–West unification heralded several years of increasingly more draconian cost containment measures, Germany has recently enacted some aspects of managed competition despite strong opposition from physicians (see Table 1–4).

As measured indexes by indices of health care outcomes (see Figure 1–2), Sweden and Canada have attained the best health care quality. Canada, however, has had great difficulty containing its costs during the past decade, partly because of its slow adoption of cost containment measures such as prospective payments to hospitals. Sweden's reforms, which emphasize increased patient choice and limited privatization of physician services, have reduced waiting lists for patient care and enhanced the provision of patient-centered care. Although formulated during an economic upturn, these reforms were implemented during an economic recession; therefore, they increased the cost of ambulatory care. Subsequent cost containment measures have eroded physicians' trust in the health care system.

As it did in Sweden, the adoption of managed competition in the United Kingdom has had some positive effects in reducing waiting lists. Moreover, its innovation of general practitioner fundholders responsible for the continuum of health care for a defined population has helped to integrate providers. Managed competition also has increased the administrative costs of care and strained physician relationships, however, especially among consultants (specialists) employed by the trust hospitals.

Turning back to the United States, President Clinton's proposed government-driven reforms met with increasing political opposition and were put aside in late 1994. Aided by the concern over the rising costs of health care, many regions in the United States rapidly adopted market-driven reforms—predominantly managed care mechanisms for financing and integrated systems or networks for delivering health care. These reforms have the most impact on reducing the demand for health care and improving the effectiveness of medical interventions across the continuum of care. Although the benefits of managed care and the effectiveness of organized delivery systems certainly can be questioned, together they can be credited with containing the aggregate costs of health care in the United States to 13.6 percent of the GDP from 1992 through 1996.[267]

Currently, although several other countries are implementing or considering elements of the U.S. managed care practices, especially utilization review, case management, and prospective payments, and the integration of health care delivery is a concern for all of these countries, the convergence between their systems and the U.S. system is limited. Emphasizing this point, Saltman and Figueras argued that the United States needs to consider both supply-side controls on, and more extensive federal regulation of, health care in order to achieve the same degree of cost containment as has been achieved in European nations.[268]

Lessons for the Future: Canada, Europe, and the United States

As the United States addresses concerns about financial access for its uninsured population while attempting to sustain its market-driven success in containing the costs of health care, three related and shared concerns may be drawn from the review of five other health care systems. These concerns are (1) rationing health care in a socially responsible fashion; (2) enabling provider-driven stewardship of health care resources; and (3) encouraging community, employer, and patient responsibility for healthy lifestyles.

Rationing Health Care in a Socially Responsible Fashion

All nations are facing the problem of rationing health care. Many of the countries examined have focused on providing access to preventive and primary care for all individuals, regardless of their ability to pay for services. In the United States, federal legislators are attempting to deal with the difficulty of balancing access to basic and elective health care services through proposed changes in Medicare and Medicaid. Health care services researchers now realize that providing access to a rudimentary level of health care and supportive services still may produce inequities in health care outcomes, however, even in those countries such as Sweden with low degrees of economic differences.[269]

Moreover, questions are arising about the primary care gatekeeping model for controlling access to care in the United States, the United Kingdom, and the Netherlands, despite its successes in containing costs. Part of the reason for dissatisfaction may be that the rapidly aging populations in these and other countries need care systems oriented toward chronic diseases and the continuum of care. Clearly, the United States and other industrial countries must ensure that their citizens have the appropriate level of care. Hence, policy makers should examine carefully those explicit attempts to ration care, including the Oregon Health Plan in the United States, the policy for establishing basic care in the Netherlands, and the recommendations of the Swedish Priorities Commission to establish guidelines for priority groups, as well as clinical and administrative priorities.[270]

Enabling Provider-Driven Stewardship of Health Care Resources

As managed care continues to dominate the marketplace for health care in the United States, it has brought renewed interest in empowering physicians to be stewards of health care resources. Initiatives in Sweden, the United Kingdom, and the Netherlands directed toward physician participation in management decision making are explicit attempts to change the structure of hospital–physician relationships, as well as to extend physician relationships with rehabilitative and long-term care organizations. These initiatives parallel the call for clinical integration of organized delivery systems in the United States.

European interest in the quality management of health across the continuum of care means that health care professionals other than physicians are being asked to use wisely those health care resources under their control. Within the United States, the growth of integrated, organized systems of health care, along with the adoption of the tenets of continuous quality improvement, heightens the need to empower health care professionals to be good stewards of the limited resources for health care.

Encouraging Community, Employer, and Patient Responsibility for Healthy Lifestyles

The emphasis on preventive and primary care in the five reviewed countries does not mean that they have eliminated the health problems associated with work, social activities, and personal lifestyles. Rather, the successes in the arena of preventive health care have led these countries to focus attention on persistent health problems, the byproducts of modern life, such as sedentary habits, obesity, the abuse of alcohol and other drugs, and the widespread use of tobacco.

While the anomie associated with modern life has been acknowledged by sociologists since the seminal work of Emile Durkheim, current concerns focus on the health-related impact of stress and the social, organizational, and personal mechanisms for alleviating and coping with it.[271] Shortell and others have argued that integrated delivery systems that organize care to a community have the potential to address the social and organizational factors leading to distress and poor health,[272] and managed care has had some successes in shaping healthy lifestyles. Taken together, this mission is a new one, and it is one that public health institutions

and provider organizations in Europe and Canada now are beginning to address.[273] The effectiveness of these approaches, however, needs to be assessed so lessons can be shared across national systems of health care.

Clearly, the U.S. health care system can benefit from looking at the successes and failures within other systems. The insular focus of many of the health care reform discussions now under way misses the opportunity to gain perspective and insight from other health care systems. Certainly, it is hoped that policy makers and all health care stakeholders will begin to take a look around the world in order to improve the financing, organizing, and delivery of health care in the United States.

NOTES

1. S.M. Shortell et al., "The New World of Managed Care: Creating Organized Delivery Systems," *Health Affairs* 13, no. 1 (1994): 46–64.

2. S.M. Shortell et al., *Remaking Health Care in America: Building Organized Delivery Systems* (San Francisco: Jossey-Bass, Publishers, 1996).

3. J.D. Blair et al., *Medical Group Practices Face the Uncertain Future: Challenges, Opportunities and Strategies* (Englewood, CO: Center for Research in Ambulatory Health Care Administration, 1995).

4. D.C. Coddington et al., *Making Integrated Health Care Work* (Englewood, CO: Center for Research in Ambulatory Health Care Administration, 1996).

5. D.A. Rublee and M. Schneider, "International Health Spending Comparisons," *Health Affairs* 10, no. 3 (1991): 187–198.

6. G.J. Scheiber et al., "Health Care Systems in Twenty-Four Countries," *Health Affairs* 10, no. 3 (1991): 22–38.

7. M.D. Smith et al., "Taking the Public's Pulse on Health System Reform," *Health Affairs* 11, no. 2 (1992): 125–133.

8. J.N. Edwards et al., "Small Business and the National Health Care Reform Debate," *Health Affairs* 11, no. 1 (1992): 164–173.

9. M.A. Peterson et al., "Momentum toward Health Care Reform in the U.S. Senate," *Journal of Health Politics, Policy and Law* 17, no. 3 (1992): 553–573.

10. D.V. Himmelstein et al., "The Vanishing Health Care Safety Net: New Data on Uninsured Americans," *International Journal of Health Services* 22, no. 3 (1992): 381–396.

11. I. Hellander et al., "The Growing Epidemic of Uninsurance: New Data on the Health Insurance Coverage of Americans," *International Journal of Health Services* 25, no. 3 (1995): 377–392.

12. Organization for Economic Cooperation and Development, *Health Care Systems in Transition: The Search for Efficiency, Social Policy Studies No. 7* (Paris: OECD, 1990). (Also published as the 1989 Annual Supplement, *Health Care Financing Review*.)

13. K.R. Levit et al., "National Health Spending Trends in 1996," *Health Affairs* 17, no. 1 (1998): 35–51.

14. J.R. Gabel et al., "Small Employers and Their Health Benefits, 1988–1996: An Awkward Adolescence," *Health Affairs* 16, no. 5 (1997): 103–110.

15. D. Chollet, "Employer-Based Health Insurance in a Changing Work Force," *Health Affairs* 13, no. 2 (1994): 315–326.

16. Intergovernmental Health Policy Project, *State Legislative Update* (Washington, DC: The George Washington University, 1996).

17. Medical Group Management Association, *State Health Policy Reference* (Englewood, CO: Medical Group Management Association, 1996).

18. F.J. Hellinger, "The Expanding Scope of State Legislation," *Journal of the American Medical Association* 276, no. 13 (1996): 1065–1070.

19. R. Priester, "A Values Framework for Health System Reform," *Health Affairs* 11, no. 1 (1992): 84–107.

20. M.L. Barer and R.G. Evans, "Interpreting Canada: Models, Mind-Sets, and Myths," *Health Affairs* 11, no. 1 (1992): 44–61.

21. P.M. Danzon, "Hidden Overhead Costs: Is Canada's System Less Expensive?" *Health Affairs* 11, no. 1 (1992): 21–43.

22. C.D. Naylor, "A Different View of Queues in Ontario," *Health Affairs* 10, no. 3 (1991): 110–128.

23. J.F. Sheils et al., "O Canada: Do We Expect Too Much from Its Health System?" *Health Affairs* 11, no. 1 (1992): 7–20.

24. J.W. Hurst, "Reform of Health Care in Germany," *Health Care Financing Review* 12, no. 3 (1991): 73–86.

25. J.W. Hurst, "Reforming Health Care in Seven European Nations," *Health Affairs* 10, no. 3 (1991): 7–21.

26. B. Jönsson, "What Can Americans Learn from Europeans?" in Organization for Economic Cooperation and Development, *Health Care Systems in Transition: The Search for Efficiency, Social Policy Studies No. 7* (Paris: OECD, 1990), 87–101.

27. Schieber et al., "Health Care Systems in Twenty-Four Countries."

28. B. Abel-Smith, "Cost Containment and New Priorities in the European Community," *The Milbank Quarterly* 70, no. 3 (1992): 393–416.

29. B. Starfield, "Primary Care and Health: A Cross-National Comparison," *Journal of the American Medical Association* 266, no. 16 (1991): 2268–2271.

30. Himmelstein et al., "The Vanishing Health Care Safety Net."

31. T.P. Weil, "A Universal Access Plan: A Step toward National Health Insurance?" *Hospital & Health Services Administration* 37, no. 1 (1992): 37–51.

32. Starfield, "Primary Care and Health."

33. Ibid.

34. J. Schieber et al., "Health Spending, Delivery, and Outcomes in OECD Countries," *Health Affairs* 12, no. 2 (1993): 120–129.

35. C.D. Naylor et al., "Canadian Medicare: Prognosis Guarded," *Canadian Medical Association Journal* 153, no. 3 (1995): 285–289.

36. C. Sakala, "The Development of National Medical Care Programs in the United Kingdom and Canada: Applicability to Current Conditions in the United States," *Journal of Health Politics, Policy and Law* 15, no. 4 (1990): 709–753.

37. M. Taylor, *Health Insurance and Canadian Public Policy: The Seven Decisions That Created the Canadian Health Insurance System* (Montreal: McGill–Queen's University Press, 1978).

38. E. Neuschler, *Canadian Health Care: The Implications of Public Health Insurance* (Washington, DC: Health Insurance Association of America, 1990).

39. M.I. Roemer, *National Strategies for Health Care Organization: A World Overview* (Ann Arbor, MI: Health Administration Press, 1985).

40. Sakala, "The Development of National Medical Care Programs."

41. T.J. Litman and L.S. Robins, *Health Politics and Policy* (New York: John Wiley & Sons, 1984).

42. H.E. Scully, "Medicare: The Canadian Experience," *Annals of Thoracic Surgery* 52 (1991): 390–396.

43. D. Coburn, "State Authority, Medical Dominance, and Trends in the Regulation of the Health Professions: The Ontario Case," *Social Science and Medicine* 37, no. 2 (1993): 129–138.

44. Sakala, "The Development of National Medical Care Programs."

45. Litman and Robins, *Health Politics and Policy*.

46. Coburn, "State Authority."

47. Neuschler, *Canadian Health Care*.

48. Sakala, "The Development of National Medical Care Programs."

49. Coburn, "State Authority."

50. M.B. Decter, "Canadian Hospitals in Transformation," *Medical Care* 35, no. 10 (1997): OS70–OS75.

51. Neuschler, *Canadian Health Care*.

52. C. Gray, "Visions of Our Health Care Future: Is a Parallel Private System the Answer?" *Canadian*

Medical Association Journal 154, no. 7 (1996): 1084–1087.

53. C. Carruthers, "Saying Goodbye to Canada's Single-Payer System," *Canadian Medical Association Journal* 152, no. 5 (1995): 731–733.

54. Health and Welfare Canada, *Notes on Hospital Financing in Canada* (Ottawa: Minister of Supply and Services, 1987).

55. J. Shamian and E.Y. Lightstone, "Hospital Restructuring Initiatives in Canada," *Medical Care* 35, no. 10 (1997): OS62–OS69.

56. Ibid.

57. Decter, "Canadian Hospitals in Transformation."

58. Shamian and Lightstone, "Hospital Restructuring Initiatives in Canada."

59. W.J. Mackillop et al., "A Comparison of Delays in the Treatment of Cancer with Radiation in Canada and the United States," *International Journal of Radiation Oncology Biology Physics* 32, no. 2 (1995): 531–539.

60. R. Cairney, "Health Care Reform Comes to Alberta: We're Making This Up As We Go Along," *Canadian Medical Association Journal* 152, no. 11 (1995): 1861–1863.

61. Carruthers, "Saying Goodbye to Canada's Single-Payer System."

62. Decter, "Canadian Hospitals in Transformation."

63. Health and Welfare Canada, *Notes on Hospital Financing in Canada.*

64. Health and Welfare Canada, *Health Personnel in Canada in 1987* (Ottawa: Minister of Supply and Services, 1988).

65. M. Rachlis and C. Kushner, *Second Opinion: What's Wrong with Canada's Health Care System and How To Fix It* (Toronto: HarperCollins, 1989).

66. Decter, "Canadian Hospitals in Transformation."

67. J. David, "Health Care a Major Topic for Canadian Public Policy Journal," *Canadian Medical Association Journal* 148, no. 10 (1993): 1806–1808.

68. T.R. Marmor, "Commentary on Canadian Health Insurance: Lessons for the United States," *International Journal of Health Services* 23, no. 1 (1993): 45–62.

69. Scully, "Medicare: The Canadian Experience."

70. Coburn, "State Authority."

71. J.K. Iglehart, "The United States Looks at Canadian Health Care," *The New England Journal of Medicine* 321, no. 25 (1989): 1767–1772.

72. Health and Welfare Canada, *Notes on Hospital Financing in Canada.*

73. R.W. Sutherland and M.J. Fulton, *Health Care in Canada: A Description and Analysis of Canadian Health Services* (Ottawa: Canadian Public Health Association, 1988).

74. Iglehart, "The United States Looks at Canadian Health Care."

75. M.M. Hagland, "Looking Abroad for Changes to the U.S. Health Care System," *Hospitals* 65, no. 10 (1991): 30–35.

76. Iglehart, "The United States Looks at Canadian Health Care."

77. Scully, "Medicare: The Canadian Experience."

78. Barer and Evans, "Interpreting Canada."

79. Danzon, "Hidden Overhead Costs."

80. Naylor, "A Different View of Queues in Ontario."

81. Sheils et al., "O Canada."

82. J.K. Iglehart, "Canada's Health Care System Faces its Problems," *New England Journal of Medicine* 322, no. 8 (1990): 562–568.

83. Marmor, "Commentary on Canadian Health Insurance."

84. Scully, "Medicare: The Canadian Experience."

85. Rachlis and Kushner, *Second Opinion.*

86. Weil, "A Universal Access Plan."

87. Naylor et al., "Canadian Medicare: Prognosis Guarded."

88. Iglehart, "Canada's Health Care System Faces Its Problems."

89. Marmor, "Commentary on Canadian Health Insurance."

90. Weil, "A Universal Access Plan."

91. Coburn, "State Authority."

92. David, "Health Care a Major Topic for Canadian Public Policy Journal."

93. Neuschler, *Canadian Health Care.*

94. A. Sepehri and R. Chernomas, "Further Refinements of Canadian/U.S. Health Cost Containment Measures," *International Journal of Health Services* 23, no. 1 (1993): 63–67.

95. Sutherland and Fulton, *Health Care in Canada.*

96. D. Swartz, "The Politics of Reform. Public Health Insurance in Canada," *International Journal of Health Services* 23, no. 2 (1993): 219–238.

97. Iglehart, "The United States Looks at Canadian Health Care."

98. Iglehart, "Canada's Health Care System Faces Its Problems."

99. Marmor, "Commentary on Canadian Health Insurance."

100. Neuschler, *Canadian Health Care.*

101. Scully, "Medicare: The Canadian Experience."

102. Iglehart, "Canada's Health Care System Faces Its Problems."

103. Scully, "Medicare: The Canadian Experience."

104. R.M. Hessler and A.C. Twaddle, "Sweden's Crises in Medical Care: Political and Legal Changes," *Journal of Health Politics, Policy and Law* 7, no. 2 (1982): 440–459.

105. A.C. Twaddle and R.M. Hessler, "Power and Change: The Case of the Swedish Commission of Inquiry on Health and Sickness Care," *Journal of Health Politics, Policy and Law* 11, no. 1 (1986): 19–40.

106. J. Calltorp, "Sweden: No Easy Choices," *British Medical Bulletin* 51, no. 4 (1995): 791–798.

107. Roemer, *National Strategies for Health Care Organization.*

108. R.B. Saltman, "Competition and Reform in the Swedish Health System," *Health Care Financing Review* 68, no. 4 (1990): 597–618.

109. Ibid.

110. Calltorp, "Sweden: No Easy Choices."

111. A.J. Heidenheimer and L.N. Johansen, "Organized Medicine and Scandinavian Professional Unionism: Hospital Policies and Exit Options in Denmark and Sweden," *Journal of Health Politics, Policy, and Law* 10, no. 2 (1985): 347–369.

112. P. Garpenby, "Health Care Reform in Sweden in the 1990s: Local Pluralism versus National Coordination," *Journal of Health Politics, Policy and Law* 20, no. 3 (1995): 695–717.

113. Swedish Institute, The Health Care System in Sweden (November 1997): 1–13, http://www.si.se/english/factsheet/health.html; accessed April 1998.

114. Saltman, "Competition and Reform in the Swedish Health System."

115. Twaddle and Hessler, "Power and Change."

116. M. Whitehead et al., "Why Is Sweden Rethinking Its NHS Style Reforms?" *British Medical Journal* 315, no. 7113 (1997): 935–939.

117. R.A. Knox, *Germany: One Nation with Health Care for All* (New York: Faulkner & Gray, 1993), 23–24.

118. W. Carr, *A History of Germany, 1815–1990* (London: Edward Arnold/Hodder & Stoughton, 1991), 136–137.

119. Knox, *Germany,* 27–28.

120. D.A. Stone, *The Limits of Professional Power: National Health Care in the Federal Republic of Germany* (Cambridge, MA: The MIT Press, 1980), 78.

121. Knox, *Germany,* 30.

122. Stone, *The Limits of Professional Power,* 50.

123. S. Leibfried and F. Tennstedt, "Health-Insurance Policy and *Berufsverbote* in the Nazi Takeover," in *Political Values and Health Care: The German Experience,* ed. D.W. Light and A. Schuller (Cambridge, MA: The MIT Press, 1986), 127–138.

124. Knox, *Germany,* 67.

125. Hurst, "Reform of Health Care in Germany," 77–78.

126. Knox, *Germany,* 48.

127. Hurst, "Reform of Health Care in Germany," 74.

128. Ibid., 77.

129. Ibid., 78.

130. Ibid., 77.

131. Knox, *Germany,* 53.

132. Ibid., 263.

133. Hurst, "Reform of Health Care in Germany," 84.

134. Ibid.

135. Ibid.

136. M. Schneider, "Health Care Cost Containment in the Federal Republic of Germany," *Health Care Financing Review* 12, no. 3 (1991): 100.

137. Hurst, "Reform of Health Care in Germany," 84.

138. Ibid.

139. Ibid.

140. Knox, *Germany,* 69.

141. R. Busse and F.W. Schwartz, "Financing Reforms in the German Hospital Sector: From Full Cost Cover Principle to Prospective Case Fees," *Medical Care* 35, no. 10 (1997 Supplement): OS40-OS49.

142. Ibid, OS47.

143. M. Hoopman et al., "Effects of the German 1993 Health Reform Law upon Primary Care Practitioners' Individual Performance: Results from an

Empirical Study in Sentinel Practices," *Journal of Epidemiology and Community Health* 49, Supplement 1 (1995): 33–36.

144. Sakala, "The Development of National Medical Care Programs," 714, 718.

145. Roemer, *National Strategies for Health Care Organization*, 171.

146. Ibid., 171–172.

147. Ibid., 172–173.

148. Sakala, "The Development of National Medical Care Programs," 715, 718, 731.

149. T.A. Madden, "The Reform of the British National Health Services," *Journal of Public Health Policy* 12, no. 3 (1991): 378–396.

150. W. Beveridge, *Social Insurance and Allied Service* [American edition] (New York: Macmillan Co., 1942), 158.

151. Roemer, *National Strategies for Health Care Organization*, 173–174.

152. R. Murley, "A Tale of Turbulent Times," *British Medical Journal* 289, no. 6460 (1984): 1783.

153. Roemer, *National Strategies for Health Care Organization*, 174.

154. Ibid., 174–175.

155. Ibid., 176–178.

156. Ibid., 178.

157. Ibid., 179.

158. Ibid., 188.

159. Ibid., 183–184.

160. Ibid., 187.

161. Ibid., 187–188.

162. Ibid.

163. Ibid., 186.

164. Ibid., 190.

165. J.K. Iglehart, "Conference Report: Health Systems in Three Nations," *Health Affairs* 10, no. 3 (1991): 255.

166. Madden, "The Reform of the British National Health Services," 380.

167. Ibid., 381.

168. Ibid., 379.

169. Hurst, "Reforming Health Care in Seven European Nations."

170. A.C. Enthoven, "Internal Market Reform of the British Health Service," *Health Affairs* 10, no. 3 (1991): 60–70.

171. A.C. Enthoven, "What Can Europeans Learn from Americans?" in Organization for Economic Cooperation and Development, *Health Care Systems in Transition: The Search for Efficiency, Social Policy Studies No. 7* (Paris: OECD, 1990), 57–71.

172. Enthoven, "Internal Market Reform of the British Health Service."

173. P. Day and R. Klein, "Britain's Health Care Experiment," *Health Affairs* 10, no. 3 (1991): 22–38.

174. Enthoven, "What Can Europeans Learn from Americans?"

175. Enthoven, "Internal Market Reform of the British Health Service."

176. B. Kirkman-Liff and E. Schneller, "The Resource Management Initiative in the English National Health System," *Health Care Management Review* 17, no. 2 (1992): 59–70.

177. Ibid.

178. G. de Wildt et al., "Research into Purchasing Health Care: Time To Face the Challenge," *Journal of Epidemiology and Community Health* 50, no. 6 (1996): 611–612.

179. Day and Klein, "Britain's Health Care Experiment."

180. Enthoven, "What Can Europeans Learn from Americans?"

181. Enthoven, "Internal Market Reform of the British Health Service."

182. Kirkman-Liff and Schneller, "The Resource Management Initiative in the English National Health System."

183. N. Lunt et al., "Staying Single in the 1990s: Single-Handed Practitioners in the New National Health Service," *Social Science and Medicine* 45, no. 3 (1997): 341–349.

184. Ibid., 343.

185. M. Drummond et al., "Economic Evaluation under Managed Competition: Evidence from the UK," *Social Science and Medicine* 45, no. 4 (1997): 583–595.

186. Ibid.

187. Ibid.

188. S. Iliffe, "The Modernisation of General Practice in the UK: 1980 to 1995 and Beyond," *Postgraduate Medical Journal* 72 (1996): 201–206.

189. "Health Inequality: The UK's Biggest Issue," *Lancet* 349, no. 9060 (1997): 1185.

190. R. Filinson, "Legislating Community Care: The British Experience, with U.S. Comparisons," *The Gerontologist* 37, no. 3 (1997): 335.

191. A.M. Pollock, "The Future of Health Care in the United Kingdom," *British Medical Journal* 306, no. 6894 (1993): 1703–1704.

192. C. Ham, "How Go the NHS Reforms?" *British Medical Journal* 306, no. 6870 (1993): 78.

193. J. Buchan et al., "Health Sector Reform and Trends in the United Kingdom Hospital Workforce," *Medical Care* 35, no. 10 (1997 Supplement): OS143–OS150.

194. Ibid, OS149.

195. Department of Health, National Health Services, *The New NHS White Paper* (1997) <http://www.official-documents.co.uk/documents/doh/newnhs/wpaper.htm>

196. F.T. Schut, "Workable Competition in Health Care: Prospects for the Dutch Design," *Social Science and Medicine* 35, no. 12 (1992): 1445–1455.

197. J. van der Gaag et al., "The Netherlands," in *Advances in Health Economics and Health Services Research, Supplement 1: Comparative Health Systems* (Greenwich, CT: JAI Press, 1990), 28–41.

198. Schut, "Workable Competition in Health Care," 1450.

199. van der Gaag et al., "The Netherlands," 28, 33.

200. Ibid., 28.

201. Schut, "Workable Competition in Health Care," 1446.

202. E. Van Doorslaer et al., "The Netherlands," in *Equity in the Finance and Delivery of Health Care: An International Perspective,* ed. E. Van Doorslaer et al. (Oxford: Oxford University Press, 1993), 168.

203. van der Gaag et al., "The Netherlands," 28.

204. Van Doorslaer et al., "The Netherlands," 167–168.

205. van der Gaag et al., "The Netherlands," 28–29.

206. Schut, "Workable Competition in Health Care," 1451.

207. Ibid., 1447.

208. van der Gaag et al., "The Netherlands," 29.

209. Schut, "Workable Competition in Health Care," 1447.

210. Ibid., 1446.

211. Hurst, "Reforming Health Care in Seven European Nations," 11.

212. Van Doorslaer et al., "The Netherlands," 168.

213. van der Gaag et al., "The Netherlands," 30.

214. Van Doorslaer et al., "The Netherlands," 170–173.

215. Schut, "Workable Competition in Health Care," 1446.

216. Van Doorslaer et al., "The Netherlands," 169.

217. van der Gaag et al., "The Netherlands," 28–29.

218. R.M. Lapré and A.A. de Roo, "Medical Specialist Manpower Planning in the Netherlands," *Health Policy* 15 (1990): 163–187.

219. Hurst, "Reforming Health Care in Seven European Nations."

220. Jönsson, "What Can Americans Learn from Europeans?"

221. van der Gaag et al., "The Netherlands," 28.

222. Schut, "Workable Competition in Health Care," 1452.

223. Ibid., 1449.

224. Ibid., 1446.

225. van der Gaag et al., "The Netherlands," 37.

226. F.F.H. Rutten, "Market Strategies for Publicly Financed Health Care Systems," *Health Policy* 7 (1987): 135–148.

227. Schut, "Workable Competition in Health Care," 1447.

228. Enthoven, "What Can Europeans Learn from Americans?" 68.

229. A.C. Enthoven, "The 1987 Professor Dr. F. de Vries Lectures," in *Theory and Practice of Managed Competition in Health Care Finance,* ed. A.C. Enthoven (New York: North Holland Publishing Company, 1988).

230. Schut, "Workable Competition in Health Care," 1447–1448.

231. Enthoven, "What Can Europeans Learn from Americans?"

232. Hurst, "Reforming Health Care in Seven European Nations."

233. B. Kirkman-Liff and W. van de Ven, "Improving Efficiency in the Dutch Health Care System: Current Innovations and Future Options," *Health Policy* 13, no. 1 (1989): 35–53.

234. Schut, "Workable Competition in Health Care," 1447–1454.

235. van der Gaag et al., "The Netherlands," 37–39.

236. R.H.J. ter Meulen, "Limiting Solidarity in the Netherlands: A Two-Tier System on the Way," *Journal of Medicine and Philosophy* 20 (1995): 607–616.

237. A. Jacobs, "Seeing Difference: Market Health Reform in Europe," *Journal of Health Politics, Policy and Law* 23, no. 1 (1998): 2–33.

238. Ibid.

239. Ibid.

240. G.J. Van der Wilt, "Towards a Two Tier Health System in the Netherlands: How To Put Theory into Practice," *Journal of Medicine and Philosophy* 20 (1995): 617–630.

241. G.F. Anderson, "In Search of Value," *Health Affairs* 16, no. 2 (1997): 164, 170.

242. E. Elsinga and F.F.H. Rutten, "Economic Evaluation in Support of National Health Policy: The Case of the Netherlands," *Social Science and Medicine* 45, no. 4 (1997): 605–620.

243. I.M.B. Bongers et al., "Socio-Economic Differences in General Practitioner and Outpatient Specialist Care in the Netherlands: A Matter of Health Insurance?" *Social Science and Medicine* 44, no. 8 (1997): 1161–1168.

244. Schut, "Workable Competition in Health Care," 1449.

245. ter Meulen, "Limiting Solidarity in the Netherlands," 608.

246. Schut, "Workable Competition in Health Care," 1453.

247. H. Maarse et al., "The Reform of Hospital Care in the Netherlands," *Medical Care* 35, no. 10 (1997 Supplement): OS26–OS39.

248. Schut, "Workable Competition in Health Care," 1451.

249. P. Dwyer and P. Oster, "We'll Need Hillary Clinton in Holland," *Business Week,* 8 November 1993, 72–73.

250. R.J. Blendon et al., "Reform Lessons Learned from Physicians in Three Nations," *Health Affairs* 12, no. 3 (1993): 194–203.

251. G.T. Savage et al., "An Exploratory Study of Hospital Manager–Physician–Nurse Relationships in the United Kingdom and the Netherlands," in *Proceedings of the Southern Management Association,* ed. M. Schnake (Valdosta, GA: Southern Management Association, 1993), 500–502.

252. U.E. Reinhardt, "Reorganizing the Financial Flows in U.S. Health Care," *Health Affairs* 12 (Supplement 1993): 172–193.

253. Jönsson, "What Can Americans Learn from Europeans?"

254. "Managed Competition: Health Reform American Style?" *Health Affairs* 12 (Supplement 1993): 7–228.

255. S.H. Altman and A.B. Cohen, "The Need for a National Global Budget," *Health Affairs* 12 (Supplement 1993): 194–203.

256. Hurst, "Reforming Health Care in Seven European Nations."

257. Ibid.

258. Enthoven, "Internal Market Reform of the British Health Service."

259. R.G. Evans and M.L. Barer, "Response: The American Predicament," in Organization for Economic Cooperation and Development, *Health Care Systems in Transition: The Search for Efficiency, Social Policy Studies No. 7* (Paris: OECD, 1990), 80–85.

260. Jönsson, "What Can Americans Learn from Europeans?"

261. Day and Klein, "Britain's Health Care Experiment."

262. A. I. Kabcenell et al., "Importing a Model of Hospital Quality from The Netherlands," *Health Affairs* 10, no. 3 (1991): 240–245.

263. Kirkman-Liff and Schneller, "The Resource Management Initiative in the English National Health System."

264. R.B. Saltman and J. Figueras, "Analyzing the Evidence on European Health Care Reforms," *Health Affairs* 17, no. 2 (1998): 85–108.

265. C. Ham, "Health Care Reform," *British Medical Journal* 306, no. 6887 (1993): 122–124.

266. U.E. Reinhardt, "Response: What Can Americans Learn from Europeans?" in Organization for Economic Cooperation and Development, *Health Care Systems in Transition: The Search for Efficiency, Social Policy Studies No. 7* (Paris: OECD, 1990), 105–112.

267. Levit et al., "National Health Spending Trends in 1996."

268. Saltman and Figueras, "Analyzing the Evidence."

269. J.P. Makenbach et al., "Socioeconomic Inequali-

ties in Morbidity and Mortality in Western Europe," *Lancet* 349 (1997): 1655–1659.

270. M. McKee and J. Figueras, "Setting Priorities: Can Britain Learn from Sweden?" *British Medical Journal* 312, no. 7032 (1996): 691–694.

271. J. Siegrist, "Reciprocity in Basic Social Exchange and Health: Can We Reconcile Person-Based with Population-Based Psychosomatic Research?" *Journal of Psychosomatic Research* 20, no. 10 (1998): In press.

272. Shortell et al., *Remaking Health Care in America*.

273. Saltman and Figueras, "Analyzing the Evidence."

GRANT T. SAVAGE, PhD, is Associate Professor of Management (College of Business Administration) and Associate Professor of Health Organization Management (School of Medicine) at Texas Tech University. In addition to serving as the director of the master's and doctoral programs in Health Organization Management, Professor Savage is the Associate Chair of the Health Organization Management Department in the School of Medicine and the lead faculty member in the College of Business Administration's MD/MBA joint degree program with the School of Medicine at the Texas Tech Medical Center. Professor Savage co-directs the Strategic Leadership Institute, a joint venture of the Center for Healthcare Strategy with the American College of Medical Practice Executives. With his colleagues John Blair and Myron Fottler, Grant is a co-editor of *Advances in Health Care Management*, an annual research volume published by JAI Press. He has published widely in the fields of communication, management, and health care management. Professor Savage's PhD and master's degree are from Ohio State University.

MARK L. HOELSCHER, MBA, is a doctoral student in management at Texas Tech University. He teaches business ethics and stakeholder management. Before taking his present position, he spent 20 years in management in the environmental/governmental field. Ground water quality protection, particularly in rural areas, has been one of his major concerns. His research interests include business ethics and stewardship theory, especially as they relate to health care reforms.

ELIZABETH W. WALKER, RN, MBA, is a registered nurse with certification in cardiac care, oncology/chemotherapy, and psychiatric nursing. She is a doctoral candidate in the College of Business Administration at Texas Tech University, concentrating in health organization management and business ethics. She has taught courses in management, business ethics, labor relations, and administrative policy. She has also participated in team teaching of biomedical ethics at the Texas Tech School of Medicine. Her writing and research interests include conflict management, international and domestic health care reform, total quality management, ethics, and organizational change and relationships. She received her MBA with a concentration in Health Organization Management from Texas Tech University.

Chapter 2

Multiprovider Systems

Myron D. Fottler and Donna Malvey

No health care system in the world has undergone as much structural change as has that of the United States over the past three decades. It has been suggested that the extent and the swiftness of structural change in U.S. hospitals are unprecedented in postindustrial society.[1] Some have characterized this change as fundamental and perhaps revolutionary. Nowhere is this more evident than in the transition to organized health care delivery systems. The previous cottage industry of individual, freestanding hospitals has become a complex web of systems, alliances, and networks. In large part, expectations of how managed care will reshape the industry and how organizations will ultimately respond have influenced many of the recent changes.[2,3]

The development of hospital systems in the United States initially encompassed the horizontal integration of facilities and resulted in the creation of multihospital systems that provided similar acute care services in multiple locations. Later, system capability expanded through vertical integration and diversification into activities that may or may not be related to a hospital's inpatient acute care business. More recently, expansion has reflected "virtual" integration that involves relationships based on contracts.[4] This system development reflects the transformation of multiprovider systems from providers of acute care to providers that are capable of addressing a continuum of health care needs.

Given this evolution and varied arrangements and structures, multihospital systems have been redefined as organized or integrated health care delivery systems.

Until recently, any discussion of systems focused prominently on comparing the functions and performance of organized health care delivery systems with those of independent freestanding institutions. However, systems have become dominant in health care, with more than 50 percent of hospitals belonging to systems and the remainder involved in some type of collaborative relationship.[5] Thus, the following questions and issues should be addressed:

- How and why have multihospital health care systems evolved and changed over time, and how are they expected to change in the future?
- How does the performance of not-for-profit systems compare to the performance of investor-owned systems?

- What factors are expected to contribute to profitability and success? Do functions such as governance, human resources, and information systems make a difference in performance?
- What has been the impact of horizontal, vertical, and virtual integration?
- Why are not-for-profit systems entering into partnerships with investor-owned chains?
- What managerial recommendations concerning systems can be made?

HEALTH CARE SYSTEM DEVELOPMENT

A variety of environmental forces have shaped the delivery of health care services and brought about variations in the development of hospital systems. Preeminent among these forces has been the shift in the industry from an emphasis on providing hospital services to an emphasis on furnishing health care services. An aging population, the increasing demand for chronic care, and new technologies that support alternative delivery systems have focused attention on a broader spectrum of health care services.[6,7] Subsequent to this shift has been the recognition that the market for health care services is local rather than national in nature.[8,9] Indeed, industry performance has indicated that patients tend to feel allegiance to local hospitals and not to national hospital chains.[10] Thus, consumer choice at the local and regional level has emerged as a powerful influence in the delivery of health care services.

The expansion of system capacity through horizontal integration has been declining, and this decline has been attributed primarily to economic forces. Specifically, rising health care costs, the shift to a risk-based payment system such as the prospective payment system (PPS), and other cost containment efforts

and regulations have negatively influenced the horizontal growth of hospital systems. Moreover, these forces have precipitated a trend toward economic concentration, consolidation, and vertical integration.[11]

Although the economic concentration of hospitals is not a new trend and has its origins in the 1970s with the growth of investor-owned hospital systems, the shift toward a local and regional orientation is radically different. Risk-based payment has compelled systems to consolidate, downsize, and divest because a large inventory of hospitals is no longer profitable.[12] Furthermore, government policies that in the past essentially subsidized hospital acquisitions through reimbursement of much of the acquisition cost now discourage horizontal integration by limiting reimbursement of capital expenditures for investments in facilities.[13] While there has been concern that industry trends seem to be influenced unduly by financial gain, there is some optimism that emphasis on vertically integrated regional strategies will refocus attention on patients and quality of care issues.[14] Conspicuously absent has been the goal of improving the quality or access to health care services for local community residents. Yet this will be a primary focus of the U.S. health care system over the next decade. Systems may need to realign their goals to this underlying reality.

A diversity of arrangements represents the configuration of U.S. hospitals, including alliances, joint ventures, federations, consortiums, networks, and systems. All of these arrangements involve partnerships and shared activities. It is expected, however, that systems will continue to predominate and ultimately will represent 80 percent of all U.S. hospitals.[15]

Shortell has argued that most systems have formed as a defense against an increasingly uncertain, complex, and hostile environment.[16] The primary motivations have been to maintain or gain market share by becoming more competitive, to increase access to needed capital, to gain exposure to new ideas, and to further career development opportunities for system personnel. The primary force behind industry consolidation has been the search for economies of scale and economic gain.

To understand the evolution of health care systems fully, it is necessary to examine both the external and the internal environments of hospitals (Exhibit 2–1). In the mid-1960s the number of systems began to increase dramatically in all ownership categories.[17] By 1980, the number had grown phenomenally to a total of 267 systems, containing 30.7 percent of all nonfederal community hospitals and 35 percent of their beds. The success and rapid expansion of horizontally integrated multihospital systems originated in a cost-based payment system and a price-insensitive environment that encouraged and rewarded system growth. Medicare reimbursement essentially provided coverage of costs and a reasonable return on investments. Consequently, systems could purchase high-cost, inefficient hospitals in diverse locations with little risk of failure.[18,19] In addition, investor-owned systems gained access to capital markets by their ability to issue stock and used this financial resource to underwrite their acquisitions.[20]

Although both investor-owned and not-for-profit systems pursued horizontal integration, their levels of economic concentration were distinct. Not-for-profit systems accumulated fewer hospitals per system and were less geographically dispersed, while their investor-owned counterparts tended to be larger, more geographically dispersed, and dominated by a few large systems.[21]

After the advent of prospective payment in the mid-1980s, organizations began to re-structure, vertical integration increased, and diversification efforts focused on developing a continuum of care at the local or regional level. The failure of health care reform at the national level and the growing impact of managed care have characterized the decade of the 1990s. As competition has accelerated, organizations have responded by documenting the cost and quality of the care that they provide and by creating both owned and virtually integrated delivery systems.

Just as the health care system has evolved through stages as outlined in Exhibit 2–1, multiprovider systems have evolved through stages.[22] In the first stage, patient/outpatient care is the "core business," and two or more hospitals affiliate, consolidate services, or merge within a given market typically to achieve economies of scale (i.e., horizontal integration). In the second stage, the core hospital activities branch off into both forward vertical integration activities, such as physician group practices, and backward vertical integration activities, such as ownership of pharmacies and medical equipment companies. In this stage, there is relatively little coordination of activities across the system. The first two stages occurred from the 1970s to the mid-1980s.

The third stage involves efforts to coordinate and optimize physician primary care networks, satellite clinics, home health care agencies, and components of the continuum of care. However, the core business remains acute inpatient care, and the other activities generally feed or support the acute care business. The fourth stage represents a radical departure in that disease prevention and/or health promotion replaces acute inpatient care as the core business for primary care. The goal of the system is to accept the risk for the health status of populations served, with incentives to keep the population well. Shortell, Gillies, and Devers believed most

Exhibit 2–1 Environmental Factors Affecting Health Care Industry and Resulting Strategic Responses of Hospitals by Time Period

External Economic, Political, and Social Environment	*Internal Environment of Health Care Organizations*	*Resulting Strategic Responses*
Pre-1965 (Charitable/Technological Era)		
• Favorable reimbursement • Lack of competition • Plentiful philanthropic support • Favorable political environment • Minimal government regulation • Public support • Increasing physician and personnel specialization	• Rapid growth • Expanding technology • Rising costs • Treatment of medical disease	• Expansion/growth of autonomous, freestanding hospitals • Emphasis on community welfare
1965–1983 (Fee-for-Service/Cost-Based Reimbursement)		
• Substantial increase in the number of physicians • Increased competition • Decline in philanthropic support • Less favorable political environment • Government reimbursement through Medicare and Medicaid	• Slowing of individual growth • Duplication of technology • Outdated facilities • Increase in debt financing • Decline of political influence • Excess capacity • Increased rate of rising costs	• Horizontal integration • Consolidation of autonomous hospital systems • Growth of systems for the sake of growth • Debt financing of acquisitions • Diversification
1984–1993 (Prospective Payment)		
• Continuous hostile political environment • Less favorable reimbursement environment • Increased business and consumer concern with health care costs • Increased price competition • Aging population	• Lower profits • Downsizing • Job redesign • Excess capacity • Shift from inpatient to outpatient care • Decentralized decision making • Growth of professional management	• Greater differentiation of system strategies • Organizational restructuring • Vertical integration • Local and regional system orientation • Divestiture of unwanted facilities • Development of continuum of care at regional/local level

continues

Exhibit 2–1 continued

Post-1993 (Health Care Reform and Managed Care Initiatives)

- Increased competition
- Increased domination by managed care organizations and other purchasers
- Failed federal health care reform
- Increase in federal and state mandates
- Incremental attempts at political reform
- Conflicts of managed care organizations, with patients and providers

- Reengineering
- Downsizing
- Continued quality improvement
- Continued shift to outpatient care

- Continued organization restructuring
- Creation of both owned and virtual organized delivery systems
- Competition based on documented cost and quality

systems were in stages 2 or 3 in 1995.[23] This situation continues to apply in 1998.

SYSTEM MEMBERSHIP

Tables 2–1 and 2–2 provide descriptive information on systems in 1992 and 1997. The number of systems increased approximately 19 percent, from 250 in 1985 to 309 in 1992. The number of systems then declined to 280 between 1992 and 1997, however, as consolidation affected the industry. During 1992, there were 2,873 hospitals affiliated with systems. In 1997, this trend continued, as the number of system hospitals increased to 2,909.

Table 2–1 identifies the number of systems by type of organizational control. Not-for-profit systems continue to predominate in terms of numbers. Approximately 80 percent

Table 2–1 Multihospital Health Care Systems in 1992 and 1997, by Type of Organizational Control

	Number and Percent of Systems	
Type of Control	*1992*	*1997*
Catholic (Roman) church-related	71 (23.0)	55 (19.6)
Other church related	15 (4.9)	13 (4.7)
Other not-for-profit	163 (52.7)	163 (58.2)
Investor-owned	55 (17.8)	44 (15.7)
Federal government	5 (1.6)	5 (1.8)
Total	309 (100.0)	280 (100.0)

Source: Adapted with permission from *1992 AHA Guide*, Healthcare InfoSource, Inc., A Subsidiary of the American Hospital Association, © 1992; and *1996/97 AHA Guide*, Healthcare InfoSource, Inc., A Subsidiary of the American Hospital Association, © 1997.

of systems were not-for-profit (249 of 309) in 1992, while 18 percent were investor-owned and 2 percent were government-affiliated. Approximately 28 percent were church-related, and 53 percent were other not-for-profit. By 1997, the church-related and investor-owned systems had declined to 24 percent and 16 percent, respectively.

Table 2–2 provides a breakdown of the number of systems that own, lease, sponsor, or contract-manage hospitals/other providers for both 1992 and 1997. Only about 20 percent of systems owned, leased, sponsored *and* contract-managed (62 of 309) health care facilities in 1992. The other 80 percent owned, leased, or sponsored (77 percent) facilities, *or* they only contract-managed (3 percent) facilities. By 1997, there was little change in these percentages. In addition, there were no significant differences based on type of ownership.

Because the vertical integration of organized delivery systems is a relatively recent phenomenon, there is little descriptive evidence available on the extent to which systems have vertically integrated. However, there appears to be a trend toward less vertical integration and more virtual integrative initiatives involving networks of contracts.[24]

There is also little descriptive evidence related to other diversification activities of system hospitals.

Table 2–3 indicates the number of hospitals and hospital beds in multiprovider systems in 1997. Church-related systems accounted for 20 percent of system hospitals and 24 percent of hospital beds, indicating that they were above average in bed size. Other not-for-profit systems accounted for 30 percent of system hospitals and 35 percent of hospital beds. Investor-owned systems accounted for 40 percent of system hospitals and 27 percent of hospital beds, indicating that they were associated with smaller facilities. Finally, the federal government accounted for 10 percent of system hospitals and 13 percent of hospital beds.

With more than 50 percent of hospitals belonging to systems (defined as a common corporate ownership) and most of the remaining hospitals being members of alliances of one form or another, the question of the advantages and disadvantages of independent, freestanding hospitals is no longer relevant.[25] The "market" has spoken and it seems to be saying that independent, freestanding institutions are not competitive with systems (either owned or "virtual"). This appears to be at

---

Table 2–2 Multihospital Health Care Systems in 1992 and 1997

	1992		1997	
	Number	*Percent*	*Number*	*Percent*
Systems that own, lease, or sponsor	238	77.0	225	80.3
Systems that only contract-manage	9	2.9	3	1.1
Systems that own, lease, sponsor, and contract-manage	62	20.1	52	18.6
TOTAL	309	100.0	280	100.0

Source: Data from *1992 AHA Guide*, p. B3, © 1992, American Hospital Association; and *1996/97 AHA Guide*, p. B62, © 1997, American Hospital Association.

Table 2–3 Hospitals and Beds in Multiprovider Systems in 1997 by Type of Ownership and Control

Type of Ownership and Control	Hospitals		Beds	
	Number	Percent	Number	Percent
Catholic church–related	516	17.2	113,327	20.8
Other church-related	93	3.1	19,514	3.6
Other not-for-profit	905	30.2	189,276	34.8
Investor-owned	1,188	39.6	148,429	27.3
Federal government	295	9.8	73,042	13.4
TOTAL	2,997	100.0	543,588	100.0

Source: Reprinted with permission from *1996/97 AHA Guide*, Healthcare InfoSource, Inc., A Subsidiary of the American Hospital Association, © 1997.

odds with the existing literature, which provides little evidence on the relative performance of the different arrangements, whether it is a system-affiliated or independent facility, or what type of system it is (e.g., those organized by hospitals, insurance corporations, or physician groups). Furthermore, a recent study of Florida hospitals by Tennyson and Fottler indicates that system hospitals have no advantage over freestanding hospitals in terms of their financial returns.[26] Other evidence seems to suggest that hospitals join systems primarily to improve their market position relative to their rivals' position in the local markets.[27]

Multiprovider systems of the 1980s, which emphasized administrative economies of scale and engaged in a variety of diversification activities, seemed to add value on almost any dimension of performance.[28] They tended to represent loose collections of hospitals that engaged in relatively unrelated diversification of services. They lacked "systemness" in that they did not behave as a system in which each operating unit understood its strategic role relative to other units of the system. Possibly, environmental and

market pressures were not severe enough to require more integrative behavior at the time.

In most parts of the United States, the pressure for integration has increased with the increased pressure of managed care, the growth of capitated payment, added competition, and state and national health care reform initiatives. As a result, many systems have come to the realization that a system is an integrated, clinical continuum of care for a defined population with an ability to provide cost, quality, and outcome data for purposes of accountability. Understanding what a system is and being able to implement that understanding are two different things, however.

In 1996, the average system operated 11.8 hospitals, earned operating income of $50.8 million on total net patient revenues of $687.4 million (an operating profit margin of 4 percent), and reported total assets of $948.8 billion.[29] These figures had all increased significantly over previous years. For-profit systems were nearly nine times the size of not-for-profit systems, operating an average of 64 hospitals with $3.8 billion in assets, compared to the not-for-profit systems' 715 hospitals and $819.6 million in assets.

Strong growth also occurred in systems' nonhospital operations. A total of 114 systems reported owning group practices with a total of 12,406 employed physicians in 1996, a 27 percent growth from 1995.[30] The goal of most systems is to provide a broad range of "cradle to grave care and services," including preventive care, rehabilitation, prenatal and elder care, and a full array of health insurance products. Systems hope to build a freestanding, financially viable, self-supporting health care delivery network in each region where they compete.

There were three major differences found between the for-profit and the not-for-profit public sector systems.[31] First, for-profit systems were allocating a greater share of their operating budgets to management information systems (6 percent compared to 4 percent in the not-for-profit sector). Second, for-profit systems were financing their expansions with considerably more debt. The ratio of long-term debt to total assets averaged 46 percent for the for-profit systems, compared to 32 percent in the not-for-profit system. As long as the return on investment is greater than the interest on the debt, borrowing increases shareholder value in for-profit systems. Third, as a percentage of net patient revenues, the charity care provided by the not-for-profit hospitals was greater (3 percent) than that of for-profit systems (1.1 percent).

A rapidly changing environment and the legacy of the diagnosis-related group (DRG) system and other risk-based payment methods motivated both hospitals and physicians away from joint ventures and toward the development of fully integrated vertical networks representing comprehensive health care systems in the late 1980s. In the early 1980s, hospitals and physicians had formed joint ventures that typically allowed for medical care and services to be provided outside the hospital's facility as well as outside the traditional medical staff structure. Although many of these joint ventures succeeded, there were also many notable failures.

In the 1990s, few joint ventures have been formed because they have become especially risky and expensive, and they create regulatory and legal problems for providers.[32] In addition, many providers now consider joint ventures transitional organizational arrangements or intermediate steps in the integrative process. Constraints from changes in reimbursement policies and cost controls have intensified pressure on hospitals to gain vertical control and influence over physician practice patterns.[33] Meanwhile, physicians' declining incomes and access to capital have precluded their aggressive pursuit of physician joint ventures.[34] Such ventures are also on the wane because the economic motivations of physicians are increasingly diverging from one another; changes in reimbursement policies are affecting different specialists differently.[35]

THE IMPACT OF MANAGED CARE

The advent of managed care appears to be driving providers more and more toward integration. Health care executives who had previously been marginally aware of market share have entered into a variety of organizational arrangements that promise continued growth and survival in highly competitive managed care markets. They have instituted integrative strategies aimed at improving the market and organizational powers of their system relative to those of its competitors. Montague Brown, a leading health care industry expert, has explained that being positioned for survival in a managed care market may represent the crown jewel of purpose of major national alliances. Furthermore, he predicted that regional multiprovider systems are the best positioned organizations to become providers of choice for managed care or other types of direct contracting arrangements.[36] Evidence from health care studies confirms that hospitals are joining local systems primarily as a competitive response.[37]

In large part, much of the impact of managed care results from expectations about how managed care will reshape the health care industry and how organizations will respond to these changes. For example, it has been reported that in markets dominated by managed care systems, providers are pursuing complete vertical integration more rapidly than in other markets, because they believe it will help them compete effectively—even though there is no compelling evidence that vertical integration provides a competitive advantage.[38] Similarly, academic medical centers increasingly are entering into strategic alliances and other collaborative relationships because they anticipate that integration will make them more competitive in a managed care environment and will assist them in preserving the educational and research missions of their institutions.[39] Boston's Massachusetts General Hospital and Brigham Women's Hospital, two leading academic medical centers and fierce competitors, merged with the expectation that the resulting partnership would enable them to be more competitive on cost and quality in managed care markets. A merger typically creates possibilities for efficiencies by making it possible to consolidate hospital services such as finance and human resources, as well as to downsize clinical staffs.[40]

Managed care organizations have continued to revise the mechanisms by which they actually manage costs. They initially relied on price discounts to achieve savings. Because price discounts did not completely control costs, managed care organizations then moved to include utilization management. Ultimately, they have come to depend on capitated payment methods to achieve substantial efficiencies.[41] As a result, systems have come to expect managed care organizations to select providers who promised the most efficient and cost-effective delivery of a comprehensive range of services. Thus, competing in managed care markets called for these multiprovider organizations to gain control over such things as physician practice patterns and resource utilization, because these elements play an essential role in determining cost.[42,43]

Effect on Physicians and Hospitals

Managed care has eroded the patient care market for both physicians and hospitals. In addition, managed care represents an intervention in day-to-day medical treatment that physicians view as threatening to their autonomy and incomes.[44] Many independent practitioners are approaching hospitals and medical centers, asking to be acquired or given employment contracts, because they recognize that the health services market is becoming increasingly oriented toward managed care.[45] Physicians believe that hospital ownership of medical practices is preferable to managed care because this arrangement can be organized under structures that allow the physician to retain some control over medical practice.[46] In many circumstances, managed care is driving physicians and hospitals to integrate fully into single structures such as physician–hospital organizations or foundations that can gain leverage in negotiating managed care contracts or can contract directly with employers to provide medical services.

Managed care also is influencing systems to acquire and/or manage group practices. Previously, physicians actively sought integration with hospitals, although most hospitals, with the exception of larger hospitals, did not aggressively attempt to acquire group practices. When hospitals did enter into formal affiliation arrangements with physician group practices, it typically was through an employment arrangement rather than a contractual one.[47]

Although many hospitals and physicians are looking for more permanent and enduring vertically integrated structures to accommodate their relationships, needs, and joint activities, others are looking for less permanent and more flexible relationships in the form of virtual integration. In California, for example, where unmanaged indemnity insurance no longer exists, organizational change is proceeding at an accelerated rate. In this context, complex ownership and contractual relationships with hospitals and outside specialists make up the core of an emerging health care delivery system based on capitated care.[48]

Effect on Systems

Many hospital systems have been accelerating the development of delivery systems that are capable of providing health care services to a large number of people on a capitated basis. They have purchased medical clinics, other hospitals, and even prepaid managed care organizations. Some systems are aligning themselves with insurers in order to expand their markets. However, many systems have little experience in capitated contract arrangements.[49] In addition, investor-owned systems are seeking alliances with not-for-profit systems in order to respond to the trend toward managed care.

A 1995 *Modern Healthcare* survey revealed that greater numbers of investor-owned chains were buying tax-exempt hospitals. Merging institutions of different ownership types is not common, but it has the advantage of increasing patient volume and

providing leverage that enhances negotiation for managed care contracts.[50] Also investor-owned systems have found that they lack many of the costly services and departments, such as obstetrics and emergency departments, that are needed to make them full-service organizations that can compete for managed care contracts. Thus, they hope to acquire these costly services through affiliation with not-for-profit systems.

Although not-for-profit systems have not shown much enthusiasm for forming alliances with investor-owned systems, this attitude appears to be shifting. In the past, the thinking was that the image of investor-owned systems as high-cost providers could negatively affect affiliated not-for-profit systems in their efforts to obtain managed care contracts or in their negotiations with third-party payers. Even though the gap in charges for services rendered is narrowing between not-for-profit and investor-owned systems, it appears that consumers, employers, and insurers continue to perceive investor-owned systems as high-cost providers.[51] Not-for-profit systems, however, can expect significant advantages in aligning with investor-owned chains. For example, in 1996, the not-for-profit San Diego, California–based Sharp Health Care negotiated a 50/50 joint venture with Columbia/HCA. Although four of Sharp's six hospitals will assume for-profit status, the parent entity will retain its not-for-profit status. The anticipated benefits for Sharp include access to financial assistance and financial markets, as well as added management capabilities for controlling utilization and physician costs.

Managed care has had a tremendous impact on health care in the United States. It has introduced incentives that call for patients to receive the appropriate type and amount of health care service, which generally will involve settings outside the hospital.[52] Health care executives must adopt a different perspective or viewpoint of the health care delivery system. They must shift their thinking and outlook toward organizing a delivery system around other facilities, such as outpatient offices, sub- and postacute care facilities, patient homes, and home health care.[53] Thus, managed care creates incentives for hospitals to look outside their walls for the most cost-effective means of providing health care services. Systems that can provide comprehensive services and can demonstrate high quality and cost-effectiveness will be "winners" in the emerging health care environment. Systems or individual providers that are unable or unwilling to move in this direction may well be among the "losers" over the next decade.[54]

As noted in Exhibit 2–1, stage 1 (pre-1965) predated the development of systems. Stage 2 (1965–1983) was a period of development and unbridled expansion of systems. Hospitals began to integrate horizontally by consolidating into organized health care delivery systems. Stage 3 (1984–1993) began with the implementation of prospective payment, declining system profits, downsizing, and restructuring. Prospective payment essentially reshaped the health care landscape by introducing price competition to the health care equation. It transformed hospital reimbursement for services, thereby altering financial incentives. Stage 4 (post-1993) heralds a period of reconfiguration, rebuilding, and redesign of systems. During this time, health care reform and managed care initiatives have become the driving forces behind broad and sweeping changes in the health care industry. Chaos and creativity are the norms, as traditional boundaries disappear and competition gives way to collaboration. The focus is now on the provision of comprehensive health care services at the regional and local levels.

SYSTEM INTEGRATION

As systems have developed, they have evolved from horizontal, to vertical, to "virtual" integration. Integration is horizontal when hospitals buy other hospitals to become multihospital systems. Integration is vertical when hospitals (or other institutions) purchase or sign contracts with other health care organizations that are "upstream" or "downstream" from the original institution. For example, a hospital may purchase physician group practices to increase referrals to their inpatient services. Finally, "virtual" integration refers to horizontally or vertically integrated systems that are based primarily on a series of contracts rather than common ownership.

Horizontal Integration

Most systems during the 1980s could be characterized as horizontally integrated. Such systems were expected to offer hospitals several advantages:

- increased access to capital markets
- reduction in duplication of services
- economies of scale
- improved productivity and operating efficiencies
- access to management expertise
- increased personnel benefits, including career mobility, recruitment, and retention
- improved patient access through geographical integration of various levels of care
- improvement in quality through increased volume of services for specialized personnel
- increased political power to deal with planning, regulation, and reimbursement issues

The pursuit of horizontal integration by hospitals has been attributed in part to hospitals' attempts to deal with an increasingly complex and often hostile environment that created intense financial pressures and risks that threatened institutional survival.[55] System affiliation offered hospitals opportunities to reduce or diversify certain facility-specific risks. Hospitals could gain management expertise, access to capital, and improve their overall performance.

As it turns out, the only advantage that system hospitals have demonstrated is an increase in labor productivity through more efficient use of personnel; investor-owned systems appear to maximize labor productivity more than not-for-profit systems. Because cost-based reimbursement offered few incentives to systems to operate efficiently, there were no rewards for reducing costs.[56–58] Instead, systems found that they were able to enhance their performance by "using size and scale to drive certain economies or to respond to certain opportunities such as competitive contracting."[59] Many of the proposed benefits of economies of scale in systems may actually be limited, as certain diseconomies of scale have been associated with extremely high corporate overhead expenditures.[60–62]

According to health care analysts, hospital systems generally have failed to integrate fully and have been unable to perform as systems rather than as collections of facilities.[63] Horizontal integration represents only the integration of hospital administrative services, however. In order for a system to be fully and functionally integrated, clinical services must be vertically integrated within the system.[64] Thus, horizontal and vertical integration may both be necessary for systems truly to behave as systems.

The absence of shared or common institutional interests may contribute to systems' inability to integrate completely. Although not-for-profit systems have been more likely to select members based on commonality of missions, investor-owned systems have tended to be more sensitive to existing market conditions, the local economy, and payer mix.[65,66] Furthermore, many hospitals have formed or joined systems to obtain access to expertise on regulatory matters and to enjoy advantages in the political environment. Affiliated hospitals can establish a political presence through name recognition, a coordinated message, and the financial ability to retain political advisors.[67,68]

However, systems affiliation cannot be expected to reduce risks related to general economic conditions or the overall health care industry.[69] System hospitals have not demonstrated any advantage over nonsystem hospitals in terms of their ability to respond to changes in the health care industry, such as the PPS.[70] Combined with rapidly rising costs and increasing price sensitivity by consumers, employers, and insurers, the PPS has provided the impetus for diversification. By shifting to the hospital the financial consequences of the medical care provided in the institution, the PPS has created a powerful incentive for systems to control costs and to establish interdependencies among hospitals, physicians, and a variety of other service providers and payers.[71] Because system hospital costs tended to be higher than those of nonsystem hospitals under cost-based reimbursement, systems have experienced intense financial pressures under the PPS to reduce costs if they were to remain competitive. Investor-owned systems have been especially challenged, because their costs were typically higher pre-PPS than those of either not-for-profit systems or freestanding hospitals.[72]

Most analyses provide little support for the cost-reducing promises of horizontal integration. After comparing the 1988 performance of independent and system hospitals in California, Dranove and Shanley found that systems are no more able to exploit economies of scale than are independent hospitals.[73] They found that the benefits of horizontally integrated hospital systems are more in their ability to market themselves than in the economies they achieve. Another analysis of the short-run performance of 92 hospital mergers in the 1980s did not show dramatic improvements in operating efficiencies.[74] Moreover, merged hospital facilities have raised prices at increased rates, especially in smaller cities with less competition,[75] because nobody is in a position to step forward to stop them.

Horizontal integration strategies dominated system development during the late 1960s, continued through the mid-1980s, and have diminished in significance with the implementation of PPS and the cost reduction programs of other payers. There are likely to be fewer systems purchasing hospitals in the future because of the financial disincentives and the increased risk.[76] In addition, there may actually be a saturation point for system horizontal integration, and that hospital acquisition should be selective. Selection factors have been shown to include market characteristics, mission compatibility, and facility management. Thus, the potential for horizontal integration as a strategy will be limited to financing mechanisms and selective acquisitions.[77]

Vertical Integration

Diversification through the integration of clinical services transforms a horizontally integrated system into a vertically integrated one. Vertical integration involves incorporating within the organization either stages of production (backward integration) or distribution channels (forward integration) that were formerly handled through arm's length transactions with other organizations.[78]

A vertically integrated system is described as offering "a broad range of patient care and support services operated in a functionally unified manner. The range of services offered may include preacute, acute, and post acute care organized around an acute hospital. Alternatively, a delivery system might specialize in offering a range of services related solely to long-term care, mental health care, or some other specialized area."[79] The intended purpose of vertical integration is to increase the comprehensiveness and continuity of care, while simultaneously controlling the channels or demand for health care services. Thus, vertical integration emphasizes connecting patient services with different stages in the health care delivery process.[80]

Vertical integration can occur through a variety of arrangements:

- internal development of new services
- acquisition of another organization or service
- merger
- lease or sale
- franchise
- joint venture
- contractual agreements
- informal agreements or affiliations
- insurance programs[81]

Although more hospital systems are becoming vertically integrated, the experience is mixed.[82] Government scrutiny by the Federal Trade Commission to ensure that integration does not lead to monopolistic or noncompetitive arrangements inhibits vertical integration. In addition, physicians may resist vertical integration because it allows the system to channel referrals among physicians and facilities,[83] and it gives the system control over demand.[84] Finally, the problems involved in moving sick people through a dispersed system of care may complicate vertical integration, as all services will not necessarily be available at one site.[85]

Diversification

During the 1980s, diversification occurred primarily in non–acute care services. Its purpose was to compensate hospitals that were losing revenues under the PPS by generating revenue through new sources. In many instances, hospitals diversified into a wide range of businesses that were completely unrelated to health care, such as dude ranches and travel agencies. Many diversification efforts failed during this decade, in part because management was unprepared to manage services unrelated to the hospital's core business of acute care. In the 1990s, the purpose of diversification shifted from generating revenues to offering health care services that reduce hospital costs.[86]

Diversification strategies in the health care industry have mirrored the turbulence and uncertainty in the environment; they have involved introducing new services and deleting others on a trial-and-error basis. Some efforts have been more successful than others.[87] It has become apparent that diversification activities related to the hospital's core business, such as ambulatory care and physician joint ventures, tend to be more profitable than those that are only partially or totally unrelated to acute care.[88] Furthermore, after more than a decade of experience with diversification, experts now recommend that the diversification activity should generate, at a minimum, at least 10 percent of total revenues to be considered a worthwhile investment.[89] Although hospitals were pursuing diversification prior to the implementation of the PPS, there has been only a modest increase in these activities post-PPS. It has been suggested that a lack of capital has retarded diversification efforts.[90] Some experts believe that the failed diversification activities of the 1980s have made managers more cautious.[91] Many of the national chains have been diverting individual activities to clean up their balance sheets and move out of markets in which they have perceived weakness.

Approximately one-third of rural hospitals are affiliated with systems either through ownership, lease, or contract management arrangements,[92] but evidence suggests that the PPS has changed the strategic value of system affiliation for rural hospitals. Specifically, affiliation with a system does not increase a rural hospital's chances for survival. In fact, affiliation with an investor-owned system may actually increase a rural hospital's likelihood of closing. Investor-owned rural hospitals that affiliate with investor-owned systems are less likely to close, but investor-owned rural hospitals that affiliate with not-for-profit systems increase their risk of closure. Thus, investor-owned system affiliation may be a reasonable strategy, but only for a rather limited group of rural hospitals that includes small, investor-owned facilities.[93]

Regionalization

Investor-owned systems initially pursued vertical integration on a national scale, but these attempts were not successful. The national companies learned that uniform corporate policies are not always sensitive to state and local market and reimbursement differences. Thus, these systems have shifted their vertical integration efforts to a smaller scale that includes regional and local approaches.[94] In addition, investor-owned systems have pursued strategies involving downsizing, divestiture, and consolidation. In 1987, the largest investor-owned system, Hospital Corporation of America (HCA) spun off approximately 25 percent of its hospitals, and the second largest investor-owned system, Humana, reported a less than 1 percent increase in the number of operating beds. Almost all investor-owned systems have sold off their European hospitals.[95,96] Some industry analysts believe that not-for-profit systems are better positioned to achieve vertical integration because, unlike their investor-owned counterparts, they are smaller in scale and less geographically dispersed.[97]

The trend toward regionalization recognized that 99 percent of health care services delivered in the United States will take place within the region in which the patient resides. Thus, systems are shifting their focus to establish predominance in local and regional markets rather than national ones.[98] The role of larger investor-owned systems is declining, and the proprietary sector is growing through small local and regional investor-owned systems, many of which are newly established systems.[99] Vertical integration is consistent with the trend toward regionalization because it concentrates resources in local markets.

As a result of all these factors, an industry that was once moving toward rapid consolidation through national chain ownership appears to be moving now toward regionally based operators with strong local ties.[100] The acquisition activities of not-for-profit organizations, hospitals, and small regional operators reflect this change in direction. Many in the field now believe that vertically integrated regional delivery systems with an emphasis on primary care and preventive medicine will prove to be the best approach to providing health care services. The focus will be on the development of a continuum of care that incorporates a range of services from preventive to long-term care.

Virtual Integration

Medical practices will continue to experience a hyperturbulent environment in the years ahead as consolidation of the health care industry continues apace. Yet it is not at all obvious that tightly coupled, fully integrated systems are the wave of the future. It is difficult to manage a system that provides many different products or services in many different markets. It is impossible for managers of fully integrated systems to understand all the different products and services and their markets. For this reason, tight coupling and high degrees of vertical integration are not increasing in other parts of U.S. industry. In fact, "decoupling" is occurring as corporations struggle to focus on their "core competencies." For example, U.S. Air has been struggling since the merger of six different carriers between 1968 and 1989. The problem is that U.S. Air has never been operationally and culturally integrated.

It is true that health care providers will need to be part of a larger organization that provides a wide range of consumer and employer choices, "one-stop shopping," economies of scale, cost-effectiveness, clinical quality, and service quality. It is not true that the only way to achieve these goals is through participation in a fully integrated system.

The advantage of a vertically integrated delivery system or network (IDS/N) is that unified ownership allows for coordinated adaptations to changing environmental circumstances.[101] In principle, vertical integration provides a unity of control and direction that allows the IDS/N to focus all the energies of the subunits on the same goals and strategies. There is a single mission statement, hierarchy of authority, and "bottom line." The unity of purpose is essential under managed care (as it is currently structured) and underlies the drive toward vertically integrated delivery systems that incorporate primary care physicians, specialty panels, hospitals, and managed care organizations.

The advantages of virtual integration, that is, integration through contractual relations (more loosely coupled systems) lie in its potential for autonomous adaptation to changing environmental circumstances.[102] Organizational independence preserves the risks and rewards for efficient performance. Although coordination may result from negotiated authority, it must involve collaboration (i.e., creating new value), a dense web of interpersonal connections based on trust, and partners willing to nurture the collaborative relationship rather than simply trying to control it.

If vertical integration worked in practice the way it works in principle, then markets and contracts would be rare.[103] The health care system could be structured as one large administered bureaucracy with centralized planning, centralized resource allocation, a single purpose, and a single process. Vertically integrated systems suffer from two weaknesses, however: incentive attenuation and influence costs. Vertical integration replaces the entrepreneurship of the owner-managed medical practice with administrative hierarchies where managers and clinicians are paid largely by salary. It also greatly increases influence costs, defined as the effect of internal struggles for control over resources by various incumbent constituencies (e.g., primary care physicians, specialists, managed care organizations, hospitals, system managers). At the extreme, the virtually integrated system or network could resemble public bureaucracies with a civil service mentality.

Because there is practically no hard evidence of the superiority of any one approach to structuring, it is prudent to proceed with caution. Much of the activity seen in the industry today is an imitation of the actions or presumed actions of others. The downside of all of the emphasis on new acquisitions, new enrollment, and restructuring has been that the consumer has been "lost in the shuffle." In the future, consumer choice of providers should increase rather than decrease.[104] Therefore, systems that do not provide open access to plans and broad networks of providers will be at a competitive disadvantage.

In the future environment, it is likely to be risky for providers to rely on exclusive partnerships, because the winners and losers are unknown. Rather, the emphasis should be on patient satisfaction, patient retention, flexibility, the availability of options for consumers, minimal paperwork, and multiple capitated contracts/partnerships for providers. Already, cost-oriented providers, like Humana, are shifting to a user-friendly philosophy that emphasizes quality and patient satisfaction.

One model for the future is for large medical groups to contract with managed care organizations to provide the full spectrum of medical services to a defined population on a capitated basis. In California, these groups have been growing rapidly.[105] The physician groups are part of a physician network, but are not part of an IDS/N. In essence, they are a "virtual network" established by contract with no common ownership or merging of assets. The fact that these medical groups manage utilization through their own medical directors and physician committees fosters a cooperative relationship rather than the adversarial one often found when outside managed care organizations monitor physician utilization and performance. Utilization in these networks is significantly below California and national benchmarks.

No one structure is necessarily the final answer. There are multiple possible paths to achieve increased integration and coordination of clinical services under managed care, and individual market dynamics will determine the appropriate level and structure of integration. Multiprovider systems face a trade-off between the advantages of coordinated adaptation through vertical integration and the advantages of autonomous adaptation through contractual networks. The current hyperturbulence and lack of definitive evidence makes it difficult to predict eventual outcomes. It also indicates the potential downside of giving up autonomy and/or making large capital investments in a vertically integrated (owned) system. The trend today, both within and outside of health care, is toward more contractual relationships and less vertical integration.

SYSTEM PERFORMANCE

The horizontally integrated multihospital systems of the 1980s did not function as true systems. They tended to function as a loose collection of unrelated operating units that were not integrated strategically. That is, each operating unit did not comprehend its strategic relationship relative to other operating units in the system. Ultimately, however, there was integrative pressure on these systems. The growth of managed care, implementation of capitated payment systems, and the influence of health care reform initiatives compelled systems to integrate more fully and to focus on an integrated continuum of care that promised accountability for cost, quality, and outcomes.[106,107]

Although capitated payment methods are expected to significantly affect organizational performance, there is little evidence as yet to demonstrate this influence. Under the fee-for-service method of payment, services that cost more brought in more revenue. With capitation, revenues are received on a monthly per capita basis, irrespective of the amount and type of services used. Profitability consequently depends on the ability to win health maintenance organization (HMO) contracts, to attract patients, and to manage care in a way that keeps expenditures beneath the capitated

rate of payment.[108,109] The competition for contracts suggests that there will be frequent shifts in market share.

Systems have demonstrated a continuing ability to outperform their nonsystem counterparts financially. In one study, it was noted that hospital staffing costs in systems decreased 25 percent through the sharing of services.[110] Many health care analysts, however, believe that, other than efficiencies in labor productivity related primarily to having fewer full-time equivalent employees and lower turnover, system hospitals have not demonstrated comparative advantages over nonsystem hospitals.[111-113] Furthermore, while system hospitals have greater opportunities to reduce their costs through sharing administrative services such as legal, data processing, and accounting services, the overhead costs involved in managing these and other activities have been extremely high. Even so, the sharing of services among system member institutions geographically situated in proximity to one another may reduce costs by avoiding or eliminating the duplication of necessary, but marginally profitable (or unprofitable) services.[114] Many investor-owned chains have looked to mergers to create cost savings. For example, Columbia expected its merger with Healthtrust in 1994 to save $125 million annually through increased volume discounts and reduced overhead expenses.[115]

Despite certain potential cost-saving benefits, primarily in the areas of purchasing and reduction of duplicate services, the creation and expansion of a system can also increase costs. As a system increases or anticipates increasing in size, its executives spend a significant amount of time on planning, policy enforcement, and related activities. They have less time available to devote to the day-to-day conduct of the system's business affairs or the delivery of health care services. Then the executives either overextend themselves trying to accomplish both present activities and future planning, or they hire new administrators to whom they delegate day-to-day operations. The quality of management may suffer and/or costs may rise. The better performing systems keep a very tight rein on corporate staff costs.[116]

Managed care has increased administrative responsibilities, as it requires monitoring and evaluating patient satisfaction, documenting a variety of aspects of quality of care, keeping track of a variety of contractual obligations and their subsequent transaction costs, and managing the use of both clinical and administrative resources.[117] These new responsibilities call for sophisticated information systems, which are expensive. In addition, high costs may be a function of additional administrative controls necessary to manage medical resources across institutions.[118–120]

In spite of the reductions in reimbursements and the pressures to control costs, systems have enjoyed profits and growth for almost a decade. Investor-owned or for-profit systems appear to have experienced increases in operating profits for the period 1987–1996, according to *Modern Healthcare* surveys. In fact, they outperformed not-for-profit systems in 1994 and, again, in 1995. During this 2-year period, investor-owned systems posted double digit profits, while not-for-profit systems actually experienced declining profits, according to *Modern Healthcare* surveys.[121,122] Not-for-profit systems appear to be making a comeback, however. According to *Modern Healthcare*'s 1996 survey, not-for-profit systems took a slight lead over investor-owned systems and experienced a growth rate of 12 percent compared with 11.3 percent reported by the for-profit chains. It appears that despite the increased pressures and competition, both not-for-profit and investor-owned systems have successfully adapted to managed care environments.[123]

The transition to managed care has involved strategies that position systems to compete effectively in highly volatile and unpredictable markets. Investor-owned systems initiated growth strategies, such as mergers. *Modern Healthcare* surveys reported that in 1994, investor-owned systems became the fastest growing sector by adding dozens of facilities to their chains. Mergers fueled the investor-owned profits, and Columbia grew through mergers to become the largest system in the United States with the exception of the Department of Veterans Affairs. During 1993–1994, Columbia merged with large for-profit chains, including Galen Healthcare, HCA, and Healthtrust. In addition, they began to add tax-exempt, not-for-profit hospitals and systems.[124–126]

Not-for-profit systems began to pursue expansion strategies in 1996, according to *Modern Healthcare* surveys. They focused on smaller rural and suburban facilities. Roman Catholic health care systems, the most aggressive in expanding their systems, experienced double digit growth rates. While not-for-profit systems became more aggressive in acquiring facilities, the investor-owned systems appeared to be slowing down. In 1996, for example, Columbia/HCA experienced a growth rate of eight hospitals or only 3 percent.[127]

Public systems, however, continue to lose money, but at a lower level, according to *Modern Healthcare* surveys. In the past, their losses were attributable mainly to the poor financial performance of public systems in New York City and Los Angeles. More recently, however, the losses appear to be more evenly distributed.[128]

Median hospital profit margins vary by system status and bed size. Smaller hospitals are less profitable than their larger counterparts. Large, investor-owned system hospitals are the most profitable,[129] primarily because of their higher prices, lower staffing levels, and lower wages.[130,131] In general, system hospitals may be more profitable because they have a more pro-active strategic orientation than do independent hospitals.[132] As noted earlier, however, when other factors are controlled, system membership does *not* appear to enhance financial returns.[133]

CHARACTERISTICS OF SYSTEMS

Corporate Structure

The existence of a corporate structure may be the most obvious characteristic that distinguishes a system hospital from a freestanding institution. Systems have an organizational structure that consists of a corporate or systemwide component and a field component of facility managers. At the institutional level, system ownership determines reporting relationships. Within investor-owned systems, the facility's chief executive officer (CEO) usually reports to a corporate officer. In not-for-profit systems, the facility's CEO may report to a hospital board of trustees, a corporate board of directors, or less typically, to a system corporate executive.[134] With the move toward vertical integration, system organizational structure becomes even more complicated, as the linkages become incorporated into that structure.

When systems began to form, there were no textbook models to follow. The investor-owned systems had already developed a corporate structure, but it was based on ownership of the majority of hospitals in the system. The not-for-profit systems learned to create structures largely as they went along.[135] As systems grew, they experienced problems with expanding corporate staffs, bureaucracy, and conflicts of interest between the corporate and field components. The potential for conflict generated is not arithmetic, it is logarithmic.[136] One study of nursing home administrators indicated that those who were part of systems and reported to corporate offices experienced more stress and role conflict than did their counterparts in freestanding facilities.[137] Systems require managers who have superior mediation skills in order to respond to these challenges.[138]

Governance

Despite the unprecedented, rapid, and dramatic upheaval in the health care industry, governance of hospitals remains basically unchanged. For systems, the lack of development in governance is particularly problematic, because governance must occur at a variety of levels in order to meet both systemwide and institutional needs. The presence of multiple governing boards to address multiple needs at various levels often causes conflict, enlarges the bureaucracy, and leads to power struggles. It has been suggested that systems should recognize governance on two levels: (1) the organizational or strategic level of governance where systemwide decisions and policies are considered, and (2) the operational governance level that addresses local operations of institutions and should be advisory to institutional management. As the work of system facilities depends on the degree of success achieved through operational governance, this level should be subsumed under systemwide governance.[139]

Systems have tended to rely on three models of governance. The most popular model, the parent holding company model, is also the most decentralized. Although it has a systemwide governing board, it also has a separate governing board for each institution. The second model is a modified parent holding company model, in which there is one systemwide governing board with advisory boards at the institutional level. Systems that represent large numbers of hospitals tend to use these two models. Systems affiliated with religious organizations are more likely to adopt the parent holding company model, while the investor-owned systems tend to favor the modified parent holding company model. The third model is the corporate model, which consists of one systemwide board with no other boards at any other level. The major advantage of this governance structure is its simplicity and clear lines of authority. Systems that have small numbers of hospitals tend to use this model; often, they are not-for-profit or public systems.[140]

The type of governance model in use has not been found to influence the strategic decision making for which systemwide boards assume responsibility. In decision making at the institutional level, however, the type of governance model appears to be influential. The parent holding company model tends to leave hospital-level decisions to the hospital governing boards, while the modified parent holding company model seems to give all boards equal involvement in most hospital-level decisions. The corporate model demonstrates greater involvement by the system-wide board in hospital decisions.[141]

The Joint Commission on Accreditation of Healthcare Organizations has recognized system governance for its complexity, primarily through changes in standards for governing boards. In 1986, the standards were upgraded to reflect the complex responsibilities that result from an increase in the number of boards and the dynamic relationships that exist between these boards and all levels of the organization. Specifically, if there are multilevels of governance, the Joint Commission requires mechanisms to ensure communication and participation at all levels. In particular, these mechanisms must ensure that medical staff have the ability to communicate and participate at all levels of governance in matters involving patient care.[142]

The transition from hospitals, to multihospital systems, to organized delivery systems, to community care networks will require profound changes in governance.[143] The structures and processes of governance suited to one type of organization probably will not work equally well in others. Although there is a great deal of experimentation in the approaches that systems have been using, there are as yet no definitive models to suggest what governance structures and processes are likely to work best under differing conditions. It is clear, however, that all board members need to understand their vision for the system, plans for future structural change, and the activities of other systems with their governance. It is also important to build trust among all the system components by changing their internal incentives to reflect concern for system performance and by promoting communication/information exchange across all system components and levels of governance. Finally, the system's multiple boards need a clear definition of governance roles, responsibilities, and authority.

Human Resources Management

Because health care systems are exceedingly complex and diverse organizational arrangements, human resources management may be among their greatest challenges. These systems require significant numbers of highly skilled and specialized personnel at a variety of levels. Systems also offer opportunities not found in nonsystem hospitals. They can develop staff-sharing programs between hospitals that not only reduce personnel expenses, but also provide the potential for quality improvements. In addition, systems may have a name recognition that facilitates recruitment of personnel. A comprehensive personnel data bank can provide system members with a pool of qualified applicants. Systems also represent variety, mobility, and job security for employees who can move to different jobs within the system.

The development of career ladders within a system can enhance the system's ability to attract and retain personnel. Promotions and transfers can occur without the employee exiting the system. A corporate office can also provide individual facilities with human resources expertise that they would not be able to afford otherwise. Finally, representing large numbers of employees can facilitate the development of more comprehensive and less expensive benefits packages that are attractive both to employees and to the system's budget.[144]

During 1992, system downsizing contributed to the increased profitability of both investor-owned and not-for-profit systems. Downsizing may be easier to manage in a system hospital than in a freestanding facility, because systems have more opportunities to move staff around within the system and, thus, are better able to protect employees' economic security. The stability of employment at one facility within the system can provide job openings for employees displaced by staff reductions at another system facility.[145]

Employees in systems, however, do face the stress of being exposed to the effects of vertical and horizontal integration. Almost no research has investigated the effect of mergers, acquisitions, and other strategies on employees, nor is there a human resources model to deal effectively with the effects of system development on employees. Human resources managers must deal with system changes and ensure that employees are recognized as assets within the system.[146]

Compensation for system executives reflects the complexity and responsibility of system management. Multihospital system executives earn more than their counterparts in freestanding hospitals and have continued to earn more rapid salary increases.[147] Systems also find advantages in reduced CEO turnover. CEOs have high-risk relationships with medical staff and boards, and they often lose their jobs because of failing relationships. In a system, the CEO can move to another facility, and the system does not lose an important management resource.[148]

One of the major challenges for a system is to align the interests of physicians with those of the system and promote physician participation.[149] Physicians may have the greatest opportunities to influence standards of care in systems. Investor-owned systems, in particular, have promoted physician participation in governance.[150] Yet, physician loyalties often are associated with the individual facility rather than with the larger system. Increasing the numbers of physician administrators within the system, increasing the numbers of physicians on corporate boards, and improving communication with physicians may improve physician loyalty.[151]

The most profitable and efficient systems appear to operate with fewer people on their management staffs and pay higher than average salaries to their employees. Financially successful systems have reported spending about one-third more on human resources, planning, marketing, and public relations, compared with their lower performing counterparts.[152] In theory, these advantages should exist for all systems. In practice, many systems restrict themselves to only certain subcategories of personnel. For example, some religious organization–associated systems require or prefer their executives to be practicing members of the religious organization. This obviously restricts the talent pool, as does the practice of paying "below the market" in systems affiliated with religious organizations.

In addition, the development and enforcement of appropriate standards of professional qualifications and job performance are crucial to the success of systems. The development and operation of a system are complex and require significant numbers of highly skilled and specialized personnel. The system needs to set and enforce appropriate standards of qualifications and performance and then recruit individuals who can meet these standards. If this is not done, the anticipated advantages will not be achieved.

Financial Management

Finances have to be centralized in a system. When seeking long-term debt or equity funds, investors are likely to insist on involving *all* of the related organization's assets. The system needs to approve budget, capital expenditures beyond a given amount, sale or purchase of property, and changes in rate structures.

System hospitals vary in the financial responsibilities of CEOs for capital management. Typically, CEOs of individual institutions in investor-owned systems have a reduced role in creating capital; that function normally resides with corporate officers. In both investor-owned and not-for-profit systems, expenditures that extend beyond yearly budgets routinely require corporate approval. Furthermore, the capital approval process may differ according to system ownership. Investor-owned hospitals tend to rely on authorization from the corporate office, and not-for-profit systems usually require approval from both the hospital level and systemwide governing boards.[153] The success of capital management influences the cost and pricing structure and ultimately the ability of the facility to be competitive within its own defined market segment;[154] therefore, capital allocation has a prominent position in system management.

Allocating Capital

The traditional capital allocation approaches, which focus on discounted cash flow, net present value, and internal rate of return, may be inappropriate for multihospital health care systems. For systems, shaping capital structure involves a systemwide vision and the integration of local and corporate needs in a way that extends beyond the normal capital budget process.[155] The system includes different facilities having different needs and facing different risks. Several facilities can be located in very distinct markets with different financial performance trends and different future potentials, as well as widely diverse facility, management, and medical staff characteristics.[156] A multifactored model that incorporates varying needs and risks, and originates in the Capital Asset Pricing Model, can be derived to allocate capital among a variety of member institutions.[157]

Of particular importance to systems is the concept of a system level mission fund. A member institution may receive a significant subsidy from the system to continue its mission. The institution would not be able to survive without this funding. As in a single institution, systems can establish allocations to mission activities based on either an ongoing cash flow subsidy or the endowment model. Often, a combination approach can be employed.[158]

Perhaps the most distinctive and important economic advantage of a system in terms of its capital allocation strategy is the system's ability to minimize the amount of aggregate safety stock that is required to protect the system. Safety stock represents a powerful advantage that reflects a system's ability to reduce or even eliminate specific risks to individual facilities through diversification of risk across multiple facilities. Thus, as the number of facilities in the system increases, the importance of a single facility's performance declines, and the contribution to safety stock can also be reduced. For systems, this reduction in safety stock requirements frees capital for allocation at other levels within the system and represents a substantial economic benefit.[159]

Systems should also focus on hospital growth pools that are similar in conceptualization to growth pools at the individual level, but include both system level and hospital level risk pools. After making all allocations, systems should assign the remaining capital to this pool in order to provide funding for system level initiatives such as vertical integration and other diversification activities.[160]

Because the capital allocation process in a system involves both corporate and facility participation, it requires the support of a strong system culture; communication among all participants to the process; an incentive system that associates hospital management's compensation with the overall performance of the system, as well as the individual performance of the facility; appropriate management and financial systems; an effective budgeting process; and an implementation plan.[161]

Financial Difficulties Within a System

Bankruptcy presents special problems for systems and their members. "When dealing with a financially troubled hospital that is part of a multihospital system, the problems seem to multiply geometrically."[162] Legal and practical problems arise from the existence of multiple boards and overlapping memberships on these boards. Fiduciary obligations of board members can conflict, especially when an action appropriate for one institution may not be beneficial to the system. Board members with multiple loyalties can be dis-

ruptive. Furthermore, statutes and case law of a particular state may support the community or individual hospital interests over the system interests.[163]

Systems have earned higher bond ratings than freestanding institutions and have shown stability in ratings over time, both important considerations for systems. This performance has been attributed to a system's ability to diversify risk and size. Rating agencies tend to measure successful systems performance by centralized operations and mechanisms for monitoring planning, budgeting, and capital expenditures of system members.[164]

Systems have the potential to increase interest earnings through a cash sweep, a technique designed to eliminate the time lag between receiving and investing funds. It involves a daily electronic withdrawal of funds from all hospital operating accounts and the placement of these funds in one central account where the interest begins accruing immediately. This technique allows the system to eliminate the problem of idle cash in local banks.[165]

Systems also have access to pooled financing that permits a member institution to use financial resources that would be otherwise unavailable. The financial markets have appeared to favor systems as sounder credit risks than independent freestanding facilities. Empirical evidence indicates that systems have generally received higher credit ratings than most independent hospitals.[166] There can be disadvantages to this type of financing, however. Member institutions may have to submit their assets as collateral, and the system, overall, may find that it is subordinating its long-term financial goals and depleting its assets in its efforts to strengthen the financial position of weaker, less responsible member institutions.[167]

However, the advantage may prove disadvantageous to the system's more financially healthy member institutions if their assets are depleted to support the needs or excesses of the system's weaker or less-responsible members. To the extent financing is available from outside sources, the stronger facilities still may be forced to pledge or otherwise encumber their assets to support the debt-financed operations and activities of the system. The separate long-range plans and goals of stronger member institutions may be subordinated and harmed to shore up other system institutions and to honor pledges and guarantees.[168]

Financially weaker institutions within the system may incur even greater detriment if the system functions inefficiently or becomes overleveraged. High interest, debt service costs, and fees for system corporate services may negatively affect the survival prospects of weaker institutions to a greater degree than the more stable units.

Management Innovation

The upheaval in the health care environment has created a variety of pressures for managers, who are now expected to contain costs without jeopardizing quality of care, downsize while simultaneously increasing productivity, and maintain good relationships with medical staffs that have grown increasingly wary of management interference in patient care issues. As expectations for what managers can accomplish increase, so does the demand for managerial innovation. Given the growth of systems and the complexity of these organizations, it is important that these systems promote managerial innovation.

Systems have the organizational resources to encourage managerial innovation. While freestanding hospitals are connected only through ad hoc relationships, systems have the benefit of group norms and more formal relationships that can be helpful in imple-

menting innovation. Moreover, systems have routinized communication channels that promote the diffusion of innovation. Mature systems, in particular, are likely to foster managerial innovation. As a system matures, it recognizes the importance and value of communications and works to build channels and mechanisms that encourage the sharing of information. Mature systems also usually have a larger resource base from which to implement new programs.[169]

Technology Assessment

With the rapid increase in technology development and pressures to contain costs without decreasing the quality of health care services, institutions are focusing attention on evaluating new technologies. Unlike single facilities, systems must address the needs of multiple facilities that are frequently in multiple locations. Thus, decisions on technologies can occur at the interregional level and involve broader standards of assessment. When the organization extends beyond the local community, community standards may not be appropriate.[170]

The dilemma for systems depends on the extent of decentralization within the organization. A highly centralized system can assist individual hospitals in technology assessment, but the resulting guidelines for adopting or implementing the new technology may be inconsistent with community standards. A decentralized system, on the other hand, can allow local facilities to assess technology within the context of the facility's environment. This approach can lead to expensive duplication, however.

Risk Management

Systems are positioned to take advantage of legislation that regulates financing mechanisms for insurance. Increasingly, systems are obtaining liability and other insurance coverages through alternative methods of financing. In particular, risk retention groups, a financing mechanism authorized by the Federal Risk Retention Act of 1986, offer systems unique opportunities for a reliable and stable source of liability protection. These groups are essentially insurance companies formed by institutions with similar interests, such as hospitals, to provide any casualty coverage, except workers' compensation. All policyholders must also be stockholders. Unlike traditional insurance companies, which must conform to the regulations of each state in which they operate, risk retention groups are able to operate nationwide once licensed in one state.

Captive insurance companies, another alternative to traditional insurance companies, write coverage for only one employer or one group of employers. Seven states have created tax laws that allow systems to take advantage of this arrangement.[171]

Marketing

Although little is known about the practice of marketing in systems, a study of marketing in multihospital systems revealed minimal differences between investor-owned systems and not-for-profit systems.[172] Marketing staffs were larger in investor-owned systems, however, where marketing responsibilities are more likely to be formally specified within the organization chart. The larger staffs tended to be associated with a decentralized approach to marketing. In contrast, not-for-profit systems reported smaller marketing staffs and employed a more centralized reporting structure for the marketing function. Overall, investor-owned and not-for-profit systems demonstrated remarkable similarities in patterns of influence over mar-

keting mix, the status of marketing information systems, and attitudes toward marketing. The move by not-for-profit systems to a more aggressive and bottom line orientation may have made marketing less distinctive in the two types of systems.

It has become evident in marketing that most hospital markets remain local or regional in nature. Local and regional systems have higher levels of market control in distinct areas than do larger more geographically dispersed investor-owned systems.[173] The trend toward system strategies that focus on regional and vertical integration is likely to influence marketing efforts in systems.

Information Systems

Increasingly, systems are facing new information requirements to accommodate strategies that involve downsizing, reorganization, restructuring, and divestitures, as well as demands by payers for information on the costs of health care services. The management of information within systems must facilitate communication between a diversity of operations and across a variety of facilities.[174] In systems, the trend is toward centralizing information systems with information systems managers reporting either to the CEO or to executive officers in charge of operations or finance. These managers typically face expanded responsibilities that include telephone systems, management engineering, and data communications. In addition, they have increasingly become involved in the implementation of alternative delivery systems through the development of systemwide clinical and managerial information systems. The growth of information systems management within hospital systems reflects the growing requirements and information needs of diversification and integration strategies.[175]

Health care systems linking hospitals, physicians, insurers, employers, and others form the foundation of most health care reform proposals. Shared information on health outcomes and costs of care will help identify and encourage the most efficient forms of care. This requires the development of a health information network.[176] Such an information network would help to direct patients to the most appropriate settings and reduce redundancies.

MANAGERIAL IMPLICATIONS

The growth and development of multiprovider health care systems in the United States have been characterized by the integration of services and the economic concentration and consolidation of resources. The transition to organized delivery systems reflected the horizontal integration of facilities that began with investor-owned acquisitions in the late 1960s. Investor-owned systems entered into multihospital system arrangements because they had access to capital markets and because federal reimbursement encouraged and rewarded growth. Not-for-profit hospitals began to integrate horizontally in the mid-1970s in response to competition from investor-owned chains and the regulatory effects of state certificate-of-need legislation and rate review programs.[177] Until the mid-1980s, the primary difference between investor-owned and not-for-profit systems was one of magnitude. Investor-owned systems concentrated on national markets and evolved into large national multihospital systems, whereas the not-for-profit systems focused on local and regional markets.

The implementation of the PPS, the shift of DRGs or risk-based payment systems, and the increasing price sensitivity of both consumers and employers precipitated the transformation of multihospital systems to multiprovider health care systems. Today's systems are characterized by trends toward vertical integration, regionalization, and related diversification. These new systems represent more than a collection of hospitals; they offer a continuum of health care services that extends beyond acute patient care.

Managed care spread throughout the U.S. health care industry primarily as an effort to reform health care financing, but ultimately it is likely to have its most significant impact in revolutionizing health care organization.[178] With more than 50 percent of hospitals belonging to some type of system and most of the remaining hospitals being members of some type of alliance, it is clear that there are many ways to organize. The fundamental question concerns the types of systems, networks, and alliances that are best able to compete effectively and deliver cost-effective care. At this time, however, there is no definitive answer to this question, because there is almost no evidence associating different types of organized arrangements with successful performance or failure.

Similarities are replacing differences between investor-owned and not-for-profit systems. In general, not-for-profit systems are behaving more like investor-owned systems as they focus on profitability, the external environment, and competitive strategies. Not-for-profit hospitals have established for-profit subsidiaries and are engaged in selling services to other hospitals for a profit. Today's not-for-profit multihospital health care system is a healthy competitor that is narrowing the profitability gap with investor-owned systems.[179]

Meanwhile, the large investor-owned system shifted its focus. In the 1970s, investor-owned systems looked to build large national chains. This changed in the 1980s when investor-owned systems pursued regional growth strategies in response to the PPS, DRGs, and the introduction of risk-based payment systems. In the 1980s, with the recognition that health care is a local business and that survival depends on dominance in local and regional markets, the investor-owned systems gravitated toward growth in smaller local and regional markets and moved out of markets where they were poor competitors. These systems streamlined, reorganized, refinanced, and divested themselves of unprofitable and, for the most part, unrelated activities in the 1980s.

In the 1990s, investor-owned systems embarked on aggressive expansion programs. Columbia/HCA, in particular, reflects the shifting trend toward becoming large national chains. By pursuing growth strategies, Columbia/HCA in 1995 became the largest nongovernmental health care system in the United States. The impetus behind its growth reflects many of the pressures of managed care. First, growth attracts partners who want to grow along with the system, such as suppliers, physicians, and others. Second, volume and dominance in a market create negotiating leverage for managed care contracts and can intimidate smaller competitors. Furthermore, large national chains that establish themselves as dominant players in certain markets can keep other systems out because the capital requirements to compete with them would be prohibitive.[180,181] Growth strategies that involve mergers also are expected to assist systems in competing more effectively, because they can reduce many overhead and administrative expenses and eliminate duplicate services and high-cost technologies.

A careful analysis of the effects of integration shows that big, vertically integrated, investor-owned health care organizations are often clumsy and slow to innovate.[182] They are difficult to manage, as they require significant cash infusions and massive managerial efforts to keep their components networked. They typically act to suppress competition and are unresponsive to local communities. Consequently, the results of vertically integrated health care organizations have been disappointing. According to one survey, only 17 percent of hospitals that purchased physician practices achieved a positive return.[183] By 1996, several systems were selling either total or partial interest in their HMOs. Of the 37 HMOs owned by vertically integrated systems, 10 had posted losses and 8 experienced declines in net income.[184] Finally, a study of 12 health care organizations that were in the early stages of vertical integration was also discouraging as it showed low levels of physician–system integration and clinical integration.[185] The systems themselves usually attribute their problems to a lack of managerial skill for operations such as physician group practices and managed care organizations.[186] Conrad and Dowling explained the failure of vertical integration as follows: "Because many of the organizations considering vertical integration are acute hospital systems, expertise may be lacking at both the corporate and institutional levels. Yet expertise—in evaluating and negotiating . . . and in managing new services—is often the single most important ingredient in success."[187]

The future of health care systems is highly speculative, given the volatility of managed care markets and future initiatives for health care reform. As the government's role in health care expands, these systems become more vulnerable to shifts in government policy. Furthermore, there remains the question of public systems and their repeated record of poor financial performance. Can these systems benefit from the experiences that have led both investor-owned and not-for-profit systems to success, or are these public systems casualties of the success of these other systems? Are public systems the new dumping grounds for unprofitable patients? Finally, there is the matter of systemness. Shortell criticized multihospital systems for their inability to perform as systems.[188] Will the focus on vertical integration, diversification, and regionalization increase the ability of multihospital health care systems to function as true systems? It seems likely that most multiprovider health care systems will emerge successfully from their "growing pains" and continue to solidify their position in the health care market as long as they are "virtually" integrated rather than vertically integrated.

Risk has identified several key trends relevant to systems existing in most areas of the United States.[189] First, health care will be purchased primarily on a local or regional basis. Quality and value will be increasingly important to purchasers. Second, managed care will encompass a significant majority of the population. Third, fewer resources will be available to deliver care, and the delivery of health care will continue to shift from acute care to ambulatory settings. Barry noted the importance of a system CEO being a "change agent" in this future environment: "Those who can understand and embrace change; those who can transform traditional but key values to tomorrow's environment; those who can educate their boards of trustees, medical communities, and the community at large; and those who can 'right size' the production activities of their organizations, and provide both high quality and cost-effective services will be the winners of tomorrow."[190]

RECOMMENDATIONS

- Health care executives in multiprovider health care systems need to allow flexibility for member institutions to respond to specific local markets while providing a clearly articulated and well understood vision for the system.
- System leaders must face the formidable task of proving to the member institutions that the system adds value, that its leaders are competent, and that they are capable of achieving the anticipated system advantages and resultant long-term benefits for the local unit.
- Each system should develop a detailed mission statement and set of behavioral norms (i.e., culture) shared by each facility within the system in order to enhance cohesiveness.
- Each system should develop a formal strategic plan for the system with input and a high degree of interaction among the corporate office and institutions in all geographic regions.
- Each system should develop a strategic human resource plan, including staffing, training and development, performance appraisal, and compensation.
- Each system should develop a system-wide management information system, quality assurance plan, market research, and guidelines for new products/services and bulk purchases that are utilized by each hospital; beyond these corporate services, the emphasis should be on autonomy and individualization of member institutions.
- Each system should develop and implement explicit measures for quality of care, patient satisfaction, efficiency, and community benefit, and then provide these data to purchasers and other key stakeholders.
- Each system should strive to achieve sufficient local market penetration/market share and vertical integration along a continuum of care on a local or regional basis.
- Each system should develop effective physician bonding strategies at the local,

regional, and corporate levels with incentives for physicians to make cost-effective decisions with the best long-term impact on patients.

- Each system should emphasize the process of developing health care in a managed care mode rather than simply the management of hospitals or acute care delivery.
- Each system should develop an organizational structure that is simple, lean, flat, responsive, customer-driven, risk-taking, and focused.
- Governance at the corporate level should be strategic in nature, whereas governance at the institutional level should be operational in nature and focused on local community/region needs and concerns.
- Systems should provide formal and informal education for those responsible for governance at all levels in the system.
- Systems should provide a clear definition of governance roles, responsibilities, and authority among the system and institutional boards of its component parts.
- Systems should move toward consolidation of management layers by combining corporate functions and decentralizing decision making where possible.
- Systems should move toward a single organized medical staff with shared values and a common culture.
- Systems should identify one or more discrete geographically defined service areas with large enough populations to support the provision of a full range of services and delivery settings.
- Systems should rigorously test clinical protocols and methodologies to determine the most cost-efficient and effective ways of providing care.
- Systems should centralize registration and medical record functions to make their networks more user-friendly and

decrease unnecessary duplication of tests.

- Systems should provide the leadership required to get the individual units of a system to think in terms of overall system performance rather than just in terms of the particular unit's performance.
- Systems should integrate their medical staffs into all phases of system planning and management.
- Only institutions that fit a particular culture and strategy should be invited to join or remain a member of the system.
- Systems should "right size" the various components of their delivery systems to respond to the health needs of the community.
- Systems should align physician incentives and achieve clinical integration across the continuum of care.
- Systems should develop information systems to support the integration of clinical and managerial information.
- Systems should use their mission and values as a guide in making difficult trade-off decisions.
- Systems should change their incentive structures to reflect concern for performance of the system as a whole, not just the individual components.
- Systems should develop broadly based "balanced scorecards" to evaluate their performance.
- Systems should own fewer facilities and contract for most services so that they are "virtually" integrated rather than vertically integrated.
- Systems should buy or contract for services only if the additions will add value to the systems' customers and are compatible with the existing mission, values, goals, and culture.
- Systems should allow the individual operating units within the system to have sufficient autonomy to be responsive to the needs of their local customers.

NOTES

1. S.M. Shortell, "The Evolution of Multihospital Systems: Unfulfilled Promises and Self-fulfilling Prophesies," *Medical Care Review* 45, no. 2 (1988): 177–214.

2. R.D. Luke et al., "Local Markets and Systems: Hospital Consolidations in Metropolitan Areas," *Health Services Research* 30, no. 4 (1995): 555–575.

3. M. Brown, "Mergers, Not Working, and Vertical Integration: Managed Care and Investor-owned Hospitals," *Health Care Management Review* 21, no. 1 (1996): 29–37.

4. J.C. Robinson and L. Casalino, "Vertical Integration and Organizational Networks in Health Care," *Health Affairs* 15, no. 1 (1996): 7–22.

5. S.M. Shortell et al., *Remaking Health Care in America* (San Francisco: Jossey-Bass, 1996).

6. S.D. Smith and P.M. Virgil, "Multihospital Systems: Applying Corporate Structures and Strategies," *A Future of Consequence: The Manager's Role in Health Services*, ed. G.L. Filerman (Princeton, NJ: Princeton University Press, 1989): 54–75.

7. D.A. Conrad and W.L. Dowling, "Vertical Integration in Health Services: Theory and Managerial Implications," *Health Care Management Review* 15, no. 4 (1990): 9–22.

8. L.R. Kaiser, "The Future of Multihospital Systems," *Topics in Health Care Financing* 18, no. 4 (1992): 32–45.

9. R.R. Risk, "Multihospital Systems: The Turning Point," *Topics in Health Care Financing* 18, no. 3 (1992): 46–53.

10. D.M. Kinzer, "Twelve Laws of Hospital Interaction," *Health Care Management Review* 15, no. 2 (1990): 15–19.

11. W.D. White, "The 'Corporatization' of U.S. Hospitals: What We Can Learn from the Nineteenth Century Industrial Experience," *International Journal of Health Services* 20, no. 1 (1990): 85–113.

12. J. Nemes, "For-Profit Chains Look Beyond the Bottom Line," *Modern Healthcare* 20, no. 10 (March 12, 1990): 27–36.

13. M.J. McCue et al., "An Assessment of Hospital Acquisition Prices," *Inquiry* 25 (1988): 290–296.

14. Shortell, "The Evolution of Multihospital Systems," 179.

15. Ibid., 192.

16. Ibid., 177–214.

17. White, "The 'Corporatization' of U.S. Hospitals," 102.

18. Risk, "Multihospital Systems: The Turning Point," 46–47.

19. Kaiser, "The Future of Multihospital Systems," 35.

20. Smith and Virgil, "Multihospital Systems," 54–55.

21. White, "The 'Corporatization' of U.S. Hospitals," 102.

22. S.M. Shortell et al., "Reinventing the American Hospital," *The Milbank Quarterly* 73, no. 2 (1995): 131–160.

23. Ibid.

24. Robinson and Casalino, "Vertical Integration," 7.

25. Shortell et al., "Reinventing the American Hospital."

26. D.L. Tennyson and M.D. Fottler, "Does System Membership Enhance Financial Returns in Hospitals?" *Best Paper Proceedings of the Academy of Management* (1997): 123–127.

27. Luke et al., "Local Markets and Systems."

28. Shortell et al., "Reinventing the American Hospital."

29. B. Japsen and L. Scott, "System Growth: A Close Race," *Modern Healthcare* 27, no. 25 (1997): 51–68.

30. Ibid.

31. Ibid.

32. G. Borzo, "Closer Ties with Physicians Skirt Safe Harbor Fears," *Health Care Strategic Management* 10, no. 11 (1992): 19–22.

33. C.K. Jacobson, "A Conceptual Framework for Evaluating Venture Opportunities Between Hospitals and Physicians," *Health Services Management Research* 2 (1989): 204–212.

34. J. Johnson, "Dynamic Diversification, Hospitals Pursue Physician Alliances, 'Seamless' Care," *Hospitals* 66, no. 3 (1992): 20–26.

35. D.A. Rublee and R. Rosenfield, "Organizational Aspects of Physician Joint Ventures," *American Journal of Medicine* 82 (1987): 518–524.

36. Brown, "Mergers, Not Working, and Vertical Integration," 33–37.

37. Luke et al., "Local Markets and Systems," 571.

38. Borzo, "Closer Ties with Physicians."

39. S. Andreopoulos, "The Folly of Teaching Hospital Mergers," *New England Journal of Medicine* 336, no. 1 (1997): 61–64.

40. A. Barnett, "The Partners Merger," *Hospital and Health Networks* (June 5, 1995): 46–50.

41. Shortell et al., "Reinventing the American Hospital," 133.

42. Brown, "Mergers, Not Working, and Vertical Integration."

43. Shortell et al., "Reinventing the American Hospital."

44. Jacobson, "A Conceptual Framework."

45. J. Montague, "Straight Talk: Doctor-driven Systems Tell How They've Gained Physician Allies," *Hospitals & Health Networks* 67, no. 13 (1993): 22–27.

46. J. Unland, "Group Practices and Hospital Affiliation of Medical Practices," *Health Care Strategic Management* 11, no. 3 (1993): 15–19.

47. D. Burda, "Most Hospitals Slow To Join with Group Practices," *Modern Healthcare* 23, no. 34 (1993): 33.

48. Robinson and Casalino, "Vertical Integration," 8.

49. P.J. Kenkel, "Filling up Beds No Longer the Name of the System Game," *Modern Healthcare* 23, no. 37 (1993): 39–48.

50. J. Greene and S. Lutz, "A Down Year at Not-for-profits; For-profits soar," *Modern Healthcare* 25, no. 25 (1995): 43–63.

51. J. Nemes, "For-profit Hospitals Waving Goodbye to Era of High Prices," *Modern Healthcare* 23, no. 12 (1993): 33–34, 37.

52. Shortell et al., "Reinventing the American Hospital," 133.

53. Robinson and Casalino, "Vertical Integration."

54. Brown, "Mergers, Not Working, and Vertical Integration."

55. Shortell, "The Evolution of Multihospital Systems," 180.

56. A.M. Sear, "Comparison of Efficiency and Profitability of Investor-owned Multihospital Systems with Not-for-profit Hospitals," *Health Care Management Review* 16, no. 2 (1991): 31–37.

57. Shortell, "The Evolution of Multihospital Systems," 183.

58. T.L. Ramirez, "Introduction to Multihospital Systems," *Topics in Health Care Financing* 18, no. 4 (1992): 1–23.

59. Risk, "Multihospital Systems: The Turning Point," 47.

60. W.O. Cleverly, "Financial and Operating Performance of Systems: Voluntary Versus Investor-owned," *Topics in Health Care Financing* 18, no. 4 (1992): 63–73.

61. Ramirez, "Introduction to Multihospital Systems," 9–10.

62. Shortell, "The Evolution of Multihospital Systems," 181.

63. Ibid., 177–178, 180.

64. R.E. Toomey and R.K. Toomey, "The Role of Governing Boards in Multihospital Systems," *Health Care Management Review* 18, no. 1 (1993): 21–30.

65. McCue et al., "An Assessment of Hospital Acquisition Prices," 294–295.

66. Shortell, "The Evolution of Multihospital Systems," 178.

67. White, "The 'Corporatization' of U.S. Hospitals," 105.

68. Ramirez, "Introduction to Multihospital Systems," 7.

69. R.D. Federa and T.R. Miller, "Capital Allocation Techniques," *Topics in Health Care Financing* 19, no. 1 (1992): 68–78.

70. Risk, "Multihospital Systems: The Turning Point," 47.

71. Conrad and Dowling, "Vertical Integration in Health Services," 12–13.

72. Cleverly, "Financial and Operating Performance of Systems," 67–69.

73. D. Dranove and M. Shanley, "Cost Reduction or Reputational Enhancement as Motive for Mergers: The Logic of Multihospital Systems," *Strategic Management Journal* 16, no. 1 (1995): 72.

74. J.A. Alexander et al., "The Short-term Effects of Mergers on Hospital Operations," *Health Services Research* 30, no. 6 (1996): 828–847.

75. J. Greene, "Merger Monopoly," *Modern Healthcare* (December 5, 1994): 38–46.

76. McCue et al., "An Assessment of Hospital Acquisition Prices," 295.

77. J.A. Alexander and M.A. Morrisey, "Hospital Selection into Multihospital Systems: The Effect of Market, Management, and Mission," *Medical Care* 26, no. 2 (1988): 159–176.

78. Shortell, "The Evolution of Multihospital Systems," 207.

79. Conrad and Dowling, "Vertical Integration in Health Services," 10.

80. Ibid.

81. Ibid., 11.

82. M. Brown and B.P. McCool, "Health Care Systems: Predictions for the Future," *Health Care Management Review* 15, no. 3 (1990): 87–94.

83. F.K. Ackerman, III, "The Movement toward Vertically-Integrated Regional Health Systems," *Health Care Management Review* 17, no. 3 (1992): 81–88.

84. Conrad and Dowling, "Vertical Integration in Health Services," 12–14.

85. Ackerman, "The Movement toward Vertically-Integrated Regional Health Systems," 85.

86. J. Greene, "Diversification, Take Two," *Modern Healthcare* 23, no. 28 (1993): 28–30.

87. J.A. Alexander, "Diversification Behavior of Multihospital Systems: Patterns of Change, 1983–1985," *Hospital and Health Services Administration* 35, no. 1 (1990): 83–102.

88. S.M. Shortell, "Diversification Strategy Benefits Innovative Leader," *Modern Healthcare* 20, no. 10 (1990): 38.

89. Greene, "Diversification, Take Two," 28–29.

90. Alexander, "Diversification Behavior of Multihospital Systems," 97–98.

91. Greene, "Diversification, Take Two," 28–29.

92. G.T. Savage et al., "Urban-rural Hospital Affiliations: Assessing Control, Fit and Stakeholder Issues Strategically," *Health Care Management Review* 17, no. 1 (1992): 35–49.

93. M.T. Halpern et al., "Multihospital System Affiliation as a Survival Strategy for Rural Hospitals under the Prospective Payment System," *Journal of Rural Health* 8, no. 2 (1992): 93–105.

94. White, "The 'Corporatization' of U.S. Hospitals," 105.

95. Ibid.

96. J. Nemes, "U.S. Hospital Chains Retreat from Europe," *Modern Healthcare* 21, no. 36 (September 9, 1991): 39–40.

97. White, "The 'Corporatization' of U.S. Hospitals," 103.

98. Brown and McCool, "Health Care Systems: Predictions," 89–90.

99. White, "The 'Corporatization' of U.S. Hospitals," 102–103.

100. J.K. Piper and H.G. Collier, "Multifacilities Move toward Regional Orientation," *Provider* 16, no. 6 (1990): 18, 20–21.

101. Robinson and Casalino, "Vertical Integration."

102. Ibid.

103. Ibid.

104. Health Care Advisory Board, *Emerging from Shadows: Resurgence to Prosperity* (Washington, DC: 1995).

105. Robinson and Casalino, "Vertical Integration."

106. Shortell, "The Evolution of Multihospital Systems."

107. Shortell et al., "Reinventing the American Hospital," 130–139.

108. Robinson and Casalino, "Vertical Integration."

109. Shortell et al., "Reinventing the American Hospital," 133.

110. J. Williams, "Successful Multis Keep Staff Costs to a Minimum," *Hospitals* 60, no. 10 (1986): 38–40.

111. L.R. Tucker and R.A. Zaremba, "Organizational Control and the Status of Marketing in Multihospital Systems," *Health Care Management Review* 16, no. 1 (1991): 41–56.

112. Shortell, "The Evolution of Multihospital Systems," 183.

113. D. Dranove et al., "Are Multihospital Systems More Efficient?" *Health Affairs* 15, no. 1 (1996): 100–104.

114. Ramirez, "Introduction to Multihospital Systems," 1–23.

115. Greene and Lutz, "A Down Year at Not-for-profits."

116. J. Greene, "Healthcare Systems' Newest Balancing Act: 'Doing More with Less,'" *Modern Healthcare* 22, no. 39 (1992): 52, 54, 56–58.

117. Robinson and Casalino, "Vertical Integration."

118. Ramirez, "Introduction to Multihospital Systems," 5.

119. Cleverly, "Financial and Operating Performance of Systems," 68.

120. Dranove et al., "Are Multihospital Systems More Efficient?" 102.

121. Greene and Lutz, "A Down Year at Not-for-profits."

122. J. Greene and S. Lutz, "A Tale of Two Ownership Sectors," *Modern Healthcare* 16, no. 18 (1996): 61–81.

123. Japsen and Scott, "System Growth."

124. J. Greene and S. Lutz, "Systems Post Fourth Straight Year of Income Growth," *Modern Healthcare* 24, no. 19 (1994): 36–63.

125. Greene and Lutz, "A Down Year at Not-for-profits."

126. Green and Lutz, "A Tale of Two Ownership Sectors."

127. Japsen and Scott, "System Growth."

128. Ibid.

129. R. Essner, *Compendium of Health Economics* (Little Falls, NJ: Health Learning Systems, 1993), 24.

130. Cleverly, "Financial and Operating Performance of Systems," 63–73.

131. Sear, "Comparison of Efficiency and Profitability," 31–37.

132. G.O. Ginn, "Organizational and Environmental Determinants of Hospital Strategy," *Hospital and Health Services Administration* 37, no. 3 (1992): 291–302.

133. Tennyson and Fottler, "Does System Membership Enhance Financial Returns in Hospitals?"

134. Smith and Virgil, "Multihospital Systems," 59–61.

135. Kaiser, "The Future of Multihospital Systems," 36.

136. Ibid.

137. G.M. McGee et al., "The Impact of Corporatization on Administrator Stress in Nursing Homes, *Health Services Management Research* 5, no. 1 (1992): 54–65.

138. Kaiser, "The Future of Multihospital Systems," 43.

139. Toomey and Toomey, "The Role of Governing Boards," 23–24.

140. L.L. Morlock and J.A. Alexander, "Models of Governance in Multihospital Systems: Implications for Hospitals and System-level Decision-making," *Medical Care* 24, no. 12 (1986): 1118–1135.

141. Morlock and Alexander, "Models of Governance," 1122–1123, 1125–1129.

142. Ibid., 1134.

143. J.A. Alexander et al., "The Challenge of Governing Integrated Delivery Systems," *Health Care Management Review* 20, no. 4 (1995): 69–81.

144. Ramirez, "Introduction to Multihospital Systems," 5–6, 11.

145. T. McLaughlin, "Finding Jobs for 1200 Laid-off Employees: Health One's Goal," *Hospitals* 66, no. 1 (1992): 43–44.

146. G.H. Kaye, "Multis, mergers, acquisitions, and the healthcare provider," *Nursing Management* 20, no. 4 (1989): 54–62.

147. T. Droste, "Multihospital Executives Continue To Earn More," *Hospitals* 63, no. 15 (1989): 74.

148. Smith and Virgil, "Multihospital Systems," 66–69.

149. D. Gregory, "Strategic Alliances between Physicians and Hospitals in Multihospital Systems," *Hospital and Health Services Administration* 37, no. 2 (1992): 247–258.

150. L. Burns et al., "The Impact of Corporate Structures on Physician Inclusion and Participation," *Medical Care* 27, no. 10 (1989): 967–982.

151. M.T. Koska, "Systems Fight Uphill Battle To Gain Physician Loyalty," *Hospitals* 64, no. 6 (1990): 60, 62.

152. Greene, "Healthcare Systems' Newest Balancing Act," 56, 58.

153. Smith and Virgil, "Multihospital Systems," 64.

154. G.F. Schwartz and C.T. Stone, "Strategic Acquisitions by Academic Medical Centers: The Jefferson Experience as Operational Paradigm," *Health Care Management Review* 16, no. 2 (1991): 39–47.

155. R.M. Albertina and T.F. Bakewell, "Allocating Capital Systemwide," *Health Progress* 70, no. 4 (1989): 26–32.

156. Federa and Miller, "Capital Allocation Techniques," 72.

157. Albertina and Bakewell, "Allocating Capital Systemwide," 26, 21.

158. Federa and Miller, "Capital Allocation Techniques," 68–69, 73–74.

159. Ibid., 74–75.

160. Ibid., 75.

161. Ibid., 77–78.

162. L. Gerber and F.I. Feinstein, "When the System Can't Save the Hospital: A Practical Overview of Workouts and Bankruptcy Alternatives," *Topics in Health Care Financing* 18, no. 4 (1992): 46–62.

163. Ibid., 50–51.

164. H.J. Anderson, "Sizing up Systems: Researchers To Test Performance Measures," *Hospitals* 65, no. 20 (1991): 33–34.

165. A.T. Solovy, "Multis Sweep Cash, Boost Investment Income," *Hospitals* 62, no. 5 (1988): 74–75.

166. Ramirez, "Introduction to Multihospital Systems," 6.

167. Ibid., 6–7.

168. Ibid., 12.

169. M.M. McKinney et al., "Paths and Pacemakers: Innovation Diffusion Networks in Multihospital Systems and Alliances," *Health Care Management Review* 16, no. 1 (1991): 17–23.

170. P. McGuire, "Kaiser Permanente's New Technologies Committee: An Approach to Assessing Technology," *Quality Review Bulletin* 16, no. 6 (1990): 240–242.

171. S. Taravella, "Risk Management: Frustrated Healthcare Systems Seek Alternatives to Traditional Insurance," *Modern Healthcare* 18, no. 20 (1988): 30–32, 36, 41.

172. Tucker and Zaremba, "Organizational Control and the Status of Marketing," 47, 53–54.

173. White, "The 'Corporatization' of U.S. Hospitals," 103.

174. T.L. Werner, "A New Approach to Decision Support at Adventist Hospital System/Sunbelt," *Computers in Healthcare* 11, no. 3 (1990): 49–50.

175. M. Hurwitz, "Multis Move To Centralize IS Decisions," *Hospitals* 62, no. 5 (1988): 75.

176. K. Lumsdon, "Holding Networks Together: Shared Information Will Be Glue for Reformed Health System," *Hospitals* 7, no. 4 (1993): 26–27.

177. Shortell, "The Evolution of Multihospital Systems," 178.

178. Robinson and Casalino, "Vertical Integration," 8.

179. M.D. Hiller, "Ethics and Health Care Administration: Issues in Education and Practice," *Journal of Health Administration Education* 2, no. 2 (1984): 147–192.

180. Greene and Lutz, "A Tale of Two Ownership Sectors."

181. Japsen and Scott, "System Growth."

182. R. Herzlinger, *Market Driven Health Care* (Reading, MA: Addison-Wesley Publishing Co., 1997).

183. M.C. Jaklevic, "Buying Doctor's Practices Often Leads to Red Ink," *Modern Healthcare* 26, no. 25 (1996): 39.

184. L. Kertesz, "Systems Begin Pruning HMOs from Holdings," *Modern Healthcare* 26, no. 27 (1996): 77.

185. R.R. Gillies, "Conceptualizing and Measuring Integration," *Hospital and Health Services Administration* 38, no. 4 (1993): 484.

186. Kertesz, "Systems Begin Pruning HMOs."

187. Conrad and Dowling, "Vertical Integration in Health Services," 21.

188. Shortell, "The Evolution of Multihospital Systems," 177–214.

189. Risk, "Multihospital Systems: The Turning Point," 46–53.

190. D.R. Barry, "Commentary: Are Hospitals and Their Boards up to These Challenges?" *Health Care Management Review* 20, no. 1 (1995): 40–92.

MYRON D. FOTTLER, PHD, is a Professor and Director of the PhD Program in Health Services Administration at the University of Alabama at Birmingham. He has authored or co-authored 11 books, 20 book chapters, and more than 100 journal articles in most of the major management and health service journals. His most recent book (co-authored with John D. Blair) is *Strategic Leadership for Medical Groups: Navigating Your Strategic Web* (1998). He received his MBA from Boston University and his PhD in business from Columbia University.

DONNA MALVEY, PHD, is an Assistant Professor of Health Administration in the College of Public Health at the University of South Florida in Tampa. Her area of expertise is the strategic management of health services organizations. Past experience includes teaching courses in labor relations and health care organizations and management. In addition, she has served as the executive director of a national trade association representing health professionals and as a congressional aide. She has co-authored articles on negotiation, the administration of the labor relations contract, and the development of comprehensive state level databases to ensure adequacy of health care professionals. Dr. Malvey received her PhD in health services administration at the University of Alabama at Birmingham and her master's degree in health services administration from George Washington University.

Chapter 3

The Legal Structure of Health Care Delivery

Robert H. Rosenfield

Throughout most of U.S. history, the legal structure of health care delivery was based exclusively on an interaction between individuals. Individual patients interacted with individual physicians; care was provided in the home; there was no insurance. Today, however, the legal structure of health care delivery is based almost as exclusively on an interaction between entities. Corporations or governments decide what care is delivered, to whom, and by whom. The physicians who provide care are likely to be employed by a large medical group that is likely to be owned by an organized delivery system or managed by a large, publicly traded company.

The evolution from individual to institutional interaction has taken a long time, although the pace of change accelerated dramatically in the closing decades of the twentieth century. While the future legal structure of health care delivery involves institutions, it is not at all clear what form those institutions will take. Will they be charitable in character? Will the proprietary form predominate? Will physician groups dominate the key players? Will they combine physician, facility, and insurance functions?

A key question is whether these changes will result in better health care. It is possible that the new system will combine the efficiency of the corporate sector with the com-

passion of the charitable world. It also is possible that the system will exhibit less attractive traits. Whatever the outcome, contemporary health care professionals will be leaders in a system that differs greatly from anything that has existed previously in the United States or in any other country. It is a grand experiment, and the stakes are high.

THE CHARITABLE MODEL AND THE WORKSHOP MODEL

In the past, people were born at home, got sick at home, had children at home, and died at home. The earliest hospitals arose to meet the needs of the poor and the transient who had no homes. Because patients could not pay and health care insurance did not exist, early hospitals were organized as charities. Typically, religious organizations sponsored them. Physicians practicing in early hospitals did not expect payment for their services. Only when a physician provided services in a patient's home (or later in the physician's office) did the physician expect payment. As a result, very few physicians ever practiced in a hospital, and early hospitals did not experience any sense of dependence on physicians or physician referrals. This combination of circumstances in which individual patients interacted with individual physicians and charitable hospitals provided care to the poor free of charge was widespread in Western civilization for nearly 1,000 years. This combination of arrangements and characteristics can be called the charitable model.

The charitable model was replaced during the Industrial Revolution. Important scientific and technological discoveries made it possible for physicians to perform surgery with a degree of safety and comfort that created a rapidly growing market for paying patients. These technological discoveries led directly to a major change in the legal structure of health care delivery. Physicians could not perform surgery in the patient's home. Moreover, the ability of a physician to attract paying patients substantially increased the physician's professional and social standing. It also made hospitals dependent on physician referrals for their financial stability. Thus, a new set of institutions emerged to meet the needs of patients paying for surgical and diagnostic services that could be provided only on a centralized basis. In keeping with its industrial heritage, this new structure became known as the workshop model.

The workshop model had two essential features. The first was the continued charitable ownership of hospital facilities. The second was the economic interdependence of hospitals and physicians, a major departure from the charitable model. Hospitals no longer could depend on charitable funds to meet the financial needs of their facilities. Just as physicians had to rely on hospitals to provide facilities for certain kinds of care, hospitals had to rely on the willingness and ability of physicians to attract paying patients and to perform services at their facility, as opposed to another. This interdependence produced constant shifts of power between physicians and hospitals. Physicians often encouraged the construction of multiple hospitals and sought medical staff privileges at each of them.

Many physicians even built their own hospitals in the years following World War II. Physicians also sought legal protection for their professional independence. The "corporate practice of medicine doctrine" precluded hospitals in most states from employing physicians.

One of the most important legacies of the workshop model grew out of these two features. That legacy was the indifference of many physicians to the cost or volume of the resources that they consumed or applied in the course of treating patients in a hospital. As the leading hospitals were charitable during this period, physicians had no ownership interest in them. Lacking any financial interests in the hospitals and being aware, as were the hospitals, that they could shift referrals of patients to competing hospitals, many physicians demanded the latest and most expensive technology, highest nursing staff ratios, and the most expensive medications and prostheses.

The workshop model came into existence around the turn of the nineteenth century. It lasted until the late 1980s. Although it did not last as long as the charitable model, it was far more stable than anything seen since.

THE ORGANIZED DELIVERY SYSTEM MODEL

The demise of the workshop model began in the summer of 1982. With the United States suffering through the most severe economic contraction since the Great Depression, public and private decision makers focused on the need to control rising health care costs. The summer of 1982 saw the adoption of legislation that effectively ended cost-based reimbursement to hospitals for Medicare patients and replaced it with prospective payment, based on diagnosis-related groups. Also that summer, California became the first state to make it possible for insurance companies to offer economic incentives for patients to seek health care exclusively from hospitals and physicians that offered discounts to the insurers. The state laws that universally had precluded insurance companies from offering such inducements, the so-called freedom of choice laws, disappeared shortly after the adoption of the California legislation, and the rapid growth of managed care followed. One of the most important aspects of the rise of managed care was the reduction in the power of physicians to control patients and hospital referrals. This combination of economic pressures forced workshop model hospitals to reexamine their most fundamental assumptions. This reexamination led to the replacement of the workshop model with the organized delivery system model.

Consolidation and Collaboration

Perhaps the earliest step taken by hospital executives toward consolidation and collaboration was to combine the market power of formerly competing charitable hospitals into a single legal structure. Consolidated providers can conduct negotiations with newly aggressive insurers more effectively, especially in health care perhaps because of consumers' perceptions that certain hospitals provide better care than others. Carriers cannot hope to sell insurance policies in certain markets unless those leading hospitals are going to be available to policyholders. Thus, multihospital systems soon replaced the freestanding charitable hospital as the norm.

Consolidating hospitals into systems also reduced the power of physicians to play one institution against another. There would be less likelihood in a consolidated environment that a physician could maintain privileges at hospitals in different systems. It also became far more difficult for individual physician-owned hospitals to compete with large systems, and proprietary hospital chains absorbed most physician-owned hospitals in the 1970s and 1980s. From the physician's perspective, loss of power relative to the hospital was one of the most disturbing aspects of the demise of the workshop model. It could be argued that most of the developments in the legal structure of health care delivery since the 1980s have represented an attempt by physicians to deal with this fundamental change. Physicians have approached this power shift in a number of ways. Some of them have sought employment with hospitals. Others have created large groupings of physicians to try to create countervailing sources of leverage. Still others have tried to acquire ambulatory care facilities and divert important revenues from the hospitals.

Following the consolidation that took place in the 1980s and 1990s, a major metropolitan area might have had 3 to 4 organized delivery systems instead of 10 to 15 independent workshop model institutions. Each system retained a workshop model structure for its physicians, however. It was typical for a system to have thousands of physicians legally organized as small group and solo practitioners, making the negotiation of managed care contracts with physicians a much more complex problem for insurance companies than the negotiation of such contracts with hospitals. From the physician's perspective, the need for collective action was great. Insurance companies offering managed care products might not allow individual physicians an opportunity to negotiate for a contract at all or, if they did, a chance to alter either the terms or the price at which their services would be provided.

Although it might be relatively easy for physicians to determine the effect that granting a discount from their customary charges to a particular carrier would have on their practice, managed care contracts soon became extremely complex. Negotiating these contracts without the help of professionals became virtually impossible. The carriers were not limiting themselves to negotiating prices. They were playing a more active role in supervising the care that was provided. Pre-admission certification, concurrent reviews, and retrospective reviews all became part of the landscape during this period. Physicians resented the intrusion of insurance bureaucrats into the physician–patient relationship and sought authority from the carriers to manage the care themselves. Only a comprehensive organization could hope to obtain consent from the carriers to carry out these functions on a delegated basis, however.

The solution to all of these problems was the independent practice (or provider) association (IPA). IPAs formed rapidly in the late 1980s and early 1990s. IPAs are associations of independent practices formed for the purpose of negotiating managed care contracts with carriers and public payers. IPAs usually have two forms: a professional corporation and a nonprofit corporation with numerous "members."

The two IPA forms have important features in common. First, neither of them actually provides care. Instead they "arrange for" care to be provided by independent physicians and small medical groups that contract with the IPA. Second, the contracts with physicians are typically nonexclusive, short-term arrangements that can be terminated on 60 to 90 days' notice. Contracting physicians are free to negotiate for patients with other IPAs or directly with the insurance companies. These features developed in response to the concerns of many physicians that IPAs would erode the traditions of professional autonomy.

By definition, IPAs represent only physician interests. Physicians traditionally have

been responsible for a lower proportion of health care costs than hospitals. This arrangement led to a tendency of carriers to negotiate first with leading hospitals in a given market and only later turn to the relevant IPAs to negotiate a payment schedule for physician services. From a carrier's perspective, it does not matter whether the hospital or the IPA gets a "better deal." The carrier's interest is the overall contract price and the allocation of risk. From the perspective of the hospital and the IPA, however, the question of who gets a better deal is of great importance. To reduce the risk that hospitals and IPAs will pursue conflicting negotiations with carriers, many organized delivery systems created physician–hospital organizations (PHOs) in the 1980s and early 1990s. These entities are joint ventures formed by hospitals and IPAs to coordinate the negotiation of managed care contracts with insurance companies. Typically, PHOs are organized as for-profit entities. Business corporations and later limited liability companies are the most common forms. The physicians and the hospital share equally in the ownership and governance of PHOs. Often, an IPA holds the physician interest in the PHO.

Early organized delivery systems, then, had three characteristics: multiple hospitals, partial horizontal physician integration through IPAs, and the collaboration of hospital and physician negotiating postures through the PHO. The basic premise of these early arrangements was that managed care would mean little more than negotiating a discount from customary charges. It soon became clear, however, that discounts were not an effective cost containment strategy. Many providers simply increased prices prior to granting discounts. More important, discounts did not reduce the number or type of procedures performed. To reduce health care costs, many employers and insurance companies concluded, it would be necessary to change the way that medicine is practiced. Fortunately, for many people, such a method already existed. It was called "gatekeeper capitation." The insurance companies that used it were called health maintenance organizations (HMOs).

Gatekeeper Capitation

The concept behind gatekeeper capitation is simple. Those principally responsible for continued health care cost increases were believed to be the specialist physicians: cardiologists, oncologists, orthopedists, and their colleagues. If patients could be weaned away from specialists and the high-technology diagnostic and surgical services that they provided, health care cost increases could be curbed.

Under gatekeeper capitation, patients are required to select a primary care physician from a list provided by the HMO. The patient must see that primary care physician for all his or her health care needs. If the patient believes that specialist care is necessary, he or she must obtain a referral from the primary care physician. To keep the number of specialist referrals under control, the HMO may offer the gatekeeper primary care physician financial incentives to limit specialist referrals. These incentives may range from relatively modest bonus payments to requirements that the primary care physician pay for all specialist care out of the per capita (or capitation) payments that the physician or the physician's group received from the HMO. The ultimate weapon, of course, is the possible refusal of the carrier to renew the primary care physician's contract in subsequent years if the carrier deems the number of specialist referrals excessive.

By the mid-1990s, many hospital and physician leaders were concerned that gatekeeper capitation was going to become the norm in the United States. Gatekeeper capitation was becoming widespread in California, and many people viewed California as a leader in health care innovation. Many trends in managed care (including the formation of HMOs, IPAs, and preferred provider organizations) had first appeared in California. In addition, the Clinton Administration, as it took shape in late 1992, indicated that one its first priorities was going to be reform of the health care delivery system. As the Clinton Plan evolved, it seemed to many observers that the entire population would have coverage under some form of managed care and that gatekeeper capitation was going to be a key ingredient in many of the plans that would be offered. These factors led to major changes in the organized delivery system model. Systems established under this model pursued HMO licenses in order to regain some of the profit and power that appeared to be passing to the HMOs. They also embarked on an intense effort to acquire primary care practices in the hope of controlling the physicians who were likely to become the gatekeepers of the future. This effort to hire primary care practitioners represented a fundamental departure from one of the key features of the workshop model. From this point forward, the medical community surrounding most hospitals consisted of two types of physicians: those who were employed and those who were not.

Some specialist physicians were concerned about the rapid consolidation of primary care that was taking place. As a result, a number of large multispecialty groups and some large single-specialty groups also acquired primary care practices during this period. By and large, however, specialists did not have anything approaching the capital resources that the organized delivery systems possessed. When the dust started to settle in the late 1990s, most organized delivery systems had acquired large numbers of primary care practices. They paid the physicians cash for their practices and offered them employment contracts of varying length, typically 3 to 5 years. Many of them received flat salaries or income guarantees.

Hospital-Affiliated Group Practices

The legal structures used by organized delivery systems to administer their primary care practices, known as hospital-affiliated group practices (HAGPs), generally take one of two forms, which are equally prevalent. In the first form, the hospital directly employs the primary care physicians. In the second form, a specialized corporate subsidiary becomes their employer. There are other models in existence. A few hospitals have created management service organization (MSO) subsidiaries that acquire the business assets of a medical practice and employ all the administrative personnel needed to perform claims processing, billing, patient scheduling, and other important management functions. These subsidiaries enter into long-term (30 to 40 years) management contracts with a new professional corporation that employs the physicians. A final form, which is common only in California, with a few examples in Alabama and Tennessee, is the foundation model. Under this model, a nonprofit corporation (called a foundation in California) acquires all the business assets of a medical practice and then contracts medical care with a new professional corporation, which employs the physicians. Unlike the MSO model, the foundation model does not sell management services to a professional corporation. Instead, the foundation is actually the provider of care and purchases professional services on an exclusive basis from the professional corporation.

The dominant forms of HAGP models (i.e., direct employment of physicians and the wholly owned subsidiary variation) have several strengths in common. First, they link the physicians directly to a substantial source of capital. To the extent that physicians need capital for satellite office expansion, new medical equipment, or information systems, for example, a hospital owner should be able to provide sufficient capital. Second, transactions involving the acquisition of a practice and employment of the physicians by an HAGP generally provide the physicians with substantial up-front payments and considerable income protection. Third, physicians employed by an HAGP have every reason to be confident that the hospital will make every effort to see that the HAGP is a participating provider in all managed care contracts to which the hospital is a party. These are substantial advantages that make the HAGP an attractive alternative for primary care physicians in the mid-1990s.

Initially, hospitals also saw substantial advantages in HAGPs. First, hospitals were attracted to the obvious control that this form gave them over the flow of patients in their communities. At least in theory, physicians employed by an HAGP could be instructed to refer their patients to specialists who were loyal to the sponsoring hospital. In addition, managed care contracts that relied on gatekeeper capitation could serve as a basis for determining not only which specialists would receive the most patients, but also how much they would be paid and how much risk they would take (through subcapitation arrangements). Second, hospitals assumed that acquiring primary care practices would provide them with substantial leverage in negotiating with managed care companies, especially those in which the primary care physician was viewed as the key to cost containment. It would be particularly difficult to exclude from a provider network large primary care practices with substantial visibility within a community. Moreover, those large in size with significant management capability might provide the carrier with added assurance that its subscribers would receive uniform, high-quality care at a reasonable price.

The mature organized delivery system model seemed to offer a comprehensive response to the problems facing providers in the mid-1990s. It combined a comprehensive network of physicians (IPA) with the hospital's negotiating strength (PHO), while simultaneously consolidating and controlling primary care physicians (HAGPs) and offering an insurance product to minimize dependence on third party carriers (HMOs). Unfortunately, the architects of this model soon found themselves facing challenges that did not exist in the early 1990s.

New Challenges

One fundamental challenge facing the mature organized delivery system model has been that its principal economic assumption proved to be incorrect. The Clinton Administration's plan for health care reform failed to gain congressional approval. Even more important, capitated patients in California soon began complaining about restrictions on their access to specialists and the inconvenience of having to deal with gatekeepers, and California HMOs were finding that sales of gatekeeper products were slowing dramatically. Suddenly, it seemed that subscribers were willing to pay more to preserve the freedom of choice that they had enjoyed in the days of fee-for-service medical care.

As a result, new insurance products have begun to enter the market. Among the most significant are so-called open access plans. These plans eliminate the gatekeeper entirely. Subscribers are promised access to any

specialist in the carrier's network at any time. Some commentators wonder how these new insurance products will control costs. For the time being, however, the pendulum appears to have swung away from capitation and back toward freedom of choice.

The implications of this renewed emphasis on freedom for consumers to seek care from specialists are profound. In the first place, it means that the massive investment of organized delivery systems in primary care practices is even less likely to produce the financial returns or the power that originally had been contemplated. Furthermore, it appears that hospitals have focused on the wrong type of physician as a business partner. The renewed emphasis on freedom of choice means that specialists, not primary care physicians, are going to have the most to say about how and where care is delivered in the foreseeable future. Moreover, they are going to have the principal say in how much that care is going to cost. Doing business with specialists is going to be a difficult task, however. This is a highly fragmented field, and the demographics of specialty care pose particular challenges.

While there is some dispute over the details, the United States seems to have more specialist physicians than it needs (Table 3–1). In fact, there may be massive surpluses in some of the most important specialties. It seems likely that this surplus is going to get worse for the foreseeable future (Figure 3–1). The number of physicians practicing in the United States will probably continue to rise through the early years of the next century. Two-thirds of these physicians are likely to be specialists if current trends continue.

The increased competition facing specialists from the growth in their numbers will translate into lower incomes for physicians unless one of two things happens. First, specialists will have to supplement their income

Table 3–1 Excess Number of Specialists

	Minneapolis	U.S.	Excess (Deficit)
PCPs	70.9	66	(7%)
All Specialists	100.6	121.7	21%
Cardiologists	4.1	5.7	39%
Anesthesiologists	7.6	9.9	29%
General Surgeons	7.8	9.7	24%
Urologists	2.6	3.3	27%

Source: Data from Bernstein Research.

derived from patient care with investment income derived from the ownership of ancillary testing or surgical equipment and facilities. In order to acquire the size necessary to bear these capital risks and ensure sufficient refer- ral volume, they will have to consolidate their practices. Second, specialists will have to develop the management and information systems capability to satisfy the demands of carriers who will seek to contract with specialist

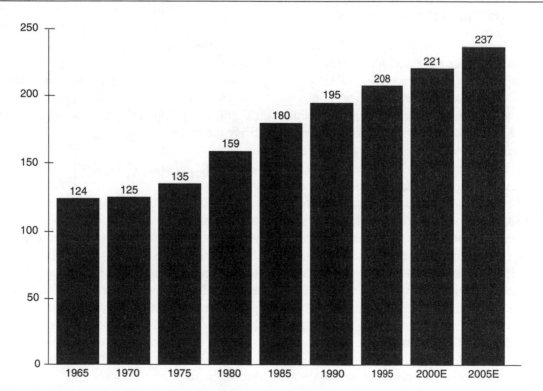

Figure 3–1 Physicians Practicing in the United States per 100,000 Population. *Source:* Data from Bernstein Research.

groups on a wide variety of bases in an attempt to reduce medical costs and improve quality of care. This alternative will also require consolidation and substantial capital investment.

This combination of demographic pressures and consolidation opportunities is one of the greatest challenges facing the health care delivery system in the United States today. The way in which the organized delivery system model responds to this "specialist challenge" will influence the shape of health care delivery in the next century. Unfortunately, the current configuration of the organized delivery system model does not appear well positioned to meet this challenge.

A CRITIQUE OF THE ORGANIZED DELIVERY SYSTEM MODEL

Results of Initial Efforts

As elements of the organized delivery system model, IPAs have achieved a great many of the purposes for which they were designed. They have permitted large numbers of physicians to contract with managed care companies without forcing them to abandon independent practice. They also have had some success in getting physicians accustomed to the idea of having their care patterns monitored by peers. These successes do not mean that IPAs will be effective in meeting the specialist challenge, however. First, IPAs do not have capital and are unlikely to be able to raise it. Generally, an IPA raises capital from individual physicians, who typically make a modest, one-time payment for their equity or nonequity interest. The formation and start-up phases of the IPA's existence consume much of that amount. Without capital, an IPA cannot consolidate specialist practices to obtain economies of scale or centralize ancillary and outpatient surgical procedures to pre-

serve specialists' incomes. Second, the leadership of IPAs is diffuse. Many different specialties demand representation at the board level, and it is difficult for IPAs to develop strategies that do not appear to favor one group of specialists over another. Finally, IPAs are very public environments. Few specialists want to have detailed financial information concerning their practices available to IPA management, much less the IPA board, as it may lead to a loss of confidentiality and a possible loss of referral volume.

PHOs are no better positioned to meet the specialist challenge than are IPAs. Indeed, most PHOs are shell entities that simply provide a formal link between IPAs and hospitals. They have few assets, and they cannot acquire capital. One of the central features of the PHO is the 50/50 balance between IPA and hospital interests. Yet this feature precludes the PHO from becoming a meaningful change agent with respect to specialists. Furthermore, charitable hospitals cannot contribute more capital than their 50 percent partner IPAs are willing to contribute without violating the Internal Revenue Code or turning the organization into something entirely different.

Experience with HAGPs

It would be natural to focus on hospital-affiliated primary care group practices as the most likely to evolve into a structure that could consolidate and control specialists. After all, some of these group practices already employ dozens, in some cases, hundreds, of physicians. Unfortunately, experience with HAGPs has been decidedly mixed. Many systems are reluctant to repeat this experience in seeking to address the challenges presented by uneasy specialists.

Although initially attractive to primary care physicians and hospitals alike, HAGPs have produced a number of unpleasant surprises. Most hospitals have found the capital cost associated with acquiring medical practices to be tremendous. A typical purchase price was $175,000 per physician, although many systems paid much more. Even at $175,000, hospitals have to spend $17,500,000 in acquiring a network of 100 primary care physicians. Moreover, the initial capital outlay was often not the end of the capital spending, because primary care practices typically lacked sophisticated information systems. In addition, many consultants began advising hospitals to consolidate solo and small group primary care practices by providing facilities that would handle five to seven physicians at one time. These facilities may cut costs and promote efficiency, but they also require additional capital outlays.

If HAGPs had been profitable from the outset, substantial capital expenditures might not have been a serious problem. Few hospital executives expected high margins, but even fewer of them anticipated the operating losses that have accompanied the use of HAGPs. It is not unusual to find HAGPs that are losing between $100,000 and $150,000 per primary care physician per year. In some cases, HAGP losses have represented more than half of the bottom line of an entire system.

Several factors have contributed to these losses. First, hospitals using the HAGP form quickly learned that they had no legal choice but to provide the same pension plan benefits to acquired physicians and their employees that the hospital had provided historically to hospital employees, even though primary care physicians and their employees typically have no pension benefits at all. Second, many hospitals provided physician employees with fixed or guaranteed compensation arrangements, which placed the hospitals at risk for declines in productivity by physicians who

were insulated for the first time from the pressures of the marketplace. Only a small reduction in effort can produce a meaningful reduction in net income.

Third, hospitals added substantial overhead costs to practices that were marginally profitable in the first place. Primary care physicians organized in small groups typically had little or no management. For example, the physicians themselves or family members did the purchasing; once consolidated into an HAGP, however, they found that they were dealing with complex and expensive bureaucracies. Without question, a good part of this new management burden was essential. If HAGPs were to provide uniform, high-quality care and produce the data necessary to achieve this management and to market the improved performance effectively, they would need sophisticated information systems and management personnel who could use it. Those costs would be in addition to the other costs associated with the acquisition and operations of a large group of former solo practitioners, however.

Faced with these losses and the impossibility of covering their capital investment through operating revenues generated by the HAGP, hospitals concluded that they could make sense of their investment only if they could trace incremental referrals and ancillary volume to these HAGP physicians. This has not proved a simple task. Most inpatient referrals come through specialists, not primary care physicians.

Hospitals are not alone in their unhappiness with HAGPs. The employed physicians have become increasingly discontented, as evidenced in their rising interest in unionization. The Service Employees International Union is one of several labor organizations seeking to organize disgruntled employed physicians and dentists. In several states, there has been litigation over the ability of physicians to avail themselves of the provisions of the National Labor Relations Act. Unions have been certified in a number of settings, and it appears inevitable that more referendums will take place in the immediate future.

Even in settings where they have not gone this far, some employed physicians are complaining about loss of professional autonomy, loss of respect from their colleagues, and fear that their compensation and even employment may not survive the sponsoring hospital's efforts to reduce the financial drain created by the HAGP. In some cases, hospitals have simply repudiated the contracts that they signed with physicians. Others are seeking renegotiations. A great many are making it clear that when existing contracts come up for renewal, some physicians will not have jobs and all others will lose their guaranteed compensation.

As HAGPs struggle with financial burdens, some federal agencies are becoming concerned about possible violations of the law. To date, the Internal Revenue Service (IRS) has been the most active agency. The IRS has challenged the tax exemption of several well-known systems over transactions involving the acquisition of physician practices. At least one system has been forced to notify bondholders that the continued tax-exempt status of its debt may be in jeopardy because of an IRS investigation. In addition, the Office of the Inspector General of the Department of Health and Human Services has been conducting a series of investigations into the abusive billing practices of physicians. Many hospitals are concerned that employed physicians may engage in "upcoding" and other questionable billing practices in order to reduce the risk that they would lose their jobs in the current financial environment. Hospital and medical school employers of physicians are at risk for civil monetary penalties, which could come to $10,000 per claim, if

they submit improper bills to Medicare. Because a single physician may generate thousands of claims to the Medicare program in a year, the risk associated with this issue is significant. As a result, hospitals are moving swiftly to implement regulatory compliance programs designed to minimize the risk that HAGP physicians could submit false bills. These programs are expensive, however, and will either increase the financial drain associated with the HAGP or force an increase in prices. All in all, it seems unlikely that the HAGP will provide an answer to the specialist challenge.

The organized delivery system model also has failed to alter a key legacy of the workshop model. That legacy is the economic indifference of physicians to the hospital cost consequences of their patient care decisions. Although primary care physicians may have become employees of organized delivery system model hospitals, specialists have not. Yet, the specialists decide when to admit a patient, what tests or procedures to perform in the case of that patient, and when to discharge the patient. Without an economic incentive to reduce costs and improve outcomes in hospitals, it may be difficult for specialists to focus on optimum efficiency in patient care.

PHYSICIAN PRACTICE MANAGEMENT COMPANIES

As the opportunities for capitation failed to materialize on a national basis, the opportunity to generate revenues from the ownership or management of single-specialty practices began to receive attention. Thus, a new type of business has now emerged to meet the specialist challenge; this new type of business is called a physician practice management company (PPM). It seems clear that these companies will remain a presence in health care delivery for the foreseeable future.

The presence of single-specialty PPMs threatens to destabilize the primacy of the hospital's role in the health care delivery system, notwithstanding the hospital's current monopoly on inpatient care in most markets and its "success" in acquiring primary care practices. A central question for hospitals in the late 1990s is whether to ignore PPM efforts to consolidate specialists in their markets or to try to create alternatives for specialists that might be more acceptable both to the hospital and to the communities that they serve. There are legal structures that permit hospitals to offer reasonable alternatives to the PPMs, but they represent dramatic departures from the way in which hospitals and physicians have related to one another in the past. They are also largely untested at this time.

Many PPMs understand the need to consolidate, capitalize, and effectively manage the nation's specialist physician practices. They rarely claim to be able to reduce practice expenses, however. They generally recognize that adding sophisticated information systems, marketing, contracting, and forecasting capability will increase costs, but they theorize that if these costs can be spread over a large number of practices, they will be less burdensome.

The key to understanding most PPM goals and objectives is to appreciate their focus on revenue growth. One way to achieve this growth is to expand the medical groups being managed, either by hiring more physicians of the type already predominant in the group or by hiring physicians in complementary specialties who currently receive referrals from the group being managed. PPMs may also seek managed care contracts from HMOs or self-insuring employers for care in the specialty being managed; such contracts can expand patient volume dramatically. The most successful approach to revenue growth at the moment involves building surgical and ancillary revenue-generating facilities that can provide the same services hospitals currently provide. This poses a substantial challenge and threat to hospitals.

A wide variety of PPM-sponsored facilities have emerged throughout the United States. Most, if not all of them, have physician investors who are in a position to refer patients for surgery or ancillary tests to those facilities. Perhaps the most elaborate examples of PPM-sponsored facilities are the heart hospitals built by MedCath. Another PPM, HealthSouth Corporation, is already the largest operator of ambulatory surgical centers in the United States. Less well-known PPMs are developing birthing centers, imaging centers, gastrointestinal laboratories, and outpatient cancer treatment centers. PPMs also have both private and public sources of financing that make it possible for them to acquire practices and build facilities and systems at a rapid rate. For many specialists facing the need to invest substantial amounts in their practices, this ready access to capital can be an important advantage. Finally, successful PPMs create opportunities for physicians to convert the value of their practices to cash. Most PPMs pay a combination of cash, notes, and PPM stock to medical groups that agree to be managed or acquired by them. If the PPM is able to meet its financial goals and succeeds in issuing shares to the public, the physician shareholders can then sell their shares at a substantial price. Recent bankruptcies of many PPMs raise concerns about their abilities to achieve their goals.

Without question, the emergence of the PPM as a consolidator of medical practices and developer of new ancillary and outpatient (and inpatient) capacity has the ability to alter the health care landscape. Successful PPMs probably will divert substantial ancillary and outpatient revenues from hospitals. Indeed, it is possible to imagine a future in which hospitals will function primarily as a place where patients with complex conditions and little insurance will be sent for treatment after their referring physicians have concluded that it would not be in the physicians' financial interest to refer them to the facilities owned or operated and managed by a PPM. If PPMs take a larger role in health care delivery, there are a number of possible outcomes:

- The PPM-sponsored facilities may provide superior specialty care, as they will have a much more narrow focus than facilities operated by a general hospital. Moreover, they will have access to large databases that incorporate experience from all similar facilities nationwide.
- It will be more difficult for a local hospital to avoid raising prices for the services that it provides if it loses high-margin revenue in ancillary and outpatient services. Yet, the resistance of insurance companies and local businesses to price increases could lead to an erosion of margins and a decline in the hospital's ability to provide quality service in all areas.
- Patients will not receive coordinated care. The narrow focus of PPM facilities on one type of illness or procedure will complicate the process of ensuring that all the patient's needs are met.
- PPMs rarely work with hospitals to reduce inpatient costs and improve patient outcomes. They are natural competitors, not collaborators. This reality perpetuates one of the worst elements of the workshop model and the organized delivery system model, namely, their failure to harmonize the economic incentives of hospital and physician.
- The emergence of a string of narrowly focused health care "boutiques" probably will strengthen the hand of the insurance companies, as they will be the only institutions in a position to contract with all of the "boutiques" and present employers and employees with a comprehensive package of care.

Elements of the charitable model are evident in these possible outcomes. If physicians and PPMs divert profitable patients to places of treatment owned by the PPMs, the hospital will become dependent on various forms of charity. Physicians will have less and less to do with hospitals, and their patient populations will again become largely poor and transient.

These changes have serious implications, and there are indications that some already are occurring. However, an alternative scenario is also possible. If the nation's hospitals can offer a credible alternative to the PPMs, the health care delivery system may evolve in new directions. It is by no means clear that hospitals will be able to do this. While hospitals and physicians long have regarded each other with deep suspicion, it is clear that hospitals will attempt to offer an alternative.

NEW DIRECTIONS

If hospitals are to create an alternative to large emerging physician groups and PPMs, the first question must be, What legal structures would be helpful in achieving this goal? New structures and approaches are probably required.

Many of the problems that organized delivery systems are having with HAGPs stem from the very concept of practice purchases. Buying physician practices does several things that detract from the long-term viability of a hospital–physician combination. First, it removes hospital capital from the system. Hospitals that are going to invest capital in physician practices are in a better position to meet market challenges and risks if that capital stays in the business rather than going into the pockets of the physicians at closing. Second, if the physicians receive an initial cash payment and then become employees, partners in the new structure do not have an equal investment in their joint future. It is essential that future hospital–physician legal structures harmonize the interests of all parties to the fullest extent possible. If one party is at risk and the other is not, decisions concerning capital investment, staffing, and the like may be poor or even unfair.

One of the greatest failings of the HAGP experience has been the inability of hospitals to harmonize their economic incentives with those of the physicians. Indeed, primary care physicians are rarely in a position to influence hospital costs because they do not admit patients to hospital facilities; that is the role of the specialists. Moreover, by paying primary care physicians on a straight salary basis, hospitals contribute to the indifference that some physicians demonstrate about what is happening outside their offices. Flat salaries also do little to curb physician appetites for more administrative support, higher salaries, and greater benefits for all concerned.

Traditionally, hospitals have been scrupulous about preserving their power to decide how to staff and run their facilities. Physicians have been equally concerned about their autonomy. From the consumer's perspective, however, hospitals and physicians constitute a single business. Maintaining an artificial separation between the hospital component and the physician component greatly complicates the process of purchasing care, prevents the parties from creating a single comprehensive data set and combining their collective experience and instincts about what would work better and reduce costs, and makes it more difficult to eliminate duplicate functions.

The following models are legally possible. They also appear to be politically and economically attractive to a wide spectrum of specialists and hospitals. The first model is the least comprehensive and least capable of producing substantial income and investment returns. It is the easiest to implement, however, and involves the smallest change in existing forms. The succeeding models present much more substantial economic opportunities, but they also involve far more change in the status quo and, consequently, far more political risk.

MSO Model A

The purpose of MSO Model A is to create a durable relationship between a hospital and one or more medical groups by aligning the political and economic incentives of the principals. In attempting to achieve this objective, MSO Model A effects the fewest changes in existing hospital and physician operations and relationships of any model. Like all the models, MSO Model A creates a single entity that allows a hospital and one or more groups of specialist physicians to share some of the economic rewards of efficient patient care. MSO Model A also establishes a single board of directors that has the authority to set policies (i.e., to establish treatment protocols for more efficient care and to negotiate managed care contracting relationships) that apply both to the hospital and the medical groups.

In MSO Model A, the hospital and a medical group form a new legal entity (probably a limited liability company) to act as the MSO (Figure 3–2). The MSO enters into management service agreements with both the hospital and the medical group. This arrangement gives the specialists a voice in the management of the department in which they treat patients, while also giving the hospital a com-

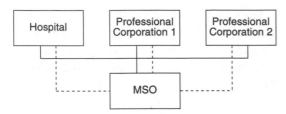

Figure 3–2 MSO Model A. The solid lines represent ownership, and the dotted lines represent a contractual relationship.

parable voice in the operations of the medical group.

The hospital and the medical group receive a 50 percent equity interest in the MSO in exchange for equal cash capital contributions. Neither the hospital nor the medical group makes any noncash contributions; each retains its respective business assets. The aggregate capital contributed to the MSO is a function of its capital needs (based on a business plan) and the parties' respective willingness to make such contributions. For example, if the parties decide that the MSO should engage in capital-intensive management services (e.g., information services), aggregate capital requirements would be significant. Although a physician group may be resistant to making a significant cash capital contribution, MSO Model A may enable the medical groups to gain a partner to assist in funding its capital requirements.

Under their respective management agreements, the hospital and the medical group would pay fair market value for services rendered. The level and type of services provided depend on where the hospital and the medical group perceive opportunities for the MSO to add value—through economies of scale, improvement of operating efficiencies in providing patient care, or elsewhere. Although MSO Model A does not create a significant equity appreciation opportunity for

its shareholders, it provides economic benefits in the form of better coordination of care, lower costs, and perhaps some modest distributions.

The strengths of MSO Model A originate primarily in the coordinated efforts it permits with only minimal changes to the hospital and physician status quo. These attributes fit in well with a strategy of trying to keep an initial transaction with the medical groups simple. MSO Model A permits the participants to achieve joint governance and management of their efforts in a given specialty and creates a limited opportunity for each owner to participate in economic rewards for improvements in efficiency, reductions in cost per case, and other benefits. In addition, this model does not require a significant upfront capital investment in the venture from either the hospital or a medical group; because the participants transfer no business assets to the MSO, it is easy to unwind. Thus, the political and financial commitment of the parties required to pursue MSO Model A is minimal and clearly less than required in any other model addressed by this section. As MSO Model A will not own significant assets or require meaningful capital, it does present its shareholders with minimal financial risk. Under MSO Model A, the decision-making authority of the MSO is limited. The medical group retains its separate and independent status, and continues to have its existing responsibilities for hiring, firing, and compensating physicians without direct hospital involvement.

MSO Model A also has several weaknesses, again primarily as a result of the minimal changes that the model makes to the status quo. Because MSO Model A does not require either party to make a significant political or financial commitment to the MSO, there is an increased risk that neither party will invest the political capital necessary to make it through challenging times. As noted earlier, the medical group may be reluctant to make a significant cash contribution to the MSO, which may leave the MSO with minimal capital resources. MSO Model A does not provide an opportunity for equity appreciation. Moreover, since the medical group does not contribute its assets to the MSO, there is no "exit strategy" for physicians who wish to liquidate unrealized equity appreciation in the medical group at a "market multiple" (a formula for determining the value of a business by multiplying its net income by a number). Because the medical group owns 50 percent of the equity in the MSO and the hospital owns 50 percent, the MSO necessarily has a governance structure that requires cooperation between the venture partners to effect its business plan. If the medical group and the hospital cannot achieve consensus decision making or reach a decision at inception that one party will have the right to control certain decision-making processes, this model may produce gridlock.

MSO Model B

Like MSO Model A, MSO Model B is intended to align incentives between a hospital and its physicians through the creation of a single entity and a single board of directors with the authority to set patient care policies (Figure 3–3). In MSO Model B, however, the medical group transfers all its nonprofessional business assets to the MSO, in a tax-free transaction, in exchange for an equity interest. The physicians themselves become employees of a new professional corporation. That professional corporation enters into a comprehensive, long-term management agreement with the MSO to manage its practice. This type of transaction, involving a tax-free asset transfer and a long-term management contract, is comparable to those entered

into by many PPMs. The hospital contributes cash or a combination of cash, assets, and revenue streams to the MSO in exchange for its interest. In addition, the hospital contracts with the MSO for management of a particular department.

The hospital and the medical group form a new corporation to act as the MSO. A corporation, as opposed to a limited liability company, is necessary to facilitate the tax-free transfer of the medical group's assets (assuming that the medical groups are incorporated). The hospital management agreement is identical to that in MSO Model A. The MSO's management services agreement with the medical group in MSO Model B is comprehensive, however, because the MSO owns all the nonprofessional business assets of the medical group.

To the extent possible, the hospital and the medical group each receive a 50 percent equity interest in the MSO in exchange for equal capital contributions. Because the hospital can contribute cash to match the value of the medical group's contribution of its nonprofessional assets, MSO Model B can have greater capital resources than MSO Model A, as well as a greater ability to undertake a

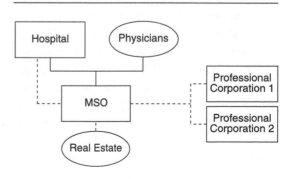

Figure 3–3 MSO Model B. The solid lines represent ownership, and the dotted lines represent a contractual relationship. Real Estate represents a nonprofessional asset to be transferred.

more ambitious business plan, including but not limited to investment in information systems, acquisitions, and provision of services to other medical groups. Thus, MSO Model B's significant equity value may increase if the organization is successful.

MSO Model B requires both parties to make a more significant commitment to the MSO venture than does MSO Model A. At least with respect to the medical group, MSO Model B also requires a more extensive contractual commitment in that the MSO will actually own the assets and employ all the nonprofessional personnel associated with the medical group's practice. This more extensive commitment should provide more "glue" to keep the parties together when challenges arise.

Medical groups do not and generally cannot buy out their shareholders for market value. The presence of the hospital as an equity partner creates the possibility of an exit strategy for physicians on retirement, however. If the hospital or the joint venture is willing, it could purchase the MSO shares of retiring physicians for fair market value. This appears to be a very attractive feature of these new partnership transactions.

Under MSO Model B, the MSO is in charge of the day-to-day business management of the medical group. Nonetheless, the professional corporations in this model retain their separate and independent status, and they continue to have their existing responsibilities for hiring, firing, and compensating physicians without direct or indirect hospital involvement. The most difficult thing about MSO Model B from the physicians' perspective is that it requires a significant shift of professional fee income from the professional corporations to the MSO. Most PPM transactions are structured in this way. The following example illustrates this point:

When NewCo, a newly formed corporation made up of physicians, transfers its nonprofessional assets to the MSO, this transaction is structured as a tax-free reorganization. In order to accomplish this (assuming that the transferring entity is a corporation), the professional assets are transferred to a newly formed, wholly owned subsidiary. This new subsidiary must have no "value" (as the IRS defines that term) in order to make the reorganization tax-free. To avoid value in the new professional corporation (PC), the MSO must keep all revenue from medical activities, less the amount equal to what NewCo would be required to pay a nonshareholder physician specialist, multiplied by the number of physicians in the group. For example, if there are 11 physicians in the group and the appraisal firm determines that fair compensation for an employed nonshareholding specialist in that group is $200,000 per year, the payment from the MSO to NewCo is limited to $2,200,000 (11 × $200,000). The 11 physicians can divide this aggregate payment among themselves if they see fit, but this could involve a reduction in PC W-2 compensation for some physicians. It is true, however, that these same physicians will receive distributions from the MSO. Some of them also may receive compensation from the MSO for services as executives and medical directors. If the hospital contributes revenue streams for its equity interest in the MSO, it should be possible for the physicians to be kept whole through a combination of MSO distributions, executive compensation, and PC compensation. This approach is complicated, but it does make business and tax sense.

Like MSO Model A, MSO Model B necessarily has a governance structure that will require cooperation between the venture partners to effect its business plan. If the hospital and the medical group physicians cannot achieve consensus decision making or reach a decision at inception that one party will have the right to control certain decision-making processes, this model may also produce gridlock.

Under MSO Model B, the MSO contracts with the hospital for management of a particular department. Many federal statutes constrain the parties' flexibility in structuring the compensation arrangement between the MSO and the hospital. Incentive compensation may be paid on the achievement of agreed upon performance objectives (such as lowering costs per case), but overall payments cannot exceed the fair market value. To be fair, the incentive component of these payments should probably remain a relatively modest percentage of the whole.

Medical Group Joint Venture Model

Like the MSO models, the medical group joint venture model is intended to align incentives between the hospital and physician owners of a medical group through the creation of a single entity (Figure 3–4). Unlike the MSO models, however, depending on state law, this model may create a joint venture that actually employs physicians to provide care. These joint venture physicians manage inpatient activity in the same specialty at the hospital. In addition, the hospital partner transfers (probably by lease) outpatient and ancillary businesses in exchange for its equity interest. This transfer must be made for fair market value to avoid a number of legal and regulatory problem areas. Consequently, the medical group joint venture model effects much greater change in the status quo than either the MSO Model A or the MSO Model B.

Perhaps the most important advantage of the joint venture model is the extent to which it brings the incentives of the hospital into harmony with those of the physicians. Although the management fees that the joint venture group can earn from managing the hospital inpatient service are limited to the fair market value of the services provided, this limitation does not apply to the services provided by the joint venture's outpatient and ancillary businesses. With respect to these important activities, the physicians are joint owners. As the joint venture corporation must pay the hospital for the value of this business, the physician owners (as well as the hospital co-owner) profit only to the extent that the joint venture corporation can increase the revenues and reduce the costs of these businesses. Nevertheless, this is still an important opportunity, and it is one that the physicians will be able to obtain without having to bear the risk of duplicating the outpatient and ancillary facilities already owned by the hospital.

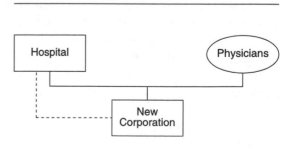

Figure 3–4 Medical Group Joint Venture Model. The solid lines represent ownership, and the dotted lines represent a contractual relationship.

The medical group joint venture model requires both parties to make a more significant financial commitment to the joint venture than do either of the MSO models. The joint venture corporation will be managing (1) the medical group's practices, (2) certain of the hospital ancillary and outpatient businesses, and (3) the inpatient activities of the hospital in a particular setting. These extensive commitments may provide an incentive to keep the parties together when challenges arise. On the other hand, it may not be easy for either party to undertake such commitments. The medical group's contribution, because it includes both the professional and the nonprofessional assets of the group, should have a greater value than that made in connection with the MSO models. Thus, for the medical group joint venture model, the hospital probably must come up with more dollars as its capital investment relative to that required under the MSO models. The greater amount should permit capital investments in facilities and infrastructure that may not otherwise be possible.

Under the medical group joint venture model, equity ownership is divided equally between the medical groups in the aggregate and the hospital. Accordingly, as is the case with all the models, the joint venture corporation necessarily has a governance structure that requires cooperation between the venture partners to effect its business plan. Furthermore, such shared governance extends to greater areas of responsibility than under the MSO models, thereby increasing the risks of loss of control to the parties.

The medical group joint venture model achieves limited integration of the respective businesses of the hospital and the medical groups. A management contract links the economics of the hospital inpatient business in the specialty under consideration to the joint venture. It is extremely complicated to create a joint venture that integrates the inpatient as well as the outpatient and ancillary activities of a hospital with a medical group, however. Accordingly, the medical group joint venture model may be the only practical alternative available.

One final disadvantage of this model is that, from a regulatory perspective, the joint venture must constitute a true medical group. It will not be possible for physicians to invest in this model if they are not at least part-time employees of the joint venture.

The Hospital Model

The most extensive form of integration of a health care facility with physicians is the hospital model (Figure 3–5). In this model, as in the medical group joint venture model, the medical groups contribute their respective nonprofessional business assets to the joint entity. The hospital leases its inpatient, outpatient, and ancillary businesses in the groups' specialty to the same entity, which applies for an acute care hospital license and becomes, in effect, a new hospital. As in the case of the medical group joint venture model, the transferring hospital must be compensated for the fair market value of the businesses transferred to the joint venture. Thus, the new hospital is essentially a new single-specialty hospital operated within an existing charitable hospital of the hospital health care system.

Creating a new "hospital within a hospital" is not a simple undertaking. For charitable hospitals, it is particularly challenging. Facilities leased to the new hospital are subject to property taxes in most jurisdictions. Tax-exempt debt financing on facilities and equipment leased to the new hospital may have to be completely or partially refinanced. A new medical staff must be created, with

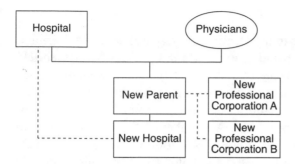

Figure 3–5 Hospital Model. The solid lines represent ownership, and the dotted lines represent a contractual relationship. New Parent represents the legal entity that owns all the stock in New Hospital.

active membership limited to those who practice in the new hospital. Establishing a new hospital model should create significant opportunities for economic credentialing and the development of patient treatment protocols that are not possible in the political environment of a general acute care hospital medical staff.

From the perspective of physician owners, the hospital model offers both the greatest risk and the greatest potential reward. The size of the inpatient business is so much larger than the outpatient and ancillary business that even a small improvement in efficiency translates into important financial returns. For example, if the total direct operating expense of a particular specialty department is $30 million per year, a 1 percent reduction in those expenses produces a $300,000 bottom line. The consistent achievement of revenue growth and expense reduction can produce substantial equity value for the owners. Current appraisals of these businesses use earnings multiples of 7 to 9. Thus, a hospital model joint venture that creates $1 million per year of net income will have an equity value of $7 million to $9 million. Most important, the physician own-

ers need not rely on a public offering and the success of a national PPM strategy to access this value. The joint venture group will agree to buy the physicians' interest for fair market value on retirement.

A combination of a hospital and physicians in the hospital model can achieve some things that have never been possible under the charitable model, the workshop model, or the organized delivery system model. First, this model creates long-term economic incentives for physicians to reduce hospital costs and improve patient care outcomes. Second, a combination of a hospital and organized physician groups can provide care in multiple specialties at the same time. It is not necessary to shift to a new "boutique" for each illness or diagnostic test. Third, a combined system can create a single, comprehensive information system, which facilitates the coordination of efforts and makes it possible to identify opportunities for higher value health care. It also enables the new hospital to demonstrate the value of its care to employers and insurance companies. In addition, the new structure reduces the amount of new construction and duplication of facilities that would occur if PPMs, or the specialists themselves, created competing new facilities.

Finally, but perhaps most important, if hospitals can succeed in creating a new business model that integrates specialty care, these joint venture organizations with their hospital-affiliated primary care physicians may be able to approach employers directly with proposals for health care delivery that would eliminate the insurance companies and HMOs from the picture. This possibility will not please the insurance industry, but it may provide substantial cost savings by eliminating the profit margins and administrative costs that many patients and employers are starting to question.

ROBERT H. ROSENFIELD, LLB, LLM, is a partner in the Health Law Department of McDermott, Will & Emery. He has more than 22 years of experience in the health law field. Mr. Rosenfield has served as counsel to a wide variety of health care organizations, including academic medical centers, organized delivery systems, physician practice management companies, physician–hospital organizations, independent practice association, and medical groups. He also has represented state, county, and district health care providers. A member of the American Health Lawyers Association and the California Association of Hospital Attorneys, Mr. Rosenfield received his LLB degree from Harvard Law School in 1967 and holds an LLM degree from the London School of Economics and Political Science. He is admitted to practice in California and New York.

Chapter 4

Business Combinations in the Health Care Field: Legal Implications

Norton L. Travis, Loreen A. Peritz, Hayden S. Wool, and Greg E. Bloom

The current uncertain environment in the health care industry—caused by factors such as the advent of managed care, health care reform, declining inpatient admissions, federal payment limitations, and rising costs—has led many hospitals and other health care providers to seek to increase their market share by diversifying the scope of the health care services that they are capable of delivering. One mechanism frequently used by hospitals and other health care providers to achieve this goal is to join with other providers in offering integrated health care services to patients. For this purpose, health care providers may enter into a business combination, such as a joint venture, merger, or other type of affiliation. These types of arrangements, however, almost always raise concerns under the federal and state fraud and abuse laws, as well as under the antitrust and tax laws. It is essential, therefore, to structure business combinations in the health care field carefully to avoid the significant adverse consequences of violating these laws.

HYPOTHETICAL

Drs. Black, White, and Green (the Physician-Partners) are cardiologists in private practice and have been granted privileges at Memorial Hospital, a not-for-profit hospital. The Physician-Partners entered into a contract arrangement with Memorial whereby they agreed to provide, on an exclusive basis, all of the cardiology services required by the hospital. In return for such services, each Physician-Partner receives a fixed salary from Memorial. In addition, each Physician-Partner receives a bonus of 25 percent of the revenues generated by Memorial as a result of patients referred to Memorial by that Physician-Partner.

The Physician-Partners also are partners in a joint venture that owns and operates an imaging center called Scans-R-Us. Each Physician-Partner owns a 25 percent interest in Scans-R-Us. There is a fourth partner who holds the remaining 25 percent interest in Scans-R-Us, but she is not involved in the health care field.

Because it is the closest imaging center to their practice, the Physician-Partners almost always refer patients who need imaging services to Scans-R-Us. In fact, more than 50 percent of the revenue generated by Scans-R-Us is attributable to patients referred by the Physician-Partners.

Dr. Brown is an employee of Scans-R-Us. The center pays him a fixed salary, plus a 10 percent bonus of the revenue generated by

Scans-R-Us as a result of the patients that he refers.

Scans-R-Us is considering acquiring another imaging center. Because Scans-R-Us and the to-be-acquired imaging center are the only imaging centers that provide certain specialized imaging services within a 100-mile radius, the Physician-Partners are quite anxious to go forward with the acquisition, expecting that they will be able to control the market with respect to these services. Using the following legal information, consider if the previously described facts present a problem with respect to the Physician-Partners, Scans-R-Us, Memorial, or Dr. Brown.

FEDERAL MEDICARE/MEDICAID FRAUD AND ABUSE AND ANTIKICKBACK REGULATIONS

The federal Medicare/Medicaid fraud and abuse laws prohibit both the submission of false claims and the payment of a kickback in exchange for the referral of patients.[1] Basically, if a health care provider submits a claim for reimbursement under the Medicare/Medicaid programs that he or she knows or has reason to know is false or fraudulent, then the provider may be liable for a violation of the federal False Claims Act.[2] False claims include not only claims for services not rendered, but also claims that the provider knows or has reason to know do not comply with the applicable laws or regulations. A violation of the False Claims Act may subject the provider to treble damages, plus a penalty of between $5,000 and $10,000 per claim. False claims also may subject providers to the penalties and sanctions that are contained in other state and federal statutes that are applicable to fraud cases generally, such as mail and wire fraud statutes, the Racketeer Influenced and Corrupt Organizations statute, and money laundering statutes.

While it is fairly easy to define the meaning of a false claim, it usually is more difficult to determine when an illegal payment or kickback has been made in conjunction with the provision of services to Medicare/Medicaid beneficiaries. The federal antikickback laws prohibit direct or indirect offers, payments, solicitations, or the receipt of remuneration to induce the referral of Medicare/Medicaid patients or to induce the purchasing, leasing, ordering, or arranging for any good, facility, service, or item paid for by the Medicare/Medicaid programs. An individual who is found to have violated the antikickback laws may be guilty of a felony and subject to imprisonment for up to 5 years and a fine of up to $25,000.[3]

In 1987, Congress enacted the Medicare and Medicaid Patient and Program Protection Act of 1987[4] (the Patient Protection Act). This law grants the Office of the Inspector General (OIG)—the prosecutorial branch of the Department of Health and Human Services—the authority to impose civil sanctions for a violation of the antikickback laws. Under the Patient Protection Act, the OIG generally must exclude any individual from participation in the Medicare/Medicaid programs for a minimum of 5 years if that individual has been convicted of a criminal offense relating to the delivery of an item or service in the Medicare/Medicaid programs. During this 5-year period, Medicare/Medicaid will make no payment for any services rendered, ordered, or prescribed by the excluded individual.[5] In addition to this mandatory exclusion, the OIG has the authority to permissibly exclude a practitioner from participation in the Medicare/Medicaid programs should certain events occur, such as the practitioner's conviction for fraud or financial misconduct, the revocation of the practitioner's professional license, or the practitioner's failure to grant the OIG access to his or her records and documents.[6]

With respect to the hypothetical set forth earlier, both Memorial and the Physician-Partners could be liable for a violation of the antikickback laws. While it is permissible for Memorial to pay the Physician-Partners a fixed, fair-market-value salary, and even a bonus, for the cardiology services that the Physician-Partners provide, Memorial may not in any way base such compensation on the volume of referrals made by the Physician-Partners. Thus, because the 25 percent bonus paid by Memorial to each of the Physician-Partners is directly related to that physician's volume of referrals to Memorial, both Memorial and the Physician-Partners are potentially liable under the antikickback laws.

The *Greber* Case

Probably the most famous, and certainly the most controversial, case interpreting antikickback laws is *United States v. Greber.*[7] Dr. Greber, a board-certified cardiologist, was the president and owner of Cardio-Med, a company that supplied a device capable of monitoring a patient's cardiac activity. In connection with the use of this device by Medicare patients, Dr. Greber made payments to referring cardiologists, supposedly for their interpretation of the tapes that the medical device produced. In fact, Dr. Greber, not the referring cardiologists, interpreted the tapes. The court concluded that the payments to the cardiologists were actually for the purpose of inducing referrals. On appeal, the federal circuit court concluded that even if the purpose of Cardio-Med's payments to the cardiologists was to compensate them for professional services, the antikickback laws were violated if one purpose of such payments was to induce referrals.[8]

Because of this one-purpose rule and other cases similar to *Greber,* every financial arrangement between those who refer business and those who provide items or services eligible for reimbursement under the Medicare/Medicaid programs warrants careful scrutiny. If any purpose for which a payment is made is to induce referrals, the payment may be unlawful under the antikickback laws. Even if the primary purpose of a payment is permissible (such as the provision of necessary medical services), the individuals making and receiving the payment are subject to prosecution under the antikickback laws if the payment is also found to have the incidental purpose of inducing referrals.

The Safe Harbor Regulations

A direct payment to a health care provider for a referral clearly violates the antikickback laws. The 25 percent bonus paid by Memorial to the Physician-Partners falls under this general prohibition. It is less clear, however, whether a physician may refer a patient to an entity or other provider in which he or she has an ownership interest or other financial relationship and, thus, would indirectly benefit from the referral. Because the antikickback laws are broadly drafted (by including both direct and indirect payments), it is often difficult to determine when a particular arrangement is prohibited.

As a result, the health care industry sought guidelines within which to evaluate proposed transactions in relation to the antikickback laws. The Patient Protection Act mandated that the OIG promulgate regulations specifying safe harbors (i.e., business combinations that are permissible under the antikickback laws).[9] In formulating the safe harbor regulations, the federal government realized that many joint ventures and other arrangements among health care providers and suppliers are legitimate enterprises that provide needed health care services. Therefore, the antikickback laws, together with the safe harbor regulations, do not absolutely prohibit business combinations in the health care field; however, they significantly limit the way that such a venture may be structured.

If the structure of a proposed health care business combination adheres to all applicable safe harbor guidelines, the parties to the transaction are exempt from civil and criminal prosecution under the antikickback laws. If the transaction does not conform to the safe harbor guidelines, the transaction is not necessarily illegal, but neither are the parties assured that they will be immune from prosecution and the civil and criminal sanctions that have been described. If more than one safe harbor is applicable, the transaction must fit within each to enjoy safe harbor status.

The safe harbor regulations cover the following areas: investment interests, space rental, equipment rental, personal service and management contracts, sale of practice, referral services, warranties and discounts, employment relationships, group purchasing organizations, and waiver of certain insurance benefits. Those structuring health care business combinations often rely on the investment interests safe harbor, which protects investments in both public and private companies under certain conditions. If an investment is in an entity that within the previous fiscal year or 12-month period had undepreciated net tangible health care assets of at least $50 million, safe harbor protection exists if (1) the investment represents the purchase of securities registered with the Securities and Exchange Commission; (2) the interest is acquired on terms equally available to the public through trading on a national security exchange; (3) the marketing of items or services to investors is the same as to non-investors; (4) the investment is not achieved through a loan or guarantee by the entity in which the investment is made; and (5) the re-

turn on the investment is proportional to the amount invested.[10]

Not surprisingly, most health care joint ventures do not meet the $50 million threshold or involve publicly traded companies, but instead, involve private organizations. If an investment is in a private company or entity, it must meet all of the following guidelines to fall within the private company safe harbor: (1) no more than 40 percent of any class of investment in the entity may be held by individuals or other entities in a position to refer Medicare/Medicaid patients or provide goods or services to the entity; (2) no more than 40 percent of the gross revenues of the entity may be derived from referrals, items, or services provided by investors in the entity; (3) the entity may not loan the investor the funds to make the investment or guarantee the investment; (4) the return from the investment must be proportional to the amount of the investment (and *not* tied to patient referrals); (5) the entity may not market its services more vigorously to investors than to the public in general; (6) the investment must be made available on the same terms to those who are in a position to refer patients as to those who are not; and (7) the investment terms cannot relate in any way to referrals.[11]

The first two tests—commonly referred to as the 60/40 tests—are clearly the most problematic. If more than 40 percent of the investors of any class either refer patients or provide any services to the entity, safe harbor protection is not available. Similarly, if more than 40 percent of the total revenue is derived from the investors in the entity—either individually or as a whole—the transaction is not protected by a safe harbor.

If a particular business combination between health care providers does not fall within the boundaries of a safe harbor, those involved should first determine if they can alter the structure of the combination to achieve such compliance. If restructuring is not possible, they must decide if the benefits of the combination outweigh the considerable risks that they must assume in going forward without the protection of a safe harbor. As in any antikickback analysis, the key issue is whether any purpose of the venture is to induce referrals.

The Physician-Partners in the hypothetical probably could *not* legally refer Medicare/Medicaid patients to Scans-R-Us. Their investment in Scans-R-Us would fail both 60/40 tests because (1) more than 40 percent of the Scans-R-Us investors are in a position to refer patients to Scans-R-Us; and (2) more than 40 percent of the Scans-R-Us revenue originates in referrals by investors in Scans-R-Us.

PHYSICIAN SELF-REFERRAL—THE STARK LAW

The Ethics in Patient Referrals Act of 1989,[12] more commonly known as the Stark Law (named for its author Congressman Fortney "Pete" Stark), prohibits a physician from referring Medicare/Medicaid patients for certain designated health care services to entities in which the physician (or anyone in the physician's immediate family) has a financial interest.[13] Unlike the antikickback regulations, which apply to health care providers in general, this law applies only to physicians (which the law defines to include dentists, podiatrists, and chiropractors). Congress enacted the Stark Law because it was concerned that physicians might refer a patient to a facility in which they had an ownership interest, rather than to a facility that would provide the best care to the patient. Congress also believed that self-referrals could lead to overutilization by physicians ordering medical services not because of the patient's medical condition, but because of

their interest in the profitability of the diagnostic/therapeutic facility.

The Stark Law attempts to provide physicians with a "bright line" rule so that they will know in advance what types of business arrangements are prohibited. A financial relationship is defined under the Stark Law as (1) an "ownership or investment interest" in an entity that "may be through equity, debt, or other means and includes an interest in an entity that holds an ownership or investment interest in any entity providing the designated health service"; or (2) a compensation arrangement, which is "any arrangement involving any remuneration between a physician (or an immediate family member of such physician) and an entity. . . ." [14] A "referral" is defined as the request by a physician for an item or service payable under the Medicare/Medicaid program or for a consultation with another physician and any test or procedure ordered or performed by or under the supervision of that other physician.[15] Referral also includes the request or establishment of a plan of care by a physician that includes the provision of designated health care service.

The types of designated health care services that are covered under the Stark Law are clinical laboratory services, physical therapy services, occupational therapy services, radiology services (including magnetic resonance imaging, computed tomography scans, and ultrasound services), radiation therapy services, durable medical equipment, parenteral and enteral nutrients, equipment and supplies, prosthetics, orthotics and prosthetic devices, home health services, outpatient prescription drugs, and inpatient and outpatient hospital services.[16]

Clearly, the prohibitions against referrals set forth in the Stark Law have a significant impact on the structuring of business arrangements with physicians. Most important, by including a prohibition against referrals for inpatient and outpatient hospital services, virtually any physician–hospital business arrangement could potentially violate the Stark Law. The Stark Law contains several exceptions to its prohibition against referrals, however. A referral is not considered to be in violation of the Stark Law if the referral is to another physician in the same group practice as the referring physician, if the referral is for the provision of certain in-office ancillary services other than durable medical equipment, or if the referral is to a prepaid plan as defined in the Stark Law.[17]

In addition, there are specific exceptions relating to the ownership/investment interest and compensation/lease arrangement prohibitions. With respect to ownership/investment interests, the Stark Law permits physician referrals to companies with publicly traded securities, to hospitals in Puerto Rico, to rural providers (as defined in the Stark Law), and to a hospital where the referring physician has privileges and the ownership or investment interest is in the hospital itself, rather than a subdivision of the hospital.[18] Furthermore, the Stark Law does not prohibit referrals to an entity if the referring physician has entered into a written lease agreement with that entity for the rental of office space or equipment for an amount that is based on fair market value and in no way relates to the volume or value of referrals between the parties. The lease must provide for a term of at least 1 year, and the space and equipment may not exceed what is reasonable and necessary for the legitimate business purposes of the lessee and must be used exclusively by the lessee when used by the lessee (except that the use of common office space areas is permitted on a pro rata basis).

Referrals also are permissible if a bona fide employment relationship exists between the parties, so long as (1) the employment is for identifiable services and (2) the compensation is consistent with fair market value and has no connection to the volume or value of referrals. There also are exceptions relating to remuneration provided to a physician by a hospital that is unrelated to the provision of designated health care services, physician incentive plan arrangements, isolated transactions (such as a one-time sale of property or practice), group practice arrangements under which designated services are provided by the group but billed by the hospital, and payments made by a physician for items and services.[19]

Penalties under the Stark Law include denial of payment, a forced refunding of any amount collected in violation of the prohibition of referrals, a civil money penalty of up to $15,000 for each claim or payment for services rendered pursuant to a prohibited referral, and a civil money penalty of up to $100,000 for each unlawful arrangement or scheme.[20]

Both federal and state authorities have the jurisdiction to investigate and impose sanctions for Medicare/Medicaid fraud. At the federal level, the Department of Justice can prosecute health care fraud under a number of criminal statutes. Also, as explained earlier, OIG has the authority to assess civil monetary penalties and to exclude from the Medicare/Medicaid programs any person or entity convicted of a criminal offense relating to Medicare/Medicaid fraud or found to have committed other specified acts.

In addition, state licensing boards can suspend or revoke the licenses of physicians and other health care providers upon a conviction of fraud or a similar offense. Furthermore, many states have enacted statutes similar to the Stark Law to prohibit certain physician self-referrals. In New York, for example, a physician may not refer patients to an entity with which he or she has a financial relationship for any of the following: clinical laboratory services, X-ray and imaging services, or pharmacy services. Unlike the federal Stark Law, the New York statute prohibits referrals for these services regardless of the patient's source of payment.[21]

The Stark Law precludes the investment of the Physician-Partners in Scans-R-Us, because it prohibits a physician from referring any Medicare/Medicaid patient for certain specified health care services to an entity in which the physician has a financial interest. Simply refraining from referring Medicare/Medicaid patients to Scans-R-Us, however, will not be permitted in those states with a state Stark Law (such as New York's law) that prohibits this type of referral whether or not the patient is a Medicare/Medicaid recipient. Consequently, the Physician-Partners will probably be forced to divest themselves of their interests in Scans-R-Us.

In the case of Dr. Brown, the Scans-R-Us employee, it at first appears that he can refer patients to Scans-R-Us, even though he has a compensation arrangement with the imaging center. The law allows an individual to refer patients to a health care entity with which he or she has a compensation arrangement if a bona fide employment relationship exists between the parties. This is true with respect to Dr. Brown and Scans-R-Us. A portion of his compensation, however, is a 10 percent bonus, which is tied to the volume of Dr. Brown's referrals to Scans-R-Us. The Stark Law prohibits this business arrangement.

ANTITRUST IN THE HEALTH CARE INDUSTRY

The purpose of the antitrust laws is to protect and promote competition. As many providers who have been competitors are responding to changes in the health care system by merging or consolidating, many of these mergers may adversely affect competition and, thereby, violate the antitrust laws.[22]

Previously, a merger between two not-for-profit hospitals was believed to be immune from prosecution under the antitrust laws. This is no longer true, however. With the increasing number of such mergers taking place, scrutiny by the Federal Trade Commission, the Department of Justice, and state antitrust agencies (e.g., Attorneys General) has increased in the last few years.

For antitrust purposes, the definition of mergers is quite broad. Basically, any time a business combination results in common control by a single entity or group, a merger has occurred. Even the formation of a new group practice among formerly independent physicians would constitute a merger under this definition. Mergers have three economic effects that are of concern in an antitrust analysis. First, a merger consolidates market power; that is, with fewer competitors, organizations have an increased ability to raise the price above or decrease the quality below a competitive level without losing customers (or patients). Second, a merger increases concentration in the market; if there are fewer competitors, it becomes easier for organizations to collude in such matters as price fixing. Third, the merger may have some positive effects, such as creating economies of scale and scope that permit greater output with fewer resources. Accordingly, in any antitrust analysis of a merger, the negative, anticompetitive effects of the merger must be balanced against the positive, procompetitive effects of the merger.

Federal Antitrust Statutes

Mergers in the health care industry may face challenges under Section 7 of the Clayton Act, Section 1 of the Sherman Act, or comparable state antitrust laws. Section 7 of the Clayton Act specifically addresses business consolidations and prohibits an acquisition whose effects "may be substantially to lessen competition or to tend to create a monopoly."[23] In order to prove a Section 7 claim, the plaintiff must define the specific product or service that is the subject of the claim, as well as the geographic market where the anticompetitive activity is taking place. Consequently, a merger between parties who either do not provide the same goods or services, or who do not supply such goods or services to the same market, will not adversely affect competition and there will be no antitrust violation. If the plaintiff can establish that a business consolidation will consolidate market power within the geographic market to such an extent that those providing the specified product may raise prices, decrease output, or reduce quality, and that even after such actions, customers will be unable to substitute another product or supplier of the product easily, then a Section 7 claim may be established.

Section 1 of the Sherman Act prohibits "every contract, combination . . . or conspiracy, in restraint of trade or commerce among the several states."[24] A person who is alleging a violation of Section 1 of the Sherman Act must establish that (1) there is an agreement, conspiracy, or combination among two or more persons or distinct business entities; (2) the intent of the agreement, conspiracy, or combination is to harm or unreasonably restrain competition; and (3) the agreement, conspiracy, or combination actually causes injury to competition beyond its impact on the plaintiff, within a field of commerce in which the plaintiff is engaged. The first element, proof of conspiracy, requires concerted action among two or more independent entities; that is, for a conspiracy to exist, there must be an agreement between at least two independent parties. Courts generally hold that officers, employees, and agents of a corporation and wholly owned subsidiaries of a corporation are legally incapable of

conspiring with each other.[25] Therefore, there is no Sherman Act liability for intracorporate agreements.

To show the second element of a Sherman Act claim, an individual must demonstrate that the competitors intended to adhere to an agreement that was designed to achieve an unlawful, anticompetitive objective. Finally, the person arguing that an antitrust violation has occurred must show that the conspiracy actually produced an anticompetitive effect. Establishing an anticompetitive effect generally requires identifying the relevant geographic and product markets and proving the effect of the restraint within these markets, or showing actual detrimental effects on competition (e.g., output decreases or price increases occurring after the formation of the conspiracy). Because the primary purpose of the antitrust laws is to protect competition, not individual competitors, the fact that a particular merger or other business arrangement harms an individual competitor will give rise to antitrust liability only if it also has an adverse effect on competition in general.

Hart–Scott–Rodino Reporting Requirements

The Hart–Scott–Rodino Antitrust Improvement Act requires that certain mergers and consolidations be reported to the Federal Trade Commission and the Department of Justice before the transaction is consummated.[26] The purpose of this law is to give these agencies the opportunity to investigate a business consolidation if they believe that such an investigation is warranted. The law does not require that all mergers or other consolidations be reported. It is necessary to report a business consolidation only if (1) the acquiring party has total assets or annual net sales of at least $100 million and the acquired party has total assets of at least $10 million, or the acquiring party has total assets or annual net sales of at least $10 million and the acquired party has total assets or annual net sales of at least $100 million; and (2) the acquiring party is acquiring 15 percent or more of the acquired party's assets of voting securities or the purchase price or fair market value of assets to be acquired is $15 million or more.[27] Although many mergers in the health care field do not meet these tests and need not be reported under the Hart–Scott–Rodino law, most hospital mergers must comply with Hart–Scott–Rodino filing requirements.

Antitrust Safety Zones

In August of 1996, the Department of Justice and the Federal Trade Commission issued a joint statement outlining their new antitrust enforcement policies concerning business consolidations and mergers in the health care area. With respect to hospital mergers and other business arrangements between entities in the health care field, these two federal agencies created antitrust safety zones similar in concept to the safe harbors promulgated in connection with the Medicare/Medicaid fraud and abuse regulations. Therefore, if a particular arrangement or transaction falls within one of these safety zones, the agencies will not challenge the arrangement as violative of the antitrust laws except under extraordinary circumstances. As with fraud and abuse safe harbors, an arrangement falling outside the safety zones does not necessarily violate the antitrust law, but those involved in the transaction cannot be certain that they will not be prosecuted.

Safety zones created by the agencies' statement include hospital joint ventures involving high technology or other expensive health care equipment, a physician's provision of information to purchasers of health care ser-

vices, hospital exchanges of price and cost information, joint purchasing arrangements among health care providers, and physician network joint ventures. With respect to the hospital merger safety zone, the Department of Justice and the Federal Trade Commission will not challenge any merger between two general acute care hospitals when one of the hospitals (1) has had an average of fewer than 100 licensed beds over the 3 most recent years, (2) has had an average daily inpatient census of fewer than 40 patients over the 3 most recent years, and (3) is more than 5 years old. As stated previously, mergers that do not fall within the safety zone are not necessarily anticompetitive. In fact, as explained in the joint statement, arrangements that (1) do not increase the likelihood of the exercise of market power, either because strong competitors exist postmerger or because the merging hospitals were sufficiently differentiated; (2) allow the hospitals to realize significant cost savings that would not otherwise be realized; or (3) eliminate a hospital that would likely fail, removing its assets from the market, are not likely to be considered troublesome.

The Scans-R-Us acquisition of a nearby imaging center may raise concerns under the antitrust laws. The Physician-Partners are interested in this acquisition because it will enable them to control the market with respect to certain imaging services. The federal antitrust agencies could conclude that this market consolidation would allow the Physician-Partners to raise prices on these services at will because, if the acquisition were consummated, there would be no competing imaging center within a 100-mile radius. As a result, individuals requiring these specific imaging services could not easily turn to a competing imaging center, even if Scans-R-Us tripled its prices or dramatically increased its turnaround time for imaging services.

TAX EXEMPTION ISSUES

Under the regulations of the Internal Revenue Service (IRS), a tax-exempt entity must provide a public benefit to the community and not a private benefit to those operating or affiliated with the entity. Specifically, the IRS private inurement prohibition mandates that no part of the net earnings of a tax-exempt entity may inure to the benefit of a private individual.[28] The IRS private benefit prohibition states that a tax-exempt entity may not serve a private rather than a public interest.[29] If a hospital or any other tax-exempt entity violates either the private inurement or the private benefit prohibition, it could lose its tax-exempt status or be subject to intermediate sanctions, which may include stiff penalties against the individuals who participate in these challenged arrangements (including hospital employees).[30]

The IRS found in the past that as long as a hospital–physician relationship was conducted on an arm's length basis, and the hospital and physician received value for services rendered, such a relationship would not affect a hospital's tax-exempt status. In 1991, however, the IRS stated in a General Counsel Memorandum that if such relationships appear to violate the fraud and abuse/antikickback regulations, they may also be violating the private inurement or private benefit prohibitions under the tax regulations.[31] Thus, if a particular arrangement confers benefits on a private individual that are so substantial and excessive that the arrangement inures to the benefit of that individual rather than to the benefit of the tax-exempt entity, a private-inurement violation would exist. Similarly, if such an arrangement is interpreted as serving only a private interest rather than a public interest (with only an incidental private benefit), a private benefit violation would exist. In either case, the tax-exempt entity would run the risk of forfeiting its tax-exempt status or be subject to intermediate sanctions.

With respect to the exclusive contract for cardiology services between Memorial and the Physician-Partners, careful analysis is necessary to ensure that the financial terms of the arrangement are not so favorable to the Physician-Partners that it can be interpreted to inure to their benefit rather than to the benefit of Memorial. Otherwise, Memorial can risk forfeiting its tax-exempt status.

In defending such relationships, a hospital must be able to demonstrate that its arrangement serves the community through the hospital and that any private benefit is incidental to the community benefit. If a hospital–physician relationship presents a fraud and abuse/antikickback problem, it is increasingly likely that it could also subject the hospital to the loss of its tax-exempt status. Therefore, hospitals should closely examine such relationships with both the fraud and abuse and the community benefit standards in mind.

OTHER LEGAL CONSIDERATIONS

Many other legal factors warrant consideration while a health care business combination is still in the planning stages. For example, the parties must determine if a certificate of need is necessary. Although the law varies from state to state, a health care facility generally must seek a certificate of need before it may commence new construction or renovation of an existing structure. A certificate of need usually must be in place before a health care facility makes a significant capital expenditure.

Also, it is essential to discuss the tax consequences of the transaction throughout the planning and implementation of a business combination. If the business combination will create a new entity, the parties must determine if the entity will be for-profit or not-for-profit, and must consider the tax consequences of this determination both to the entity itself and to the parties involved in the transaction. An entity that is to be not-for-profit must obtain the appropriate federal, state, and local exemptions. As obtaining these exemptions often takes a significant amount of time, the process should begin as soon as the decision to seek tax exempt status is made. Finally, the private inurement and private benefit prohibitions must be considered both prior to structuring a transaction and during the operation of the tax-exempt entity.

Another regulatory issue that must be addressed before the consummation of a business combination is whether any securities will be issued and, if so, whether registration will be required under the federal or state securities laws. The definition of *security* under the federal laws is very broad and includes not only stock and partnership interests, but also "participation in any profit sharing arrangement."[32] Because this definition is so broad and because every issuance of securities must be either registered with the Securities Exchange Commission or issued pursuant to an exemption from registration, the parties to any business combination must determine whether registration is mandatory or whether some exemption is available.[33] As registration is a very expensive and time-consuming process, it is wise to rely on an exemption from registration whenever possible.

Finally, the parties to a health care business combination should consider if the transaction will violate any state corporate practice of medicine laws. These laws prohibit the practice of medicine by an unlicensed entity. In New York, for example, a business corporation may not provide physicians' services without certificate-of-need approval.[34] The parties to a business combination in the health care field must constantly keep in mind that the goals of the venture can be achieved only within the regulatory framework governing such ventures.

NOTES

1. Social Security Act § 1128(b), 42 U.S.C. § 1320a-7.

2. 31 U.S.C. § 3729 et seq.

3. 42 U.S.C. § 1320a-7b(1).

4. 42 U.S.C. § 1320a-7.

5. The consequences of exclusion are far-reaching. For example, an excluded physician generally is not permitted to admit Medicare/Medicaid patients to a hospital, because the hospital is not entitled to payment under the Medicare/Medicaid programs for any services ordered by the excluded physician.

6. 42 U.S.C. § 1320a-7b.

7. 760 F.2d 68 (3d Cir. 1985), *cert. denied*, 474 U.S. 988 (1985).

8. *See* 760 F.2d at 72.

9. 42 C.F.R. § 1001.950 et seq.

10. 42 C.F.R. § 1001.952(a).

11. 42 C.F.R. § 1001.952(a).

12. Social Security Act § 1877, 42 U.S.C. § 1395nn, amended by Pub. L. No. 103-432 (1994).

13. Section 13624 of the Omnibus Budget Recommendation Act of 1993, enacted on August 10, 1993, expanded aspects of the Stark prohibition to Medicaid by denying federal financial participation payments to states under the Medicaid program for referrals that violate the Stark provisions. 42 U.S.C. § 1395nn.

14. 42 U.S.C. § 1395nn(a)(2), (h)(1).

15. 42 U.S.C. § 1395nn(h).

16. 42 U.S.C. § 1395nn(a).

17. 42 U.S.C. § 1395nn(b).

18. 42 U.S.C. § 1395nn(d).

19. 42 U.S.C. §1395nn(e).

20. 42 U.S.C. § 1395nn(g).

21. N.Y. Pub Health Law § 238-a.

22. *See, e.g.*, United States v. Rockford Mem'l Corp., 898 F.2d 1278 (7th Cir. 1990), *cert. denied*, 498 U.S. 920 (1990), holding that § 7 of the Clayton Act applies to not-for-profit corporations.

23. Clayton Act § 7, 15 U.S.C. § 18.

24. Sherman Act § 1, 15 U.S.C. § 1.

25. *Copperweld Corp. v. Independence Tube Corp.*, 467 U.S. 752 (1984).

26. 15 U.S.C. § 18.

27. 15 U.S.C. § 18.

28. 26 C.F.R. § 1.501(c)(3)-l (c)(2).

29. 26 C.F.R. § 1.501(c)(3)-l (d)(1)(ii).

30. I.R.C. §§ 501(c)(3) & 4958.

31. Gen. Couns. Mem. 39,862 (November 21, 1991).

32. 15 U.S.C. § 77a(l) (1981).

33. 15 U.S.C. § 77c.

34. N.Y. EDUC. LAW § 6531.

NORTON L. TRAVIS, JD, is one of the founders of Garfunkel, Wild & Travis, PC, and a Managing Director of the firm. Mr. Travis devotes his efforts to the general representation of numerous hospitals, physician groups, physician associates, and other health care–related business organizations. Recently he was appointed a member of the American Medical Association's Physician Advisory Network. In addition, he is a member of the American Academy of Healthcare Attorneys, the National Health Lawyers Association, the American Bar Association (Antitrust and Litigation Sections and the Forum Committee on Health Law) and the New York State Bar Association (Antitrust and Health Law Divisions). Mr. Travis is the author of numerous articles of medical–legal import and lectures frequently on a host of medical–legal subjects. He received his JD with distinction from the Hofstra University School of Law.

LOREEN A. PERITZ, JD, is currently counsel at The Guardian Life Insurance Company of America. She is responsible for the legal aspects of the company's managed care strategic alliances. Prior to joining Guardian, Ms. Peritz was a member of the health care group at Garfunkel, Wild & Travis, PC. She graduated from the Washington College of Law at American University, where she served as a member of *American University Law Review*.

HAYDEN S. WOOL, JD, is a member of the Board of Directors of Garfunkel, Wild & Travis, PC. He devotes his efforts to the general representation of numerous hospitals, physician groups, physician associations, and other health care–related business organizations. He is a member of the National Health Lawyers Association, and the American Bar Association (Antitrust Section and the ABA Forum Committee on Health Law). Mr. Wool is also a member of the New York State Bar Association (Health Law Division). Mr. Wool is a graduate of Albany Law School of Union University, where he served as a member and comment editor of the *Albany Law Review*.

GREG E. BLOOM, CPA, JD, also a member of the Board of Directors of Garfunkel, Wild & Travis, PC, specializes in the representation of hospitals, physician groups, physician associations, and other health care–related business organizations. Earlier, he had specialized in corporate and securities law at Kelley Drye & Warren. He is a certified public accountant and a member of the New York Bar Association. He is a graduate of Fordham University School of Law, where he was a member of the *Urban Law Journal*.

Chapter 5

Strategic Planning for Health Care Provider Organizations

E. Gordon Whyte and John D. Blair

Evidence of the rapidly changing health care environment is everywhere. For example, it appears in the recent rise and fall of Columbia/HCA, in the continuing amalgamation of the giants in the managed care arena, and in the ever unpredictable health policy making of the U.S. Congress and state legislatures around the nation. In addition, the marketplace continues to send confusing and conflicting messages about the relative importance of cost, access, and quality. Sachs divided today's managed care into two models: the economic model and the medical care model.[1] Both focus on the reduction of cost, but each takes a different approach. The economic model attempts to squeeze waste out of the system by emphasizing monitoring and control of the services rendered by providers; the medical care model, by emphasizing wellness and prophylaxis. Entering into the cost–access–quality conundrum is the role of choice and selection in the delivery and purchase of health care services. Sachs suggested a new model, called the "focused care" model, that takes the consumer into account more than does either of the other two.

Clarke describes the important role of derived demand in attracting and retaining satisfied customers (see Chapter 7). She describes derived demand as a two-stage marketing process. The marketer must develop a set of products and services to appeal not merely to the immediate customer (i.e., the purchaser of the service) but to the customer of the immediate customer. The customer of the immediate customer, no matter which model is used, is the patient. Today patients want more choice. All these factors—rapidly changing environment, shifting marketplace pressures, evolution of the managed care segment of the health care industry, the reentry of consumer choice—are increasing tensions between and among the providers, purchasers, and recipients of health care services.

As Blair and colleagues point out (see Chapter 6), much of the recent health care literature is championing the development of organized delivery systems. The rapid growth of these systems and networks is changing the "strategic web of stakeholder relationships." Much of the initial activity in forming organized delivery systems was an effort to appeal to a perceived desire for "one-stop shopping" by the purchasers of health care services. A system that provided all things great and small in health care was thought to be in a better position in the managed care environment. More recently, however, Shortell and associates have led the way in recognizing the efficiencies, flexibility, and maneuverability of virtually integrated systems, in which an organization does not have to own all the services in order to deliver all the services needed or wanted by any of the growing number of purchasers of health care services (the immediate customers) and the patients (the customers of the immediate customers).[2] Virtually integrated delivery systems consist of a wide variety of strategic alliances and partnerships among provider organizations and units bound together by contractual agreements rather than by the ownership of assets.

As providers and purchasers align themselves and form partnerships for the delivery of various services, it becomes increasingly difficult for any given organization to define its position in the marketplace, its competitors, and its partners.

Stakeholders can shift from internal to external and back again, depending on the service or geographic area involved. In fact, organizations can find themselves partners in one venture and competitors in another, simultaneously. Today's potentially overlapping strategic alliances and partnerships blur lines of affiliation and divide loyalties.

According to Shortell and associates,[3] a system's readiness to perform is dependent on its ability to define the population that it is to serve; identify the population's needs; and align the system's clinical, managerial, and governance functions. The hub of the capability wheel is the system's information system. Shortell noted that information systems are the "least developed aspect of the community health care management system concept . . . and that this underdevelopment slows down achievement of the other components of the system."[4]

The tasks of database development, management, and conversion into information

systems are growing in their importance to health care systems. Sophisticated information systems will allow the health care system, whether asset-based or virtual, to know its population of present and future customers, their wants and needs, their patterns of use, and the state of their health as individuals and as a group. Data will facilitate decision making about disease management, prevention services, and the prevalence of chronic and acute disease in the population. Therefore, today's health care systems must know how to collect data, what data to collect, and how to analyze and use the data once they are in the system. Despite their importance, however, databases cannot replace the critical role of the human factor in the planning and marketing of the health care services. They cannot replace judgment based on experience, knowledge, and thinking—strategic thinking.

STRATEGIC THINKING

The current U.S. health care system has not resulted from a coordinated planning effort that carefully considered strategically developed alternatives. Rather, the system has grown out of a variety of responses to a range of market forces. Health care organizations have changed direction as an outcome of their individual responses to specific interpretations of their missions and their assessment of the opportunities that exist in their particular environment.

Health care provider organizations must assess the future in terms of their ability to meet the expectations of a better informed public and a more active, diversified group of purchasers of care and services. In addition, the fact that government is assigning itself a larger role in controlling the growth of the system calls for constant monitoring by providers. Finally, the relationship between hospitals and physicians, long considered the linchpin of the health care system, is changing as well. Physicians now perceive that their preeminent role as the primary customers of hospitals and the driving force of the system as a whole is eroding through the growing influence of managed care organizations, and as a result, their authority to direct the care of their patients within the system is decreasing.

The convergence of these factors and other changes in the current health care environment have caused health care provider organizations to discern more fully the necessity of addressing and understanding the environment in which they must interact and deliver their services. The forces in the environment are compelling the system to change rather than allowing the system to assess and change itself. In other words, the paradigm of the health care delivery system and the environment in which the system operates are being changed for the industry rather than by the industry.

Without an awareness of how their organization affects other organizations and is, in turn, affected by other organizations and other forces in the environment, health care managers run a risk of developing plans that are myopic and, thus, ineffective management tools. It is essential that health care managers conceptualize their organizations in systems terms. As they do this, they will begin to measure each decision that they make in terms of its ramifications in and on the environment. This conceptualization is the basic component of strategic thinking.

PREPARATION FOR THE STRATEGIC PLANNING PROCESS

Selecting the Participants

Selection of the individuals who will serve on what generally is called the Strategic Plan-

ning Committee is vital to the success of the process and, by extension, to the success and survival of the organization. They will have a direct impact on the future of the organization. These decision makers will review the mission statement; interpret the planning information; and analyze the strengths, weaknesses, opportunities, and threats (SWOTs). They will set the course and direction that the organization will follow for the foreseeable future.

It is rare that someone from outside the organization is selected for participation at this level, with the exception of a paid strategic planning consultant. Because of the importance of these individuals and the power that they will exercise over and within the organization, maneuvering or outright campaigning for a position on this committee is common among governing body members, as well as executive staff. Some individuals, because of their positions, must be included (e.g., chair of the governing body, chief executive officer, chief operations officer, chief financial officer). However, every effort should be made to choose other individuals who have been identified as strategic thinkers in the organization. In all cases, a stakeholder assessment will assist the person selecting the planning committee members in evaluating the strengths, power bases, and values of the individuals selected.

Developing a Mission Statement

Every health care provider organization has a purpose for existing. Although it may seem that the nature of the health care industry would make defining the purpose of a health care provider organization a simple undertaking, a simplistic approach to defining purpose can lead an organization to a false sense of directedness. The purpose of a hospital in the current environment is not what it once was, nor can it be assumed that all hospitals have the same purpose. Likewise, the nature and purpose of each organized delivery system are developed individually. Therefore, every organization should express its purpose in a clearly composed set of statements, a mission statement.

Since early in the history of this country, emphasis has been on the provision of the highest quality of care at virtually any price. Expectations of the marketplace were in large part set by the providers. Physicians and hospitals told the patients and, by extension, the community what they should expect in terms of outcomes and cost of medical services. When stakeholder expectations were controlled by the provider organizations, it was a relatively simple task for the organization to define its mission to meet the expectations that were prescribed. In today's environment, however, the marketplace and organizational stakeholders are more informed and vocal. They set their own expectations. Additionally, as Clarke points out (see Chapter 7), until there is greater stabilization of the systems and networks, the identification of the competitors may be possible only in the short run.

In order to arrive at a comprehensive definition of the mission of an organized health care delivery system or its health care provider organizations, it is necessary to consider the various needs and goals of the key stakeholders. Without assessment of and input from these groups and individuals, the organization may misstate its mission and thereby run the risk of misdirecting its efforts. Analysis of the turbulent environment in which organized delivery systems and health care provider organizations find themselves today reveals an increase in the complexity of stakeholder relationships and a growth in the number of active stakeholders. In the recent past, hospital administrators

might have been able to describe their stakeholders simply as board members, medical staff members, patients, some payers, and a few key vendors. This is no longer the case. Today's stakeholder relationships are likely to be much more complex. Careful management of the relationships with those individuals and groups that have significant interests in and are significantly affected by the actions and decisions of the health care provider organization transforms these complex relationships into logical, systematic frameworks that encourage the pro-active integration of the organization with the environment.[5] By evaluating the needs and goals of the key stakeholders, the organization is better able to develop a clear definition of its mission and specific strategies for carrying out that mission.

To know its real mission, an organization must be able to answer the question, What business are we in? The answer to this question should be unique for virtually every health care provider organization in every setting and every community. Descriptions of the business of a hospital, physician group practice, nursing home, home health care agency, or organized delivery system can vary greatly, depending on such things as ownership, location, competition, state of the economy, politics, availability of technology, ethics, and the values of the people in leadership positions within the organization. Often, believing that their organization's mission is obvious, leaders are unwilling to spend the time necessary to define that mission. Mission often is taken for granted and dismissed as being obvious. Yet, when they do occur, detailed discussions usually reveal differing opinions.

The mission statement becomes the basis for all other planning, at all levels. The key to successful planning and goal attainment is clear organizational direction based on a coherent mission that is rooted in a strong set of mutually held organizational values. One of the most frequently cited examples of the success of a value-based, mission-driven organization is the Disney Corporation. The inculturation process required of new Disney employees is extensive and thorough. The key to Disney's success is not the process through which employees go, but the values and coherent mission of the organization. So, while the Disney process is replicative, it will succeed only over the long haul in an organization that adapts the process to its own values and mission.

Getting to the Strategic Level

Perhaps the most difficult phase of the strategic planning process is defining exactly what strategic planning is, why strategic thinking is required for success, and how accomplishing both can be successful only if implementation is instituted through strategic management. Many health care executives believe that the use of a strategic approach to operations, including strategic thinking, planning, and managing, enhances the survival of their organizations. The adoption of a strategic approach creates linkages between philosophical underpinnings, organizational culture, operational direction, and financial decision making. These crucial linkages open a clear path to the ultimate success of the organization through fulfillment of its mission and the attainment of its goals.

The strategic approach to operation is applicable at all levels of an organization. At the organizational base, the strategic approach requires each manager to have a thorough understanding of his or her particular unit and the specific environment in which the unit operates. In order to contribute to the good of the whole organization, the unit's relationship with its environment should be central to every action taken. By extension, senior managers must recognize and consider the association between the organization and its external environment, realizing that this relationship is fundamental to each action taken by the organization as a whole.

Failure to recognize the nature and particular characteristics of the operating environment of a particular institution can result in policy directives and programs that are doomed to failure. For example, a national chain of nursing homes that uses standardized monthly menus designed to provide adequate nutrition and reduce cost through the use of large purchasing contracts will quickly come to understand that while it may be more expedient and efficient to plan and purchase dietary items this way, the palates of New Jersey residents are very different from those of Louisiana residents. Either the residents of one of the homes will be dissatisfied, or perhaps all of the residents in both homes will be dissatisfied. It is essential to consider the needs of the particular market (environment) and the stakeholders in that market.

Defining Strategy

There is a growing interest in strategy in the health care sector today. In order to move a health care organization toward thinking, planning, and managing strategically, executives must first agree on what strategy means. Strategy is an approach to thinking, planning, and decision making in a business situation that requires a manager to know, understand, accept, and support the mission of the organization (or unit within an organization) and to relate that mission to the environment in which decisions will be implemented. The driving force behind strategic thinking, planning, and managing is the organization's mission.

All organizations have goals. Articulated or not, the goals act as a point of reference in thoughtful decision making. However, many goals are set to accommodate a short-term interest; to appease or please a superior; or to comply with organizational policy, established procedure, or outside regulations. These constraints, when joined with personality, values, and management style, can cause a manager to make decisions and act in a manner that Lindbloom described as "muddling through."[6] When they use the muddling through approach, managers make decisions that are guided more by the specifics of a particular situation than by agreed upon goals developed through a formalized planning process and previous strategy selection. Managers who muddle are constrained by "how things are." In contrast, a strategic approach forces a manager to know "how things are" and to make decisions in support of "how things could be" or "must be" in order to fulfill the organization's mission in its defined environment.

As a result of ongoing monitoring, a manager who uses a strategic approach has a thorough understanding of the internal and external environments and uses this collection of information to make decisions that will advance the organization toward mission fulfillment. Information generated through the monitoring process is both quantitative and qualitative in nature. Both are needed in the decision-making process. Managers must make sound decisions that are based on feelings, impressions, and opinions, as well as on quantitative data developed by the system's information system. Throughout the process, decisions are made with consideration given to both environment and mission.

According to Shrivastava,[7] strategy is not simply a means of making an organization more financially successful. It is a way of making the organization more useful and productive to society, which, in turn, will enable it to prosper.

STRATEGIC PLANNING PROCESS

Organized delivery systems and their health care provider organizations frequently begin their planning processes, strategic or otherwise, by creating a set of desired goals. With this set of goals as the guiding light, managers proceed to "back into" the planning process. In other words, they ask the question, What do we need to do to accomplish these goals?

In a strategic approach to planning, the process begins with an in-depth assessment of the organization, its mission, and its environment. There is an attitude of openness and willingness to challenge conventional wisdom and the existing paradigms. Strategic thinking enables a manager to consider how to change the environment rather than simply reacting to it. Changing the paradigm and/or adjusting to the environment requires time, effort, resources, creativity, and risk taking. This is the nature of strategic planning. It encourages the manager to ask, "How can we further our mission given this collection of information?" rather than "What do we have to do to reach these goals?" This approach challenges a manager to be pro-active, think creatively, and set aggressive goals.

The strategic planning process is a series of connected steps through which an organization assesses its mission, internal strengths and weaknesses, and external opportunities and threats; identifies goals and objectives; develops alternative strategies for attaining those goals; selects the best combination of strategies; and monitors the organizational behavior and progress toward mission fulfillment through goal attainment. There is nothing fixed about the number of steps in the process. Each organization will divide the process into a different number of steps, and each probably will change the process each time it is repeated to conform to the current organizational structure and the environment in which the planning is being done.

Step One: Planning the Process

The first step in any strategic planning process is to develop a road map through the planning process itself, often referred to as the "plan to plan." In this phase, those individuals responsible for directing and guiding the strategic planning process assist the leaders of the organization in deciding the following:

- the committee structure to be used in developing the planning data, assessing the resulting information, and selecting the strategies to be implemented
- the methodology to be used in gathering data (e.g., primary or secondary collection)
- the members of the planning team(s) (i.e., which administrators, medical staff members, governing body representatives, and department heads will participate and at what level)
- the frequency of the meetings to be held by each team and committee, a specific time frame for completion of each assigned task, and a schedule of the meeting times for each committee and team
- the expected duration of the entire planning process, calculated with an emphasis on thoroughness and clarity rather than speed

An example of a plan to plan is shown in Table 5–1. Not only are the various steps clearly delineated, but also there is an approximate time frame allotted to each step and a designated person(s) responsible for its completion.

Step Two: Assessing the Mission Statement

As noted earlier, the value-based mission statement is the foundation on which the rest of the strategic planning process is built. Because the individuals who participate in the mission assessment process usually are also key stakeholders, it is essential that they share a core set of values and purposes. Without these underpinnings, there is an increased risk that each individual will respond to and act in reference to personal interests, which may not be consistent with the interests of the other group members and with the purpose of the organization.

Members of the governing body and upper management levels in the organization usually conduct the mission assessment. This process is infinitely more complicated when the organization is a virtually integrated delivery system. It is common to find that the fundamental missions of the partnering organizations are not necessarily consistent with one another. Because it is nearly impossible to rely on the individual mission statements of the respective partners in this situation, the need for redefinition of the virtual system's mission becomes even greater. Conducting this step of the strategic planning process in a retreat format allows for the greatest level of attention and participation by organization leadership. The end result is a shared sense of purpose that will facilitate the subsequent strategic decision making.

Step Three: Conducting the Environmental Assessment

Internal staff generally conduct both external and internal environmental assessments

Table 5–1 Planning the Planning Process

Planning Steps	Time Frame	Responsible Person(s)
1. Develop a planning procedure and gain agreement from key individuals.	Two meetings held within two weeks	Administrator, planning director, and planning consultant
2. Assess organizational mission statement.	Two-day retreat	Administrator, board chair, and physician representative
3. Assess external environment.	Six weeks	Planning director, planning consultant, and planning staff
4. Assess internal environment.	Six weeks (simultaneous with external environment)	Planning director, planning consultant, and planning staff
5. Develop organizational goals.	Two weeks following circulation of internal and external assessment data	Administrator, board planning committee, planning director, and planning consultant
6. Formulate strategic options for accomplishing each goal.	One month after agreement on organizational goals	Administrator, planning director, planning consultant, board planning committee, and staff planning teams
7. Select and develop strategic options to be implemented.	One week after formulation of strategic options	Administrator, planning director, planning consultant, and board planning committee
8. Approve the strategic plan with specific options, costs, and estimated implementation dates supplied by the governing body.	First board meeting following final selection of strategic options	Governing body
9. Develop action plan and implementation schedule for each chosen strategic option.	Varies with the complexity of each option. However, no longer than one month will be allowed any option.	Administrator, planning director, and various department heads

under the guidance and supervision of the person charged with shepherding the strategic planning process. There are two overriding characteristics of successful external and internal assessments: thoroughness and usefulness.

The data search should begin with an assessment of the organization's information system and its ability to provide existing data in a meaningful form, as well as its ability to handle the collection and manipulation of any new data generated in the external and internal assessment process. The search for the data to be used must be well organized. Every important element of the environment warrants investigation. Once the staff are confident that they have collected all available data necessary for strategic planning purposes, they should then configure those data into formats that make them understandable for the individuals who will be making decisions.

In many cases, ensuring that every participant understands the assessments will require several different presentation formats. Some individuals more readily grasp information presented in visual formats, such as bar graphs and pie charts, while others prefer tables and lists. Still others want written detailed reports. It is the responsibility of the staff who have collected the data to report them in a way that is useful to each decision maker involved in the process.

In converting the external and internal data into information, the staff compile a list of the organization's internal strengths and weaknesses, and the opportunities and threats that exist in the external environment. This task is referred to as a SWOT analysis. It is not uncommon in such an analysis to find the list of internal strengths and weaknesses much longer and more detailed than the list of external opportunities and threats. This frequently happens because most staff members are more familiar with their own organization than they are with the external environment, and the data are more readily available. Also, there are finely tuned, well-known formulas for analyzing and interpreting internal data. As a result, health care system executives are generally more comfortable interpreting balance sheets than they are interpreting political climates.

External Environment

Assessing the external environment in today's turbulent times takes a high level of attention to detail and an ability to assimilate a large quantity of data with significant gaps. The goal of this assessment is to understand more fully the position of the organization in its environment. Duncan and others have developed specific objectives for this phase of the process that will help to ensure the development of the best possible environmental description.[8] These objectives are as follows:

1. to classify and order information flows generated by outside organizations
2. to identify and analyze current important issues that will affect the organization
3. to detect and analyze the weak signals of emerging issues that will affect the organization
4. to speculate on the likely future issues that will have a significant impact on the organization
5. to provide organized information for the development of the organization's purpose, mission, objectives, internal assessment, and strategy
6. to foster strategic thinking throughout the organization

Through external environmental assessment, those involved in the strategic planning process can identify the potential threats and opportunities for the organization. The external environment can be systematically assessed using the following taxonomy as a guide:

1. macro-environment: major trends and events taking place outside of the specific environment in which the organization operates (e.g., the global economy, industry trends, national economic indicators).

2. regulatory environment: recent or expected changes in the myriad of regulations that directly affect the organization.

3. economic environment: trends, events, and economic indicators that are specific to the marketplace in which the organization operates. Also included in this area is an assessment of the growth, strength, and impact of managed care arrangements on the delivery of health care services in the marketplace.

4. social environment: public health status of the marketplace, health impacts of generalized social behaviors (e.g., poor diet, sexually transmitted disease, smoking, substance and alcohol abuse). Also included in this area is an assessment of the demographic changes and trends in the marketplace.

5. political environment: factors such as recently enacted or pending legislation at the local, state, and federal levels.

6. competitive environment: strengths and weaknesses of the organizations and individuals who are seeking to provide the same or similar services to the organization's targeted segments. Also included in this area is an assessment of any recent or expected changes in strategic alliances among providers in the marketplace.

7. technological environment: recent advances in pharmaceuticals, genetics, and high-technology equipment, as well as the knowledge base, skills, and talents of the organization's workforce pools.

8. consumer environment: consumer preferences, purchase behaviors.

The external environmental assessment should clarify those specific aspects of the environment that affect the organization to-day and in the foreseeable future. Therefore, it is necessary for the strategic planning teams to develop methodologies that are appropriate for forecasting significant events and trends. Regardless of how thorough and sophisticated the forecasting techniques, they do not foretell the future. They can only provide strategic decision makers with the best available information and the best strategic thinking of the individuals involved in the planning process.

Internal Assessment

Through a structured internal assessment, a health care provider organization will become aware of its strengths and weaknesses. Conducting such an assessment in the strategic planning process is sometimes difficult, however, for a couple of reasons. First, it can be organizationally and personally painful to make a detailed self-evaluation. Second, as with the preconceived notions surrounding the mission statement, some health care executives feel that they already know the strengths and weaknesses of their organizations.

Not only does the internal assessment identify organizational strengths and weaknesses, but also it evaluates them in relation to the specific external opportunities and threats that have been identified. The matching of strengths and weaknesses with opportunities and threats exposes critical information that subsequently will be used in the development of strategic alternatives. To facilitate the internal assessment, the organization can be divided into 10 operating components. Each component is first assessed on an individual basis. Then the component is evaluated relative to the other components in the organization. The 10 components evaluated in the internal assessment are

1. management: the number of levels, strength of each level as a whole and

the individuals in that level, management skills, and formal delegation of decision-making authority.

2. human resources: skill levels in technical areas, availability of appropriately prepared personnel, recruitment and retention track record, and efficiency in scheduling.

3. finance: availability and use of capital funds, use of operating revenues, ratio analyses, budget variances, and internal control mechanisms.

4. marketing: characteristics of current patients, such as payer source, acuity, demographics, origin, and destination; referral sources; review of the current level of usage of services or product lines offered; channels or mechanisms for service delivery; promotional techniques; and success rates of each.

5. clinical systems: output measures of volume and quality, level of technology available, level of technology needed, and skills and knowledge base of clinicians.

6. organizational structure: linkage of human resources, technologies, marketing, and management talent.

7. organizational culture: value system and behavioral expectations that support the mission.

8. physical plant: constraint or facilitation of future growth and change.

9. information systems: ability to link the financial, clinical, and marketing information systems.

10. leadership abilities: demonstrated leadership of the organization's senior and executive managers, the governing body, and department and section heads. This is a particularly sensitive area and is, unfortunately, frequently left out of the process.

Most of these components require the gathering and assessment of both quantitative and qualitative data. In the internal assessment phase, as in all other phases of the strategic planning process, the ability of the decision makers to exercise judgment in evaluating and prioritizing the information is as critical as the collection of the data itself.

Step Four: Conducting a Strategic Stakeholder Analysis

This is the point in the strategic planning process where the strategic stakeholder assessment process is conducted as described by Blair and colleagues in the following chapter.

Step Five: Setting Goals and Objectives

For the purposes of strategic planning as discussed in this chapter, there is little difference between goals and objectives. They are end points that the organization plans to reach in a specified period of time. They have three characteristics. First, goals are reachable, although not necessarily easily reachable; they should be challenging in order to motivate staff and employees to work toward them. Second, goals must be verifiable. The goals need not always be discretely measurable or quantifiable, but it is absolutely essential that there be a clearly defined means for demonstrating whether the goal was reached at the end of the agreed upon time period. Third, goals must be specific and explicit. They must establish specific outcomes that will contribute to the fulfillment of the organizational mission. Furthermore, their accomplishment must be the explicit responsibility of particular individuals or groups within the organization.

Goals flow from the matching of organizational strengths and weaknesses with environmental opportunities and threats. The goals should reflect, in reachable, verifiable, specific, and explicit terms, the organization's efforts to maximize its strengths and avail itself of the opportunities, while minimizing its acknowledged weaknesses and defending itself against identified threats.

There is no generally accepted guideline to the number of goals that an organization should set. Setting too many goals can have the effect of making some or all of them unreachable, however, because they will suffer from a lack of attention and activity. In addition, setting too many goals can overextend an organization's financial and human resources. Employees are motivated by their successes in reaching their goals, and organizations flourish as a result of motivated employees accomplishing agreed upon goals.

Setting the strategic goals for the organization is the single most important step in the entire strategic planning process. Every step that has preceded goal selection has served as preparation for making these decisions. Every step that follows goal selection will be directed at moving the organization toward the fulfillment of its mission. The selection of the goals is a function of the thoroughness of the data collection and the conversion of the data into information. The successful accomplishment of the goals is a function of the strategic thinking abilities of the involved decision maker.

Step Six: Formulating Strategic Options

Once the goals have been set, the organization develops the means for relating them to the environment. These means are the strategies. In this phase in the strategic planning process, the planning teams or planning committee may use techniques such as brainstorming and planning retreats, among others. In addition to statistical forecasting,

Zentner suggested that health care provider organizations use scenarios in planning.[9] In the construction of alternative scenarios, planners combine selected environmental factors into a wide spectrum of possible situations to assist decision makers in assessing the consequences of alternative decisions.

The purpose of this step is to develop a list of realistic strategies that could lead to the accomplishment of each organizational goal. In some instances, the lists may be extensive; in others, limited. If the planning team seems unable to generate more than one strategy for a given goal, there may be a predetermined decision about the strategy to be used to accomplish that particular goal. That predetermined strategy should not be accepted without serious discussion and evaluation.

Each proposed strategy not only should address a specific goal, but also should take into consideration specific stakeholders. For instance, an urban hospital that is going to consider a rural outreach strategy as a means of increasing inpatient referrals to its cardiology unit must simultaneously consider the willingness of its cardiology staff to accept referrals from that area and the possible reactions of the physicians in the targeted rural community.

Alternative strategies can be categorized into three types:

1. practical alternatives that can receive immediate approval and are easily implementable
2. incremental alternatives whose implementation in some sequence will lead to eventual accomplishment of the goals
3. radical alternatives that will require significant change in the organization, but implementation of which will result in rapid movement toward goal attainment

Neither the number nor the type of alternative strategies is important. The fact that each suggested strategy is realistic, implementable, and stakeholder-based is very important.

Step Seven: Selecting and Developing the Strategies

It is important that the selection of the strategies to be implemented be a separate step from the development of the alternative strategies. If strategy selection is part of the option development step, each option will be evaluated at the time it is suggested. This instantaneous evaluation retards the production of alternatives, because team members become fearful of the immediate rejection of their alternative ideas. By separating the two steps, each alternative receives its due consideration, and participants are more likely to contribute to the process.

The development of the specific procedures and actions required to implement the strategies should originate in the assessment of the desired goals and the potential impacts of the selected strategies on the various stakeholders in the organization. Each stakeholder has expectations for the organization that the strategies are going to affect. Managers in health care provider organizations must anticipate the reactions of the stakeholders to the proposed strategies and manage the various stakeholder relationships in a manner that capitalizes on stakeholder support and minimizes their opposition.

Drucker warned planners of four common mistakes at this stage of the strategic planning process.[10]

1. failure to test the new strategy before full implementation. There are many techniques that can be used to test a strategy, including pilot projects, focus groups, and in-depth stakeholder interviews.

2. "righteous arrogance." Almost every strategy will require some modification as the planning process progresses. Refusal to make the necessary changes because that is not the way it was conceived or proposed can result in the elimination of a potentially successful strategy. The planning committee needs to "own" the accepted strategy, and the person who contributed the original proposal needs to relinquish personal ownership of the idea.

3. failure to develop and propose radical strategies. The proposed strategies should not all be modifications of the way business is done at any particular moment. There comes a time when it is necessary to design a strategy for the specific requirements of a job.

4. the assumption that there is just one right strategy for each goal and that the role of the planning committee is to determine which one is correct. There may be several equally right strategies, and the role of the committee is to select the one that will accomplish the goal in the most efficient and effective manner, taking into consideration the mission and the stakeholders involved.

Finally, Drucker offered these words of advice when selecting a new strategy for implementation: "If at first you don't succeed, try once more. Then do something else."[11] He noted that often a new strategy will not work the first time. Before abandoning the entire strategy, the organization should assess the reason for the failure and attempt to fix it. This assessment and willingness to modify strategy will intensify an organization's commitment to a selected strategy because the individuals involved will know that it is not simply a matter of making it work the first time. It is a matter of making it work in the end.

Step Eight: Developing the Implementation Plan

As part of the implementation plan, the organization assigns specific responsibility for each strategy to an individual or group within the organization. Each strategy is also assigned a timeline and a completion date. The plan for implementation should be presented in a format that is similar to the "plan to plan" shown in Table 5–1.

In some cases, an organization establishes important checkpoints to measure movement during the implementation process. In all cases, organizations monitor and evaluate progress in some way. The evaluation of the strategies has the effect of causing the organization to monitor and evaluate the environment as well. This kind of feedback allows the organization to evaluate the effectiveness of its selected strategies continuously and to make adjustments as deemed necessary. Adjustments may range from minor tinkering with the action plan or timelines to complete abandonment of the strategy and/or adoption of a new strategy in extreme cases.

ROLE OF THE PLANNING DIRECTOR AND DEPARTMENT

Whether a member of the staff or a paid professional planning consultant, the planning director is not responsible for the plan. Furthermore, it is not the responsibility of the planning department to produce an annual update of the strategic plan. The role of the planning director is to facilitate and guide the process. A successful planning director does not feel a psychological ownership of the planning document. Rather, that person, together with the members of the planning staff, feels the "thrill of success" as a result of completing the process and obtaining a commitment from the key stakeholders in the organization to the successful implementation of the strategies.

Almost all organizations must decide whether to use an outside consultant at some point. In general, it is prudent to seek the help of an outside consultant the first few times through the strategic planning process. This outsider will be more objective about the work being done and will be in a stronger position to ensure that deadlines are met and that everyone who is supposed to be involved continues to participate. Furthermore, the consultant will bring technical and professional expertise to the organization that often is not available in the early attempts at the process.

CONCLUSION

Organized delivery systems and their health care provider organizations are struggling to survive in a dynamic and sometimes dangerous environment. This situation requires an approach to the management of these organizations that goes beyond the institutional boundaries of the past. These organizations must realize that they are not only part of the health care delivery system, but also part of the larger ecosystem in the United States; thus, national and international issues affect them.

Strategic planning is one part of a new approach to running health care provider organizations in this environment—strategic management. Through the use of strategic management, specifically strategic planning, an organization is able to develop a sensitivity to both its external and its internal environments. This environmental sensitivity allows organizations to evaluate their relationships with their individual stakeholders and develop plans to manage those relationships strategically.

The basis for strategic planning and management is an organizationwide dedication to fulfilling the mission of the organization. This shared dedication creates a cohesiveness that ensures consistent decision making directed toward the survival and success of the organization in today's turbulent environment.

NOTES

1. M.A. Sachs, "Managed Care: The Next Generation," *Frontiers in Health Services Management* 14, no. 1, (1997).
2. S.M. Shortell et al., *Remaking Health Care in America: Building Organized Delivery Systems* (San Francisco: Jossey-Bass, Publishers, 1996).
3. Ibid.
4. Ibid.
5. J.D. Blair and M.D. Fottler, *Challenges in Health Care Management: Strategic Perspectives for Managing Key Stakeholders* (San Francisco: Jossey-Bass, Publishers, 1990), 2–3.
6. C.E. Lindbloom, "The Science of Muddling Through," *Public Administration Review* (Spring 1959): 79–88.
7. P. Shrivastava, *Strategic Management: Concepts and Practices* (Cincinnati, OH: Southwestern Publishing Co., 1994), 6.
8. W.J. Duncan et al., *Strategic Management of Health Care Organizations* (Boston: PWS-Kent Publishing Co., 1992), 75.
9. R.D. Zentner, "Scenarios: A Planning Tool for Health Care Organizations," *Hospital & Health Services Administration* (Summer 1991): 211–222.
10. P.F. Drucker, *Managing the Non-Profit Organization: Principles and Practices* (New York: Harper-Business, 1990), 69–71.
11. Ibid.

E. GORDON WHYTE, MHA, PHD, is Vice Chairman and Director of Master Programs, Department of Health Systems Management, in the School of Public Health and Tropical Medicine at Tulane University Medical Center. He also is President of Gordon Whyte and Associates, a health care planning and marketing consulting firm. Dr. Whyte has previously served as Vice President of Strategic Planning and Marketing at St. Mary of the Plains Hospital, Lubbock, Texas; and Administrator of HealthSouth Rehabilitation Center of New Orleans. A licensed nursing facility administrator, he received his master's degree from Trinity University in 1975 and his PhD from the University of Mississippi in 1985.

JOHN D. BLAIR, PHD, is the Trinity Company Professor in Management and Health Care Strategy for the College of Business Administration (and the School of Medicine) at Texas Tech University. He currently serves as the Coordinator of the Area of Management (Department Chair) and has served as the Chair of the Health Care Administration Division of the National Academy of Management. He is also the founding Director of the Center for Health Care Strategy and an editor of *Advances in Health Care Management*, a new JAI Press series. His most recent books include *Strategic Leadership for Medical Groups: Navigating Your Strategic Web* (1998); *Challenges in Military Health Care* (1993); and *Challenges in Health Care Management: Strategic Perspectives for Managing Key Stakeholders* (1990). He received his PhD from the University of Michigan in 1975.

Chapter 6

Strategic Management of Stakeholder Relationships

John D. Blair, G. Tyge Payne, Timothy M. Rotarius, Carlton J. Whitehead, and E. Gordon Whyte

The health care environment is undergoing fundamental and somewhat revolutionary changes. Even without the proposed government changes, reform is occurring. The ultimate effect of this reform—whether mandated by the government, driven by private sector initiatives such as managed care, or produced by the demands of powerful buyer groups for more health care for less money—is unknown. It is certain to affect the future of the industry, however, by leading to increasingly complex, integrated organizations and networks.

The leaders of these new organizations must manage an increasingly complex web of relationships with a growing number of active, powerful, and sometimes competing stakeholders (i.e., any individuals, groups, or organizations that have a stake in the decisions and actions of an organization and attempt to influence those decisions and actions). These stakeholders exert an influence on every health care management issue, and managers must recognize and evaluate these relationships for their potential to support or threaten the organization and its competitive goals.

Much of the emerging health care literature champions the development of organized health care networks and systems as the fundamental strategy for facing the uncertain future created by health care reform. Managers, seeking to position their organizations for optimal strategic responsiveness to a still poorly understood future, have turned to linkages with others that have often been competitors or adversaries. Thus, hospitals, physicians, and health care plans are creating vertically integrated organizations and systems.[1-8] This emergence of rapidly growing organized delivery systems and networks has changed the strategic web, that complex set of interrelated relationships, within which health care organizations find themselves.[9] Therefore, because the nature of those relationships is constantly changing, the need for managers to engage in effective strategic management of stakeholder relationships is more crucial now than ever before.

Today's strategic stakeholder management tools must be sophisticated and powerful if executives are to lead their health care organizations effectively, as the strategic web of health care relationships can become extremely complicated. For example, Figure 6–1 depicts a private, tertiary care hospital (Hospital A) that, as part of an integrating system (System A), is contemplating a strategic alliance with a cardiology group (Group

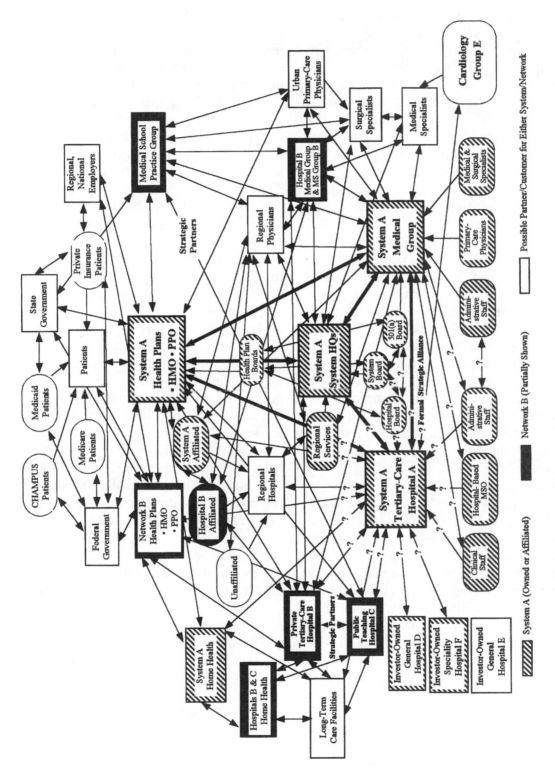

Figure 6–1 The Evolving Strategic Web for the Tertiary Care Hospital within an Integrating Regional System, a Simplified Model

E). Strategic alliances of this sort often are formed to allow for the attainment of some overall competitive goal. Also identified in Figure 6–1 is a myriad of other relationships that come into play because of this contemplated strategic alliance. What initially would have been viewed as a simple, dyadic relationship has mushroomed into a large number of key relationships (notice that only key relationships are shown in this strategic web figure, not all the relationships) that need to be acknowledged, addressed, and managed.

Figure 6–1 shows many key relationships. Those relationships that are highlighted with question marks are used as examples throughout this chapter. These are relationships that need to be examined in light of a strategic alliance between Hospital A and Cardiology Group E. As can easily be seen, there is an array of relationships between the hospital and the stakeholders that can be changed or called into question through the formalization of just one specific strategic alliance. The key relationships that Hospital A has with its stakeholders represent a pattern of formal and informal, interconnected stakeholder relationships.

Many hospitals already are forming or have formed one or more strategic alliances with physicians—both in primary care and in medical or surgical specialties. Some hospitals have even formed alliances with both physicians and health care plans in order to present a more fully organized health care system. Many of these newly created relationships have forced organizations to match the ever-changing environment. Unique opportunities exist to explore the consequences of creating and managing relationships among key hospital, physician, and health care plan stakeholders.

Few organizations have a fully developed, articulated strategic approach for managing their key stakeholder relationships. In most organizations, the stakeholder management perspectives of the executives are incomplete at best, and their approaches to stakeholder relationship assessment and management are haphazard. At worst, organizations have absolutely no systematic and effective stakeholder management approach. (Health care leaders require a detailed, overall approach, however, along with specific tools and techniques.) The strategic relationship management approach to stakeholders provides a means of properly identifying all the players, their roles, and their level of stake in the network.[10–15] In other words, it can help identify those areas in which there are likely to be significant opportunities for cooperation or risks of conflict among key network stakeholders.

Health care executives can develop more productive relationships with the key people —employees, physicians, community leaders, hospitals, competitors, managed care organizations, and others—who hold a stake in the management decisions of health care organizations. The examples used throughout this chapter are those varied and complex relationships that affect a specific type of health care organization—hospitals. The steps in this approach to strategic stakeholder management include the following:

- Identify all relevant external, interface, and internal stakeholders.
- Diagnose each stakeholder in terms of potential for threat and potential for cooperation.
- Ensure that the diagnosis for each stakeholder relationship is relevant for the specific issue facing the organization (e.g., the emerging issue of increasing hospital–physician integration through an alliance with a specialty physician group).
- Classify each stakeholder relationship as

mixed blessing, supportive, nonsupportive, or marginal.

- Formulate generic strategies for the management of each stakeholder relationship: involve the supportive stakeholder; collaborate with the mixed blessing stakeholder; defend against the nonsupportive stakeholder; and monitor the marginal stakeholder.
- Implement these generic strategies by developing specific implementation tactics and programs for each strategy–stakeholder combination.
- Evaluate the managerial implications of effectively managing stakeholder relationships from a strategic point of view.
- Identify which employees, as internal stakeholders, should be involved in the implementation process.

IDENTIFICATION OF ORGANIZATIONAL STAKEHOLDERS

Exhibit 6–1 provides a listing of the typical stakeholders for a large U.S. hospital, divided into three distinct stakeholder groups: external, interface, and internal. Whereas the internal and interface stakeholders often are at least partly supportive of the hospital, many of the external stakeholders may be neutral, nonsupportive, or even openly hostile.[16] A health care organization must respond to a large number and a wide variety of external stakeholders. They fall into three categories in their relationship to the organization: (1) those that provide inputs into the organization, (2) those that compete with it, and (3) those that have a particular special interest in how the organization functions. The first category includes suppliers, patients, third-party payers, and the financial community. The relationship between the organization and these

external stakeholders is a symbiotic one, as the organization depends on them for its very survival. (The degree of dependence of the organization on these stakeholders depends on the number and relative attractiveness of alternative providers of similar services.) In turn, these stakeholders depend on the organization to take their outputs. Without the organization or others like it, the stakeholders providing inputs could not survive. Consequently, the relationship between the organization and the stakeholders that provide necessary inputs is one of mutual dependence. As such, the two parties cannot, or do not want to, do without one another. They may experience conflict in finding ways to cooperate, however. For example, conflict may develop between a hospital and its patients over the price charged for certain services, but neither wishes to sever all relationships with the other.

The competing external stakeholders seek to attract the focal organization's dependents. These competitors may be direct competitors for patients (e.g., other hospitals), or they may be competing for skilled personnel (e.g., related health care organizations). Competitors do not necessarily need one another to survive. While cooperation between hospitals and their competitors has increased in recent years, so, too, has competition. Competitiveness, rather than cooperation, best defines the nature of the relationship most of the time.

External stakeholders in the third category, special interest groups, are concerned with those aspects of the organization's operations that affect their interests. The major special interest groups that relate to hospitals are government regulatory agencies, private accrediting associations, professional associations, labor unions, the media, the local community, and various political action groups. Because of the nature of the special interest, conflict most often defines the nature of this relation-

Exhibit 6–1 Stakeholders for Typical Large Hospital

A. **External Stakeholders**
1. Competitors
   - Other hospitals
     Private, not-for-profit
     Public
     Investor-owned
   - Physician practices (for outpatient services)
   - Other alternatives, e.g., freestanding outpatient surgery, diagnostic, or instant care centers
2. Related Health Care Organizations
   - Other hospitals in region (noncompetitors)
     Private, not-for-profit
     Public
     Investor-owned
   - Physician practices
     Solo
     Single-specialty medical group
     Multispecialty medical group
   - Nursing homes
   - Pharmacies
   - Home health agencies
3. Government Regulatory/Licensing Agencies
   - Federal
   - State
   - Local
4. Private Accreditation Associations
   - e.g., Joint Commission on Accreditation of Healthcare Organizations
5. Professional Associations
   - e.g., for certification of hospital professionals
     National
     State
     Local
6. Unions
   - National/international
   - Local
7. Patients
   - Private pay patients

- Insured patients
  Direct contract with employer
  Through contract with managed care organization
  Pay through prospective payment
  Pay at full rate
  Pay at discounted rate
  Pay through capitation
- Indigent patients
  Residents
  Nonresidents
- Patient families

8. Third-Party Payers
   - Governments
     Federal
     State
     Local
   - Regional employers
     Through indemnity insurance
     Through managed care contract
     Through direct contract
   - Business coalitions
   - Insurance companies
   - Managed care organizations (as purchasers of hospital services)
9. Hospital Suppliers
10. Media
    - Local
    - National
11. Financial Community
    - Including joint venture investment partners
12. Special Interest Groups
    - e.g., American Association of Retired Persons, veterans' organizations for VA hospitals, or Alcoholics Anonymous for psychiatric/substance abuse programs
13. Religious Organizations
    - Denominational organizations, e.g., synods or dioceses
    - Local churches/synagogues
    - Pastors/priests/rabbis

continues

Exhibit 6–1 continued

14. Local Community

B. Interface Stakeholders
1. Nonmanagement Medical Staff
   - On staff only at this hospital
   - Also on staff at other hospitals
   - Partners in joint-venture with hospital
2. Hospital Board
   - Trustees with policy authority
   - Advisory only
3. Parent Companies/Organizations/
   Religious Orders
4. Stockholders/Taxpayers/Contributors
5. Related Health Care Organizations (e.g.,
   as part of integrated delivery system)
   - Other hospitals in regional network
        Private, not-for-profit
        Public
        Investor-owned
   - Physician practices as strategic
        partners in alliance
        Solo

Single-specialty medical group
Multispecialty medical group
Group's own internal stakeholders
   as *indirect* stakeholders:
      Administrative staff
      Primary care physicians
      Medical specialists
      Surgical specialists

C. Internal Stakeholders
1. Management
   - Top managers
   - Physician managers/medical director
   - Nonclinical managers (e.g., market-
     ing, financial, regional services,
     practice management services)
   - Clinical functional managers
   - Clinical product line managers
2. Nonmanagement Employees
   - Professional
   - Paraprofessional
   - Support personnel

Source: Adapted from *Challenges in Health Care Management: Strategic Perspectives for Managing Key Stakeholders* by J.D. Blair and M.D. Fottler, pp. 81–83, with permission of Jossey-Bass, Publishers, © 1990.

ship. Compromise and, in some cases, overt collaboration generally resolve the conflict.

In Figure 6–1, Long-Term Care Facilities; Network B Health Plans; and Hospitals B, C, D, E, and F are all representative of external stakeholders for Hospital A.

Some stakeholders function on the interface between the organization and its environment. The major categories of interface stakeholders include the medical staff; the hospital board of trustees; the corporate office of the parent company; organizations as part of an integrated delivery system or network; and stockholders, taxpayers, or other contributors. These tend to be among the most powerful stakeholders in health care organizations, but are easily misunderstood because they are thought of as "us" or "them" when they are both—and neither.

The organization must offer each interface stakeholder sufficient inducements to continue to make appropriate contributions, but the lack of such things as a structured human resource system or adequate management authority can make it difficult to provide such inducements. Even so, the organization may offer professional autonomy (medical staff), institutional prestige or political contacts (hospital board), good financial returns (corporate office), access (taxpayers), and special services or benefits (contributors). Specific examples of interface stakeholders for Hospital A on Figure 6–1 include: System A Health Plans, Group A, the Hospital Board, and System A Affiliated Regional Hospitals.

Finally, internal stakeholders operate almost entirely within the generally accepted bounds of the organization and typically include management, professional, and nonprofessional staff. Management attempts to provide internal stakeholders with sufficient inducements to gain continual contributions from them. The stakeholders determine whether the inducements are sufficient for the contributions that they are required to make, partly on the basis of alternative inducement/contribution offers received from competitive organizations. Unless both the organization and the stakeholder believe an agreement will be mutually beneficial and of fair value (relative to alternatives), there will be no agreement. When resources are scarce, the exchange partners can be expected to attempt to obtain as high an inducement as possible while giving as low a contribution as possible. The organization may restructure the situation (i.e., offer a better compensation and benefit package) to induce or persuade employees to make the needed contribution. Alternatively, individuals in the organization may engage in manipulation, bargaining, and coalition activity in order to protect both their own interests and that of the coalition (including unions or professional associations) to which they belong. In Figure 6–1, the rounded corners on the boxes identify internal stakeholders to their respective focal organizations. The internal stakeholders to Hospital A include the Clinical Staff, the Hospital-Based Management Service Organization, and the Administrative Staff.

Clearly, health care organizations do not face just one or a few stakeholders. Rather, health care executives must learn to manage a portfolio of stakeholder relationships. It is vital that the leaders of health care organizations see the strategic implications of these stakeholder portfolios. No longer can specific functional managers be concerned only with those stakeholders that fall within their functional responsibilities. Instead, these managers must be cognizant of all the other relationships that are influenced by their one-on-one specific stakeholder episodes. The challenge facing health care organization executives is the creation of consistency and effectiveness in all of these individual stakeholder episodes.

DIAGNOSIS OF KEY STAKEHOLDER RELATIONSHIPS

To manage stakeholder relationships strategically, health care managers must be involved in a continuous process of internal and external scanning. They must go beyond the traditional issues in strategic management, such as the likely actions of competitors or the attractiveness of different markets. They must also look for those external, interface, and internal stakeholders that are likely to influence the organization's decisions. As noted earlier, managers must make two critical assessments about these stakeholders: (1) their potential to threaten the organization and (2) their potential to cooperate with it.[17,18]

Stakeholder's Potential for Threat

Hostility or threat appears as a key variable in several formulations of organization–environment–strategy relationships.[19] Physicians, for example, are often explicitly identified as a group that does or could apply extensive pressure on hospitals, thereby having an impact on the hospital's effective strategic management.[20,21] Looking at the current anticipated threat inherent in the relationship with a particular stakeholder or group of stakeholders is similar to developing a worst case scenario and protects managers from unpleasant surprises.

Stakeholder power and its relevance for any particular issue confronting the organization's managers determine the stakeholder's potential for threat. Power is primarily a function of the dependence of the organization on the stakeholder.[22] Generally, the more dependent the organization, the more powerful the stakeholder. For example, the power of physicians is a function of the hospital's dependence on those physicians for patients, alternative sources of patients, the use of hospital beds, and the provision of hospital services. Such power introduces a clear potential to threaten the organization by denying it needed resources and providing them to another, such as a competitor.

A health care organization's managers need to anticipate and evaluate systematically the actual or potential threats in its relationships with stakeholders and, in some cases, evaluate threats that face their supportive stakeholders. These threats may focus on obtaining inducements from the organization that may or may not be provided. The desired inducements may include financial resources, participation in decision making, and enactment of particular organizational policies. Alternatively, these threats may focus on undermining the fundamental viability of the organization.

Stakeholder's Potential for Cooperation

The level of cooperation in an organization's relationship with its stakeholders clearly directs attention to potential stakeholder management strategies that go beyond the merely defensive or offensive in confronting stakeholder pressures. Diagnosing this dimension suggests the potential for using more cooperative strategies that focus on the actual or potential contributions that are valued and needed by the organization. For example, two competitors who are facing a common threat of discontributions from a given stakeholder, such as a third competitor

who has purchased a helicopter to aid in rural market penetration, may well be potential allies in counteracting such a move through a joint venture helicopter of their own.

Similarly, competitors may join together to reduce the bargaining power of preferred provider organizations (PPOs), which have been able to demand price concessions from hospitals in markets where several hospitals compete for market share. With unprofitable hospitals falling by the wayside, however, the remaining hospitals can merge. Such a merger leaves the PPO in a very weak position since there is only one dominant organization with which to negotiate and the PPO cannot threaten to send its members elsewhere. While the Antitrust Division of the Department of Justice is carefully monitoring these types of mergers, both the public and regulators are increasingly aware that in order to meet the three criteria of reasonable cost, high quality, and ready access, these types of mergers may be necessary. Health care executives need to anticipate the likely reaction of regulators—who represent the public's stake—regarding prospective mergers.

The stakeholder's dependence on the organization and its relevance for any particular issue facing the organization determine the stakeholder's cooperative potential. Generally, the more dependent the stakeholder on the organization, the higher the potential for cooperation. Often, however, the organization and the stakeholder are very interdependent. For example, in a small town with one hospital and a limited number of physicians, the hospital and the physicians usually have high levels of mutual dependence. Although the hospital may encounter potential threats from some physicians who send patients to another hospital in a larger city, it may also have cooperation from most other physicians who want to keep their patients in the community.

Factors Affecting the Potentials for Threat and Cooperation

Health care executives should examine a variety of factors that can affect the level of a stakeholder's potential for threat or cooperation. Table 6–1 focuses on four major factors: relative power, control of resources, coalition formation, and likelihood and supportiveness of potential stakeholder action. For each factor, two different basic situations are possible. Generally, only one situation from each will apply to a given organization's relationship with a particular stakeholder, unless the stakeholder is likely to take both supportive and nonsupportive actions or is likely to form a coalition with both the organization and other stakeholders that are potentially nonsupportive to the organization. After looking at the probable impact of the relevant situation on overall threatening or cooperative potential, a manager must make a qualitative judgment to weigh the relative importance of the four factors in making the final stakeholder relationship diagnosis most appropriate for that organization at that time.

Exactly how a factor will affect the potential for threat or cooperation depends on (1) the specific context and history of the organization's relations with that stakeholder and (2) the historical and contextual relations with other key stakeholders in the organization. For example, a hospital manager may be able to assess the threatening or cooperative

Table 6–1 Stakeholder Relationship Assessments: Impact of Specific Assessments on Stakeholder's Potentials To Threaten and/or To Cooperate

Relationship Assessment Factor	Stakeholder's Potential To Threaten Your Organization...	Stakeholder's Potential To Cooperate with Your Organization...
If stakeholder is more powerful than your organization, then...	Increases	Either
If stakeholder is less powerful than your organization, then...	Decreases	Increases
If stakeholder controls key resources (needed by your organization), then...	Increases	Increases
If stakeholder does not control key resources, then...	Decreases	Either
If stakeholder is likely to form coalition with your organization, then...	Decreases	Increases
If stakeholder is unlikely to form coalition with your organization, then...	Either	Decreases
If stakeholder is likely to form coalition excluding your organization, then...	Increases	Decreases
If stakeholder is unlikely to form coalition excluding your organization, then...	Decreases	Either

Source: Reprinted from *Challenges in Health Care Management: Strategic Perspectives for Managing Key Stakeholders* by J.D. Blair and M.D. Fottler, p. 126, with permission of Jossey-Bass, Publishers, © 1990.

potential of the medical staff only in the context of how competing institutions are managing their medical staffs and how the organization has treated its medical staff in the past. By carefully considering the factors in Table 6–1, executives can fine-tune their analyses and management of stakeholders.

Federal, state, and local governments can influence organizations in at least two different ways: through political actions and through regulations. Governments use political activities to alter the strategic decisions that organizations make (e.g., antitrust issues vis-à-vis physician–hospital alliances). On the other hand, regulations cause organizations to change operational activities (e.g., Medicare forms and rules).

EMERGING LEVELS OF INTEGRATION IN HEALTH CARE DELIVERY

A wide range of possible organizational forms exists in today's turbulent health care environment. A model by Coddington, Moore, and Fischer highlighted six basic structural forms of both vertically and horizontally organized systems (1) physician–physician, (2) physician–hospital, (3) physician–health plan, (4) hospital–hospital, (5) hospital–health plan, and (6) physician–hospital–health plan.[23] Each form occurs at different stages of integration—early-stage, mid-stage, or later-stage.

According to this model, integration among physicians ranges from early-stage independent practice associations (IPAs) and physician-only management service organizations (MSOs) to mid-stage integration of large single-specialty or multispecialty groups (which may serve as a basis for fully organized systems). Integration between hospitals and physicians ranges from hospital-based MSOs (early-stage) to shared equity physi-

cian–hospital organizations (PHOs). Integration forms among hospitals are considered primarily early-stage integration. These three forms of integration (i.e., physician–physician, physician–hospital and hospital–hospital) are useful for classifying typical health care delivery systems in the United States. One other major player must be added to the integration puzzle in order to reach the fully organized health care system, however. That third player is the health plan. Only when the health plan is integrated at a high level with the PHO-type organization will an organizational form be created that can meet all the health care needs of a given population.

The final three forms of integration in the model developed by Coddington and associates include the health plan—hospital–health plan, physician–health plan, and physician–hospital–health plan. In each case, the addition of the health plan in the health care delivery system increases the extent of integration. Most hospital–health plan forms occur at early- to mid-stage levels; physician–health plan and physician–hospital–health plan forms, at mid- to later-stage levels of integration.

As physicians become more integrated among themselves and as health plans begin to integrate with hospitals and/or physicians, the necessity of effective strategic stakeholder management becomes apparent. For example, what happens when physicians initiate their own physician–physician integration? Their power relative to the hospital becomes stronger, and they become more of a threat to the hospital. Hospital management must understand this phenomenon fully in order to manage their strategic issues effectively.

In addition, hospital executives need to understand how their direct competitors use these new organizational forms to their own best interests. For example, as competition becomes more and more integrated, all the organizational players need to have carefully designed stakeholder management strategies in order to stay competitive. The closer a hospital moves toward the fully integrated health care system, the better prepared that hospital is, both strategically and opportunistically, to deal with the environment.

TYPES OF STAKEHOLDER RELATIONSHIPS

The two dimensions—potential for threat and potential for cooperation—make it possible to characterize four types of health care stakeholder relationships (Figure 6–2).[24] There is a dynamic process occurring at all times, however. Stakeholder relationships initially categorized in one cell might be moved to another cell as a result of what the organization does or does not do, what stakeholders do or do not do, what new information the organization has that would change the classification, and what issue currently faces the organization and its stakeholders.

One stakeholder can be both a direct and an indirect stakeholder. A direct stakeholder deals directly with the organization. An indirect stakeholder is still a stakeholder, but exerts influence through an intermediary. In Figure 6–1, there are several stakeholders who hold this double distinction. For example, Regional Hospitals and Cardiology Group E are both direct and indirect stakeholders of Hospital A.

Type 1: The Mixed Blessing Stakeholder Relationship

With mixed blessing stakeholder relationships, the health care executive faces a situation in which the stakeholder ranks high on both types of potential: threat and cooperation. Normally, relationships of the mixed blessing type include not only those with the medical staff, but also those with other physicians not on the staff, insurance companies, insured patients, and hospitals with complementary, but not competing, services. Physician–hospital relationships probably are the clearest example of this type of relationship. Although physicians can and do provide many services that benefit hospitals, physicians also can threaten hospitals because of their general control over admissions, the utilization and provision of different services, and the quality of care. In addition, physician–entrepreneurs can create organizations and alliances that threaten the hospital.

Some special interest group relationships also are a mixed blessing. For example, groups such as Alcoholics Anonymous influence substance abuse programs at hospitals. These groups have a significant stake in the hospital's program and its therapeutic ap-

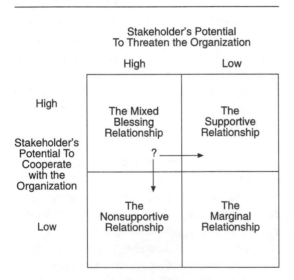

Figure 6–2 Stakeholder Relationship Diagnoses Based on Pattern of Relationship Assessments. *Source:* Reprinted with permission from J. Blair and M. Fottler, *Strategic Leadership for Medical Groups: Navigating Your Strategic Web*, © 1998, Jossey-Bass, Publishers.

proach. Such groups can either enhance referrals to the program or can undermine the program, thereby having a great impact on its clinical and financial viability.

Figure 6–2 also shows a question mark and two arrows under the mixed blessing relationship type. One arrow is directed toward the type 2, supportive relationship. The other is pointed at the type 3, nonsupportive relationship. These arrows imply that a mixed blessing relationship could become either more or less supportive. Later in this chapter, appropriate relationship management strategies for each type are discussed.

Some of the relationships highlighted in Figure 6–1 (highlighting refers to those relationships that have a question mark) are those between Hospital A and mixed blessing stakeholders. In this example, Hospital A recognizes two different kinds of mixed blessing stakeholders: direct and indirect. Cardiology Group E is a classic example of a direct mixed blessing stakeholder for Hospital A. Even though Hospital A is contemplating a strategic alliance with Group E, the physicians are still of the mixed blessing variety of relationships.

Relationships with competing institutions such as regional hospitals also can be mixed blessings. These regional hospitals represent the rural-type health care provider facilities in the region surrounding Hospital A. Because of their referral ties, affiliated regional hospitals indicate potential for cooperation. Because the regional hospitals also compete directly with Hospital A, they also are a potential for threat, even if the regional hospitals happen to be relatively minor competitors.

Relationships of health care providers with government agencies and patients are indirect mixed blessing relationships. Since each of these relationships is often supportive in a direct sense, the introduction of an intermediary (i.e., a managed care organization) obvi-ously creates some potential for threat that does not exist when these stakeholders are dealing directly with the provider. This potential for threat may arise from the historical conflict of interests between the hospital and the managed care organization; it may come from the very nature of the intermediary, which attempts to control or influence this indirect stakeholder relationship.

Type 2: The Supportive Stakeholder Relationship

The ideal stakeholder relationship is one that supports the organization's goals and actions. Managers wish all their relationships were of this type. Such a stakeholder is low on potential threat, but high on potential cooperation. For example, the relationships of a well managed hospital with its board of trustees, its managers, its staff employees, its parent company, the local community, and nursing homes are of this type. In many large medical centers with multiple health care facilities, a common support facility such as a power plant, laundry, or parking consortium typifies the concept of the supportive stakeholder relationship.

In the continuing example of Hospital A, several supportive stakeholder relationships surface. Assuming Hospital A does not have its own rehabilitation facility, Hospital F, which is a rehabilitation specialty hospital, would be in a supportive relationship because Hospital A feels little or no direct competitive threat from Hospital F. In fact, Hospital F has every reason to be supportive to Hospital A in the hopes of maintaining a good referral contact. However, if Hospital A did have a rehabilitation facility or was planning on adding one, then Hospital F would cease to be a supportive relationship and would likely become a nonsupportive one due to the competitive nature of their relationship.

Although government agencies and patients may have mixed blessing relationships with hospitals in the indirect sense, they have supportive relationships with hospitals from the perspective of their direct relationships. Both groups desire to have available the services that the hospital provides when they need them. Therefore, governments and patients tend to be supportive, because they have everything to gain by being supportive. Clearly, the same stakeholder can assume different stakeholder postures, according to the contextual or situation attributes of the stakeholder issue.

Type 3: The Nonsupportive Stakeholder Relationship

The most distressing stakeholder relationships for an organization and its managers are the nonsupportive ones. They are high on potential for threat, but low on potential for cooperation. Typical nonsupportive relationships for hospitals include those with competing hospitals, freestanding alternatives such as urgicenters or surgicenters, employee unions, the federal government, other government regulatory agencies, indigent patients, the news media, and employer coalitions. Special interest groups may often prove to be nonsupportive, as in the case of pro-life demonstrations that have slowed or halted normal business, particularly for ambulatory women's centers.

Figure 6–1 shows several examples of major nonsupportive relationships, including that with the Medical School Practice Group and competing Hospital B, which is part of its own integrating network. Both of these stakeholders have similar types of relationships with Hospital A. For example, they both try to manage the same key stakeholders as Hospital A, which sets up confrontational types of behaviors. The Medical School Practice Group is clearly a nonsupportive relationship through its strategic partnership with the Public Teaching Hospital C. While not in direct competition, as is the case with Hospital B, it principally refers patients to a competing hospital (which is a high threat to Hospital A largely due to its strategic relationship with the competing network), leaving little room for any cooperative agreements.

If, however, agreements could be made with the Medical School Practice Group to partner with Hospital A instead, a new referral source could be established and the competition's network simultaneously damaged. This presents the major strategic issues facing today's health care executives: how to manage nonsupportive relationships effectively today so that those same stakeholders will be less threatening and more cooperative in the future.

Type 4: The Marginal Stakeholder Relationship

Although marginal stakeholders may have a stake in the organization and its decisions, most issues do not affect them. Thus, marginal stakeholder relationships are high on neither threatening nor cooperative potential. For a well run hospital, typical relationships of this kind may include those with volunteer groups in the community, stockholders or taxpayers, and professional associations for employees. Certain issues such as cost containment or access to care could activate one or more of these stakeholders, however, increasing their potential for either threat or cooperation.

Figure 6–1 shows a marginal stakeholder relationship in that between Hospital A and Hospital E. This investor-owned hospital is a small-scale general facility that does not directly compete at the large-scale tertiary care level with Hospital A. It should be noted that

Hospital E is not affiliated or identified as a key relationship with any other stakeholder shown on the web figure. Therefore, it is not perceived as being either cooperative or threatening. For reasons such as geographic location, quality of medical staff, and deteriorating physical plant, Hospital E is not viewed as playing an important part of the strategic plans of any other organization depicted in the figure. This more than likely resulted from Hospital E's mismanagement of its relationships or its lack of unique strategic value as a partner.

Issue-Specific Stakeholder Relationship Diagnosis

The most important issues facing organizations and their managers at a given time change constantly. Of all the possible stakeholders for a given health care organization, the particular ones that are relevant to its managers depend on the corporate/competitive strategies being pursued, as well as on the specific issue. The stakeholders concerned with cost containment will be different from those concerned with access to health care. The diagnosis of the relevant stakeholder relationships in terms of the four types will probably be different on these two issues as well.

For example, System A Medical Group performs important duties to maintain the vital links between Hospital A and the patients being seen by group physicians. In this capacity, System A Medical Group is clearly in a supportive type of relationship with Hospital A, acting as a "supplier" to Hospital A. Given the issue-specific scenario of Hospital A's attempt to form a strategic alliance with Cardiology Group E, however, System A Medical Group now faces the introduction of Group E into its company's (Systems A's) network. The introduction of the physicians from Group E may threaten the smooth operations

and referral patterns of System A Medical Group, since Cardiology Group E may have previously been viewed as a direct competitor. In other words, the potential strategic alliance between Hospital A and Group E may challenge the way that the System A Medical Group traditionally conducts business. Therefore, the System A Medical Group may react harshly and choose to become a less supportive stakeholder regarding this specific issue.

The inherent issue in classifying stakeholder relationships into a typology suggests that relationship diagnosis is an ongoing activity for health care managers. They cannot assume that a stakeholder supportive on one issue will be supportive on every issue, nor that a stakeholder nonsupportive on one issue will be nonsupportive on another. Moreover, whatever the classification of a particular relationship on a specific issue, explicitly classifying stakeholder relationships brings inadvertent managerial biases to the surface. For example, if a manager identifies all relationships for any particular issue as nonsupportive, then the manager should critically examine his or her assessment of the relationship between the organization and its stakeholders. If a manager always thinks of a particular stakeholder as threatening, the manager may be missing opportunities for capitalizing on potential for cooperation; similarly, a manager who always sees a stakeholder as cooperative may be running the risk of underestimating the potential for threat on a specific issue.

GENERIC STRATEGIES FOR STAKEHOLDER RELATIONSHIP MANAGEMENT

Stakeholder relationship diagnosis of the type attempted in Figure 6–2 suggests some generic strategies for managing relationships with different levels of potential for threat and for cooperation. Each of the strategies presented in Figure 6–3 can be either proactive or reactive. Since executives continually manage a wide variety of stakeholder relationships (in terms of their potential for threat and cooperation), all executives need to use a combination of strategies at any one time.

Strategy 1: Collaborate Cautiously in the Mixed Blessing Relationship

The best way to manage the mixed blessing relationship, high on the dimensions of both potential threat and potential cooperation, may be cautious collaboration. The goal of this strategy is to turn mixed blessing relationships into supportive relationships. If executives seek to maximize their stakeholders' potential for cooperation, these potentially threatening stakeholders will find their sup-

portive endeavors make it more difficult for them to oppose the organization.

For example, the proposed strategic alliance between Hospital A and Cardiology Group E (see Figure 6–1) represents a collaborative strategy. If this alliance took the form of a joint cardiology diagnostic and care center, such collaboration effectively stops the cardiology physicians, with whom the hospital has a mixed blessing relationship, from building a center themselves and, thus, competing with hospital-based invasive cardiology or diagnostic procedures. The hospital can contribute its name and capital resources, while the physicians will presumably send their patients to the hospital when inpatient services are needed. Both the hospital and the physicians potentially will benefit.

If Hospital A can use creative contracting covenants to ensure some form of referral pattern from the regional hospitals, Hospital A has again effectively used the collaborative strategy. However, these contractual covenants could be viewed as a defensive posture of the organization. The use of this kind of collaborative strategy requires caution because of the inherent instability of mixed blessing stakeholder relationships vis-à-vis the organization. Therefore, the collaboration strategy used with them may well determine the long-term stakeholder–organization relationship. In other words, if this type of stakeholder relationship is not properly managed through the use of a cautious collaborative strategy, the unstableness of these types of relationships could turn a mixed blessing relationship into a nonsupportive one.

Stakeholder's Potential
To Reduce Stakeholder Threat

	High	Low
High Stakeholder's Potential To Enhance Stakeholder Cooperation **Low**	Collaborate Cautiously *in the Mixed Blessing Relationship*	Involve Trustingly *in the Supportive Relationship*
	Defend Proactively *in the Nonsupportive Relationship*	Monitor Efficiently *in the Marginal Relationship*

Figure 6–3 Strategies for Managing Stakeholder Relationships. *Source:* Reprinted with permission from J. Blair and M. Fottler, *Strategic Leadership for Medical Groups: Navigating Your Strategic Web,* © 1998, Jossey-Bass, Publishers.

Strategy 2: Involve Trustingly in the Supportive Relationship

Because supportive stakeholders pose a low potential for threat, they are likely to be ignored as a relationship to be managed; therefore, their cooperative potential may be ignored as well. By involving supportive stakeholders in relevant issues, however, health care executives can maximally capitalize on these stakeholders' cooperative potential.

It is important to distinguish between collaborating with a stakeholder and involving a stakeholder. Collaboration and "win–win" strategies often are prescribed as the basic solution to problems in health care management, but the collaborative relationship is often confused with the involving relationship. Involvement and collaboration are different, however. Involvement further activates or enhances the supportive capability of an already supportive stakeholder; the emphasis is not on reducing threat, since its potential is low. It has a higher level of trust (and lack of risk) on the part of the organization. Collaboration, on the other hand, involves much more of a give and take on the parts of the organization and the stakeholder. It includes an element of caution due to the high potential for threat inherent in mixed blessing stakeholder relationships and may require the organization to give up or expend certain key resources or change important policies to gain stakeholder support either by decreasing threat and/or by increasing cooperation. Collaboration may even have a defensive element to protect the organization against potential threat.

Managers can operationalize the involvement strategy by using participative management techniques, by decentralizing authority to clinical managers, or by engaging in other tactics to increase the decision-making participation of these stakeholders. For example, hospital management may invite clinical managers to participate in the analysis and planning for the elimination of redundant programs. The clinical managers are more likely to become committed to achieving such an organizational objective if they have been involved in establishing it. The success of this type of strategy requires managers to enlarge their vision of ways to further involve supportive stakeholders in higher levels of cooperation.

Nonmanagerial professional and support employees represent another class of relationships that belong in this category and for whom an involving strategy might be effective.[25,26] Employees do not pose a great deal of direct threat to the organization, although union activism, the perception of poor third-shift conditions, or human resource shortages can make their continued service problematic under certain circumstances. Yet, their cooperative potential may not have been fully tapped.

At this time, many group practices and hospitals are explicitly involving their supportive employees and in-house volunteer stakeholders in strategies by training them to manage mixed blessing relationships, such as those with funded patients, patient families, and physicians. Guest or customer relations programs are designed to enhance the management of one or more potentially threatening stakeholders by increasing the cooperative potential of a key internal stakeholder. Another involving relationship management technique is the "womb to tomb" marketing approach to caring for patients.

Another explicitly strategic utilization of involvement systematically links human resource management systems and practices to overall strategic management. Called strategic human resource management, the technique has only recently been introduced into the field of health care management.[27,28] It is very consistent with the strategic relationship management approach, because it increases involvement of a generally supportive internal stakeholder (employees) in furthering the strategic goals of the organization.

Hospital executives need to be aware of physician perceptions when entering into alliances with physicians. From a hospital perspective, relationships with physicians generally are considered to be mixed blessing relationships, and hospital executives often use involvement strategies to manage them. This can strain the hospital–physician relationship. For example, if a hospital buys a physician practice, all the physicians become employees of the hospital. If hospital executives try to exert typical hierarchical authority and typical involvement strategies over the physicians in the newly acquired practice, the physicians will most likely rebel. Even if the physicians have become employees of the hospital, they may view themselves as partners in the venture. As such, they would expect to be involved in strategic decision making at the highest levels. This is a classic case of the hospital misdiagnosing the physician–stakeholder relationship as nonthreatening and supportive, when, in fact, it is a powerful mixed blessing.

Strategy 3: Defend Proactively in the Nonsupportive Relationship

Stakeholder relationships with high threatening potential but low cooperative potential are best managed through a proactive defensive strategy. Relationships with the federal government and indigent patients are nonsupportive stakeholder relationships for most health care organizations. In terms of Kotter's framework on external dependence, the defensive strategy tries to reduce the dependence that forms the basis for the stakeholders' interest in the organization.[29] In stakeholder terms, a defensive strategy involves proactively preventing the stakeholder from imposing costs—or other disincentives—on the organizations. Health care executives should not attempt to eliminate totally their dependence on nonsupportive relationships, however. Such efforts are doomed, either failing outright or creating a negative image for the organization. For example, trying to sever all ties with the federal government is counterproductive if a hospital hopes to market to older patients. Also, the public and the local government will almost surely take a negative view of a public hospital that tries to deny access to all indigent patients.

For example, given the regulations hospitals face, their most appropriate defensive tactic in dealing with the federal government's regulatory agencies is to explore ways of complying with the demands imposed by the federal government at the least possible cost. Diagnosis-related groups (DRGs) that produce a surplus for the hospitals define their areas of distinctive competence. Hence, hospital executives might adopt a case-mix approach to the delivery of health care, modifying the services they offer based on cost and process accounting. Investing in more effective management information systems and specialized medical records "grouper" software, and recruiting and paying for more highly skilled medical records personnel are all part of this defensive strategy vis-à-vis a nonsupportive, demanding third-party payer and/or regulator.

This generic strategy also can drive out or reduce competition. For example, Hospital A (Figure 6–1) might be able to drive out competition from Hospital B (another private tertiary care hospital) by securing a monopoly over a particular market segment through further PPO contracting. On the other hand, to reduce competition with urgicenters or surgicenters, Hospital A could build new ambulatory facilities or restructure existing facilities. In these examples of the defensive strategy, the connection of stakeholder management to broader strategic management is very clear, involving many traditional marketing and strategic notions for handling competitors.

Relationships with indigent patients often are thought of as nonsupportive with hospitals, especially county facilities. As a defensive strategy to reduce the use of expensive emergency department facilities by these types of patients, a county hospital could open more primary care clinics in surrounding regions and inform the indigent population about the services provided at the clinics. Such an approach might change these nonsupportive relationships to mixed blessing relationships. While the stakeholders still would be high on threatening potential, at least there would now be some element of cooperative potential.

Strategy 4: Monitor Efficiently in the Marginal Relationship

Monitoring helps manage those marginal relationships in which the potential for both threat and cooperation is low. For example, numerous special interest groups are opposed to certain procedures, such as abortion or the placement of artificial implants, or are concerned about certain patient groups, such as the aged. Typically, these groups have only a marginal stake in the activities of the organization and affect operations only indirectly by advocating a specific moral or ethical viewpoint. Relationships with taxpayers and stockholders are also marginal. In essence, marginal relationships are unstable; they can move into any one of the other three types of relationships if the particular issue is of enough importance to the organization.

Often, relationships with patient families are considered marginal. Leaving this key marginal relationship unmonitored ignores the possibility of developing a supportive relationship that can make a decisive difference in the course of patient care. In addition, dissatisfied patient families that go unnoticed potentially can cause significant problems for an organization. Assigning specific responsibility for monitoring this relationship to a member of the patient care team can avert disaster for the organization's management.

The underlying philosophy for managing these marginal relationships is proactively maintaining the status quo, while keeping the use of financial resources and management time to a minimum. Executives address issues on an ad hoc basis, and their general thrust is to "let sleeping dogs lie." Keeping them asleep, however, may require an organization to engage in ongoing public relations activities and to be sensitive to issues that could make these groups an actual threat.

Stakeholders in marginal relationships should be minimally satisfied in most cases. What it takes to keep a particular marginal stakeholder minimally satisfied may increase over time, thus necessitating greater involvement of managerial time and other organizational resources. Managers must monitor such expenditures of inducements or disinducements to determine whether they have become excessive or whether they are perhaps inadequate because the marginal stakeholder has become a key stakeholder, in general or on a particular issue.

An Overarching Relationship Management Strategy

In addition to using the four strategies specifically tailored for relationships in the four diagnostic categories, health care executives may employ an overarching strategy to move the relationships from a less favorable category to a more favorable one. Then the relationship can be managed by means of the generic strategy most appropriate for that new diagnostic category. For example, rather than simply defending itself against the news media as a nonsupportive relationship, a hospital could implement an aggressive program of external relations to foster openness with the media. If successful, the program could change the news media relationship to a less threatening category, such as a marginal relationship, and allow it to be managed by means of a monitoring strategy. If the hospital is willing to invest enough time, energy, skill, and money in the effort, the media relationship might even become a supportive one.

In the continuing example of Hospital A (Figure 6–1), the proposed strategic alliance with a mixed blessing stakeholder (Cardiology Group E) can present an opportunity for Hospital A. If Hospital A effectively manages Group E with a collaborative strategy, such as building a cardiology center for the group of physicians, Hospital A also may have successfully turned a mixed blessing relationship into a less threatening supportive one.

Even if mixed blessing relationships are collaboratively managed, they may not become supportive relationships. Every player in this new era of health care delivery is not voluntarily becoming involved and integrated. Thus, stakeholders do not always react as the strategy suggests. Furthermore, although organizations can create structural integration (i.e., strategic integration) fairly early, the new structure may not work without social and cultural integration (i.e., tactical integration) as well.

Of course, stakeholders generally do not just sit still and allow themselves to be managed. Stakeholders who are powerful and, hence, threatening are as likely to try to manage organizational relationships as vice versa. Many organizations and their stakeholders engage in continuous management and countermanagement strategies. To manage these relationships prudently and effectively, executives should periodically repeat the procedures to identify stakeholders and match their relationship diagnoses with appropriate strategies.

STRATEGY IMPLEMENTATION AND OUTCOMES

Given the importance of key stakeholder relationships for an organization's overall business strategy, the successful implementation of the stakeholder management concept should provide the organization with a competitive advantage. At best, the relationship management perspectives of hospital executives are incomplete, and their approaches to stakeholder assessment are underdeveloped and haphazard. At worst, these executives display a total lack of explicit awareness of, and involvement in, a systematic and effective relationship management approach.[30] It is essential to develop systematic and strategic stakeholder approaches—integrated with still broader relationship management issues. A key issue in all strategic action is the implementation of the planned and articulated strategy.

With a consistent and conscientious relationship management implementation strategy, a quite fully organized health care system can develop. For example, the three necessary components of organized delivery networks are shown in Figure 6–1: a hospital, a large multispecialty physician group, and a health plan. A fourth component, the System A Headquarters, is the coordinating centerpiece for the primary system components.

The shading of the boxes (as the legend shows) represents the hospital's different stakeholders and the nature of their relationships, given the strategic alliance among the components of Hospital A, Group A, and System A Health Plans. Assuming all the various stakeholder relationships are effectively managed and formalized into this specific vertical integration, the original patterns (prior to system integration) of informal, but interconnected, stakeholder relationships now serve to structure network relationships and systems.

The organized delivery system still has embedded within it many formal and informal networks (Figure 6–1). Even with the formal development of this organized health care delivery system, however, sophisticated health care executives know that new stakeholder challenges have been raised. Stronger competitors (by virtue of the network), and new and varied partners have emerged. The health care delivery system is more complex and complicated than ever before. The number of relationships has grown geometrically. No longer do the old, internally oriented human resources approaches to solving production problems suffice.

Executives at Hospital A do not have the same level of hierarchical control, and the hospital can no longer be independent as a result of developing alliances. The overall power of the hospital has increased, but at significant cost to independence and control. Executives must coordinate with and be acceptable to strategic partners. All of this requires the development of additional tactics and stakeholder management strategies to manage these more complex and radically changing relationships.

In Figure 6–1, the formation of systems and networks has effectively divided the entire health care delivery system for the area represented into three components: those or-

ganizations affiliated with System A; those organizations affiliated with the emerging Network B; and those organizations that have yet to be included in either system/network, but that are possible partners for either system/network. As a direct competitor and nonsupportive stakeholder for Hospital A, Hospital B has attempted to imitate the successful strategic alliance of System A by establishing its own strategic alliances. Hospital A is not content with being the first to form a health care network, however. On the contrary, Hospital A hopes to maintain that lead in strategic alliance formation.

In contemplating a strategic alliance with Cardiology Group E (an independently owned and unaffiliated specialty group), Hospital A executives should consider the impact such an alliance would have on internal system relationships (System A owned and affiliated) and on direct competitors (Network B owned and affiliated). They should also consider the possibility that if Hospital A does not make an alliance with Cardiology Group E, Hospital B might do so. If the proposed strategic alliance is formalized, a joint strategy team composed primarily of administrative staff from Hospital A and Cardiology Group E should be developed to facilitate the smooth transition of Hospital A and Group E from a mixed blessing stakeholder relationship to a strongly supportive one. Additionally, representatives from the other system components, primarily from the System A Medical Group, should be part of this team to ensure that the real and important issues of System A, as a whole, are being met.

With the consummation of a strategic alliance, the administrative staffs are in mutually supportive relationships and are now strategically involved in each other's organizations. The formalization of a strategic alliance does not mean that all the employees and managers of each respective organization will instantly function as supportive stakeholders, however. Rather, relationship management tactics such as joint strategic teams composed of players from both fields are necessary in order to begin the process of jointly facing the new challenges in the environment.

MANAGERIAL RESPONSIBILITY FOR STAKEHOLDER RELATIONSHIPS

It would be a mistake to assume that the chief executive officer or any other single individual manages all the diverse stakeholder relationships in today's health care system. Instead, the evolution of some of these organizations has seen the development of management specialists whose major purpose is to manage particular relationships. In some organizations, for example, a medical staff director or Vice President for Medical Affairs has the major responsibility for managing the medical staff relationship. Nonetheless, others, including the chief executive officer, are available to help handle nonroutine problems.

In the continuing example shown in Figure 6–1, four executives typically devote much of their time to managing several key relationships. Their roles are typical of managers who have responsibilities for several stakeholder relationships. The Director of Physician Practice Management Services, for example, is responsible for developing a physician–provider network capable of delivering health care to the insured patient base in an efficient, cost-effective manner. This person also is integrally involved in medical staff development and recruiting. The Director of Regional Services can work collaboratively with the Director of Physician Practice Management Services to provide service to regional physicians affiliated with rural

hospitals in Hospital A's regional network.

The chief financial officer and the Vice President of Marketing will work closely with Hospital A's network partner, the health plan, which functions as a managed care organization. By forming this health care delivery network, Hospital A has assumed a much greater portion of the system's financial risk than it previously had. For example, with capitation, the hospital agrees to treat all the patients in a given population for a preset amount of money. If a patient's medical bills exceed this preset amount, the health care providers absorb the excess cost. As a result of this increased financial risk, the chief financial officer is quite involved with the network risk management functions. The Vice President of Marketing has direct responsibility for promoting Hospital A's interests (both individually and in the network). The "all-in-one" concept of health care delivery is still new to the purchasers of health care, and a key responsibility of the Vice President of Marketing is to counter any actions by competing health care networks. Each of these specific hospital executives must let go of the old hospital mentality of "filling beds" and thinking, "If we own it, we can control it." Instead, they must embrace the new health care network mentality of providing the highest quality, easiest access, and most cost-effective health care for a given population.

Stakeholder webs that show the potential opportunities and responsibilities of each stakeholder manager can aid in managers' understanding of the strategic stakeholder process. Based on the general stakeholder web developed during stakeholder assessment, this technique provides a way to incorporate relationship management into an executive's job description. It aids in clarifying and communicating unique and overlapping managerial roles and responsibilities. Obviously, the development of these webs requires some agreement among the various managers concerning who will manage which stakeholders on which issues. This process typically involves internal negotiations and the development of organizational policies and procedures.

CONCLUSION

To survive the turbulent and revolutionary changes facing the health care industry, health care executives must better manage their external, interface, and internal stakeholder relationships. Organizations have to rethink their strategies and operations as they face increasing and potentially conflicting demands for effectiveness and efficiency from these stakeholders.

To satisfy key stakeholders, managers must make two critical assessments about these relationships: their potential to threaten the organization and their potential to cooperate with it. When determining the stakeholder's orientation, managers should account for factors such as control of resources, relative power, likelihood and supportiveness of potential stakeholder action, and coalition formation. These factors should be interpreted in light of the specific context and history of the organization's relations with it and other key stakeholder relationships influencing the organization as well as that stakeholder.

Incorrectly categorizing a stakeholder relationship into the wrong classification type is, in itself, indicative of a lack of stakeholder relationship expertise. If a relationship is incorrectly classified, the chosen strategy for managing that relationship will be wrong also. Using the wrong strategic stakeholder relationship strategy can be very detrimental to an organization. Incorrectly classified relationships will be more likely to move from

whichever type they are to a type that has a greater potential for threat, coupled with even less potential for cooperation.

As an overarching strategy, managers should try to change their organization's relationships with each stakeholder from a less favorable category to a more favorable one. Then, the relationship can be managed using the generic strategy most appropriate for that "new" diagnostic category.

Executives need to do more than merely identify stakeholders or react to stakeholder demands. They must proactively develop or enhance their organization's capacity for the strategic management of stakeholder relationships. They need to satisfy their key relationships by offering appropriate inducements in exchange for essential contributions. Executives also should monitor their marginal relationships so that they do not become key nonsupportive relationships and confront the organization with undesired discontributions.

In order to manage stakeholder relationships effectively, health care executives must recognize that the implementation of strategic stakeholder management strategies requires a thorough understanding of negotiation strategies.[31-33] Clearly, to survive in the future, organizations should establish goals for their relationships with current and potential stakeholders as part of the strategic management process.[34-37] Such goal setting should include clear analyses and consideration of both the organization's and the stakeholder's goals.

Even with effective strategic management of stakeholder activities, health care executives will face many challenges. The unpredictable and, yes, exciting times are not over for the health care industry. Government reforms will continue; employer coalitions will gain in strength and demand concessions from health care providers and administrators; managed care will become a stronger force. Those health care organizations that take an active lead in managing their stakeholder relationships and that consciously build stakeholder relationships into their strategic plans will increase the accuracy of their relationship diagnoses and will begin to gain from the effectiveness of their strategies for managing stakeholder relationships.

NOTES

1. Arthur Andersen and Co., *Best Practices Report on Physician/Hospital Integration—An Overview* (Arthur Andersen and Co., 1993).

2. J.D. Blair et al., "Achieving Competitive Advantage through and within Integrated Health Care Networks: Synthesizing and Applying Firm Resource and Stakeholder Management Theory" (Unpublished manuscript, Area of Management, Texas Tech University, Lubbock, TX, 1994).

3. B. Borys and D.B. Jemison, "Hybrid Arrangements as Strategic Alliances: Theoretical Issues in Organizational Combinations," *Academy of Management Review* 14, no. 2 (1989): 234–249.

4. L.R. Burns and D.R. Thorpe, "Trends and Models in Physician–Hospital Organization," *Health Care Management Review* 18, no. 4 (1993): 7–20.

5. R. Gillies et al., "Conceptualizing and Measuring Integration: Findings from the Health Systems Integration Study," *Hospital & Health Services Administration* 38, no. 4 (1993): 467–489.

6. P.R. Kongstvedt and D.W. Plocher, "Integrated Health Care Delivery Systems," in *Essentials of Managed Health Care*, ed. P.R. Kongstvedt (Gaithersburg, MD: Aspen Publishers, 1997).

7. S.M. Shortell et al., "Creating Organized Delivery Systems: The Barriers and Facilitators," *Hospital & Health Services Administration* 38, no. 4 (1993): 447–466.

8. S.M. Shortell et al., *Remaking Health Care in America: Building Organized Delivery Systems* (San Francisco: Jossey-Bass, Publishers, 1996).

9. J.D. Blair and M.D. Fottler, *Leadership Challenges and Strategic Choices: Navigating Health Care's Strategic Web* (San Francisco: Jossey-Bass, Publishers, 1998).

10. J.D. Blair and M.D. Fottler, *Challenges in Health Care Management: Strategic Perspectives for Managing Key Stakeholders* (San Francisco: Jossey-Bass, Publishers, 1990).

11. J.D. Blair et al., "A Stakeholder Management Perspective on Military Health Care," *Armed Forces & Society*, 18, no. 4 (1992): 548–575.

12. M.D. Fottler et al., "Assessing Key Stakeholders: Who Matters to Hospitals and Why?" *Hospital & Health Services Administration* 34, no. 4 (1989): 525–546.

13. R.E. Freeman, *Strategic Management: A Stakeholder Approach* (Marshfield, MA: Pitman Publishing, 1994).

14. R.O. Mason and J.J. Mitroff, *Challenging Strategic Planning Assumptions* (New York: John Wiley & Sons, 1981).

15. G.T. Savage et al., "Strategies for Assessing and Managing Stakeholders," *Academy of Management Executives* 5, no. 2 (1991): 61–75.

16. Blair and Fottler, *Challenges in Health Care Management.*

17. J.D. Blair and C.J. Whitehead, "Too Many on the Seesaw: Stakeholder Diagnosis and Management for Hospitals," *Hospitals and Health Services Management* 33, no. 2 (1988): 152–156.

18. Freeman, *Strategic Management.*

19. D. Miller and P.H. Friesen, "Archetypes of Strategy Formulation," *Management Science* 24 (1978): 921–933.

20. J.D. Blair and K.B. Boal, "Strategy Formation Processes in Health Care Organizations: A Context-Specific Examination of Context-Free Strategy Issues," *Journal of Management* 17, no. 2 (1991): 305–344.

21. S.M. Shortell et al., *Strategic Choices for America's Hospitals: Managing Change in Turbulent Times* (San Francisco: Jossey-Bass, Publishers, 1990).

22. J. Pfeffer and G. Salancik, *The External Control of Organizations: A Resource Dependence Perspective* (New York: Harper & Row, 1978).

23. D.C. Coddington et al., *Making Integrated Health Care Work* (Englewood, CO: CRAHCA, 1996).

24. Blair and Whitehead, "Too Many on the Seesaw."

25. Blair and Fottler, *Leadership Challenges and Strategic Choices.*

26. Blair and Fottler, *Challenges in Health Care Management.*

27. M.D. Fottler et al., eds., *Strategic Management of Human Resources in Health Services Organizations* (New York: John Wiley & Sons, 1988).

28. M.D. Fottler et al., "Achieving Competitive Advantage through Strategic Human Resources Management," *Hospital & Health Services Administration* 35, no. 3 (1990): 341–363.

29. J.P. Kotter, "Managing External Dependence," *Academy of Management Review* 4, no. 1 (1979): 87–92.

30. Blair and Fottler, *Challenges in Health Care Management.*

31. Blair and Fottler, *Challenges in Health Care Management*, Chapter 5.

32. J.D. Blair et al., "A Strategic Approach for Negotiating with Hospital Stakeholders," *Health Care Management Review* 14, no. 1 (1989): 13–23.

33. G.T. Savage and J.D. Blair, "The Importance of Relationships in Hospital Negotiation Strategies," *Hospital & Health Services Administration* 34, no. 2 (1989): 231–253.

34. Blair and Boal, "Strategy Formation Processes in Health Care Organizations."

35. M.E. Porter, *Competitive Advantage* (New York: Free Press, 1985).

36. M.E. Porter, *Competitive Strategy* (New York: Free Press, 1980).

37. Shortell et al., *Strategic Choices for America's Hospitals.*

JOHN D. BLAIR, PhD, is the Trinity Company Professor in Management and Health Care Strategy for the College of Business Administration (and the School of Medicine) at Texas Tech University. He currently serves as the Coordinator of the Area of Management (Department Chair). He is also the founding Director of the Center for Health Care Strategy and an editor of *Advances in Health Care Management*, a new JAI Press series. He has also served as the chair of the Health Care Administration Division of the National Academy of Management. His most recent books include *Strategic Leadership for Medical Groups: Navigating Your Strategic Web* (1988); *Challenges in Military Health Care* (1993); and *Challenges in Health Care Management: Strategic Perspectives for Managing Key Stakeholders* (1990). He received his PhD from the University of Michigan in 1975.

G. TYGE PAYNE, MBA, RPH, is a PhD student in Strategic Management in the College of Business Administration at Texas Tech University. He serves as the Project Coordinator for the Center for Health Care Strategy, a joint venture of the College of Business Administration and School of Medicine at Texas Tech University. He also is the assistant editor of *Advances in Health Care Management*, a new JAI Press series. In addition to his service as the Assistant Field Experience Director for the Health Organization Management (HOM) graduate program at Texas Tech, he has held positions as a registered pharmacist in both institutional and retail settings. He received his MBA from Texas Tech University.

TIMOTHY M. ROTARIUS, PhD, is Assistant Professor of Health Services Administration at the University of Central Florida. Dr. Rotarius does research on integrated delivery systems and other complex structural relationships between health care organizations. He has numerous publications and research awards, and he has been a medical group administrator. Dr. Rotarius received his PhD in strategic management from Texas Tech University.

CARLTON J. WHITEHEAD, MBA, PhD, is a Professor of Management in the College of Business Administration, Texas Tech University, and Professor of Health Organization Management, School of Medicine, Texas Tech University Health Sciences Center. Since the fall of 1994, he has served as Associate Dean of the College of Business Administration at Texas Tech. In addition, he is a research associate in the Center for Health Care Strategy and Associate Director, Texas Center for Productivity and Quality of Work Life. Dr. Whitehead has published extensively and participated actively in professional organizations. He received his PhD in management from Louisiana State University.

E. GORDON WHYTE, MHA, PhD, is Vice Chairman and Director of Master Programs, Department of Health Systems Management, in the School of Public Health and Tropical Medicine at Tulane University Medical Center. He also is President of Gordon Whyte and Associates, a health care planning and marketing consulting firm. Dr. Whyte has previously served as Vice President of Strategic Planning and Marketing at St. Mary of the Plains Hospital, Lubbock, Texas; and Administrator of HealthSouth Rehabilitation Center of New Orleans. A licensed nursing facility administrator, he received his master's degree from Trinity University in 1975 and his PhD from the University of Mississippi in 1985.

Chapter 7

Marketing Health Care Services

Roberta N. Clarke

Slowly, marketing is evolving into a more sophisticated management function in health care organizations. Too often, it erroneously has been introduced into health care organizations as a "quick fix," a speedy, simple way to address an increasingly competitive health care environment. Some unfortunately still perceive it as glorified public relations (which overlaps the promotional aspects of marketing), a very important tactical tool and often an undervalued function itself, but not in any way the equivalent of marketing. Others, particularly managed care organizations, defined it largely in terms of sales and promotional activities. Far too often, health care organizations have created their own definitions of health care marketing without taking into account the data collection and analytical components of marketing. As a result, they either have developed marketing strategy in a vacuum or, possibly worse, have failed to develop a cohesive and comprehensive marketing strategy at all.

To perform marketing as it should be performed, it is necessary first to have a clear understanding of what it is. One of the leading experts in the field defines marketing in the following way: "Marketing is a social and managerial process by which individuals and groups obtain what they need and want through creating, offering, and exchanging products of value with others."[1] In order to carry out this process, marketers rely on the tools called the marketing mix: product and/or service, price, promotion, and place (also thought of as distribution and access). Often, the promotional component of marketing, which includes (but is not limited to) advertising, collateral materials, direct mail, websites, events, selling, and price promotion, has been mistaken for the equivalent of marketing. All the tools in the marketing mix must be considered together in developing a marketing strategy, however, as they are closely interrelated. To rely on one or two marketing tools to the exclusion of the others is to invite disaster. The marketing mix can be viewed as a jigsaw puzzle; unless all the pieces of the puzzle are in place, the puzzle is not complete. It takes only one tool in the marketing mix, one piece of the puzzle, to be out of place for the marketing strategy to fail.

As marketing sophistication in health care has increased, resulting in greater recognition of the analytical component of the marketing function, the use of marketing intelligence and the performance of market research have become more common. Health care organizations, therefore, can better understand their market; their competition; the operational performance of their own organization and the impact of that performance on their customers; and the regulatory, technological, legal, and health care environments within which they must function. Furthermore, their increasing use of marketing performance benchmarks allows them to evaluate the effectiveness of their marketing efforts.

Marketing is a process that involves performance of market research; assessment of internal performance; an environmental market scan; the collection of marketing intelligence and other relevant data; careful analysis of all available data, coupled with consideration of the organization's strategic plan; and finally, the development of marketing strategy and tactical marketing plans. Ultimately, there must be an evaluation of the results of marketing efforts in order to improve future investment in the marketing function. There is a tendency to confuse marketing with strategic planning. A strategic plan relies heavily on market planning, which may explain the confusion. Strategic planning is the effort to align the organization's mission, resources, and capabilities with its external environment, its current and potential markets, and its competition. It not only must extend beyond marketing planning to include financial, human resource, technological, regulatory, operational, and information system considerations, but also must build on the values and mission of the organization.

There is consensus among marketers that data collection and analysis should precede marketing strategy, which should then be followed by marketing plan development, implementation, and control. Health care marketers are not in agreement, however, about whether marketing should have a heavy consumer focus or instead emphasize business-to-business marketing. Nor do they agree on the value of and relationship between customer satisfaction and customer loyalty, or on the appropriate allocation of resources between customer attraction and cus-

tomer retention. These are key issues for any organization. If the mission statement and strategic plan of the health care organization do not address these considerations—and many of them do not—then the marketing efforts may be focused on goals that do not reflect the values of the organization.

MARKETING MISSION AND OBJECTIVES

The function of health care marketing is difficult to define. The seemingly inexorable movement toward a predominantly managed care and capitated environment has turned the traditional mission and objectives for marketing upside down. Although health care marketing efforts historically have attempted to increase the volume and usage of hospitals, medical practices, nursing homes, and other medical care providers, the current and future objectives of most health care providers may be to minimize volume or use and, as a result, cost.

Success may no longer be defined in terms of high occupancy rates and a high volume of patients or procedures, but in terms of the ability to keep the cost of "covered lives" low. As managed care organizations and employers continue to transfer the capitated risk for patients onto the providers with whom they contract, these providers will likely assume a "womb to tomb" approach to caring for patients. They can then apply marketing to a variety of tasks, from promoting patient compliance (i.e., encouraging patients to follow through with all their physicians' instructions with regard to medications, exercise, lifestyle, and so on) to educating patients about the appropriate time to see the physician.

Volume will continue to be an objective for health care marketers. Managed care organizations will aim to increase the size of their memberships, and hospitals, after downsizing, will aim to maintain a high occupancy level in order to cover their fixed costs. Similarly, providers will seek to attract a sufficient quantity of patients to maintain an acceptable level of quality in performing certain surgical and other procedures. Anyone who defines the marketing objectives of a health care organization as simply seeking to increase volume has underestimated the complexity of the new health care marketplace. The necessity of conceptualizing organizations as parts of larger systems requires a recognition of the multiple and sometimes conflicting marketing objectives.

One of the tasks, then, of the marketing function is to define carefully the full range of its objectives. A health maintenance organization (HMO) must simultaneously seek a high volume of membership and foster a low volume of usage. Even this is simplistic, however. It is necessary to encourage visits for preventive care and early diagnosis of disease, but to discourage visits for certain nonacute symptoms, such as sore throats that are likely to disappear by themselves with no treatment within a week. Each of these objectives, even if directed at the same market or individual customer, may require a different marketing strategy.

THE COMPETITION DEFINED

The same complexity in the health care environment that leads to multiple marketing missions and objectives also requires a more systematic and sophisticated approach to defining the competition. A competitor is often defined as any organization that lessens the likelihood of another organization achieving its desired marketing exchange. Previously, hospitals competed with other hospitals, and nursing homes competed with other nursing homes, for example. Even so, however, there was some overlap between types of providers. An inpatient psychiatric unit of an acute care hospital might have competed with a freestanding psychiatric hospital; physical therapists, chiropractors, and orthopedic surgeons might all have competed for the same patient with chronic acute low back pain.

The formation of systems expands those included in the definition of competitors. Moreover, the uncertainty of future organized health care delivery membership in these systems makes it unclear who may be a current competitor, but a future collaborator. This makes it more difficult to invest in competitive positioning strategies or to develop strengths and competencies based on a competitor's strengths and weaknesses.

The Changing Environment

The current health care environment promises confusion in identifying the competition. Not only do organizations have to ask themselves, "What business are we in?" but also they have to ask about the competition: "What businesses are they in? What businesses will they be adding tomorrow? Which providers and organizations that contract with us now will choose to contract with our competitors tomorrow?" This difficulty in defining long-term competitors arises even when managed care does not play a significant role in the competitive environment. The pressure to increase revenues and cut costs led to bitter competition between two hospitals in Louisiana that had been peacefully coexisting with each other and with their shared medical staffs. In addition, entrepreneurial efforts by physicians placed them in direct competition with one or both of the hospitals.[2]

The vertical integration of a variety of health care organizations into systems can make competition of customers. For example, an HMO with which one hospital used to contract may now contract in the same service area with a competing hospital, making the two former allies competitors. Yet, it may not be wise for the hospital to launch a marketing offensive against that HMO, because it might once again contract with the hospital in the future. Few health care vertical integration relationships specify exclusivity; the relationship of the HMO with the competing hospital does not prevent it from once again developing a relationship with the first hospital as well.

Alternatively, organizations that were once ardent competitors may become part of the same system. Sometimes, they continue to offer the same services that they provided before becoming part of a system; other times, the system expects them to complement each other rather than compete. The former instance is an example of a federation, the latter of a partnership. An even more extreme competitive change is the merger of two or more former competitors. Such mergers abound as health care providers and managed care organizations conclude, at least for the time being, that the greater size, geographic coverage, and service coverage produced by a merger make them more marketable. It is not clear that this is true, however. Gabel noted that the mergers and acquisitions in managed care, the shift from vertically integrated staff models to virtually integrated network models, and the increased patient cost sharing (including capitating primary care physicians) have not improved patient satisfaction or quality of care.[3] The dramatic growth of Columbia/HCA appeared to demonstrate the benefits of significant acquisitions until the sweeping probes of their Medicare billing practices, their recruitment of and incentives offered to physicians, and their home health care operations suggested otherwise.

In the long term, the widely held belief that the larger merged entities function more effectively and are more marketable may not hold true, particularly if several network members provide poor-quality services and, thus, potential customers elect other networks. Many networks may be trading away long-term marketability for short-term assumed economies of scale and presumed competitive advantage. The economies of scale that a number of merged health care organizations have expected have not always materialized in the basic services that they provide. As Anders and Winslow pointed out, citing the $50 million loss in 1997 of Kaiser, the giant in the managed care industry, "Some of the industry's biggest names are racking up losses, grappling with unexpected rises in medical bills, struggling to absorb costly mergers and squirming under a backlash from consumers, doctors and politicians. Wall Street is fearful and unhappy."[4]

Smaller merged entities may not offer marketing advantages either. The heavy cross-functional dependence of many medical specialties and services, for example, prevented two hospitals that had formally merged from eliminating certain specialties from one hospital and placing them solely in the other, originally a goal of the merger in order to cut costs. Both hospitals needed infectious disease, cardiology, nephrology, endocrinology, psychiatry, otolaryngology, and other diagnostic and treatment capabilities in-house for their inpatients. The inconvenience, cost, and possible clinical repercussions of having to move a patient from one hospital to the other because the necessary diagnostic equipment was not available in the first prevented the hospitals from eliminating the services as they had initially planned. This scenario has been repeated around the United States.

The more common result of hospital mergers has been essentially to eliminate one of the hospitals as an acute care hospital. The eliminated hospital may become a substance abuse center, rehabilitation provider, walk-in facility, chronic care center, congregate living quarters for the elderly, or a housing center for needy women and infants, for example. These are valuable services for which there may be more demand than for the acute care services that the hospital facility used to provide. This process is not one of merging with the competition, however, as much as it is a process of eliminating the competition. The weakest hospitals begin to provide non–acute care services, while the stronger hospitals with which they merged remain in the acute care business. The merger of hospitals with more equal status is less likely to result in the closure of one of them, but it is not yet proved that there are significant economies of scale to be achieved when these hospitals both continue to operate as acute care facilities.

Mergers outside the health care industry may provide a glimpse of the future. The period of high flying mergers and acquisitions that characterized the 1980s in the general commercial sector within a decade led to a less than exciting and sometimes traumatic period of divestitures and fraudulent conveyances.[5] Businesses that had merged later discovered that the gains expected from the mergers were not to be found. Although no one yet knows if the health care industry will exhibit the same cycle of merger followed by divestiture, it is already clear that these arrangements do not necessarily guarantee an increased flow of patients and/or members. There are still excess beds and excess physicians in specific areas; as a result, organizations still must compete for patients and members. Until provider networks become more stable, the naming of competitors may be possible only on a short-term basis.

Analysis of Competitive Position

The development of a good marketing strategy requires an analysis of the organization's competitive position. Customer-oriented analysis is one possibility; this approach involves determining who the customers are, what benefits and values they seek, and how well the organization is providing those benefits and values to the customers compared to how well the competition is doing so. Then, if one or more of the competitors are doing a better job of delivering the desired benefits to the customer, the organization investigates further to determine which of the competitors' activities it needs to emulate or, if possible, surpass in order to equal or exceed the competition.

Competitor-oriented analysis, a second form of competitive analysis, involves benchmarking. With this technique, the organization regularly compares its performance on key performance attributes and benefits desired by the customer against the "best in class." Benchmarking allows the organization to get a sense of context; it provides the organization with answers to questions such as, Where do we stand in the marketplace? How far behind the strongest or best competitors are we? What will it take for us to draw ourselves up to an equal level of performance with our best competitors?

Another useful tool is a perceptual map. Along a two-axis grid, an organization positions itself and its competitors according to the variables that the two axes represent (Figure 7–1). For example, consumers often compare hospitals on the basis of whether they are teaching hospitals (or whether they do tertiary care) or community hospitals (which provide nontertiary basic acute care). They also often compare hospitals on the basis of their nursing and support staff care being friendly, warm, and responsive. Through the use of market research, a hospital can ask a sample of consumers in its service area to rate it and its competing hospitals on these two attributes. Then, using these research findings, the hospital can position all the hospitals that the consumers rated along these two axes (see Figure 7–1). In addition, the hospital can, with further research, determine where the consumer segments in the market are positioned. For example, the people inside the oval marked <1> care primarily about being in a tertiary care or teaching hospital, even if that means not receiving the friendliest or warmest care. For them, a community hospital, such as hospitals E, F, or G would not be satisfactory. Those who fall inside the oval marked <3> prefer to go to the local community hospital. They obviously trust the community hospital to provide adequate acute care, and they want the friendliness and warmth that they feel a community hospital is more likely to provide. Clearly, this would be the segment to which hospital E would appeal. Those in the oval

marked <2> are not willing to sacrifice either friendly, warm care, nor do they want to forgo the capacity for tertiary care. Hospital B best meets their needs, followed by hospital D. In comparing the position of the consumer segments with the position of the various hospitals on the perceptual map, it becomes apparent that hospitals C, F, and G may want to modify their positioning in the marketplace to attract a larger portion of the existing market segments.

BUSINESS-TO-BUSINESS   MARKETING

The need to market to businesses and organizations, referred to as industrial, business-to-business, or organizational marketing, remains as strong as ever. Whether the target

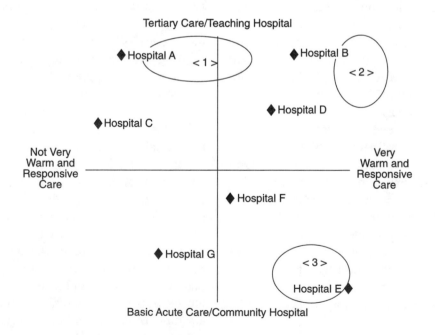

Figure 7–1 Perceptual Map

market consists of employers, the government, insurers, physician groups, or managed care organizations, the nature of business-to-business marketing remains the same: marketers must be skilled in organizational analysis in order to understand to whom to sell and what to sell. Failure to identify the decision-making unit or buying center, as it is called in a business-to-business marketing setting, is likely to result in unsuccessful marketing efforts. Thus, marketers must know who within the organization plays the roles of initiator, influencer, decider, purchaser, gatekeeper, and user.

Historically, for example, pharmaceutical companies hired salespeople to sell existing and new drugs to physicians, who then prescribed or recommended them to their patients. In this scenario, the physician was the decider, and the patient was the user (and often the purchaser as well). Increasingly, however, organizational health care providers such as hospitals and managed care organizations are examining the cost and efficacy of the various drugs available and using their findings to create formularies that specify the drugs that their physicians may prescribe. The individuals who select drugs for the formularies (e.g., infectious disease physicians, pharmacists, quality assurance nurses) are now the initial deciders. The practicing physician can decide on a drug only within the limited set of formulary drugs. A pharmaceutical company that continued to sell its drugs only to physicians and did not attempt to address the formularies might unnecessarily lose significant business. Pharmacy benefit managers, who are often employed by pharmaceutical companies charged with containing pharmaceutical costs for a managed care or insurance entity, continue to sell to physicians; in recognition of the influence and decision-making power of hospital and managed care organizations in the purchase of pharmaceuticals, their marketing efforts remain within the limits of the drugs approved for the formulary.

A buyflow map permits a more systematic analysis of a buying center. It traces the buying process through the customer's recognition of need that presumably must be met through the purchase of a good or service, specification of a technical product or service, potential supplier identification, solicitation of proposals, selection of a supplier, negotiation of the final contract, and performance evaluation. The map identifies who, within the customer's organization, participates in each step of the process, in what order each person affects the process, and where the process slows and may need the further attention of the supplier (marketer).

Organizational buyers are fewer in number than are consumers (individual buyers), but they represent larger overall volumes of purchases. For example, a physician can sell more *Streptococcus* test services to an HMO than to an individual consumer or family within 1 year. Because of the smaller number of business buyers, the investment in analyzing their buying center behavior may be less, even though the potential purchase volumes are greater. The analysis of an organization's buying centers may take at least two forms. "Snowball" research within the target organization entails asking the individuals within the organization thought to be involved in the purchase to identify all others within the organization who might also influence the particular purchase. The analysis proceeds by determining the role that each named individual plays, soliciting from those individuals more names, identifying the roles of those newly named, and continuing until no new names are given. The sum of this type of information usually allows the marketer to detect who plays what role in the decision-making unit/buying center.

Focus group research is the other most common source of information in organizational analysis. This approach generally involves a number of similar organizations rather than just one. For example, a medical software company that had traditionally sold its products to the hospital market was planning to enter the managed care market with a new type of software. Within the hospital market, the company knew that the decider was most often the planner. The title *planner* was not a common one in most HMOs and preferred provider organizations, however, and the company was uncertain who should be the target of its promotion and personal selling. Therefore, the company held six focus groups with a variety of people in different jobs at a number of managed care organizations in order to assess who would be the likeliest deciders and influencers in the purchase of this new product.

The expansion of the marketing of certain health care products is going beyond traditional organizational buyers to include consumers. The reclassification of certain previously ethical drugs (those that consumers could buy only with a prescription from a physician) to over-the-counter (OTC) drugs and the decreasing influence of physicians over which drugs may be prescribed for a patient (because of managed care plan formularies) have resulted in a dramatic explosion in pharmaceutical advertising directed to consumers. Even before Rogaine, the product used to treat hair loss and baldness, was changed from an ethical drug to an OTC drug, it was being advertised directly to the consumer with the exhortation to "ask your doctor" about the medication. Mail order catalogues sent to consumers now carry products, such as special chairs for arthritic patients, that used to be available only through specialty retailers or other organizational sellers. Marketers whose expertise had in the past been limited only to organizational selling must learn how to market directly to consumers.

DERIVED DEMAND

Some marketers believe that consumer marketing should not require as much attention as does business-to-business marketing in the health care marketplace. They rationalize that employers make the first choice of health plans, before the individual employees are given any purchase choices, and that health plan members must choose their physicians or hospitals from panels approved by their health plan. Therefore, they conclude that the individual plays a less significant role in health care purchase decisions.

This set of beliefs does not take into account derived demand. For example, a hospital is trying to convince the management of an HMO new to the area that it should be the HMO's primary hospital. Although factors such as the hospital's willingness to negotiate on price and the extent to which it can provide the full range of medical care will influence the HMO, the desirability of the hospital to potential HMO members is a key consideration. If the potential HMO members consider the hospital unacceptable as the HMO's primary hospital, then the HMO itself will be a less attractive health plan and will have difficulty enrolling members. The HMO derives its demand in part from the attractiveness of the hospital(s) to which it sends patients, as well as from the physicians who are on its panel.

In essence, derived demand requires a two-stage marketing process. The marketer must develop a set of products and services to appeal not only to the immediate customer, but also to the customer of the immediate customer. A large medical group practice can make itself attractive to a managed care organization by agreeing to significant discounts. To reduce costs sufficiently to permit these discounts, however, the medical group may understaff and, as a result, deny quick access to all but the sickest patients. While the discounts initially may be appealing to the managed care organization, the lack of access would soon become apparent to the patients, would make the medical practice unattractive to them, and would cause them to steer away from this practice in future enrollment periods. Thus, the managed care organization would derive little long-term demand from consumers through contracting with this practice. Ultimately, with little derived demand, this practice would become unattractive to the managed care organization.

With the right information available, derived demand offers marketers an opportunity to influence business-to-business buyer behavior. Any health care provider (of significant size) that can produce credible market research to establish consumer preference for its services within its target market area is in a good position to negotiate with managed care organizations, with other organizational buyers, and with potential contract partners; the stated consumer preference indicates that the provider can bring to the organization derived demand for its services. Similarly, managed care organizations do their own consumer preference research to identify the providers that are so attractive to consumers that their presence on the managed care provider list overwhelms the need for a significant discount from them.

The key to using derived demand is information—market research data on consumer preferences and on consumers' intended use or purchase behavior. The relatively unsophisticated research that continues to characterize many health care marketing efforts does not uncover derived demand very well. Asking consumers if they prefer hospital A to

hospital B may establish a preference for one over the other, but it does not assess any trade-off that consumers may be willing to make, such as accepting the less preferred provider for a specified dollar lower premium or more convenient location. To capture this level of information, it is probably necessary to do a trade-off analysis, commonly called conjoint measurement. This market research methodology requires the identification of those variables that appear most likely to affect a buyer's purchase decision (in a specific, not generic, type of purchase situation). These variables include those that make it possible to measure the attractiveness to the consumer at different levels, such as a $3.00 vs. $5.00 vs. $10.00 co-pay per visit. Each of the variables, at different levels, is combined with other variables and presented as a package to the consumer interviewee, who is asked to assess the attractiveness of the overall package. For example, a shortened version of two packages for an HMO might be

Option A
- $3.00 co-pay
- Primary care visits with nurse-practitioner
- Acute illness appointments available within 48 hours
- Admits to most preferred hospital in the area

Option B
- $10.00 co-pay
- Primary care visits with a physician
- Acute illness appointments available within 24 hours
- Admits to moderately preferred hospital in the area

The consumer is asked to rate the preferability of several of these packages. Using an algorithm, conjoint analysis can determine which variables at which levels prove to be most attractive to the consumer, and when to trade off one variable for another. Most health care organizations do not have the capability to carry out this type of market research in-house, but market research firms should be qualified to do so. Over time, health care marketers may add this type of research to their expected set of skills. Other research approaches, recommended by Berry and Parasuraman, include transactional surveys, which focus on customers' most recent service experiences with the organization rather than the totality of their experiences; mystery shopping in both one's own and competing services to evaluate the quality of services delivered; focus group interviews; service reviews (a formal process of periodic visits with customers to discuss the service relationship); customer complaint and inquiry systems; employee field reporting and surveys; and a system to track and analyze operating data, such as service response times and waiting times.[6]

Some network managers have failed to take derived demand into account. For some, the natural tendency has been to put together the lowest cost hospitals and practices. As a result, their provider list may have no tertiary care facilities, nor the local women's health center, and specialty children's hospital, for example. The network managers' assumption underlying this choice of providers is that low cost will outweigh all other considerations. For many potential members, however, cost is secondary to access to preferred high-quality providers. Moreover, if those for whom cost is the primary concern find, once in the network, that they are unhappy with the quality of the services, they are likely at the next enrollment period to search out another network or managed care organization, even at a slightly greater cost. Failure to consider derived demand may be effective in the short run, but is likely to create a higher turnover of customers in the long run.

CONSUMER BEHAVIOR: INFORMATION SEARCH AND USE

The rapidly increasing availability of health care information is likely to change the way that consumers make their health care choices. In the early 1990s, employers were beginning to collect information that they could share with their employees. For example, three large employers (GTE, Digital Equipment, and Xerox) surveyed a sizable sample of their employees regarding their satisfaction with their health care providers, including managed care organizations, and reported the results to all geographically relevant employees.[7] This "report card" on health care providers and managed care organizations presumably allowed employees to compare these organizations intelligently and make informed choices. The National Committee on Quality Assurance (NCQA) has been producing report cards on managed care plans since the mid-1990s, reporting on rates of Cesarean section, rates of mammography in women over the age of 50, rates of use of other early disease detection methodologies, and member satisfaction. Local magazines in cities such as Philadelphia and Boston provide an annual list of the best regional physicians and hospitals. The Massachusetts Department of Public Health offers ratings of all the state's skilled nursing facilities on its Web site and updates them every 6 months, based on semiannual surveys of the facilities. Many other sources have added or are adding themselves to the list of health care information providers.

From a marketing and consumer behavior perspective, the implications are enormous. Historically, the dissonance reduction model of consumer behavior, under which consumers make a high involvement (i.e., very important) decision with very little information, has characterized most annual health care enrollment or purchase behavior. To assure themselves that they are not making the wrong decision, consumers often choose what they perceive to be the safe choice: the most well-known organization, the organization recommended by the benefits clerk (the most immediately available expert to someone who is enrolling in a health care plan at work), or the organization in which they have already been enrolled, where the feeling of safety is based on personal experience. Rarely have consumers incorporated valid, objective, and comprehensive provider and insurance carrier information into their decision-making process,[8] in no small part because the information has not been available.

Availability of Information

The growing availability of new information on health care providers and carriers suggests that a far larger portion of the population will behave, or at least try to behave, according to the complex buying behavior model. The basic assumption of the model is that all purchase behavior is information based; consumers compare and contrast purchase alternatives, form intelligent opinions regarding the alternatives, and purchase based on these informed opinions. For those able to analyze the somewhat complex information related to health care plans, the option to behave according to the complex buying behavior model may now be available. For example, the New Jersey utility, the Public Service Electric & Gas Company, and Digital Equipment have put information about their health care plans on-line. Using interactive computer technology, employees can do research and obtain information about the health care plans, such as their report cards;

employees can even determine which physicians in the health care plans are willing to take more patients and sign up for the physician of their choice. Marketers should be sensitive to consumers' desire for data and should constantly be attuned to what the data say about the quality of the organization's health care services. For the marketer, this database should be a welcome addition (if it does not already exist) to the tools used for continuous quality improvement.

Unfortunately, it is clear that consumers are not receiving all the information that they want. Moreover, some of the attributes important to the consumer, such as the denial of access to a specialist when it is necessary, are difficult to measure. Consumer self-reports of needing to see a specialist may be inflated; patients may think they need a specialist when, in fact, they do not. The reporting organization, on the other hand, has an incentive to downplay the number of reports of denied access to specialists. Because the task of measuring a void, of measuring what did not happen, is usually more difficult than measuring what did happen, this information is generally not reported.

It also appears that consumers are not using many of the data provided to them. In their study, Tumlinson and associates provided a wide range of information to consumers.[9] These researchers found that, while consumers consider specific plan benefits, premium costs, and out-of-pocket costs essential information when choosing a health care plan, they seldom use such information as the ratings of plans by independent experts, the percentage of members who are satisfied with the overall plan, and comparisons in the convenience of the administrative paperwork. Other research has shown that consumers do not use much of the information provided, particularly if it cannot be easily and readily understood.[10,11] Hibbard and associates discovered that even employers, that is, the managers within companies who were responsible for selecting health care plans for the company's employees and who should have been knowledgeable about health care plan data, did not use much of the information made available to them, nor did they seek out other information that could have allowed for a more informed purchase choice.[12] Therefore, it appears that, even if far more data were available, health care purchasers may continue to act according to the dissonance reduction model.

Integrity and Validity of Information

Much depends not only on the availability of the data, but also on the integrity and validity of the information. For example, there is a great deal of generic health care and medical data on the Internet. It can empower patients and give them a great deal of information about their diagnoses and potential treatments, but it can also mislead them. No one is charged with reviewing studies or data cited on the Internet, as there is in the case of medical journals; yet, one of the two most common reasons for logging on to the Internet is to obtain health information. Currently, there is no way to judge how much of this information is correct and how much may do harm.[13]

Another problem arises if the aggregation of health care data changes its meaning. For example, health care services are of variable quality. An aggregation or collapsing of the data makes them easier for everyone to use; some of the consumers report excellent experiences, while others report terrible experiences, which could average out simply to mediocre experiences. Failure to note the extremes could easily mislead those who wish to use and are capable of using the full range of data. A health care organization with a bimodal distribution of satisfaction ratings could hide the high level of dissatisfaction on the low end by reporting only means or medians.

It may be difficult to promulgate objective information. One method of reporting that can help to overcome this problem is to provide not only the means and medians, but also more complete information on the unaggregated data: How many answer categories were there? What percentage of the respondents fell into the lowest category? What percentage fell into the highest category? A survey of customer satisfaction ratings with answers ranging from 1 to 5 (where 1 is extremely satisfied and 5 is extremely dissatisfied), may show a mean rating of 3 for both HMO A and HMO B. This may suggest that the HMOs are performing similarly in terms of satisfying the customer. If only 2 percent of those rating HMO A responded by rating it a 5, but 14 percent of those rating HMO B gave it a rating of 5, the potential customer may be far more likely to experience extreme dissatisfaction in HMO B than in HMO A.

Some marketers may find themselves under pressure to use the data to portray their health care organization in the best possible light, even if that portrayal is misleading. In this scenario, a marketer takes the single best rating or set of ratings and positions the organization on that one rating or set while ignoring the other ratings. For example, a hospital may receive very high ratings on nursing care while receiving average or below-average ratings on maintaining its physical plant, having up-to-date diagnostic equipment, having a wide array of specialists, and providing coordinated care. The hospital management, in the interests of best representing the hospital, may then advertise that the hospital provides some of the best nursing care in the area.

From a policy perspective, the danger is that many consumers will rely on the advertisements, which may represent predigested information, rather than on the full body of information available. Few advertisements are likely to provide information that portrays the organization negatively, after all; the job of advertising is generally to sell the organization, not to demarket it. (Demarketing is the act of making a product, service, or organization less marketable.) The subjugation of available and/or required data from informing the consumer to selling the consumer has been a common practice in other industries and can be expected in the health care industry as the government, employers, or other outside bodies require the collection of an outcome and satisfaction database. While the consumer and employer may wish to use the collected data and act by the complex buying behavior model, the act of analyzing large amounts of data is foreign to most people. The natural tendency is to substitute the predigested data, as presented in an advertising form or in an oversimplified format by the data collectors.

It is not yet reasonable to assume that the relevant data will be available. One of the big problems in reporting customer quality perceptions and satisfaction data is the failure of senior management in many health care organizations to budget for the measurement of the data.[14] New requirements by the government, by accrediting organizations, or by employers force health care organizations to budget for the collection of such data, but because this is relatively new for most health care organizations, the data measures may not be standardized from organization to organization. What one hospital or HMO labels as a condition leading to high consumer satisfaction (e.g., a 30-minute wait for urgent care) may be labeled as unacceptable by another hospital or HMO. These differences make it even more difficult for consumers to compare and contrast health care organizations intelligently.

As a result, the dissonance reduction model is likely to remain the predominant model of consumer behavior in the health care field as it is in many other industries. Most people do not have the capacity or the desire to wade through the data and turn them into usable information, or they do not trust the integrity of the data. The health care industry does not yet have an independent, unbiased agency that can collect information agreed upon as the most relevant, objectively analyze it, and present it in a trustworthy predigested format.

CONSUMER BEHAVIOR: DIFFERENTIATION

Markets are fond of saying that three things matter to consumers and, therefore, could act as differentiators: cost, quality, and access. Definitions of quality are anything but consistent across health care studies and health care consumers. The way in which the NCQA measures quality includes a number of early disease detection tests that are largely irrelevant to most consumers, for example. The measures of service quality that are now standard in the service marketing literature do not apply particularly well to health care settings. Even the definition of access may mean different things to different people. One person may speak of access as the ability to get an appointment with the physician on the same day; someone else may mean the ability to see a specialist at will; and a third may define access as the ability to find a physician who is willing to take new patients and whose office is closer than 30 minutes away.

Clearly, these and other factors can differentiate one provider or insurer from another. For a health care plan, the composition of benefit packages is one source of differentiation. Does it include drug coverage? Does it allow self-referral to an obstetrician–gynecologist? To what hospitals can plan members be admitted? Many of these provisions can allow for differentiation between plans and can give the consumer (and employer) a real choice. In geographic areas where the benefit packages of the different health care plans are quite similar and the panel of physicians and hospitals offered are nearly the same, consumers seeking points of differentiation between plans will have to rely more heavily on satisfaction and service attributes, on location of physicians and facilities, and on other factors that the plan chooses to use for differentiation purposes, such as free membership in a health club. The implications for marketers are that they must attend to those areas where they can effectively differentiate themselves.

Price as a Differentiator

One of the easiest areas of differentiation conceptually involves pricing. It does not require extensive advertising, promotion, and education to demonstrate a lower price. The ability to maintain a competitively low price is dependent on having a low cost structure, however. If a low cost structure does not result from significant re-engineering of the service process so as to continue to deliver a consumer-perceived high quality of service, but rather results from limited coverage, denial of access to services, long waits, and so on, differentiation on the basis of pricing will be advantageous only in the short run. Members dissatisfied with the level and quality of service will opt to join competing plans (even though they may be higher priced) in the next re-enrollment period.

From a marketing standpoint, the ability to differentiate on price means that price-sensitive consumers are given the choice of buying less service or lower quality (at least lower perceived quality) for less money; con-

versely, price-insensitive consumers are given the choice of buying more and paying more for the choice. Also, true innovation, which may entail vastly different prices (both higher and lower) is possible. The result should heighten the ability of organizations to differentiate themselves and should enhance consumer choice.

This approach supports the concept of customer-responsive marketing. It allows the organization to segment the market; develop a product, package, or set of services that meets particularly well the needs and wants of that specific segment; and to differentiate itself from its competitors. Unfortunately, the marketplace has not yet focused on quality or access as much as it has focused on price in the past. Therefore, price competition has been fierce, and differentiation on the basis of factors other than price has been limited. One of the few well-known health care organizations that did differentiate in other ways was Oxford Health (prior to the bad publicity that it received when the failure of its computer systems to keep up with its growth caused prolonged delays in payments to its contracted providers). Oxford Health gained a significantly differentiated reputation in part due to the broad access to alternative medicine providers allowed to its members at a time when few other managed care plans covered alternative providers in any significant way.

In reality, pricing decisions are not nearly as straightforward in the health care industry as in most other industries. Regulations often dictate prices for health care services, for example, and retroactive denials of payment after the delivery of services are common. Normally, organizations set a price floor (below which the price does not fall) at the cost of producing the service. As in most service environments, fixed costs are high for health care, while variable costs are low. Determining the full cost of a service can be quite difficult, since it involves a somewhat arbitrary distribution of fixed costs among the various services that share the fixed costs of overhead. Because each organization can allocate overhead in a different way and competitors have different overhead structures, different providers of service have different costs for any specific service. Health care providers face fierce price competition in many parts of the United States and often feel compelled to try to match the low price of their competitors. If they are unsure of the full cost of the service in question, they may price the service below its true fixed cost in order to match competing prices. Furthermore, if regulated prices are based on the market's low prices, which arose from a mix of fierce price competition and uncertainty about services' full costs, then these low prices will be regulated into long-term existence.

The decreasing amount of cross-subsidization in the health care market exacerbates the problem. Historically, those who had "good" insurance (usually fee-for-service or, until diagnosis-related groups [DRGs], Medicare) cross-subsidized those with "poor" insurance (e.g., Medicaid) and those without insurance. Those with "good" insurance paid a higher price for the same procedure, room, or diagnostic test, thus compensating for those with "poor" insurance. This cross-subsidization was viewed as serving the public good, ensuring that all who needed health care would receive it. As more health care providers came to see themselves as businesses and as price competition intensified, health care organizations sought increasingly to price their services as low as possible in order to make themselves as marketable as possible. This left little room for cross-subsidization.

Yet another way in which pricing decisions are not straightforward in health care is evident in the way in which health care organizations try to raise their prices by segment-ing patients according to their insurance coverage. For example, Wildwood Health Care Center, an Indianapolis nursing home owned by Vencor, Inc., the fourth largest nursing home in the United States, had a significant number of nursing home patients who were covered by Medicaid. Wildwood indicated that it was losing money on these patients, however, because Medicaid was willing to pay only $82 per day. Because Wildwood could not persuade Medicaid to raise the reimbursement to be closer to the $125 per day that private pay patients paid, Wildwood sought to raise the aggregate price mix of its patients by forcing out its Medicaid residents. It then planned to admit only private pay patients in the future so that all its patients would then be paying $125 per day.[15] Their inability to change regulated prices, thus, may cause health care organizations to aim their marketing strategies at those segments of the market whose prices or reimbursement rates are already the most favorable. In this way, some health care providers differentiate themselves on price indirectly by directly targeting well reimbursed market segments.

Other Sources of Differentiation

Health care plans also compete on the basis of location, customer service, and distribution/access issues. Location is the most obvious issue; physician practices, hospitals, outpatient facilities, and other health care providers make choices relative to the areas in which the served market works and lives. Acquisition of other providers and plans has become a fast-growing mode of expanding geographically within the health care market in the recent past. Convenience of location is clearly one of the key decision factors that people use in selecting their health care providers and in the decision to stay with those providers.

Implicitly, many health care plans now are differentiating themselves by serving certain market segments particularly well. Disease management programs single out those with a specific condition (e.g., asthma or diabetes) and provide specialized services related to that condition. This is an application of one-to-one marketing and is dependent on information systems that can collect member information to identify those in need of specific services. For example, a program that focused on asthmatic patients would keep track of such occurrences as how many times an asthmatic patient needed to go to hospital emergency departments within a 6-month period and how many times the patient had filled a daily medication (to help determine if the patient was using the medication as often as prescribed) and tailor its services to that patient. Someone who had paid multiple visits to emergency departments in a short period of time probably would need more training in how to use the small diagnostic instrument that allows the patient to assess his or her air intake and how to use the inhaler medications that can arrest the development of the asthma incident before it requires an emergency department visit.

Health care providers who contract with managed care plans seek to differentiate themselves to employers, to managed care plans, and to consumers. The ways in which they differentiate their services should vary according to the audience. Although a hospital's ability to capture data on resources used in serving its employees may impress an employer, the employees may see little value in these data and want information instead on the postsurgical therapies offered by the hospital. Again, using the power of the computer, a hospital can engage in one-to-one segmentation to differentiate itself. It can, for example, identify all patients coming for breast cancer surgery and arrange for all those pa-

tients to talk to a volunteer from Reach for Recovery, to receive literature on breast reconstruction if they have had a mastectomy, and to consult a representative from the local store that specializes in clothing for patients who have undergone breast surgery. Hospitals also are differentiated in some cases on the basis of characteristics inherent in their incorporation, such as Catholic, Jewish, Adventist, public city, private psychiatric hospital, or specialty children's hospitals.

CUSTOMER RETENTION

Many consumers feel that they must remain with their current health insurance or managed care organization in the belief that a pre-existing condition precludes them from switching to a different provider organization. The promise of the Health Insurance Portability and Accountability Act, a law that was intended to guarantee consumers continued health care insurance when they changed jobs, has not been fulfilled because the premiums have been exorbitant and some insurance companies have discouraged their agents from writing these policies. As a result, many consumers who appear to be highly loyal to a health care provider or plan may simply fear losing their coverage. If the health care system ever develops in a way that allows these captive consumers to switch from one plan to another without penalty, health care plans would have a greater incentive to keep their members satisfied and their marketers would have to work harder at maintaining a high enrollment level.

The belief that consumers have few options because many employers have in the past limited the number of options available to their employees is not fully correct. According to *Business & Health*, "Managed care has not put an end to choice. . . . Nationwide, nearly two out of three workers whose employers provide health coverage had a choice of plans. Even many employees whose firms offered only one health plan had options. According to the AAHP (American Association of Health Plans), 90 percent had coverage with a non-network component."[16] Consumers who have more choices switch plans more often. Since the choice of health care plan is a high-involvement decision, however, consumers must be convinced through advertising, personal selling, word of mouth, or some other form of promotion that their new choice of health care plan is a safe choice.

Historically, the marketing efforts of health care providers, health insurers, and health maintenance plans have appeared to focus more intently on attracting patients, customers, and members than on retaining them. Hospitals and medical group practices that have formally engaged in marketing have relied heavily on tactics such as promotion and advertising to the detriment of the more strategic functions of marketing. Insurers and health maintenance plans have done the same, with an additionally heavy use of sales personnel to market the product. Managed care penetration has now reached such a high level, however, that it no longer draws its new members from the indemnity sector, but rather draws them from other managed care plans during re-enrollment periods. Also, the advent of Medicare managed care allows the Medicare recipient to switch health care plans and providers. Taken together, these events challenge health care organizations to find new ways to retain patients and members. No amount of advertising, promotion, and selling can retain a customer who is unhappy with a service; promoting great nursing care or short waits will not counteract a patient's own experience of nonempathic and abrupt delivery of care. The focus of marketing efforts, if retention is the goal, shifts away from advertis-

ing, promotion, and selling to the provision of visibly good service quality.

Service marketers and academics in the last 10 years have been trying to measure and quantify service quality. Parasuraman and associates devised a now well accepted model of service quality that has been applied to health care settings with mixed results.[17–19] Although this model, called the SERVQUAL instrument, may not apply fully to health care settings as it was developed, it is likely to fit health care consumer behavior better with modification over time. It measures constructs such as reliability, responsibility, tangibles, assurance, and empathy. Once its measures are better related to health care consumers' satisfaction, marketers will be able to rely on it and on other validated measures of customer-defined quality in their search for ways to retain customers.

Those in health care marketing often fail to examine the consumer decision to stay with a provider. Even though it costs five times as much to capture a new customer as to keep an existing one,[20] most health care organizations continue to define marketing as encouraging trial (capturing new patients or members) rather than retaining members. This is not a wise choice fiscally, given the higher cost of attracting new customers. Greater effort should be directed toward retaining existing customers.

One reason for the failure of health care organizations to address customer retention is that most do not have information systems designed to identify retention variables.[21] It is the rare hospital, group medical practice, or outpatient rehabilitation facility, for example, that can easily produce a list of patients who have been using its services for more than 2 years and those who have used them for less than 1 year. Even managed care plans, which have annual enrollment periods that make it easier to distinguish years of use, cannot generally identify those who have voluntarily disenrolled. If an organization cannot identify those who have chosen to go elsewhere (presumably to a competitor), then the organization cannot learn from them what it can do better in the future so as to keep its members (or patients).

Customer service and a variety of service marketing issues, such as managing the service process experience so that the customer can project a positive outcome based on a positive process experience, have become a major focus of total quality management efforts. Most larger health care organizations have instituted total quality management, continuous quality improvement, or some other form of patient/member–based re-engineering process management that is designed to deliver a seamless service and, if introduced to the organization correctly, to build long-term relationships with its customers rather than a series of one-time transactions. Very often, only those with authority over the operations of the organization can solve what marketing research identifies as dissatisfaction caused by poor service. If patients are kept waiting for an average of 2 hours to get a laboratory test, the marketing resolution of the dissatisfaction requires modifying the operational component by expanding the capacity of the laboratory (e.g., adding technicians, space, equipment, information systems, or some combination of these).

The area of distribution and access is only one of the battlefields where the fight to retain customers will be fought. The concept of access always has been a sensitive one to consumers of health care. Time access is a constant and consistent source of irritation, if not anger, in health care market research; waiting for an appointment, waiting for a procedure or test, and waiting for the results of tests all have caused great customer dissatisfaction and have conveyed a sense of poor service.

The continuing movement of most of the marketplace into managed care, where one of the primary cost-saving measures is based on denial of access (presumably in the positive sense of forgoing unnecessary care or substituting equally adequate, but less expensive care), expands the sensitivity of the issue of threatened access. Denial of access is most often seen as negative, such as denial of access to choice of provider, denial of access to any specialist without the gatekeeper's approval, or denial of tests deemed to be too expensive for 98 percent of cases. Health care organizations have seen and can expect to see much higher levels of dissatisfaction stemming from perceived (or real) access problems. Some managed care organizations already have sensed this and have removed the barriers that prevent members from seeking medical specialist care on their own, without having first to seek the permission and referral of their primary care physicians.

Physicians, too, have become highly sensitive and vocal about denial of access. In great numbers, they have described to their patients and the press the barriers presented by the managed care gatekeepers whose job it is to assess the need for tests, procedures, and care, supposedly in the interests of the patients. The physicians often view the gatekeepers as those who deny patients needed care in the fiscal interests of the organization. In fact, the denial of access may be based on a legitimate recognition that unnecessary tests and care are driving up health care costs. Anecdotally, consumer dissatisfaction stems from real fears of improper denial of access. In market research, consumers say things such as "What if an X-ray can't show the problem, and I really do need an MRI?" "What if my physician is right, and I really do need this surgery?" "What if my physician gives up too easily and doesn't fight for the surgery I need?" When gatekeepers are young, inexperienced, and possibly not well trained in specialty areas, denial of access becomes not only a marketing and retention problem, but also an ethical and clinical problem that cuts to the very heart of the health care business and the practice of good medicine. If a patient seek alternative opinions from non-network physicians who disagree with the initial conclusions of the patient's plan physician, the result may be conflict and potential liability.

The marketing task in addressing retention is to explain denials of access to consumers and physicians in such a way that they can appreciate and agree with the decision, assuming that the rationale to deny is wise. Alternatively, the task is to examine the denial process to ascertain that denials are not, in fact, inappropriate. Unless this is done, dissatisfaction may be manifested not only through increasing retention problems, but also through medical malpractice suits and angry verbal assaults in the press. Either way, the health care organization places itself in long-term fiscal jeopardy if its retention rates drop dramatically.

CUSTOMER SATISFACTION

Many of the regional and national health care accrediting organizations require the health care organizations that they accredit to collect and share customer satisfaction information. The obvious assumption is that organizations want to satisfy their customers and should do so. It is not yet clear, however, whether customer satisfaction correlates with customer retention; that is, are satisfied customers loyal customers? There is anecdotal information to suggest that the correlation might not be as high as one would expect it.

Service Recovery

Dissatisfied customers have the potential not only to go to a competitor, but also have the potential to spread negative word-of-mouth about the organization's services. Instead of being a missionary (one who speaks enthusiastically in favor of the organization and recommends it to others), a dissatisfied customer is more likely to be a terrorist (one who says negative things about the organization and tries to dissuade people from using its services). The cost of counteracting the efforts of a terrorist can be quite high. The advertising and promotion undertaken by the organization do not have nearly the credibility of a former or current customer who can cite specific instances of bad service. Therefore, it is in the organization's best interests to keep its customers happy.

Keeping customers happy is not merely a matter of providing the routinely good service that customers expect. The real test of a service organization's ability to satisfy its customers is its ability to solve problems. No organization is perfect; all organizations sooner or later make a mistake or inadvertently provide poor service. The true test of an organization's service competence is its ability to recover after a service problem occurs.[22] It is essential to anticipate service problems rather than simply to respond to them. Management must decide in advance the amount of flexibility that employees should have to solve customer problems on the spot and the amount of resources that should be available to employees for the purposes of service recovery.

Some organizations do not believe that their employees are capable of responding to service problems appropriately. In these organizations, a customer who feels that a service has been of poor quality must tell not only the front-line employee of the problem, but also the employee's immediate superior and anyone else in the chain of command who must be part of the problem resolution effort. This repeated explanation of the source of dissatisfaction, often two or more times, runs contrary to good problem resolution or service recovery, which dictates that the customer should have the problem resolved as quickly as possible. Each time the customer has to "tell the story" about the problem without obtaining resolution of the problem, the customer becomes increasingly uncertain that the problem will be resolved; customers frequently will resort to magnifying the problem in telling it to the next level in the organization in the hope that maybe this time it will be resolved. Any person who has suffered through this process is ripe to become a terrorist in communicating about this organization.

In contrast, good service recovery organizations provide both flexibility and resources at the front line so that problems can be solved or addressed in a fashion that satisfies the customer immediately. In order for this approach to work effectively, the organization must inculcate its employees with an understanding that an important part of their job is to recognize and solve customer problems—whatever it takes. Educating employees to the concept of the lifetime value of a customer supports this outlook. If an HMO member stays with that HMO for an average of 10 years, bringing in an average of $1,200 a year, then the lifetime value of the member is $12,000. If a member of the HMO becomes upset because she spent $15 ($30 round trip) for taxi fare to be on time for her doctor's appointment, only to find that the physician was not in that day and no one thought to call her, it makes sense, given her long-term value to the HMO of $12,000, to reimburse her for the $30 taxi fare. The trade-off of $30 in order

not to risk $12,000 seems more than reasonable for the service recovery.

Measurement of Customer Satisfaction

Ways of measuring customer satisfaction vary, as do the reasons for measuring satisfaction. First, many health care providers have started to measure customer satisfaction more aggressively in the late 1990s because of the requirements of accrediting organizations and employers. Often, these accrediting organizations require the use of standardized measures to allow comparisons across health care facilities. While this requirement has obvious value, it also has drawbacks. Standardized measures are usually generic in nature so that they apply equally well to all the health care organizations using them; however, generic measures are generally so broad and nonspecific that they do not give the health care organization enough information to identify and correct problems revealed in the customer satisfaction research. For example, a poor rating on a patient survey for the Joint Commission on Accreditation of Healthcare Organizations may alert a hospital to the fact that there was a problem, but may not indicate what the specific problem was, thereby limiting the hospital's ability to correct the problem. Thus, although standardized customer satisfaction studies are valuable for the purposes of providing industry report cards with needed information, they are not generally managerially useful.

Second, satisfaction is known to be in part a function of the amount of choice the customer had in the purchase decision.[23] Thus, satisfaction ratings are likely to be lower among health care plan members whose employers gave them no choice of health care plan than among members who had at least some choice of plan, even if only one other choice. This then raises the question, exactly what is being measured in customer satisfaction research? Choice at the time of purchase becomes one of the key items reflected in customer satisfaction studies rather than customer satisfaction with the organization's performance after purchase.

Third, the interpretation of customer satisfaction research often focuses on the nature of the customers. Medicare managed care plans, for example, have recently been prone to explain their low patient satisfaction ratings as a function of the age of the people who are the subjects of the research. Their assumption is that older people are, by definition, more dissatisfied. Studies have shown, however, that patient or member characteristics account for only 9 percent of the variations in customer service research; the rest is due to the performance characteristics of the organization itself.[24]

Fourth, some satisfaction studies in the health care industry have biased the response categories by loading them too heavily in the positive direction. For questions such as "How satisfied are you with your care?" for example, they have provided the answer categories: highly satisfied, somewhat satisfied, satisfied, not satisfied. Because the respondent has three positive (satisfied) categories from which to choose and only one negative category, there is a bias toward a positive response. The willingness of many in the industry to interpret any of the top three categories as satisfied exacerbates the problem. The public has become cynical about the multitude of managed care plan advertisements claiming 94 percent, 95 percent, 98 percent (and so on) customer satisfaction levels. In reality, only those who answer in the most positive response category are truly satisfied and likely to return to the organization for services. More than half of those in the second highest category can be expected to defect to a competitor. Obviously, customer satisfaction studies are neither simple to devise nor simple to interpret; when performed correctly with the appropriate expertise, however, they can be quite valuable.

DATA-DRIVEN MARKETING

Correctly performed marketing always has been data driven. A marketing function that is fully supported will be given the tools with which to do its job. Insufficient data support, whether for internal data capture and analysis; for market research; or for market, competitive, and other external data analysis, cuts at the very heart of the marketing function. Health care organizations that hope to thrive in the future must expect to position marketing not only as a creative function but also as a data-driven, analytical, and strategic function.

NOTES

1. P. Kotler, *Marketing Management: Analysis, Planning, Implementation, and Control*, 9th ed. (Englewood Cliffs, NJ: Prentice Hall, 1997), 9.

2. M. Langley, "Hospitals and Doctors Fight for Same Dollars in a Louisiana Town: New Iberia Physicians Set Up Facilities To Nab Revenue Institutions Normally Get," *Wall Street Journal*, November 25, 1997, A1.

3. J. Gabel, "Ten Ways HMOs Have Changed During the 1990s," *Health Affairs* 16, no. 3 (1997): 134–145.

4. G. Anders and R. Winslow, "HMOs' Woes Reflect Conflicting Demands of American Public," *Wall Street Journal*, December 22, 1997, A1.

5. A. Michel and I. Shaked, *Takeover Madness: Corporate America Fights Back* (New York: John Wiley & Sons, 1986).

6. L. Berry and A. Parasuraman, "Listening to the

Customer—the Concept of a Service-Quality Information System," *Sloan Management Review* (Spring 1997): 65–76.

7. R. Winslow, "Three Big Firms Survey Workers To Evaluate, Improve Health Care," *Wall Street Journal*, October 8, 1993, B3.

8. H. Smith and R. Rogers, "Factors Influencing Consumers' Selection of Health Insurance Carriers," *Journal of Health Care Marketing* (December 1986): 86–98.

9. A. Tumlinson et al., "Choosing a Health Plan: What Information Will Consumers Use?" *Health Affairs* (May/June 1997): 229–238.

10. J. Hibbard and J. Jewett, "What Type of Quality Information Do Consumers Want in a Health Care Report Card?" *Medical Care Research and Review* 53, no. 1 (1996): 28–47.

11. J. Hibbard and J. Jewett, "Will Quality Report Cards Help Consumers?" *Health Affairs* (May/June 1997): 218–228.

12. J. Hibbard et al., "Choosing a Health Plan: Do Large Employers Use the Data?" *Health Affairs* (December 1997): 47–63.

13. R. Ackerman, "Computer Briefs: You Can't Believe Everything You Read on the Web," *Journal of Medical Practice Management* (October 1997): 88–89.

14. A. Woodside, "What Is Quality and How Much Does It Really Matter?" *Journal of Health Care Marketing* 11, no. 4 (1991): 61–67.

15. M. Moss and C. Adams, "Evictees Relish Nursing Homes' Reversal," *Wall Street Journal*, April 21, 1998, B1, B12.

16. "Data Watch—Employee Choice: Alive and Well," *Business & Health* (February 1998): 58.

17. A. Parasuraman et al., "A Conceptual Model of Service Quality and Its Implications for Future Research," *Journal of Marketing* 49, no. 2 (1985): 41–50.

18. R. Shewchuk et al., "In Search of Service Quality Measures: Some Questions Regarding Psychometric Properties," *Health Services Management Research* 4, no. 1 (1991): 65–75.

19. D. Headley and S. Miller, "Measuring Service Quality and Its Relationship to Future Consumer Behavior," *Journal of Health Care Marketing* 13, no. 4 (1993): 32–41.

20. Kotler, *Marketing Management*, 47.

21. R. Clarke, "The First Step in Addressing Voluntary Disenrollment," *The Health Care Strategist* (December 1997): 7–9.

22. Spreng et al., "Service Recovery: Impact on Satisfaction and Intentions," *Journal of Services Marketing* (Spring 1995): 49–58.

23. R. Ullman et al., "Satisfaction and Choice: A View from the Plans," *Health Affairs* (May/June 1997): 209–217.

24. R. Clarke, Measuring Consumer Satisfaction (Paper presented at the Health Care Policy and Regulation Workshop, Rutgers University, December 9, 1994).

ROBERTA N. CLARKE, DBA, is Associate Professor and former Chairman of the Department of Marketing at Boston University's School of Management. She is the past President of the Society for Healthcare Planning and Marketing, a professional society affiliated with the American Hospital Association. She has been teaching health care marketing courses at Boston University's Health Care Management Program since January 1974, and her executive and graduate student audiences range from health care and nonprofit to high technology, communications, and service industries. Professor Clarke has served on the editorial review board of the *Journal of Healthcare Marketing* since its inception and is on the editorial boards of many other health care publications. With Philip Kotler, she co-authored *Marketing for Health Care Organizations*, considered to be the leading text in the field of health care marketing. Professor Clarke received her master's and doctorate from the Harvard Graduate School of Business Administration.

Chapter 8

Financial Management of Organized Health Care Delivery Systems

Leslie G. Eldenburg, Eldon L. Schafer, and Dwight J. Zulauf

Managing the financial viability of a health care organization involves a collection of processes or subsystems to obtain funds for the organization and to make optimal use of those funds once obtained. Financial management includes the following functions: design and operation of the financial information system; financial planning, reporting, and control; and providing information for decision making.

FINANCIAL INFORMATION NEEDS

Financial information must be generated for several purposes, some for external needs and some for internal needs:

- Entity financial statements prepared in accordance with generally accepted accounting principles (GAAP) are required for external reporting to stockholders and creditors; although not required, they generally are prepared for the board of directors as well.
- The financial information required for state and federal regulatory agencies generally focuses on cost data.
- Management needs information to plan the resources and to evaluate performance. Information is needed for segments or responsibility centers as well as for the entity as a whole.

- Management needs information for short-run decisions, such as determining prices, volume, and mix of services to be offered.
- Management also needs information to make long-range investment decisions involving large expenditures that have long lives; however, the financial information system generally provides very little information relevant to specific long-range decisions.

Accounting information generally falls into two broad classifications: financial accounting and management accounting. Financial accounting is concerned with the preparation and content of the conventional financial statements. The Financial Accounting Standards Board issues GAAP, which prescribe the form, content, and measurements of the financial statements for external reporting. For internal reporting, there are no similar principles, but most health care organizations follow the same accounting standards for both external and internal reporting. The major exception is in ambulatory care organizations, particularly physician groups.

Conventional financial statements include the financial position statement (balance sheet), operating statement (income statement), and the cash flow statement.

The financial position statement shows what the organization owns (assets), what the organization owes to outsiders (liabilities), and the resulting owners' equity (net assets). The operating statement (income statement) shows the revenues and expenses of the organization and the resulting net income or loss for a period of time. This statement is sometimes called by its older title, the profit and loss statement. The cash flow statement shows the cash flows from operating activities, investing activities, and financing activities for a period of time and the resulting change in cash balance.

Management accounting addresses the internal information needs for financial planning, control, and decision making. Health care executives are responsible for planning, implementing, and reporting the use of their organization's resources consistent with an established mission and the resulting strategic plan. Owners or governing boards review both plans and reported results to be certain that the mission of their health care organization is being fulfilled.

A decision is efficient if its benefits exceed its costs. Health care organizations must be able to identify, measure, and compare the benefits and costs attributable to particular kinds of decisions. Decisions fall into two general types; long-range decisions involve the addition or replacement of long-term capacity, while short-range decisions involve the use of existing capacity over a short period of time, usually 1 year, or less. The information needs and decision criteria for long-range and short-range decisions are very different.

This chapter is presented in three major sections. The first discusses the three conventional financial statements, and financial statements for an integrated health care organization are presented and analyzed. The second section discusses long-range decisions

that involve the acquisition or replacement of resources that have long lives. The most common example is the acquisition of equipment or buildings. The third section deals with decisions involving the use of existing capacity over a short period of time. The most common short-range decisions involve what fees to charge and what volume and mix of services to offer. Most decisions take place within some segment of the health care organization, such as a hospital, an ambulatory center, or a physician group. It is important to ensure that decisions are consistent with the strategy or mission of the organized health care delivery organization, as well as its individual segments.

UNDERSTANDING FINANCIAL STATEMENTS

Financial statements work from a basic accounting model or equation:

$$\text{Assets} = \text{Liabilities} + \text{Owners' Equity}$$

This is the framework of the balance sheet, and other financial statements show changes to this model. For example, the income statement shows changes in owners' equity due to operations, and the statement of cash flows explains changes in cash. This basic model and the financial statements have evolved over centuries of use.

Financial statements prepared in conformity with GAAP follow a generally uniform format. GAAP require the use of accrual accounting and have prescribed the type, format, measurements, and disclosures in general purpose financial statements. In accrual basis financial statements, as required by GAAP, revenue is recognized when service is performed, regardless of when cash is collected, and expenses are recognized when resources are consumed in providing that service, regardless of when cash is paid. Hospitals and many other health care organizations long have used accrual accounting. Until recently, however, physician and other ambulatory care groups have generally used cash basis accounting. In cash basis accounting, revenues are recognized when cash is collected, and expenses are recognized when cash is paid. As organized health care delivery systems acquire them, these physician groups generally change from cash to accrual basis accounting to be consistent with the rest of the system's accounting policies. A significant segment of the health care industry still uses cash basis accounting, however, and the management of an organized health care delivery system should understand both types of statements.

TYPES OF FINANCIAL STATEMENTS

The following financial statements are adapted from a large, organized health care delivery system that includes hospitals, acute care centers, outpatient care centers, physician practices, and a foundation. The amounts are adjusted to maintain anonymity, but all financial relationships remain.

Statement of Financial Position

The combined statement of financial position or balance sheet for the sample health system combines the balance sheets of all the entities in the system (Exhibit 8–1). Intercompany transactions, such as an amount payable in the balance sheet of a hospital and a receivable in the balance sheet of a physician group, have been eliminated. Assets and liabilities are classified into types to provide a better understanding of the organization's financial position and to allow computation of ratios and other comparisons in analyzing the financial statements. Four types of assets are included in the statement of financial position:

1. Current assets (i.e., cash and those assets expected to be converted into cash or consumed in the normal course of operations within a year). These assets are expected to be used to pay current liabilities and operating costs of the organization.
2. Limited use assets (i.e., cash and other assets held for specified purposes in the future). The use of these assets is restricted by the board, by donors, or by some other agreement. Restricted assets are common in not-for-profit organizations.
3. Property, plant, and equipment (i.e., tangible, long-lived assets used in the operations of the organization). Any assets held for future use are classified as limited use assets. These assets are depreciated over their useful life.
4. Other assets (i.e., expenditures that will be amortized (expensed) over some future period of time, such as bond issue costs).

Liabilities are present obligations to parties outside the entity that arise from past events and are payable in the future. The statement of financial position for this health system includes three types of liabilities:

1. Current liabilities (i.e., liabilities due within 1 year, the same period used to measure current assets). Current liabilities are used in several analytical ratios.
2. Accrued pension and medical malpractice liabilities. GAAP require the recognition of the costs and liabilities from postretirement benefits. This system also has recognized a possible liability arising from self-insuring for medical malpractice.
3. Long-term liabilities (i.e., liabilities that are due beyond the time period

Exhibit 8–1 Sample Health System: Combined Statement of Financial Position (for the Year Ended December 31, 1998)

	1997 ($000)	1998 ($000)
ASSETS		
Current Assets		
Cash and cash equivalents	3,371	4,891
Investments	59,671	112,833
Accounts receivable (less allowance for doubtful accounts of $6,673)	44,026	47,508
Inventories	3,805	3,962
Limited use assets—required for current liabilities	3,312	3,310
Prepare expenses and other current assets	3,972	1,900
Total current assets	118,158	174,406
Limited Use Assets, net of current position:		
By board for future use	50,571	43,672
Under bond indenture agreement	13,419	13,328
Under self-insurance arrangement	9,904	2,710
Donor-restricted	19,892	21,706
Total limited use assets	93,786	81,415
Property, Plant, and Equipment		
Land and improvements	17,300	18,018
Buildings	158,121	162,365
Equipment	126,318	140,195
Total	301,739	320,579
Less accumulated depreciation	(118,212)	(138,050)
Net	183,528	182,529
Construction in progress	6,701	6,489
Net property, plant, and equipment	190,229	189,018
Other Assets		
Unamortized bond issue cost	4,988	4,735
Other	9,983	8,364
Total other assets	14,971	13,100
Total Assets	$417,144	$457,938
LIABILITIES AND NET ASSETS		
Current Liabilities		
Accounts payable and accrued expenses	$34,844	$45,343
Accrued interest payable	3,909	3,475
Estimated third-party payer settlements	4,700	8,754
Current portion of long-term debt	4,985	4,664
Total current liabilities	48,438	62,236
Accrued Pension and Medical Malpractice Liabilities	18,836	16,121
Long-Term Debt, net of current portion	145,693	141,104
Total Liabilities	212,967	219,461
Net Assets		
Unrestricted	184,490	216,948
Temporarily restricted	6,510	6,617
Permanently restricted	13,177	14,913
Total net assets	204,177	238,477
Total Liabilities and Net Assets	$417,144	$457,938

Source: Anonymous.

used for current liabilities). All long-term liabilities are measured as the present value of future cash flows to retire the obligation. This system has long-term accruals and long-term debt.

The form of Owners' Equity depends on the nature of the corporation. In a for-profit corporation, the owners' equity includes contributed capital, representing the par or stated value of the stock issued and the additional amounts paid by the stockholder investors, and earned capital, the earnings less distribution to stockholders since the corporation was formed. Because there are no "investors" in a not-for-profit corporation, the difference between assets and liabilities in this type of corporation is described as net assets. These net assets must be classified to reflect certain restrictions on the assets of the organization, however.

Statement of Operations

The sample system's statement of operations or income statement combines the operating statements of the various organizations included in this system (Exhibit 8–2). Intercompany transactions, such as the sale of goods or services between organizations, have been eliminated. The statement includes

1. *revenue* (i.e., the value of services provided and goods sold to patients, whether or not cash has been collected). An estimate of bad debts to reflect patient billings that will not be collected is included in expenses.
2. *expenses* (i.e., the consumption of resources in providing services and goods to patients, regardless of when cash is paid). Some expenses, such as depreciation, involve estimates of the cost of long-lived assets amortized dur-

Exhibit 8–2 Sample Health System Combined Statement of Operations (for the Year Ended December 31, 1998)

	($000)
Revenue	
Net patient service revenue	288,322
Other	6,612
Total revenue	294,934
Expenses	
Salaries and wages	130,619
Employee benefits	27,546
Supplies	36,365
Depreciation and amortization	20,853
Interest	9,678
Provision for bad debts	9,608
Other	57,635
Total expenses	292,305
Income from Operations	2,629
Nonoperating Gains (Losses)	
Unrestricted contributions and fund raising activities	3,564
Income on investments	16,037
Other	(3,747)
Total nonoperating gains, net	15,854
Net Income	18,484

Source: Anonymous.

ing this period. Others, such as pension expenses, represent an estimate of payments to be made in the future.
3. *income from operations.* Operating income is a key measure of the performance of the health care organization; it is the excess (deficiency) of revenues over expenses. Unless there are significant nonoperating gains or donations, income from operations must be positive over time to provide the funds to replace assets and grow.
4. *nonoperating gains* (losses) (i.e., the gains and losses from donations or other activities, such as income from

investments, that do not involve the delivery of health care to patients).

Statement of Cash Flows

The changes in cash during the accounting periods are shown on the statement of cash flows (Exhibit 8–3). Three types of cash flows are identified: operating, investing, and financing.

Cash flows from operating activities include cash collected from providing health care services, cash paid for expenses, and cash paid for interest and taxes. In practice, an organization may use either of two forms to present cash flows from operations. The

Exhibit 8–3 Sample Health System: Combined Statements of Cash Flows (for the Year Ended December 31, 1998)

	($000)
Operating Activities	
Change in net assets	34,300
Adjustments to reconcile change in net assets to net cash provided by operations:	
Depreciation and amortization	20,905
Other	2,918
Realized and unrealized losses on investments	(13,191)
Cumulative effect of accounting change	(10,358)
Restricted contributions	(4,300)
Cash provided (used) by changes in operating assets and liabilities:	
Accounts receivable	(3,483)
Inventories, prepaid expenses and other assets	1,901
Accounts payable and accrued expenses	8,977
Estimated third-party payer settlements	4,054
Accrued pension and medical malpractice liabilities	(2,715)
Net cash provided by operating activities	39,010
Investing Activities	
Purchase of property, plant, and equipment, net	(19,058)
Purchase of other long-term productive assets	(581)
Change in investments and limited use assets	(17,241)
Net cash used by investing activities	(36,880)
Financing Activities	
Repayment of long-term debt	(4,910)
Restricted contributions	4,300
Net cash used by financing activities	(610)
Net Increase in Cash and Cash Equivalents	1,520
Cash and Cash Equivalents	
Beginning of year	3,371
End of year	4,891

Source: Anonymous.

indirect method, used by this system and most other organizations with external reporting requirements, begins with net income or loss from the operating statement and removes any accrual transactions (such as billings not collected, expenses on account, and depreciation) that do not involve cash. This leaves only cash transactions related to operating activities. Although the indirect method is very difficult to understand for those who are not accountants, its use is widespread because it reconciles net income in the operating statement with cash from operations in the cash flow statement.

The direct method simply shows the amount of cash collected from patients and the amount paid for expenses, interest, and taxes. Although the direct method is easier to understand, it is seldom used for external reporting. The following cash flows, which were constructed from financial statements, illustrate the direct method of presenting cash flows:

	($000)
Cash collected from patients	$285,897
Cash from contributions	3,564
Cash from investments	12,929
Cash payments for expenses	(253,188)
Cash payments for interest	(10,112)
Cash flow from operations	39,010

The cash from operations is the same by both methods, $39,010.

Cash flows from investing activities include cash flows from buying and selling assets, including plant, property, equipment, and investments. Cash flows from financing activities include borrowings, repayment of debt, cash from equity investors, and dividends.

Statement of Changes in Net Assets

For external reporting, GAAP require an explanation of the changes in owners' equity (net assets in not-for-profit organizations). The reconciliation may be in the form of a statement or in a footnote (Exhibit 8–4). This system has three classes of net assets, based on whether there are any restrictions on the assets and, if so, the type of restrictions. Some of the assets have temporary restrictions, usually imposed by the board of directors, and some assets have permanent restrictions imposed by the donor of the assets.

Cash and Accrual Accounting

The acquisition of physician groups presents a unique set of problems for an organized health care delivery system. Because they often use cash basis accounting, the financial statements do not always provide all relevant financial information about the groups. Often, the commitments made by the organized delivery system to the acquired physician group result in financial surprises. The cash basis financial statements of the physician groups sometimes do not provide a basis for reliable projections on the accrual basis of accounting.

Exhibits 8–5 and 8–6 illustrate the differences in accounting methods that lead to problems. They record 11 transactions in a worksheet with columns representing balance sheet accounts and rows representing transactions. The balance sheet and income statement are generated from the column totals, which show ending balances for each account. The statement of cash flows is generated from an analysis of the cash column. The set of transactions used for both the accrual and cash basis examples follow:

1. The physicians invest $250,000 in the medical practice.
2. Supplies and insurance are prepaid at $50,000.
3. Equipment at $1 million is purchased

Exhibit 8–4 Sample Health System: Combined Statement of Changes in Net Assets (for the Year Ended December 31, 1998)

	($000)
Unrestricted Net Assets	
Balance, beginning of year	184,490
Net income	18,484
Increase in net unrealized gains on investments	2,986
Net assets released from restrictions—Capital acquisitions	789
Cumulative effect of accounting change	10,199
Increase in unrestricted net assets	32,458
Balance, end of year	216,948
Temporarily Restricted Net Assets	
Balance, beginning of year	6,510
Contributions	3,741
Income on investments	274
Increase in net unrealized gains on investments	46
Net assets released from restrictions—Capital acquisitions	(789)
Net assets released from restrictions	(3,324)
Cumulative effect of accounting change	159
Increase in temporarily restricted assets	107
Balance, end of year	6,617
Permanently Restricted Net Assets	
Balance, beginning of year	13,177
Contributions	559
Income on investments	1,101
Increase in net unrealized gains on investments	76
Increase in permanently restricted net assets	1,736
Balance, end of year	14,913
Total Net Assets	238,477

Source: Anonymous.

with $50,000 as the down payment and the balance on a note payable. (It is assumed that the facilities are rented with rent included among operating expenses.)

4. Patients are billed for $1 million during the accounting period.

5. Expenses are incurred on accounts payable of $50,000.

6. Cash is collected from patients in the amount of $800,000.

7. Expenses are paid in cash for $500,000.

8. Payments are made on accounts payable in the amount of $30,000.

9. A principal payment is made on the note payable in the amount of $100,000.

10. Depreciation on equipment for the period is $100,000.

11. Distributions to physicians for the period are $300,000.

Exhibit 8–5 Accrual Basis Financial Statements

TRANSACTIONS FOR ACCRUAL BASIS FINANCIAL STATEMENTS ($000)

Tran	Explanation	Cash Flow Statement	Cash	Patient Receivable	Prepayment	Equipment	Accounts Payable	Note Payable	Capital Stock	Revenue	Expense
1	Investment by owners	F	250						250		
2	Supplies and insurance	O	(50)		50						
3	Purchase equipment	I	(50)			1,000		950			
4	Billings to patients			1,000						1,000	
5	Expenses on account						50				(50)
6	Collect on account	O	800	(800)							
7	Pay expenses	O	(500)								(500)
8	Pay on account	O	(30)				(30)				
9	Pay on note	F	(100)					(100)			
10	Equipment depreciation					(100)					(100)
11	Distribution to physicians		(300)								(300)
			20	200	50	900	20	850	250	1,000	(950)

INCOME STATEMENT

Revenue from patients	$1,000
Operating expenses	(950)
Net income (loss)	$ 50

BALANCE SHEET

ASSETS

Cash	$ 20
Patient receivables	200
Prepayments	50
Equipment	900
	$1,170

LIABILITIES AND OWNERS' EQUITY

Accounts payable	$ 20
Note payable	850
Total liabilities	870
Capital stock	250
Retained earnings	50
Total owners' equity	300
Total	$1,170

CASH FLOW STATEMENT

Cash from operations:	
Collections from patients	$ 800
Payment of expenses	(580)
Distributions to physicians	(300)
Total	(80)
Cash from investing	(50)
Cash from financing:	
Investment by owners	250
Payment on lease	(100)
Total	150
Change in cash	20
Beginning cash balance	—
Ending cash balance	$ 20

Exhibit 8–6 Cash Basis Financial Statements

TRANSACTIONS FOR CASH BASIS FINANCIAL STATEMENTS ($000)

Tran	Explanation	Cash Flow Statement	Assets		Liabilities	Owners' Equity		
			Cash	Equipment	Note Payable	Capital Stock	Revenue	Expense
1	Investment by owners	F	250			250		
2	Supplies and insurance	O	(50)					(50)
3	Purchase equipment	I	(50)	1,000	950			
4	No entry							
5	No entry							
6	Collect on account	O	800				800	
7	Pay expenses	O	(500)					(500)
8	Pay on account	O	(30)					(30)
9	Payment on note	F	(100)		(100)			
10	Equipment depreciation			(100)				(100)
11	Distribution to physicians	O	(300)					(300)
			20	900	850	250	800	(980)

INCOME STATEMENT

Revenue from patients	$ 800
Operating expenses	(980)
Net income (loss)	$ (180)

CASH FLOW STATEMENT

Cash from operations:	
Collections from patients	$ 800
Payment of expenses	(580)
Distributions to physicians	(300)
Total	(80)
Cash from investing	(50)
Cash from financing:	
Investment by owners	250
Payment on lease	(100)
Total	150
Change in cash	20
Beginning cash balance	—
Ending cash balance	$ 20

BALANCE SHEET

ASSETS	
Cash	$ 20
Equipment	900
Total	$ 920

LIABILITIES AND OWNERS' EQUITY	
Note payable	850
Total liabilities	850
Capital stock	250
Retained earnings	(180)
Total owners' equity	70
Total	$ 920

In Exhibit 8–5, all 11 transactions are recorded on the accrual basis. In the column next to cash, the cash flow transactions used to prepare the cash flow statement are identified as financing activities, cash flows related to investment by owners, borrowing and repayment of debt; operating activities, cash flows related to providing service to patients; or investing activities, cash flows involving purchase and sale of assets and investments.

In Exhibit 8–6, the transactions are recorded on the cash basis. Only cash collections are recognized as revenue. Receivables are not recorded in the accounts. Only cash payments for operations are recognized as expenses. Accounts payable are not recorded in the accounts. Depreciation is recognized in both systems, however.

Accrual basis financial statements are presented in Exhibit 8–5 and cash basis financial statements are presented in Exhibit 8–6. Transactions 4 and 5, relating to billings to patients and expenses on account, are not recorded on the cash basis. The payments for supplies (Transaction 2) and payments on account (Transaction 8) are recorded as expenses in the cash basis, but involve asset or liability accounts on the accrual basis.

There are significant differences in the balance sheets and income statements. On the accrual basis, revenues are $1,000,000; expenses are $950,000; and net income is $50,000. On the cash basis, revenues are $800,000; expenses are $980,000; resulting in a loss of $180,000. On the accrual basis balance sheet, assets are $1,170,000; liabilities are $870,000; leaving net assets of $300,000. On the cash basis balance sheet, however, the patient receivables, prepayments, and accounts payable are omitted, leaving assets of $920,000 and liabilities of $850.000. The difference in income is exaggerated because there are no beginning balances of receivables or payables in the first

period of a new business. In subsequent years, this difference will be smaller. On a monthly basis, wide differences will occur if billings fluctuate during the year. Because of the lag in collections, the month of highest collections often occurs in the month of lowest billings, and there is often a shortage of cash in the month of highest billings.

The statement of cash flows is the same for both bases of accounting because only cash is involved. In the cash basis statements, the net loss in the income statements ($180,000) is larger than the cash used by operations in the cash flow statement ($80,000) only because depreciation ($100,000) is included in the income statement, but does not involve cash. Because of receivables, payables, and other accrual accounts, there always will be differences between net income and cash flow from operations on the accrual basis. In the cash flow statement for the sample health system discussed earlier (see Exhibit 8–3), these accrual measurements were identified when cash flow from operations was computed by the indirect method.

Patient receivables, generally the major asset in physician group practices, are omitted from the balance sheet on the cash basis requiring that physician groups must provide supplemental information for creditors in a loan transaction, for buyers in the sale of the practice, and for physicians involved in the admission or withdrawal of a physician. This particularly is true when dealing with a party that has no experience with cash basis accounting.

These accrual and cash basis examples represent the extremes in the accounting measurements. In practice, few organizations use a full cash basis. Instead, most use a modified cash basis system that recognizes some accrual basis measurements (e.g., vacation pay) and some cash basis measurements. The modified cash basis reduces the differences between accrual and cash measurements, and it provides more consistent financial results.

SEGMENT OR RESPONSIBILITY CENTER REPORTING

Financial statements for external reporting are prepared for the organized health care delivery system as a whole. While these statements may provide creditors, other external users, and the board of directors with an overall picture of the health care system, they are not useful to operating management for evaluating financial performance. Operating management needs statements for each responsibility center in the organization, that is, for any organizational segment for which financial data are accumulated and reported. For example, the sample health system shows a net income of about $18 million for the entity as a whole. A study of the income statements of the various responsibility centers shows wide differences in incomes of individual responsibility centers, however, ranging from a net income of about $18 million to a net loss of about $17 million (Exhibit 8–7).

Types of Responsibility Centers

The identification of responsibility centers is the first step in determining the full cost of services to patients. There are three types of responsibility centers for the purposes of reporting financial information (Table 8–1):

1. Cost centers are responsibility centers that do not serve patients directly and, therefore, have no revenue. Only costs may be traced to cost centers, and they must be allocated to profit centers to generate the full cost of services to patients. They are evaluated based on their ability to minimize costs. Examples of cost centers include: administration, occupancy, medical records, food service, and laundry.

2. Profit or contribution centers are responsibility centers that perform a service directly to patients. Both revenues and costs directly related to the service provided to patients can be traced to profit centers. Costs of cost centers may be allocated to profit centers to generate a full cost for setting fees. Profit centers are evaluated on their ability to control costs and to generate a satisfactory income. Examples of profit centers are laboratory, radiology, pharmacy, surgery, patient rooms, and medical specialties.

3. Investment centers have responsibility for costs, revenues, and management of assets employed. The identification of investment centers is generally limited to an entire entity, such as the entire health care system, or a major segment such as a hospital, an ambulatory care center, or a physician group. In addition to evaluation based on cost containment or profitability, the investment center may be evaluated by the global measure of return on investment. These cost centers differ in the amount of financial information that may be traced to each one and they differ in the criteria by which performance can be measured.

An organized health care delivery system has a variety of responsibility centers. The entire system entity is an investment center that may be evaluated by return on investment, as well as by profitability and cost containment measures. The nine major responsibility centers of this system are all investment centers with responsibility for revenues, costs, and assets employed, except the corpo-

Exhibit 8–7 Sample Health System: Responsibility Center Operating Report ($000) (for the Year Ended December 31, 1998)

	Metrocare Medical Center								
	Metro General Hospital	Metro Children's Hospital	Support Services	Metro Hospital	Metrocare Health Services	Metrocare Physician Network	Urgent Care Centers	Other Medical Services	Metrocare Foundation
PATIENT SERVICE REVENUE									
Daily patient services—inpatient	$ 63,625	$ 6,545	—	$ 5,069	$—	$—	$—	$—	$—
Professional services—inpatient	81,709	10,956	—	19,282	—	1,020	—	—	—
Daily patient services—outpatient	1,456	628	—	332	—	—	3,209	—	—
Professional services—outpatient	75,896	20,844	—	41,191	—	64,355	—	—	—
Capitation	891	123	—	—	33,851	827	—	—	—
TOTAL	223,577	39,097	—	65,875	33,851	66,202	3,209	—	—
DEDUCTIONS FROM REVENUE									
Contractual adjustments	72,573	8,983	—	25,932	—	18,334	636	—	—
Charity care	2,889	836	—	520	—	104	—	—	—
TOTAL	75,462	9,819	—	26,452	—	18,438	636	—	—
NET PATIENT SERVICE REVENUE	148,115	29,278	—	39,422	33,851	47,764	2,573	—	—
OTHER OPERATING REVENUE									
Hospital services	688	168	1,446	937	785	2,114	—	—	—
Other	—	55	47	—	137	—	—	867	—
TOTAL	688	222	1,493	937	922	2,114	—	867	—
TOTAL OPERATING REVENUE	148,803	29,501	1,493	40,359	34,773	49,878	2,573	867	—
OPERATING EXPENSES									
Salaries and wages	48,065	12,693	9,420	13,480	11,408	33,711	1,804	37	—
Employee benefits	3,905	992	7,970	2,596	4,541	7,294	245	3	—
Supplies	20,901	1,538	2,248	5,846	735	4,936	149	10	—
Depreciation	10,541	817	782	2,217	3,422	2,543	191	340	—
Interest	8,085	—	—	1,075	—	126	—	392	—
Provision for bad debts	4,942	1,002	—	1,226	23	2,275	138	—	—
Corporate office services	32,620	6,838	(22,365)	3,177	(25,645)	4,934	210	45	—
Other expenses	2,734	4,277	3,563	3,826	44,843	10,733	869	290	—
TOTAL	131,795	28,157	1,618	33,442	39,328	66,553	3,606	1,117	—
INCOME (LOSS) FROM OPERATIONS	17,009	1,344	(125)	6,917	(4,554)	(16,675)	(1,034)	(250)	—
NONOPERATING REVENUE									
Unrestricted gifts	571	3,109	134	18	3	—	—	—	(510)
Income on investments	746	(17)	(11)	130	12,679	—	—	—	2,429
Other income/(loss)	88	—	—	(1)	(3,873)	—	—	67	1
TOTAL	1,405	3,092	123	147	8,809	—	—	67	1,921
EXCESS OF REVENUES	$ 18,414	$ 4,436	$(2)	$ 7,064	$4,255	$(16,675)	$(1,034)	$(183)	$1,921
Assets Employed	306,305	41,142	—	34,330	226,963	66,043	2,455	3,047	36,697

Source: Anonymous.

Table 8–1 Types of Responsibility Centers

Type	Examples	Nonfinancial Measures of Performance	Traceability of Financial Information	Financial Measures of Performance	Evaluation Criterion
Cost center	Corporate supports, administration, occupancy, medical records, laundry, food service	Time spent, resources used, units of output	Total costs, costs per unit of output	Amount of costs: actual vs. budget, actual vs. previous period	Minimize costs; minimize dollars of cost per unit of activity
Profit or contribution center	Laboratory, radiology, pharmacy, surgery, patient rooms, medical specialties	Number of patients served, time spent, resources used, units of output	Total revenue, total costs, profit or contribution	Amount contributed by responsibility center to cover common costs and provide a profit	Maximize profit or contribution, maximize profit per unit of activity, control costs
Investment center	Entire system, hospital, ambulatory surgery center, medical group	Number of patients served, time spent, resources used, units of output	Total revenue, total costs, profit or contribution, assets employed	Return on assets employed, also measures cited above	Maximize return on assets employed

rate support center, which is a cost center that provides services to other entities in the system (see Exhibit 8–7). The physician network involves a number of physician group practices, each of which could be identified as an investment center.

For planning, control, and evaluation of their operations, each of the nine responsibility centers has identified a number of profit and cost centers. For example, one of the hospitals has identified 78 responsibility centers. Of those, 43 are cost centers that provide services to the 35 profit centers. In each profit center, the full cost of the various services provided to patients includes the direct costs traceable to the profit center, as well as the indirect costs of the other cost centers that support the profit center. The costs allocated from supporting cost centers to a profit center should be based on the quantity of resources used rather than on an arbitrary allocation process. Much of the regulatory reporting involves the identification and management of costs in responsibility centers.

Evaluation of Responsibility Centers

A comprehensive budget provides the framework for setting priorities, allocating resources, and monitoring financial performance. It includes an operating budget (also called profit plan), a cash budget, a projected balance sheet, and a capital budget (Figure 8–1). The comprehensive budget for the entire health care organization originates in the budgets of the various segments or responsibility centers. Its development is an iterative process, in which the results of the combining process repeatedly are compared with the goals and objectives of the entire health care organization.

The heart of any financial planning and control system is the operating budget, for it reflects the planned activity levels, the pricing or fee structure, and the cost structure of a responsibility center of the health care entity. The operating budget may be considered a static budget, in that it establishes only one level of activity at the beginning of the budget year. The activity level in the operating budget drives the rest of the comprehensive budget, however.

Although the operating budget may serve as a valuable planning tool, it may be misleading as a performance evaluation tool if the actual activity has varied significantly from the planned level of activity. For example, a hospital projected 1,000 patient days with average daily fees of $1,000. The fixed expenses were projected to be $700,000 for the year, and variable expenses were estimated to be $250 per patient day. (Variable expenses change in direct proportion to changes in activity, but fixed expenses do not change as activity changes.) Actual revenue during the year was $1,090,000, as the hospital incurred 1,100 patient days; fixed expenses were $720,000, and variable expenses were $300,000.

In Exhibit 8–8, the actual operating results are compared with two budgets: the operating budget at the level projected at the beginning of the year and a performance budget based upon the actual level of operations. The operating budget projected an income of $50,000, while the income statement showed an actual income of $70,000, a favorable variance of $20,000. This is misleading, because the variances represent an increase in volume, which was favorable; and changes in price and spending, which were unfavorable. The income should be higher than $50,000 when there are 10 percent more patient days than planned, but it is not possible to determine how much higher it should be with only a static budget. A comparison of actual results to the static operating budget does not make it possible to separate the effect of increased

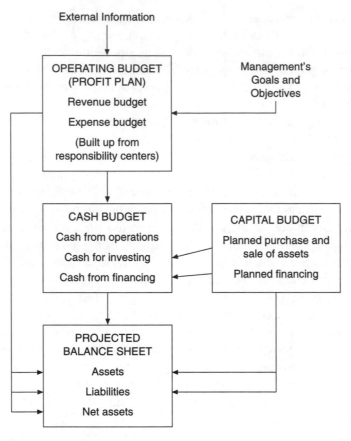

Figure 8–1 Comprehensive Budget

volume from the effect of price and spending variances.

A performance budget, prepared after the period, shows what revenues, expenses, and income should be for this hospital at 1,100 patient days (see Exhibit 8–8). With many fixed expenses, a small change in volume results in a large change in income. The performance budget indicates that income should have been $125,000 if the hospital had maintained its fee structure and its cost structure. Revenue should have increased by $100,000 (100 days × $1,000); the variable expenses should have increased by $25,000 (100 days × $250), but fixed expenses should have remained unchanged. According to a compari-

son of the actual results to the performance budget, the differences now reflect only price and spending variances. Apparently, fees were reduced, and both variable and fixed expenses were higher than they should have been. A summary of the difference between income in the operating budget and actual income follows:

Budgeted income in operating budget	$50,000
Variance due to volume ($125,000 – $50,000)	$75,000
Variance due to fee reduction ($1,100,000 – $1,090,000)	(10,000)

Variance due to spending
($1,020,000 – $975,000) (45,000) 20,000
Actual income $70,000

This very simple example shows that the operating budget may be misleading in an attempt to evaluate actual performance when there has been a significant change in volume. When there is a large change in volume, a difference in income will depend upon the cost structure—how much is fixed and how much is variable. This is referred to as operating leverage.

Exhibit 8–9 presents the operating report for one of the sample system's hospitals. The operating budget reflects management's estimates of activity, the pricing structure, and the cost structure planned for 1998. Patient service revenue was projected to be about $215 million; deductions from revenue, $79 million; other operating revenue, $2 million; operating expenses, $98 million; allocated corporate services, $34 million; and nonoperating revenue, $800,000, resulting in an excess of revenue over expenses of about $6 million.

The performance budget reflects the pricing structure and cost structure for the actual activity levels. It appears that total patient

Exhibit 8–8 Comparison of Actual to Budget

COMPARISON OF ACTUAL TO OPERATING BUDGET

	Operating Budget	Actual	Variances
Patient days	1,000	1,100	100
Patient revenue	$1,000,000	$1,090,000	$90,000
Operating expenses:			
Variable expenses	250,000	300,000	(50,000)
Fixed expenses	700,000	720,000	(20,000)
Total	950,000	1,020,000	(70,000)
Operating income	$ 50,000	$ 70,000	$20,000

COMPARISON OF ACTUAL TO PERFORMANCE BUDGET

	Operating Budget	Performance Budget	Actual	Variances
Patient days	1,000	1,100	1,100	0
Patient revenue	$1,000,000	$1,100,000	$1,090,000	$(10,000)
Operating expenses:				
Variable expenses	250,000	275,000	300,000	(25,000)
Fixed expenses	700,000	700,000	720,000	(20,000)
Total	950,000	975,000	1,020,000	(45,000)
Operating income	$ 50,000	$ 125,000	$ 70,000	$(55,000)

Exhibit 8–9 Sample Health System: Hospital Operating Report ($000) (for the Year Ended December 31, 1998)

	Operating Budget	Performance Budget	Actual	% Change Due to Activity	Variance from Performance Budget	
					Amount	Percent
					(unf)	– = unf
Patient service revenue	$215,624	$221,107	$223,577	3%	$2,470	1%
Deductions from revenue	79,269	81,280	75,462	3%	5,818	7%
Net patient service revenue	136,355	139,827	148,115	3%	8,288	6%
Other operating revenue	1,795	1,795	1,646	0%	(149)	–8%
Total operating revenue	138,150	141,622	149,761	3%	8,139	6%
Operating expenses						
Salaries and wages	46,351	48,207	48,065	4%	142	0%
Supplies	19,261	19,764	20,901	3%	(1,138)	–6%
Professional fees	3,129	3,198	2,807	2%	391	12%
Employee benefits	3,859	4,001	3,905	4%	96	2%
Lease and rental fees	386	386	519	0%	(133)	–35%
Interest	8,653	8,653	8,085	0%	568	7%
Depreciation and amortization	10,689	10,689	10,541	0%	148	1%
Provision for bad debts	4,977	5,104	4,942	3%	162	3%
Other operating costs	1,191	1,191	(592)	0%	1,783	150%
TOTAL	98,497	101,193	99,174	3%	2,019	2%
Income (loss) from operations	39,653	40,429	50,587	2%	10,158	25%
Allocated corporate services	34,140	34,397	32,620	1%	1,777	5%
Net income	5,513	6,032	17,967	9%	11,935	198%
Nonoperating revenue	837	837	834	0%	(3)	–0%
Excess of revenues over expenses	$6,350	$6,869	$18,801	8%	$11,932	174%

Source: Anonymous.

revenue increased about 3 percent. Expenses with some variable component increased about 3 percent, labor-related cost increased about 4 percent, and allocated corporate services increased only 1 percent. Expenses that were only fixed remained unchanged. The excess of revenue over expenses in the performance budget is about the same as that in the operating budget.

Except for small items (e.g., lease and rental fees), the variances from the performance budget are nearly all favorable and not very large. The combination of a 6 percent favorable variance in total operating revenue, a 2 percent favorable variance in operating expenses, and a favorable variance in allocated corporate costs led to an actual net income that was nearly three times the net income in the performance budget. Because the budgeted net income was very low, about $6 million, the small variances in revenues and costs resulted in a net income of about $18 million.

A performance budget, also called a flexible budget, is necessary when activity varies significantly from that estimated for the operating budget. In this situation, the operating budget is not a relevant basis on which to evaluate performance.

ANALYSIS OF FINANCIAL STATEMENTS

Creditors, long-term lenders, governing boards, regulators, and donors or investors are vitally concerned with changes in the financial status of the health care organizations with which they are associated. This is true whether the organization is not-for-profit or investor-owned. Estaugh noted the convergence of fiscal focus of both not-for-profit and for-profit hospitals: "Managers in both sectors are equally anxious about generating capital to secure a better future for their institutions."[1] In order to do this, they must not only achieve continued profitability, but also maintain short-term liquidity and long-term solvency.

Among the important tools used to evaluate an organization's financial health are financial ratios. Although the ratios themselves do not provide answers, they alert their user to areas that require deeper analysis. A single ratio for a single period gathers meaning when a comparison with the same measures for previous years reveals a trend or indicates compliance with an industry standard, for example.

Measures of Profitability

Maintaining profitability in a health care organization is important for a number of reasons:

- If operations are to provide funding for the expansion of patient service capacity, those operations must be profitable. Even at the break-even point, a health care organization will not be able to maintain current capacity because inflation has resulted in higher replacement costs.
- Other than donations or subsidies, profits are the only way to build up owners' equity (net assets). Increased owners' equity (net assets) will lead to a better bond or mortgage rating when it is necessary to finance expansion with long-term debt. This will decrease future interest charges and, hence, overall debt service costs.
- A for-profit organization must achieve profitability to pay dividends and to provide growth for stockholders.

The following three profitability ratios— profit margin, return on assets employed, and return on equity—are computed from the sample health system's financial statements.

The profit margin indicates how much of each revenue dollar is net income. To understand changes in this ratio over time, it is necessary to examine changes in revenues and expenses. Profit margin is computed as follows (see Exhibit 8–2):

Profit Margin = Net Income / Total Revenue
= $18,484 / $294,934 = 6.27%

The return on assets employed provides an indication of how much each dollar of assets earns on an after-tax income basis during a given period of time. A global measurement, return on assets, encompasses all financial factors of an organization: revenues, expenses, and assets. It is the basic measure of an investment center. Obviously, not-for-profit organizations that own no for-profit affiliates need not deduct income taxes to arrive at net income. For either for-profit or not-for-profit health care organizations, if the "bottom line" is negative, assets and owners' equity are declining. (See Exhibits 8–1 and 8–2.)

Return on Assets = Net Income / Average
Total Assets = $18,484 / (($417,144 +
$457,938) / 2) = 4.22%

Overemphasis on this ratio may cause managers to postpone investments in new assets and other important, but discretionary, expenditures, such as maintenance or training. Return on assets may be broken into a profitability component (profit margin) and an asset management component (asset turnover) that will provide management with a better insight into the causes of changes in this ratio. Return on assets may be computed as follows (see Exhibits 8–1 and 8–2):

Return on Assets = Profit Margin ×
Asset Turnover

Return on Assets = (Net Income / Revenue)
× (Revenue / Average Total Assets) =
($18,484 / $294,934) × (($294,934 /
(($417,144 + $457,938) / 2)) =
6.27% × .67 = 4.20%

Given the components of profit margin and asset turnover that make up return on assets, there are four major ways to improve profitability: (1) Increase revenues by more than expenses, (2) decrease expenses by more than a decrease in revenue, (3) generate more dollars of revenue while maintaining or increasing the net margin, and (4) decrease assets employed.

Traditionally, investors have placed more emphasis on return on equity than on return on assets, as owners' equity represents the owners' interest in the organization. Return on equity is computed as follows (see Exhibits 8–1 and 8–2):

Return on Equity = Net Income / Owners'
Equity or Net Assets = $18,484 /
(($204,177 + $238,477) / 2) = 8.35%

In summary, profitability ratios attempt to measure an organization's ability to generate sufficient funds from operations to provide an acceptable return to owners. Although a not-for-profit organization does not have owners in the sense of for-profit organizations, it must maintain itself. It must replace assets as they wear out, replace old technology with new, and sustain some rate of growth.

Measures of Short-Term Liquidity Risks

External parties who are concerned with the financial health of an organization usually compute financial ratios based on the historical data in the financial statements to determine the organization's debt-paying ability. Long-term lenders may require that the health care organization maintain minimum ratios as an assurance that the organization can meet current interest and principal payments. Bankers and other short-term creditors also look to a number of financial ratios to make decisions about granting credit. There are several useful short-term liquidity risk ratios: the current ratio, the average days receivables outstanding, and the cash flow from operations compared with the average current liabilities.

The current ratio is computed by dividing current assets by current liabilities. Although this ratio may be "improved" on the date of the balance sheet by a number of ingenious window dressing techniques, empirical studies have found it to have strong predictive power in bond issue defaults and bankruptcy.[2] (See Exhibit 8–1.)

Current Ratio = Current Assets / Current Liabilities = $174,406 / $62,236 = 2.80 to 1

The system's current ratio appears to be very satisfactory as of the balance sheet date. It indicates that the system has $2.80 of current assets for each $1.00 of current liabilities. Comparison should be made with past years and with standard ratios for the health care industry.

One of the current assets that is a step away from being converted to cash is the amount of patient receivables. On the balance sheet date, this amount is divided by the average amount of patient revenue per day over the period. The result is the estimate of time to convert receivables into cash. (See Exhibits 8–1 and 8–2.)

Days Receivable Outstanding = Patient Receivables / Patient Revenue / 365 days =

= $47,508 / ($288,322/365) = 60 days

The system's days in receivables averaged 60 days in 1998. Because several different entities are involved (e.g., hospitals, physician groups), this aggregate number may be difficult to interpret. It should be compared with the patient payment policies established by the system.

The ratio of operating cash flows to current liabilities in financially healthy organizations tends to be .4 or more in financially healthy organizations.[3] (See Exhibits 8–1 and 8–3.)

Operating Cash Flows to Current Liabilities = Operating Cash Flow / Average Current Liabilities = $39,010 / (($48,438 + $62,236)/2) = .70

In summary, the system's current financial position appears to be very strong. A current ratio of 2.80 to 1, 60 days of patient receivables outstanding, and an operating cash flow to current liabilities of .7 all indicate financial strength.

Measures of Long-Term Liquidity Risks

As indicated earlier, financial ratios based on the financial statements are very important to both external creditors and investors of health care organizations or any other firm using the capital markets. Four ratios are of particular importance to long-term creditors and owners: the financial leverage ratio, the debt/equity ratio, the debt/plant ratio, and the debt service ratio.

The financial leverage ratio is a comparison of the total assets employed in relation to the total capital provided by owners' equity. The point of financial leverage is that the system is using long-term debt to finance $219 million of assets. Interest payments on this debt already have been deducted in arriving at the $18 million in net income, leaving the entire $18 million of net income as a return on owners' equity, which represents the nondebt portion of the capital. (See Exhibit 8–1.)

Financial Leverage Ratio = Total Assets / Total Owners' Equity (Net Assets) = $457,938 / $238,477 = 1.92

A simple explanation of the difference between return on assets and return on equity is that the total asset amount is used to compute the return on assets, and the owners' equity amount is used to compute the return on owners' equity. The return on equity is higher than the return on assets (8.35 percent as compared to 4.22 percent) because this system is using financial leverage. It is using debt to finance $219 million of its assets. Return on equity may be reconciled with return on assets as follows:

$$\text{Return on Equity} =$$
$$\text{Return on Assets} \times \text{Financial Leverage} =$$
$$4.22\% \times 1.92 \text{ times} = 8.10\%$$

(Note: The difference between 8.35% and 8.10% is due to rounding errors.)

The good news about using financial leverage is that the return on equity is magnified when debt-financed assets are earning more than the after-tax cost of interest expense. If debt-financed assets are earning less than their fixed interest charges, however, decreases in return on equity also are magnified. This is bad news for the owners' profitability and risk position.

The debt/equity and the debt/plant ratios are of particular interest to present and potential long-term lenders. In their debt covenants, lenders often insist that the ratio of long-term debt to owner's equity be maintained at less than 1 to 1, that is, debt must be less than equity. A higher ratio indicates that the long-term creditors have provided more money than the owners to finance the organization and that the cushion for owners to absorb losses before they affect lenders is less than 50 percent. Lenders also are focused on a financial safety cushion when they ask for a limit on the amount of long-term debt as a percentage of property, plant, and equipment (see Exhibit 8–1).

Long-Term Debt / Owners' Equity Ratio = Long-Term Debt / Owners' Equity (Net Assets) = $141,104 / $238,477 = .59 to 1

Long-Term Debt / Plant Ratio = Long-Term Debt / Property, Plant, and Equipment = $141,104 / $189,018 = 74.7%

This system's debt/equity ratio is much less than 1 to 1, but its debt/plant ratio appears a bit high. If these ratios were close to the critical limit in the lending agencies, they could deter growth of both plant and debt. In the balance sheet, however, this system is carrying investments in an amount more than $50 million larger than the previous year and a limited use asset available to the board for future use of more than $43 million. If these funds are held for future plant or equipment acquisition, both amounts may be used in interpreting the plant ratio.

The debt service ratio is important for both short-term risk evaluation and long-term solvency. Current interest and principal installments require immediate cash payments when they fall due. The ratio divides cash flow available to pay interest and principal during the period by the required interest and principal payment amounts. (See Exhibit 8–3).

Debt Service Ratio = (Cash Flow from Operations + Interest Payments + Payments on Long-Term Debt Principal) / (Interest Payments + Payments on Long-Term Debt Principal) = ($39,010 + $10,130 + $4,910) / ($10,130 + $4,910) = 3.59 to 1

The debt service ratio appears very satisfactory for this system, as the cash flow available to service the long-term debt is 3.59 times the amount required.

Profitability of Segments of the Organized Delivery System

The ratios computed to this point have concerned the overall system from an external vantage point. Operating management must evaluate individual segments or responsibility centers, however. Because the segments identified in Exhibit 8–7 are investment centers (with one exception), both profit margin and return on assets may be used as evaluation measures.

For the business segments in Exhibit 8–7, the profit margins are computed as follows:

General Hospital =
$18,414 / $148,803 = 12.37%

Children's Hospital =
$4,436 / $29,501 = 15.04%

Hospital =
$7,064 / $40,359 = 17.50%

Health Services =
$4,255 / $34,773 = 12.24%

Physician Network =
$(16,675) / $49,878 = (33.43%)

Urgent Care Centers =
$(1,034) / $2,573 = (40.19%)

Other Medical Services =
$(183) / $867 = (21.11%)

The wide range of profit margins for the individual segments explains the low overall profit margin of 6.27 percent for this system.

Return on assets employed for the profitable segments is as follows:

Return on Assets =
Profit Margin × Asset Turnover

General Hospital =
($18,414 / $148,803) × ($148,803 / $306,305) = 12.37% × .49 times = 6.06%

Children's Hospital =
($4,436 / $29,501) × ($29,501 / 41,142) = 15.04% × .72 times = 10.83%

Hospital =
($7,064 / $40,359) × ($40,359 / $34,330) = 17.50% × 1.18 times = 20.65%

Health Services = ($4,255 / $34,773) × ($34,773 / $226,963) = 12.24% × .15 times = 1.84%

Acquisition of new assets will cause the return on assets to drop; however, tracking margin and asset turnover separately should show that the asset turnover falls, but the profit margin remains the same. Over time, the separation will provide the manager with a better explanation for increases or decreases in the return on assets.

In summary, a health care organization can evaluate how well it has carried out its financial management strategies by computing and evaluating a number of financial ratios. The principal purpose of a financial ratio is to facilitate comparisons of relationships over time in the same entity, or with other health care entities or norms. Although there are many possible ratios, they tend to fall into three critical areas of analysis: profitability, liquidity, and solvency.

FINANCIAL MANAGEMENT PRACTICES IN HEALTH CARE ORGANIZATIONS

The term *benchmarking* is often used to refer to the continuous process of measuring products, services, and activities against the best levels of performance. To determine these best levels of performance, an organization may use internal benchmarking information or external benchmarking information gathered from similar organizations or from consulting firms that offer benchmarking services. Benchmarking involves both financial and nonfinancial data. Financial information, such as the ratios computed earlier, are more important at the level of the entity or major responsibility center. At lower levels in the organization, nonfinancial information becomes more useful.

The hospital industry has a number of firms that specialize in producing benchmark information for departments, services, products, and activities undertaken by hospitals. Using cost information submitted by hospitals to various U.S. regulatory bodies, these consultants generate reports that compare a hospital with numerous other U.S. hospitals. Hospital administrators use these reports to direct attention to areas with above average costs. The reliability of individual hospital cost data used in these benchmark reports varies widely, as many hospitals have not refined their cost accounting systems. In addition, the cost allocation process that a hospital uses greatly affects benchmarking information. Nonfinancial factors that need to be analyzed include perceived quality of service to patients, success rate of procedures and operations, and satisfaction of employees and physicians. Benchmarking information is a valuable source for developing best practices within individual organizations. Health care organizations that have no counterparts with which to share information can develop internal benchmarks and identify practices that facilitate services in the most cost-effective manner.

Another tool available to hospital administrators for measuring the total business unit performance is a balanced scorecard, a set of performance measures and targets that reflect an organization's performance with respect to its various stakeholders (e.g., customers, employees, business partners, community members). The word *balanced* is used because for many years, performance was measured primarily from a financial or cost-containment perspective. During the late 1980s and early 1990s, however, the focus of many organizations shifted from the financial perspective only to include quality and customer concerns. The balanced scorecard concept is an attempt to balance the focus of an organization between financial and other relevant performance measures. Health care organizations typically have multiple objectives, so balanced scorecards that incorporate both financial and nonfinancial performance measurements are especially useful.

The balanced scorecard translates mission and strategy into objectives and performance measures from four perspectives:[4]

1. The financial perspective, as discussed, continues with emphasis upon operating margin and return on assets employed.
2. In the customer perspective, organizations identify the customer and market segments in which they expect to compete and devise measures of performance for these targeted segments. The performance measures emphasize customer satisfaction, customer retention, new customer acquisition, and market share in the targeted segments.
3. The internal business perspective focuses on the processes within the organization that will have the greatest impact on delivering value to the customer.
4. The learning and growth perspective targets the development of people, information technology, and systems necessary for delivering value to the customers and other stakeholders in the organization.

FINANCIAL STATEMENTS IN REVIEW

This section discussed the preparation, content, and evaluation of conventional financial statements. The balance sheet presents the financial position of an entity at a given point of time. It presents the assets, liabilities, and owners' equity of the entity. The operating statement measures the revenues and expenses and resulting income in providing services to patients. The cash flow statement identifies changes in cash due to operating, investing, and financing activities. Cash and accrual bases of measurements for physician groups were demonstrated and discussed. Financial statements of an actual integrated health care organization were presented.

It is necessary, for operating management, to evaluate financial performance for the various responsibility centers in the organization. Responsibility centers may be classified as cost centers that are evaluated on how well costs were contained, as profit centers that are evaluated on the amount of profit earned, or investment centers that are evaluated on the return on assets employed. The concept of a performance or flexible budget was used to evaluate performance when actual activity differs significantly from planned activity.

Analysis of financial statements was examined from the perspective of ratio analysis. Ratios analyzing profitability, liquidity, and solvency were computed and discussed. Ratios gain more meaning when they are compared with data from past periods and with data from similar organizations.

In an organized health care delivery system, the board of directors and senior management determine the corporate strategy and set the goals and objectives to be followed by the organization and its various entities. In a decentralized organization, decisions consistent with the corporate strategies, goals, and objectives are made at the segment or responsibility center level.

Decisions fall into two general classifications. Long-range decisions involve the addition or replacement of capacity with long lives, while short-range decisions involve the use of existing capacity. The information needs and decision criteria for long-range and short-range decisions are very different.

LONG-RANGE DECISIONS

One of the most common examples of a health care organization's long-range decision is the acquisition of equipment or buildings. Because of this investment, the capacity of the organization changes, and the delivery of health care is more comprehensive. The health care organization is able to provide a greater range of services or, in some way, has the capacity to do something that was not previously possible.

Most of the information needed to measure the benefits and costs attributable to long-range decisions cannot be generated from the accounting system for two reasons. First, the decision relates to the future and often involves the acquisition of unique assets. Unless the new activity resembles an activity in the past, information about the past obtained from the accounting system will not be relevant to the decision. Second, because of the long periods of time affected by the decision, the health care organization should be concerned with cash flows—not accounting measurements of income. It is important to know when cash is invested and consequently unavailable for other purposes and when cash will be recovered and therefore available for other purposes. Both the amount and timing of cash flows are important in measuring the benefits and costs of a long-range decision. The length of time involved in long-range decisions makes it essential to take the time value of money into account.

Concept of Time Value of Money

The time value of money is the difference in value between having a dollar in hand today and receiving a dollar at some future time. As a result of the long period of time involved in most long-range decisions, it may take several years to realize fully the benefits of most long-range decisions. Table 8–2 illustrates the time value of money by showing the growth of $1,000 invested at the beginning of year 1 and earning interest at the rate of 10 percent compounded annually.

Two concepts are important in explaining the time value of money: future value and present value. Future value is the amount to which a given amount of cash invested now will grow at the end of a given period of time when compounded at a given rate of interest. In Table 8–2, for example, the future value of $1,000, compounded at 10 percent, is $1,100 at the end of 1 year, $1,210 at the end of 2 years, and $1,331 at the end of 3 years.

A second concept involving time value of money is to value all cash flows in terms of the present time—present value. Present value is the amount of money that must be invested now to accumulate to a given amount of money at some future date when compounded at some given rate of interest. In the example, $1,000 is the present value of $1,100 to be received at the end of 1 year, compounded at 10 percent.

Future and present values allow the comparison of any two or more dollar amounts of cash paid or received at different points of time. The two amounts can be measured in terms of future value (i.e., what they are worth at some future time), or they can be measured in terms of present value (i.e., what

they are worth today). Because an investment is being made today, however, it is much easier to understand and to work with present values than to deal in future values.

Present Value Tables

For the concept of present value to be useful, it is necessary to have a way of computing the present value of any amount of cash at any future point. The present value of $1 may be computed by dividing each present value by its future value. For example, the present value of $1 to be received at the end of Year 1 is $.909 ($1,000 / $1,100). This present value factor may then be multiplied by any amount to be received 1 year from now. In Table 8–3, the present value of $1.00 compounded at 10 percent is computed for each of 3 years. These present value factors are used for single payments or receipts of cash.

Application of Present Values in Decision Making

If it is necessary to earn 10 percent on an investment, which of the following investments is acceptable?

1. Invest $2,000 now and receive $2,400 at the end of 2 years.
2. Invest $2,000 now and receive $1,200 at the end of Year 1, $800 at the end of Year 2, and $400 at the end of Year 3.
3. Invest $2,000 now and receive $400 at the end of Year 1, $800 at the end of Year 2, and $1,200 at the end of Year 3.
4. Invest $2,000 now and receive $800 at the end of each of the next 3 years.

All four investments involve $2,000 of cash outflows and $2,400 of cash inflows. Timing of the inflows, however, is different in each case (Exhibit 8–10).

To earn exactly a 10 percent return, the present value of cash inflows and cash out-

---

Table 8–2 Compounding Interest To Determine Present Value

	Investment at Beginning of Period	Interest (10%)	Investment at End of Period
Year 1	$1,000	$100	$1,100
Year 2	$1,100	$110	$1,210
Year 3	$1,210	$121	$1,331

Table 8–3 Development of Present Value Factors

Period of Time	Present Value/ Future Value	Present Value of $1	Present Value of an Annuity of $1
One year	$1,000/$1,100	.909	.909
Two years	$1,000/$1,210	.826	1.735 (.909 + .826)
Three years	$1,000/$1,331	.751	2.486 (1.735 + .751)

flows must be equal. For Investment A, the present value of cash inflows is only $1,982, while the present value of cash outflows is $2,000. Therefore, Investment A earns less than 10 percent and should be rejected. For Investment B, the present value of cash in-

flows is $2,052, while the present value of cash outflows is only $2,000. Therefore, Investment B earns more than 10 percent and should be accepted. Like Investment A, the cash inflows of Investments C and D are less than the cash outflows, and both should be

---

Exhibit 8–10 Present Value of Investments

INVESTMENT A
Present value of cash outflows $(1,000)
Present value of cash inflows:
  Year 1—$0 × .909 = $ —
  Year 2—$1,200 × .826 = $991
  Year 3—$0 × .751 = $ — $ 991

INVESTMENT B
Present value of cash outflows $(1,000)
Present value of cash inflows:
  Year 1—$600 × .909 = $545
  Year 2—$400 × .826 = $330
  Year 3—$200 × .751 = $150 $ 1,025

INVESTMENT C
Present value of cash outflows $(1,000)
Present value of cash inflows:
  Year 1—$200 × .909 = $182
  Year 2—$400 × .826 = $330
  Year 3—$600 × .751 = $451 $ 963

INVESTMENT D
Present value of cash outflows $(1,000)
Present value of cash inflows:
  Year 1—$400 × .909 = $364
  Year 2—$400 × .826 = $330
  Year 3—$400 × .751 = $300 $ 994

rejected. In each case, the cash flow for each year was multiplied by the appropriate present value factor.

An easier calculation is possible for an annuity, when the stream of future cash flows is equal and occurs at equal intervals of time. The present value of an annuity may be computed in either of two ways. First, with the present value factors for $1, the cash flow for each year may be multiplied by its appropriate cash flow factor. Second, with the present value factor for an annuity of $1 (see right-hand column in Table 8–3), the present value factor for Year 3 may be multiplied by one periodic amount in the annuity ($800 × 2.486 = $1,989). The present value factors for an annuity are determined by cumulating the present value factors for single amounts.

The process of computing the present value of future cash flows is called *discounting*. Amounts to be received or paid in the future are discounted to their present values. This process is often called *discounted cash flow analysis*. All discounted cash flow techniques use the same basic approach in identifying cash flows and computing present values; they differ only in the way that the results are presented.

Long-Range Decision Rule

A long-range decision rule may now be formulated. *A long-range decision is favorable if the incremental discounted cash inflows attributable to the investment proposal are equal to or greater than the incremental discounted cash outflows attributable to the investment.*[5]

Techniques That Satisfy the Long-Range Decision Rule

Three techniques satisfy the long-range decision rule. They use the same data and tools of analysis, but they vary in the way that the

decision criteria are stated. In the first technique, discounted cash outflows are deducted from discounted cash inflows; the difference is called net present value. If the net present value is zero, the project has earned exactly the predefined rate of return used as the discount rate and should be accepted. A positive net present value shows that the project earned more than the predetermined rate of return and should be accepted; a negative net present value shows that the project earned less than the predetermined rate of return and should be rejected. The net present value of the investments in Exhibit 8–10 are Investment A, ($18) [$1,982 – ($2,000)]; Investment B, $52 [$2,052 – ($2,000)]; Investment C, ($74) [$1,926 – ($2,000)]; and Investment D, ($11) [$1,989 – ($2,000)]. Only Investment B has a positive net present value and should be accepted.

When the second method, the profitability index or discounted benefit cost ratio, is used, the discounted cash inflows are divided by the discounted cash outflows to show the dollars of discounted benefits for each dollar of discounted cost. The profitability indexes for each of the investments in Exhibit 8–10 are Investment A, $0.991 [$1,982 / $2,000]; Investment B, $1.025 [$2,052 / $2,000]; Investment C, $.963 [$1,926 / $2,000]; and Investment D, $.994 [$1,989 / $2,000]. Only Investment B will return more than $1.00 of discounted benefits for each $1.00 of discounted costs.

The third method, the internal rate of return method, involves computing the actual rate of return by the investment instead of using a predefined rate of return. A minimum acceptable rate of return, the cutoff rate, must be set. Any investment project earning less than the cutoff rate should be rejected; any investment project earning at or above the cutoff rate should be accepted. The internal rate of return may be computed in one of two ways, depending on the nature of the cash flows. For example, what is the internal rate of return for a piece of equipment with an initial cost of $31,270 and annual cash inflows of $10,000 for 5 years? This approach involves two steps. First, determine the present value factor that equates the initial cash inflow and the stream of cash outflows ($31,270 = $10,000 × 3.127). Second, find the present value factor computed in the first step in Appendix 8–A, Present Value of an Annuity of $1 in the 5-year row. The present value factor of 3.127 is found in the 8-percent column and the 5-year row, indicating an internal rate of return of 8 percent. If the computed present value factor falls between two values in the table, it will be necessary to estimate the actual rate of return by interpolating between the two columns in the table. If the future cash inflows are not in a single amount (as in Investment A) or in an annuity (as in Investment D), a trial and error method must be used. When the net present value is zero, the internal rate of return is exactly equal to the predefined discount rate. To determine the internal rate of return, it is necessary to compute this at different rates until a net present value of zero is achieved. This can be a very tedious process. An easier approach is to use the internal rate of return function on a computer spreadsheet. Exhibit 8–11 illustrates the three methods with Excel on the basis of an investment of $31,270 and annual cash inflows of $10,000 for 5 years.

Information Relevant to Long-Range Decisions

Data needed to apply the long-range decision rule are the amount and timing of cash outflows, the amount and timing of cash inflows, and a discount rate to measure the time value of money.

Relevant cash outflows are incremental cash outflows over the life of the project that are directly traceable to the investment, regardless of what they are called. Cash outflows generally involve a large initial cash outflow for the acquisition of the asset and include maintenance, income taxes, and other cash outflows traceable to the project. Additional working capital to support the increased activity must be included as cash outflows as they occur and treated as cash inflows as they are recovered. When an investment decision involves any non-cash resources, such as present equipment, presently owned by the organization, the relevant "cost" is the cash value of the asset, not the book value or the balance of undepreciated cost carried in the accounting records.

Relevant cash inflows are the incremental cash inflows over the life of the investment, regardless of what the particular cash inflow is called. All cash inflows, including cash from service to patients, annual cost savings from new equipment, and estimated salvage value from the disposal of the asset at the end of its estimated useful life are treated as cash inflows.

In not-for-profit health care organizations or in physician practices that have as a goal the paying of no income taxes, taxes are not relevant to any decision. For-profit organizations must be concerned with income taxes, however. Any income taxes paid as a result of a long-range decision must be considered a cash outflow. The amount of taxes to be paid in a given year will be affected by depreciation of the assets acquired, as well as cash inflows and cash outflows from the operation of the asset.

The tax code is very complex. The amount of depreciation allowed for recovery of an expenditure for long-lived assets depends on three factors:

1. depreciation method. The tax code provides a specified schedule based on the

Exhibit 8–11 Discounted Cash Flow Analysis Using a Spreadsheet

	A	B	C	D
1				
2				
3				
4	Period	Cash Flows		NET PRESENT VALUE
5				Net present value of future cash flows less investment
6	0 (now)	$(31,270)		=NPV(Discount rate, Range of future cash flows) / Investment
7	1	$10,000		=NPV(.10,B7:B11)+B6
8	2	$10,000		=37,908 – 31,270 = $6,638
9	3	$10,000		
10	4	$10,000		PROFITABILITY INDEX
11	5	$10,000		Net present value of future cash flows divided by investment
12				=NPV(Discount rate, Range of future cash flows) / Investment
13				=NPV(.10,B7:B11) / B6
14				=37,908 / 31,270 = $1.21 per dollar of discounted investment
15				
16				INTERNAL RATE OF RETURN
17				Rate of return that produces a zero net present value
18				=IRR(Range of all cash flows, Guess rate)
19				=IRR(B6:B11,.10) = 18%
20				
21	Note: The NPV function computes the net present value of future cash flows. It assumes
22	the first flow is at the end of Period 1. Therefore, it is necessary to deduct the investment
23	from the present value of the future cash flows.
24	The IRR function assumes that the first cash flow is at the beginning of the first period (or
25	the end of period zero). It is necessary to provide a guess rate as a starting point in
26	computing net present value. The function performs several iterations to reach a net present
27	value of zero. The actual rate of return is reached when the net present value is zero.
28				

declining balance method or allows the straight-line method.

2. recovery period. The tax code identifies a number of property classes with a specified cost recovery schedule.

3. first-year convention. The tax code allows a choice between treating the asset as having been placed in service mid-year (half-year convention) or as having been placed in service in the middle of the quarter in which the asset was acquired.

Table 8–4 presents the depreciation percentages allowed for a piece of equipment with an asset class of 5 years that was pur-

Table 8–4 Asset Recovery Allowances for Taxes: Five-Year Asset Class

Year	Half-year Convention	Quarterly Convention (1st qtr.)	Straight-line
1	20.00%	35.00%	20.00%
2	32.00%	26.00%	20.00%
3	19.20%	15.60%	20.00%
4	11.52%	11.01%	20.00%
5	11.52%	11.01%	20.00%
6	5.76%	1.38%	

Source: Reprinted from Internal Revenue Service.

chased the first day of the year. The five-year property class applies to assets with a life of more than 4 years, but less than 10 years, including automobiles, trucks, property used in research or experimentation, computers and peripheral equipment, and office equipment. Actually, the 5-year class extends over 6 years. If the asset is held less than 6 years, the schedule will be followed to the point of disposal with the balance of the undepreciated cost (less salvage) expensed in the year of disposal. An organization may expense up to $18,500 of the cost of tangible property in the year an asset is acquired if the total qualifying asset purchases in the year are less than $200,000.

Exhibit 8–12 shows the tax impact on the acquisition of a piece of equipment costing $50,000, with a 5-year life and no salvage value. The new equipment will reduce annual operating expenses by $8,000 and will generate additional patient billings of $16,000 per year. The before-tax cash flows for this asset are the investment of $50,000 now and cash inflows of $24,000 each year. The after-tax cash flows change by the tax reduction (cash inflow) in year 1 of $1,934 as well as the tax payments in Years 2 through 5. The example (i.e., Exhibit 8–12) expenses $18,500 of the

equipment in the first year and uses the 5-year cost recovery schedule. The use of the cost recovery schedule results in a postponement of the taxes when compared with using the straight-line method. Any postponement of cash outflows or advancement of cash inflows increases the present value of the project and makes it more favorable. Clearly, the determination of the tax effect of an investment project is very complex, and provisions must be considered.

The discount rate is the rate of return desired by the particular health care organization. It is composed of three elements: a risk-free rate of return, expected inflation, and the degree of risk. The appropriate discount rate in determining the present value of an investment is the weighted average cost of capital, that is, the weighted average of the expected returns to be provided on equity capital and long-term debt capital. The weights are determined by the percentages of debt capital and equity capital. The weighted average cost of capital is computed as follows:

Weighted Average Cost of Capital =
After-tax Cost of Debt Capital ×
(Proportion of Debt Capital/Total Capital) +
Cost of Equity Capital × (Proportion of
Equity Capital/Total Capital)

When prices are increasing at a 2-percent or lower annual rate, it is safe to ignore the impact of inflation on most long-range decisions. It is necessary to consider the impact of a high rate of inflation in projecting cash flows over the life of a project, however, and to adjust these estimates for the impact of anticipated price changes. There are several cash flows (e.g., salaries, supplies, maintenance, fees charged to patients), and the appropriate rate of price changes should be applied to each cash flow. The discount rate, if properly determined, already has taken inflation into account, because investors' required

Exhibit 8–12 Impact of Taxes on Long-Range Decision

		Years				
	0 (Now)	1	2	3	4	5
Before-tax cash flows:						
Cash outflows:						
1. Purchase of equipment	$(50,000)					
Cash inflows:						
1. Annual cost savings		$8,000	$8,000	$8,000	$8,000	$8,000
2. Additional patient billings		16,000	16,000	16,000	16,000	16,000
Total annual cash flows	$(50,000)	$24,000	$24,000	$24,000	$24,000	$24,000
Present value factor 10%	1.000	0.909	0.825	0.751	0.683	0.621
Present value of cash flows	$(50,000)	$21,816	$19,800	$18,024	$16,392	$14,904
Net present value	$40,936					
After-tax cash flows:						
Cash outflows:						
1. Purchase of equipment	$(50,000)					
2. Payment of taxes		$1,934	$(5,534)	$(6,680)	$(7,186)	$(7,034)
Cash inflows:						
1. Annual cost savings		8,000	8,000	8,000	8,000	8,000
2. Additional patient billings		16,000	16,000	16,000	16,000	16,000
Total annual cash flows	$(50,000)	$25,934	$18,466	$17,320	$16,814	$16,966
Present value factor 10%	1.000	0.909	0.825	0.751	0.683	0.621
Present value of cash flows	$(50,000)	$23,574	$15,234	$13,007	$11,484	$10,536
Net present value	$23,836					
Computation of income taxes:						
Annual cost savings		$8,000	$8,000	$8,000	$8,000	$8,000
Additional patient billings		16,000	16,000	16,000	16,000	16,000
Total		$24,000	$24,000	$24,000	$24,000	$24,000
Depreciation:						
First-year expensing		18,500				
Year 1—$31,500 x 35.00%		11,025				
Year 2—$31,500 x 26.00%			8,190			
Year 3—$31,500 x 15.60%				4,914		
Year 4—$31,500 x 11.01%					3,468	
Year 5—Balance of cost						3,903
Taxable income (loss)		$(5,525)	$15,810	$19,086	$20,532	$20,097
Income tax, payment (refund)						
35% rate		$(1,934)	$5,534	$6,680	$7,186	$7,034

rate of return includes their expectation of inflation.

Techniques That Do Not Satisfy the Long-Range Decision Rule

Two investment techniques that do not involve the time value of money and, therefore, do not satisfy the long-range decision rule are in widespread use. These methods are the payback period and the accounting rate of return. They are simple, easy to use, and easily understood. However, because they do not consider the time value of money, they do not always identify the best choice.

Of the techniques of investment analysis examined in this chapter, the payback period method is the simplest; it has been widely used in ambulatory health care organizations. With this method, the question is simple: How soon will the initial investment be recovered? The payback period method calculates the amount of time that the projected cash inflows will recover the initial investment. All cash inflows after the recovery of the initial investment are ignored. Calculation of the payback period in Table 8–5 for the four investment projects examined earlier (see Exhibit 8–10) shows a range from 1⅚ years to 2⅔ years. If this organization requires a cutoff time period of less than 2 years, only Investment A is acceptable. In-

vestment B would probably be accepted, but Investments C and D would be rejected. In this illustration, Investment A was found unacceptable by the net present value method, but evaluated as the best project under the payback period method.

The major deficiency in the payback period method is that it does not take into account the profitability or the life of the investment beyond the payback period. For example, the following two investments have the same payback period, but substantially different net present values:

	Investment S	Investment T
Initial investment	$100,000	$50,000
Annual cash inflow	$ 50,000	$25,000
Estimated useful life	2 years	5 years
Payback period	2 years	2 years
Net present value at 10%	$(13,223)	$40,770

When there is a high degree of risk associated with the investment or when the rate of obsolescence is high, the payback method provides an excellent supplement to the discounted cash flow methods. When two or more projects meet the rate of return criterion, the better investment is the one with the shortest payback period.

In the accounting rate of return method, accounting income rather than cash flows is used to compute a rate of return for a particu-

Table 8–5 Illustration of Payback Period

Investment	Investment Amount	Period			Payback Period
		1	2	3	
A	$2,000	—	2,400	—	1 5/6 years
B	$2,000	1,200	800	400	2 years
C	$2,000	400	800	1,200	2 2/3 years
D	$2,000	800	800	800	2 1/2 years

lar investment. It is computed as follows:

$$\text{Accounting Rate of Return} = \text{Average Annual Accounting Income} / \text{Initial Investment}$$

Because average income is used, all investments with equal lives, equal total income, and equal initial investments are evaluated the same, regardless of when the cash is recovered. The accounting rate of return is computed in Table 8–6 for the four investments examined earlier. As in the payback method, the accounting rate of return method shows the highest value for Investment A because of its shorter life. Investments B, C, and D have identical accounting rates of return because average cash revenues and average costs for the 3-year period are the same. Their net present values are different, however.

The accounting rate of return uses accounting measurements and therefore is consistent with the accounting records. Most health care organizations that use this method do so because it is easily understood, but it is not a good long-range decision-making technique.

Long-Range Decision Illustration

The following example comes from an actual organized health care delivery system. The names, location, and some key amounts are disguised to maintain the anonymity of the organizations involved.

As a part of its newly developed strategic plan, the sample health system proposes to acquire ownership of the resources that it uses to provide services to its patients. For some time, the system has had a joint venture and partnership with Radiology Unlimited, a radiology group adjacent to the system's hospitals. Radiology Unlimited operates three businesses in a building that it owns. These businesses share common areas and personnel, and the radiology group provides professional radiology services for each business. A joint venture of Radiology Unlimited and the health system, called MRI, provides magnetic resonance imaging and stereotactic breast biopsy service; the health system owns one-third and Radiology Unlimited owns two-thirds of MRI. The system and Radiology Unlimited are partners in the third business, called CT, which provides computed tomography scanning services; the system owns two-thirds, and Radiology Unlimited owns one-third of CT.

The health system has offered to purchase the technical component of Radiology Unlimited's practice and Radiology Unlimited's equity in MRI and CT. The radiologists are to form a hospital-based radiology group, performing its own billing. Long-term agreements with the system will ensure continuing patient referrals to the group, and a management contract will be obtained to control the hospital-owned imaging center. The system

Table 8–6 Illustration of Accounting Rate of Return

Investment	Average Inflows	Straight-Line Depreciation	Annual Income	Initial Investment	Accounting Rate of Return
A	$1,200	$1,000	$200	$2,000	10.0%
B	$800	$667	$133	$2,000	6.7%
C	$800	$667	$133	$2,000	6.7%
D	$800	$667	$133	$2,000	6.7%

has agreed to pay the fair market value of the three businesses. The fair market value will be determined as the replacement cost of the assets for the technical component of Radiology Unlimited, and the present value of future cash flows for Radiology Unlimited's equity in MRI and CT.

The system contracted with the health care consultant from a major accounting firm to perform the present value analysis for MRI and CT. They also contracted with a certified appraiser to determine the replacement cost of the technical component of Radiology Unlimited. Both the system and Radiology Unlimited agreed to provide all information requested by the consultants.

Cash flows were projected from 1998 through 2002, at which time operations are expected to reach a level of normal long-term growth. Tables 8–7 and 8–8 show the determination of the present value of MRI and CT, respectively. The projections in these tables use a time horizon of 20 years. The certified appraiser set the appraisal of the technical as-

Table 8–7 Determination of Present Value of MRI

	Cash Inflows	Cash Outflows				
Year	Operating Revenues	Operating Expenses*	Estimated Taxes	Working Capital Additions	Capital Expend.	Net Cash Flows
1998	$1,381,700	$600,865	$271,367	$1,255	$5,000	$503,213
1999	1,425,720	617,640	280,903	7,483	5,000	514,694
2000	1,464,540	633,967	288,776	6,599	5,000	530,198
2001	1,503,040	650,237	296,556	6,545	5,000	544,702
2002	1,531,720	666,050	301,060	4,876	5,000	554,734
2003	1,531,720	666,050	301,060	4,876	5,000	554,734
2004	1,531,720	666,050	301,060	4,876	5,000	554,734
2005	1,531,720	666,050	301,060	4,876	5,000	554,734
2006	1,531,720	666,050	301,060	4,876	5,000	554,734
2007	1,531,720	666,050	301,060	4,876	5,000	554,734
2008	1,531,720	666,050	301,060	4,876	5,000	554,734
2009	1,531,720	666,050	301,060	4,876	5,000	554,734
2010	1,531,720	666,050	301,060	4,876	5,000	554,734
2011	1,531,720	666,050	301,060	4,876	5,000	554,734
2012	1,531,720	666,050	301,060	4,876	5,000	554,734
2013	1,531,720	666,050	301,060	4,876	5,000	554,734
2014	1,531,720	666,050	301,060	4,876	5,000	554,734
2015	1,531,720	666,050	301,060	4,876	5,000	554,734
2016	1,531,720	666,050	301,060	4,876	5,000	554,734
2017	1,531,720	666,050	301,060	4,876	5,000	554,734

*Excluding depreciation.
Present value of net cash flows = NPV(.15, range of net cash flows) = $3,375,318
Present value of net cash flows = NPV(.12, range of net cash flows) = $4,041,794
Source: Anonymous.

Table 8–8 Determination of Present Value of CT

	Cash Inflows		Cash Outflows			
Year	Operating Revenues	Operating Expenses*	Estimated Taxes	Working Capital Additions	Capital Expend.	Net Cash Flows
1998	$2,441,400	$933,936	$398,112	$(9,655)	$5,000	$1,114,007
1999	2,447,170	946,780	411,387	961	5,000	1,083,042
2000	2,452,200	959,523	424,437	855	5,000	1,062,385
2001	2,452,550	973,842	435,298	60	5,000	1,038,350
2002	2,452,440	988,160	442,498	(19)	107,000	914,801
2003	2,452,440	988,160	442,498	(19)	107,000	914,801
2004	2,452,440	988,160	442,498	(19)	107,000	914,801
2005	2,452,440	988,160	442,498	(19)	107,000	914,801
2006	2,452,440	988,160	442,498	(19)	107,000	914,801
2007	2,452,440	988,160	442,498	(19)	107,000	914,801
2008	2,452,440	988,160	442,498	(19)	107,000	914,801
2009	2,452,440	988,160	442,498	(19)	107,000	914,801
2010	2,452,440	988,160	442,498	(19)	107,000	914,801
2011	2,452,440	988,160	442,498	(19)	107,000	914,801
2012	2,452,440	988,160	442,498	(19)	107,000	914,801
2013	2,452,440	988,160	442,498	(19)	107,000	914,801
2014	2,452,440	988,160	442,498	(19)	107,000	914,801
2015	2,452,440	988,160	442,498	(19)	107,000	914,801
2016	2,452,440	988,160	442,498	(19)	107,000	914,801
2017	2,452,440	988,160	442,498	(19)	107,000	914,801

*Excluding depreciation.
Present value of net cash flows = NPV(.15, range of net cash flows) = $6,194,158
Present value of net cash flows = NPV(.12, range of net cash flows) = $7,328,603
Source: Anonymous.

---

sets at approximately $1 million, an amount agreed to by both sides. The offering price by the system was set as follows:

Replacement cost of assets of Radiology Unlimited	$1,000,000
Present value of MRI (2/3 of $3,375,318)	2,250,212
Present value of CT (1/3 of $6,194,158)	2,067,719
Total purchase price	$5,317,931

The radiologists analyzed the assumptions of the valuation performed by the accounting firm and took exception to the 15 percent discount rate. The exceptions involved the consultants' assumptions about the capital structure and risk adjustments. The consultant had used an average of the capital structures of comparable health care organizations to develop a 1 to 3 debt to equity ratio for weights in computing the cost of capital, but the radiologists argued that the capital structure should reflect the industry average or cost of capital for the buyer. As to risk adjustment, the radiologists argued that the projections of future cash flows already reflect probable reimbursement under managed care. In doing the build-up method of determining a discount rate, the consultant included an additional factor for reimbursement risks. Thus, the radiologists argued that this risk was included twice in the valuation. Under these circumstances, they suggested a discount rate of 10 percent to 12 percent. The entities to be acquired are well established ventures with little competition and, therefore, low risk. In an economic environment of low inflation (2 percent) and low business risk, the radiologists argued that a lower discount rate is appropriate.

The use of a 12 percent discount rate would have produced a purchase price of $6,137,397, a figure $819,466 above the consultant's price of $5,317,931 using a 15 percent discount rate. Clearly, it is very important to select a proper discount rate. There are two general ways of determining the appropriate discount rate for measuring the present value of future cash flows. The first approach, used by the consultant for the health system, involves the weighted average cost of capital. The second approach involves the opportunity cost of the funds to be invested. As a general rule, the minimum rate of return on a particular investment should not be less than the cost of acquiring and maintaining the entity's capital resources.

The consultant for the system and Radiology Unlimited felt that the appropriate discount rate in valuing an investment is the weighted average cost of capital. This rate is the weighted average of the expected returns on equity capital and long-term debt capital. The weights are determined by the projected long-term debt/equity position. The weighted average cost of capital has three components:

1. *capital structure, the proportion of debt and equity.* The consultant used a capital structure of 33 percent debt and 67 percent equity, basing this decision on an average capital structure of seven large diversified health care companies.

2. *cost of debt capital.* The average rate on borrowed funds was set at 7.3 percent, based on "yield in percent per annum" for corporate Baa bonds, published by the Federal Reserve Statistical Release at December 31, 1997. This yields an after-tax cost of debt of 4.7 percent calculated as follows:

$$7.3\% \times (1-35.0\%) = 4.7\%$$
(assuming a tax rate of 35%)

3. *cost of equity capital.* The consultant estimated the cost of equity capital by using the capital asset pricing model (CAPM), which is measured as follows:

Equity Rate of Return = Rf + (ERP × B) + SSRP + CR

where Rf = risk-free rate (i.e., the 20-year Treasury bond yield at 6.02 percent).

ERP = equity risk premium (i.e., the large company stock total returns minus long-term government bond income returns as reported in Ibbotson and Associates 1997 Yearbook). ERP equaled 7.5 percent in the 1997 Yearbook.

B = Beta (i.e., a coefficient that relates a specific company's risk to the average risk of a group of stocks, such as the Standard & Poors 500). The overall market is equal to a beta of 1. The consultant computed the beta for MRI and CT at 1.05, approximately equal to the average in the market.

SSRP = small stock risk premium. Investors in small capitalization stocks have historically earned a premium over large capitalization stocks. A small size premium was added to the cost of equity to reflect the investment characteristics of the imaging businesses relative to selected comparable companies. The premium of 5.78 percent was drawn from Ibbotson and Associates 1996 Yearbook.

CR = company-specific risk premium. A specific risk premium of 0.5 percent was developed from the consultant's evaluation of management depth, market position, access to capital markets, public vs. private ownership, and management projections.

Equity Rate of Return for MRI and CT
= 6.02% + (7.5% × 1.05) + 5.78% + 0.5% = 20.02%

Exhibit 8–13 presents the calculation of the weighted average cost of capital for the investment project. Clearly, this example demonstrates, for long-range decisions, the importance of accuracy in estimating cash flows, the timing of these cash flows, and the key role of the discount rate employed. Lack of reasonably correct information for any of these variables may produce a poor long-range decision.

LONG-RANGE DECISIONS IN REVIEW

The long-range decision-making process is not well developed in many health care organizations. This chapter advances a long-range decision criterion that incorporates theoretically superior decision criteria. This methodology is appropriate for all levels in the health care organization. It states that an investment is economically sound if the discounted incremental cash inflows equal or exceed the discounted incremental cash outflows attributable to the investment. Information needed to apply the long-range decision criterion is the incremental cash inflows and outflows projected for each investment alternative and a discount rate that reflects the cost of capital of the health care organization. All cash flows directly traced to the investment proposal are relevant.

Three techniques satisfy the long-range decision criterion. They are the net present value method, the profitability index, and the internal rate of return. They differ only in the way the decision criterion is applied.

Determination of the proper discount rate is critical for the use of discounted cash flow techniques. The illustration in this chapter

Exhibit 8–13 Computation of Weighted Average Cost of Capital

	Cost of Capital		Capital Structure	Total
Cost of Debt	4.70%	×	33%	1.55%
Cost of Equity	20.20%	×	67%	13.53%
Total Weighted Average Cost of Capital				15.08%
Concluded Weighted Average Cost of Capital				15.00%

Source: Anonymous.

shows the effect of using a high discount rate. As the discount rate is increased, the present value of future cash flows is decreased. The appropriate discount rate in valuing an investment is the weighted average cost of capital.

Two techniques that do not satisfy the long-range decision criterion are in widespread use. They are the payback method and the accounting rate of return. Both are simple, easily understood, and easily computed. The payback method is an excellent supplement to the net present value method if the project involves a significant degree of risk, or if there is a high rate of obsolescence.

SHORT-RANGE DECISIONS

To accomplish their goals, objectives, and strategic plans, health care organizations must make both long- and short-range decisions. It is generally most effective if those at the responsibility center level make the short-range decisions.

Fixed and Variable Costs

Costs change for a variety of reasons: people simply spend more, inflation occurs, quality or volumes of service vary. Changes in quality must be dealt with on a case-by-case basis. Changes in cost due to changes in inflation and volume are easiest to accommodate. The behavior of costs as volume changes involves the determination of fixed and variable costs. The most basic information for planning, decision making, and evaluation of performance in the short run is an understanding of the underlying behavior of costs as activity changes for an organization, a department, or a service.

Economists model cost behavior as shown in Figure 8–2. In this model, fixed costs are the intercept, and variable costs are the

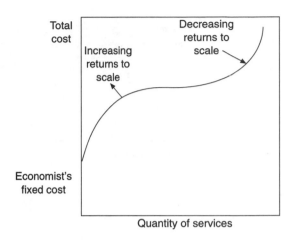

Figure 8–2 An Economist's Cost Curve

change in slope. Economists' cost curves are idealizations. The organization gains increasing returns to scale at low levels of activity, then goes through a range of stable operations, and finally incurs decreasing returns to scale as capacity is approached. In actuality, cost curves are likely to be jagged rather than smooth. Many costs come in "lumps." For example, to go from serving 2,000 patients to 2,001 patients may mean that another health care provider will go on the payroll.

Accountants use an approximation of the real cost curve. Because most operations are in the stable portion of the economist's cost curve, accountants assume that cost is a linear function of volume (Figure 8–3). The cost function that accountants use is $C = a + b(q)$, where C is total cost, a represents total fixed cost, b represents the variable cost per unit of service, and q represents units of service. In using this cost function, accountants make several assumptions. Fixed costs are assumed to remain fixed within a relevant range, reflecting the past experience of the organization. Both variable costs per unit of service and the service mix are assumed to remain constant within the relevant range. To the extent that a variable cost (e.g., supplies) de-

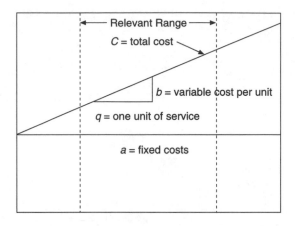

Figure 8–3 An Accountant's Cost Curve

creases with volume discounts, or other fixed or variable costs change due to forces other than volume, these cost behavior assumptions may not reflect actual operations. Accountants assume that the linear function represents cost accurately enough to permit appropriate short-term decisions, however.

Very seldom is the accounting system designed to provide fixed and variable costs.

Therefore, total cost must be separated into its fixed and variable portions to use the linear cost function. Accountants have developed two practical means for determining cost behavior patterns: inspection of accounts and study of past cost behavior patterns. The methods differ with the sources of data used.

Inspection of Accounts. The most intuitive method of determining whether a cost is fixed or variable is to examine the nature of each cost in the chart of accounts. Many costs are fixed or variable by their very nature. Because inspection is both intuitive and arbitrary, it is subject to some degree of error. For those situations in which analysis is not very sensitive to error in classification of fixed and variable costs, however, this method may provide a quick and inexpensive measure of cost behavior.

Even if data for only one period are available, a cost function can be developed by using the inspection of accounts method. For example, an analysis of the accounts for the Community Health Center in Exhibit 8–14 would probably identify salaries and admin-

Exhibit 8–14 Community Health Center Operating Statement for 1997

		Fixed Expenses	*Variable Expenses*
Patient visits	10,000		
Revenue:			
Patient fees	$750,000		
Donations and grants	950,000		
Total revenue	1,700,000		
Expenses:			
Salaries	900,000	$ 900,000	
Drugs	400,000		$400,000
Administration	350,000	350,000	
Contributed services	150,000		150,000
Total expenses	1,800,000	$1,250,000	$550,000
Excess of expenses over revenue	$(100,000)		

istrative costs as fixed, drugs and contributed services costs as variable. With 10,000 patient visits, the average variable cost per patient visit is $55 ($550,000 / 10,000). The cost function is $C = \$1,250,000 + \$55q$. This cost function can be used to estimate costs at any level of activity. If the number of patient visits is expected to be 10,500 in 1998, the total cost is estimated to be $1,250,000 + ($55 × 10,500) = $1,827,500.

Study of Past Data.   Analysis of past experience assumes that past data are accurate and that future cost behavior patterns will be like past cost behavior patterns. Several methods can be used to determine cost behavior patterns. Among them are: the scattergraph approach, in which data points are plotted on a graph across time; regression analysis, which fits a line to several observations statistically; and the high–low point method, which fits a line to two data points.

To illustrate the separation of past cost data into fixed and variable costs, Table 8–9 presents cost and volume relationships for supplies and patient visits within a clinic setting. When these data points are plotted across time in Figure 8–4, there appears to be a linear relationship between the cost of supplies and the number of patient visits. A line may be fit to the scattergraph by visual inspection so that approximately half the data points lie above the line and approximately half lie below the line. The point where the line crosses the vertical axis is the estimate of fixed costs, and the slope of the line is the estimate of variable cost per patient visit. A scattergraph should be used to determine whether a linear relationship exists or whether unusual observations exist. If a linear relationship exists, regression analysis is an appropriate tool for determining cost behavior. Abnormal observations identified by examining the scattergraph may be dropped from the data to allow a better fit when regression analysis is used.

The most accurate method for determining fixed and variable costs is regression analysis. Least squares regression selects the single straight line that minimizes the sum of the squared deviations from the line. Regression analysis may be performed with any current spreadsheet package, such as Excel or Lotus. Although it may be performed with a small number of observations, statisticians caution that if the number of observations drops below 15, regression analysis is not the appropriate tool.

Exhibit 8–15 presents the regression summary output from the data for supplies and patient visits (see Table 8–9). The key regression output data are shaded. The intercept coefficient in this regression is $884, reflecting the fixed portion of total supplies cost. The X Variable 1 coefficient is $0.52, reflecting the slope of the regression line and representing the variable supplies cost per patient visit. Therefore, the cost function for supplies is $C = \$884 + \$0.52q$. This cost function may be

Table 8–9 Cost and Volume Data for Cost-Behavior Analysis

Month	Cost of Supplies	Patient Visits
January	$1,120	500
February	$1,310	660
March	$1,380	1,040
April	$1,100	850
May	$1,610	1,240
June	$1,700	940
July	$1,770	1,560
August	$1,500	1,440
September	$1,970	1,710
October	$2,100	1,950
November	$1,660	1,840
December	$1,500	1,650
January	$1,400	1,340
February	$1,760	1,380
March	$1,420	1,170

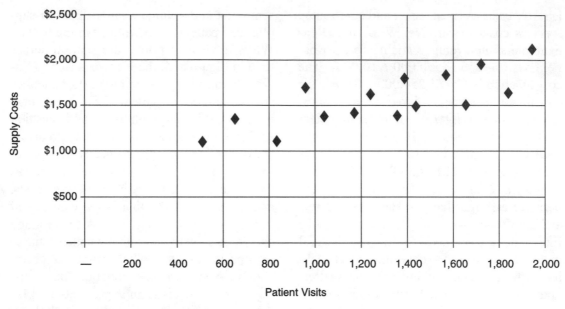

Figure 8–4 Plot of Supply Cost Against Number of Patient Visits

Exhibit 8–15 Regression Analysis for Supplies in Relation to Patient Visits

SUMMARY OUTPUT

Regression Statistics

Multiple R	0.78591283
R Square	0.61765897
Adjusted R Square	0.58824812
Standard Error	182.119724
Observations	15

ANOVA

	df	SS	MS	F	Significance F
Regression	1	696554.611	696554.611	21.0010594	0.00051362
Residual	13	431178.722	33167.594		
Total	14	1127733.33			

	Coefficients	Standard Error	t Statistic	P-value
Intercept	884.026826	153.434217	5.76160159	6.5815E-05
X Variable 1	0.52099624	0.11368783	4.58269128	0.00051362

used to estimate total supplies costs at any level of activity within the relevant range. For example, the estimate of total supplies costs at 1,500 patient visits is $C = \$884 + (0.52 \times 1,500) = \$1,664$.

The regression analysis output gives an adjusted R square statistic that indicates the percentage of the change in supplies that is explained by changes in the number of patient visits. In this example, the figure is 58 percent. An R square of less than 50 percent indicates one of two things. Either the cost is primarily fixed and changes in a stepwise fashion, or the choice of the volume measure is not strongly related to cost. Plotting the data helps to identify scatter patterns for which regression results will produce misleading cost functions. Ideally, the plots fall in a perfectly straight line, and the R square is 1.00, indicating that changes in the number of patient visits explain 100 percent of the variation in supplies costs. This does not happen in practice, however. An examination of the plot for supplies costs and the R square of 0.58 shows a great deal of variation in the cost behavior pattern, and any cost estimates may be subject to considerable error.

Some potential problems arise when managers attempt to use regression analysis to develop a cost function. If the accounting system records the costs of supplies as expenses when purchased rather than when used, for example, regression analysis will not provide an accurate representation of the relationship between costs and changes in volumes. A regression analysis of supplies costs in an intensive care unit at one of the sample health system's hospitals resulted in an R square of only 5 percent. During the year, the hospital was expensing intensive care supplies when purchased. Therefore, the resulting monthly supplies cost was not useful in planning or evaluating operations. Moreover, total costs in many health care organizations are mostly fixed costs. If the variable costs are a very small proportion of total cost, regression analysis will not reflect the large jumps in fixed costs as capacity limits are reached.

When there are too few data points to perform regression analysis, the high–low method can be used. A representative high point and a representative low point are used in the calculations. From the data in Table 8–9, for example, the highest activity (1,950 patient visits with $2,100 of cost) and the lowest activity (500 patient visits with $1,120 of cost) are selected. Variable cost is calculated as the change in cost over the change in volume:

$$\text{Variable Cost} = (\$2,100 - \$1,120) / (1,950 - 500) = \$0.68 \text{ per Patient Visit}$$

To determine fixed cost, the high total cost is used with $0.68 substituted for variable cost and 1,950 for quantity. Substituting these values into the equation

$$\text{Total Cost} = \text{Fixed Cost} + (\text{Variable Cost per Visit} \times \text{Patient Visits})$$

and solving for fixed costs

$$\$2,100 = \text{Fixed Cost} + (\$0.68 \times 1,950)$$
$$\text{Fixed Cost } \$774$$

Using the high–low method, the cost equation is

$$C = \$774 + (\$0.68q)$$

When the results from the high–low method are compared to the results of the regression analysis, fixed costs are higher for regression ($884) and the variable cost lower ($0.52) for regression than for the high–low method. Regression is a more accurate analytical tool because it uses all of the data points, whereas the high–low method uses only two points; furthermore, these may not reflect normal levels of operations. Also, unfortunately, there is no measure like the R square to show the goodness of fit of the cost equation.

Cost–Volume–Profit Analysis

Underlying most short-range decisions, cost–volume–profit analysis provides a framework for evaluation of performance when the organization faces significant changes in volume. It involves the impact of a change in activity on costs and profit.

The total cost function developed for the Community Health Center can be considered a flexible budget or performance budget for determining whether the health center is operating in an efficient manner. If 10,500 patients were served in 1998 and the actual costs were $1,900,000 (variable costs $625,000 and fixed costs $1,275,000), then the Community Health Center overspent by $72,500.

	1997 Actual	Performance Budget	1998 Actual	Variance
Patients served	10,000	10,500	10,500	0
Variable costs	$ 550,000	$ 577,500	$ 625,000	($47,500)
Fixed costs	$1,250,000	$1,250,000	$1,275,000	($25,000)
Total costs	$1,800,000	$1,827,500	$1,900,000	($72,500)

Using a flexible budget in which costs are divided into fixed and variable is the most accurate method of measuring performance. It is preferable to the comparison of a static budget set at a particular level of operations that is compared to the actual costs at a different level of operations.

Cost–Volume–Profit Analysis Through Graphs

The easiest way to visualize and understand cost–volume–profit analysis is through a break-even chart. Such a chart shows much more than the point at which an organization will break even. It provides a picture of the profit or loss at all levels of activity within the relevant range of activity.

For example, a hospital has a small laboratory that has shown a loss for some time. The October operating statement is presented in Exhibit 8–16. Fixed costs total $14,000 per month, and variable costs are $5,700 ($3 × 1,900 tests). Management is looking for ways to eliminate the loss and construct a break-even chart (Figure 8–5). The break-even point, where the total revenue line crosses the

---

Exhibit 8–16 Laboratory Operating Statement for October

		Variable Costs	Fixed Costs
Number of tests	1,900		
Gross charges	$19,000		
Operating expenses:			
Wages and benefits	5,760		$5,760
Supplies	3,800	$3,800	
Other variable costs	1,900	1,900	
Depreciation	500		500
Allocated costs	7,740		7,740
Total	19,700	$5,700	$14,000
Operating income (loss)	$(700)		

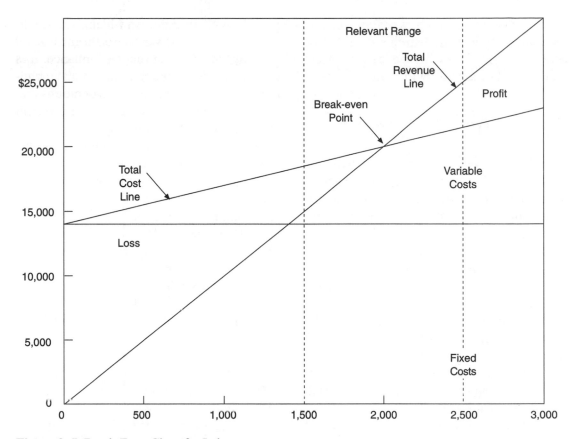

Figure 8–5 Break-Even Chart for Laboratory

total cost line, is 2,000 tests. The laboratory is currently operating at the level of 1,900 tests per month, showing a loss of $700. From the break-even chart, it is possible to estimate the profit or loss at any level of activity within the relevant range.

In a fee-for-service setting, there is a strong motivation to increase patient visits to show a profit or reduce a loss. The break-even chart for a mature health maintenance organization (HMO) shows just the opposite (Figure 8–6). With a constant membership in a mature HMO and no co-payments, the revenue line on a capitation basis is flat. The total cost line is similar to the total cost line in a fee-for-service setting, however. The HMO will show a

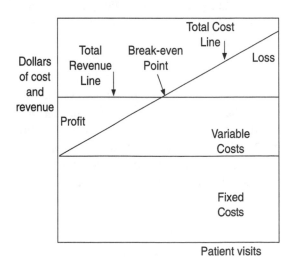

Figure 8–6 Break-Even Chart for a Mature HMO

profit if it keeps its members healthy, thereby reducing patient visits. In this case, a low level of patient visits will produce a profit and a high level of activity will result in a lower profit or a loss.

Cost–Value–Profit Analysis Through Equations

The break-even point may be determined by equation, dividing the total fixed costs by the contribution margin per unit. The contribution margin is the difference between revenue and variable costs. In the laboratory example, the fee is $10 per test ($19,000 / 1,900). The variable cost per test is $3 ($5,700 / 1,900). Each test thus generates a contribution margin of $7 ($10 − $3) toward covering fixed costs and providing a profit. The break-even point is 2,000 tests ($14,000 / $7). Each test beyond 2,000 will generate $7 of income because fixed costs are covered at 2,000 tests. Each test below 2,000 will result in an additional loss of $7.

The number of tests to generate a desired profit can be determined by dividing the contribution margin per unit into the sum of fixed costs and desired profit. If the management wants to show a profit of $700, the laboratory must perform 2,100 tests [($14,000 + $700) / $7].

This equation may be adapted to determine the dollar amount of revenue needed to break even or to generate a given amount of income even when a single measure of volume is not available. In the laboratory example, the number of tests was used as the measure of volume. If the laboratory conducts a variety of tests that consume different amounts of variable costs, it is possible to determine the overall break-even point in dollars of revenue by using the contribution margin ratio. The contribution margin ratio is the ratio of contribution margin to revenue. In this case, the contribution margin ratio is 70 percent ($7 /

$10). The break-even point in dollars of revenue is $20,000 ($14,000 / 70 percent).

Identifying the fixed and variable costs and computing the average contribution margin ratio make it possible to perform a cost–volume–profit analysis for the overall health care system. Although the contribution margin ratio may vary greatly among the various segments of an organized health care delivery system, it is still a useful tool of analysis. For example, if the contribution margin ratio of each segment is known, the analyst at the overall organization level may determine the impact of a change in activity in any segment on the overall organization profit. If a hospital has a contribution margin ratio of 20 percent, an increase of $100,000 in revenue should increase profit by $20,000. If a laboratory has a contribution margin ratio of 40 percent, an increase of $100,000 in revenue should increase profit by $40,000.

Contribution margin is a very useful concept in short-range decisions. Fixed costs are constant in the short term within the relevant range, so analysts can ignore fixed costs and focus on contribution margin in many short-range decisions. For example, what would be the impact on the laboratory's loss in Exhibit 8–16 if the hospital contracted with another health care organization to perform 300 tests per month at $6 per test? The contribution margin per unit on these tests would be $3 per test ($6 − $3), and the contract would add $900 to income, or change the $700 loss to a $200 profit. Any price above variable cost per unit of service will generate a positive contribution margin and, therefore, increase profits.

At some point, capacity constraints must be considered. If the special contract pushes the laboratory's level of services over current capacity, we may have to add personnel to relax the capacity constraint. Another important factor to consider is whether these special contract patients are part of the laboratory's current business. If they are, the relevant costs must include the portion of fixed costs that will be lost because regular business will decrease. Sometimes, other opportunities may arise, and the cost of these opportunities also warrants consideration.

Relaxing a constrained resource is another short-term decision that managers often face. If the firm is operating beyond the break-even point, regular operations are covering all the fixed costs. Therefore, all the contribution margin that occurs when the constraint is relaxed is available to pay for the resources needed to relax the constraint. Often, the contribution margin is unexpectedly large. For example, if the laboratory is operating at 2,000 tests per month and facing a labor constraint, the laboratory could afford to pay up to $1,400 ($7 contribution margin × 200 tests) to hire additional personnel and serve an additional 200 patients. In the short run, managers often underestimate the amount of money available to relax a constrained resource.

Establishment of Fees

In the short term, managers may set the price for a special order to generate some contribution margin. On this type of contract, they should seek to maximize total dollars of contribution margin. Over time, however, they cannot ignore fixed costs; they must cover all costs of providing a service and generating a desired income. Most reimbursement mechanisms are based upon covering the full cost of providing a service. To determine cost-based fees, the health care organization must be able to establish the full cost for each procedure or class of procedures, including the direct cost of providing the service and a fair share of other indirect costs.

Pricing for the Community Health Center can be analyzed with this flexible budget (see Exhibit 8–14). Fees this period were $750,000 for 10,000 patient visits, for an average fee of $75. The contribution margin per patient visit is $20 ($75 − $55). For every patient visit, $20 is available to cover fixed cost and then add to "income." The flexible budget can be written as

$$I = G + (p - v)q - F$$

where I is income, G represents grants and donations, and p reflects price. This type of flexible budget is used in cost–volume–profit analysis by forecasting the variables included in the analysis. For example, if grants and donations are expected to decrease in the next period, the price of services may be raised to compensate. Thus, if donations and grants are expected to drop to $850,000 and patient visits increase to 12,000, the estimated income is

$$I = \$850,000 + [(\$75 - \$55) \times 12,000] - \$1,250,000 = (\$160,000)$$

The loss (excess of expenses over revenues) is expected to increase to $160,000. To cover all costs, the Community Health Center must increase fees by $13.33 per visit ($160,000 / 12,000), arriving at a new fee of $88.33 ($75.00 + $13.33).

This flexible budget does not incorporate the effect on demand of price changes. If the new price is not competitive, volumes may decrease, and the anticipated revenue from patient fees will be less than expected. In the prediction of future volumes, the sensitivity of demand to price must also be predicted and incorporated explicitly.

Activity-Based Costing To Measure the Full Cost of Services

Organizations in the manufacturing sector developed activity-based costing to provide the full cost of products and services in a complex setting. Historically, manufacturers have used a single overhead rate to allocate indirect costs to products and services, usually on the basis of direct labor. A single plantwide overhead rate cannot reflect the complexities of automation and other modern manufacturing techniques, however, and products with a high labor content were overcosted while products in complex manufacturing processes with automation were undercosted.

When firms use activity-based costing, they must first analyze production processes to determine the many activities that drive production costs. Once a set of cost pools and drivers has been determined, standards can be set and costs allocated to products and services using the activity as an allocation base. The resulting full cost of a product or service then reflects the level of complexity involved. For example, after tracking the cost of purchasing all of its materials and supplies, a firm can designate the number of purchase invoices as the activity that drives these costs. This results in a cost per unit for the activity of purchasing. Those products and services requiring many purchases will bear the additional costs.

Activity-based costing treats all costs as variable costs in the long run, although fixed costs remain fixed in short-term decision making (such as pricing and product emphasis). The fully allocated cost under activity-based costing does not reflect the large changes in fixed costs needed to expand capacity, and it overestimates (sometimes substantially) the marginal cost of providing additional service when there is excess capacity. Hence, activity-based costing can lead to suboptimal decisions in any service organization characterized by a large proportion of fixed cost.

Health care organizations are characterized by large fixed costs, regardless of the activities undertaken. When Noreen and

Soderstrom examined a sample of hospital overhead costs for an average of 108 hospitals over a 15-year period, they found, on average, that 80 percent of costs were fixed and that an activity-based costing model overstated their marginal costs by more than 40 percent.[6] Because of the preponderance of fixed costs in health care organizations, activity-based costing is appropriate for setting and monitoring efficiency variances (i.e., analyzing time and procedures used in an activity) and determining full cost for fee setting when the organization is at capacity, but its poor estimates of marginal cost make it inappropriate for decision making involving changes in activity. In health care organizations, marginal cost may be very small until capacity becomes an issue. As volumes of service increase, fixed costs will increase in large increments at some point (e.g., the cost of hiring another full-time service provider).

Decision To Drop an Activity

When an activity or service has been showing a loss and there is no way to reduce the loss, the health care organization may face the decision of whether to drop the activity or service. In the earlier laboratory example (see Exhibit 8–16), the hospital management may try to determine how much the hospital can save by eliminating the unprofitable laboratory. Although fixed costs are generally irrelevant in short-term decisions, the hospital must know which costs will be avoided by dropping the laboratory service and which costs will continue. The hospital administrator then approaches a pathologist with an offer to sell the laboratory. The pathologist agrees to purchase the equipment at its undepreciated cost and pay the hospital a monthly rental of $3,000. An examination of the avoidable and unavoidable costs of dropping the laboratory indicates that the hospital will not incur

$2,000 of the costs allocated to the laboratory (e.g., occupancy, administration) if it drops the laboratory service (Exhibit 8–17). However, $5,740 of allocated fixed costs are unavoidable and will continue if the laboratory is sold. The rental income of $3,000 will not fully offset the $5,740 of unavoidable allocated fixed costs; thus, the effect of selling the laboratory is to lose $2,740 per month.

Operating Leverage

Many health care organizations are characterized by a large percentage of fixed costs, which leads to a high degree of operating leverage. Operating leverage reflects the proportion of costs that are fixed and is an important concept for health care service managers and accountants to understand. When operating leverage is high, profits will vary a great deal as volume varies. Operating leverage is unimportant if revenues are based on cost, because payment will always exceed cost. When revenues are based on volume rather than cost, however, profits become highly variable when operating leverage is high.

A simple example can illustrate how changes in the proportion of fixed costs affect earnings variability under a flat-fee per patient reimbursement scheme. A hospital has two departments, Department A and Department B. Fixed costs in Department A are $100, and variable costs per patient are $5. If 25 patients receive services during a particular period, the cost per patient is $9 ($100 / 25 patients + $5). If reimbursement is on a flat-fee basis at $10 per patient, the income will be $25. If the patient volume drops to 20 patients during the next period, the cost per patient becomes $10 ($100 / 20 patients + $5). If reimbursement is still $10 per patient, the department just breaks even.

Department B has total costs similar to those of Department A, but Department B has lower fixed costs, $75 per period, and higher variable costs, $6 per patient. The total cost for the treatment of 25 patients is $225 [($75 + ($6 x 25 patients)]. With a reimbursement of $10 per patient, the total reimbursement is $250 and earnings are $25, the same as for Department A. When volume drops to 20 patients, however, the total cost in Department B is only $195 [($75 + ($6 x 20 patients)]. Reimbursement is $200 ($10 x $20), and the department has earnings of $5 rather than just breaking even as in Department A. Thus, lower operating leverage (the fixed portion of costs) reduces earnings variability.

Exhibit 8–17 Illustration of Decision To Drop a Service

Type of Expense	Cost Behavior	Amount	Avoidable	Unavoidable
Wages and benefits	Fixed	$5,760	$5,760	
Supplies	Variable	3,800	3,800	
Other variable costs	Variable	1,900	1,900	
Depreciation	Fixed	500	500	
Allocated costs	Fixed	7,740	2,000	$5,740
Total		$19,700	$13,960	$5,740

Use of Information from Regulatory Reports for Decisions

Health care organizations must gather information for regulatory reports. Consequently, they often design their internal accounting systems to produce the required information. Unfortunately, these reporting systems are not designed to provide relevant information for the wide variety of decisions that managers must make. Managers need to consider carefully the types of decisions that they make and develop appropriate accounting techniques and systems to support their decision-making process fully.

Target Costing

The Japanese developed target costing for the manufacturing sector. Although target costing is used primarily in manufacturing, the principles are certainly applicable to health care and service sectors. Target costing is a cost control method that takes place at the design phase of new product development. After a market survey, a target price is set and a target cost calculated. The decision to produce that product is based on whether it is possible to meet the target cost. Thus, cost control is built into the production process at the outset. As the design team develops a new product, they consider trade-offs in price, functionality, and quality to meet a product's target cost.

As health care and not-for-profit organizations focus on cost containment, they can develop new services or product lines at a price that will maximize volumes. Using techniques that analyze the relevant time and costs to provide a particular service, health care organizations can develop a production plan to provide the service at a specified target cost. Because a large proportion of cost is fixed in many health care and service organizations, capacity levels have a greater impact on the variability of costs in any service product. If a firm has ample capacity, fixed cost will not be part of the target cost. If there are capacity limits, however, the costs of increasing capacity or using capacity more efficiently enter into the target cost.

SHORT-RANGE DECISIONS IN REVIEW

Fixed and variable costs relate to how costs behave as volume changes. Avoidable and unavoidable costs relate to what happens when an activity or service is dropped. Direct and indirect costs relate to determining a full cost of a service or product. Different information needs must be considered in the design of the accounting system. A system designed to provide information for regulatory reports may not provide the relevant information for many short-range decisions.

CONCLUSION

Accounting information falls into two broad classifications: financial accounting and management accounting. GAAP require the presentation of three financial statements—the financial position statement (balance sheet), the operating statement (income statement), and the cash flow statement. All three statements are presented to stockholders and creditors and to the health care organization's board of directors. Operating management within an organized health care organization needs financial statements for responsibility centers. Evaluation of operations for responsibility centers requires the development of a performance or flexible budget if actual volume varies significantly from planned volume.

The discounted cash flow approach is appropriate for long-range decisions at any level in the health care organization. The superior method for evaluating the decision to acquire long-term assets considers the time value of money. A long-range decision is favorable if the incremental discounted cash inflows attributable to the investment proposal are equal to or greater than the incremental discounted cash outflows attributable to the investment. In practice, the payback method and accounting rate of return method are used because they are simple and easy to apply but may lead to less desirable decisions.

Short-range decisions involve the fees to charge, and the volume and mix of services to provide with existing capacity. The most basic information for short-range decisions involves the behavior of costs as activity changes. Variable costs change in proportion to changes in volume, and fixed costs remain unchanged with changes in volume. Because fixed costs do not change with changes in activity, the concept of contribution margin (the difference between price and variable costs) is useful in many short-range decisions.

In most health care organizations, a very large percentage of total costs are fixed in nature, causing wide swings in income as volume changes. The concept of operating leverage (the extent of fixed costs in the organization) must be understood by management at all levels of the organization.

NOTES

1. S.R. Estaugh, *Health Care Finance* (New York: Auburn House, 1992), 416.

2. C.P. Stickney, *Financial Reporting and Statement Analysis* (New York: Dryden Press, 1996), 119.

3. Stickney, *Financial Reporting and Statement Analysis*, 120.

4. R.S. Kaplan and A.A. Atkinson, *Advanced Management Accounting* (Englewood Cliffs, NJ: Prentice Hall, 1998), 367–380.

5. D.T. DeCoster et al., *Management Accounting*, 4th ed. (New York: John Wiley & Sons, 1988).

6. E. Noreen and N. Soderstrom, "The Accuracy of Proportional Cost Models: Evidence from Hospital Service Departments," *Review of Accounting Studies* 2 (1997): 89–114.

LESLIE G. ELDENBURG, CPA, PHD, has been an Assistant Professor of Accounting at the University of Arizona since 1993. She is also a Certified Public Accountant. Her research areas are health care accounting and managerial accounting issues in an international setting. Her research papers have been published in academic accounting journals, as well as in *Healthcare Financial Management* and *Controllers Quarterly*. Before she began her academic career, she worked in the finance department at Virginia Mason Hospital in Seattle. She received her doctorate in accounting from the University of Washington in 1991.

ELDON L. SCHAFER, CPA, PHD, is Professor Emeritus at Pacific Lutheran University. With teaching interests in management accounting systems, he has been a faculty member or visiting faculty member at the University of Nebraska, California State University—San Jose, Syracuse University, University of Washington, Massey University in New Zealand, University of Southeast Asia in Macao, Riga Technical University in Latvia, and most recently at the University of Arizona. He has also served as a consultant to the Washington State Hospital Commission and on the board of an HMO. Dr. Schafer has co-authored a number of books in management accounting and health care administration. He holds a master's degree and a doctorate from the University of Nebraska, and he is a Certified Public Accountant in Nebraska.

DWIGHT J. ZULAUF, PHD, is Professor Emeritus and the founding dean of the School of Business Administration at Pacific Lutheran University. His teaching has focused primarily on undergraduate and graduate accounting courses. He has been a Visiting Professor at Riga Technical University, Massey University in New Zealand, University of Minnesota, University of Washington, and California State University—Long Beach, and he is Professor Emeritus at Humboldt State University. Over the years, he has served on the boards of a number of organizations providing health care in the state of Washington, including the Good Samaritan Hospital, the Pierce County Health Council, Lutheran Social Services of Southwest Washington, and the Health Systems Agency. He has also been a consultant to the Washington State Hospital Commission. Currently, he is serving on the Board of Visitors of the Children's Therapy Unit of Good Samaritan Hospital. Dr. Zulauf has co-authored three books in accounting systems for medical groups. He holds a master's degree from Columbia University and a doctorate from the University of Minnesota. In addition, he is a Certified Public Accountant in the state of Washington.

Appendix 8–A

Present Value Tables

$$PV = \frac{1}{(1 + \gamma)n}$$

PRESENT VALUE OF $1

Period	2%	4%	6%	8%	10%	12%	14%	16%	18%	20%	22%	24%	26%	28%	30%	35%	40%	45%	50%
1	0.980	0.962	0.943	0.926	0.909	0.893	0.877	0.862	0.847	0.833	0.820	0.806	0.794	0.781	0.769	0.741	0.714	0.690	0.667
2	0.961	0.925	0.890	0.857	0.826	0.797	0.769	0.743	0.718	0.694	0.672	0.650	0.630	0.610	0.592	0.549	0.510	0.476	0.444
3	0.942	0.889	0.840	0.794	0.751	0.712	0.675	0.641	0.609	0.579	0.551	0.524	0.500	0.477	0.455	0.406	0.364	0.328	0.296
4	0.924	0.855	0.792	0.735	0.683	0.636	0.592	0.552	0.516	0.482	0.451	0.423	0.397	0.373	0.350	0.301	0.260	0.226	0.198
5	0.906	0.822	0.747	0.681	0.621	0.567	0.519	0.476	0.437	0.402	0.370	0.341	0.315	0.291	0.269	0.223	0.186	0.156	0.132
6	0.888	0.790	0.705	0.630	0.564	0.507	0.456	0.410	0.370	0.335	0.303	0.275	0.250	0.227	0.207	0.165	0.133	0.108	0.088
7	0.871	0.760	0.665	0.583	0.513	0.452	0.400	0.354	0.314	0.279	0.249	0.222	0.198	0.178	0.159	0.122	0.095	0.074	0.059
8	0.853	0.731	0.627	0.540	0.467	0.404	0.351	0.305	0.266	0.233	0.204	0.179	0.157	0.139	0.123	0.091	0.068	0.051	0.039
9	0.837	0.703	0.592	0.500	0.424	0.361	0.308	0.263	0.225	0.194	0.167	0.144	0.125	0.108	0.094	0.067	0.048	0.035	0.026
10	0.820	0.676	0.558	0.463	0.386	0.322	0.270	0.227	0.191	0.162	0.137	0.116	0.099	0.085	0.073	0.050	0.035	0.024	0.017
11	0.804	0.650	0.527	0.429	0.350	0.287	0.237	0.195	0.162	0.135	0.112	0.094	0.079	0.066	0.056	0.037	0.025	0.017	0.012
12	0.788	0.625	0.497	0.397	0.319	0.257	0.208	0.168	0.137	0.112	0.092	0.076	0.062	0.052	0.043	0.027	0.018	0.012	0.008
13	0.773	0.601	0.469	0.368	0.290	0.229	0.182	0.145	0.116	0.093	0.075	0.061	0.050	0.040	0.033	0.020	0.013	0.008	0.005
14	0.758	0.577	0.442	0.340	0.263	0.205	0.160	0.125	0.099	0.079	0.062	0.049	0.039	0.032	0.025	0.015	0.009	0.006	0.003
15	0.743	0.555	0.417	0.315	0.239	0.183	0.140	0.108	0.084	0.065	0.051	0.040	0.031	0.025	0.020	0.011	0.006	0.004	0.002
16	0.728	0.534	0.394	0.292	0.218	0.163	0.123	0.093	0.071	0.054	0.042	0.032	0.025	0.019	0.015	0.008	0.005	0.003	0.002
17	0.714	0.513	0.371	0.270	0.198	0.146	0.108	0.080	0.060	0.045	0.034	0.026	0.020	0.015	0.012	0.006	0.003	0.002	0.001
18	0.700	0.494	0.350	0.250	0.180	0.130	0.095	0.069	0.051	0.038	0.028	0.021	0.016	0.012	0.009	0.005	0.002	0.001	0.001
19	0.686	0.475	0.331	0.232	0.164	0.116	0.083	0.060	0.043	0.031	0.023	0.017	0.012	0.009	0.007	0.003	0.002	0.001	0.001
20	0.673	0.456	0.312	0.215	0.149	0.104	0.073	0.051	0.037	0.026	0.019	0.014	0.010	0.007	0.005	0.002	0.001	0.001	
21	0.660	0.439	0.294	0.199	0.135	0.093	0.064	0.044	0.031	0.022	0.015	0.011	0.008	0.006	0.004	0.002	0.001		
22	0.647	0.422	0.278	0.184	0.123	0.083	0.056	0.038	0.026	0.018	0.013	0.009	0.006	0.004	0.003	0.001	0.001		
23	0.634	0.406	0.262	0.170	0.112	0.074	0.049	0.033	0.022	0.015	0.010	0.007	0.005	0.003	0.002	0.001			
24	0.622	0.390	0.247	0.158	0.102	0.066	0.043	0.028	0.019	0.013	0.008	0.006	0.004	0.003	0.002	0.001			
25	0.610	0.375	0.233	0.146	0.092	0.059	0.038	0.024	0.016	0.010	0.007	0.005	0.003	0.002	0.001	0.001			
30	0.552	0.308	0.174	0.099	0.057	0.033	0.020	0.012	0.007	0.004	0.003	0.002	0.001						
35	0.500	0.253	0.130	0.068	0.036	0.019	0.010	0.006	0.003	0.002	0.001	0.001							
40	0.453	0.208	0.097	0.046	0.022	0.011	0.005	0.003	0.002	0.001									
45	0.410	0.171	0.073	0.031	0.014	0.006	0.003	0.001	0.001										
50	0.372	0.141	0.054	0.021	0.009	0.003	0.001	0.001											

$$PV = \frac{1 + (1 + \gamma)^n}{\gamma}$$

PRESENT VALUE OF AN ANNUITY OF $1

Period	2%	4%	6%	8%	10%	12%	14%	16%	18%	20%	22%	24%	26%	28%	30%	35%	40%	45%	50%
1	0.980	0.962	0.943	0.926	0.909	0.893	0.877	0.862	0.847	0.833	0.820	0.806	0.794	0.781	0.769	0.741	0.714	0.690	0.667
2	1.942	1.886	1.833	1.783	1.736	1.690	1.647	1.605	1.566	1.528	1.492	1.457	1.424	1.392	1.361	1.289	1.224	1.165	1.111
3	2.884	2.775	2.673	2.577	2.486	2.402	2.322	2.246	2.174	2.106	2.042	1.981	1.923	1.868	1.816	1.696	1.589	1.493	1.407
4	3.808	3.630	3.465	3.312	3.170	3.037	2.914	2.798	2.690	2.589	2.494	2.404	2.320	2.241	2.166	1.997	1.849	1.720	1.605
5	4.713	4.452	4.212	3.993	3.791	3.605	3.433	3.274	3.127	2.991	2.864	2.745	2.635	2.532	2.436	2.220	2.035	1.876	1.737
6	5.601	5.242	4.917	4.623	4.355	4.111	3.889	3.685	3.498	3.326	3.167	3.020	2.885	2.759	2.643	2.385	2.168	1.983	1.824
7	6.472	6.002	5.582	5.206	4.868	4.564	4.288	4.039	3.812	3.605	3.416	3.242	3.083	2.937	2.802	2.508	2.263	2.057	1.883
8	7.325	6.733	6.210	5.747	5.335	4.968	4.639	4.344	4.078	3.837	3.619	3.421	3.241	3.076	2.925	2.598	2.331	2.109	1.922
9	8.162	7.435	6.802	6.247	5.759	5.328	4.946	4.607	4.303	4.031	3.786	3.566	3.366	3.184	3.019	2.665	2.379	2.144	1.948
10	8.983	8.111	7.360	6.710	6.145	5.650	5.216	4.833	4.494	4.192	3.923	3.682	3.465	3.269	3.092	2.715	2.414	2.168	1.965
11	9.787	8.760	7.887	7.139	6.495	5.938	5.453	5.029	4.656	4.327	4.035	3.776	3.543	3.335	3.147	2.752	2.438	2.185	1.977
12	10.575	9.385	8.384	7.536	6.814	6.194	5.660	5.197	4.793	4.439	4.127	3.851	3.606	3.387	3.190	2.779	2.456	2.196	1.985
13	11.348	9.986	8.853	7.904	7.103	6.424	5.842	5.342	4.910	4.533	4.203	3.912	3.656	3.427	3.223	2.799	2.469	2.204	1.990
14	12.106	10.563	9.295	8.244	7.367	6.628	6.002	5.468	5.008	4.611	4.265	3.962	3.695	3.459	3.249	2.814	2.478	2.210	1.993
15	12.849	11.118	9.712	8.559	7.606	6.811	6.142	5.575	5.092	4.675	4.315	4.001	3.726	3.483	3.268	2.825	2.484	2.214	1.995
16	13.578	11.652	10.106	8.851	7.824	6.974	6.265	5.668	5.162	4.730	4.357	4.033	3.751	3.503	3.283	2.834	2.489	2.216	1.997
17	14.292	12.166	10.477	9.122	8.022	7.120	6.373	5.749	5.222	4.775	4.391	4.059	3.771	3.518	3.295	2.840	2.492	2.218	1.998
18	14.992	12.659	10.828	9.372	8.201	7.250	6.467	5.818	5.273	4.812	4.419	4.080	3.786	3.529	3.304	2.844	2.494	2.219	1.999
19	15.678	13.134	11.158	9.604	8.365	7.366	6.550	5.877	5.316	4.843	4.442	4.097	3.799	3.539	3.311	2.848	2.496	2.220	1.999
20	16.351	13.590	11.470	9.818	8.514	7.469	6.623	5.929	5.353	4.870	4.460	4.110	3.808	3.546	3.316	2.850	2.497	2.221	1.999
21	17.011	14.029	11.764	10.017	8.649	7.562	6.687	5.973	5.384	4.891	4.476	4.121	3.816	3.551	3.320	2.852	2.498	2.221	2.000
22	17.658	14.451	12.042	10.201	8.772	7.645	6.743	6.011	5.410	4.909	4.488	4.130	3.822	3.556	3.323	2.853	2.498	2.222	2.000
23	18.292	14.857	12.303	10.371	8.883	7.718	6.792	6.044	5.432	4.925	4.499	4.137	3.827	3.559	3.325	2.854	2.499	2.222	2.000
24	18.914	15.247	12.550	10.529	8.985	7.784	6.835	6.073	5.451	4.937	4.507	4.143	3.831	3.562	3.327	2.855	2.499	2.222	2.000
25	19.523	15.622	12.783	10.675	9.077	7.843	6.873	6.097	5.467	4.948	4.514	4.147	3.834	3.564	3.329	2.856	2.499	2.222	2.000
30	22.396	17.292	13.765	11.258	9.427	8.055	7.003	6.177	5.517	4.979	4.534	4.160	3.842	3.569	3.332	2.857	2.500	2.222	2.000
35	24.999	18.665	14.498	11.655	9.644	8.176	7.070	6.215	5.539	4.992	4.541	4.164	3.845	3.571	3.333	2.857	2.500	2.222	2.000
40	27.355	19.793	15.046	11.925	9.779	8.244	7.105	6.233	5.548	4.997	4.544	4.166	3.846	3.571	3.333	2.857	2.500	2.222	2.000
45	29.490	20.720	15.456	12.108	9.863	8.283	7.123	6.244	5.552	4.999	4.545	4.166	3.846	3.571	3.333	2.857	2.500	2.222	2.000
50	31.424	21.482	15.762	12.233	9.915	8.304	7.133	6.246	5.554	4.999	4.545	4.167	3.846	3.571	3.333	2.857	2.500	2.222	2.000

Chapter 9

Planning Health Care Facilities and Managing the Development Process

James E. Hosking

BACKGROUND

The Hill-Burton Hospital Survey and Construction Act of 1946 encouraged construction of health care facilities by recognizing that voluntary hospitals needed capital support for renovation and expansion of hospital facilities. Consequently, many new hospitals and hospital expansion programs were completed during the 1950s and the early 1960s. Starting in the late 1960s, through a series of health planning laws, the emphasis within government programs shifted from supporting hospital construction to controlling it. With the enactment of Public Law 89-749 in 1966, construction and expansion became reviewable in terms of areawide need rather than institutional need. Subsequent laws refined this process of comprehensive health planning. Public Laws 90-174 and 92-603 initiated 1122 reviews, and Public Law 93-641 set up the Certificate of Need (CON) process mandating state review of major health care capital expenditures and new services.

In the 1980s, demands for greater convenience, an increased supply of physicians, new technologies, and continued cost pressures led to a major shift to ambulatory services and new competition for traditional hospitals. Solo physicians formed large, single, or multispecialty groups and added diagnostic services to their offices. Entrepreneurial physicians and investors formed partnerships to build and operate freestanding surgery, cancer centers, and diagnostic centers in direct competition with local hospitals.

A major impetus for the ambulatory shift was the enactment of the Medicare prospective payment system in 1983. Under this system, hospitals are paid a predetermined amount for Medicare inpatients based on diagnosis-related groups (DRGs) regardless of costs. Initially, capital costs continued to be cost reimbursed; however, in 1992, capital costs began being phased into the DRG payment. Thus, a fixed payment per DRG must be allocated to cover capital costs, as well as operating expenses, depreciation, and interest charges. Similarly, states have begun basing Medicaid payments on DRGs and/or capitating eligible patient populations. Additionally, ambulatory DRGs (APGs) are being implemented to fix payment for ambulatory patients. Over the past 20 years, the incentives for health care providers to build and expand have changed to manage and control capital expenditures.

Because of the shifting market and government incentives, state CON reviews of major capital expenditures and new programs and services have been eased or eliminated in many states. The value of CONs will continue to be debated as entrepreneurs attempt to enter new markets while existing providers protect their franchises.

FACILITY PLANNING IN HEALTH CARE SYSTEMS

As a result of the shrinking inpatient market, limited financial resources, diverse competition, and the increasing prominence of managed care organizations, health care providers are joining forces in networks and systems, and the number of independent hospitals is falling rapidly. Thus, a major facility-planning focus for the new millennium will be reallocating the existing physical resources of independent facilities into a cost-effective organized delivery system with multiple campuses that provide a continuum of care from wellness/fitness centers and primary care centers to tertiary referral hospitals and skilled nursing centers. Downsizing and patient care redesign will continue to be factors for the next several years; however, it will be difficult to achieve significant additional savings without considering facility changes.

With the flurry of merger activity in the early 1990s, many new organized delivery systems were formed and significant operational savings were promised in order to gain community and regulatory approval for the mergers. Many of these new systems initially have focused on organizational issues, such as the consolidation of administrative and support services. In most cases, limited con-

solidation of major clinical programs has occurred. One of the major difficulties with clinical service consolidation is inadequate physical capacity to consolidate programs at one site. As many institutions will not be able to achieve the promised savings without consolidation of major clinical services, construction activity should increase by the turn of the century.

A major consideration in clinical services consolidation and/or development is the balance between geographic coverage and economies of scale. A larger, high-volume program is typically more efficient and cost-effective, but organizations must determine the distances that their patients are willing to travel, as well their vulnerability to existing or new competition. As systems evaluate the possibility of vertical expansion, they also should consider alternatives to full control and ownership, such as strategic alliances or joint ventures with existing service providers or specialty providers that may consider entering the market. Alternatives to ownership may include leasing existing buildings, working with developers on a "build-to-suit" basis, or even the sale/lease back of existing facilities to raise capital for other needs. Integrating strategic, operations, financial, facility, and equipment planning is more important today than ever before, as limited capital resources must support strategic system initiatives.

In most cases, systems have allowed individual hospitals to select their own planning and design team, determine facility priorities, and manage their own processes. Typically, the only direct system input has been prioritizing capital expenditures at the system level and allocating capital to individual hospitals based on system priorities rather than individual hospital priorities. As organized delivery systems evolve, however, it appears that more facility-planning activities will be centralized. Most systems will develop corporate departments responsible for all planning, design, and construction activities. In most cases, department staff select and manage external health care facility–planning teams, but design and construction professionals on staff may handle smaller projects. An alternative approach gaining some acceptance is to outsource all planning, design, and construction management activities to one or more firms for a fixed period of years. In this case, the outside professionals act as the in-house department, even though they are employees of other firms.

FUTURE FACILITY PLANNING TRENDS

In response to the limitations on financial resources, attention has turned to modernizing facilities rather than replacing them. For example, inpatient areas have been retrofitted for ambulatory care and alternative uses, and freestanding delivery sites have been established to maintain/develop market areas and make services more convenient to patients. This trend of downsizing inpatient capacity and expanding outpatient care will continue. Additionally, hospital and alternative care providers will continue to expand home care programs, possibly preventive care, and elder care services to complete the continuum of care—particularly if capitation is expanded as a payment mechanism.

Continuing change in the health care environment and evolution toward organized delivery systems will affect facilities development for the next decade. Several general trends will be observed as systems level facility planning evolves:

* *Changing Inpatient Care Delivery.* To attain cost-effective operations while providing better care for more acutely ill patients and segregating patients according to their special needs and preferences, hospitals are increasingly turning to private rooms. Additionally, as fewer patients are admitted and their stays are shorter, those left in the hospital are more likely to need critical care; thus, a larger percentage of beds are being monitored and designed for critical care. Several hospitals have established universal rooms sized and planned to meet the needs of multilevels of care. Also, more services are being brought to the patient rather than the patient being brought to the services. These and other factors have significantly increased the support space required on patient care units.

* *Continuing Technological Advances.* Flexibility will continue to gain importance in facility planning. In the 1960s, hospitals had to accommodate nuclear medicine; in the 1970s, computed tomography scanners; and in the 1980s, magnetic resonance imaging. In the 1990s, new technological advances have continued to make new demands on facilities. Advances in information technology have enhanced satellite testing/diagnosis, for example, and will continue to play a major role in the future with filmless radiology departments, integrated computerized medical records, noninvasive surgery, and telediagnostics to link remote sites to specialists and expensive technology. Information technology also allows more staff members (e.g., transcriptionists) to work at home and makes it possible for others (e.g., radiologists) to be available around the clock without leaving home. To accommodate new technology, facilities must have maximum remodeling flexibility and expansion capability.

* *Return-on-Investment Orientation.* Be-

cause it is no longer permissible to pass capital costs through to payers, managers of health care facilities review potential projects more carefully. Facility projects implementing strategic objectives or reducing operating costs will have priority over routine modernization projects. In order to remain competitive, investments in physical plant and equipment are necessary, but prudence in reviewing such investments and allocating funds is essential. Before initiating a construction project, hospital administrators will be more likely to evaluate alternatives to facilities expansion, such as extended hours of operation to increase room equipment capacity and utilization management to reduce demand. In addition to the initial costs, operating costs must be considered in the selection of building systems and the design of patient care units and ancillary services. Life cycle costing identifies cost-saving opportunities that may require larger initial investments to reduce operating costs and conserve scarce resources over an extended period of time.

- *Consolidation of Services at Both System and Hospital Levels.* Over the years, health care has become more specialized; small clinical and nonclinical services have developed throughout institutions. Similarly, organizations have created additional layers of management. Downsizing and redesigning activities are likely to consolidate or eliminate many of the small departments of today to maximize efficiency and reduce the duplication of facilities and support staff. For example, facility planning will focus on grouping reception, waiting, and staff areas for multiple departments. The reduction in department management positions will reduce office space require-

ments. Additionally, the use of more open landscape furniture will save space and increase flexibility. With the shift of decision making to the system level, more services will be consolidated across the system. Services will be duplicated primarily to provide geographic coverage and attain strategic advantage.

- *Outsourcing.* Hospitals historically have maintained an on-site laundry, warehouse, kitchen, central supply, and pharmacy. To reduce costs, some hospitals have closed their in-house laundries, and many hospitals have begun to implement "just-in-time" warehouse policies. A just-in-time policy is when a supplier warehouses supplies and delivers them to the provider on a frequent and as-needed basis. These trends will intensify as a result of hospital consolidations into organized delivery systems. Systems also will look for ways to reduce costs further in these areas by outsourcing; they may contract with off-site central reprocessing vendors, use prepared meals or depend on shared production kitchens, and implement just-in-time pharmacy systems (potentially run by the hospital system). Similarly, they may outsource records management, facility management, or business office functions. Reducing their direct involvement in many business and support activities allows them to focus on their core competencies.

- *Increasing Space Requirements.* Over the past several decades, the number of square feet required for each bed in a hospital has increased to accommodate new services and programs. Traditionally, this square foot per bed figure was computed by dividing the total square feet of the hospital by the number of beds. Never a truly representative figure, the concept has become outmoded as more services are provided on an outpatient basis or away from the hospital altogether in freestanding facilities. Thus, it is more accurate to seek the most efficient use of space for technology and treatment purposes by projecting square footage in terms of service utilization. The space to accommodate outpatients in many departments is greater than that required for inpatients. Outpatients need space to change into a gown, go through the preparation process, undergo the procedure, and recover in the department, while many of the same activities for inpatients can take place in the patient's room. Thus, the shift of services to an outpatient basis does not necessarily decrease the overall need for space.

- *Geographic Market Coverage.* As managed care continues to reduce inpatient utilization, the emerging organized delivery systems are searching for ways to maintain/increase market share and serve target market areas better by bringing services to patients and tying physicians to their systems. Many systems have used a significant amount of the capital resources previously allocated to hospital facilities development to purchasing physician practices and facilities, recruiting new physicians and placing them in target market areas in leased space, or developing ambulatory care/primary care facilities. Additionally, organized delivery systems own and manage numerous office buildings around the market (often more a liability than an asset). Geographic market coverage will continue to be important to demonstrate to managed care companies that a hospital's services and physicians are conveniently located to attract additional subscribers to their plan.

- *Continued Proliferation of Freestanding Facilities.* In the 1990s, major facility development issues have involved not only the retrofitting of inpatient facilities, but also the development of freestanding alternative health care delivery centers (e.g., urgent care centers, primary care centers, ambulatory surgery centers, birthing centers, wellness centers). These alternative health care delivery centers, designed for the treatment of ambulatory, non–life-threatening conditions that need not be treated in a hospital, represent the health care industry's response to the population's growing health care consumerism, managed care, concern about rising hospital costs, and interest in convenience and greater participation in the care of family members. Another factor in the development of alternative health care delivery centers has been the significant competition among physicians and hospitals in metropolitan areas. Physicians are seeking new ways to maintain or create a patient base. Under managed care, more independent physicians have joined together in large group practices. In order to maintain their current income, they will need to review operations and make better use of their physical facilities. Additionally, physicians must compete with hospitals and other physicians for profitable ambulatory care services by catering to consumer desires for evening and weekend hours, house calls, or out-of-hospital deliveries.

FACILITY DEVELOPMENT PROCESS

The increasing cost pressures on health care providers mandate an ongoing planning process to anticipate market initiatives and guide development plans. A strategic plan at

the system (i.e., corporate) level should outline the goals and vision of the system; highlight strengths, weaknesses, threats, and opportunities; address alternative scenarios of
market-based directions; and establish priorities for program development that should be
the basis of physical development.

It is recommended that, in the future, facility planning take place at the corporate level
in organized delivery systems. Therefore,
once the system's strategic plan is established, the physical facilities–planning process can begin to address the facility requirements of each delivery site in the system in an
orderly and progressive manner. Without organizational approval and support for the strategic plan, the facility-planning process may
have no focus and can meander on tangential
issues, lengthening the overall process.

The two major phases of the facility development process, planning/design and construction, evolve through many separate, but
interrelated, activities that can be grouped
into two major categories—facility planning
and implementation planning. Facility planning is the process of planning, designing,
and building the physical facility. Implementation planning involves related management
and operational activities, such as ensuring
financing, planning operations, selecting
equipment and furniture, and obtaining the
regulatory approvals that are necessary for
facility planning to proceed in a timely manner. Generically, this process applies to all
types of health care facilities; however, the
complexity, time frame, and regulatory approvals may vary significantly. Figure 9–1
outlines a generic schedule of the facility development process for a hospital project with
an approximate time frame for each activity.
The sequence and duration of each of these
activities vary somewhat, depending on
project scope, complexity, and implementation strategy.

Working with a qualified external planning
team and following the guidelines of a reasonable schedule, the role of the organized
delivery system management in the process is
to review, comment, and make timely decisions on the team's recommendations. This
review-and-response interaction among the
various parties may require administrative
and board decisions before each phase of activity begins.

Facility Planning

There are seven major steps in the facilities
planning process. The sequence of the activities varies according to the development
strategy employed.

Master Site and Facility Planning

A master plan establishes a framework for
addressing a system's potential site and facility needs over an undefined period. With a
sound master site and facility plan, the system
can respond to rapid growth or to the need to
replace existing facilities in a phased and
logical manner. The system's master site and
facility plan should take into account several
key items:

- Needs of all delivery sites in the organized delivery system
- Interdepartmental relationships within
  those sites
- Flow of patients, visitors, staff, and supplies throughout the system and within
  those sites
- Site development, including parking
  needs and traffic patterns
- Other current and planned facilities on
  the campus, such as an ambulatory care
  center, physicians' office building, long-
  term care facility, parking structure, and
  specialty centers
- A functional and engineering evaluation

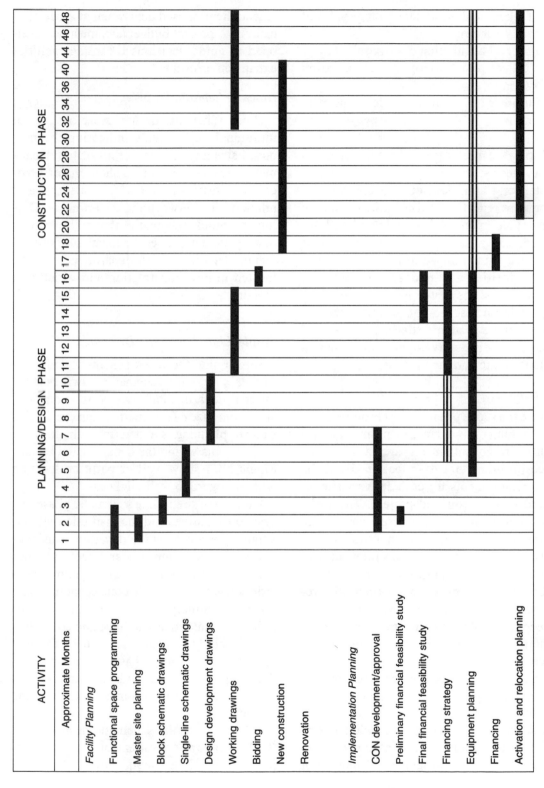

Figure 9–1 Stages in the Facility Development Process. *Source:* Copyright 1987, James E. Hosking.

of the immediate and long-range value of
each structure

- Property acquisition or disposal
- Vertical and horizontal transportation
  systems
- Future expansion of services and programs

During the master site and facility planning
phase, the system managers approve a fundamental long-term development concept, development priorities, and potential phasing of
that development. Once reviewed and approved, the master site and facility plan is
used in conjunction with the system's program priorities and budget constraints to
identify the scope of the initial phase of the
proposed projects. Program priorities that are
defined in the system's strategic plan should
guide the facility development priorities in
the master site and facility plan.

Functional Space Programming

Once the scope of the project is defined, the
system management or, in many cases, a
health care consultant prepares a functional
space program that describes in detail the
space requirements for each delivery site included in the proposed project. The functional space program addresses current and
future activities, outlines operational concepts, reviews past and projects future utilization and staffing, outlines room-by-room
space needs, identifies major proximity requirements and planning considerations, and
conceptually illustrates internal interdepartmental and intradepartmental organization of
space.

During the functional space programming
phase, the system managers determine the
delivery sites to be included in the project;
review the future program, utilization, operational systems, and staffing assumptions in
the functional space program; and approve or

amend the proposed departmental space allocations. A project budget also must be developed to guide decisions regarding facilities
expansion priorities.

Block Schematic Drawings

Block schematic drawings are outlines of
individual departments indicating the proposed size and location of all of the departments. The drawings also show major vertical and horizontal traffic patterns and
relationships between the departments. During the block schematic phase, the system
management approves the location of departments, deciding which departments will be
located in new construction and which will
remain "as is" or expand in existing buildings.

Single-Line Schematic Drawings

Developing the block schematic drawings
further, single-line schematic drawings show
internal departmental layouts, relationships,
and room sizes. The main emphasis in this
stage of planning is to determine the location
of the rooms within the departmental blocks.
Single lines show wall or partition location
without regard to wall thickness.

During the single-line schematic phase, the
system executives and the institution administrators, particularly the department managers, review and approve architectural floor
plans (departmental layouts), preliminary exterior elevations, generic equipment lists, and
other preliminary design concepts. At this
point, adequate square footage and cost information should be available for the CON and
preliminary financial feasibility analysis so
that the project scope can be adjusted as necessary to avoid problems in later stages of the
project.

At the end of the schematic design stage,
the health care consultant or architect prepares room data sheets outlining recom-

mended building systems criteria for communications; lighting; heating, ventilation, and air conditioning; medical gas; and equipment considerations that will be defined in the design development process.

Design Development Drawings

Refining the single-line schematics, design development plans show wall thicknesses and locations of built-in equipment and casework, as well as mechanical, electrical, structural, and architectural systems required within the individual rooms in the project. Also at this time, the equipment consultant prepares equipment specifications and provides "cutsheets" for the architects and engineers to illustrate equipment layouts and utility requirements.

During the design development phase, the system executives and the institution managers, in particular the department managers, review and approve room details, outline specifications, room finishes, and design refinements. For example, they consider the number and location of medical gas outlets; locations, width, and type of doors; types of heating, ventilation, and air conditioning systems; details of casework; and selection of windows and exterior materials.

Working Drawings/Construction Documents

In the working drawing stage, architectural details are refined to meet the requirements of the departments that were outlined in the design development drawings. For example, mechanical, electrical, and plumbing systems are sized. During this phase, the system and institution managers review and approve the working drawings and final specifications before they are released to potential contractors for bidding. Typically, this phase involves only limited participation at the departmental level of the institution.

Construction

The last major phase of the facility development process is the actual construction of the new and/or renovated facilities. The construction or renovation activities are scheduled so as to minimize the interruption of normal operations, although they may interfere with or restrict some institutional functions. During the construction phase, the system and the institution executives need to minimize change orders—both owner- and contractor-initiated—plan for occupancy of the new building, and procure medical equipment and furnishings.

Implementation Planning

Simultaneously with physical facilities planning, design, and construction, implementation planning activities occur. The sequence of its basic activities varies, depending on the facility development strategy, internal management capabilities, and external factors of the organized health care delivery system.

Certificate-of-Need Development

In many states, a CON must be submitted to the state and regional review agencies to seek approval for any new or upgraded facility. The application must be timed to permit the facility development schedule to proceed without major interruptions. Generally, the system submits the application after approving the block schematic plans; however, some states require single-line schematic drawings.

The system must develop a strategy to move the CON through the review process with minimal delays and compromises. Some states require applications to be batched and submitted according to a predetermined schedule. Because this requirement could affect the overall project schedule, management must consider it to ensure that the project is not delayed.

Financial Feasibility Study and Financing Strategy

An evaluation of the system's financial operations is necessary to determine its debt capacity. Based on this evaluation, management develops a strategy to finance the projects at a reasonable cost while providing flexibility to respond to future capital needs. In order to prepare the financial feasibility study, the system executives, often with the assistance of an external planning team, develop an overall project budget identifying all project-related costs, including professional fees (e.g., attorney fees), land acquisition, equipment, financing, and construction. In organized health care delivery systems that have centralized the facility-planning function, financial feasibility analyses are likely to be done internally.

The system needs to determine how it will fund these development projects and other capital requirements of the master plan. A preliminary feasibility study, performed early in the project, examines major assumptions regarding construction costs, utilization, and interest rates so that the project scope can be adjusted as necessary with minimal loss of time and effort. The final feasibility study, performed after the receipt of construction bids, focuses on actual interest rates at the time of financing. If the project involves bond financing, additional consultants such as underwriters and bond counsel will be necessary to prepare documents and help sell the bonds.

Medical Equipment Planning

Evaluating existing equipment, determining what can be relocated, and deciding what additional equipment will be needed for the new and/or renovated facilities are essential activities. They should begin as early as possible so that the initial project budget and CON application can accurately reflect equipment needs. Once defined, equipment requirements must be communicated to the architects and engineers to ensure that room sizes, layouts, and utilities are adequate to accommodate the equipment.

As technology becomes more sophisticated, medical equipment consumes a greater percentage of a health care system's overall capital budget. Appropriate planning may require external assistance to ensure objective determination of reuse, proper lead times for timely installation, adequate planning information, and competitive pricing.

Facility Activation and Occupancy Planning

Thorough planning is necessary for the smooth opening and activation of the new and/or renovated facilities. Development of operational systems, determination of staffing levels and staff recruitment plans, definition of relocation strategies, equipment installation schedules, and development of a building activation schedule all occur during this activity. Management engineers are important participants in this process. Careful planning facilitates a smooth transition to and maximum effectiveness of the new and/or renovated facilities once they are occupied.

FUNCTIONAL CONSIDERATIONS IN FACILITY PLANNING

Whether evaluating the adequacy of existing facilities or considering new construction, planners must take some functional facility-planning considerations into account. Primary planning considerations include separating patient, service, and public traffic flow; maximizing operating efficiencies; providing for future expansion; and optimizing functional relationships and patient flow among sites of service in an organized delivery system.

In analyzing the functional needs of a service, it is important to consider these major factors that influence utilization:

- Scope of services
- Operations (e.g., hours of operation, policies of scheduling certain tests on certain days, or special room designation in surgery)
- Equipment (e.g., automated versus manual equipment, dedicated versus multiuse equipment, potential new technology)
- Staffing (e.g., full-time versus part-time, maximum number of people on the primary shift)
- Workload (e.g., projected inpatient/outpatient mix, procedure mix, clinical protocols, capitation)
- Competition (e.g., likelihood of new providers or existing hospitals and physician groups developing competing services)
- Current operations and future facility plans of other health care delivery sites in the system

Managers can use these and the following considerations both to evaluate existing facilities and to determine the long-term use of the system's physical assets.

Patient Care Units

Hospitals traditionally have been developed around the primary unit, the patient bed. Complete patient care services should integrate 28 to 36 patient beds into effective and efficient patient care units. Although an equal mix of private and semiprivate (two-bed) rooms has historically been appropriate, the increasing acuity of inpatients, patient desire for privacy, and the desire for flexibility over time shifted the mix toward all private designs for the 1990s.

Patient care units should be located in a patient tower served by a central elevator core. Ideally, two to three patient care units are located on one level so that they can share some common support services. If two or more patient care units are on the same level, traffic should not have to pass through one unit to reach the other.

Today, many hospitals are implementing patient-centered care and redesigning patient care delivery systems, typically by decentralizing some medical and administrative ancillaries on the nursing floors. Although this is the current trend for patient unit design, long-term flexibility is necessary to avoid costly errors. With the significant shift from inpatient to outpatient care, hospitals today must also develop facilities around the new primary unit, the ambulatory visit, and focus services near convenient parking and ambulatory entrance facilities.

Medical Ancillary Services

It is best to locate medical ancillary facilities in an area where they can be expanded independently as necessary. Major medical ancillary departments that are expensive to relocate, such as radiology, laboratory, surgery, emergency, and central reprocessing, should be located by exterior walls and next to "soft" areas (e.g., office areas) that can be converted inexpensively to other uses. In organized health care delivery systems, some ancillary services should be available at independent sites to serve patients and physicians more efficiently than if they are hospital focused.

The outpatient and inpatient mix served by each service requires consideration. With the trend to ambulatory care, depending on volume, separate inpatient and outpatient ancillary services may be necessary, especially if many physicians are practicing in or adjacent to the hospital and if the volume of service is high enough to justify duplicate staffing and equipment.

Although campus-based ambulatory care centers proliferated in the late 1980s, most of the ambulatory care development today is strategically located off-site in key market areas. In many cases, hospitals are consolidating inpatient and outpatient services to achieve economies of scale and operational flexibilities. Some organizations are taking planning a step further physically and organizationally, eliminating numerous departmental "silos," which fragment patient service and create duplication of support services. Multidisciplinary diagnostic centers provide the services of multiple departments to both inpatients and outpatients in one convenient area.

Elevators and Transportation Systems

Generally, patient, service, and visitor/personnel elevators should be segregated, but centralized, to maximize flexibility during peak load times. This is a very important consideration, particularly when elevators are out of service. If the elevators are centralized, a single malfunctioning elevator will not greatly disrupt traffic patterns and service within the central transportation core. Flexibility in terms of size is also an important consideration. All patient/service elevators should be large enough to carry a hospital bed with an orthopedic frame. Patient/service elevators should not be visible from the public areas.

Materials transportation systems also merit consideration. With the increased use of hospital information systems, the need for pneumatic tubes or dumbwaiters for paper docu-

mentation is decreasing. Similarly, efficient materials management and unit-dose pharmacy systems reduce the need for automated tote-box and cart-type systems. Although automated materials transportation systems are generally expensive to install and maintain, management should not rule them out as impractical or too expensive without a full life cycle cost analysis. In assessing materials transport alternatives, it is important to make sure that floor-to-floor heights are adequate to accommodate the system.

Traffic Patterns

Ideally, travel through any institution in the system, particularly patient travel, requires only one elevator trip. Thus, it is desirable to locate all ancillary services so that a patient can reach them from any nursing unit by traveling in one elevator. This principle also holds true for outpatients, who should be able to arrive at one central point and easily move on to the appropriate service. General horizontal circulation patterns should be planned to separate service and public traffic.

Travel Distance

Minimizing the distance that patients and personnel travel from one department or one site in the system to another will reduce operating costs. Generally, all hospitals require a two- or three-level ancillary base with the bed towers located above to minimize these distances. Some hospitals have separated medical ancillaries, bed towers, and support services into distinct buildings built to different building codes to reduce initial construction costs.

Relationships Between Departments

Interdepartmental relationships require considerable attention in planning a major facilities expansion or replacement (Figure 9–2). Ideally, all services should be centrally located and adjacent to the elevator core, but some compromises must be made. In order to reduce operating costs, hospitals should consider grouping smaller departments to share support areas, such as reception and waiting, locker/lounge areas, and conference rooms.

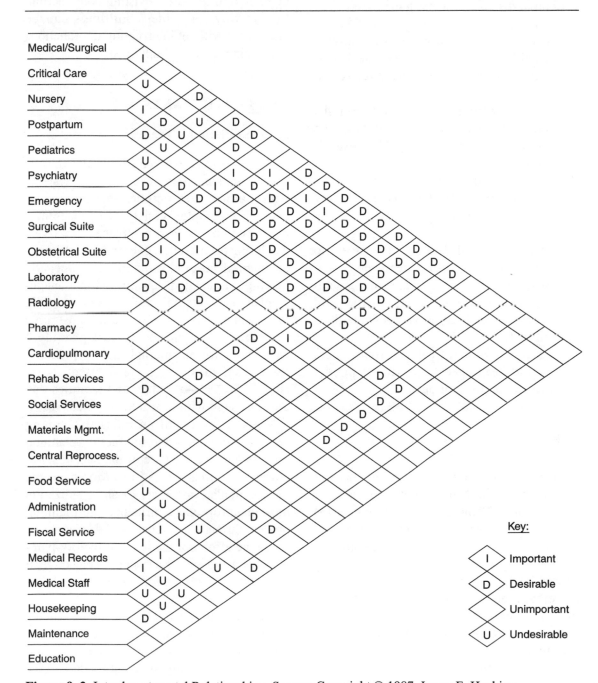

Figure 9–2 Interdepartmental Relationships. *Source:* Copyright © 1987, James E. Hosking.

Intradepartmental Design

The internal design of the various departments should meet similar criteria for service, patient, and staff traffic separation:

- The patient reception and waiting area should be near the entrance of the department, but it should not open directly into work areas.
- Gowned waiting areas should be near the treatment spaces. Patients should not be required to walk through public areas after gowning.
- To maximize privacy, toilet rooms should open off the corridors; they should not open directly into waiting spaces.
- Staff lounges should not be adjacent to patient waiting areas or treatment areas.
- Storage and utility spaces should be designed to maximize flexibility and should have a minimal amount of built-in cabinets.
- Examination and treatment room doors should be hinged to maximize patient privacy as the door opens.

Entrances

Ideally, there are six distinct entrances at each site: (1) the main entrance for patients and visitors, (2) the employee entrance, (3) the physicians' entrance, (4) the emergency entrance, (5) the outpatient entrance, and (6) the receiving entrance. Appropriate parking should be readily available at each. Furthermore, these entrances should direct the traffic into the appropriate elevator core and circulation system of the hospital. It is also necessary to direct traffic from one delivery site in a system to another.

Facility Replacement

To allow for an orderly progression of facility replacement, new construction should be related to the latest existing construction. In this way, the oldest buildings can be phased out without interrupting the functions housed in the newer buildings.

KEY PARTICIPANTS

Internal Planning Team

Hospitals have evolved from isolated, self-sustaining, single-site institutions to systems with multicampus facilities that provide an extremely complex variety of services in a highly competitive marketplace. The overwhelming proliferation of external influences on internal hospital programs and decision making has created new roles for management at every internal administrative level. In facility planning activities, the administrative decision-making process must provide a framework for an internal facility-planning team's activities, which are focused toward an end product—a system and facilities that are consistent with institutional objectives.

Many members of an internal planning team do not understand the facility-planning process and are unaware of the decisions required at various stages in it. Moreover, the more articulate members of an organization may inappropriately influence the planning process through "personalized" decisions. To focus the efforts of the internal facility-planning team and ensure a system perspective, it is necessary to do the following:

- Educate internal planning team members (e.g., board of trustees, medical staff, department managers, in-house planners) about the facility planning process.

- Define the management level at which project decisions are to be made.
- Organize the facility-planning team to facilitate decision making and implementation.
- Establish a communication mechanism to disseminate planning decisions and prevent the reintroduction of issues that already have been resolved.

The organizational structure of the internal planning team changes as system complexities change. The scope and nature of the project ultimately determine the team needed to plan and implement the project. Power struggles are inevitable as managers attempt to direct more project resources to their departments at the expense of other departments. A well managed system should be able to maintain project control at a corporate level during such inevitable conflicts.

Members of the Internal Planning Team

The organization and, therefore, the decision-making process for facility planning should not differ from the decision-making process for daily operations. Information gathering and consensus building provide a critical basis for final, administrative decision making. The information gathered is weighed and evaluated, but not every suggestion can or should be incorporated into the final facility plan; thus, informed decision making is essential.

Governing Board. For all practical purposes, the governing board has full authority and responsibility at all stages in the physical facility–planning process and is free to delegate all or portions of the decision-making responsibility to management of the organization. In the facility-planning process, the board has these major responsibilities:

- Establishing the basic objectives of the functional space program through approval of the strategic plan, as well as the master site and facility plan
- Hiring an appropriate external planning team and ultimately auditing its performance and approving its actions
- Approving the capital program budget and overseeing its control
- Signing contracts or delegating the ability to do so, and approving change orders relating to the construction project

Chief Executive Officer of the System. The major responsibilities of the system's chief executive officer (CEO) in the facility-planning process are no different from those in the system's operations. The CEO, by virtue of his or her responsibility for the system's operations, must make or approve all plans for physical facility implementation as they affect the operating mode of the institution. In turn, however, the CEO should delegate specific responsibility for facility planning to the operations staff in the affected delivery sites of the system.

Because capital development programs have a significant impact on the system's operating costs, the CEO should not delegate them to a lower organizational level. To ensure provision of the best input for critical decisions, the CEO should select an experienced and knowledgeable internal or external planning team to provide the technical input required for proper administrative decision making.

Medical Staff. Although physician influence in hospitals varies, the physician is usually an individual entrepreneur who has significant control over the utilization of a health care facility. As both the provider and consumer of health care services, the physician is a major force in initiating facility development programs. Thus, the medical staff is likely to have a strong effect on the facility-planning, decision-making process.

In this process, the physician's primary role is to provide appropriate technical input about the requirements of a specific program or service. The most effective method of securing this input may be through the existing medical staff committee structure or, as appropriate, through a single ad hoc medical staff planning committee established specifically to advise management and the external planning team. The input and output of an ad hoc committee should fall within the context of the pre-established project constraints.

User Groups. Typically, key staff members and physicians associated with a particular facility or department make up the user groups. They can play an important advisory role in the facility-planning process, providing input on specific department space, equipment needs, and design concepts. Although they sometimes have decision-making authority, most user groups are advisory only, and the decision-making/control function remains with the CEO or his or her designate. The establishment of specific facility planning user groups depends on the scope and magnitude of a particular project.

System Planner. Given the complexities of management today, many organized health care delivery systems have a staff planning department to support the CEO. The system planner not only may serve as the prime source of the system's input to the facility development process, but also may convey the information that ultimately forms the basis for management decisions. Another invaluable role of the planner is to communicate management decisions pertinent to the project to the entire hospital organization.

Framework for Controlling Time and Input. The ultimate success of a physical facility plan depends on control of time, the func-

tional space program, and design criteria. The best method to help a system's internal planning team understand its role, project time frames, and the facility activation process is the critical path method. A properly developed critical path outlines the necessary tasks, the internal planning team's role, and the time frame necessary to complete a particular planning sequence. The critical path is a road map for scheduling that educates the internal planning team members about the project sequence, team members' roles, the decision-making process, and current project status.

The functional space program and design criteria are crucial elements in project control. Appropriate input from the internal planning team members is necessary in developing these control documents. Proper project direction from management, timing, and organization will elicit the required internal planning team inputs and create a dynamic, positive planning attitude, thereby ensuring proper control and project direction.

Facility-planning projects are series of controlled compromises accomplished within the constraints of time, money, and strategic program planning. The internal planning team's role and relative input to the decision-making process vary by individual perception and level within the organization. Ultimately, however, the CEO is responsible to the governing board for implementing the facility plan.

External Planning Team

In most cases, a single health care facility cannot rely on internal resources augmented by an architect/engineer to conceive, orchestrate, implement, and activate a major facility development program. A team of professional external resource people is generally necessary to manage the project properly. In an organized health care delivery system that has centralized facility planning, the need for an external planning team changes.

Qualified external planning team members are involved in several similar projects each year and know the best approaches and options to streamline the planning process. In addition, time constraints associated with an external approval process mandate tight project control, and external professionals, being experienced in the process, are able to provide that control. A comprehensive external team includes a facility-planning consultant, equipment-planning consultant, archi-

tect/engineer, financial advisor, financial feasibility consultant, fund-raiser, construction manager, legal counsel, and underwriter (see Appendix 9–A for a description of their responsibilities). The external team's precise composition is directly dependent on the project complexity and the expertise of the internal team.

The selection and control of the external planning team influence the project outcome and its cost. Every project undergoes early changes to avoid cost overruns. The eventual outcome of a facility development plan is based on cumulative decisions, and the possi-

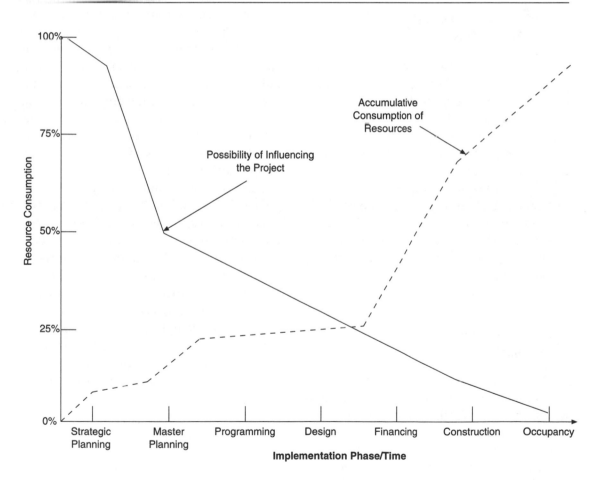

Figure 9–3 Conceptual Diagram of Resource Consumption. *Source:* Copyright © 1987, James E. Hosking.

bility of influencing a project is reduced as time progresses (Figure 9–3). A poorly run project can cost millions of dollars in construction delays, change orders, and operating costs over the life of the project. For example, an inefficiently organized department, or an over- or undersized department, creates operating problems and increases personnel costs. A poorly engineered facility generates high maintenance expenses and/or operating costs. An improperly located building or department may preclude future expansion. A poorly executed financing plan may limit future capital development opportunities.

DESIGN AND CONSTRUCTION APPROACHES

Despite competition and cost constraint pressures, health care systems will continue to be built, upgraded, and expanded. Furthermore, existing health care facilities will continue to be replaced to comply with codes, maintain accreditation, and gain a competitive advantage. A variety of facility construction alternatives are available; each affects owner control, building quality, project duration, and, ultimately, project cost. The major facility implementation alternatives are the traditional approach, the team approach, the design/build approach, and the project management approach.

Traditional Plan/Design/Bid/Build Approach

In the traditional and most common method of building, an owner, under separate contracts, engages a facility-planning consultant and an architect/engineer to plan and design a building. They prepare a functional space program, as well as a set of working drawings and specifications. Bids are requested for the project on a lump sum basis. In soliciting competitive bids, the owner typically awards the contract for construction to the lowest bidder. This sequential process allows for the establishment of a fixed construction figure before committing to the building implementation.

Team or Fast Track Approach

In the team approach, as in the traditional approach, the owner contracts with a facility-planning consultant, an architect/engineer, and a construction manager to develop and implement a building program. To ensure that the construction is completed in the shortest possible time, however, the process and planning team are organized to implement the building program in an expeditious manner. For example, the design and construction phases are typically overlapped, rather than done in sequence as in the traditional approach. Also, the construction manager may guarantee a fixed cost—guaranteed maximum price—for the project early in the development process if the scope of the project is clearly defined.

The greatest advantage of the team approach is that it minimizes planning and construction times. Construction begins before the completion of all working drawings. Logical groupings of building elements are offered for bids at various stages of the project. Excavation, off-site utilities, and foundations may be prepared as a complete bid package, for example, and be awarded before completion of the total design of the project. Depending on project requirements, each of these bid packages may be competitively bid or negotiated.

Design/Build Approach

A simple description of the design/build or "turnkey" approach is that a developer or single party undertakes the entire responsibility for delivering a project to the owner. Although there are many variations, the developer or single party usually acquires or is provided the land, designs and builds the project under one financial transaction, and delivers a final product to the owner. This approach relieves the owner of all management and coordination responsibility.

The design/build approach is typically less time-consuming than the traditional approach. Generally, the vendor negotiates contracts with local suppliers, eliminating the need for competitive bids. The vendor must stay within a pre-established budget and, thus, must make cost-effective design decisions in order to develop the building within the originally guaranteed cost.

A disadvantage of this approach is that, if the budget has been set before completion of design and construction documents, the owner has little or no control over cost-cutting measures or construction standards. Typically, there is limited enforceable documentation describing the end product or building. The owner knows what the project is going to cost, but not what the end result will be. Although short-run capital costs may be lower, long-term operating costs can be greater.

Project Management Approach

Because of the complexity of today's facility planning projects, many experts believe that the traditional approach for developing, planning, and financing health care construction is no longer effective or responsive to the current health care environment. This belief has led to the development of the project management approach.

The project management approach to facility implementation requires the assembling of an appropriate group of professionals to implement a project. A single spokesperson is responsible to the institution for project implementation. This new specialist, the project manager, is under contract to the institution to coordinate and manage the professionals in the various disciplines involved, act as the institution's advocate by reporting to the institution's governing body, and develop the strategy and accountability of every planning and implementation function. A project manager provides an understanding of each professional's contribution to the project, knowledge of concurrent task scheduling, management communication skills, and an ability to interpret and solve problems. The project management process is a contracted extension of institution management that, although typically used in a team approach, can also be used in a traditional approach.

Review of Alternatives

From the owner's perspective, each of these alternatives has a different impact on the institution's organization, and no single alternative is best for all projects. The alternative can be evaluated objectively and subjectively according to the following criteria:

- owner's authority
- project fees
- project costs
- project duration
- building quality
- checks and balances
- owner coordination
- owner control
- owner liability

For projects costing less than $5 million, a traditional approach or a design/build approach provides an advantage to the owner, provided that proper controls can be maintained to ensure value in the final product. In a major building program, one costing $10 million or more, or a complicated renovation project requiring phased construction, the team approach is typically the most cost-effective. The team approach can be organized either through separate contracts with an owner or through a project manager. The concept has been used for years in industry, and the many cost constraints in the health care industry today have intensified its application to the health care field.

CONCLUSION

Several major factors—managed care, physician–hospital relationships, health care competition, changes in the payment system, and the consumer movement—are creating permanent changes in health care delivery. Systems must retool and adjust through a constant reexamination of their strengths, weaknesses, opportunities, and threats. To be successful, CEOs will need to monitor new developments and strategic options, and to take decisive action to stay ahead of the competition. Although facility-planning decisions may not be as important as other strategic initiatives, the development and deployment of capital resources will continue to be a significant factor in the overall success of a health care institution. With today's shrinking capital availability and increasing demands for capital, meeting facility needs will require creative solutions.

JAMES E. HOSKING, MBA, FAAHC, is a Vice President of TriBrook/AM&G LLC, consulting primarily in the areas of facility master planning, functional space programming, business and program development, and ambulatory care planning. In more than 25 years of health care consulting experience, Mr. Hosking has worked with community hospitals, academic health science centers, physician groups, and health care systems on a variety of facilities, strategy, and operations assignments.

He is a Fellow in the American Association of Healthcare Consultants and the Healthcare Information and Management Systems Society, as well as a Diplomate in the American College of Healthcare Executives. Additionally, Mr. Hosking has authored three book chapters and published numerous articles in national health care publications. He holds a master's degree in business administration, with a concentration in hospital administration and finance, from the University of Chicago.

Appendix 9–A

Potential External Team Members and Responsibilities

A simple project may be implemented solely with an architect/engineering firm, whereas a complex project may require a comprehensive team. Health care expertise requirements, program complexity, the external planning environment, and project implementation requirements determine the makeup of the external team. The relative roles, responsibilities, and tasks of team members must be identified at project inception. Particular expertise should be sought and controlled with respect to overall project direction.

FACILITY-PLANNING CONSULTANT

The facility-planning consultant's primary role is to define the required departmental space and the inter- and intra-relationships necessary to optimize cost-effective operations (functional planning). He or she provides management skills relating to project implementation, thereby translating the institution's program objectives into space requirements and operationally effective designs, as well as providing operational and systems expertise through building activation. The consultant's recommendations are based on a review of the institution's strategic plan, program plans, and forecasts of departmental workloads, staffing, and operating and management systems.

In some cases, the facility-planning consultant or an independent project manager coordinates the activities of all external professional team members, monitors the budget and schedule, and integrates internal and external planning team decisions from project definition to final activation. In general, a qualified health care planning consultant understands tasks necessary for project implementation and the outputs required of various external team members throughout the process.

The facility-planning consultant may be independent or may represent a health care consulting firm that takes a broader health care planning role in assisting the institution in defining its overall project scope. During the external approval phase, a health care consultant may make valuable recommendations in project strategy and in dealing with the planning agency. The health care consultant brings a working knowledge of the approval process, case histories of similar situations, and an understanding of the discipline necessary to implement the project.

EQUIPMENT-PLANNING CONSULTANT

Historically, equipment planning was handled by the institution's purchasing department in consultation with individual departments. However, the ever-increasing sophistication of technology, emphasis on cost containment, and required coordination of department needs demand that management assume the responsibility of inventorying and evaluating existing equipment, preparing and monitoring equipment lists and budgets, preparing specifications, and coordinating procurement and installation. This process usually demands time and expertise not available within today's downsized hospital or system organization.

CONSTRUCTION MANAGER

A qualified construction manager provides multiple levels of input to a facility project. During the external approval process, the construction manager is responsible for developing credible construction cost inputs for submittal documentation. This costing is based on the program definition provided by the institution, the facility planning consultant, and the architect/engineer. The construction manager provides input into cost-benefit analyses of alternative construction techniques and assists the project team in maximizing facility development within the limits of an approved project scope and budget. The construction manager also may be called on to render a guaranteed maximum price for financing purposes or a phased construction process and may act as an owner/agent in the construction process.

During construction, the construction manager receives bids, schedules work, coordinates subcontractors, and manages the construction program to minimize construction time and provide the earliest possible occupancy.

ARCHITECT/ENGINEER

The architect is responsible for translating the functional space program into an operationally cost-effective design maximizing the reuse of existing physical resources. The engineer develops the infrastructure (structural, mechanical, electrical, and plumbing systems) necessary to appropriately support the architect's design. In many cases, the architect and engineer are a single firm; however, it is just as likely for the engineering services to be provided by independent single or multiple engineering firms.

The regulatory process and innovative methods of project implementation have changed the traditional role of an architect/engineer. The regulatory approval process requires that major project decisions be made in early design because the institution will have to live within a maximum capital expenditure. Decisions regarding the inclusion of a pneumatic tube system or air conditioning of an old building will have to be made during the schematic phase of the process. A phased construction approach also has changed the traditional role of an architect/engineer, requiring that certain design packages be developed and bid before all working drawings are complete.

Many states require submission of single-line schematics for regulatory review, whereas others require only block schematic drawings. It is important to ascertain the requirements specific to a state so that the drawings can be developed to the minimum level of detail required. The level of detail on drawings submitted in the approval process should be minimized to reduce the institution's initial financial exposure when regulatory denial is possible. Although drawing detail may be minimal for the approval phase, the architectural/engineering firm must participate actively in defining project scope and design criteria for costing purposes.

LEGAL COUNSEL

In today's health care environment, legal counsel is necessary from the preliminary project definition phase through approval and activation. The role of legal counsel varies, depending upon the local environment, the political structure of the regulatory process, community acceptance of the project, and project complexity. Several types of legal counsel may be required, including attorneys specializing in reimbursement, regulatory processes, and financing (bond counsel).

FUND-RAISER

A fund-raiser has several distinct roles. The first is to develop the feasibility study to estimate fund-raising potential. This study measures community support, and it can be utilized as part of the external regulatory approval process. A fund-raiser would also be involved in managing the campaign if the institution commits itself to a fund drive.

FINANCIAL ADVISOR/FINANCIAL CONSULTANT

Most major construction projects require external financial advice. Financial consulting tasks begin with preparation of a preliminary financial capability study outlining the effects of the proposed project on a system's fiscal structure. The financial consultant assesses the debt capacity and debt limitations of the systems, the probable effect of refinancing existing debt, and the effect of the project on the system's operating costs. The consultant also makes an assessment of financing the proposed project in the money market. Using existing and proposed program analysis and workload projections, the financial advisor verifies previous consulting analyses and conducts required financial studies.

The financial consultant's role varies in each project phase. During the approval process, the consultant tests demand figures, assists management in preparing operating budgets, and develops a preliminary capability study for submission with the application. During the implementation process, the consultant monitors overall operations and, as permanent financing is secured, prepares the financial feasibility study to be submitted with public offering documents.

UNDERWRITER

Underwriters sell money to an organization for a fee. In most major facility projects, an underwriter is involved for financing unless there is a possibility of private placement (e.g., a direct, negotiated sale). An underwriter's role generally does not begin until interim or permanent financing is sought. The underwriter can assist the system in the regulatory process by assessing the system's financial status and bond rating probabilities and establishing an effective interest rate for budget purposes. The underwriter's major input is required while developing the financing instrument and actual bond sale. Systems must exercise caution in developing the financing instrument in order to preserve flexibility for future capital development projects.

Chapter 10

Financing of Health Care Facilities

Geoffrey B. Shields and Debra J. Schnebel

In light of a consolidating industry and the resulting demands for capital, it is becoming increasingly necessary for health care institutions and their chief financial officers (CFOs) to consider an assortment of financing techniques. Techniques that must be examined include tax-exempt and taxable bond financing, public offerings and private placements of taxable debt, limited partnerships, limited liability companies, joint ventures, and sales of streams of business to unrelated institutions. In addition, public equity financing is a major source of financing for large for-profit corporations.

The amount of equity capital raised through partnerships, limited liability companies, joint ventures, and stock offerings during the last few years has been significant. The rate of initial public offerings of stock is an indication of new business development. As presented in Table 10–1, initial public offerings of stock issued by health care companies have raised significant equity capital, but the amount is small compared to debt offerings during the same period.

TAX-EXEMPT FINANCINGS

In recent years, not-for-profit health care providers have gained access to the capital markets primarily through tax-exempt financing.[1] Health care institutions that qualify as organizations described in Section 501(c)(3) of the Internal Revenue Code of 1986 (IRC), as amended, and are exempt from tax under Section 501(a) of the IRC may borrow on a tax-exempt basis (i.e., the interest on the bonds is not includable in the gross income of the owners thereof for federal income tax purposes).

The IRC permits states, municipalities, and other local government units to issue tax-exempt bonds and to loan the proceeds of such issues to Section 501(c)(3) organizations for qualifying uses. The issuer loans the proceeds of the bonds to the hospital. The hospital's payments to the issuer on such a loan are used by the issuer to pay the principal of and interest on the bonds. The bonds are so-called revenue bonds; that is, the bonds are payable solely from the revenues received by the issuer from the borrowing organization and are not a general obligation of the issuer.

As a general rule, tax-exempt financing is available to a not-for-profit institution for capital expenditures in connection with its charitable activities. Such an institution may use bond proceeds for activities that do not constitute unrelated trades or businesses. No more than 5 percent of the proceeds of the bond issue may be used for (1) facilities used in an unrelated trade or business, (2) facilities

Table 10–1 Initial Public Offerings of Health Care Company Stock

Date Range	Proceeds (millions)	Market Share	No. of Issues
1982	21.5	0.3	2
1983	405.2	5.4	33
1984	127.5	1.7	17
1985	210.0	2.8	15
1986	223.5	3.0	18
1987	231.4	3.1	15
1988	56.9	0.8	5
1989	149.9	2.0	7
1990	86.6	1.1	8
1991	1,740.9	23.0	39
1992	1,291.5	17.1	37
1993	391.5	5.2	16
1994	452.5	6.0	19
1995	1,055.2	13.9	24
1996	704.0	9.3	21
1997 (thru 9/1)	419.4	5.5	15
Industry Totals	7,567.5	100*	291

*0.2% rounding error.

Source: Courtesy of Securities Data Company.

used by a nonexempt person, and (3) costs of issuing the bonds.

In addition, the state law that authorizes the issuance of the bonds by the government unit circumscribes the permissible uses of the bond proceeds. In general, a not-for-profit institution can apply the proceeds of tax-exempt bonds to pay, or to reimburse itself, for capital expenditures relating to a hospital, nursing home, or other health care facility. Under recent IRC regulations, an institution may seek reimbursement for expenditures incurred within 18 months before the date of issuance of the bonds, provided that the institution has not previously financed such expenditures and the issuer or the health care facility has, prior to the incurrence of such expenditures, declared its intent in a resolution of its board, to finance such expenditures.

Tax-exempt bonds also can be used to refund existing debt, either taxable or tax-exempt, the proceeds of which had been applied toward eligible uses. A refunding occurs when the institution applies the proceeds of the new issue to the payment of an existing debt. This refunding releases the institution from the covenants in the existing debt's documents and permits it to renegotiate the structure and the covenants with respect to the new issue. In addition, if there have been changes in the capital markets, such as a decrease in interest rates, the institution may achieve debt service savings.

Typically, tax-exempt bonds that bear a fixed rate of interest provide for a no-call period during which the bonds cannot be prepaid. On a 30-year bond issue, the no-call period is generally 10 years. Generally, such long-term bonds may be advance refunded.

In an advance refunding, the institution deposits the proceeds of the new debt in an escrow account and invests them in a portfolio of government securities. The cash flow of principal and interest from the escrow portfolio is designed to match the debt service requirement on the existing, or refunded, debt. Thus, although the refunded bonds remain outstanding, the escrow account provides the payments on the refunded bonds, and the institution is free of the obligations associated with those bonds. In order to achieve a legal defeasance (i.e., a discharge from the obligations) of the documents in connection with the refunding of the existing debt, those documents must specifically provide for such. The Tax Reform Act of 1986, however, imposed restrictions on advance refundings. Generally, bonds issued before 1986 may be advance refunded only twice; however, any pre-1986 bonds may be advance refunded at least once after March 14, 1986. Bonds issued after 1985 may be advance refunded only once.

Finance Team

When a health care institution decides to raise capital externally, it should begin by assembling its finance team. First, a hospital or organized delivery system should identify who on its staff will be responsible for the day-to-day activity related to the financing. Typically, that person is the CFO. In order for the financing to reflect the needs and desires of the institution, the CFO should play an active role in the financing process as spokesperson for the borrower, and the financing process will take a great deal of that person's time. It also will require input from other hospital personnel and departments. The chief executive officer (CEO) and the board of directors are ultimately responsible for approving the finance plan. Planning personnel must participate in identifying, describing, and providing details of the cost of the project to be financed. Also, in preparing the information to be disclosed in the offering document, staff members must collect and digest a significant amount of data and documentation regarding diverse aspects of the institution.

An investment banker is a key member of the finance team. Often, a panel of managers and board members choose the investment banker from a select group of bankers who have made written and oral presentations. The organization should look for an investment banker with experience in health care finance. A banker familiar with the health care industry, with the legal restrictions on hospitals and tax-exempt financing, and with the market revenue bonds can provide valuable input into the structuring of the financing and will facilitate the financing process. Most important, however, the banker must be someone in whom the key participants have confidence. He or she should have a particular interest in the institution and its financing needs, because the finance plan should be tailored to those specific needs. In a public offering, the investment banker acts as underwriter, or purchaser, of the bonds, ensuring that the bonds are sold and the financing consummated. Thus, the borrower should request and review each banker's experience with financings for similar institutions, comparing the respective interest costs and fees.

The underwriter has legal counsel, whose role is to ensure that the offering and sale of the bonds comply with federal and state securities laws. Thus, the underwriter's counsel is responsible for preparing the offering document that provides full disclosure of the transactions, the bonds, the issuer, and the borrower. The borrower also has legal representation, either the borrower's general counsel or special counsel experienced in tax-exempt finance. The borrower's counsel must provide assurances to the other participants regarding the tax-exempt status of the institution, the validity of certain corporate actions, and the adequacy of disclosure of the hospital's operations. In addition, the borrower's counsel represents the hospital in negotiations regarding the structure of the financing and the covenants to be contained in the documents.

A state, municipality, or other government unit must issue the bonds in order for them to be tax-exempt. In any given jurisdiction, there may be one or more eligible issuers. Several states have created state financing authorities to issue bonds on behalf of qualifying health care institutions. In other cases, a municipality or a local government unit has authority to issue bonds on behalf of such institutions. The authority and powers granted to issuers, the experience of issuers, and the extent of issuers' involvement vary widely. When a choice of issuers is available, the borrower's counsel and the investment banker can explain the disadvantages and advantages of using each issuer and aid the institution in selecting the appropriate issuer. The issuer retains a bond counsel who is responsible for drafting the legal documents. In addition, the bond counsel renders the opinion that the bonds are legally and validly issued and that the interest on the bonds is exempt from federal income taxation and any state taxation, where applicable.

The borrower's auditors must also be involved in this process. They assist in the preparation of certain financial information to be included in the offering document and consent to the use of the audited financial statements, accompanied by the auditor's letter, in such an offering document. In addition, the auditors must provide written assurance or give "comfort" with respect to changes in the organization's financial condition up to the date of the issuance of the bonds.

In certain cases, it may be necessary to obtain a feasibility study that sets forth the projected operational and financial performance of the health care institution. Feasibility studies were commonly used in the past for borrowing, but are now generally limited to continuing care facility and nursing home borrowing. A feasibility study for a hospital may be necessary if (1) the hospital is undertaking a major project that is anticipated to have a substantial impact on its operational or financial performance; (2) some change in the marketplace, such as the addition of a new hospital to the service area, is anticipated to have a substantial impact on the hospital's operational or financial performance; or (3) questions arise about the continuing financial viability of the hospital and its ability to pay on the debt. In general, projected operational and financial data must be prepared for review by the rating agencies, investors, and/or credit issuers. In many cases where a study is not necessary, an independent evaluation can be beneficial. Whether to prepare a feasibility study is a judgment call based on the strength of the institution and the nature of any changes occurring within the institution or in its marketplace.

Financing Process

Once the finance team is assembled, the financing process typically takes 2 to 3 months. During this period, the finance team undertakes a "due diligence" review, which involves a substantive review of all significant matters that affect the borrower. First, the various lawyers review numerous documents, including corporate documents, material contracts (e.g., loan documents, leases, union contracts, insurance policies), physician contracts, supply contracts, and management contracts. In addition, the finance team conducts interviews of key hospital personnel, including the CEO, the CFO, a member of the Board, and a member of the medical staff. The purpose of this extensive review process is to ensure that the disclosure in the offering document is accurate in all material respects and does not omit a material fact.

Concurrently, the documentation for the financing progresses. The bond counsel prepares drafts of bond documents to reflect the structure of the issue and any particular needs or concerns of the borrower. Generally, there are several drafts of the documents to ensure the legal documentation properly reflects the needs and desires of the hospital. Also, the underwriter's counsel prepares the offering document. Diverse members of borrower's management assemble the information—for example, the history of the borrower, governance, services, medical staff, affiliations, demographics of the service area, market share data, utilization statistics, and other miscellaneous information—to be disclosed in the offering document. A careful review of this information is essential to ensure its accuracy and completeness.

The borrower must also prepare documentation, including historical financial information, utilization statistics, and financial projections, for presentation to and analysis by the rating agencies and/or prospective issuers of credit enhancement (bond insurers and/or banks issuing letters of credit). Generally, the key management personnel, a member of the board, and a member of the medical staff make an oral presentation for each rating agency and/or credit enhancer, during which they highlight the strengths of the institution and respond to any questions or concerns of the rating agency and/or credit enhancer. Although the rating agencies and credit enhancers put significant emphasis on the quantifiable criteria, subjective impressions contribute to the determination of a rating.

Structuring the Issue

When a health care institution considers a financing, a number of questions arise.

- How much debt should be incurred?
- What is the project being financed?
- Should any existing debt be refinanced?
- What should the maturity of the debt be?
- Should the interest be at a fixed rate or variable rate?
- What is the credit or security for the debt?
- Should credit enhancement be obtained?

Choosing the appropriate financing vehicle for an institution requires a careful review of the borrower's current capital needs, its operational and financial strengths and weaknesses, and its future plans. The finance team, particularly the investment banker, can provide borrower's management and board with the objective factors to consider in selecting a finance plan. In addition, the team can analyze the risks and rewards of alternative financing plans in relation to the borrower's particular needs and goals, and can then present a recommendation. It is important that management have input in this process to ensure full consideration of the borrower's current and future plans, to evaluate the potential impact of the finance plan on the borrower, and to ensure that the finance plan coincides with the borrower's needs and desires.

Tax-Exempt Financing Methods

Tax-exempt financing traditionally has offered organizations a ready source of long-term, relatively low-cost capital. Until the mid-1980s, virtually all tax-exempt health care bond issues were fixed rate financings, with a term of approximately 30 years. A major portion of those dollars represented the hard construction costs of major renovations and expansion, additional nursing towers, and satellite hospital facilities. The long-term, fixed rate financing assisted the hospital in its financial planning by "fixing" its cost of capital. This approach also enabled the organizations to conform to the old accounting adage that the term of the financing should match the life of the assets.

Variable Rate Demand Bonds

Since the mid-1980s, many borrowers have issued variable rate demand bonds (VRDBs) in order to take advantage of the low interest rates available in the short-term market. The nominal maturity of the VRDB is long-term, frequently 30 years. The interest rate on the bonds is based on the short-term market, however, and fluctuates in accordance with the designated adjustment period and index selected. In order to attract investors to these short-term rates, the borrower gives the investor the right to tender the bond for purchase at a designated period, either 1 day, 7 days, 1 month, 3 months, 6 months, a year, or several years. The "put" period generally coincides with the pricing period. Typically, any bonds tendered are remarketed to and purchased by other investors.

With VRDBs, the investor requires assurance that funds will be available to pay the purchase price of the tendered bonds if they cannot be remarketed. Most hospitals, therefore, are required to provide some form of liquidity/credit enhancement, such as an irrevocable bank letter of credit to provide liquidity and credit enhancement or a line of credit for liquidity with an insurance policy to provide credit enhancement. The promise of a deep-pocket financial institution to buy "put" or "tendered" VRDBs is referred to as "liquidity facility." Unlike a "credit facility," as described below, a liquidity facility will not be available upon certain defaults of the

borrower, including bankruptcy. The term of the liquidity facility is usually limited to 3 to 5 years, with the exception of renewals.

The borrower accepts certain risks in using VRDBs. As noted earlier, these bonds are subject to the fluctuation in short-term tax-exempt rates. If an aberration in the capital markets makes it impossible to remarket the bonds, it will be necessary to purchase tendered bonds by drawing on the liquidity facility. Repayment to the liquidity issuer will generally result in higher interest costs—typically, the bank's prime rate—and a shorter amortization period (i.e., on demand or over a period of several years). Such an event can substantially increase the hospital's annual debt service costs. Although the VRDB issue is rated on the basis of the credit/liquidity facility, the rating agencies analyze the hospital's ability to repay the debt in this worst case scenario in evaluating outstanding ratings on existing debt or in rating any subsequent debt issued on the hospital's credit.

Upon the expiration of the liquidity facility, the VRDBs no longer can be marketed at short-term rates unless the facility is renewed or a replacement liquidity facility is obtained. Generally, VRDB issues are structured to provide for conversion to a fixed interest rate at the option of the borrower when such conversion will not affect the tax-exempt status of the bonds. Because of these inherent risks in variable rate financing and the impact on the borrower's credit ratings, VRDBs are usually recommended only for those with stronger, at least A-rated credits.

Investment bankers continue to develop new financing techniques and structures. The devices and structures take on many different forms to address the investment requirements of specific classes of investors. In some cases, the new financing devices are available only to those that have stronger credits and are undertaking larger financings (i.e., $50 million or more). Invariably, they require more complex documentation. A borrower's patience in undertaking the more complex financings can be rewarded by quantifiable dollar savings when properly structured, however.

Some of the financing products require the borrower to hedge any variability in interest rates with an interest rate swap with the underwriter or other third party. When swap agreements are employed, the borrower must determine what, if any, additional risks the borrower may bear.

- Is the swap a perfect hedge for the bonds? In other words, are the payments on the swap based on the same market index and at the same intervals as the bonds, under all contingencies?
- Is the borrower taking the credit risk of the counterparty on the swap agreement? In other words, if there is a default by the other party on the swap agreement, is the borrower still liable on the bonds?
- If liable, is the borrower comfortable with assuming the credit risk of the counterparty?
- Do the cost savings outweigh this potential additional risk?

It is imperative that a borrower and its counsel fully understand the structure and the additional risks, if any, that the structure presents in order to evaluate properly the alternative financing methods and make the appropriate selection for the needs and circumstances.

Security

The property of the borrower, such as real estate, equipment, stocks, or revenues may serve as security for the obligation of the borrower to repay the loan from the issuer. Entities with stronger credit may be able to issue unsecured debt, which is not secured by any property or revenues of the institution. In the event of bankruptcy, the holder of such an obligation is a general credit of the borrower, subordinate to any secured party. Fairly restrictive negative pledge provisions, which restrict the borrower's ability to grant a prior security interest in its assets to other creditors, usually accompany unsecured debt. The negative pledge should not be drafted as an absolute prohibition against prior liens, but rather as a limitation, for example, a provision that the hospital may encumber not more than 10 percent of its assets. Such a restriction provides protection to the investor and yet allows the borrower some flexibility in its future capital financing.

Security may consist of a pledge of the gross revenues of the corporation, coupled with a negative pledge. As a practical matter, the revenues pledge does not affect organization operations so long as the organization is not in default or in bankruptcy. Many documents provide, however, that in the event of a default or of bankruptcy, the trustee may direct that the revenues of the borrower be deposited with the trustee. By controlling the borrower's cash flow, the trustee effectively gains control of the borrower's operations. It is preferable to avoid such a requirement, but if it cannot be avoided, its application should be limited specifically to events of payment default and/or bankruptcy.

Health care entities with weaker credit or specific legal requirements may have to secure their debt through a mortgage on their property. The security interest includes all or part of the real property, as well as existing and after-acquired buildings and equipment. If a mortgage is required, the property to be pledged should be narrowly defined. If possible, it is in the borrower's interest to exclude property that is not integral to the operation of its facilities (e.g., office buildings, vacant lots, parking garages) to preserve flexibility and to facilitate future borrowings or corporate restructurings. The mortgage should also contain provisions that allow for the release of obsolete and/or unsuitable equipment and the substitution of alternate collateral.

Master Indenture

A financing instrument that provides a mechanism for consolidating the credit of the participating corporations and for developing a legal framework for the future borrowings of each such participant, a master indenture model is most useful for a multi-hospital system, restructured hospital (e.g., a holding company family of corporations), and a hospital planning to restructure. The structure provides a network of cross-guarantees among the participating corporations that permit a pooling of the credit while maintaining the legally distinct corporations. Thus, it establishes a common framework for multiple borrowings by several entities; offers a mechanism for incurring various types of debt, whether taxable or tax-exempt; and provides a uniform set of covenants applicable to all participants. Ideally, all participants and all debt conform to the standards of the master indenture. Often, however, investors and credit issuers in specific financings demand specific covenants—in addition to the provisions of the master indenture.

The master indenture may impose operating requirements and restrictions on each of the participants in the group. Because hospitals have traditionally had the stronger credit, the covenants in the master indenture have been in large part designed to address the operations and financial conditions of hospitals. Such restrictions and limitations may not be appropriate for corporations engaged in other businesses, whether or not they are health care–related.

Corporate Debenture Model

Several of the financially strongest not-for-profit hospital systems have used a corporate debenture structure for borrowing. In this structure, the parent holding company borrows the money and loans it to the controlled affiliates. Unlike the typical master indenture model, the corporate debenture model has no cross-guarantees of payment of the bond indebtedness by affiliates or subsidiaries of the parent holding company. The parent holding company must agree, however, to maintain control (by contract, corporate governance, or state ownership) over affiliates and subsidiaries that are included as part of the corporate credit and to ensure their compliance with the covenants and restrictions of the indenture, including the transfer of funds to the parent holding company, to permit the parent holding company to pay debt service on the bond indebtedness.

Credit Enhancement

The ratings awarded to health care institutions by the rating agencies have, on average, been declining. The advent of the prospective payment system for Medicare, alternate delivery systems, and the resulting increased competition among hospitals for a declining number of patient days have made investors and rating agencies wary. In addition, the uncertainty of the health care market as a result of the possibility of health care reform has made investors increasingly cautious.

The purpose of credit enhancement of bonds is to provide the bondholder with security in addition to the credit of the hospital. For a specified fee, the credit issuer promises to pay the bondholder upon a payment default by the health care borrower. Typically, such credit facility has been in the form of a letter of credit from an AA- or AAA-rated bank or a municipal bond insurance policy issued by an

AAA-rated insurance company. The credit facility is used to raise the rating on the bonds. A higher rating makes it possible to sell the bonds at a lower interest cost in the marketplace and provides a broader market for them. Most hospitals that have variable rate financing must obtain credit enhancement. The cost of the credit support is one of the costs of the transaction that enables the hospital to take advantage of short-term interest rates. It is essential to take these costs of credit support into account when determining the appropriate financing structure to pursue.

The decision to provide credit enhancement for a fixed rate, long-term bond issue is primarily an economic one. Does the interest rate saving that results from the higher credit rating more than compensate for the credit issuer's fees? For most hospitals with an AA or lower rating, the answer to this question has been, Yes.

Restrictive Covenants

In the debt documents, the borrower is required to agree to comply with various restrictions on its operations. The restrictions are designed to ensure the continuation of the borrower's ability to generate revenues and preserve assets. Covenants in health care financings are fairly standard, although they have evolved to reflect changes in the health care industry. To some extent, the provisions in a document can be tailored to meet the specific circumstances of the hospital. The covenants provide the rating agencies, credit issuers, and/or investors with assurance that the borrower's credit quality will be maintained. Any significant weakening of the covenants will alter the market's perception of the credit and perhaps result in a higher interest rate. Thus, the negotiation of covenants requires a balancing of the hospital's desire for flexibility and the market's demand for credit protec-

tion. As noted earlier, the highest rated health care systems using the corporate debenture model (those rated AA) have been able to borrow based on a simple promise to pay, with virtually no financial or operating covenants.

Additional Indebtedness

In order to protect the creditor's access to revenues and assets, there is often a restriction on the hospital's ability to incur additional debt. Typically, debt is defined to include capitalized leases and guaranties of the obligations of other persons. Standard provisions related to additional debt are based on the hospital's historical or projected ability to generate sufficient revenues to pay debt service. In addition, the documents may provide for a minimum level of debt that can be incurred without meeting any financial performance tests. Specific provisions also may be included regarding variable rate indebtedness, refunding indebtedness, completion indebtedness, and short-term indebtedness.

Transfer of Assets

Because of the many corporate reorganizations undertaken in response to the changing health care environment, hospitals have desired the ability to transfer assets to provide seed capital to affiliates or to capitalize joint ventures. In order to preserve the assets necessary to repay the debt, however, documents often specifically restrict a hospital's ability to carry out such transfers of assets. The typical provision permits transfer of up to a specified percentage (e.g., 5 percent) of organization assets in any 12-month period. In addition, transfers may be permissible if an organization meets specified debt service coverage tests or if the organization makes the transfer for fair consideration. Also, an exception can be made for specific transfers of cash or assets that are contemplated at the time of the financing. Under a master indenture, transfers among participants can be made without limit.

Mergers

Standard provisions permit mergers only if certain financial tests relating to the net worth and debt service coverage of the surviving entity are met and if, after the consummation of the merger, there would be no default. In addition, an opinion of bond counsel that the merger would not adversely affect the exemption from federal income taxation of interest payable on the bonds may be required. Under a master indenture, mergers among participants are not restricted.

Rate Covenant

In a rate covenant, the hospital agrees to set its rates so as to generate sufficient revenues to pay the debt service on the bonds. In addition, the hospital agrees that if its debt service coverage drops below a specified level (typically in the range of 1.10 to 1.25 coverage of maximum annual debt service by cash flow), the health care system will retain an independent consultant to make recommendations regarding ways to achieve appropriate coverage. The health care system further agrees to follow such recommendations to the extent feasible. The requirement to retain a consultant may be waived if laws or regulations, such as those regarding rate review, prevent the hospital from maintaining the specified coverage.

Insurance

In some cases, the documents set forth specific requirements for insurance coverage of the hospital's property and the operation thereof against casualties, contingencies, and risks, including public and professional liability. It is in the hospital's interest to avoid setting specific dollar limitations on this cov-

erage. One such approach provides that the health care system maintain insurance in the forms and amounts that are customary in the case of corporations engaged in the same or similar activities and similarly situated, and are adequate to protect its property and operations. The hospital may be required to obtain an annual report certifying adequate insurance coverage from an insurance consultant that serves the hospital's program. Self-insurance is also generally acceptable; a typical covenant provides for self-insurance if an insurance consultant determines that self-insurance is prudent under the circumstances.

POOLED FINANCING

A number of statewide and county health care facility financing authorities have established pooled financing programs. The authorities issue bonds and hold the proceeds as a pool of funds available to loan to health care institutions for eligible purposes. The pooled programs offer the institutions an opportunity to participate in an existing issue without going through the lengthy financing process.

The 1986 tax act severely restricted the availability of pooled financing by prohibiting "blind pools" (i.e., pools of money borrowed prior to identification of and commitment by each of the ultimate borrowers from the pool). Many of the pre-1986 pools provide for recycling the principal of the loans taken from the pools, however, so some blind pool money remains available as an alternative to other types of financing.

The typical pool bond issue provides for loans at a variable interest rate with maturities up to 7 years. The loan proceeds must be used for capital expenditures, generally the purchase of equipment. These debt instruments impose the same risks as a single hospital issue of variable rate debt with respect to the fluctuation of interest rates and the marketability of tendered bonds. In addition, the hospital must consider the impact of repaying the debt over 7 years. When the amount of money borrowed is substantial, the relatively high annual debt service may effectively restrict the hospital's ability to incur any additional debt in the future. As with a variable rate issue by a single hospital, the bond issue must be supported by a liquidity/credit facility. The issuer of the liquidity/credit facility has the power to accept or reject the hospitals that want to participate in pooled financing. In some cases, a hospital may be required to obtain a letter of credit in order to participate.

The clear advantage of the pooled program to a participating hospital is its simplicity. The hospital can participate in a financing that has already been structured, which minimizes the financing time and effort. This can also be a disadvantage, however, because it virtually eliminates the hospital's ability to structure the financing to meet its particular circumstances. In some cases, a hospital may still be able to negotiate specific covenants with the credit facility issuer, but generally not to the same extent as in a single hospital financing.

The pooled financing can also accomplish significant economies of scale because the participating hospitals share issuance expenses. These savings, however, can be minimized or eliminated if the hospital must obtain a letter of credit in order to participate. In addition, under certain circumstances, the hospital's share of expenses may be disproportionately high if the bond proceeds are not loaned out in a timely manner.

The terms of the pooling of the financing structure warrant a careful review. To what extent is one borrower liable if another borrower defaults in its debt service payments? In general, pools are structured so that a hospital has no direct liability for a nonpayment by another, but all earnings on the funds held by the trustee administering the pool may be available to make up a nonpayment by any borrower. Typically, each hospital receives a credit against its debt service payments for its pro rata share of any such earnings. If such earnings instead are applied to make payments for a defaulting borrower, a hospital suffers an economic loss.

Each organization must review the specific provisions of the pool(s) available to it and the appropriateness of the pool to meet its capital needs. In addition, the hospital should review any existing debt documents to make sure the participation in the pooled program will not unduly restrict its future flexibility.

TAXABLE BONDS

Although tax-exempt financing has accounted for the great bulk of their financing, not-for-profit hospitals may borrow money on a taxable basis for a variety of reasons: (1) for working capital or other purposes for which tax-exempt financing is not permitted, (2) for financing of their for-profit affiliates, and (3) for loans in small amounts for which the high costs of tax-exempt financing are unappealing. The obvious difference between taxable and tax-exempt financing is the difference in the interest rates. Because the interest on tax-exempt bonds is exempt from federal income taxes and, in some cases, state income taxes, that interest rate can be correspondingly lower than the interest rate on taxable bonds.

There are other noteworthy differences between the markets for taxable bonds and those for tax-exempt bonds, however. For the most part, taxable hospital bonds have been privately placed with institutional investors, including insurance companies, pension funds, and banks. The terms of the financing have been tailored to meet the demands of these investors. Typically, therefore, the maturities of taxable hospital bonds have been

15 or 20 years, compared to the 30-year maturities for tax-exempt bonds. The amortization of the principal over this shorter time period substantially increases the annual debt service requirements.

In a private placement, the borrower and the investor negotiate the covenants of the debt instrument directly. The covenants in taxable and tax-exempt financings are very similar, except that the covenants in taxable bonds are generally more restrictive and may include certain asset-based covenants, such as a debt:total capital ratio and a liquidity ratio. In some cases, a mortgage may be required. When the number of bondholders is limited, however, it may be easier to obtain their consent to amendments to the debt instruments. Institutional investors are selective in their investments, and many have limited their investments to entities with better credit (at least A ratings).

Federal and state laws and regulations do not restrict the use of proceeds of taxable bonds. Legally, these proceeds can be used for any creditworthy purpose. Thus, taxable bonds provide a source of money for activities and/or entities that cannot be funded through tax-exempt financing. For example, taxable debt may be the only source of financing for office buildings and venture opportunities. Investors in speculative ventures often seek a participation or equity position in the venture, however.

EQUITY FINANCING AS A CAPITAL-RAISING TECHNIQUE

It has become common for two or more institutions to combine their capital, expertise, and market access to enter into joint health care ventures. Joint ventures normally take the form of either a business corporation, a limited liability company, or a partnership. Equity offerings of stock, member interests, or partnership interests can also be used to raise capital from passive investors. In a business corporation, the various investors buy stock and control the corporation by electing members to a board of directors. Structuring a venture as a corporation has the advantage of limiting the liability of the shareholders to the value of their shares of stock and permits the accumulation of capital at the corporate level. A major disadvantage is that the earnings of the corporation are taxed not only at the corporate level, but also at the shareholder level when dividends are paid.

In a partnership (or limited liability corporation), as opposed to a business corporation, there is no federal income tax at the partnership level, and profits and losses are deemed to be received by the partners in the year earned. A general partner, designated as such by the partnership agreement, usually assumes responsibility for management; in a general partnership with more than one general partner, a partnership committee may exercise control of management, selecting the managers of the partnership and meeting periodically with them.

There are several advantages to raising money through a partnership, limited liability company, or stock offering, rather than through the issuance of debt:

- Ability to raise capital. If the enterprise is attractive and there is a good chance for future capital gains, then capital can be raised at a fairly high multiple of expected earnings.
- No interest debt burden. No fixed interest payments are required on partnership, member, or stock interests in the firm, which frees a venture from the burden of paying interest during its start-up years when there is often a loss.
- Leverage. By improving the net worth and debt:equity ratio through the offering

of equity, a company enhances its ability to raise additional capital through debt.

- Acquisitions. In a stock company, stock can be used to acquire assets, partnership interests, or stock in another venture. Thus, the need to raise cash is held to a minimum.
- Personal incentive. Stock, member, and partnership interests and options can be structured to provide incentives for management. Such an incentive can be a valuable tool in attracting and holding top-flight management personnel.

Perhaps the major disadvantage of using equity to raise capital is the dilution of ownership interest that results. In a successful venture, the percentage of earnings that must go to the investing equity partner is substantially higher than the percentage of earnings that is necessary to pay off indebtedness. Dilution of ownership also means that minority shareowners may insist on participating in the management of the business. This can raise problems for management, particularly if business is not going well.

Joint Venture Structures

Among health care providers, a joint venture is a particularly effective means of sharing services to ensure a minimum of overlap and a wise expenditure of capital. Joint ventures are also effective in starting up new ventures that require a larger purchasing base or market area. When several health care providers participate in the joint venture, they themselves can provide not only the seed capital, but also the initial market for the joint venture products or services.

Physician–Hospital Joint Ventures

Although physician–hospital joint ventures have various purposes, they all require care-

ful attention to a variety of proscribing laws, including those involving the avoidance of private inurement or private benefit for the physicians, avoidance of fraud and abuse (impermissible referral requirements), and Stark law issues. Physician–hospital organizations (PHOs) have become a very common joint venture mechanism for vertical integration of health care services, however. Typically, physicians and hospitals use PHOs to market their services jointly to managed care companies and large employers. In general, PHOs are structured as business corporations in which the physicians either individually or, more often, jointly through a professional corporation hold a portion of the stock while the hospitals involved hold a portion of the stock.

Such ventures are sometimes used to finance health maintenance organizations, ambulatory surgery centers, and specialized hospitals, such as psychiatric and drug abuse hospitals. In these joint ventures, the non-hospital entity often brings particular expertise to the transaction, and the hospital provides its service area reputation, staff, and sometimes, space within the hospital facility. Usually, all participating groups make capital contributions.

Hospital–Hospital Joint Ventures

A hospital system (either for-profit or not-for-profit) can gain access to a new service area at a minimal cost through a hospital–hospital joint venture. Generally, the proprietary chain contributes its expertise and cash, and the hospital provides market access and facilities. Often, establishment of the joint venture is a multistep process. The institutions first enter into a contract for management to be provided by the proprietary hospital. This is followed by a joint venture and finally by purchase of the hospital by the proprietary system.

The IRC specifically limits the duration and compensation for management contracts in which a nonowning entity can manage tax-exempt, bond-financed property. These restrictions warrant careful attention in negotiating management contracts. As in a physician–hospital joint venture, expert tax counsel is essential early in the structuring process of a hospital–hospital joint venture to address the many tax and other regulatory issues that arise.

Legal Issues: Control and Liability Exposure

Corporate Form

The business corporation acts of most states typically grant shareholders of corporations the right to approve major changes proposed by the corporation's board of directors, such as amendments to articles of incorporation, mergers, consolidation, and sale of all or substantially all of the corporation's assets. On other matters, such as an election of directors, state laws commonly permit corporations to vary shareholders' voting rights. Therefore, the bylaws of a joint venture corporation may define each shareholder's voting rights with respect to the election of directors. For example, each joint venturer may be given the right to elect a certain number of directors; the number of directors that each joint venturer is entitled to elect may or may not be in proportion to the joint venturer's percentage of ownership of the corporation.

Subject to the provisions of the relevant state's corporation law, the shareholders of the joint venture corporation also may establish, in written shareholder and stock subscription agreements, certain restrictions on the shareholders' ability to transfer the corporation's stock and their obligation to make additional capital contributions.

Partnership Form

The Uniform Partnership Act, adopted in all 50 states, and the Uniform Limited Partnership Act, adopted in a majority of states, give all general partners in a general or limited partnership the right to direct involvement in the partnership's day-to-day business affairs. Both acts allow joint ventures to vary their statutory rights and responsibilities in written partnership agreements, however. Therefore, if there is more than one general partner, the partners can, through contract, decide which responsibilities will belong to which partner. The partnership agreement normally requires that all general partners vote on certain major partnership decisions. General partners have unlimited obligation for partnership liabilities.

Limited Liability Company

A more recent form of legal entity, a limited liability company establishes limits on the liability of the investors, or members. For federal income tax purposes, the limited liability company generally is treated as a partnership. (State tax treatment varies, but not all states permit pass-through treatment for a limited liability company.) The management of the limited liability company, which is the subject of a contract or operating agreement, depends on the particular situation. Its structure may take the form of management by all members (similar to a general partnership), management by a managing member (similar to a limited partnership), or management by a board of directors representing or elected by the members (similar to a corporation). Because of this flexibility, the limited liability of the members, and the treatment as a partnership for federal income tax purposes, the limited liability company structure has become popular in joint ventures. In states that tax limited liability companies, a common structure is a limited partnership with a limited liability company as the sole general partner.

Federal Income Taxation

A Business Corporation

As noted earlier, unless a corporation qualifies as a Section 501(c)(3) corporation, a limited liability corporation, a professional corporation, or a Subchapter-S (small business) corporation, its income is taxed twice—once at the corporate level and once at the shareholder level when dividends are passed out to the shareholders. If the corporation formed as a joint venture is a for-profit business corporation, participating Section 501(c)(3) institutions should not be concerned about the impact of the corporation on their Section 501(c)(3) status so long as the joint venture functions as a separate and distinct corporation and the exempt organization's participation in the governance and profits of the corporation is in proportion to its capital contributions to the corporation.

Dividends paid to a Section 501(c)(3) tax-exempt organization by its taxable subsidiary are not taxed as unrelated business income so long as the Internal Revenue Service (IRS) does not consider the subsidiary to be a mere instrumentality of the exempt parent. If its participation in a taxable joint venture corporation is properly structured, a tax-exempt organization can avoid federal income taxation of dividends paid to it by the corporation.

The IRS does scrutinize a taxable joint venture corporation to determine whether the tax-exempt shareholder receives a return from the corporation's net profits that is proportionate to its capital contribution to the corporation. If, for example, the IRS finds that the tax-exempt shareholder purchases 50 percent of the corporation's stock, but receives only 40 percent of the corporation's dividends, it will consider the tax-exempt shareholder's capital contribution to be, in part, the transfer of tax-exempt assets to a taxable entity (the taxable shareholder) in violation of the prohibition in Section 501(c)(3) against private inurement. A similar problem can arise when the taxable joint venturer receives a disproportionate share of the corporation's income through payment schemes other than stock dividends, such as an unreasonable bonus plan for a taxable shareholder who is also an employee of or contractor to the corporation. The tax-exempt shareholder must be certain that the joint venture corporation is organized so that each participant's share of return from equity is proportionate to equity contributed, and that no other payment mechanisms exist in the organization that unfairly distribute income to taxable participants.

Careful attention to the treatment of management contract revenue is important when calculating the true return participation in earnings. Also, it is necessary to address the question of a "control premium." The IRS's principal concern with respect to the involvement of an exempt organization in any for-profit venture with private individuals or taxable entities is whether earnings rightfully due the exempt organization will inure to the benefit of a private investor. Therefore, to avoid an inurement violation, an exempt organization should require that the profits of the corporation be distributed to it in proportion to its capital contribution to the corporation.

Partnership and Limited Liability Corporation

As noted earlier, a partnership is not a taxable entity under the IRS. Instead, profits and losses are passed on to each of the partners. Thus, the nonexempt partners may benefit directly from the partnership's losses, deductions, and credits without incurring a tax at the partnership level. These advantages of a partnership have certain limitations, however. First, partners must pay taxes on their allocable share of partnership income, regardless of whether they actually receive the income. Second, a partner may deduct its share of partnership losses only to the extent of the basis of its partnership interest. Generally, a partner's basis is equal to the amount of cash and the cost of any other property contributed to the partnership, as well as its share of partnership liability for which it is "at risk." A partner's basis is increased by the partner's share of undistributed income and is decreased when cash or property is distributed or losses incurred. Under certain, but not all, circumstances, the partners may carry forward unused losses indefinitely for as long as they own a partnership interest.

Private inurement rules of Section 501(c)(3) also require that an exempt general partner receive distributions of partnership income in proportion to its capital contribution to the partnership. Therefore, for example, if the exempt general partner contributes 50 percent of the total initial capital of the general partnership, it must receive 50 percent of the partnership income distributions. Furthermore, the exempt general partner must receive a credit toward its capital contribution equal to the fair market value of any property other than cash that it contributes to the partnership. Also, if a nonexempt general partner is appointed the managing general partner, the management fee must be reasonable compensation for the services performed. An inflated management fee would artificially reduce the income and funds available for distribution to the general partner or partners, effectively resulting in a disproportionate share in favor of the nonexempt partner.

If the business conducted by a general partner is considered unrelated to the Section 501(c)(3) purposes of an exempt general part-

ner, that partner must include its share of the gross income of the partnership—whether or not it is distributed—and its share of the partnership deductions directly connected with such gross income in computing its total unrelated business taxable income. The exempt partner must also carefully monitor the amount of unrelated business taxable income it generates from participation in one or more joint ventures to ensure that such income does not outweigh the income generated from its charitable activities and thereby threaten its Section 501(c)(3) exemption.

SALE AS A CAPITAL-RAISING TECHNIQUE

Redeployment of assets through the sale of one or more of an organized delivery system's hospitals or one of a restructured system's companies may be the best means available for raising capital for the corporation's remaining businesses. Before making a sale, a system should undertake a careful appraisal of the value of the asset to be sold. Investment banking firms use a wide variety of market value tests to determine this value. These include price earnings multiples enjoyed by publicly held companies engaged in the business of the enterprise to be sold, confidential information of the price paid in similar transactions, and real estate appraisals. Often, these appraisal firms can provide advice about restructuring the enterprise to be sold in order to enhance its value. In addition, the tax implications for both the buyer and the seller require careful consideration. The participants will work to avoid tax on the transaction, if possible, and the tax basis of the purchased property may be of importance to the buyer. Again, the involvement of a tax expert early in the structuring of the sale is prudent.

CONVERSION

Perhaps the most dramatic type of restructuring is a conversion from not-for-profit to for-profit form.[2] California and Wisconsin have special conversion statutes that permit not-for-profit institutions to convert to for-profit institutions on payment of the going concern value of the enterprise to the state or to a not-for-profit charitable institution. In other states, conversion is accomplished through a leveraged buy-out mechanism; this technique involves the creation of a shell business corporation that then buys the assets of the not-for-profit corporation.

In conversions, the major concern is that the price paid for the assets of the not-for-profit institution is sufficient so that the attorney general of the state will not challenge the transaction as a violation of the charitable trust doctrine, *cy-près*, or the state's not-for-profit act. Normally, preclearance is sought from the office of the attorney general; in the case of conversions of HMOs, the approval of the state department of insurance is also sought.

For enterprises that can entertain high price-earning multiples upon conversion, a conversion to for-profit form can be a very effective way to gain access to capital at a minimum price, because once the enterprise is in for-profit business corporation form, it can issue stock.

PRIVATE PLACEMENTS AND PUBLIC OFFERINGS OF SECURITIES

Both state and federal laws heavily regulate the issuance of securities, whether through partnership participations, limited liability corporation shares, shares of business corporation stock, warrants, or bonds. State securities laws, often referred to as "blue sky" laws, were enacted for the most part earlier this century to protect the public from the sale of "lots in the blue sky." The primary concerns of state securities laws were the registration of securities, of securities brokers, and of investment advisors and the prohibition of fraud. Since the passage of the federal National Securities Markets Improvement Act of 1996 (NSMIA), the Securities and Exchange Commission (SEC) has pre-empted many state functions. Although still required, state filings are considered to be "Notice of Intention to Sell" filings, and states are prohibited from the merit review of offerings and requests for information other than that required by the SEC. For example, Regulation D, Rule 506 offerings are considered "covered securities" and states can require only the filing of the Form D as filed with the SEC and a fee. Investment company shares are also "covered securities" under NSMIA, and only a notice and fee filing with the states is necessary.

The NSMIA has also affected investment advisor registration in the states. Investment advisors with $25 million or more under management register with the SEC and are not required to register with the states. A notice filing and a fee may be required in a state where the investment advisor has a place of business. Most state securities laws do provide for exemption from registration of certain types of securities and certain transactions. The debt securities of Section 501(c)(3) organizations and tax-exempt bonds are generally exempt from registration requirements under state securities laws.

The Federal Securities Act of 1933 governs the primary and secondary distribution of securities. Ownership interests in joint ventures and syndications are regarded as securities within the meaning of Section 5 of the 1933 Act, as are stock and bond issues. The 1933 Act was enacted in response to the stock market crash of 1929. Congressional inquiries into the events surrounding Black Tuesday uncovered the widespread practice of distributing securities to investors without any disclosure of information that could aid the investor in his or her decision making. The 1933 Act, therefore, was enacted to provide full disclosure of the character of securities sold in interstate and foreign commerce and to prevent frauds in their sale.

In drafting the provisions of the 1933 Act, Congress recognized the burdens that its regulation requirements might place on certain distributions of securities. Accordingly, it provided registration exemptions for certain securities and certain types of transactions. Among the transactions exempted from registration were the securities issued by Section 501(c)(3) organizations, tax-exempt bonds, and those securities included in the private placement exemption of Section 4(2) of the 1933 Act. Over the years, both the courts and commentators found Section 4(2) lacking in specificity, and in 1982, the SEC enacted Regulation D to provide new, specific private offering guidelines. Section 4(2) and Regulation D provide exemptions from registration for certain sales to wealthy, sophisticated individuals and institutions, and for very small offerings.

Before issuing securities, an entity should retain expert securities counsel to determine whether the offering can be made on an ex-empt basis and the very expensive process of federal registration thus avoided. Securities counsel should also be asked to advise the institution about compliance with state blue sky laws, as an issue that is exempt from federal registration is not necessarily exempt from state registration.

Securities counsel and the institution's investment banker should also provide advice on the advantages of a publicly registered offering of securities. Those that can be freely traded provide management with certain substantial advantages in their employee incentive plans, their ability to acquire other companies, and their ability to raise large amounts of capital. On the other hand, public registration under the 1933 Act subjects a company to cumbersome and expensive ongoing public disclosure requirements.[3]

CONCLUSION

As with many other aspects of the health care industry, health care financing is in a period of rapid change. Equity financing, use of limited partnerships, taxable debt issuance, and the use of tax-exempt debt are all techniques that a CFO must master in order to be able to apply the least cost available technique for raising capital to the various opportunities that arise in today's complex financial climate.

NOTES

1. For a more technical discussion of tax-exempt financing for health care institutions, see S.B. Kite, *Tax-Exempt Financing for Health Care Organizations* (Washington, DC: Bureau of National Affairs, 1996).

2. For a detailed description of conversion from not-for-profit to for-profit form, see K.C. Dunn et al., "The Dynamics of Leverage Buy-Outs, Conversion, and Corporate Reorganizations of Not-for-Profit Health Care Institutions," *Topics in Health Care Financing* 12, no. 3 (1986): 19–35.

3. For a detailed discussion of private and public offering of securities, see *Topics in Health Care Financing* 12, no. 3 (1986).

GEOFFREY B. SHIELDS, JD, is a securities and health care lawyer at Gardner, Carton & Douglas, a leading health care law firm based in Chicago and Washington, D.C. He has edited four books and written more than 35 articles dealing with health care finance, mergers, and acquisitions. He is a graduate of Harvard College and Yale Law School.

DEBRA J. SCHNEBEL, MBA, JD, is a partner in the corporate department of Gardner, Carton & Douglas. She practices in the area of corporate and securities law, primarily in commercial lending and private placements. She is a Fellow of the American College of Investment Counsel. Ms. Schnebel received her law degree from the Northwestern University School of Law and her MBA from the University of Chicago.

Chapter 11

Human Resources Management

Norman Metzger

Social forecaster John Naisbeth points to the biggest challenge of all for those who will be in human resources management in the early part of the twenty-first century: it is the need to reconceptualize roles. Change will be the order of the day. New technology; robots; electronic workstations; and local, regional, and international communication networks will change the work arena. The most dramatic change of all will be the rapid decline in rigidly defined jobs. The concept of work in the twenty-first century will not be the same as that which was prevalent in the twentieth century. Organizational structures will be as unfamiliar to us as those in the twentieth century were to individuals familiar with nineteenth-century organizational patterns.

Naisbeth's predictions certainly are applicable to the rapidly evolving health care industry, in which few solo hospitals and physicians may exist in the future. Health delivery systems, comprised of organizations (e.g., hospitals, physician groups, surgery centers) that historically may have had little to do with one another (and, in fact, may have been competitors) will challenge future generations of managers and human resource professionals.

HUMAN RESOURCES MANAGEMENT: HISTORICAL BACKGROUND

The earliest work relationships were based upon the principle of slavery. Masters owned and commanded as many workers as they financially could support. There was very little concern about inefficient use of labor, and slaves were available if one had the resources to feed them. Slave owners assumed many of the functions that one associates with modern personnel administration, e.g., recruitment (the cruel but efficient method of enslaving and transporting able-bodied workers), training, housing, catering, and industrial medicine. The one discipline that was conspicuously absent was collective bargaining.

The serf system developed in the agriculturally based society of the Middle Ages. Such workers were not chattel, but were attached to the land that they worked. It was not until the advent of the handicraft system, the true forerunner of modern industrial society, that a more sophisticated approach to training and management developed. This new approach was a system of craftsmen who took on younger men as apprentices and taught them a trade. Apprentices were paid little, if any, wages and lived with their masters. However, they could aspire to, and often reach, journeyman status. Indeed, if they could save money and purchase a few tools, they could start their own business. Craft guilds developed from this system. These associations regulated the quality of materials, wages paid, and terms and conditions of apprenticeship training. Personnel management in the handicraft system was the responsibility of the master craftsman.

During the Industrial Revolution, the status of the worker changed dramatically. The enormous expansion of markets, much more sophisticated and efficient transportation, and the continuous development and improvement of machines that replaced hand tools and steam power multiplied the efforts of individual workers. New social and economic classes emerged, and wage earners for the first time formed a distinct class. Slowly, but perceptibly, a changing attitude toward the worker evolved. A growing emphasis was placed on personal and individual values. Because workers could move to new areas where free land was available, for the first time employers realized that a dissatisfied employee could leave the job and become an independent landowner or farmer.

Personnel management did not become a distinct discipline until the development of large organizations, in which a great number of people came to work together. Paternalistic at first, the discipline was then geared to prevent or undermine unions; finally, it evolved into a professional approach to the managing of labor. It started slowly and was initially limited to specific employment departments. B.F. Goodrich developed the first employment department in 1900. A labor department was formed in 1902 at National Cash Register. In 1910 Plimpton Press had a full-fledged personnel department. The growing emergence of personnel departments in organizations was pointed out in a 1920 book by Ordway Tead and Henry C. Metcalf, *Personnel Administration: Its Principles and Practices:* ". . . [T]he fundamental reason for the development of a separate administrative division for the direction of the human relations is a growing recognition that people are endowed with characteristics different from those of machines or of raw materials. And if people are to be directed in ways which give best results, the direction must be specialized just as direction in the other major fields of management has been specialized."[1]

Tead and Metcalf were early observers of the growing importance of personnel administration as a management science. They certainly were precocious in their acknowledgment that "it is manifestly true that in the majority of corporations production is today affected adversely not so much because of technical inadequacies as because of the failure of managers to recognize that workers are human beings who demand the considerate treatment which only intelligence and insight regarding human nature can suggest."[2]

Two factors—welfarism and the scientific management school—contributed to the institution of a formal employment management department in U.S. industrial plants. Welfarism, more commonly termed "paternalism," was a movement active in both society at large and within the industrial world in the 1920s. It was aimed at improving the general tenor of American life and the living standards of the poor and unfortunate by ameliorating hard working conditions. Under this general rubric, managements made available various facilities, such as libraries and recreational activities; offered financial assistance for education; provided medical care; and instituted hygienic measures for their workers.[3] Personnel or employment departments had the responsibility of literally buying employee loyalty through the development and administration of a host of different types of welfare plans, most of them aimed at curbing union membership and keeping labor costs at a minimum. In addition, during the period of the 1920s many states passed workers' compensation laws, which became a prime force in causing employers to take positive steps to reduce and prevent work injuries and to organize company health programs.

The scientific management school was a product of many industrial engineers, but none more important than Frederick M. Taylor, who claimed that hidden waste in an organization and the resulting costs were caused by the inefficient use of labor. He introduced the concept of standardization of equipment and conditions, so that work could be more efficiently performed. Taylor believed that workers needed to be "won over" and "led" by management, and he was firmly committed to the legitimacy of management's unshared hegemony over the work process and workplace.

Taylor's theories had a great effect on the development of the field of professional personnel management. Although he cannot be identified as the father of modern personnel administration, his insistence that management must pay attention to matters such as employee selection, training, and compensation programs was indeed a basic element from which modern human resources management developed. However, his quantitative approach to human relations has been greatly discredited by the labor industrial psychologists—the behavioral scientists—and his motives are still suspect.

Elton Mayo and F.J. Roethlisberger made an enormous contribution to the development of modern human resources management. Their research at the Hawthorne plant of the Western Electric Company recognized complex working relationships that had been previously overlooked. They found that workers tend to cluster together in informal groups in order to fill a void in their lives that results from the lack of attention paid by the modern industrial organization to their basic need for cooperation and comradeship. Many years later Rensis Likert and Daniel Katz[4] conducted research that supported the important role managers play in the success of an organization. Employee-centered supervisors— those that were cooperative, reasonable, and exercised a democratic management style— were more successful than production-centered supervisors who were more defensive and authoritarian. Frederick Herzberg[5] saw the human desire for achievement as a critical element in the efficient operation of any institution. He concluded that management's great deficiency is its failure to capitalize on this desire.

Finally, A.H. Maslow made significant contributions to the understanding of worker needs. His research indicated that, although the thwarting of unimportant desires produces no psychological results, thwarting of a basically important need does have a psychological effect. He established that there are at least five sets of goals or basic needs: physiological, safety, love, esteem, and self-actualization. These basic goals are related to each other and arranged in a hierarchy of importance. When a need is fairly well satisfied, the next higher need emerges. He therefore concluded that the human being is a perpetually wanting animal.[6] Building on Maslow's work, behavioral scientists in general see the worker as having personal and social as well as economic needs. In this view, the worker does not want to be paid for merely doing what he or she is told, but also wants to satisfy, through the work, a need for security, independence, participation, and growth. This perspective is the basis of human resources management as practiced successfully in many hospitals throughout the country.

The profession of personnel management involves the development, application, and evaluation of policies, procedures, methods, and, most importantly, programs—broadbased and continuing—relating to the individual in the organization. The field of human resources management is eclectic, drawing from many other disciplines, such as sociology, economics, psychology, and law.

FUNCTIONS AND RESPONSIBILITIES OF THE HUMAN RESOURCES DEPARTMENT

The health care field is both unique and complex. Over 300 distinct jobs or major job classifications can be identified in the hospital industry. The industry's workforce is predominantly female; it is comparatively young, with a majority of workers under 35; it is highly fragmented, compartmentalized by function and occupation, with between 50 and 70 departments in most major short-term hospitals. It is slightly more organized by unions than general industries throughout the United States (unions still win more elections in the health care industry than they do in the general industry elections throughout the United States). In short, the hospital industry is huge and labor-intensive.

More than half of the U.S. workforce now consists of minorities, recent immigrants, and women. White males are a statistical minority. White males will make up only 15 percent of the increase in the workforce over the next 10 years. The fastest growing segment of the U.S. population is over 85 and the fastest growing segment of the workforce is between the ages of 45 and 64. The changes in the makeup of the workforce have affected the health care industry (Table 11–1). With the

presence of more women and minorities in management positions, the industry is experiencing a group with a fresh perspective of the workplace. These are employees who want to be involved in decision making about their jobs. Changes in employee perspectives must be juxtaposed with the downsizing that many health care organizations have experienced in the past decade. Many boards of trustees and chief executive officers have come to understand the need to restructure the work environment. Health care institutions are becoming leaner, flatter, and far more flexible. Notwithstanding the limited budgets now in effect in many health care institutions, there is a far greater investment in human resources than in the past. Incentive systems that are different from traditional compensation programs are prevalent. The need to build trust between management and its employees had come to the fore. With all these changes, the role of the human resources department has been transformed radically from guarding management prerogatives, to developing a caring and nurturing environment.

To manage this labor-intensive industry, a human resources department should fulfill many of the following functions:

1. *Human resources planning*
   • job analysis; job descriptions
   • planning of staffing levels
   • establishment of workforce plans and policies: determination of workforce objectives and inventory of current workforce
   • job evaluation: establishing comparative worth of each job, wage surveys, and classification and pricing of jobs
   • wage and salary administration: designing records and information systems, control of the table of organization, designing and administering merit programs, and processing forms

Table 11–1 The Workforce in 2005, Fastest-Growing Health Care Occupations, 1990–2005

	Employment*		
Occupation	*1990*	*Percent 2005*	*Increase*
Home health aides	287	550	91.7
Paralegals	90	167	85.2
Systems analysts	463	829	78.9
Personal/home care aides	103	183	76.7
Physical therapists	88	155	76.0
Medical assistants	165	287	73.9
Radiologic technologists	149	252	69.5
Medical secretaries	232	390	68.3
Physical therapy assts.	45	74	64.0
Surgical technologists	38	59	55.2
Medical records technicians	52	80	54.3
Respiratory therapists	60	91	52.1
Child care workers	725	1,078	48.8
Registered nurses	1,727	2,494	44.4
Nursing aides/orderlies	1,274	1,826	43.4
LPNs	644	913	41.9

Who's entering the workforce?

Hispanics: a 75% increase
Asians and others: a 74% increase
Blacks: a 32% increase
Women: a 26% increase

Who's leaving the workforce?

White, non-Hispanic males: 82% of those leaving

*Numbers in thousands

Source: Bureau of Labor Statistics: *Monthly Labor Review*, November 1991, Vol. 114, No. 11; and Kutscher, Ronald E. "New BLS projections: findings and implications." *Monthly Labor Review*, November 1991, Vol. 114, No. 11.

2. *Employment*
   • identifying sources of supply: public and private agencies, search organizations, and specialized agencies (retired individuals and handicapped)
   • selection: design of forms
   • interviewing, testing, and reference checks
   • referral for pre-employment physicals
   • maintenance of records and turnover statistics

3. *Induction and orientation*
   • design of staff orientation program
   • coordination of line orientation program
   • processing for benefits
   • follow up: probationary period

4. *Benefits administration*
   • processing of new employees
   • maintenance of records
   • design of plans
   • policing Employee Retirement Income

Security Act (ERISA) requirements
- trusteeship of various plans
5. *Personnel training and development*
- design and coordination of skills training and management development programs
- assessment centers
- administration of tuition refund program
6. *Evaluation and motivation of workforce*
- design and administration of performance evaluation program
- design and administration of incentive program
- coordination of quality of work life program
- training of management in motivational skills
- design and implementation of job enrichment program
- design and coordination of employee communication programs
- administration of employee newsletter
7. *Labor relations*
- collective bargaining
- contract administration: discipline and discharge administration, grievance and arbitration procedures, and National Labor Relations Board (NLRB) hearings
- affirmative action programs and equal employment opportunity (EEO) provisions
8. *Health and safety responsibility*
- physical examinations
- safety and health education programs
- Occupational Safety and Health Act (OSHA) requirements
9. *Employee recreation and activities*
- employee housing, food service, and recreational programs
10. Human resources policies
- design and administration

- implementation of recommended changes
11. *Outplacement*
- retiree programs, including services for terminated employees and counseling services

Human Resources Planning

The need for scientific wage determination in hospitals and organized delivery systems is no longer in question. Dissatisfaction about wages has three separate causes: inequities among wage rates paid within classifications and among classifications that employees consider similar to their own, individual or group pressure for higher earning power, and inappropriate market positioning. Hospitals and health systems have come to accept that a sound method of establishing wages is through job evaluation. Job evaluation has three purposes: to determine the relative worth of the various jobs in the system, to establish a wage scale that incorporates fair differentials among jobs, and to correct pay inequities where necessary. When defensible job rates are established on a quasi-scientific and logical basis, the issue of compensation is removed from the world of conjecture, arbitrariness, and subjectivity and personalized rates are abolished. By establishing a formal wage pattern that conforms to hospital wage rates in the area and in general with community wage rates, job evaluation is a key tool for the administration in meeting competition.

Job Analysis

Job analysis is the scientific determination of the actual nature of a specific job. Each of the tasks that make up the job is studied, as well as the skills, knowledge, abilities, and responsibilities required of the worker. Job analysis examines the job as it is—its duties, responsibilities, working conditions, and relationship to other jobs. There are three steps in the analysis of any job: identifying the job completely and accurately, describing the tasks of the job, and indicating the requirements for a successful performance.

Through a job analysis job facts are secured for the following purposes:

- *Job evaluation:* The facts assembled from a job analysis are used in the evaluation of jobs that will set the wages.
- *Selection and placement:* Job analysis results in job descriptions—specifications that are an orderly and effective guide for matching applicants to positions.
- *Performance evaluation:* Quantified job descriptions provide standards against which an employee may be rated.
- *Training:* Detailed information provided by job analysis can serve as a basis for a training department's curriculum.
- *Labor relations:* Job analysis provides specific breakdowns of duties, which can be used to answer grievances regarding the nature of the employees' responsibilities.
- *Wage and salary survey:* Job analysis provides a method of comparing rates of jobs in one institution with those in others.
- *Organizational analysis:* Job analysis can clarify lines of responsibility and authority by a detailed breakdown of each job and can indicate functional organizational positioning of jobs.

Three basic methods of obtaining information about jobs are (1) questionnaires sent to the job incumbents, which are then checked by the supervisor; (2) interviews conducted by job analysts; and (3) personal observation of the actual performance of a job by a job analyst.

Job Descriptions

Brandt states that "no single instrument is as important to effective wage and salary administration as the job description, yet there is evidence that it receives far less attention than it requires to assure either that it is properly prepared in the first place or that its uses are properly understood or directed."[7] This criticism has been addressed by modern wage and salary administration sections of hospitals' human resources departments throughout the country. Once all the requirements of a specific job are assembled, the job analyst reviews the questionnaire and notes from an interview or direct observation and organizes the information into a job description. Patten, Littlefield, and Self[8] offer these eight principles as a guide to writing effective job descriptions:

1. Arrange job duties in logical order. If a definite work cycle exists, duties may be described in chronological order. When the work cycles are irregular, more important duties must be listed first, followed by less important duties.
2. State separate duties clearly and concisely without going into such detail that the description resembles a motion analysis.
3. Start each section with an active functional verb in the present tense.
4. Use quantitative words where possible.
5. Use specific words where possible.
6. Avoid proprietary names that might make the description obsolete when equipment changes occur.
7. Determine or estimate the percentage of time spent on each activity, and indicate whether the duties are regular or occasional.
8. Limit the use of the word "may" with regard to the performance of certain duties.

Job descriptions become indispensable to the process of classifying work into management components. In order to ensure maximum agreement between supervisors and subordinates, the administration must provide well-written and up-to-date job descriptions. These descriptions must be widely publicized, and the supervisor and incumbents in each position must be in complete agreement with their contents. The descriptions are a foundation upon which to build a formal job evaluation plan, an effective and objective guide for intelligent selection and placement, and a source of detailed information for inaugurating training programs. With proper quantification, the job descriptions can also be used as a standard by which employees may be rated.

Job Evaluation

The primary objective of job evaluation is to determine the relative worth of each job in the institution according to the basic determinant of each job's requirements. Once the relationship between jobs has been established, fair pay differentials can be designed, and any existing pay inequities can be corrected.

Because a job evaluation plan ultimately may affect every worker in the hospital and because critical policy decisions must be made, it is advisable to have a representative job evaluation committee guide the effort. In the average-size hospital an excellent committee would be made up of the human resources director, the director of nursing, the building service manager, the executive engineer, and an administrative representative of the laboratories. It is essential that members of the committee and the committee as a whole be as knowledgeable as possible about the largest number of job areas in the institution. Members must be impartial and analytical as well.

Because the job evaluation plan is the cornerstone of the compensation program of the hospital or organized delivery system, it is essential that the following basic principles be agreed upon at the outset:

- Grant upward salary adjustments to currently underpaid employees to conform with the findings of the evaluation.
- Prohibit any downward salary adjustments to current employees as a result of the evaluation.
- Pay employees at rates equal to or better than the rates for positions requiring comparable skill, effort, and responsibility in the industry and the community.
- Establish and maintain fair wage differentials between jobs in all departments in terms of the value of each job to the institution.
- Pay all employees in accordance with all applicable federal and state legislation or regulations governing wages, hours, and other conditions of work.
- Follow the principle of equal pay for equal work assignments in the institution.
- Recognize and reward employees based upon their individual ability, outstanding performance, and length of service within the rate range established for the job occupied.
- Develop a plan that is objective, simple, and acceptable to the personnel affected.
- Develop a plan that is flexible and adaptable to the unique needs of the institution.

The two most commonly used types of job evaluation programs are the point method and the factor comparison method or variations thereof. Both are quantitative systems, and both consider each job one element at a time.

The point rating method measures specific features of a job using a predetermined rating scale. Job features that are most commonly measured in this method include education, experience, complexity of duties, monetary responsibility, contacts, working conditions, and, for supervisory jobs, type of supervision and the extent of supervision. Each feature has a range of degrees to which points are assigned. The sum of the points assigned to a given job indicates its relative standing among the jobs being rated. The job as a whole is not measured.

Factor comparison plans, in contrast, do not employ specific scales for job measurements. The essential ingredient of such plans is a job-to-job comparison, rather than a job to predetermined scale comparison. In this complex but flexible system, key jobs are compared to each other on the basis of several factors, including mental demands, skills, working conditions, responsibility, and physical demands. Most factor comparison plans do not exceed seven factors. This method's basic assumption is that these key jobs have correct salaries attached to them and thus represent a standard. Pooled judgments on the basis of repeated judgments of competent evaluators must be used in obtaining final figures.

Two other methods of job evaluation, which are used less frequently, are the classification method and the ranking method. The ranking method considers each job as a whole and measures each job against every other. It attempts to establish an order of relative worth. Job descriptions are necessary, but the jobs are not subdivided into factors. To use such a plan, which is applicable in smaller institutions, it is necessary to select committee members who have sufficient familiarity with a wide range of jobs.

The classification method, also known as the predetermined grading method, has been widely used in evaluating jobs in the federal and state governments. The evaluation is accomplished by preparing a set of job grades, with definitions for each grade, and classifying individual jobs in relation to how well they match the job definitions. A list of benchmark jobs, which serve as illustrations of the types of jobs that fit into the specific grade, usually accompanies each grade description. Underlying the job classification method is the basic principle that within any given range of jobs there are differences in levels of duties, responsibilities, and skills required for performance.

Wage and Salary Administration

It is important that clear policies covering wage and salary administration are developed, including the responsibilities for implementing such policies. One institution, Mount Sinai Hospital in New York, outlined such responsibilities in 1970 as follows:

- It is the responsibility of the human resources director to establish wage objectives and approve wage and salary policies, coordinate the activities involved in handling of wage matters and evaluate performances against these objectives, prepare and update job descriptions, and perform job analyses and evaluations.
- The human resources director is the executive director's designated representative for the administration of the wage and salary policies. He or she is responsible for ensuring that the approved salary and wage administration policies, programs, and procedures are administered to meet the institution's requirements; recommending changes in wage and salary objectives and policies; after classifying all jobs into their appropriate job classifications and grades according to their function requirements, establish-

ing and approving the rate of compensation that employees are to receive for the performance of work on either an hourly or salaried basis; approving all employee transfers, promotions, demotions, and merit increases; and establishing and performing periodic checks to ascertain and ensure that all employees are properly classified.

- The human resources department conducts periodic wage and salary surveys necessary for the maintenance of equitable ongoing rates for positions in the institution.
- The human resources department conducts periodic audits of the wage and salary administration program, wage objectives and policies, organizational structure for salary administration, merit rating plan, wage practices, and salary administration.

The design of appropriate forms is a key element in developing necessary controls over wages and salaries. Many organizations have computerized such forms, of which the most common is the requisition form. It is used to establish new positions, to ensure appropriate administrative approval of the legitimacy of the need, to aid in recruitment, and to initiate payroll action. It is also used for personnel replacements. The personnel action form is a document used to request changes in status, such as reclassification, transfer, salary increase, and termination. Personnel files, which may be set up either manually or computerized, are essential to ensure that the employee's work lifespan with the institution is reflected in a permanent and protected form.

In addition to other responsibilities, the wage and salary division is responsible for control over the authorized table of organiza-

tion. Other personnel reports emanating from the wage and salary division are turnover reports, seniority reports, average wage reports, and vacancy evaluation reports.

Screening and Selection: The Employment Process

As discussed in the earlier section on history of the human resources discipline, the first personnel departments, in the main, were solely concerned with the search for and selection of employees. Effective recruitment requires a determination of future needs, the clear definition and description of the types of people needed, and an evaluation and determination of methods to be used in each particular case. When the employment division within the human resources department receives a requisition, it must review the specific job requirements for this position, the profile of a successful applicant, the most productive source for finding such an applicant, and the market conditions. Most hospitals have accepted the need for centralized screening and decentralized hiring.

Recruitment

Recruitment is a proactive, positive mechanism. In order to be effective in this area the human resources director must be involved in the organizational planning function. It is not enough to know which positions are vacant; it is equally as important to anticipate the needs of the hospital in the changing health care environment.

Before establishing a sound recruitment program, sources of personnel must be identified and developed. Modern employment departments carefully research the market. Sources of recruitment include present employees, employee referrals, walk-in applicants, applicants who send in written resumes, public employment agencies, private employment agencies, retired military personnel, other retired individuals, schools and colleges, and unions.

Very often hospitals have a written policy that requires the posting of all available positions. With the increase of organized delivery systems, job posting in each institution is important. Posting provides present employees the opportunity to apply for such positions or to recommend others. An institution's present employees are an excellent source of referral of qualified applicants. Many organizations offer bonuses to present employees for recommending successful applicants for difficult-to-recruit vacancies. The largest single group of candidates is comprised of those who apply to the institution's employment office without any formal solicitation by the institution. Private employment agencies are widely used, once again for difficult-to-recruit classifications. Successful recruitment of professional positions can be achieved by visits to college campuses.

The most widely used recruitment technique is that of placing classified advertisements. The employment manager is responsible for either writing such advertisements or working with companies that specialize in such services. Such companies usually do not charge the hospital any fee higher than the institution would pay directly to the newspaper or magazine.

The physical characteristics of the employment office are critical factors in the reception of applicants because an applicant's first impression of the institution is made in there. The ease of locating it, cleanliness, space for waiting, privacy afforded during the interview, and, indeed, the cordial reception by employees in the department are remembered by applicants long after their initial contact with the institution.

Selection: Design of Forms

Recruitment is a positive function, whereas selection is a negative one. Recruitment attempts to attract as many applicants as possible; selection is a sieve through which only the most able applicants pass. The selection process has as its hallmark the effective appraisal of applicants' qualities that are indicative of job success. The process necessitates making value judgments, forecasts as to which applicant will turn into a productive employee. To aid the employment department in fulfilling such responsibility, five tools are widely used: the application blank, interview, personnel tests, reference checks, and pre-employment physicals.

Employment managers must be fully aware of federal EEO laws when selecting employees. These laws require that employment decisions, including hiring, be made solely on the basis of the worker's job qualifications or other job-related criteria. They bar the employer from considering certain general characteristics, such as race, national origin, religion, gender, and, to a lesser extent, age.[9] Federal laws specifically prohibit certain questions from being used in the interviewing process and on applications.

The primary objective of the application is comparing the applicant's qualifications with the qualifications required for the available job. Therefore, only elements that legitimately can be considered in the hiring process should be contained on it. Most applications contain the following items: identifying information, such as name, address, and telephone number; education and training; work experience; and personal references. Many state and local governments also have laws prohibiting discrimination.

Interview

No other tool is more effective in the selection process than the face-to-face interview. Peskin describes the following functions and objectives of the employment interview:

> Employment interviewing is the open exchange of information between persons of acknowledged unequal status for a mutually agreed upon purpose, conducted in a manner that elicits, clarifies, organizes or synthesizes the information to effect positively or negatively the attitudes, judgments, actions or opinions of the participants, thereby making possible an objective or rational evaluation of the appropriateness of an employee for a specific job.[10]

The interview has been described as a conversation with a purpose. It is intended to match people with jobs, elicit from the applicant data relevant to making a sound employment decision, provide the applicant with necessary information about the job, and, not the least, serve as a means of creating good feelings toward the institution.[11]

The employment section is usually responsible for preliminary screening, whereas final, in-depth interviewing is conducted by the line supervisor. The initial screening interview indicates whether the candidate is generally qualified for the job. The in-depth placement interview, conducted by the line supervisor, determines specifically whether the candidate meets the detailed requirements of the job and whether his or her work habits, attitudes, and personality are compatible with working in the institution. Job specifications and job descriptions are invaluable aids in the interview process.

An integral part of the process is the information stage in which the interviewer presents a picture of the institution and the job under discussion. It is important that the applicant fully understand the requirements of the job. Too often, employees start new jobs and find a marked difference between their initial understanding of the requirements and the actual on-the-job requirements. A study conducted on superior-subordinate communications in management concluded that:

> If a single answer can be drawn from the detailed research study into superior-subordinate communication on the managerial level in business, it is this: If one is speaking of a subordinate's specific job—his duties, the requirements he must fulfill in order to do his job well, his intelligent anticipation of future changes in his work, and the obstacles which prevent him from doing as good a job as possible—the answer is that he and his boss do not agree but differ more than they agree in almost every area.[12]

This common misunderstanding often starts at the original placement phase.

The rejection of an applicant on the basis of the screening interview should be done with as much compassion as possible. The employment function serves a public relations function as well.

Reference Checks

Reference checks are widely used, and the responsibility for carrying out this function lies with the employment section. To ensure the accuracy and sincerity of such checks, privacy and confidentiality must be guaranteed. An often-used technique for obtaining such references is to send a form letter (form card) to former employers. However, more effective means of obtaining such information are face-to-face interviews or telephone calls to former employers. Many institutions contact the applicant's last employer by telephone, using the letter or card form for earlier employers. To ensure the validity of a reference, it is imperative to attempt to obtain such information from the applicant's former immediate supervisor. Personnel records usually reflect, in references, information noted on termination forms. Such information is guarded, which often reflects the concern of a former employer about lawsuits and charges of discrimination. Many former employers are reluctant to put in writing any derogatory information about an individual who has worked for them.

An equally important responsibility is the checking of credentials. It is essential to validate education and licensure credentials directly with the issuing institution. Some employment departments require that the applicant present photostatic copies of diplomas, degrees, and licenses. Because of the responsibility that health care facilities have to protect patients, specifically in the area of ascertaining the qualifications and licensure of employees, it is critical that this process be assiduously carried out under strict controls.

Pre-Employment Physicals

The pre-employment physical should be given in advance of hire in order to eliminate the expense and embarrassment of terminating the candidate within the first few days of employment on the basis of a physical defect that might affect his or her ability to do the job. In order to be rejected on the basis of a physical disability, that disability must significantly restrict the applicant's ability to do the job. A disability that does not affect performance may not be considered in making employment decisions. Whether a particular individual with a disability is qualified depends on whether the disability is job related. Even after an employee is found by virtue of

a preemployment physical to have a job-related disability, the employer still is obligated to make reasonable accommodation without undue hardship to the operation of the facility. The applicant turned down for physical reasons should be so informed.

Affirmative Action Programs

The human resources department is responsible for ensuring the institution's compliance with EEO laws. Sometimes, in order to promote EEO, positive affirmative action is used to eliminate the effects of past discrimination, along with result-oriented activities that go beyond the establishment of neutral, nondiscriminatory merit hiring. The implementation of affirmative action programs is usually the responsibility of the human resources department. The mechanism by which an affirmative action program is developed includes (1) workforce analysis, the collection of availability statistics reflecting the available number of members of the protected class living in the organization's relevant recruitment area; (2) utilization analysis, which compares the institution's workforce statistics with the availability statistics to determine which job positions reflect underutilization of protected class members; and (3) the hiring and promotion goals wherein the institution identifies job areas of underutilization and prepares an affirmative action plan.

Personnel Testing

Many organizations find tests attractive because they appear to provide the quantitative evaluation of an applicant that does not seem to be obtained from an interview or a reference check. It is well to note that, although modern construction of tests has facilitated administration and scoring, tests are neither infallible nor universally precise. They should be combined with other selection methods and not used as the sole selection criterion.

The critical measure of tests and their application for a specific institution is their validity—whether they measure the elements tested, and whether these elements relate to job performance. Testing of the test involves its application to present employees in one's institution. For example, if the test is designed to measure job output, its validity would be determined by the regularity and consistency with which it forecasts job output. Another measure of a test's effectiveness is its reliability—the consistency with which a test measures whatever it was designed to measure. If a test is to be reliable, it must give the same measurement (score) each time it is given to the same person. When selecting a test, it is imperative that the employment department have a scientific appraisal of the test's validity and reliability to ensure fair opportunity for all those who apply.

Moreover, federal and state laws impose conditions on the use of tests in determining selection or promotion. The tests cannot be discriminatory in their construction, administration, or resultant action. The test selected to measure the qualifications of an applicant must be specifically related to the requirements of the job.

For many candidates the test is both a traumatic and important experience. It should be conducted in a professional setting. Although the institution may depend more on the interview and reference checks than on the results of tests, applicants are, in most cases, impressed with test results and feel them to be more decisive than other selection methods. Therefore, each candidate should be apprised of the role that test results play in the final selection. It is best to communicate the fact that, although test results can be an effective predictor of performance, they are not used as a substitute for good judgment. The test refines the judgment of the interviewer when added to the interview itself.

Induction and Orientation

A new employee forms permanent and, too often, irreversible attitudes toward the job, supervisor, and hospital much earlier than management believes. The management task of induction and orientation has been assigned to human resources departments, with special emphasis on the social adjustment to a new milieu. If an induction and orientation program is to succeed, it must have clearly stated and publicized objectives, must be thoroughly understood, and must be carefully planned. Such a program has four general objectives: to reinforce the employee's confidence in his or her ability to cope with the new work assignment, to communicate complete and detailed conditions of the person's employment, to inform the person of rules and regulations governing his or her employment, and to instill in the employee a feeling of pride in the hospital.

Once the objectives of the hospital's induction and orientation program have been established, a clear statement of philosophy must be publicized. What follows is an example of a sound statement of a hospital's policy on induction and orientation:

> It is the policy of the hospital to imbue a sense of "belonging" in each new employee. To this end, the administration and supervision subscribe to the following statement of principle:
> 1. Human resources are a most precious asset and require our understanding and empathy.
> 2. Each new employee who joins our hospital staff must be convinced that he or she is, indeed, welcome and needed.
> 3. All information necessary to acquaint a new employee with his

or her new job, the hospital, and his or her fellow employees must be presented at the onset of employment.

4. Total objectives of the hospital and the role the new employee plays in relation to the successful attainment of these goals must be shared with the new employee; sharing of goals does not cease with the end of the probationary period.

5. Responsibility for induction is clearly that of the line supervisor; it is a long process and may well mean the difference between average ongoing performance and exceptional performance.

The expense of a sound and effective formal induction and orientation program is infinitesimal when compared to the cost of employee turnover and inefficiency. Four principles—none of which can be compromised or neglected—underlie a successful induction program:

1. A new member of a group or an organization must go through an extensive process of adjustment, during which he or she must learn new rules and adapt old habits to the new group.

2. This adjustment can be facilitated by providing the new employee with facts relating directly to the job and to employment in the hospital as a whole.

3. The responsibility for induction and orientation must be delegated clearly to a capable member or members of the management team. Although the line employees are truly responsible for induction, the human resources department should be given a substantial part of this responsibility.

4. The process of induction does not end the first week or after the first month of employment. It must be recognized that induction and orientation is a rather long process and is, in the final analysis, the link between good selection and good job performance.

Dubin offers the following clear description of the basic task of orientation and induction:

> Orientation and indoctrination of a new member are essentially processes of acculturation. He has to learn ways of behaving, a set of standards and expectations, and a point of view largely foreign to him in their specific details, although he may be generally familiar with them in their broad outline. A great deal of the new employee's time may be spent during his early weeks and months of employment simply becoming adjusted to the organization.[13]

The important consideration in the entire induction and orientation program is to build up, as rapidly as possible in the mind of the new employee, an understanding of the organization's operation and his or her part in these operations. The premise one builds upon is that an employee who is informed—who knows the what, why, how, and when of his or her role in the large organizational structure—is likely to be more efficient, motivated, and sympathetic to the total goals of the hospital than one who does not possess this knowledge.

Some useful techniques for imparting needed information are described below.

• *Notice of employment in writing with complete details:* Such notice should be received by the employee before he or she reports to work. It is a written statement of the actual job offer, including the title of the position, a brief description of the position, the supervisor's name, the pay rate, and the reporting time and place.

- *Institutional tours:* Many successful induction programs include institutional tours to key areas.
- *Employee handbooks:* In almost all successful induction programs an employee handbook is distributed. These handbooks are essentially a statement of policy, conditions of employment obligations, and benefits. Successful orientation programs include time for the employee to review with the supervisor the handbook's contents.
- *Sponsorship system*
- *Informational lectures and films:* At the formal staff orientation, either a film developed specifically for the hospital or one about hospitals in general can be presented.

The staff induction, usually performed by the human resources department, is a formal and integral part of the orientation process. It is not unusual for key department heads to present information about their services and the role they play in the total patient care delivery system to groups of new employees.

The line induction is performed by the supervisor. It starts on the first day of employment, when the supervisor should introduce the employee to some of his or her fellow workers and carefully explain, preferably in private or at the very least in a nonpressured atmosphere, the responsibilities of the job. The fellow employee or supervisor responsible for on-the-job training takes over the next phase of the induction and orientation program. Sponsorship is a useful mechanism

for effective orientation. One of the more experienced employees in the department is asked to sponsor or be responsible for each newcomer. The experienced employee talks with the newly hired employee, joins him or her during the rest period, explains the customs and rules, and attempts to make him or her feel at home in the new work situation. The sponsor often joins the employee in his or her first lunch and escorts the employee to the time clock at the end of the workday. The sponsor should be a senior, loyal, well-motivated employee.

Many organizations establish a probationary period, a time for testing out an employee. It permits the institution the right to terminate employment of a new employee during a 30-day, 60-day, 90-day, or 6-month probationary period. Certain benefits do not start until after the probationary period.

Turnover is costly. The highest percentage of turnover occurs with new employees during their probationary periods. The human resources department is responsible for ensuring the implementation of effective induction and orientation programs that are designed to lower the turnover rate. Good habits are developed from the very start, as are bad habits. An employee who displays poor work habits during the probationary period is a bad risk for productive and efficient employment.

Performance Evaluation

Performance appraisal is a most complex and controversial area of supervisor-subordinate relationships. The development of a sound performance appraisal program is the responsibility of the human resources department.

Merrihue describes effective performance evaluation as follows:

> The supervisor who obtains the best
> from his employees is the one who

creates the best atmosphere or climate of approval within which his work group operates; he accomplishes this through the following methods:

1. He develops performance standards for his employees and sets them high to stretch employees.
2. He measures performance against these standards.
3. He consistently commands above-par performance.
4. He always lets employees know when they have performed below-par.[14]

The primary purpose of performance evaluation is the improvement of job performance by these methods:

- communicating specific standards to employees, gaining acceptance of those standards, and using those standards to measure the employee's performance
- measuring the employee's performance against the agreed-upon standards
- jointly developing with the employee a plan of action to assist the employee to overcome obstacles to his or her development and to strengthen his or her capabilities
- offering constructive suggestions and tangible assistance to the employee toward his or her development
- encouraging reactions, facing and resolving differences, and reaching a mutual understanding of the implications of the review.

The end product of the performance evaluation program is an understanding between the employee and his or her supervisor that includes the employee's understanding of what is expected of him or her, how the expectations are met, and ways to improve performance. Workers will be better motivated if they know precisely what is expected of them, if they have the opportunity to obtain assistance as needed, if they know exactly how a supervisor feels about their performance, and finally if they receive appropriate recognition when it is deserved. A successful performance evaluation program encourages employees' reactions to the evaluation and facilitates the identification of different perceptions about job performance. Evaluation provides a manager with the means of rating job performance on a more objective basis and identifying those employees who are qualified for positions with greater responsibility.

Human resources departments in hospitals and in organized delivery systems are delegated the responsibility of developing performance evaluation programs that accomplish the difficult objectives described above. Goal-oriented job descriptions are most useful in such systems. Performance evaluation must be based on clear, well-defined, and fully communicated expectations of goals.

Performance evaluation forms seem to take as many shapes as the number of institutions using them, and there is no one best method. Some of the options are described below:

- *Rating scales:* This is probably the most commonly used form. Scales are developed in a graphic or multiple-step format, which requires the supervisor to make a choice of appropriate rating along the scale. Rating is often done on various traits, such as ambition, character, cooperation, responsibility, attendance, and punctuality.
- *Checklists:* These rate various traits, but instead of using a quantitative measurement (numbers, letters) as in a rating scale, each trait is evaluated according to descriptive statements.

- *Employee comparison systems:* These do not require the use of an absolute standard as found in rating scales and checklists. Instead, the supervisor who is doing the rating is asked to compare the employee being rated with other employees being evaluated.
- *Goal setting:* This is widely used and often referred to as management by objectives. The employee is rated according to the degree to which he or she attains predetermined job goals.

No matter which form the performance evaluation takes, the goal should be to reinforce performance by a systematic assessment of observable work achievements. Most employees, if communicated to properly and given the necessary assistance, will improve their performance.

Training and Development

There are three basic goals of any training program: the acquisition of knowledge, the development of skills, and the development or modification of attitudes. These goals must be clearly defined and communicated, possibly in a policy on training, adopted by the board of trustees, and underwritten by the CEO. This policy statement should address how the training function will be carried out, who will be responsible for its administration, the types of training involved in the overall program, the relationship of line to managerial staff in the implementation of the program, and how the cost will be borne.

Training objectives are based upon specific desired outcomes, some of which follow:

- Break-in time for new employees can be reduced.
- Labor turnover can be reduced.

- Employees can be better prepared for higher positions and to assume responsibility.
- Employees can obtain heightened interest in the job and hospital, thereby increasing their job satisfaction.

Training and development is not a single-shot effort or a short-term program, but rather a continuing effort made up of a variety of programs that are developed with professional leadership and planning. The quality of patient care depends almost entirely on the knowledge, skill, and attitude of the staff delivering it. Training's potential for improving employee performance and operational effectiveness can be realized only when line managers view it as an integral part of their responsibilities, rather than a function or activity performed in a vacuum by an education or human resources department.[15] The increased participation of health system administrators, hospital administrators, and department heads in the design and implementation of training programs has significantly refined the training needs assessment picture and greatly increased the number of such programs. The trend is toward training based on operation needs, almost to the exclusion of generalized learning programs.

The human resources department is responsible for determining training needs through a needs analysis. This analysis is geared to answering these questions:

- Where are existing staffing shortages or inadequate supplies of employees who are promotable?
- Where do specific skill shortages within the organization exist?
- Where do specific skill shortages in the labor market exist?
- Which areas of service have been identi-

fied as deficient by patient complaints?
- Where is a department unable to function within the prescribed budgets?
- Where are poor morale levels?

Based on these identified needs, a reliable roster of actual skills must be assembled and a differentiation made between potential skills and actual skills.

The most prevalent form of training in hospitals and in organized delivery systems is on-the-job training, which is conducted on a one-to-one basis and often informally. The planning of such training should be a joint effort between the human resources training division and line supervision. Conferences and lectures are widely used in hospitals to effect desired training results.

LaParo[16] warns that it is absolutely essential that hospital trainers systematically analyze and assess training needs. The disciplined use of a systems approach in designing programs is a key factor in ensuring that training becomes a solution of first choice only when the root cause of an operating problem can be traced directly to a lack of job knowledge and/or skill on the part of the employee(s).

Management Development

Management development is an:

individual process involving the interaction of a man, his job, his manager, and total work environment . . . [which] results in the acquisition of new knowledge, skills, attitudes in a planned orderly manner to improve present job performance while accelerating preparation for advancement into more responsible positions.[17]

These topics are most frequently included in a management development program:

- leadership, human relations, working with people, behavioral science concepts, motivating people
- management theory and practice
- hospital policies, benefits, personnel procedures
- labor relations, labor laws and regulations, collective bargaining
- hospital organization, role of the line departments, role of the staff, staff services
- problem solving, decision making
- role of the supervisor
- safety, OSHA
- administrative procedures
- goal setting, management by objectives

Management development programs, which are usually the responsibility of the human resources department's training and development section, should offer ongoing opportunities to supervisors to improve their knowledge and increase their skills in employee relations. A critical element in the success of such programs is the initial careful selection of individuals for managerial positions.

PLACEMENT OF THE HUMAN RESOURCES DEPARTMENT IN THE INSTITUTION'S ORGANIZATIONAL STRUCTURE

To fulfill their broad spectrum of responsibilities, human resources departments have grown in size and have attracted professionally trained executives for leadership positions. Human resources directors are key members of the top administrative group in many health care systems, and most report to the CEO, reflecting the industrial model.

Placement at that top management level promotes better institutional decisions by encouraging all other administrators to give weight to human resources factors in their decision-making process. With this placement, members of the top administrative group of the institution perceive the human resources department director as having higher status than a department head or operating supervisor. In addition, with sufficiently high status the human resources administrator can effectively urge the establishment of new programs. Placed at the top of the organizational structure, human resources departments are more likely to be seen as creative and innovative, and more weight will be given to their ideas, suggestions, recommendations, and advice. Human resources professionals are valuable resource people who assist, advise, and aid the administration in solving people problems. They provide surveys, analyses, information, directions, programs, and concerns all directed toward an effective utilization and motivation of the hospital workforce.

Titles for the top human resources executives in hospitals vary considerably. In institutions with corporate structures, the individual who heads the human resources or personnel function may well be called vice president for human resources. Other titles are personnel manager, human resources manager, personnel administrator, director of human resources, director of industrial relations, director of personnel, chief of personnel, associate director for personnel, or assistant director for personnel.

Jobs that report directly to the top executive of the human resources department are employee relations manager, labor relations manager, wage and salary administrator, manager of training, employment manager, and benefits manager. Other positions in the department include managers of human re-sources research, safety, employee services, employee counseling, and housing. In other subsections of the department, one finds such positions as job analyst, employment interviewer, personnel statistician, personnel assistant, and personnel clerk. In some institutions, the health service department reports to the human resources administrator.

It is not sufficient that the vice president for human resources direct his or her own thinking and activity toward a strategic planning process. The mindset and commitment must filter throughout the human resources staff. However, there is risk of romanticizing all this "fun" activity of influencing the leadership of the organization at the expense of good, basic personnel administration. Compensation, benefits, employment, contract and regulation compliance, and other ongoing programs must be well managed.

In helping human resources staff maintain their expertise in their specialized functions, yet still assume this new kind of leadership role, these strategies for their development are recommended.

- *Provide opportunities for external education and professional affiliation.* Many educational programs, both in specific areas of human resources and in business administration, are available at reasonable cost at universities, at junior colleges, and through professional seminars. Also, membership in professional societies, such as the American Society for Healthcare Human Resources Administration or the American Society for Personnel Administration, or their local or state chapters, is not expensive and provides stimulating exchange among colleagues. A portion of the human resources budget devoted to the professional development of staff is money well spent.

- *Send human resources staff out into the hospital and the organized delivery systems to do their work.* If they do all their work in their offices, expecting employees always to come to them when they need assistance, their function will never be perceived as proactive. "Road shows" are one effective way to expose human resources staff to the environment they need to know and understand. For example, an employee relations specialist might ask to speak at various departmental meetings on subjects such as the disciplinary policy or the grievance procedure. Or people from the employment or compensation areas might do an educational road show on promotions and transfers. By having human resources staff appear in other departments, such as the laundry or a nursing conference room, respect for those functions is conveyed. This also allows the human resources staff to get more in-depth knowledge of their customers' issues.

- *Create interdisciplinary work teams.* When projects are undertaken, involve staff from a variety of human resources areas as well as from departments. For example, if an exit interview program is being developed, line managers should participate with human resources people in devising the questionnaire and deciding how the data will be used. This process assures support for the program but, more importantly, results in a product that reflects issues important to the whole organization. Other opportunities for expanding staff members' knowledge of the organization can be created in the form of ongoing committees on topics such as employee health and safety and employee recognition programs. Also, internal experts could be invited to attend human resources staff functions. A phy-

sician speaking on the research going on in the organization, a development officer talking about the hospital's reliance on fund raising, a facilities engineer describing how buildings are planned and maintained—all serve to open human resources staff's eyes to the broader scope and purposes of the organization.

- *When possible, expose human resources staff to top management and members of the board of trustees.* Hearing those who are ultimately accountable for the effectiveness of the organization reinforces the importance of its mission and the value of all employees in supporting it. If such opportunities do not exist, the human resources staff could initiate activities and events to create a dialogue throughout the hospital.

- *Teaching and mentoring are important functions in assuring that human resources staff rise to the level of competence needed to lead the organization.* They can learn the principles and mechanisms of strategic planning, and they can follow the excellent examples set by top-flight human resources executives, both within their institution and in others.[18]

Assessment Centers

Assessment centers are used to identify candidates for managerial positions. These centers perform this function more effectively than the usual appraisal procedures, because all assessees (1) have an equal opportunity to display their talents, (2) are seen under similar conditions and situations designed to bring out the particular skills and abilities needed for the position or positions for which they are being considered, and (3) are evaluated by a team of trained assessors unbiased by past associations, who are intimately familiar with the position requirements.

In using assessment centers to select applicants for management positions, the institution is primarily interested in estimating managerial potential of its employees, but centers may also produce useful training and development recommendations. The program of the assessment center should meet, as a minimum, the following specifications:

- It must validly measure management potential. Decisions made on the potential development of the individual worker must be related to actual job performance factors.
- It must have high face validity and acceptability to both the health care institution and to the person being assessed.
- It must be administered as an integral part of the hospital's staff development program. The assessment program should serve as a partial individual needs analysis, because the output reports will include information about the individual's skills that may be improved through education and development of training programs.
- It must be flexible enough to permit assessment of managerial potential at various levels and functional areas of specialization.
- It must be comprehensive enough to tap a wide variety of potential managerial characteristics. The complexity and breadth of managerial functions require an elaborate battery of measuring devices for adequate coverage.
- It must have a high payoff value in relation to investment and the cost of administration.
- It must be feasible in terms of the realities of the institution's particular organizational structure and climate, as well as be practically and theoretically sound.

As part of the assessment center method, a battery of psychological tests, including those for mental ability, numerical ability, logical thinking, and personality, is administered. A systematic pattern interview, which consists of a reservoir of preplanned questions to be asked of all candidates, usually follows the testing. The interviewer evaluates the participant on the basis of his or her actions and words in the interview. This interview is usually followed by an "in-basket exercise." This semistructured exercise is designed to measure a number of variables that together make up a large part of what is called leadership ability. In the exercise, the persons being assessed sit around a table. Observers are in attendance, but do not participate. The group is briefed on the assigned topic for discussion, or a problem is posed to the group for solution. Each participant is asked to put himself or herself in the role of an administrator in that situation. He or she must then make judgments, delegate assignments, and indicate decisions. Each observer takes notes on an assigned number of participants, assessing variables such as leadership, interpersonal relations, flexibility, oral skills, and quality of participation.

Human Resources Strategic Planning

An effective human resources strategic plan is one that supports the overall strategic plan of the organization or integrated health delivery system. This overall business plan may be one of growth or consolidation, one introducing new services or improving current programs, one of specialization or diversification. In any event, the human resources strategy and management responses must complement and enhance the possibility of a successful outcome.

Second, the strategic plan must define the organization's benefits and values. Employees at all levels must be permitted to understand the culture and contribute to the common beliefs and expectations that employees have for each other and for how their jobs should be performed, from simple phone courtesy to the detailed training of surgical teams. The blending of multiple organizations into delivery networks makes this strategic goal imperative.

Finally, the plan must encourage the development of specific and measurable objectives to determine success and to allow individuals to see results and participate in shaping and influencing these outcomes. The leadership and workforce values that emanate from the thoughtful consideration of these factors must reflect the organization's values of quality and service: how it relates to the patient; how it views itself as an organization; and how it will carry out its commitment to cost containment, service, and efficiency. The successful integration of these values in an organization requires the commitment of senior management. Management practices and attitudes need to ensure that the medical facility's labor force is seen not merely as a necessary expense, but also as a crucial asset requiring wise investment and sound management in order to realize significant return.

Before embarking on the development of a human resources strategic plan, the human resources director needs to assess the readiness of the organization to develop an effective plan. Questions that should be asked include the following:

- What are the key organization concerns or goals expressed by senior management?
- Which of these critical concerns or goals depend on human resources for success?
- How does your organization view its workforce: as an asset? as an expense?
- How would you judge your own performance and the human resources department's level of performance?

- Are you part of the senior planning group? If not, why not?
- Have you thought hard about the long-term implications of a changing health care environment for the human resources aspects of your organization?
- Are you prepared to raise, and persist in the discussion of, difficult and complex human resources issues for which there appear to be no easy or convenient solutions?

Thus, the human resources director can only model the organization's commitment to a concept that treats human resources as a valuable organizational asset to be managed for an investment return, like any other asset. By adopting this philosophy, the human resources director will be required to oversee four important responsibilities essential to a human resources strategic plan.

1. Install information systems to establish an employee database. The human resources director must ensure that the information systems and data are available to enable the organization to understand how human resources can and should be measured. These data range from a comprehensive organizational employee attitude survey to turnover statistics, benefit utilization, and work force demographics. In short, the organization must be able to measure and understand the tremendous investment that it has in a labor-intensive organization such as a hospital medical group or integrated delivery system.
2. Train and educate management and staff concerning human resources management issues. The human resources leadership must play a central role in training and developing employees and managers with regard to their approach

to human resources management. This will require consultation and support from other departments, because the human resources function will be in the unique position of articulating the organizational values and principles regarding the human resources department.

3. Participate in the development and redesign of human resources policies, procedures, and practices. The human resources director will be required to oversee and/or participate in the development or modification of organizational policies, procedures, and practices regarding human resources. These operation revisions may include the discussion and consideration of staffing patterns and compensation policies, as well as employee training programs.

4. Prioritize human resources responsibilities. The human resources director must assess and prioritize the tasks of the human resources department and his or her own functional responsibilities. A department that is awash in paperwork compliance and consumed by urgent operational issues will not be effective in a strategic environment, which requires a director to give greater emphasis to broader organizational issues and the planning necessary to achieve the desired results.[19]

Encouraging Organizational Acceptance of the Human Resources Strategic Plan

Although there is no simple blueprint for ensuring that a human resources strategic plan will be embraced by the organization, four steps are essential for a successful introduction.

1. The senior management of the organization must be involved sufficiently to develop "ownership" in the human resources strategic plan. They must have argued about, challenged, designed, and accepted a strategy of human resources principles that they feel are critical to the long-term success of the medical facility.

2. The human resources strategy must have a clarity and directness about it so that employees at all levels understand it. While a human resources strategy will be tough, of necessity, on numerous facets of the organization, the strategy must have a cohesiveness that provides a reference point for key human resources decisions and programs.

3. There must be an explicit commitment to preserve the adopted human resources principles during the communications and implementation phases. Recognizing the limitations and resistance that will exist in any organization, particularly one as diverse and complex as a health care delivery organization, it is important that management visibly demonstrate ownership of the human resources strategy. The recognition that the establishment of these key human resource principles is a multiyear effort will temper unrealistic expectations and minimize frustration.

4. The human resources function must have the credibility, influence, and expertise to allow the human resources strategy to be communicated effectively and instituted throughout the organization. Not only must the communication process allow information to flow regularly to employees, but also it must allow information from employees to reach the decision and policy

makers of the organization. This results not only in the reinforcement of, and adherence to, key human resources principles, but also in the sharing of human resources values, standards, and key organizational principles.

Figure 11–1 illustrates the strategic role of the human resources department at Yale–New Haven Hospital. The vice president of human resources coordinated the hospital's human resources management and professional staff in developing and implementing this successful strategic plan.[20]

Labor Relations

Labor relations in the health care industry are subject to a complex body of statutory, administrative, and case law. All nongovernmental health care facilities are covered by the federal labor law, the National Labor Relations Act. Once a union is certified, all matters relating to wages, hours, and working conditions, which the nonunion hospital decided without outside interference so long as its policies were in compliance with state and federal laws, must be determined through the collective bargaining process. The contract that is finally signed is, in effect, a statement of mutually agreed-upon personnel policies. The function of labor relations is usually the responsibility of the human resources director. Four specific elements of labor relations deserve attention:

1. union organizational drives—how hospitals react to such drives
2. preventive labor relations
3. collective bargaining—negotiations
4. contract administration, including disciplinary, grievance, and arbitration procedures

Most health care industry employees who join unions see them as a limited-purpose economic institution. They are searching for something that they perceive they cannot presently find in the institution. Unions are quite selective in their organizational targets because an organizational drive is costly both to the union and to the institution. Unions are less likely than in the past to mount an organizational drive based upon an invitation by large employee groups. Once determining on both a cost-effective and philosophical basis that a specific institution should be organized, the union attempts to rally employees to respond to some overt action taken by the hospital administration or professional staff, which may be perceived as unfair or unjust. The union organizer is selected either from within the institution or the union hierarchy on the basis of an ability to relate to the specific problems in that particular hospital. The organizer first attempts to establish a base within the institution by selecting employees within the organization who can be the focal point of organizing activity. Once an organizing committee has been established, the campaign moves forward. When the appropriate appeal or combination of appeals has been developed by a joint effort between the organizer and the organizing committee, handbills appear. Unions have effectively used handbills to communicate differences in benefits between the target of its effort and another institution that it had already organized. Thus, the union attempts to communicate its power by enumerating gains it has won at other institutions. Authorization cards are then solicited.

During an organizing campaign, actions of the institution and the union are specifically governed by various decisions of the NLRB. The labor relations department of a health care system must be familiar with all provi-

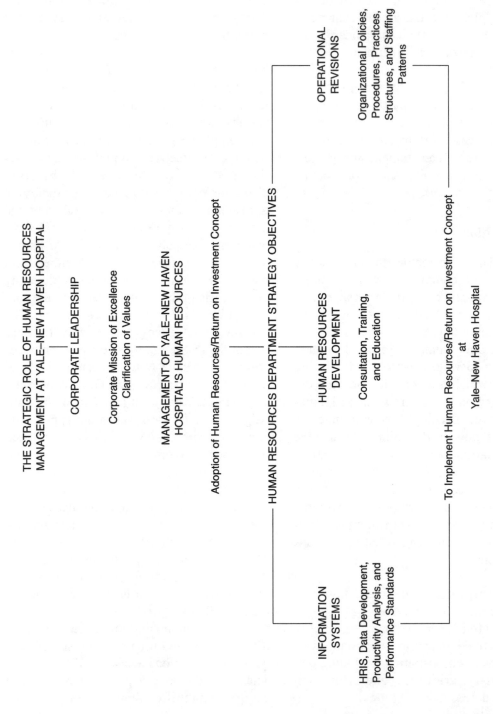

Figure 11–1 The Strategic Role of Human Resources Management at Yale–New Haven Hospital

sions of the National Labor Relations Act and decisions of the NLRB, specifically in the area of solicitation and distribution. More often than not, the desire for unionization is created by management's actions, rather than by the union. The following list states permissible and impermissible actions on the part of a hospital.

Hospitals can take the following actions:

- Explain the meaning of union recognition and the procedure to be followed.
- Encourage each member of the bargaining unit to cast his or her ballot in the election.
- Communicate to employees that they are free to vote for or against the union, despite the fact that they signed the union authorization card.
- Communicate to all employees why the administration is opposed to recognition of the union.
- Review the compensation and benefits program, pointing out the record of the administration in the past.
- Point out to employees the statements made by the union that the administration believes to be untrue and communicate the administration's own position on each of these statements.
- Prevent solicitation of membership by the union during working hours if there is a general no-solicitation rule that has been implemented assiduously in the past.
- Continue to enforce all rules and regulations in effect before the union's request for recognition.
- Send letters to employees' homes stating the administration's position and record and the administration's knowledge of the union's position.
- Discuss the possibility of strikes when hospitals become unionized and the ramifications of such strikes.

- Discuss the effect of union dues and, in general, the cost of belonging to the union.
- Discuss the position of the institution with employees individually at their work areas.
- Respond to the union's promises during the pre-election period by pointing out to employees that if the hospital were to meet union demands it might be forced to lay off employees (this statement can be made as long as the administration points out that the layoff would be an involuntary action necessitated by the union's demands).

Hospitals cannot do the following:

- Promise benefits and threaten reprisals if employees vote for or against the union or have supervisors attend union meetings to determine whether employees are participating in union activities.
- Grant wage increases or special concessions during the election period, unless the timing coincides with well-established prior practices.
- Prevent employees from wearing union buttons, except in cases where buttons are provocative or extremely large.
- Bar employee union representatives from soliciting employee membership during nonworking hours, when the solicitation does not interfere with the work of others or with patient care.
- Summon an employee into an office for private discussion about the union and the upcoming election (this does not preclude an employee from coming in voluntarily to discuss these things).
- Question employees about union matters and meetings.
- Ask employees how they intend to vote.
- Threaten layoffs because of unionization

or state that they will never negotiate with the union even if it is certified.
- Hold meetings of employees within the 24-hour period immediately preceding the election.

Discipline

Hospitals and organized delivery systems that have been organized by unions have found it necessary to establish formal labor relations divisions within their human resources departments, which are delegated the responsibility of overseeing the disciplinary, grievance, and arbitration procedures. "Management has the right to manage; employees have the right to grieve," is an old industrial relations maxim. It simply means that the power of decision is vested in management; management has the right to act. However, in acting, management must live by certain rules incorporated in the collective bargaining agreement. It has the unquestionable right to impose discipline, up to and including discharge, if it has sufficient and appropriate reasons. Yet, the burden of providing "good and just cause" for discipline rests on administration. Jules Justin, a prominent labor arbitrator, lists some noteworthy principles of corrective discipline.[21]

- To be meaningful, discipline must be corrective, not punitive.
- When you discipline one, you discipline all.
- Corrective discipline satisfies the rule of equality of treatment by enforcing equally among all employees established rules, safety practices, and responsibility on the job.
- Just cause or any other comparable standard for justifying disciplinary action under the labor contract consists of three parts:

1. Did the employee breach the rule or commit the offense charged against him or her?
2. Did the employee's act or conduct warrant corrective action or punishment?
3. Is the penalty just and appropriate to the act or offense as corrective punishment?

- The burden of proof rests upon the supervisor who must justify each of three parts listed above that make up the standard of just cause under the labor contract.

Discipline is usually meted out by oral reprimands, warning notices, suspensions, and terminations. Too often, institutions develop rules and policies that run counter to the prevailing customs operative over the years in the workplace. It is important that the rules and regulations be perceived by employees as necessary. The organization's cardinal responsibility in the disciplinary procedure is to attempt a restructuring of the employee's behavior, not to punish him or her.

The Bureau of National Affairs conducted a study of many successful policies controlling disciplinary actions; it found the following common elements:[22]

- Company rules are carefully explained to employees. Indoctrination courses, employee handbooks, bulletin notices, and many other methods of bringing rules to workers' attention are used.
- Accusations against employees are carefully considered to determine whether they are supported by facts. Witnesses are interviewed, their statements are recorded, and careful investigations are made to ensure that both sides of the story are available and are presented fairly. Circumstantial evidence is kept to a minimum in judging the facts. Person-

ality factors and unfounded assumptions are eliminated.

- A regular warning procedure is established and applied. Sometimes all warnings are in writing, with the original handed to the employee and a copy filed in the worker's record in the personnel office. Sometimes first warnings are delivered orally, but a written record of that action is filed. Warnings are given for all except the most serious offenses: those that management has made clear to everyone mean immediate discharge.

- Some companies bring the union into the disciplinary case early in the procedure. They provide copies of warning notices and advance notice of other disciplinary actions that management has to take.

- The employee's motive and reasons for the violation of rules are investigated before disciplinary action is taken. Then the penalty is adjusted to the facts: whether the employee's action was in good faith, partially justified, or totally unjustified.

- The employee's past record is taken into consideration before disciplinary action is taken. A good work record and long seniority are factors in the employee's favor, particularly where a minor and first offense is involved. Previous offenses are not used against the employee, unless the individual is reprimanded at the time they occurred or warned that they would be used in any future disciplinary action.

- Companies make sure that all management agents, particularly first-line supervisors, know the employer's disciplinary policies and procedures and observe them carefully. This is particularly important in the case of verbal warnings or informal reprimands.

- Disciplinary action short of discharge is used wherever possible.

Grievance Procedure: Resolving Employee Complaints

Many so-called grievances are informational in nature, resulting from a lack or breakdown in communication; for example, the employee misreads the rule, clause, or policy. Others result from a dissatisfaction with the rule, clause, or policy—they are gripes. However, whether they are gripes, complaints, or bona fide grievances, they must be addressed. A large majority of grievances result from a decision made and/or communicated by first-line supervisors. Therefore, if a theory of due process is to prevail, it becomes necessary to permit an employee to contest an immediate supervisor's decision and to have an avenue of recourse beyond that ruling.

The major purpose of the grievance procedure is to dispose of the grievance fairly and equitably and, where possible, reach an agreement. To do so facts must be obtained and evaluated objectively; fact finding is at the heart of the grievance procedure. The most effective grievance handling, which results in fair and equitable resolution of employee disputes, requires (1) energetic pursuit of all facts, (2) omission from the hearing procedures of preconceived ideas about the validity of the grievance, (3) a desire to dispose of the grievance by protecting the rights of the institution and of the employee, and (4) a willingness to admit that management is wrong, if that is the case.

The basic principles of grievance adjustment are as follows:[23]

- Inherent in successful grievance adjustment is a commitment to adjusting the employee's complaint properly and on its merits.

- Because the majority of grievances derive from a decision by a first-line supervisor, there must be a direct avenue of appeal beyond that ruling.

- A grievance procedure that has as its terminal step a review inside the institution is not as effective as one that provides for an outside review (arbitration) by an impartial third party.
- There should be a strong desire to resolve dissatisfaction and conflicts before they become real problems.
- Supervisors should empathize with their employees, try to understand their problems, and be able and willing to listen in a nonjudgmental fashion.
- Supervisors should balance their personal commitment to the interest of the institution with a sense of fair play on behalf of the employees.
- Employees deserve a complete and empathetic hearing of all grievances.
- The most important job in handling of grievances is obtaining the facts. Therefore, supervisors must listen attentively and encourage full discussion and defer judgment.
- Supervisors must look for the hidden agenda, look beyond the selected incident, and judge the grievance in context.
- Hasty decisions often backfire. On the other hand, the employee deserves a speedy reply.
- Supervisors should try to separate fact from opinion or impressions while investigating a grievance, consult others when appropriate, and, most importantly, check with the personnel office.
- The supervisor, after coming to a decision, should communicate it to the employee promptly, giving the reasons for the ruling and informing the person of the right to appeal an adverse outcome.
- Decisions must be made and then "sold" to the employee. The decision is less ef-

fective if the individual does not understand its rationale.
- Common sense is an essential ingredient in arriving at a decision.
- Written records are most important. They serve as a review for the supervisor to ensure consistency of grievance handling.

Management's responsibility in the administration and adjudication of grievances includes the following:

- hearing and discussing the grievance facts with the employee
- investigating the facts during and after the hearing
- formulating a decision based upon the facts
- answering the grievance

The typical grievance procedure contains four steps. In the first step the employee submits the grievance to the first-line supervisor. In many instances, the employee's representative is involved in this step. In the second step the employee and the union representative, where applicable, appeal the decision from step 1. The specific management representative at this point differs from institution to institution, but he or she should be superior of the first-line supervisor. In some organizations the personnel department handles the second step. In step 3, the employee and the union representative, where applicable, appeal the decision to a labor relations' representative of the institution. In some facilities the third step, which is the last in-house appeal, is conducted by an associate director of the institution. Step 4 is the arbitration procedure.

Some institutions prefer an informal rather than a formal grievance procedure. A lower-level employee may find it difficult to express frustrations, fears, and needs to a person in a much higher position, who appears to be isolated from the everyday problems of the rank-and-file worker. Most high-level executives find the grievance procedure activity to be an imposition on their busy schedules.

Voluntary arbitration, the terminal step in the grievance procedure and a contract dispute, is judicial in nature. When the two parties—the union and the institution—are unable to resolve a dispute by mutual agreement, they submit the particular issue to an impartial third party for resolution. The solution deriving from this procedure is final and binding on both parties.

Arbitrators are usually selected by agreement of both parties and more often than not are chosen from a national panel of arbitrators provided by the American Arbitration Association. The institution's case usually is presented by a labor attorney. Some institutions delegate the responsibility for presenting their case to the labor relations director in the human resources department.

Participatory Management: Quality Circles

The development of programs that increase worker participation will be the major challenge to human resources managers in the twenty-first century. Many studies show that when employees are given the opportunity to make more decisions about their work, they are more productive and satisfied, and their needs are fulfilled. This is most obvious when an institution undertakes a re-engineering program. Need fulfillment or frustration results directly in either constructive or defensive behavior. Dissatisfied employees do not provide the excellent level of care so desperately needed in hospitals. Such dissatisfaction leads to an ineffective workforce, costly absenteeism, and labor confrontations.

Worker participation plans must develop a spirit of cooperation and teamwork as their end-product. The critical nature of shared decision making must be sold down the line to the organization.

In one study,[24] hospital management structures were analyzed to identify the features that led to alienation of nonsupervisory personnel. The study's hypothesis was that the degree of alienation is inversely related to the degree to which nonsupervisory nursing personnel are allowed to participate in management's decisions. The results bore out the hypothesis, indicating that alienation is greater when nonsupervisory staff are not allowed to participate in the decision-making process and that inflexible bureaucratic systems tend to increase frustrations and depersonalization in staff relations, causing a loss of initiative.

In addition, many studies in the area of democratic vis-à-vis authoritarian leadership styles have generated these findings:

- The greater number of competent judges, the greater the validity of their combined judgments.
- When there is worker participation, there is a tendency for the members to sharpen and refine an idea before it is given to the group, and the group in turn is able to reject and correct ideas that escape the notice of individuals when working alone.
- Tasks that were performed through cooperation rather than competition were more efficiently accomplished, with members exhibiting a higher degree of motivation and morale.
- Group discussion under the democratic approach is more likely to alter opinions, and conversely attitudes are less likely to change under authoritarian approaches.
- Participation increases the likelihood

that a goal is set that is congruent with the group's perceived values.

- As a result of discussion of establishing goals, members are more likely to have adequate knowledge of the nature of the goal, its value to themselves, and its true attainability.

To increase worker participation, hospitals and organized delivery systems are investigating and, in some cases, implementing the quality circle process. Applying theories of behavioral scientists such as Maslow and Herzberg, Japanese industrialists introduced quality circles into manufacturing firms three decades ago and into areas where quality of service and the involvement of employees were essential. The preeminent exponent of the quality circles concept in Japan is Kaoru Ishikawa, who was a professor at the University of Tokyo. According to Ishikawa, the outcomes of quality circles include the following:

- developing oneself and others
- increasing quality awareness
- encouraging the brainpower of the workforce
- improving worker morale
- developing managerial abilities of circle leaders
- implementing and managing accepted ideas

The benefits of participatory management are still being carefully monitored in factories throughout the United States.

The concept of participatory management and its positive effects on productivity were first espoused in the early work of Elton Mayo, a professor on the faculty of the Harvard Graduate School of Business Administration. Some 60 years ago, in one of his first major studies at a Philadelphia textile mill, he analyzed the excessive labor turnover rate in one of the mill's departments. When the workers were given an opportunity to schedule their own work and rest periods, dramatic results occurred: morale improved, turnover fell, and productivity rose. Mayo concluded that these positive outcomes resulted mainly from allowing employees to participate in the managing of their own work. His seminal study at the Hawthorne Works of the Western Electric Company identified that increased productivity resulted when all employees in the experimental workroom were given a major voice in deciding the management of their own time. In addition, he pointed out that the opportunity to discuss their work problems with the interviewers gave these workers unprecedented freedom to ventilate their feelings, permitting them to view their situation more objectively and to develop positive solutions.

Six basic principles are operative in quality circles and can be applied whether an institution adopts them or not:[25]

1. Trust your employees. Expect that they will work to implement organizational goals if given a chance.
2. Build employee loyalty to the company. It will pay off.
3. Invest in training and treat employees as resources, who, if cultivated, will yield economic returns to the firm. This means developing employee skills. Long-term employee commitment to the organization is an objective.
4. Recognize employee accomplishments. Symbolic rewards mean more than you think.
5. Decentralize decision making.
6. Regard work as a cooperative effort with workers and managers doing the job together by implementing consensual decision-making processes.

Quality circles embody the principle of participatory management to its fullest. They are based on the theory that an organization's workers are closest to the problem and indeed may be part of the problem and that therefore they are best equipped to remedy it, thereby increasing their output and improving the caliber of work or service. A quality circle is a small group of 5 to 15 employees, usually from the same work area doing similar work, who meet together on a voluntary basis and discuss, with the assistance of a facilitator and leader, solutions to job-related problems. Quality circles give a broader base of employees the opportunity to speak up in an atmosphere where management is listening.

The Quality Control Institute in California, one of the several consulting organizations involved in promoting and assisting in the formation of quality circles, defines the quality circle process as follows:[26]

- *Problem identification:* Typically several problems are identified. Problem selection is a prerogative of the circle.
- *Problem analysis:* Formed by the circle with assistance, if needed, by appropriate circle experts.
- *Problem solutions or recommendations to management:* The circle makes them directly to its manager using a communication technique described as "the management presentation."

According to the Institute, circle suggestions either cost nothing or can be financed from normal department budgets. Moreover, the entire training of the circle members emphasizes that the best way to control problems is to avoid them. Quality circle programs are organized along these lines:[27]

- A quality circle effort is initiated only upon the decision of senior management.
- Initial meetings for a quality circle are held with all union, management, and supervisory personnel.
- Participation in the circle is voluntary.
- The managers who decide to try a circle and then make presentations to the hourly workers, at which participation of the hourly workers is voluntary.
- Participation of management in the circle is voluntary.

In the quality circle process, it is the individual who is important. Employee self-esteem is increased; consequently, employees are more open and do not fear a display of openness as they discuss, suggest, and set quality goals and methods for reaching these goals. An employee who participates in a quality circle is more likely to be concerned about the effectiveness of the recommendation springing from the activity and, therefore, would be more effective in monitoring the group's activities. The key to the success of a quality circle is top management's complete support and confidence in the concept.

Personnel Policies

The description of the hospital's or health system's personnel policies in a written manual is essential in obtaining understanding and commitment to those policies by the entire management team and by employees. The human resources department is responsible for the assembling of all such personnel policies into a manual. In collecting such information, careful attention to past practices must be paid, and the participation of department heads is essential. The policy manual, which must be precise, complete, and understandable, usually covers the following areas:

- *benefits:* health benefits, workers' compensation, disability, Social Security benefits, pension plan

- *compensation:* salary determination, salary increase policy, reclassifications, pay schedules, overtime pay, shift differential, on-call pay, uniform allowance, severance pay
- *disciplinary action:* guidelines, warning notice policy
- *employment:* employment standards, type of employment, probationary period
- *grievance procedure*
- *health, safety, and security*
- *hours of work and time off:* work schedule, meal and rest periods, holidays, vacation, sick leave, leave of absence
- *performance review*
- *employee recognition program*
- *seniority*
- *services and activities:* blood protection program, gift shop, recreational activities
- *termination:* retirement, resignation, discharge
- *training and development*

Benefits Administration

On average, hospitals pay the majority of the cost of individual medical coverage. Vision coverage is offered to employees in only a small number of all hospitals. About one-third of all hospitals offer short-term disability benefits to their employees. A little over half of all hospitals offer an employee assistance program to their employees. Employees usually view their total benefit plan as a means of reducing or offsetting entirely the financial loss that they can incur due to death, disability, medical expense, or retirement.

Employee benefits management is an integral part of the human resources department and requires intensive planning, close supervision, and integrated direction. Expanded health protection benefits, including dental, drug, psychiatric, and optical plans, are being developed at a faster pace than ever before and may be required to attract and retain employees. The human resources manager must become more knowledgeable about such plans.

Pension Plan

The most fundamental decision in the design of pension plans is the choice of the basic formula. Most hospital plans contain either a career-average salary or final-average pay formula. The career-average pay plan generally bases its benefits on the earnings either during each year of service or on an average of the total salary earned during a career. This approach tends to produce a lesser, albeit less expensive, benefit in an inflationary economy. Generally, the final-average pay plan bases benefits on the earnings of the participant during the last 5 years of service. The theory underlying this method is that the benefit payable at retirement is automatically inflation-proof because it is related to the average wage just before retirement. Both these plans are defined benefit plans. In contrast, in defined contribution plans the employer establishes the amount of the contribution that the institution desires to make on behalf of each participant. There is no definition of a definitely determinable benefit. The contribution may be defined as a percentage of pay or a flat annual rate per salary range. The present law—ERISA—specifies rigid eligibility, participation, vesting, and funding requirements. The benefits administrator must be thoroughly familiar with all its provisions.

Social Security benefits may be integrated into the pension benefits formula, thereby reducing the amount of money that the institution contributes to pension benefits. Not-for-profit hospitals operating under Section 501(c)(3) of the Internal Revenue Code can sponsor tax-sheltered annuity programs. Under these programs, the employer can contribute either a percentage of salary or a flat dollar amount to the annuity. The money accumulates on a tax-free basis until the annuity income is received.[28]

Preretirement Planning Programs

Many hospitals and organized delivery systems provide programs to ease employees' transition to retirement. These programs are usually offered 5 years in advance of normal retirement and are intensified in the last year before retirement. Individual counseling and group seminars focus on the psychological adjustment to retirement, benefits and financial aspects of retirement, and health considerations. They serve a morale-building function in the latter part of an employee's career in an institution.

Disability Insurance

In addition to legislated short-term disability programs, many hospitals provide long-term disability. Such plans usually begin at around 26 weeks. They contain maximum benefit levels and a coordination of benefits with other plans to eliminate duplicated coverage. The benefit levels usually are set at less than full take-home pay.

Health Insurance Plans

Hospitals and organized delivery systems offer a broad spectrum of comprehensive health insurance plans, including hospital, medical, surgical, and major medical coverage. Some large hospitals and systems have developed self-insurance plans as cost-saving devices. These are usually administered in conjunction with an umbrella policy, which covers claims in excess of a specific stop-loss and individual claim level. Plans may be administered in-house or through insurance companies. In addition to the financial advantage of administering plans in-house, the personal touch and the value of reimbursement being handled directly in the institution have

enormous morale implications. Many hospitals now provide dental, optical, and pharmaceutical benefits. These are usually offered under third-party plans, but many institutions have found, as with other insurance plans, that self-insurance is a viable option.

Other Employee Benefits

There are a myriad of employee benefit programs in addition to traditional pension and health benefits. Programs such as educational assistance, purchase discount programs, credit unions, legal and automobile insurance, banking services, and housing are among the most widely provided programs under the general rubric of employee benefits. Educational assistance programs benefit both the individuals taking advantage of such aid and the institution, inasmuch as the employee is prepared for advancement. Purchase discount programs, including car rentals, motel and hotel discounts, restaurant and sports events discounts, are very popular. Credit unions have been found to be a useful means of serving employees' banking needs. They provide checking account services, loans, and other services that ease financial burdens of employees.

Flexible Benefit Plans

These are plans that allow employees to use specific dollars assigned to benefits, in the manner that best meets their personal needs. They involve employees and their families directly in the decisions on how much to select and spend for each benefit. They provide a means for employees to know the real cost/worth of their benefits.[29]

Flex allows employees to use specific dollars to purchase benefits, thereby tailoring the plan to their personal needs. For most people the choices to date are between an indemnity plan and a health maintenance organization (HMO) or preferred provider organization (PPO) option. But they probably have never taken a hard look at benefits within the benefit plan, and that certainly is what a flex plan does.

What Is Gain Sharing?

Gain sharing is an organizational program designed to improve productivity, enhance quality, and reduce cost. The benefits that accrue from these improvements are then shared in cash with the employees who produced them. Gain sharing is a group incentive program with the emphasis of teamwork. Furthermore, gain sharing is intended to capture the numerous small savings that collectively add up to substantial savings. Further, gain sharing creates an environment for sustained, continual improvements.

The concept of gain sharing is simple. First, the organization calculates its historic rates of productivity (and, where measurable, quality). Then, new targets are set. If performance reaches the new targets, the organization and its employees share the monetary gains. Because it involves money that the institution otherwise would not have saved or earned, the program is self-funding. In this sense, it is a win-win program for both the hospital and its employees.[30]

FUTURE DIRECTION OF HUMAN RESOURCES MANAGEMENT

At the beginning of the twenty-first century, human resources departments' challenges and responsibilities will change radically. The need to develop trust, which is a particularly difficult task, will be critical. The establishment of enduring trusting relationships depends on the creation of an overall climate of justice and fairness, which will be one of the responsibilities of human resources managers. Creation of that climate may require clear, representative decision-making structures, which involve those members of the staff with the relevant interest, expertise, and credibility appropriate to the given issue.[31]

Job training and retraining will be important because many jobs will be changed by advances in technology, changing reimbursement systems, and the effects of HMOs. In addition, in organized delivery systems, economies-of-scale goals will require that certain employer categories be shared by all institutions within the system.

The human resources administrator will also occupy the position of keeper of the ethical standards of the organization. He or she must assume the role of mentor and advisor to the operating executives. The role of physicians in hospitals will change radically. Physicians will become more dependent upon hospital systems, in terms of increased competition for privileges. Women will constitute a growing percentage of physicians. Retirement issues will radically change. Employees will be retiring earlier, with recreational options far in excess of what is available today.

The computer will allow an entirely new arrangement of work. Human resources managers of the future will be expert in the use of the computer; the computer will free such managers from the maintenance function of human relations: wage and salary administration, benefits administration, and even employment. With such freedom, they can direct their maximum efforts to the essential core of human relations: building trust, building a structure of participatory management, and creating flexible and ingenious reward systems.

The most compelling challenge facing health care human resources administrators over the next several years is to identify to the industry's leadership the inextricable link between humanized work and working conditions on the one hand, and the levels of productivity that survival requires on the other. Compassionate and efficiently rendered patient care is not possible without a humanized and democratically organized work environment. Organizational health and survival need to be linked with the empowerment of health care workers. If health care administrators cannot be expected to speak and understand the language of social justice within the workplace, then they need to be spoken to in the idiom of institutional survival.

Exclusion from the essential features of patient care management and the absence of work autonomy are the two most consistently cited sources of dissatisfaction for health care workers. These factors must be seen as an instrumental part of the destructive process through which adversaries are made of our employees. Despite its historically low levels of productivity, the industry has failed to move beyond a classification structure based on fractionalized job functions that serve to routinize and de-skill job functions rather than expand them.

There are still opportunities, however, to advance the alternative model. Indeed, the failures of the present strategy may eventually make the alternatives more attractive to health care administrators, if only out of desperation. There already are several instances in which the requirements of the burgeoning marketing function have caused some health care institutions to probe the issue of job satisfaction. That this concern has emerged from a patient relations perspective rather than out of a concern for the working lives of health care workers need not deter us.

The present course is a prescription for industrial conflict and will almost certainly result in higher levels of successful union organizing, even as the proportion of unionized employees in other sectors of our economy continues to decline. More importantly, it is a prescription for failure, particularly in a more

cost-competitive and integrated delivery system environment.[32]

THE GROWTH OF MERGERS, AFFILIATIONS, ORGANIZED DELIVERY SYSTEMS, AND HMOs

It is clear that the government's drive toward universal health care coverage will be addressed by the industry in what may be called a "positioning phase." Large tertiary-care institutions are—and will continue to position themselves for the new world of health care providers by—acquiring, merging, or affiliating with institutions that will better meet the new realities. Some institutions will decrease their number of beds, look for "feeder" institutions that provide primary care, merge with other tertiary institutions in order to reduce duplication of services, and concomitantly reduce costs.

These new arrangements produce many challenges to the human resources executive. Consideration must be given to areas such as:

- compensation programs
- benefits programs
- personnel policies
- union representation/labor relations
- employment facilities
- training programs

Critical to the decision-making process in these areas of human resources, and the decisive element in such considerations, is whether the organization will centralize all or some of its human resources functions, or whether it will maintain a decentralized service.

There are clear benefits in opting for a centralized service in compensation, benefits, personnel policies, and training. Yet, regional differences can be defended. As to employment, centralization is preferred if the units are geographically close. A difficult problem may confront the new relationship in the area of union representation. Maintaining a merged multidivisional organization, where some units are unionized and similar units in another division are not, may bring a myriad of problems. In addition, a union may attempt to organize the latter unit, or petition the NLRB on the basis of an accretion to the existing similar unit, which is organized.

It should be clear that a careful consideration to merging human resources services must include legal requirements, local standards, efficiency, and cost implications. Too often such decisions to affiliate, merge, or acquire omit the input of the human resources executive. This is a mistake, which often is hastily addressed after the fact.

THE EFFECT OF MANAGED CARE ON HUMAN RESOURCES MANAGEMENT*

Managed care is the latest in a series of events and periods that have affected health care workers negatively. The difference between the events of the 1990s and ones that predate the period is that, except for the very highest level of the organization, all workers, including managers, are affected equally. These changes affect workers of other industries as well, but the effect that managed care will bring to the health care industry will be profound. The subjects of managed care and a consolidating industry are too broad to be dealt with briefly; what follows is narrow in scope.

The rapid conversion from an indemnity insurance based health care market (competition based on access and quality) to a managed care market (competition based on price

and quality) will have a significant effect on the current complexion of the health care delivery system, resulting in a major shift and realignment in the health care labor force. All elements of the health care delivery system will be affected by this change. It is essential that human resources managers understand and participate in the framing of response to these challenges.

The implication for labor relations is the potential of fundamental alienation (at all levels of the workforce) from the employer because of the insecurity of an uncertain future. This alienation will lead to mistrust and lack of confidence in leadership, loss of loyalty and identity with the institution, culminating in decreased productivity, low morale, and the very real threat that the employees will turn to a third party for protection and representation.

The spread of managed care and industry consolidation has been so rapid and unanticipated that a backlash was inevitable. George Anders, a reporter for the *Wall Street Journal*, contributed to the backlash in *Health Against Wealth*.[33] Anders argues that cost-driven managed care companies systematically are degrading the quality of medicine. Managed care generally works for people who need only routine treatments or check-ups, Anders contends, but for the seriously ill, managed care often provides *too little too late*. The reason is simple. Serious illnesses consume most of the health care dollar and, therefore, inspire managed care companies to impose daunting obstacles to aggressive treatment. The restrictions may mean good profits, he warns, but they are bad for patients. Anders' theory (and that of critics in general) is that too much of the money managed care saves *comes from* giving patients less of what they need.

Managed care's full effects are not yet clear, because the system is evolving. The idea that crass commercialism is corrupting medicine is less beguiling than it seems. Open-ended spending also was corrupting medicine and, just as important, hijacking the nation's social priorities. Although the new financial discipline is not inevitably benign, it (or something like it) is desirable. Economics alone, however, will not and should not shape managed care. More employers are demanding accountability on quality. Congress and the states are doing more regulating; they are requiring some services (mental health, for example) and outlawing some restrictions (one-day hospital discharges of new mothers, for example.) These steps may not always be wise, but they emphasize that the health care system does not exist in a political or moral vacuum.

The country is in the midst of a national phenomenon. It is a time of depression, anger, and a subliminal sense of failure. Layoffs, downsizing, and reengineering are different from those of the past. These conditions are now permanent, affecting employees who are middle class, educated, and, most importantly, seriously in debt; and they are affecting professionals and technicians who had believed they had a secure job within a financially sound institution and an expanding industry. Then came sudden change.

Anomalies and Shifting Paradigms

Since corporate America became embroiled in an acquisition frenzy, which began in the 1980s and continues, there has been first a gradual, then more rapid, decay of the trust in all organizations. For the first time managers, as well as employees, were affected. This change removed a valuable utility from the organization—the manager as a communication vehicle. Managers realized they could become victims of the corporate predator just as easily as their more vulnerable subordinates.

Employees at all levels sense the breach of trust. They feel there is no lifeline that extends from the employers. When subordinates see and hear their managers behaving like "employees," it causes the integrity of the corporate infrastructure to become dynamically unstable. One of the byproducts is the mentality of "what's in it for me?" It is difficult for managers, who are in relatively the same economic situation as their subordinates, to espouse the party line when they fear what the immediate future holds.

Human resources executives must consider problems and challenges. Faith in management is rare. How can there be faith in a manager who executes a layoff of employees and says, "This will properly adjust our staffing configuration," when 3 months later the same manager is forced to lay off employees again. Employees want to know what the plan is and when the uncertainty is going to end. Do they control their own destiny, or is the organization controlling its own destiny with little or no concern for employees? The market is fast becoming a matter of quality access to quality care. In the age of managed care continued provider consolidations, the change will not end. Employers and employees must change the way they relate to jobs if they are to survive financially as well as emotionally. The notion of having only one employer is extinct. People will be forced to change jobs, and they must be assisted with the transition. In the merged organization, how to consolidate the management groups effectively to realize the required savings from a reduced exempt budget is the core issue. The road maps of the past do not lead to the same successful results. There must be a shift in paradigms to succeed and survive.

Change is an inadequate description for what is being witnessed in the health care field. "Revolution" would not be a hyperbole; indeed it is truly descriptive of the present state of events unfolding in the field. A sober review of the ingredients of this revolution follows:

- HMOs are a growing force.
- Restraints are placed increasingly on specialty referrals and lucrative procedures.
- Primary care practitioners are assuming more responsibility for referrals and are growing in number.
- Hospitals are merging.
- Bed-closings proliferate.
- Downsizing is the order of the day.
- Greater numbers of physicians are affiliating with HMOs.
- Capitation is replacing fee for service.
- The incentive is to reduce utilization.
- There is a major shift from inpatient to outpatient care.
- There is incentive to keep labor costs down.
- Plans emerge to deal directly with employers and cut out insurance companies.

The following is a review of what may lie ahead:

- strong surviving HMOs in each regional market
- physician groups acting as HMOs
- hospitals acting as HMOs
- competing regional organized provider delivery systems; survival of the fittest
- generalists/primary care physicians having more control
- changing service areas; from city/town to region
- large employers increasing influence on controlling costs
- health care consumerism rising significantly

Table 11–2 is a helpful aid in visualizing the actual and anticipated changes.

Effects of the Health Care Revolution on Labor Relations

The article in the *New York Times*, "Prospective Labor Leaders Set To Turn to Confrontation," directs our attention to the fallout from the revolution in health care.[34] Moving from a prolonged drought in union organizing to an era of militancy and disregard for labor laws, a resolution at the American Federation of Labor and Congress of Industrial Organizations' (AFL-CIO's) national convention stated, "*We* must first organize despite the law, if we are ever to organize with the law."

It is evident that the AFL-CIO unions and the unaffiliated will take full advantage of the changes in the health care system. With job security threatened and large displacement of workers in the industry, the grounds for organization are more fertile now and in the near future than in the past 30 years.

Some of the factors to consider in forecasting union activity in the health care industry are

- Mergers present a myriad of problems.
- Layoffs will proliferate (for the first time in decades, nurses are at risk).
- Movement from inpatient care to outpatient care presents small pockets of easily organizable workers.
- Cost-saving becomes the trend; efforts to control/reduce levels of expenditure for health benefits and pension levels will be priority issues.
- Job security, in general, will be a hot issue; employer efforts to maintain or increase flexibility will be resisted and become a key organizing factor.
- Hospitals will reduce the number of beds; some will close; empty buildings will be a stark symbol of the "success" of managed care.

Table 11–2 The Changing Paradigm of Health Care

	1960	1980	2000
Core Provider	Hospital	Medical center	Health care system
Marketplace	Unstructured independent providers	Alliances and networking	Managed competition
Payers	Indemnity insurance	Mixed insurance HMOs, PPOs	Managed care companies
Reimbursement	Charged-based per diem	Cost-based DRGs	Capitation and direct contracting
Employers	Disinterest in health care	Emerging focus on cost	Strong influence on cost and delivery systems
Service Area	Neighborhood	City/town	Region
Care Focus	Inpatient services	Inpatient and outpatient	Full continuum of care
Physicians	Solo practices and shortages	Group practice overspecialization	Employed physicians, rising demand for primary care
Competition	Nonexistent	Growing market competition	Oligopoly

Courtesy of The Mount Sinai Medical Center, New York, New York.

- Employee insecurities will surface, manifesting union organizing in professional, administrative, and support personnel.
- Employee groups will seek support from politicians, "rights" groups, clergy, and unions.

The days of double digit inflation of health care costs will be a faint memory. Everything will change—the market will evolve into highly competitive regional centers. Managed care will be controlling, cost containment will be essential, and from this revolution the challenge will be to maintain/develop highly motivated and efficient workforces who will not take up the AFL-CIO's call to arms.

Some predictions, based on fact and trends, are

1. Because of inflexibility and longer response cycles, the unionized health care provider will have a more difficult time than the union-free organization surviving the transition to managed care.
2. Insecurity will increase the attractiveness of unions to employees. If unions are successful in organizing previously union-free employees, those employees will be more vulnerable because their employers will be less able to accommodate to change.
3. Labor contracts must be modified to anticipate rapidly changing forces; suc-

cessorship language will require incredible scrutiny.

4. Unions will be relentless in featuring job security as the main issue in organizing health care employees.

5. Employers need to educate employees about the realities of business before they are faced with making difficult choices.

6. Training for life after the current job is a tradeoff for less security.

7. If we cannot provide security, the short-term financial payouts to employees need to be more accommodating.

8. The primary care physician is the source of referrals to most specialists, but this may deteriorate as specialist costs are brought more into line.

9. Destinies will be managed by playing by different rules; managers need to adapt to a fast-paced changing world.

10. Nurses, as the employees most dependent on the number of hospital beds, will be affected by capitation more negatively than others.

11. Contracts need to be amended to include revisions reflective of the changing employer/employee relationship. The market is changing, so labor laws (and interpretation) should change as well, e.g., statutes need to change in order to facilitate flexibility and employee participation and to be reflective of current exigencies.

The following are recommendations to manage the changing environment:

1. Build a new culture anchored in reality and ownership. Employees should be advised that the old days will not return, and that the new environment can be tolerable for employees who are treated with dignity and respect. Every organization should strive to provide a workplace that (1) recognizes individual contribution, (2) is free of harassment for any reason, and (3) solicits input from every level of the organization because every level of the organization has a stake in success.

2. Redefine the relationship between the employer and its employees.
   • Consider two-tiered workforces where a core of employees with longer service and broader skills is more protected.
   • Investigate staffing alternatives, e.g., contract services, outsourcing, and employee leasing options.
   • Arrange multiemployer/employee sharing networks where employees split time between several different organizations.

3. Convert conventional compensation theory to new, creative methods.
   • Pay employees for "hazardous duty" because they may have a shorter career.
   • Use direct compensation programs.
   • Implement gains sharing; it is a valuable way to reward success even in a constricted environment.
   • Consider self-governance as a wage control tool.

4. Training and education will be very important.
   • Every opportunity should be taken to crosstrain employees to increase flexibility.
   • Training and updates regarding the condition of the business are a must. Communication with employees is critical.
   • Career transition training is a trade-

off for short-term employment prospects.

5. In mergers, consolidations, and acquisitions, a process of selecting and deselecting managers is prudent. An assessment center approach may provide for long-term dividends.
6. Employers who face the transition related to changes in the industry should draw on resources from outside the organization to avoid unanticipated pitfalls.

The Effects of Reengineering and Downsizing

The following are common approaches to cost reduction that can have negative effects:

- The replacement of high-priced registered nurses.
- The expectation that staff would compromise quality.
- The belief that "one size fits all."
- The belief that if costs are not reduced as planned that it is the managers' fault, and, therefore, the management team must be changed.

Rather than using the above flawed approaches to reduce costs, to succeed in a reengineering program, one must

- Identify the financial imperative—be *realistic* not *idealistic*.
- Segregate patients in appropriate size populations from a medical care perspective.
- Build the workforce around caring for these patient populations.
- Involve employees as never before.
- Include your human resource managers in the planning and implementation phases.

The failures of some mergers have been because of a lack of attention to differing corporate cultures. Still other difficult factors relate to employee discontent and insecurity, which often are discussed infrequently and/or underestimated. There are increased fears about job security, layoffs, changing job requirements, and the effects of differing benefit structures, and employee relations philosophies. Mergers can be the trigger for union organization. This situation is further accentuated when the merger brings together a unionized staff with one that has little or no union representation. Successful mergers have several things in common: constant communication regarding the positive aspects of the change; treatment of displaced/demoted employees with understanding, flexibility, and assistance; offers of early retirement opportunities and placement services; sponsorship of job fairs with career centers for displaced employees; and sensitivity to any disparate effect on minority groups.

GREAT PLACES TO WORK

Over the years, Robert Levering and Milton Moskowitz, separately and together, have studied workplaces in order to identify the characteristics of those that are considered—by employees and management—great places to work. In earlier studies hospitals were noticeable by the fact that they rarely appeared in the listing. The critical element for inclusion in the list of the best places to work has been the essential factor of employee–employer relationships. There have been some very positive changes—not the least of which is the inclusion of three hospitals among the "100 Best"—since their first study in the early 1980s. In Levering and Moskowitz's second edition of *The Hundred*

Best Companies To Work for in America, they note positive changes in five key areas:[35]

1. *More employee participation.* This growing phenomenon often develops after layoffs. The reduction in management thrusts upon employees the need to participate in reorganization programs.
2. *More sensitivity to the problems of working mothers and fathers.* Many of the companies (including three hospitals) listed in this book provide childcare options and flexible work schedules.
3. *More sharing of the wealth.* Many of those listed have profit-sharing or gain sharing programs. Beth Israel Hospital in Boston uses a version of the Scanlon Plan, a share-the-wealth scheme, wherein employees share directly in productivity gains.
4. *More fun.* Those companies and hospitals selected for inclusion in this book have employees who are enjoying themselves; the institution has a sense of humor that is not inconsistent with a serious, productive institution.
5. *More trust between management and employees.* Employees trust their supervisors and management; managers and supervisors trust their employees. Indications of such trust are the absence of time clocks; regular meetings where employees can discuss their concerns; job posting; and constant training.

The three hospitals cited as exceptional places to work were Beth Israel Hospital of Boston (listed in the top ten), Baptist Hospital of Miami, and Methodist Hospital of Houston. These institutions are the models for our industry. At a time when many health care institutions are attempting to position themselves for the coming changes inherent in health care reform legislation, we can look to these three (and many more not listed) for a clear direction of renewal and dedication toward the improvement of employee-employer relationships. A significant partner in developing and directing such a renewal will be the human resources professional.

NOTES

1. O. Tead and H.C. Metcalf, *Personnel Administration: Its Principles and Practices* (New York: McGraw-Hill, 1920), 51.
2. Ibid., 64.
3. H. Eilbert, "Development of Personnel Management in the U.S.," in *Management of the Personnel Function*, ed. Heckman and Hueneryager (Columbus, OH: Charles E. Merrill Books, Inc., 1962), 20.
4. R. Likert and D. Katz, *Motivation: The Core of Management* (New York: American Management Association, 1953), 3–25.
5. F. Herzberg, *Work and the Nature of Man* (New York: World Publishing Co., 1966).
6. A.H. Maslow, "A Theory of Human Motivation," *Psychological Review* 50 (1943): 370–396.
7. A.R. Brandt, "Describing Hourly Jobs," in *Handbook of Wage and Salary Administration*, ed. M.L. Rock (New York: McGraw-Hill, 1972), 1–11.
8. J.R. Patten et al., *Job Evaluation: Text and Cases*, 3rd ed. (Homewood, IL.: Richard D. Irwin, 1964), 93–94.
9. B. Essig and M.H. Singer, "A Brief Look at the Federal Equal Employment Opportunity Laws," in *Handbook of Health Care Human Resources Management*, ed. N. Metzger (Gaithersburg, MD: Aspen Publishers, Inc., 1981), 115.
10. D.B. Peskin, *Human Behavior in Employment Interviewing* (New York: American Management Association, 1971), 12.
11. M.M. Mandell, *Choosing the Right Man for the Job*

(New York: American Management Association, 1964), 154.

12. N.R.F. Maier et al., "Superior-Subordinate Communication in Management," in *AMA Research Study 52* (New York: American Management Association, 1961), 9.

13. R. Dubin, *The World of Work* (Englewood Cliffs, NJ: Prentice-Hall, Inc., 1950), 337.

14. W.C. Merrihue, *Managing by Communication* (New York: McGraw-Hill, 1960), 122.

15. H.C. Laparo, "Training," in *Handbook of Health Care Human Resources Management*, ed. N. Metzger (Gaithersburg, MD: Aspen Publishers, Inc., 1981), 277.

16. Ibid.

17. R.L. Desatnick, *A Concise Guide to Management Development* (New York: American Management Association, 1970), 11.

18. L. Avakian, "Human Resources Leadership—A Perspective from the Trenches," in *Handbook of Health Care Human Resources Management*, ed. N. Metzger (Gaithersburg, MD: Aspen Publishers, Inc., 1990), 47–48.

19. E.J. Dowling and E.A. Kellman, "A Case Study in Human Resources Strategic Planning," in *Handbook of Health Care Human Resources Management*, ed. N. Metzger (Gaithersburg, MD: Aspen Publishers, Inc., 1990), 29–30.

20. Ibid., 30–31.

21. J.J. Justin, *How To Manage with the Union*, Book 1 (New York: New York Industrial Workshop Seminars, Inc., 1969), 294, 295, 301, 302.

22. *Grievance Guide*, 6th ed. (Washington, DC: The Bureau of National Affairs, Inc., 1982), 5–6.

23. N. Metzger and J. Ferentino, *The Arbitration and Grievance Process* (Gaithersburg, MD: Aspen Publishers, Inc., 1983), 23–24.

24. J. LaPorte, "Participatory Management—The Technique to Alleviate Alienation of Bureaucratic Organizations" (Thesis, University of Ottawa, 1972).

25. R.E. Cole, *Work Mobility and Participation: Comparative Study of American and Japanese Industry* (Berkeley, CA: University of California Press, 1979), 84.

26. Quality Control Institute, *Quality Circles* (Red Bluff, CA: Quality Control Institute, 1987).

27. "E.P. Yager, Quality Circle: A Tool for the 80s," *Training and Development Journal* (August 1980): 60.

28. G.R. Guralnik and J.F. Sapora, "Employee Benefits Administration," in *Handbook of Health Care Human Resources Management*, ed. N. Metzger (Gaithersburg, MD: Aspen Publishers, Inc., 1981), 455–472.

29. R.E. Johnson, "Flexible Benefit Plans," in *Handbook of Health Care Human Resources Management*, ed. N. Metzger (Gaithersburg, MD: Aspen Publishers, Inc., 1990), 311, 313.

30. K.E. Romanoff and J.B. Williams, "Gainsharing," in *Handbook of Health Care Human Resources Management*, ed. N. Metzger (Gaithersburg, MD: Aspen Publishers, Inc., 1990), 147.

31. S.M. Shortell, "The Medical Staff of the Future: Replanting the Garden," in *Frontiers of Health Services Management* 1, no. 3 (1985): 3–48.

32. B. Metzger, "Human Resources Administration: An Alternative Model," in *Handbook of Health Care Human Resources Management*, ed. N. Metzger (Gaithersburg, MD: Aspen Publishers, Inc., 1990), 14.

33. G. Anders, *Health Against Wealth: HMOs and the Breakdown of Medical Trust* (Boston: Houghton Mifflin, 1996).

34. "Prospective Labor Leaders Set To Turn to Confrontation," *New York Times*, 25 October, 1995.

35. R. Levering and M. Moskowitz, *The Hundred Best Companies To Work for in America* (New York: Currency-Doubleday, 1993), xii–xiii.

NORMAN METZGER, MEd, is Edmond A. Guggenheim Professor Emeritus of Health Care Management of The Mount Sinai School of Medicine. He was for many years Vice President for Human Resources and Vice President for Labor Relations of The Mount Sinai Medical Center in New York City.

Professor Metzger is President of the Health Care Division of Adams, Nash & Haskell, Inc., a management advisory group. He is also a senior consultant for Martin H. Meisel Associates, an executive search company.

Professor Metzger was President of the League of Voluntary Hospitals and Homes of New York, and of the American Society for Healthcare Human Resources Administration (ASHHRA).

Professor Metzger is the author, co-author, and editor of 15 books, and has written over 100 articles on labor relations, personnel administration, and social behavior. In 1987, he became a recipient, for the sixth time, of the Annual Award for Literature, given by ASHHRA, in recognition for his outstanding contribution to hospital personnel administration literature.

Professor Metzger conducts management seminars and workshops on subjects such as empowerment, transformational leadership, interviewing skills, communications, labor relations, and motivational skills.

He is a founder and adjunct professor in the Graduate Program in Health Care Administration, jointly sponsored by Mount Sinai School of Medicine and Baruch College. He has been a visiting professor at over 20 universities.

Chapter 12

Health Care Information Systems: An Organized Delivery System Perspective

Joseph K.H. Tan

Despite the remarkable growth of the health computing industry and the considerable efforts dedicated to the application of health management information system solutions over the past several years,[1] unprecedented changes in the organization of health care delivery, new reimbursement schemes and negotiations for medical services, and increased competition among health care providers have generally called for a retooling of health care information system (HCIS) technologies. Health care provider organizations, including hospitals, health maintenance orga-

Portions of this chapter are adapted from J.K.H. Tan, *Health Management Information Systems: Theories, Methods, and Applications*, © 1995, Aspen Publishers, Inc.; and from J.K.H. Tan, *Health Decision Support Systems*, © 1998, Aspen Publishers, Inc.

The author acknowledges the contributions of Otamere Omoruyi, who assisted in the discussion on the intranets, and Mohammed Taqi, who assisted in the production of the figures relating to structured systems analysis and design method stages. This work is partly supported through grants to the author from the Social Sciences and Humanities Research Council and from the Vancouver Hospital and Health Sciences Centre.

nizations (HMOs), preferred provider organizations (PPOs), and independent practice associations (IPAs) will be technologically driven in the coming age of knowledge explosion. McDonald and Blum predicted that emerging information technology would have a huge effect on the changing health services sector:

> Telecommunication in the form of telephone service and elementary data communication is already critical to the operations of all aspects of the health care system. Yet this role is dwarfed by the emerging telecommunication applications that will become widely available to the health sector in the upcoming decade. . . . Presently, health care institutions and practitioners still view themselves as recipients and consumers of telecommunications. However, a new information infrastructure with a strong public network platform would recast the health sector's role in the Information Age from solely a consumer of telecommunications to a central provider of information and facilita-

tor of health information exchange within their community. The health care institutions with which the practitioner is associated could be networked to make most or all the necessary connections for its "practicing partner." This would entail access and use of the world's medical and scientific data bases, access to his or her patients' institutional records, decision-support software, communications structure for expert consultation (on a nation-wide or international basis, when needed), electronic inventory control, supplies purchasing, prescription order, and so on."[2]

As the coming century approaches, hospitals and other health care organizations will continue to face increasing pressures to redefine their roles and operations in the continuum of health service delivery. Computer hardware and telecommunication systems will continue to improve with increased emphasis on the networking of computers, the linkage of software from multiple vendors, and the development of high-capacity information storage media. A "universal" virtual and digital patient records system will make patient information electronically accessible to the health care practitioner around the clock and from any place within the confines of a networked health care provider organization infrastructure.

Meanwhile, sweeping changes will become evident in many other aspects of the health computing and telecommunications industry. Among these changes there will be innovation in and extension of health informatics and telematics concepts, accumulation of skills and training in large-scale HCIS design methodologies and project development, and advances in health computing technolo-

gies in areas such as natural language systems, neural nets, expert decision support systems, clinical information systems, group support systems, telehealth, virtual reality, the Internet and the world wide web (WWW), virtual private networks, intranets and extranets, local area networks (LANs), and wide area networks (WANs).[3–7] From an organized delivery system perspective, HCISs will bring together many of these new challenges as their role gradually evolves from that of a vehicle for health information service provision and distribution to that of a facilitator of change.

AN ORGANIZED DELIVERY SYSTEM HCIS INFRASTRUCTURE

Reform in the health care industry, just like revolutions in other information-intensive industries, is likely to further the growth of informatics and telematics. In 1996, total expenditures on information technology within the health care industry alone were estimated to range from $12 billion to $16 billion.[8] Indeed, many health care practitioners and informaticians are now predicting that this trend is likely to rise considerably because of the purported and wide-ranging potentials of information technology to reduce health care costs while simultaneously improving the quality of health care delivery. Addressing the information technology challenges for today's health care providers, Raghupathi noted:

> From a provider perspective, health maintenance organizations, which added millions of members in the past couple of years, need information to analyze the outcomes and costs of different treatment plans. Innovations range from routine hospital information systems to sophis-

ticated artificial intelligence (AI)-based clinical decision-support systems. Simultaneously, in today's information intensive society, consumers of health care want to be better informed of their health options and are, therefore, demanding easy access to relevant health information. In this context, the Internet is playing a critical role. The challenge lies in using various forms of IT [information technology] to organize, store and present health information in a timely and efficient manner for effective health-related decision-making. That means all related parties, including profit and nonprofit health care stakeholders, providers (like hospitals), payers (like insurance companies), employers, practitioners, public health officials, and educators must meet the challenge of addressing these new expectations.[9]

In meeting these challenges in a multiprovider organizational setting, today's health care providers may find the concept of an integrated organizational informational technology infrastructure useful to view, guide, and direct future HCIS developments (Figure 12–1).

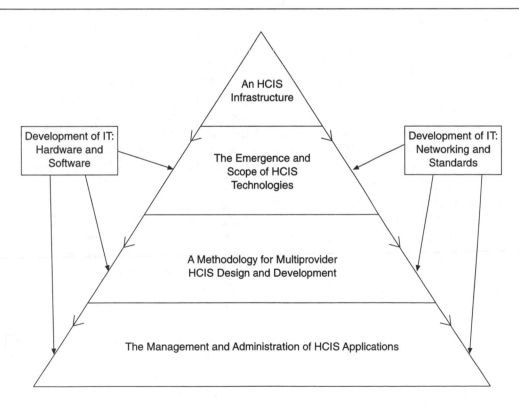

Figure 12–1 Organized Delivery System Information Technology Infrastructure for Health Care Information System (HCIS) Design and Development

Trends in Organized Health Care Delivery Systems

Just a few decades ago, the independent physician and other practitioners, and the voluntary hospitals, were the dominant forms of health care provision in North America. Today, physicians affiliated with numerous specialized organized delivery systems and multiprovider corporations (e.g., HMOs) are fast becoming the prevailing forms of health care provision. Consistent with this apparent dramatic change, several other trends are occurring at the broader health care organization levels:

- increased scale
- increased concentration, diversification, and specialization
- increased linkages among health care service organizations
- an expanded role of government
- increased managerial and consumer role, but reduced professional influence
- increased privatization and market orientation[10]

Regardless of the method used to determine the size (scale) of the health care delivery system—whether the annual health care expenditures in terms of percentage of the gross national product, the number of health care professionals per 1,000 population, the number of health care provider organizations within a specified region, or the amount of health resources employed over a given period, or some other measure—the health care industry has to date experienced dramatic growth. In the United States, for example, health care costs in 1990 consumed more than 12 percent of the gross national product, up from 4.6 percent in 1950.[11]

The increased concentration and the diversification of alternative health care mechanisms are evident in many areas. First, it is more common nowadays for physicians to work in multispecialty clinics, HMOs, and other multiprovider institutions. Second, individual hospitals have become larger, both because individual units have expanded, and because smaller hospitals are more likely to fail.[12] Third, health care organizations today are more likely to operate as part of a corporation or consortium than on their own: this trend is most apparent in the United States.[13] Fourth, health care delivery systems can expand through the addition of services that are closely related (e.g., ambulatory care programs) or simply unrelated (e.g., management of real estate). Finally, health care providers (physicians, allied health care professionals) have become more specialized. For instance, the number of recognized medical specialties, as well as the proportion of full-time physician specialists, has increased in North America since the 1930s.[14,15] Specialized facilities also have proliferated over the past few decades.

Linkages among health care organizations have increased in a variety of ways. Greater numbers of hospitals are managed under contracts, with more specialized management systems.[16] Different types of health care institutions have developed various alliances to coordinate certain facets of their activities without giving up their independent status.[17] Federal agencies have established and funded several research-oriented networks to direct the activities of independent physicians and health provider organizations.[18]

The expanded role of government is more evident in the United States than in Canada. In the United States, the government has increased its role from merely providing certification to professional providers in the 1930s to planning and aggressively marketing some form of national health care coverage in the 1990s. Across the border, the Canadian federal government, in conjunction with provincial governments, has long established a national health care coverage plan; in recent years, the government has taken an expanded role in the definition and funding of new dimensions of health and well-being, including health promotion, health care research, and palliative care.[19]

Although practitioners continue to assume a powerful role in health care organizations, the influence of managerial groups and an informed consumer population is beginning to increase. For example, the rights of patients to health care information have been extended, as encouraged by a number of health-related movements.[20] Furthermore, the notions of "health technology assessment" and "information therapy" (i.e., the belief that consumers should be empowered to make their own treatment decisions by choosing among available health options) are challenging the influence of health care providers.[21] These circumstances are ever more pressing today in view of continuing cost containment measures on the one hand and the need for improved health care quality on the other.

In the United States, increased privatization is evident in the doubling of the number of for-profit hospitals about every 10 years. It is purported that as early as 1986, 80 percent of nursing homes, as well as 35 percent of HMOs, were operating for profit.[22] In Canada, a significant number of health care clinicians, including physicians, chiropractors, physiotherapists, and other allied health care practitioners (e.g., massage therapists and acupuncturists), in British Columbia, Alberta, and Ontario have been billing their patients privately (and separately from the universal health care plan). While health care services continue to remain under the discretionary control of providers and governments (provincial in Canada), these services have become more market-oriented in recent decades as consumer influence has intensified.

Colins predicted that in addition to these far-reaching changes in the health care industry, alternative medicine and health care approaches, encompassing such diverse topics as holistic medicine, herbal-based medicines, faith healing, acupuncture, naturopathic and homeopathic healing techniques that differ from traditional, "established" medical technologies, will receive much more attention in the coming years.[23] These techniques are expected to provide alternative and complementary approaches to traditional medicine, thereby further reducing the influence of traditional medical practitioners. On the individual level, these alternative approaches include an increased awareness of illness prevention and the importance of maintaining a healthy lifestyle.

Together, these trends "have operated to reduce the uniqueness of organizational arrangements that had long distinguished" the medical care sector from other economic sectors.[24] In this sense, as it comes to resemble the business and other economic sectors more closely, the health care sector is beginning to perceive data, information, and knowledge as increasingly more valuable corporate resources rather than as isolated pools of privately owned professional properties. Technology, especially information technology, has become a strategic weapon. A new type of organizational information technology infrastructure gradually is evolving to meet these new challenges, one that promotes systems integration and information sharing.

Achievement of an Integrated HCIS Infrastructure

The move toward an integrated, multiprovider HCIS infrastructure requires not only a basic recognition of the need for systemwide architectural standards, but also the active nurturing of technological expertise and information-sharing concepts throughout the multiprovider organization. Such an organizational information technology infrastructure is necessary to coordinate and integrate individual units within the multiprovider organization in a way that maintains efficient and effective programs or services over long periods of time. If the thoughts of Murray and Trefts are extended, the development of this infrastructure means adopting a new management culture and process that embraces

> the concept of architectural standards to organization-wide [system-wide] information technology to guide the development of new system capabilities [and expertise]. These standards, as they relate to technologies, data, communications, applications, and systems, are analogous to the plumbing, heating, ventilation, air conditioning, and electrical systems standards for a new residential [or multiunit complex] construction project. Without these standards, a house is apt to run on the wrong voltage or be missing drainage pipes. Similarly, without IT [information technology] architectural standards, organization-wide systems become yet additional islands of automation, akin to existing departmental solutions in that they are useful only to a limited segment of the business.[25]

Architectural standards, in this context, become the cornerstones for an HCIS infrastructure to achieve systems integration (i.e., the relating and tying together of various subsystems in the health care delivery system). The ultimate goal of systems integration is to eliminate redundancy, fragmentation, and duplication of information and services, thereby reducing the overall costs of health care substantially. Achieving systems integration within an organized delivery system also requires a completely new management culture and process. Underlying systems integration is the need for a constant analysis of the strategic health care requirements of the population serviced by the provider organization (e.g., an increased demand in certain health care services) to act as inputs to the integrated HCIS in determining its corresponding outputs (e.g., the design of a "universal" patient records system) to provide feedback both to providers and to members of the user community. Figure 12–2 illustrates the key variables involved in systems integration within a multiprovider context.

The central component to systems integration is clearly the development of an organizational information technology infrastructure that encompasses all the stakeholders in the specific population's health care services. The major subcomponents of such an infrastructure include[26]

- data management through which all types of data from various sources are collected, consolidated, and organized in a standardized fashion for easy and accurate processing
- technology management, which entails the strategic planning, designing, engineering, controlling, monitoring, and assessing of various forms of health care technologies to achieve health care efficiency, effectiveness, and excellence
- end-user management, which is concerned with the management of user-developed applications, a phenomenon that is increasing because of the decentralization of control and management of computer resources and skills throughout an organization
- organizational task management, which focuses on the organizational functions,

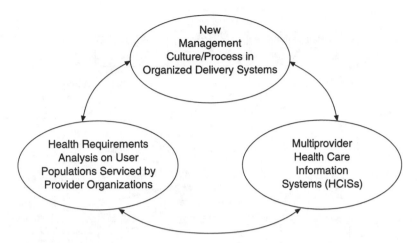

Figure 12–2 Major Variables Involved in Organized Delivery System Health Care Information System (HCIS) Integration

tasks, and activities across the organizational hierarchy, including strategic, tactical, and operational levels

The challenge in designing an appropriate multiprovider organizational information technology infrastructure is in forming an overall plan and strategy to interconnect and reconcile the ever evolving perspectives of various providers, the different stakeholders, and user groups. Halloran noted that "this technical infrastructure design process for an organization [or, a multiprovider organization] is one of the most important activities IS [or HCIS] departments can undertake in providing the enterprise with an enabling infrastructure."[27]

The potential of such an infrastructure to support the HCIS functions within a multiprovider context is shown in Figure 12–3.

Specifically, the integrated HCIS infrastructure allows such subsystems as laboratories, universities and research facilities, suppliers and drug companies to receive inputs (e.g., additional laboratory test requests, research needs, and new prescription orders)

from the HCIS, and then provide appropriate outputs (e.g., laboratory test results, research findings, and new drug information) to the HCIS, after processing the inputs and the accompanying information. In this fashion, the integrated HCIS of a multiprovider system resembles the brain in the central nervous system in terms of information gathering, decision making, and controlled information dissemination.

Advances and limitations in information technology can both provide opportunities for and impose constraints on the design of the infrastructure. There are opportunities to use technology in ways new to the organization, such as direct substitution, proceduralization, and new capabilities.[28] Direct substitution involves the replacement of old ways with new ones, such as replacing parts with a robot rather than by human hands. Proceduralization entails a greater procedural transformation of events previously performed, such as validating purchase data between supplier(s) and purchaser(s) via a networked electronic data interchange before the orders are filled rather than during delivery (i.e., only

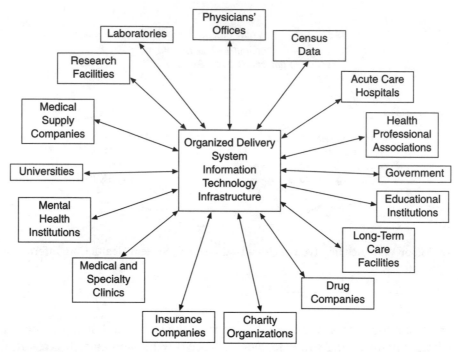

Figure 12–3 Potential of an Organized Delivery System Information Technology Infrastructure. *Source:* Adapted from J.K.H. Tan, Advances in Health Informatics and Telematics: Toward an Integrated Health Information System, *Health Management Information Systems: Theories, Methods, and Applications*, p. 276, © 1995 Aspen Publishers, Inc.

after the orders have been filled). New capabilities arise from a technology transfer that allows the organization to do things that it could not have done in the past, such as electronically publishing the organization's annual reports on its intranet rather than outsourcing the publication work.

Some aspects of existing technology infrastructure limit the possibilities for innovation and thereby deter opportunistic changes in the relevant time frame. For example, if a multiprovider health care organization partners with a certain carrier having only certain network capabilities, it will be difficult, if not impossible, for that carrier to cater to any sudden change in the organization's network-

ing capabilities. Strategic partners of the organization may use different communications standards and network protocols, for example.

The user of the technology ultimately decides on the need and appropriateness of the available HCIS infrastructure. Thus, innovation lies not only in the hands of the HCIS staff, but also in the hands of the users. Conflicts often arise when users strive to fulfill short-term needs at the expense of significant long-term HCIS development. In transferring technology to multiprovider organizational users, there may be a loss of competitive leverage. It is, therefore, the duty and responsibility of the HCIS department to ensure that all major investments, activities, and efforts related to HCIS technology development and application are consistent with a multiprovider perspective.

EMERGENCE AND SCOPE OF MULTIPROVIDER HCIS TECHNOLOGIES

In an increasingly competitive health care environment, the health care organization's efficient and effective management of data, information, and knowledge to support strategic planning, control costs, improve the quality and relevance of information for health managerial and clinical decision making, improve the quality of health care services, enhance productivity, and generate more user-friendly designs of health care products and services will become critical. This is especially true in a multiprovider organizational context. In this context, the significance of computer-based patient records in supporting the management of care is well-known.[29] Equally significant, however, are HCIS technologies such as expert systems and decision support systems technologies,[30] electronic claim processing,[31] and remote computing capabilities.[32] These technologies will enable the multiprovider organization not only to improve communications, but also to extend its cognitive understanding and organizational learning across geographic, time, social, and cultural boundaries, thus achieving the characteristics of an intelligent health care organization.[33]

Development of HCIS Technologies for an Intelligent Health Care Organization

One of the primary characteristics of an intelligent health care organization is that it continually promotes a culture of knowledge empowerment among its organizational workers.[34] In the context of a multiprovider health care organization, these workers range from the senior executives to the various professional clinical members, to the administrative and managerial personnel, to the clerical and operational staff members of various organizational units. An intelligent organization is also one that focuses on the development of effective management. In the case of health care provider organizations, expert clinical knowledge is a critical component of effective clinical management. The management of information technology in an intelligent organization is organic rather than mechanistic.[35] In terms of HCIS technologies, such an organization emphasizes systems flexibility, a systemwide focus on information technology planning and management, and the nurturing of technological expertise among staff members; there is likely to be less concern about the details of these technological processes. Finally, an intelligent health care organization is one that can accept new and emerging forms of technology as building blocks for change and implementation.[36]

In terms of the system structure of a multiprovider organization, HCIS technologies necessarily differ from traditional health maintenance information systems implementations in two fundamental ways. First, the technologies must be accessible to many more users in many more locations because the relevant information is often stored in different places and has to be drawn from diverse sources. Often, the information must then be distributed via LANs, WANs, or other highly reliable and secure means (e.g., intranets and extranets). Second, the organizational decision-making activities must frequently cut across functional areas and multiorganizational layers. Unlike traditional health management information systems that focus more or less on the individual organizational units, multiprovider organization HCISs should focus on the entire organizational structure. In this era of knowledge diffusion, therefore, effective multiprovider HCISs must involve a combination of data-based,[37] model-based,[38] and knowledge-based[39] decision support technology, as well as advanced electronic communications technology.[40]

Accordingly, multiprovider HCISs should facilitate cooperative or collaborative activities throughout the various organizational units and among individual clinicians or other workgroups (e.g., managed care teams). The new skills, new technological adaptation, new management culture, and new organizational arrangements that will follow eventually may alter the way that people communicate, share information, and interact; in addition, they may change the infrastructure of health care organizations, altering the channels of authority and responsibility. It is necessary to devise new ways to finance and pay for health care services that are consistent with these new relationships.

A group decision support system is an example of an emerging network HCIS technology that is likely to be useful in a multiprovider organizational setting. By definition, a group decision support system is an interactive, computer-based system that helps decision makers working as a group to find solutions to unstructured and semistructured problems.[41] Such systems are particularly helpful in soliciting inputs from several decision makers in committees, review panels, board meetings, task forces, and decision-making units across the various organizational levels. As shown in Figure 12–4, some of the major components of a group decision support system include

- a database as a data repository
- a model base with modeling capabilities

- a dialogue management with multiuser access
- an actual group facilitator or a specialized application program to facilitate group access
- general purpose input/output devices (e.g., terminal, voice input/output)
- central processor
- a common viewing screen
- individual monitors (for each participant)
- a network system linking together the different sites or participants

In an organized delivery system setting, group decision support systems are ideal in the solicitation of inputs from HCIS users, for example, in association with the management, evaluation, and selection of alternative solutions to complex managerial and clinical problems. Moreover, the technological architecture of such a system can change according to geographic distribution. Figure 12–4 shows a group decision support system in a decision room (e.g., board room) setting. A local decision network can be useful for participants spread over a limited geographic area. Decision makers in scattered geographic locations may require teleconferencing and videoconferencing to support remote decision making.

Decision Support and Organization Management Technologies for Organized Delivery Systems

Priorities in multiprovider HCIS development must shift from routine operational data processing to analytical group decision support systems and various other forms of health decision support systems, including clinical information systems and AI-based clinical decision support systems. These technologies will combine telecommunica-

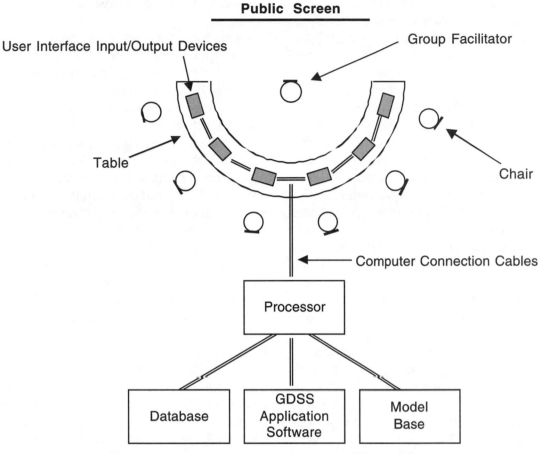

Figure 12–4 A Model of a Group Decision Support System (GDSS) and a Local Decision Network. *Source:* Adapted from J.K.H. Tan, Road Map to the Future: HMIS in the Twenty-First Century, *Health Management Information Systems: Theories, Methods, and Applications,* p. 467, © 1995, Aspen Publishers, Inc.

tion capabilities, AI techniques, and advanced modeling capabilities to support the generation of solutions to complex management and clinical problems. More specifically, these technologies can be applied to strategic management planning and clinical problem solving in new areas, such as improving the clinical performance of health care workers and comparing the costs of various treatment plans.

Expert decision support systems, which combine data, models, and knowledge bases to present the clinical users with the relevant critical information in real time, can facilitate decision making that affects the continuation of particular health care programs and treatment regimens.[42] Systems that provide intelligent feedback and alerts are already successful in some settings.[43] These decision support technologies can draw upon the knowledge of clinical experts and the development of formal models to create "automated intelligence" for the benefits of the less-than-expert users.

Until now, traditional health management information systems have dealt almost exclusively with individualized decision support and have been mostly limited to well structured decision problem situations. They have not provided the kinds of integrated information needed to make quality decisions that the government, health care providers, and patients demand. The solution lies in evolving group decision support systems and systemwide health decision support capabilities that fit appropriately into the organizational information technology infrastructure to share critical information, facilitate key decisions, and build high-quality programs that allow for the multiprovider health care organization to meet diverse internal and external needs.

From an organized delivery system perspective, the current efforts to integrate medical, financial, and administrative data and decision systems will be the environment for future group and systemwide HCIS development and implementation. The primary potential applications for these organization management technologies lie in the area of patient care, including nursing, laboratory testing, imaging, pharmacy, surgery, and emergency inpatient and outpatient services. In the administrative domain, these applications also can be useful, however, in scheduling decisions, accounting and financial decisions, facility location decisions, personnel management decisions, and quality control decisions. In the management systems domain, similar applications can address strategic planning, marketing, risk management, and quality control. With successful HCIS innovation, design, development, and implementation, the impact of these newer organization management technologies will be substantial and far-reaching; they will enhance the multiprovider health organization's efficiency, effectiveness, and productivity.

Remote Computing Networks

An important aspect of enhanced HCIS technologies for organized delivery systems is the development of remote computing capabilities. Such capabilities extend the reach of the various organizational units beyond the traditional means of health care delivery such as those used in physicians' offices and independent hospitals. For example, employees can work at home while remaining "connected" as if they had never left the premises. Patients and the public in general can have access to information they could not have obtained before. Figure 12–5 illustrates a remote computing network operating in an HCIS within a multiprovider context.

The key to this new accessibility is, of course, electronic and satellite communication. Where once the span of cable and the limits of dedicated data circuits constrained the flow of data, now desktop and palm-sized computers communicate through a variety of media, including telephone lines, cellular communication, ISDN cables, and even laser communications. Organized delivery systems need a high-speed foundation network with LANs and WANs capable of handling many different networking protocols. The foundation should also be capable of supporting data, voice, graphics and video transmissions. Thus, networking and integration will be the glue that holds HCIS technologies together in the multiprovider context.

The wide-ranging impacts of the Internet and the WWW on the diffusion of medical and clinical knowledge are already evident. Internet services include electronic mailing, newsgroups, file transfer protocols, and other information transfer and exchange services (e.g., Telnet). The Internet offers health care information to a growing population of consumers who regularly browse web pages.

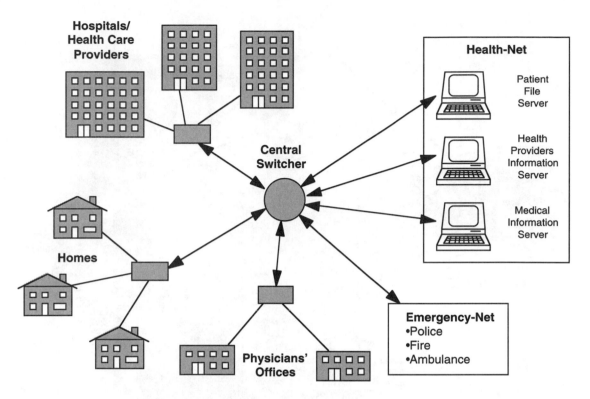

Figure 12–5 Remote Computing Network in a Multiprovider Health Care Information System. *Source:* Reprinted from J.K.H. Tan, Road Map to the Future: HMIS in the Twenty-First Century, *Health Management Information Systems: Theories, Methods, and Applications*, p. 469, © 1995, Aspen Publishers, Inc.

Furthermore, this wealth of information is available inexpensively, privately, and conveniently.[44] Beyond the Internet and the WWW are the intranets and extranets.

In essence, an intranet is a private computer network built on Internet technologies. It uses the same browsers that are necessary to view websites and the same underlying stack of protocols and open standards that enable all brands of computers and operating systems to share data and interact with each other. Whereas the Internet is an open system, an intranet is a closed network to which only authorized personnel have access. Simi-

larly, the extranet extends network access privileges only to certain partners, thereby creating a secure customer or vendor network. An example of an extranet is a health care provider organization network that allows physicians to link into the provider's network system from their offices.

The proliferation of intranets, which are replacing proprietary LAN and WAN technologies, amounts to nothing short of a revolution in how people in an organization communicate, analyze data, find information, share knowledge, and make decisions. The first stage of the revolution was the creation of the

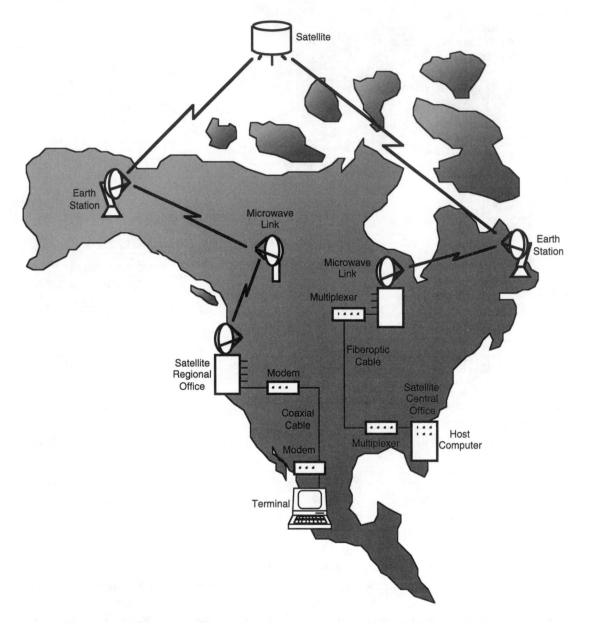

Figure 12–6 Example of the Telecommunications Media in a Wide Area Network. *Source:* Reprinted from J.K.H. Tan, A Survey of HMIS Technologies: State-of-the-Art Applications for the Health Service Delivery Industry, *Health Management Information Systems: Theories, Methods, and Applications*, p. 229, © 1995, Aspen Publishers, Inc.

LAN, which allowed computers in the same office to communicate with each other and share resources, such as a printer. This was eventually followed by the WAN, which tied computers together in different locations (Figure 12–6). Only the largest companies can afford WANs, however, because they require costly hardware and expensive, private networks of dedicated telephone lines to carry data between computers.

The intranet stage of the networked computing revolution combines LAN and WAN technologies with tools developed for the Internet. Intranets take advantage of the same hardware and software used to build, manage, and view Web sites. Unlike Web sites, however, these virtual private networks have the protection of security software (firewall) that keeps people outside the network from gaining access.[45] Because virtual private networks make use of the same communications lines that are used for the WWW, they provide all the benefits of a WAN without the costly expenses. Thus, an intranet can combine the best of the client–server paradigm of HCIS development with the brightest of Internet technologies to create a computing environment that is easy to build, easy to maintain, easy to change, easy to learn, and easy to use to connect and exchange information remotely. Moreover, compared to the cost of constructing and maintaining proprietary islands of databases and services found in most health care organizations, building an intranet is highly cost-effective.

One of the main advantages of intranets is their underlying simplicity and flexibility. It is necessary only to have one or more "servers," which can be any mix of computers, to organize, manage, and store information. Depending on the size of the organizational intranet and the number of desktops it needs to include, servers may be dedicated to one service (e.g., a mail server, transaction processor, an index server), or may carry out a variety of functions. It takes some form of network connection (such as routers and bridges, which most health care agencies already have) to connect the desktop computers and the various servers so that they can "talk." Similarly, Internet-based software can be useful in performing special services, for example, indexing the information, querying a database, or handling security.

Other Future-Oriented HCIS Applications

Increased competition will demand continuous quality improvement and the use of new and innovative HCISs to integrate clinical and financial information. Thus, many older generation health management information systems, which are essentially a mix of administrative and financial information systems, are likely to be either greatly expanded or completely replaced by more advanced HCIS applications in the near future. The multiprovider HCISs will be able to generate "electronic systems for claims processing; imaging systems to scan documents as part of the move toward a paperless environment; multimedia technology incorporating data, voices, and images for educational training of physicians, patients and remote diagnostics; speech recognition in transcription; robots in surgery; and kiosks for presenting health information to consumers and employees."[46] Figure 12–7 portrays an electronic claims processing network system within a virtual private network.

Many future-oriented HCIS applications will involve the integration of digital communications, microprocessor computing power, and network technology. The scope of these applications can range from general systems that are helpful in routine health care administration, education, and communications to domain-specific systems that facilitate strategic, managerial, and clinical decisions. As the organization management technology matures, innovations may include automated intelligent systems embedded inside devices, integrated intelligent systems among devices, and networked intelligent systems. According to Tan and associates, four categories of

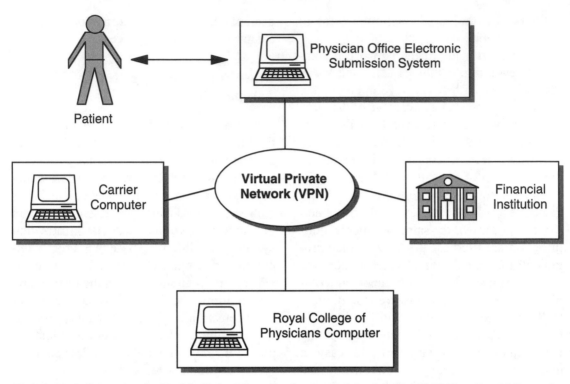

Figure 12–7 Example of a Health Claim Network. *Source:* Adapted from J.K.H. Tan, Road Map to the Future: HMIS in the Twenty-First Century, *Health Management Information Systems: Theories, Methods, and Applications*, p. 468, © 1995, Aspen Publishers, Inc.

information and decision support systems technology are likely to affect health care provider organizations significantly in the immediate future: (1) individual work support, (2) groupware, (3) advanced organization management technologies, and (4) global communications via the Internet and intranets.[47]

Altogether, these HCIS developments will enable the efficient and effective capture of clinical and organizational performance data and indicators at broader and specific levels of the health care provider organizations. From these data, quality can be effectively assessed and measured, and accountability can be efficiently monitored.

SSADM FOR MULTIPROVIDER HCIS DESIGN AND DEVELOPMENT

Given the complexity of most multiprovider HCIS projects, there is a need for guidance and direction in planning and designing such systems. One such system development methodology is the structured systems analysis and design method (SSADM).[48] It has several valuable characteristics:[49]

- comprehensiveness
- accommodation of a large number of techniques
- decomposition of work into discrete, structured steps

- flexibility to be applied in a variety of problem situations
- appropriateness for a wide range of areas
- growing significance at an international level

The Republic of Ireland, Malta, United Kingdom, Hong Kong, and Israel all have adopted SSADM as an architectural standard for large-scale information system development work within government bodies and agencies.

SSADM Defined

Generally speaking, the SSADM is a comprehensive methodology that supports both the analysis and the design phases of HCIS development, while producing deliverables that are the basis for real-time, distributed, AI-based, object-oriented, and conversational processing. It is a powerful, structured approach to system specifications for HCIS applications.

Techniques applied in the SSADM include the following:

- data flow diagrams
- logical data structure
- security, control, and audit
- user options
- entity life history
- logical dialogue design
- relational database analysis
- composite logical data design
- process outlines
- first cut data design
- program specification
- physical data control

These techniques guide the system analyst and designer in completing the procedures to be carried out within the SSADM.[50–53] Because the SSADM addresses all the possible requirements anticipated in the analysis and design phases, its documentation may not be easy and may take a considerable amount of time to complete.

Stages in the SSADM

As depicted in Figure 12–8, the SSADM consists of six stages. Stages 1 to 3 constitute the analysis phase; stages 4 to 6, the design phase. The analysis phase focuses on what business requirements are to be supported (the baseline of any computer information system), the static structure of the data as defined in an entity model, the dynamic flow of the data around the business enterprise, and the selection of appropriate business and technical options to define the scope of the application and the technical framework for the subsequent design phase. More specifically, stage 1 involves analyzing the current system, focusing on problems to be solved; stage 2 represents an attempt to enhance stage 1 deliverables through specifying additional requirements of the proposed systems, identifying solutions to the current problems, and choosing an appropriate business option for conducting the business; and stage 3 concentrates on selecting the hardware/software technological framework in which the proposed system will run. Preliminary dialogue design and entity life history analysis should also begin during the analysis phase.

The design phase deals with how the business requirements are to be supported. This phase has two parts: (1) stages 4 and 5 generate a full logical design specification through the completion of the data model, dialogue design, and entity life histories according to the business requirements; and (2) the logical design becomes in stage 6 a physical design (i.e., computer programs and a physical database), together with an application design appropriate to the selected hardware/ software environment. The database and pro-

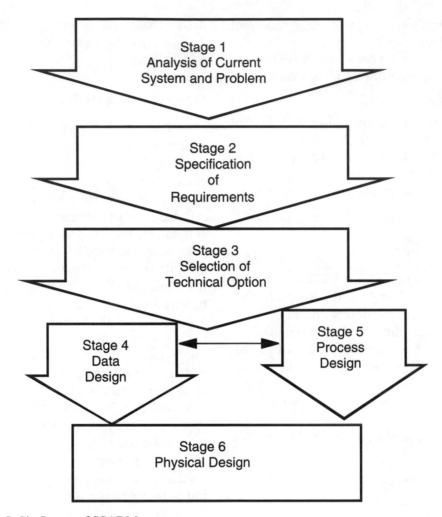

Figure 12–8 Six Stages of SSADM

grams are then optimized, if necessary, to meet the performance objectives initially defined in stage 3 and further refined at the beginning of stage 6.

The SSADM is a thorough step-by-step methodology, requiring the analyst and designer team to work hand-in-hand throughout all the stages, steps, and tasks. There are, however, three options available for organizations that want to shorten the process, thereby reducing substantial developmental costs:[54]

1. Using software aids
2. Going more quickly through the stages, steps, and tasks
3. Omitting or abbreviating some of the steps, such as the preliminary phase

Preliminary Phase: Feasibility Studies

A feasibility study is not mandatory for the SSADM, but it is a highly recommended first-step option. The purpose is to obtain information about the needs of the organization and the ways in which an information system project may address those needs. Feasibility studies are the responsibility of the project supervisory team, who must decide whether to commit the organization's resources to a proposed project. Feasibility studies are conducted in two stages using the techniques of data flow diagrams and logical data structures.[55]

Stage 1a: Problem Definition.   It is essential to have a clear understanding of the major problems and opportunities that an information system development project should address. For example, a multiprovider health care organization may have concerns about the speed and security of transmitting massive amounts of information among various providers (partners) of the organization. Also, new market opportunities may be quickly identified if the organization is networked appropriately and has adequate intranet and extranet capabilities. These problems and opportunities are identified and defined during stage 1a.

Stage 1b: Project Identification.   The goal of stage 1b is to identify and further evaluate the project outline and specification. The deliverables for this stage are the feasibility report outlining options to enable user selection and a presentation or review of the whole process for quality assurance.

If appropriate, the feasibility of developing an intranet for an organized delivery system is assessed and reported at this stage. The reasons that the current system capabilities are inadequate will be rationalized, and various aspects of the project justified. It is essential to seek strong support from both senior management and end-users, as this support is critical to ensure the eventual success of the project. Figure 12–9 shows how this preliminary phase factors into the other analysis stages of the SSADM.

Analysis Phase: Stages 1 to 3

As noted, stage 1 is concerned primarily with the preliminary phase of conducting the feasibility studies and championing the information system development project to management and user groups of the organization. The next stages include stage 2, the specification of requirements, and stage 3, the selection of technical option.

Stage 2: Specification of Requirements. The initial steps in stage 2 are to produce a logical view of the current system, by means of data flow diagrams, to define the security controls needed and to audit the system in order to produce a list of initial requirements. The next step is to consolidate a list of the problems to be eliminated and the requirements to be met by the proposed system.

At this stage, the analyst should create and thoroughly review a detailed description of the requirements for the proposed system, using techniques such as data flow diagrams, logical data structure, and entity life history. For example, the analyst who is developing an HCIS for an organized delivery system concerned about the security of its information should sample various data files (databases) that would be transmitted and show how the data (or database) processing would be secured (e.g., use of a firewall). The analyst should also detail a logical view of the data structure(s) involved. Documenting the data flow and the history of the data entity life cycle allows the analyst to gain an understanding of how the various data sources will move from one part of the organization to another. Figure 12–10 shows an example of a data flow diagram for a payroll system in a multihospital setting.

Stage 3: Selection of Technical Option. Stage 3 can be subdivided into four steps:

1. Creation of an option menu that describes the possible physical imple-

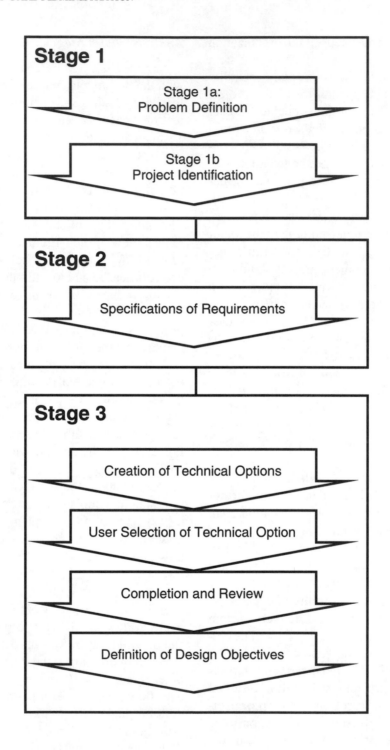

Figure 12–9 Preliminary and Analysis Phase: Stages 1 to 3

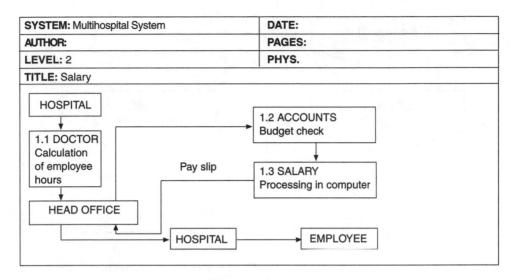

SYSTEM: Multihospital System	DATE:
AUTHOR:	PAGES:
LEVEL: 2	PHYS.
TITLE: Salary	

Figure 12–10 Example of a Data Flow Diagram for Payroll System

mentation to meet the system requirements.

2. Presentation of the technical solutions to the users, together with the provision of advisory support while the users carry out their evaluation.

3. Provision of the basics for the design phase, incorporating the effect of the selection decisions into the required system products.

4. Specification of the performance criteria that the implemented system must achieve to meet the performance target for the physical design stage. A technique employed at this stage is the physical data control.

In the case of the organized delivery system example, the analyst must consider at this stage various technical options to satisfy the specifications of the required system. For building an organizational intranet communications infrastructure, some of the technical options include developing the intranet in-house, outsourcing all or some part of the "server" maintenance work, or partnering with an outside carrier. Management and user groups are consulted regarding these options, and technical information is provided to aid the user decision-making process. Once the decision has been made, the analyst specifies the performance criteria, for example, transmission speed to be in the range of 100,000 KBs (thousands of bytes per second). Interestingly, the size of files downloaded via an intranet can easily be 1,000 to 10,000 times larger than those that can normally be downloaded from the Internet, depending on the intranet capabilities.

Although it is not essential to complete all stages in the analysis phase fully before stages 4 and 5, it is essential to complete them before stage 6, which is the physical design. As noted earlier, the analyst should work hand-in-hand with the designer throughout the various SSADM phases; in some cases, the same team works through the entire process, despite the fact that the skills required for the analysis phase may be quite different from those required for the design phase.

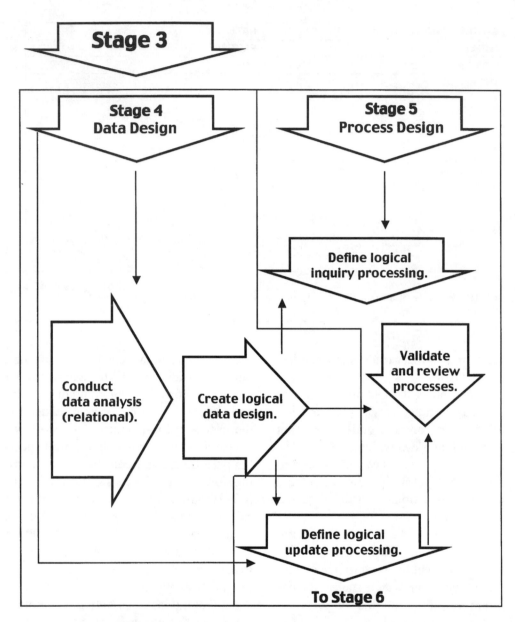

Figure 12–11 Logical Design Phase: Stages 4 and 5

Design Phase: Stages 4 to 6

Figure 12–11 depicts the steps involved in stages 4 and 5.

Stage 4: Data Design.   During stage 4, all the data sources within the system (i.e., input description, data flow, and existing document and file structures) are analyzed and reviewed thoroughly by means of the relational data analysis technique, that is, the normalization process. The results are merged with the business view of the data provided by the logical data structure to give the composite logical data design.

In the multiprovider example, the specification of database requirements that were elicited and compiled in the analysis phase would be reviewed and further consolidated in this stage. Figures 12–12 and 12–13 illustrate the normalization process applied to the "patient record" data set. Figure 12–12 shows the transition from unnormalized form to first normalized form, whereas Figure 12–13 shows the transformation from second normalized form to third normalized form.

Relational tables can also be used to list the various data (database) sources, transactional documents, file extensions, and codifications of various data elements and keys (i.e., unique identifiers). The complete logical data design, which represents a current version of the data architectural plan for the proposed system, is then finalized. In fact, it is advisable to leave room for later expansion by incorporating other potentially significant data entities (e.g., by means of dummy variables) in the database. Alternatively, these variables can be added or made available to the organization in the future.

Stage 5: Process Design. There are three key steps in stage 5: (1) designing the details of the inquiry functions, including all the necessary input/output descriptions (formats), logical dialogue outlines, and logical dialogue control functions; (2) defining the

NORMALIZATION	

SYSTEM: Multiprovider HCIS	DATE:
AUTHOR:	PAGES: 1 OF 2

DATA STRUCTURE: Patient Record	
UNF	**1NF**
Patient Name	
Patient Account No.	
Sort Code	
History ———————▶	
MSP Contribution	

Figure 12–12 Normalization Technique: First Normalized Form (1NF) for Patient Record System in Multiprovider Health Care Information System (HCIS)

NORMALIZATION	
SYSTEM: Multiprovider HCIS	**DATE:**
AUTHOR:	**PAGES:** 2 OF 2

DATA STRUCTURE: Patient Record

2NF	3NF
Patient Name	Patient Name
Patient Account No.	Patient Account No.
Sort Code	
History	
MSP Contribution	

Figure 12–13 Normalization Technique: Third Normalized Form (3NF) for Patient Record System in Multiprovider Health Care Information System (HCIS)

logical update processes, including a logical description of processing associated with each event (transaction) in the system; and (3) validating and reviewing the logical system design, including the logical model, by cross-checking the products of the processes and data design activities. Techniques used in this stage include entity life history, process outline, logical dialogue design, and relational data analysis.

To follow up the multiprovider example, stage 5, the logical "process" design stage, can be carried out simultaneously with stage 4, the logical "data" design stage. In this instance, the main tasks are concerned with specifying, documenting, and validating the processing of data elements and the databases to ensure that all the client's potential queries are dealt with appropriately.

For intranet or network database applications, the term *publishing* is common because of the request-oriented nature of such teleprocessing; the client can access the server whenever it is convenient.[56] Designs of these processing capabilities differ, depending on whether the processes are for static report publishing (i.e., server generates reports on request), query publishing (i.e., server responds to client's queries), or application publishing (i.e., server supports transaction and update processing). In the last two categories, the designer needs not only to specify the dialogues for the different queries and transactions, but also to cross-check the databases to ensure that responses will be appropriate.

Stage 6: Physical Design. Converting the logical model of stages 4 and 5 into a physical model in stage 6 contains nine different steps (Figure 12–14). In the multiprovider ex-

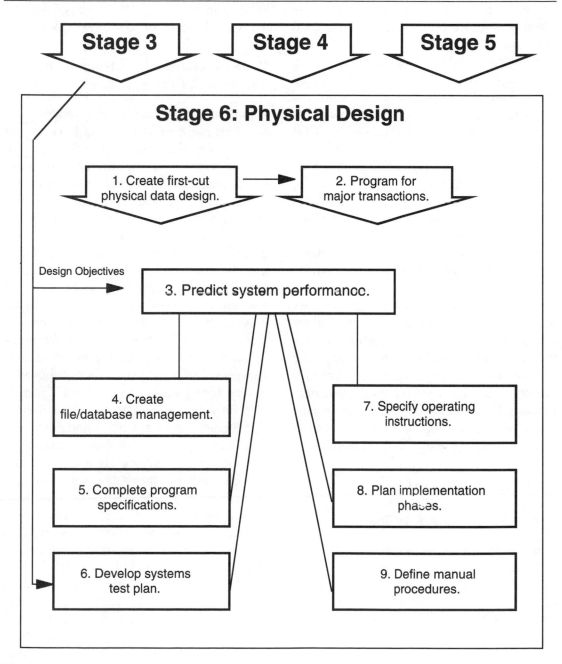

Figure 12–14 Physical Design Phase: Stage 6

ample, efforts at this stage focus on physically transforming and programming an intranet HCIS application based on the previously specified logic, data, and file-processing requirements. In terms of programming and choice of software, Microsoft's Net-Meeting software can be used to design and program the physical model, that is, the intranet application. NetMeeting supports real-time document collaboration, distributed and distance learning or training, standards-based video conferencing, and remote meetings. Other software choices include CGI (common gateway interface) with Perl (practical extraction and report language), VB-Script and Java script, and ActiveX.[57] Again, system performance criteria can be predicted and the application tested to ensure that performance standards are met.

In general, systems development methods have become increasingly accepted within the information technology industry. In the early 1980s, these large-scale methodologies were seen as the preserve of the large corporations that could afford them, not so much in the sense of money, but in the sense of the amount of time required to go formally through each stage of the methodological process. Today, attitudes have changed to the extent that many systems developers expect organizations to use well defined methods.

MANAGEMENT AND ADMINISTRATION OF MULTIPROVIDER HCISs

Just as the Industrial Revolution and its social implications changed the way of life not only of the workers, but also of the family and of society in general, so the information revolution may have similar effects. Where computers and information technology once were needed by only a few people, there is now the potential for applying information technology to every departmental level and every functional area of a health care provider organization. Technology will infuse every imaginable component of the health care system, from medical research to patient care to home care. With all the benefits that technology promises, many challenges will arise as well, however.

HCIS Implementation Challenges in an Organized Delivery System

Currently, most health care provider organizations use mainframes for a large part of their information-processing activities, but the migration from mainframes to client–server architecture has already begun in certain areas. At the heart of these changes is a challenge to develop more efficient and effective means of integrating human and computer components to meet data-handling and knowledge-processing needs. Powerful computer hardware and software alone are not enough. Successful HCIS implementation must fit the human side of the equation into these technologies. In other words, for multi-provider HCISs to be truly efficient and effective, senior management and various user groups (especially clinicians) must participate fully and actively in the HCIS design, development, and implementation process.

As a case in point, planning an intranet for an organized delivery system entails more challenges than just deciding what platform is preferable; which software tools to build or buy; whether to construct a firewall (for security) or to use some form of encryption; and how many workstations to purchase and install. More important, there are challenges faced in the strategic alignment of the HCIS mission, goals, and objectives with the corporate mission, goals, and objectives; the elimination of barriers to system integration; and the provision of user education and training, including human–computer interfacing and changes in human–human inter-action in an evolving, technologically com-plex organized delivery system environment. After all, designing a HCIS project so that it can succeed means building the right team, selecting the right content for the system, de-tailing the site management process, putting the pre- and post-launch measurements in place to gauge effectiveness and user satis-faction, developing a system promotional plan, conducting training on the uses and abuses of the organization's electronic space, and making a host of diverse other proce-dural and policy-related decisions.

According to Alavi and associates, in pre paring the health care provider organization for growth and maturation in HCIS imple-mentation, management must clearly provide three primary functions: (1) direction; (2) support; and (3) control.[58] Direction focuses on discovering and evaluating cutting edge technologies to improve organizational com-petitiveness and service excellence. Support focuses on ensuring the availability of the necessary technical assistance to organiza-tional users to facilitate intelligent decision making. Control focuses on providing a means of standardization and integration to-ward universal compatibility, as well as a means of control over the wasteful replica-tion of programming efforts.

Multiprovider organizations must over-come two classes of barriers (and challenges) in HCIS implementation: (1) barriers due to hardware/software issues and (2) barriers due to strategic and organization management is-sues. In regard to the hardware/software bar-riers, management of the health care provider organization should ensure hardware com-patibility, as all existing systems should be physically networked. If there is already a large installed base of equipment, manage-ment should direct the organization toward an "open systems" platform through careful

planning of the system transition (i.e., evolu-tionary approach); alternatively, manage-ment may decide to acquire an entirely new system that conforms to "open systems" ar-chitecture (i.e., revolutionary approach). By applying teleprocessing technology to link users' hardware and software, the organiza-tion enables its employees to share informa-tion-processing capabilities and consciously encourages them to work collaboratively rather than individually.

In regard to the strategic and organization management barriers, the health care pro-vider organization should attempt to educate employees at all levels about changing trends; engage the assistance of consultants, if necessary, who have strong HCIS leader-ship skills and a clear knowledge of the cur-rent health care and information technology environments; redefine and clarify roles and responsibilities of management in regard to HCIS implementation; and designate a new type of senior manager to oversee all HCIS investments, projects, and activities—the chief information and technology officer. This person should be responsible for strate-gically linking corporate information through new technologies with the multiprovider or-ganization's long-range plan. Essentially an internal consultant, the chief information and technology officer works to advance the state of the art in the organization's HCIS by con-tinuously scanning for new technologies in the marketplace and making recommenda-tions in areas such as advanced diagnostic devices, automated intelligence, bionics, ro-botics, "smart cards," virtual reality applica-tions, and telehealth.

Strategic Group Thinking: The New Management Culture

The increased scale, concentration, diversi-fication, specialization, managerialism, consumerism, and market orientation that have occurred in the health care industry have two primary implications for the management of health care provider organizations at this time. First, there will be a dramatic increase in information flow, brought about by rapid organizational changes in today's turbulent health care environment and by rapid technological advancements (e.g., the information highway) that have transpired to date. Second, there will be an increased need for health care professionals from different specializations to work together to provide a "managed" form of care as opposed to the longstanding "individualized" form of care.

Information will become the currency of the twenty-first century. Therefore, there will be a significant increase in the emphasis on HCIS among health care planners, managers, and even practitioners. The existing HCIS theories, methods, technologies, applications, and activities on the organization and management of health care provider institutions will significantly influence HCIS growth and development in the coming decade. The increasing need to share and exchange information among health care practitioners, government, third parties, and consumers will further intensify this trend.

Admittedly, traditional hospital management structures have tended to provide relatively routine departmentalized information management. For each department, information filters separately across various management levels, often resulting in "fragmented" and "marginalized" data. Duplications of data collection and preparation efforts tend to produce inconsistencies and potentially conflicting versions of the same data. In a multiprovider context, a new level of organizational information technology infrastructure should be implemented to coordinate the collection and processing of a networked database (or linked databases) containing

"uniquely identifiable" virtual patient records. With accurate, reliable, timely, consistent, and valid patient information, the clinician and the health care administrator will no longer have to screen and scrutinize fragmented data continually, but will be able to use the shared information and knowledge network in productive analysis.

Although many new technologies and software will be highly advanced and relatively sophisticated in the multiprovider context, the success of all HCIS projects will continue to depend on human skills. The evolution of technologies and new forms of health care organizations will mandate new and expanded skills for health care managers and administrators. In general, strategic group thinking, interdisciplinary skills, and the capability to self-learn continually will be among the most sought after skills in health care organization management.

Health care managers in organized delivery systems will continue to experience challenges in the development and the use of their skills in negotiated strategic information technology planning and management. It is expected that there soon will be a significant shortage of these skills for several reasons. First, as rapidly changing trends are causing more and more hospitals and other health care providers to join together in strategic alliances, more and more organized delivery systems are forming. This not only will enhance communications with sources external to the organization, but also will provide new opportunities for finding better ways of sharing limited resources. Second, interorganizational project teams will become more active. Projects such as community healthy lifestyle ventures that require teamwork will begin to take on a life of their own. Such interdisciplinary teams will need access to vast networks of resources and information that would not have been available within the framework of a single health care provider organization. Therefore, new skills are required to create and maintain a climate for teamwork, that is, those that foster creativity and innovation. Finally, leadership skills are needed for handling increased exchange of knowledge and ideas, and for educating and training others.

Health care professionals already are becoming more familiar with the use of new information technology, and this trend is likely to continue into the future. The proliferation of interactive systems and the rapid and easy access to information via CD-ROM technology will bring health care professionals from all specialties and different disciplines together, enhancing the integrated, managed approach to health care that is evolving so quickly today. Not all these changes will be pleasant, however. Greater emphasis on interdisciplinary and multidisciplinary approaches may sow the seeds for "turf battles" and a general "weeding out" in health care provider organizations.[59] The lack of medical standards and guidelines for ascertaining professional duties and performance accountability among various health care providers and across multiple units of health care organizations will require administrators to resolve disputes about who should perform specific procedures and use particular medical technology. Thus, it is essential to nurture good interpersonal and negotiation skills. Multiprovider health care managers will face more such challenges as technology further diffuses into the health care industry. New forms of HCIS technologies and applications will have to evolve so as to assist health care providers and managers to meet these new challenges. Indeed, the ability to meet these challenges effectively will ultimately determine organizational survival in the short term and its success in the longer term.

Open Systems Philosophy: The New Management Process

Amid the changing needs of health care managers within an organized delivery system context, the open system concept provides a framework for the development of the organized delivery system information technology infrastructure. Indeed, it is this open system philosophy that will assist management of the organized delivery system in directing the development of an HCIS infrastructure within an integrated framework.

Conceptually, the open system model has several components, including the external environment, inputs, processes, outputs, and many levels of feedback loops (Figure 12–15). Essentially, an open system is one that interacts actively with its environment.[60] In this sense, multiprovider HCISs thrive in a highly dynamic, information-intensive, and task-dependent environment. In other words, the use of HCISs helps individuals or a group of health care providers to respond and adapt to the changes that are occurring throughout the organization. Continually, the environment imposes political, legal, economic, sociodemographical, cultural, educational, or technological constraints on the tasks to be performed; these constraints dictate the data, models, and knowledge elements (inputs) needed for the various organizational tasks. The best performance results require the most appropriate processing strategies, methods, or database/model management techniques (processes). One of the chief contributions of a multiprovider HCIS infrastructure, therefore, lies in its role of facilitating the decision makers in capturing and processing the inputs intelligently.

Apart from inputs and processes, the open system model includes outputs and a series of feedback control loops. Regardless of the level at which decision making transpires,

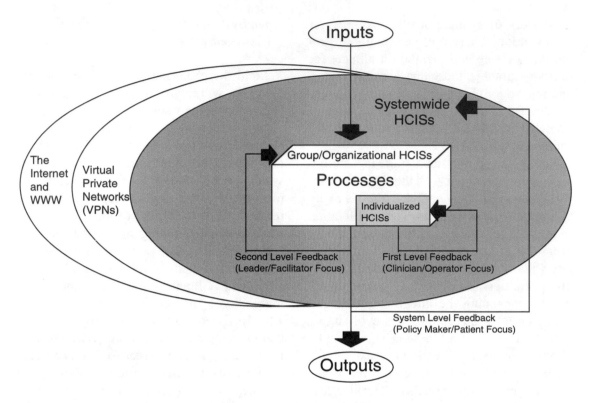

Figure 12–15 Open System Model for Developing Health Care Information Systems (HCISs) in Organized Delivery Systems. *Source:* Reprinted from J.K.H. Tan, Charting the Future of Health Decision Support Systems: Future Perspectives, Trends, and Challenges, *Health Decision Support Systems*, p. 375, © 1998 Aspen Publishers, Inc.

these outputs consist of both decision outcomes and explanations to justify those outcomes. Evaluating these outcomes is an important aspect of the open system model. Through the feedback mechanisms, the output is used to regulate the inputs of the HCIS–user system. Any discrepancy found in a comparison of the actual output with a reference standard is, in turn, used to determine the corrective or regulatory action(s) necessary. With this feedback, the whole process is then repeated.

The feedback control system highlights any inadequacies or deficiencies of the existing

HCIS–user system, such as failures in the HCIS design features. Each time a new task generates a new solution, a learning process occurs, whether in terms of changing the human side of the equation or changing the HCIS design features. Such learning allows the decision makers to enlarge and update their knowledge and skills, and to hone their decision-making strategies and problem-solving skills. Similarly, such learning will indicate any need for re-designing or re-engineering the various features of the HCISs. The capacity for adaptability and flexibility is vital, especially in highly dynamic task environments such as a multiprovider health care organization, a system that is still undergoing reform.

In summary, the open system model shifts the focus from individualized, isolated, and fragmented applications to a more integrative view based on evolving HCIS technologies to support collaborative partnerships and exchanges of information throughout higher organizational system levels. In the context of self-organizing systems,[61] the development of an HCIS infrastructure applicable to organized delivery systems provides the entire system with a powerful mechanism for storing, analyzing, and disseminating in the most appropriate form massive amounts of collected information from many sources. In this regard, it builds the bridges necessary to bring a complex, but fragmented health care system closer to a more unified, integrated one.

CONCLUSION

In this changing environment, organized delivery systems are expected to double their current HCIS expenditures from an estimated 4 percent to 5 percent of their budgets to a possible 8 percent to 10 percent, suggesting that information technology will become a driving factor in achieving competitive advantages and desired performance results.[62] The integration of isolated pools of data sets currently held individually by hospitals, physicians' offices, pharmacies, home care agencies, public health and government bodies, research units, and other health-related institutions not only will make the information more meaningful, but also will lead to lower costs and better quality care.

In the next few years, there will certainly be further unforeseen technological advances that will represent fundamental departures from the current technology. The continuation of the numerous trends in the health care delivery industry, in fact, depends heavily on

these technological advancements. Advances in client–server technology, AI-based decision support systems, hyperlink processing and computer networking, computer animation and multimedia technology, robotics, and others will drive health care provider organizations' strategic and decision making processes clear into the twenty-first century.

From an organized delivery system perspective, the need for intranets and health decision support systems is attributable to the shift in health care organization funding, combined with a shift in the way that knowledge is being shared. In the industrial economy, capital assets were steel, bricks, and machinery, but a health organization's main capital asset is the intellectual capital invested in its administrators, clinicians, and other employees. In the hands of knowledge workers, the more advanced HCISs are tools for turning ideas and information into cost-minimizing and quality-maximizing services. The new HCISs, therefore, are redrawing the structure of the relationships between individuals and their organizations. Informationally empowered employees will be proactive: they act, rather than wait to be told what to do. There is no time for further waiting, and few organizations can afford to waste more such capital assets.

In this light, the role of the information technology department will change. Programmers and systems engineers, freed from the chores of maintaining islands of information and providing intensive user support, will be able to shift their focus to new multiprovider HCIS technologies and the creation of productivity tools that improve data quality and shrink development cycles. Ultimately, these new technologies will be driving the changeover from static, hierarchical organizational structures to team-based, highly productive, learning, and intelligent organizations.

NOTES

1. J.K. Tan, *Health Management Information Systems: Theories, Methods, and Applications* (Gaithersburg, MD: Aspen Publishers, 1995).

2. M. McDonald and H. Blum, *Health in the Information Age: The Emergence of Health Oriented Telecommunication Applications* (Berkeley, CA: Environmental Science and Policy Institute, 1992), 23.

3. T.C. Rindfleisch, "Privacy, Information Technology, and Health Care," *Communications of the ACM* 40, no. 8 (1997): 92–100.

4. D. Strickland, "VR and Health Care," *Communications of the ACM* 40, no. 8 (1997): 32.

5. W.M. Detmer and E.H. Shortliffe, "Using the Internet To Improve Knowledge Diffusion in Medicine," *Communications of the ACM* 40, no. 8 (1997): 101–108.

6. D.G. Kilman and D.W. Forslund, "An International Collaboratory Based on Virtual Patient Records," *Communications of the ACM* 40, no. 8 (1997): 110–117.

7. J.G. Anderson, "Clearing the Way for Physicians' Use of Clinical Information Systems," *Communications of the ACM* 40, no. 8 (1997): 83–90.

8. W. Raghupathi, "Health Care Information Systems," *Communications of the ACM* 40, no. 8 (1997): 81–82.

9. Ibid.

10. Tan, *Health Management Information Systems*, 452–453.

11. O.W. Anderson, *Health Services as a Growth Enterprise in the United States since 1875*, 2nd ed. (Ann Arbor, MI: Health Administration Press, 1990).

12. D.R. Longo and G.A. Chase, "Structural Determinants of Hospital Closure," *Medical Care* 22 (1984): 38–40.

13. S.M. Shortell, "The Evolution of Hospital Systems: Unfulfilled Promises and Self-Fulfilling Prophesies," *Medical Care Review* 45, no. 2 (1988): 177–214.

14. American Hospital Association, *Physician Characteristics and Distribution in the U.S.: 1992 Edition* (Chicago: AMA, 1992).

15. S.M. Shortell, E.M. Morrison, and S.L. Hughes, *Strategic Choices for America's Hospitals: Managing Change in Turbulent Times* (San Francisco: Jossey-Bass, 1990).

16. M.A. Morrisey and J.A. Alexander, "Hospital Acquisition or Management Contract: A Theory of Strategic Choice," *Health Care Management Review* 12, no. 1 (1987): 21–30.

17. T.A. D'Aunno and H.S. Zuckerman, "The Emergence of Hospital Federations: An Integration of Perspectives from Organization Theory," *Medical Care Review* 44, no. 2 (1987): 323–370.

18. M.L. Fennell and R. Warnecke, *Diffusion of Medical Innovation: An Applied Network Perspective* (New York: Plenum, 1988).

19. J. Epps, *Achieving Health for All* (Ottawa: Health and Welfare Canada, 1986).

20. P. Hamilton, *Health Care Consumerism* (St. Louis, MO: C.V. Mosby, 1982).

21. J.K. Tan, ed., *Health Decision Support Systems* (Gaithersburg, MD: Aspen Publishers, 1998).

22. B.H. Gray, *For Profit Enterprise in Health Care* (Washington, DC: National Academy Press, 1986).

23. D.W. Colins, "Future Health Care: Increasing the Alternatives," *The Futurist* (May/June, 1988): 13–16.

24. W.R. Scott, "The Organization of Medical Care Services: Toward an Integrated Theoretical Model," *Medical Care Review* 50, no. 3 (1993): 275.

25. R. Murray and D. Trefts, "Building the Business of the Future: The IT Imperative," *Information Systems Management* (Fall 1992): 56–57.

26. Tan, *Health Management Information Systems*, 145–153.

27. J. Halloran, "Achieving World-Class End-User Computing," *Information Systems Management* (Fall 1993): 9.

28. T. Grusec, "Office Automation in Government Offices: Productivity and Other Myths," *Optimum* 16, no. 2 (1985): 7–24.

29. Anderson, "Clearing the Way for Physicians' Use of Clinical Information Systems."

30. E. Turban, *Decision Support and Expert Systems: Management Support Systems*, 3rd ed. (New York: Macmillan, 1993).

31. Raghupathi, "Health Care Information Systems."

32. J. Tan and J. Hanna, "Integrating Health Care with Information Technology: Knitting Patient Information through Networking," *Health Care Management Review* 19, no. 2 (1994): 72–80.

33. J. Burn and L. Caldwell, *Management of Information Systems Technology* (Hong Kong: Alfred Waller Ltd., 1990), 200.

34. Ibid.

35. A.C. Boynton et al., "The Influence of IT Management Practice on IT Use in Large Organizations," *MIS Quarterly* 18, no. 3 (1994): 115.

36. Burn and Caldwell, *Management of Information Systems Technology*.

37. C. Hertzman, "Data-Based Health Decision Support Systems: Perspectives on Population Health Data, Linked Databases and Statistical Decision Systems," in *Health Decision Support Systems*, ed. J.K. Tan (Gaithersburg, MD: Aspen Publishers, 1998).

38. R. Klimberg, "Model-Based Health Decision Support Systems: Data Envelopment Analysis (DEA) Models for Health Systems Performance Evaluation and Benchmarking," in *Health Decision Support Systems*, ed. J.K. Tan (Gaithersburg, MD: Aspen Publishers, 1998).

39. A. Kushniruk and V. Patel, "Knowledge-Based Health Decision Support Systems: Cognitive Approaches to the Extraction of Knowledge and the Understanding of Decision Support Needs in Health Care," in *Health Decision Support Systems*, ed. J.K. Tan (Gaithersburg, MD: Aspen Publishers, 1998).

40. P. Jennett et al., "Telehealth: A Frontier for Embodying Health Decision Support Systems Future," in *Health Decision Support Systems*, ed. J.K. Tan (Gaithersburg, MD: Aspen Publishers, 1998).

41. G. DeSanctis and B. Gallupe, "A Foundation for the Study of Group Decision Support Systems," *Management Science* 33, no. 5 (1987): 589–609.

42. J. Tan, "Automated Intelligence: Clinical Decision Support Systems, Expert Systems, and Expert Decision Support Systems," in *Health Decision Support Systems*, ed. J.K. Tan (Gaithersburg, MD: Aspen Publishers, 1998).

43. H.R. Warner, "Knowledge Sectors for Logical Processing of Patient Data in the HELP System," in *Proceedings of the Second Annual Symposium on Computer Applications in Medical Care*, ed. F.H. Orthner (Silver Spring, MD: IEEE Computer Society, 1984), 401–404.

44. J. Carroll and R. Broadhead, *The Internet Advantage* (Scarborough, Ontario: Prentice Hall Canada, 1995).

45. D.M. Kroenke, *Database Processing: Fundamentals, Design, and Implementation*, 6th ed. (Upper Saddle River, NJ: Prentice Hall, 1998).

46. Raghupathi, "Health Care Information Systems," 82.

47. J. Tan et al., "The Art of Macro-Micro View: Strategic Planning for Health Decision and Executive Support Systems," in *Health Decision Support Systems*, ed. J.K. Tan (Gaithersburg, MD: Aspen Publishers, 1998).

48. E. Downs et al., *Structured Systems Analysis and Design Method: Application and Context* (Englewood Cliffs, NJ: Prentice Hall, 1988).

49. E. Downs, *Structured Systems Analysis and Design Method: Application and Context* (Englewood Cliffs, NJ: Prentice Hall, 1991).

50. Tan, *Health Management Information Systems*, 173–206.

51. D. Avison and G. Fitzgerald, *Information Systems Development: Methodology, Techniques and Tools* (Boston: Blackwell Scientific Publications, 1988).

52. J. Cougar et al., eds., *Advanced System Development/Feasibility Techniques* (New York: John Wiley & Sons, 1982).

53. M. Colter, "A Comparative Examination of Systems Analysis Techniques," *MIS Quarterly* 8, no. 1 (1984): 51–66.

54. G. Longworth, *SSADM Developer's Handbook Version 3* (Manchester: NCC Publication, 1988).

55. G. Longworth, *SSADM Manual Version 3* (Manchester: NCC Publication, 1986).

56. Kroenke, *Database Processing*.

57. Ibid.

58. M. Alavi et al., "Managing End-User Computing as a Value-Added Resource," *Journal of Information Systems Management* (Summer 1988): 26–35.

59. S.L. Bloom, "Hospital Turf Battles: The Manager's Role," *Hospitals and Health Administration*, 36, no. 4 (Winter 1991): 590–599.

60. R. Lindstrom et al., "Organizational Health Decision Support Systems: The Application of Systems Concepts, Chaos Theory, Quantum Mechanics, and Self-Organizing Systems," in *Health Decision Support Systems*, ed. J.K. Tan (Gaithersburg, MD: Aspen Publishers, 1998).

61. Ibid.

62. Kroenke, *Database Processing*.

JOSEPH K.H. TAN, PHD, is Associate Professor of Health Policy and Management at the University of British Columbia, Faculty of Medicine, Canada. He currently sits on the Information Systems Advisory Committee of the Tzu Chi Institute for Complementary and Alternative Medicine, VH&HSC, and has since the Institute's inception played an active and instrumental role in creating and developing the Institute's information technological infrastructure. His primary research interests are in the theories, methods, and applications of health information technologies and health decision support systems. Dr. Tan is not only the author of *Health Management Information Systems: Theories, Methods, and Applications*, but also has served as special issue editor for *Topics in Health Information Management*.

Chapter 13

Management Engineering

Karl Bartscht

Management engineering is the practice of industrial engineering in the health care field. The name of the discipline is changed not only to encourage acceptance by health care professionals but also to indicate its application to management. The health care delivery system will continue to undergo significant changes in the next decade because of consolidations and continued pressures for reduction in health care expenditures. The major change, increased managed care, leading toward primarily capitated reimbursement, will require health care providers to ensure high value (and in some cases, low cost) services. This will be achieved through consolidation of health care providers into organized delivery systems. Management engineering tools and techniques, with particular emphasis on increased productivity, will be invaluable in achieving high value, low cost services. Hospital mergers result in downsizing, reengineering needs, and will call on the management engineer to apply long-standing, cost-control, and productive measures. These long-standing measures will be planned from the corporate levels of emerging organized delivery systems and will be implemented at all other levels. This chapter concentrates on cost control, productivity, and quality control.

The discipline of engineering is defined by the Accreditation Board for Engineering and Technology (ABET), formerly Engineers Council for Professional Development (ECPD), as the "profession in which a knowledge of the mathematical and natural sciences gained by study, experience and practice is applied with judgment to develop ways to utilize economically the materials and forces of nature for the benefit of mankind."[1] The key words in this definition are:

- mathematical and natural sciences, particularly with emphasis on a quantitative approach
- applied with judgment, implying that not everything can be quantified
- economically, implying a concern with costs

According to the American Institute of Industrial Engineers (AIIE), the special field of industrial engineering is concerned with:

the design, improvement and installation of integrated systems of people, materials, equipment and energy. It draws upon specialized knowledge and skill in the mathematical, physical and social sciences together with the principles and methods of engineering analysis and design to specify, predict and evaluate the results to be obtained from such systems. The element that is unique to industrial engineering . . . is the explicit reference to people and to the social sciences in addition to the natural sciences.[2]

The key words in this definition are:

- design/improvement and installation, implying that whether one starts from scratch or with an existing system, installation is also a part of the job
- systems of people, materials, equipment, and energy, hereafter referred to as a resource system or systems
- specify, predict, and evaluate, implying that not only is the system defined but also its expected outcomes or performance are defined and evaluation of systems operations is a part of the process

The Handbook of Industrial Engineering[3] has defined these 12 areas of industrial engineering specialization:

1. organization and job design
2. methods engineering
3. performance measurement and control of operations
4. evaluation, appraisal, and management of human resources
5. ergonomics/human factors
6. manufacturing engineering
7. quality assurance
8. engineering economy
9. facilities design

10. planning and control
11. computers and information systems
12. quantitative methods and optimization

With the exception of manufacturing engineering, all of these areas of specialization are applicable to health care systems and hospital operations. Several of them are covered in other chapters of this book, including human resource management, management information systems, quality assurance, strategic planning, materials management, and facilities planning. Quantitative management engineering methodologies and techniques are used in each of those areas.

Quality assurance, as expanded by Deming to include total quality management (TQM) and subsequently continuous quality improvement (CQI), as well as current case management and disease management efforts, are basic applications of management engineering, which has been described as the design, improvement, and installation of integrated systems of people, materials, equipment, and energy.

After briefly describing the history of the application of management engineering to the health care field, this chapter focuses on cost containment and productivity management and then briefly describes some other areas of management engineering specialization.

HISTORY

In their book, *Hospital Management Engineering: A Guide to the Improvement of Hospital Management Systems*,[4] Smalley and Freeman provide a very complete history of the use of management engineering in hospitals. They trace the history from the motion study of a surgical procedure by Frank B. Gilbreth at the turn of the century, through the dearth of hospital activity in the 1920s and 1930s, and the post–World War II period to the present. Some events of interest are the employment of the first (recorded) full-time hospital management engineer in 1952, the development of university programs for education and service in the 1950s and 1960s, and the founding of the Hospital Management Systems Society (HMSS) in 1961.

HMSS's membership first expanded from the original group of management engineers, who were primarily hospital-based or university faculty, to include administrators and consultants. Subsequently, HMSS has evolved into the Health Care Information and Systems Society (HIMSS) as it includes thousands of information system specialists.

Over 700 hospitals have organized management engineering departments, and an equal number secure management engineering services from either multihospital system programs or consulting firms.

The 1960s and 1970s

In simplest terms, management engineering is directed at increasing the utilization of system resources, either through reducing costs or increasing productivity, including throughput. As the health care environment has changed, so has the utilization of management engineering.

The first significant use and expansion of management engineering services occurred during the 1960s and 1970s. However, because hospitals were generally reimbursed on a cost basis, there was little incentive to reduce costs. Hospital management engineering efforts were directed at improving operations in problem departments utilizing engineering techniques. Examples of such efforts were improving the patient admission process and supply systems and developing employee-scheduling systems. It was rare that real economies were achieved, except in cases where accounts receivable or inventory holding costs were reduced.

As hospitals initiated more sophisticated budgeting processes, it became clear that a more objective system for determining personnel requirements than the one of "needing more personnel than we have now" was necessary. Early work at the University of Michigan in the 1960s resulted in the development of staffing methodologies:[5] quantitative, detailed, step-by-step procedures for determining personnel requirements. They were subsequently refined and modified by hospital association-sponsored efforts in order to make them easier to apply. These staffing methodologies were then applied through educational programs, booklet format, and shared data collection systems. However, the need for quantitative methodologies was still not appreciated. In general, the incentive to reduce costs was not there, except where hospital management recognized the need to contain costs by managing more effectively.

During the 1960s and 1970s the other use of management engineering that evolved was its application in planning new facilities. In particular, as hospitals increasingly utilized debt financing for replacement and expansion of facilities, ways to reduce operating costs were sought in order to pay debt service. Berg[6] reports on such an analysis that projected an annual operating savings of $4.5 million generated by the operation of more efficiently designed facilities.

The 1980s

The advent of the federal prospective payment system (PPS), combined with state Medicare and statewide/regional Blue Cross plans, changed the incentive system for hospital payment in the 1980s. The emphasis was on reducing acute hospitalization, particularly lengths of stay. Not only did lengths of stay drop during the decade, admissions fell too. Admissions dropped because of several outside influences, including physician peer review organizations and the shift of care to other settings, such as outpatient and nursing homes, and through technological advances and the increased availability of alternative settings. The result was a drop in occupancy, which resulted in excess personnel (the nursing shortage of the 1970s became a surplus in the late 1980s and early 1990s). Management engineering provides an objective approach to staffing issues that ensures that reductions occur where the change in workload is actually warranted and in a way that is sensitive to the disposition of employees.

However, hospitals were able to work the system to maximize reimbursement, with minor personnel reductions. Once personnel costs and other costs such as drugs, supplies, and food were reduced, then shifts to outpatient services resulted in increased revenues and cost shifting to the fee-for-service payers. This resulted in financial health for hospitals at the end of the 1980s.

The 1990s

Maximizing the PPS system was short-lived, when pressures to reduce health care costs became a primary issue with employers (particularly as they incurred the cost shifting arising from the perceived federal and state underpayments). In the late 1980s and the early 1990s, this resulted in the development of the new reimbursement system of managed care.

Early managed care insurers sought pure discounts in exchange for guaranteed volumes and rapid payment, but the real objec-

tive was the reduction in utilization. While PPS primarily influenced length of stay reductions, the managed care insurer has prompted further length of stay reductions, plus forced inpatient services to the outpatient setting and to the physician's office. This has been enhanced by technological advances that facilitate relocation of important services to facilities specializing in skilled nursing, home care, subacute care, and rehabilitation—all of which provide alternatives to long inpatient stays.

These changes in service settings have resulted in resource and information management problems. Resources of people, equipment, and facilities are particularly underutilized in the inpatient setting. However, they are in short supply in the ambulatory and postacute settings. Information systems that provide effective resource management are still insufficient in the inpatient setting, as well as for alternative settings. The full application of management engineering tools and techniques will be needed to solve these resource problems in the coming years.

The Future

In many ways, the real benefits of management engineering are yet to be achieved in health care operations, particularly organized delivery systems. Benefits will be achieved through realistic pricing strategies, effective information systems, and efficient facility design, with the ultimate goal by those at risk of ensuring the health of their constituents through aggressive disease management. The major objective of the PPS is to create a price-competitive health care environment by enabling purchasers of health care to solicit bids from health care providers to provide specific disease category services or total hospital care for specific population groups.

Management engineering can be used to do the following:

- reduce costs of present operations, be it for a department or a disease entity or total organized delivery systems
- provide a resource standard as a basis for a cost-accounting system to facilitate effective pricing
- provide a productivity management system to monitor and control utilization of resources
- develop care "maps" and disease management protocols

Management engineering can increase the effectiveness of information systems by applying systems design and analysis techniques for analyzing manual systems being replaced by the computer. Such techniques include:

- measure the existing systems: labor, costs, response times, storage space, etc.
- identify improvements in the manual system that could be achieved without computerization
- provide design criteria that ensure that all necessary procedures are provided and all unnecessary procedures are deleted
- monitor implementation to ensure that replaced functions are eliminated
- monitor operations to ensure that goals are met

The use of management engineering in the planning of new facilities is directed at ensuring that:

- the space plan reflects the actual amount of the space required based on projected workloads and systems
- workstations and departments are located to minimize travel

- movement, communication, and information systems satisfy current requirements and have the ability to expand to meet future needs

The application of management engineering to health care operations is a necessity for survival as the year 2000 approaches.

COST CONTAINMENT

The change in reimbursement systems from a cost base to a PPS, decrease in inpatient occupancy, and the emergence of price competition place cost containment as a top priority for all health care provider managers. Cost containment implies that (1) total operating costs are reduced, (2) labor costs, the largest cost item, are reduced, (3) costs per unit produced are reduced or at least maintained, or (4) more service is provided for the same cost; all while maintaining acceptable quality.

As defined earlier, management engineering is primarily concerned with containing or reducing operating costs. And, in the author's opinion, the cost of providing management engineering services has to be justified by a reduction in operating costs.

Labor Cost Containment Has the Largest Payoff*

Labor costs are only one part of the cost containment equation. What is important is the output that results from a labor expenditure. The ratio between output and resources

---

*The remainder of this chapter is adapted from K. Bartscht and R. Coffey, "Management Engineering—A Method To Improve Productivity," *Topics in Health Care Financing* 3, no. 3, pp. 39–62, © 1977, Aspen Publishers, Inc.

expended to obtain a desired output is also called productivity. Therefore, one approach to labor cost containment is to increase productivity. Productivity always implies a given level of quality for any output. Increased quality for the same amount of input (labor) may result in cost containment. Low quality may result in the reprocessing or redoing of the work. Further, cost containment can be achieved only if one takes the broad view or total systems approach to the organized health care delivery system under study. One may be able to maximize productivity of one department, but if doing so has adverse effects on other departments, its benefits may be outweighed by the disadvantages to the total delivery system.

Another method of labor cost containment is to replace labor, with either personnel with lesser skills or nonlabor expenditures. For example, a practical nurse may replace a registered nurse. This question—can someone at less cost do the same job?—is asked too infrequently. Automated systems (i.e., utensil washers, floor cleaning machines) and monitoring devices can also reduce labor costs. The computer to date has not yet fulfilled its labor-reduction potential. However, an effective case management information system can reduce length of stays and utilization of ancillary services and supplies. Computerization seems to reduce costs in the accounting/patient billing area, but when looking at the total systems cost (the fixed cost of computer programming, operating, and leasing equipment), it is not clear that there has been cost containment, particularly labor savings. However, outsourcing of information services may stabilize labor costs and reduce capital requirements. Labor costs also have been reduced through other types of expenditures, such as use of disposable products. Many disposable products have not only reduced labor due to the elimination of repro-

cessing but have also enabled the use of better health care techniques. Again, one must look at the total delivery cost. Disposables increase storage and disposal requirements, and, in some cases, environmental pollution.

A more significant goal in containment of labor costs is to reduce the demand for service, and in turn labor, in the first place. Is it feasible? Yes! Outpatients can be scheduled for more efficient service, preadmission procedures and outpatient surgery can eliminate certain inpatient care tasks, and proper inventory levels can eliminate handling requests. In fact, rather than a last step, the first step in any cost-containment effort should be answering the question: Do we have to do this job at all?

Finally, effective cost containment must have a long-term effect. Two key ingredients—the involvement and commitment of management, and a monitoring system to provide management with continuing, updated reports on productivity and quality— are required to sustain cost savings.

Deterrents to Labor Cost Containment

The cost-based reimbursement system has been a deterrent to labor cost containment. Current and continuing limitations on reimbursement conflict with the continuous demand for new and additional services by patients and physicians. When they are sick, patients feel that care at any cost is not too much, yet upon recovery and receipt of the bill, they may feel that the price is rarely worth the care. The physician, as manager of the care required and delivered, often ignores economic factors in pursuit of this care by misusing inpatient facilities or demanding exotic equipment and services that are provided elsewhere.

In the middle stands the health care and organized delivery system executive. In the past, as long as a hospital's cost increases were equal to those of its neighbors, there was no problem and the hospital manager could keep the physicians happy and stay financially viable. However, with PPS managed care and more competition, the executive of an organized health delivery system is feeling the pressure of holding costs on a daily basis. But what can be done?

Direction for Achievement

Clearly, equipment purchases can be delayed, and nonessential outside services dropped, but for how long? Greater numbers of health care providers are faced with fixed debt service requirements and other new expenses, such as increasing malpractice insurance premiums. There are three possible directions for containing costs:

1. increase total revenue without raising rates: do more business with the same resources
2. decrease supply costs through more effective purchasing
3. increase labor productivity

The first direction is achieved through decreasing length of stay and increasing the throughput of outpatients: more outpatients treated per hour, extended outpatient hours, Saturday and Sunday utilization, among other things. As a result, fixed assets (plant and equipment) are maximized, but this direction still requires some labor. The second direction (decreased supply costs) can be achieved through group purchasing and application of value analysis techniques. The key is to ensure that supplies do not result in increased labor costs due to greater processing or handling requirements.

The third direction is through increasing labor productivity. Although much effort has been expended in this direction, the net effect has unfortunately not always been significant, primarily due to limited applications in restricted areas. For example, a study of the housekeeping department may achieve significant reductions in its labor costs, but these improvements may be small relative to overall staffing. Gray and Steffy, in their book *Hospital Cost Containment*,[7] describe a series of cost-containment systems that show how to:

- measure, analyze, and monitor productivity
- conduct a value analysis
- organize hospital functions into a top-efficiency operation
- improve and evaluate worker performance
- institute a quality control system
- use space as efficiently as possible
- share services
- manage equipment
- audit all hospital operations
- schedule patients
- plan and control budgets
- determine the benefits of capital investments

PRODUCTIVITY MANAGEMENT

Productivity management provides the techniques that can make the greatest contribution to cost containment. Unfortunately, even with the pressures for cost containment, it is not obvious at this time that such techniques are considered standard management tools of today's health care manager, as opposed to marketing, strategic, or planning techniques. The lack of importance placed on productivity management is a major problem. Some health care providers have a policy that any expenditure over $1,000 (or $10,000) must be approved by the board. However, no approval is necessary to hire one new employee, who may cost $20,000 to $50,000 per year and may be there for 10 years. This is actually a $200,000 to $500,000 decision. The expenditure for labor must be placed in the proper perspective.

As the American Hospital Association stated in 1973, which is still true today:

> Many hospital administrative personnel have been reluctant to attack the task of managing their employees' productivity. They often are unaware of (1) the approaches and tools available to them in the trade literature, and (2) the basic techniques and steps that provide the needed foundation for effective use of the more sophisticated techniques.[8]

This reluctance was further substantiated in an Arthur Andersen study.[9] Not only are many managers not trained in productivity concepts but also they perceive their employees as loyal and hardworking. Until recently, employee salaries have been low, and their hours were long. This is no longer the case. In fact, in many areas of the country, the hospital pays the highest wages of any employer. There are also certain human characteristics that contribute to this reluctance to explore productivity management. It is always difficult to suspend or lay off employees, and there is always fear of upsetting the employees. Concerns of union activities are always present. Besides, whenever management is observing, all employees are busy. The real questions are: is this always the case, and what are they busy doing? We have reached a point in hospital productivity management at which we can no longer live with the status quo.

Cost containment achieved through improvement of productivity of ongoing operations should strive for a minimal goal of savings of 5 percent, an expected goal of 10 percent, and in many instances, a realizable goal of 15 percent in any year. This is not a one-time cost or savings but an annual savings.

The approach for improving productivity has seven steps (Figure 13–1):

1. management orientation
2. overview studies
3. productivity reporting
4. quality control
5. in-depth studies
6. performance/reward systems
7. monitoring, review, and change

Management Orientation

First, a philosophical framework must be established, which in turn should establish why productivity improvements are necessary and what benefits are expected. As Figure 13–1 suggests, the management orientation includes at least two levels—the individual department manager or supervisor and the manager's superior (and top management).

A set of objectives must next be stated. These objectives should be related to expected benefits within a certain period of time. For example:

- Objective 1: All departments will be analyzed as to existing manpower productivity levels within an 18-month period.
- Objective 2: Changes resulting in a $400,000 annual saving should be initiated within 12 months.
- Objective 3: Productivity for all departments will be reported on a monthly basis.

The objectives must also state the responsibility of top and middle management and detail the commitment and support they will

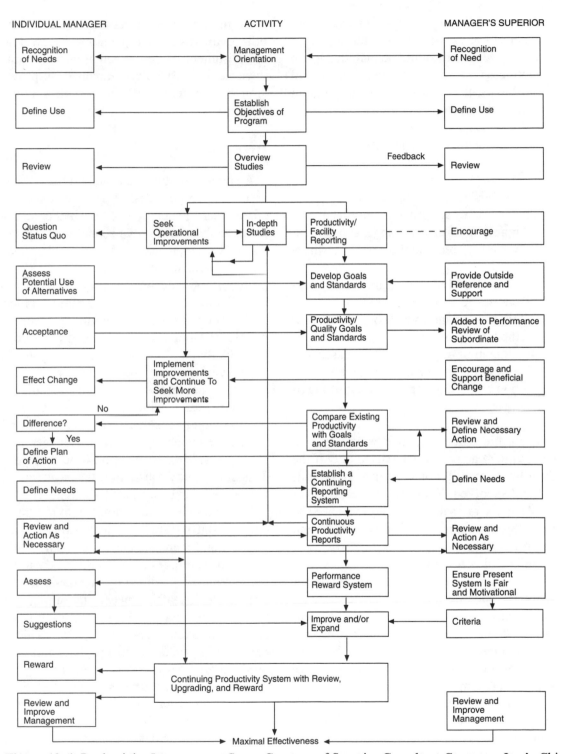

Figure 13–1 Productivity Improvement Steps. Courtesy of Superior Consultant Company, Inc.'s Chi Systems Practice, Ann Arbor, Michigan.

contribute. Finally, the costs of increasing productivity must be a consideration, so return on investment should be included in the objectives. One would not want to expend more dollars on a cost-containment program than it could return in additional service and in reduced costs.

Top management's major input focuses on four areas:

1. establishment of objectives
2. creation of an environment that allows managers to effect change, and the provision of technical assistance where needed
3. control of individual productivity increases so that they are not made at the expense of the overall organization or the quality of service
4. utilization of productivity measures to assess personnel performance evaluation and long-range planning of facilities and labor

The achievement and maintenance of cost containment goals can take place only if the department manager or supervisor is committed and involved. They can make improvements work or make sure they do not. The first step in obtaining their involvement and commitment is to explain to them why cost containment is necessary. The second step is to review goals and secure agreement on (or negotiate) specific goals for each department. The usual problem is that the establishment of a cost-containment program in a department implies that department members are not performing as expected. It is therefore important to emphasize that cost containment is a new management direction in which all managers are to be involved. Likewise, it should be emphasized that to the agreed-upon cost-containment goals will be added their

performance measures as part of their periodic evaluation by top management. The establishment of departmental cost-containment goals must be accompanied by provision of adequate staff support to achieve these goals.

Overview Study

An overview study has two purposes. First, at a relatively low cost, it provides data that enable management to decide whether an in-depth analysis will prove economically justifiable. Second, it enables the engineer or analyst to direct his or her efforts to specific problem areas during an in-depth analysis, thus minimizing the cost of the more detailed study.[10] In addition, the overview provides a profile of labor productivity and the initial baseline for a productivity reporting system.

An overview study should be directed by a person trained in the use of such a technique. If a staff person with these qualifications is not available, consultants from shared management engineering programs[11] or management consulting firms should be retained. This initial study can then be the basis for future work by existing staff (if available).

The overview study should provide three outputs: staffing analysis, quality survey, and systems and management review. The staffing analysis utilizes gross workload data and predetermined productivity standards to determine total staffing needs in comparison with existing staff. The quality survey measures performance relative to quality. This is particularly crucial to ensure that increased productivity does not have a negative impact on quality. Quality surveys are conducted by random sampling, involving observations and work counts. The systems and management review identifies and analyzes problems involving the management structure of the department and the systems, methods, and procedures for performing work. The management structure analysis looks at organization, skills, and work assignments. Systems analysis looks for duplication of effort, unnecessary steps, and imbalance of workstations.

As a result of the overview study, four directions can be pursued (Figure 13–2).

Productivity and Quality Reporting

A productivity reporting system is one part of a resource utilization management information system that measures labor productivity. The other part is the quality control system, which measures the quality of services. An effective productivity reporting system should generate a continuous—at least monthly—timely report on productivity of each department and a comparison of productivity over time to show trends; for example, this month compared to last month, this month compared to same month last year, or year to date compared to last year to date. In addition, this system should provide the following information.

Measurement of Actual Productivity in Person-Hours per Output

Actual productivity can be measured in person-hours per output or output per person-hour; these outputs are specific for each department. See the radiology example in Table 13–1. Increased labor productivity may result from:

- a decrease in person-hours invested with no change in output; staffing is reduced, decreasing both direct and indirect salary costs for the hospital
- an increase in output with no change in staff; additional services are provided with increased efficiency, avoiding additional salary costs by not having to hire more staff

Actual Productivity Compared to a Performance Goal

Actual productivity (person-hours per output) can be compared to a performance goal of person-hours per actual output.

The reason for analyzing productivity is to determine if the existing productivity level is

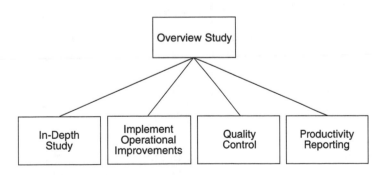

Figure 13–2 Directions Stemming from an Overview Study. *Source:* Reprinted from *Topics in Health Care Financing*, Vol. 3, No. 3, p. 44, © 1977, Aspen Publishers, Inc.

Table 13–1 Workload Unit Recording Systems: Productivity Measurement Results for Radiology (Input = Person-Hours)

Method/Component	Person-Hours Invested (Input)	Workload Units Produced (Output)	Person-Hours per Unit
Aggregate:			
Total procedures	930	1,820	0.51
Totals	930	1,820	0.51
Service specific:			
Radiography	600	1,400	0.43
Fluoroscopy	250	400	0.63
Specials	80	20	4.00
Totals	930	1,820	0.51
Procedure specific:			
Radiography			
Chest—PA & lat.	50	250	0.20
Chest—PA	30	180	0.17
•	•	•	•
•	•	•	•
•	•	•	•
Subtotal for radiography	600	1,400	0.43
Fluoroscopy			
Barium enema	20	20	1.00
Gallbladder	10	20	0.50
•	•	•	•
•	•	•	•
•	•	•	•
Subtotal for fluoroscopy	250	400	0.63
Specials			
Head angiography	30	10	3.00
•	•	•	•
•	•	•	•
•	•	•	•
Subtotal for specials	80	20	4.00
Totals	930	1,820	0.51

acceptable. One of several methods to establish a comparative value must be selected to make this judgment. A comparison of current productivity to historical performance, comparison to other institutions or groups of institutions, guidelines developed by professional societies, and measured (engineered) time standards are used most frequently.

Most comparatives provide meaningful information, which can be translated into improvement objectives, and comparisons with predetermined measured, or engineered, standards appear to be the most meaningful form of evaluation. The standards assumedly represent an objective, unbiased per-occurrence representation of labor requirements necessary to produce a single unit of output. They are unadulterated by any existing non-productive labor practices or inefficient work methods.

Measured productivity time standards can be viewed in a number of different ways. Several elemental work tasks must be performed in a department regardless of the workload unit volumes produced. Conversely, other tasks will be performed in direct proportion to the workload unit volume. Consider that the activities of a department manager require one full-time position, and staffing will not vary according to the number of procedures, tests, and so on performed. On the other hand, the number of person-hours necessary to perform procedures will depend upon the number of procedures performed. The position-hours associated with managing the department become a fixed task, and the processing of procedures a variable task.

Fixed tasks can be viewed as components of the cost of doing business. In addition to routine department management supervision, other fixed tasks include preparation of departmental statistics, administrative clerical services, daily activation and quality control of diagnostic devices, routine supplies inventory and replenishment, departmental/hospital meetings, and giving or receiving in-service educational sessions. Similarly, variable work tasks, such as scheduling appointments, prepping patients, and filing new reports, contribute directly to the production of each processed workload unit. The time required to perform each variable task may either be the same or different for each specific procedure.

Engineered productivity time standards are frequently established by developing a fixed and a variable component. The fixed component represents the labor requirements necessary to perform all fixed work tasks; the variable component, the additional resources required for each processed workload unit. All departments will have at least one fixed component. The number of variable components will relate to the level of detail reflected in the workload unit recording system. Mathematically, this relationship is expressed as follows:

$$\text{Standard time} = \text{fixed component} + \\ (\text{variable standard component} \\ \text{workload} \times \text{unit volume})$$

These time standards can be used to determine the required person-hours for processing the observed workload unit volumes over a specified period of time. The predetermined time interval between reporting cycles, the reporting period, is typically defined to coincide with the availability of data concerning inputs or outputs.

In the radiology example, if an aggregate measure of workload (total procedures) is used, one variable component appears in the equation. If the workload unit recording system uses service-specific information (radiography, fluoroscopy, and special procedures), three variable components are required. If the workload unit recording system is procedure-specific, the productivity standard equation will include as many variable components as there are specific procedures. The required person-hours for the three-alternative workload unit recording systems for a four-week period is illustrated in Table 13–2.

To determine how effectively departmental labor resources were utilized during the reporting period, required person-hours determined by using the productivity standards

Table 13–2 Workload Unit Recording Systems: Total Required Person-Hours for Radiology Procedures (Period = 4 Weeks)

Method/Component	Workload Unit Volume (Procedures)	× Productivity Standard (Hours/ Procedure)	= Required Person-Hours
Aggregate:			
Total procedures	7,640	0.41	3,122.00
Totals			3,500.00*
Service specific:			
Radiography	5,200	0.33	1,716.00
Fluoroscopy	2,378	0.50	1,189.00
Specials	62	3.50	217.00
Total required person-hours			3,500.00*
Procedure specific:			
Radiography			
Chest—PA and lateral	600	0.16	96.00
Chest—PA	520	0.13	67.60
•	•	•	•
•	•	•	•
•	•	•	•
Subtotal for radiography	5,200	0.33	1,716.00
Fluoroscopy			
Barium enema	65	0.83	53.95
Gallbladder	60	0.35	21.00
•	•	•	•
•	•	•	•
•	•	•	•
Subtotal for fluoroscopy	2,378	0.50	1,189.00
Specials			
Head angiography	22	2.60	57.20
•	•	•	•
•	•	•	•
•	•	•	•
Subtotal for specials	62	3.50	217.00
Total required person-hours			3,500.00*

*Totals include a standard time of 378 hours for fixed work tasks over a 4-week period.

can be compared to the actual person-hours used. This measure of labor utilization, the department's productivity index, is expressed as a percentage of required person-hours divided by actual person-hours. If 4,200 person-hours were utilized, the productivity index for the radiology department example presented in Table 13–2 would be calculated as:

$$\text{Productivity Index} = \frac{3,500}{4,200} \times 100 = 83.3\%$$

At this point, the value of a service- or procedure-specific workload unit recording system becomes apparent. The detailed information produced can be compared to existing staffing patterns for each major facet of departmental operations. Often, such comparisons provide the basis for staff reallocation or schedule adjustments.

The key to the development and utilization of time standards is their acceptance by the department manager. Because the measurement of work is, in most instances, a new concept to department managers, gaining this acceptance is not always an easy task. In particular, managers have realistic concerns such as the difference in patients served (age, diagnosis, cooperativeness) and the random demands for services placed on most departments. To overcome these concerns, it must be recognized that, in reality, all department managers actually are measuring work when they establish labor budgets and work schedules. From there, one proceeds to define major work activities. Time standards are applied to these major work activities. These are then modified to take into account fluctuations in workloads as caused by patients with different degrees of illness, peak and valley demands, delays, and approved time off of staff members.

In some cases, the department managers may not accept the predetermined time standards. Because the first objective is to establish a productivity reporting system, an interim time standard may be established as an initial goal. This "negotiated" time standard would then be used at the initial reporting phase.

It has been the experience of the author, as well as colleagues in the field, that the establishment of a system to report productivity is beneficial in itself. It provides a regular vehicle by which the department manager can review the performance of his or her department. As a result of this report, the department manager may initiate further studies and changes to increase productivity. Most good managers want to do a better job, and the report provides them a way of measuring improvement.

Written Reports to All Management Levels

The productivity report should be shared with all management levels: hospital, divisions within the hospital, departments within each division, and sections within each department. Figure 13–3 illustrates this concept. The report should cover the level of detail necessary at each level for effective management control.

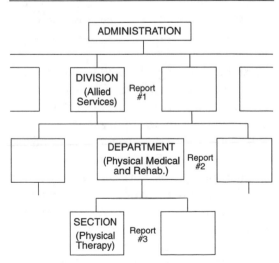

Figure 13–3 System Organization. *Source:* Reprinted from *Topics in Health Care Financing,* Vol. 3, No. 3, p. 46, © 1977, Aspen Publishers, Inc.

Exhibit 13–1 Sample of Hospital Report

```
CHI SYSTEMS                              22:35           REPHOS.L38          PAGE 1

HOSPITAL                                                ******* CHIMIS *******
                                                        ** HOSPITAL REPORT**


                              EARNED              PAID
DIVISION                      MAN-HOURS           MAN-HOURS            % PROD
HOSP ADMINISTRATION              519.000             528.000            98.3
EMPLOYEE SERVICES              14746.417           13528.000           109.0
ALLIED SERVICES               21135.314           21784.000            97.0
FISCAL SERVICES               21410.943           21834.000            98.1
SUPPORTIVE SERVICES           35482.832           32818.000           108.1
NURSING SERVICES              66734.731           68158.000            97.9
DEVELOPMENT                     173.000             177.000            97.7
PLANNING                        519.000             531.000            97.7
            TOTALS           160721.238          159358.000           100.9

- - - HISTORICAL - - -       *INDICATES CURRENT MONTH

  JAN    FEB    MAR    APR    MAY    JUN    JUL    AUG    SEP    OCT    NOV    DEC
 ── ── ── ── ── ── ── ── ── ── ── ── ── ── ── ── ── ── ── ── ── ── ── ──

PERCENT PRODUCTIVITY
  90.5   102.7  100.9*  0.0    0.0    0.0   86.2   86.0   91.9   92.0   92.3   85.6


THIS MONTH EARNED FTE   929.0
THIS MONTH PAID FTE     921.1


PAST 12 MONTHS PRODUCTIVITY    91.9
```

Courtesy of Superior Consultant Company, Inc.'s Chi Systems Practice, Ann Arbor, Michigan.

Exhibits 13–1 and 13–2 illustrate monthly reports produced under the CHIMIS productivity reporting system, for two different levels within the sample organization.

Productivity must be continuously updated because the procedures being performed (the output) change over time, new ones are added, and others are deleted. Second, as more data are developed for each department, more refined time standards can be derived by dividing certain comprehensive procedures into more specific procedures. In addition, negotiated time standards, set as initial goals, should be reviewed and revised as necessary.

QUALITY CONTROL PROGRAM

The myth that increasing productivity reduces the quality of care has limited efforts to increase productivity. Not only is this generally not true but there is also significant evidence that increased quality can be consistent with increased productivity. Common sense tells us that, if something is done correctly the first time, there is no need to repeat the effort.

The primary objectives of a quality control program are to provide:

- a quantitative measure that indicates the level of quality on a continuing basis

- positive feedback that allows corrective action to be taken
- quality assurance upon implementation of new systems, equipment, or workload revisions

Quality

The ultimate measure of the quality of the health care system is the health status of the community. Determination of quality of

---

Exhibit 13–2 Sample of Section Report

CHI SYSTEMS		22:34	REPSEC.L38	PAGE 7

HOSPITAL   —   ******* CHIMIS *******
DIVISION   —ALLIED SERVICES   ***SECTION REPORT ***
DEPARTMENT —P.M. & R.

SECTION   — PHYSICAL THERAPY

WORKLOAD UNIT	VOLUME	M-H/PROC STANDARD	EARNED MAN-HOURS	PAID MAN-HOURS	% PROD
THERAPEUTIC EXERCISE	780	0.601	468.780		
GAIT TRAINING	569	0.694	394.886		
HOT PACKS	340	0.432	146.880		
ULTRASOUND	281	0.555	155.955		
ROOM VISIT	503	0.324	162.972		
TRACTION	128	0.447	57.216		
HUBBARD–UNASSISTED	4	0.863	3.452		
HUBBARD–W/THERAPIST	7	1.202	8.414		
WHIRLPOOL–ALL	76	0.478	36.328		
EXERCISE–OTHERS	267	0.554	147.918		
MASSAGE–ALL	314	0.516	162.024		
DIATHERMY–ALL	119	0.468	55.692		
P.T. LEVELS–ALL	11	0.678	7.458		
OTHER MODALITIES	66	0.615	40.590		
FIXED			221.000		
EPI			0.000		
SECTION TOTALS			2,069.565	1,799.000	115.0

- - - HISTORICAL - - -   *INDICATES CURRENT MONTH

JAN	FEB	MAR	APR	MAY	JUN	JUL	AUG	SEP	OCT	NOV	DEC

PERCENT PRODUCTIVITY

JAN	FEB	MAR	APR	MAY	JUN	JUL	AUG	SEP	OCT	NOV	DEC
95.5	116.8	115.0*	0.0	0.0	0.0	95.6	95.5	106.1	153.3	112.8	94.8

THIS MONTH EARNED FTE   12.0
THIS MONTH PAID FTE   10.4

PAST 12 MONTHS PRODUCTIVITY   108.7

Courtesy of Superior Consultant Company, Inc.'s Chi Systems Practice, Ann Arbor, Michigan.

health in an area can be derived from indices of unnecessary disease, unnecessary disability, and unnecessary untimely death.[12] However, the relationships of such measures of quality to the services provided by specific physicians or hospital departments are undefined. Therefore, one should use measures that are more specific to the services being provided by the respective physicians or departments.

A comprehensive definition of quality is difficult to develop due to its many components and the need to determine the relative values of "good" and "bad" quality. Rather than attempt a synthesized definition of quality, existing definitions and concepts are examined to specify the dimensions of quality relevant to a quality productivity program.

Random House Dictionary defines quality as "character with respect to fineness or grade of excellence."[13] Gavett's definition of quality related to production is that "the quality of a product or service is expressed in terms of a given set of attributes that are required to meet the . . . needs for which the product or service is created."[14]

Many definitions of quality refer to quality control, which can be defined as "the sending of messages which effectively change the behavior of the recipient."[15] A more useful definition of control is "that function of the system which provides direction in conformance to plan, or in other words, the maintenance of variations from system objectives within allowable limits."[16] Components of a control system include:

- a monitored characteristic or operational variable
- a monitoring device or method
- a standard of performance for each monitored characteristic
- a comparison of actual to predetermined standard performance
- an activator that can effect change

In a quality control system, therefore, the rating of operational variables is done by comparison to standards or, at least, predetermined values of quality. The purpose of a quality control system is to give some assurance that the standards of services are maintained.

Quality control systems exist, and can be developed, for both medical care provided by physicians and for services provided by hospital departments. Some departments, such as nuclear medicine and tissue pathology, have strong medical components. Quality of medical care is monitored by the hospital's utilization review and medical audit programs. Medical record abstracting services provide information for use by the medical review committees of the hospital.

Quality of services can be measured from three perspectives: input, process, and output. A comprehensive system measures quality from all three perspectives, with an emphasis on output measures.

Input measurement involves the quality of inputs (labor, facilities, equipment, and supplies) used to provide departmental services. Input quality measurements include staff educational requirements, types of linen purchased, type of lighting installed in the operating room, and the physical characteristics of the building.

Process measurement involves the quality of the organization and the methods it uses to provide services. Assessment of process answers the question: Is the process proper or performed correctly? Methods are compared with standard procedures, and when standards do not exist or are not applicable, relative values are determined. Examples of process quality measurements include written procedures for the care of isolation patients, identification procedures for patients going to surgery, staffing schedules, sterile technique maintained in the operating room, and appropriate tagging of contaminated linen.

Output measurement involves the quality of the services provided by a department. Examples include timely delivery of drugs by the pharmacy, cleanliness of a patient's room after discharge cleaning, timely and courteous answering of telephones, and achievement of nursing care objectives.

A distinction between absolute and relative measures of quality should be made. An absolute quality measure requires no interpretation, whereas relative quality measures require interpretation and rating. The question "Does the surgical light work?" is an absolute quality measure; the light either works or not. However, the question "Is the ambient room temperature sufficient?" is relative to the activity being done and the judgment of the observer.

Measurement Variables and Standards

Measurement variables are activities on which judgment or decision can be based. Both qualitative and quantitative measurement variables can be used, but quantitative variables are less subjective. Examples of measurement variables are sterility of instrument trays, accuracy of accounting records, cleanliness of patient rooms, and person-minutes per pack.

Standards are specific values of measurement variables. Each quality and productivity measurement variable can have specific levels or standards established as acceptable or unacceptable. Examples of standards are 95 percent acceptably cleaned rooms or 5 instrument trays packed per hour.

Measurements To Develop Standards

Continuous measurement of quality is often prohibitively expensive. Therefore, quality and productivity are usually measured by sampling the measurement variable.[17] Prob-

lems to be avoided in sampling include concentrating on only one of the many quality and productivity variables, sampling only problem situations, and taking nonrepresentative samples. Three methods of avoiding these problems are to randomize the samples, take a large enough sample to be representative, and include all relevant variables in the sample.

In measuring quality and productivity, the concepts of reliability, validity, and bias must be considered. Reliability refers to the ability of two or more persons to make similar judgments on the measurement variables or for the data to be judged similarly on multiple occasions. Validity refers to the ability of the observation to measure what it is supposed to measure. Bias occurs when one judge or observer of the data systematically rates the variable differently than others.

In addition, quality and productivity measurement needs to be applicable to repetitive measurement over time, as opposed to a one-time evaluation. Measurements should also be responsive to changes in input or process during the sample interval (commonly one month). The quality question for a maintenance department "(Does the department have a preventive maintenance program?")" would always be answered "yes" if such a program existed, regardless of the performance of the program. The question "Has a minimum acceptable number of items been preventively maintained during the sampling period?" would measure departmental performance during the period.

Interaction Among Departments

In the development of measures of quality and productivity for the services provided by the various functional units or departments within the hospital, the point is eventually reached where the performance of a given element of service is dependent upon some other element previously performed by another department or functional unit. Before the laboratory can be expected to run a battery of tests on a sample of blood, it must first receive a requisition for this service from nursing or from a physician. Most of the time, responsibilities for required prior services can be assigned to either one of the two units directly involved. However, there are some instances in which a third party or element enters the picture. These are the "network" systems. Consider the situation in which an X-ray examination is requested for an inpatient. All forms have been properly processed. Before the examination can occur, however, the patient must be transported from his or her bed to the X-ray department, a function that belongs neither to nursing, the X-ray department, nor to the physician. The network system here is patient transportation, which is likely handled by a patient transport or messenger service, and its own quality of performance can be measured as an individual functioning unit. Other network systems include communications (verbal and physical; hard copy, electronic, recorded), material supply (procurement, reprocessing, storage, distribution), education, and equipment and facility maintenance. The responsibility for the operation of each network system can, in fact, be assigned to some functioning unit or individual, and the performance of that responsibility can be measured.

When interaction among departments does not involve a third party, the concern becomes the accurate definition of the department's interface with another department and the determination of where one department's responsibility ends and that of the other begins. The quality and productivity measurement variables must then be defined consistently with the interface definition so that monitoring and reporting will be appropriate.

Relationship of Quality and Productivity

The relationship of quality and productivity is neither easily determined nor consistent; it varies with the levels of quality and productivity and the procedures used by the hospital.

Beginning with the current quality level and current productivity, both can usually be increased to some point. At that point, they cannot be simultaneously increased, but other alternatives are (1) increasing quality at the same productivity level, (2) increasing productivity at the same quality level, (3) increasing productivity while decreasing quality, and (4) decreasing both quality and productivity. The difficulty is knowing at what quality and productivity level the hospital is currently functioning and monitoring where it is on future dates.

Providing this information is a major reason for a quality-productivity program that simultaneously measures and integrates quality and productivity. Then, as changes in either level are planned, the impact on the other can be determined.

The following examples demonstrate increases in both productivity (decreasing cost) and quality. Most of these involve several departments, emphasizing the importance of interdepartmental effects on quality and productivity.

Pharmacy Ordering

In some hospitals, physicians write pharmacy orders on the patients' charts. These orders are then transcribed by a ward clerk, checked by the head nurse, and sent to the pharmacy to be filled. Changing the system so that a computerized copy of the physician's order is sent directly to the pharmacy decreases errors of interpretation of the physician's order, thereby increasing quality, and reduces staff time needed to transcribe and verify the physician's order, which can increase productivity or decrease cost.

Early Admission Testing

Traditionally hospitals have admitted patients to their rooms, orders for admission tests are written by the physicians, and then the patient receives the admission tests. Earlier admission testing both reduces cost and improves quality. Earlier testing is done one of two ways: on the day of admission before the patient reaches his or her bed (early testing—ET) or before the day of admission (preadmission testing—PAT). ET and PAT often improve quality because physicians receive test results earlier, reducing the probability of surgery or other action being taken before test results are available. Costs are also decreased by reducing the length of stay of patients[18,19] and reducing the amount of time needed to escort patients from patient floors to testing areas.

Paging System

Many institutions take advantage of paging systems for their communication needs. Quality is improved by reducing response time of services required by patients. Physicians, nurses, and others can be reached in emergencies or other situations. Productivity is improved by reducing walking time and delays.

Coordinated Admission and Surgery Scheduling

Close coordination of admission scheduling and surgery scheduling is very important for surgery patients. This can be done several different ways, but the advantages are similar. Quality is improved when fewer schedule changes and cancellations result in less patient and physician disruption. Productivity is improved by reducing the personnel time needed to schedule and reschedule both admissions and surgery. The probability of unused surgical time due to last-minute cancellations is also reduced. The shift to outpatient surgical sites has further influenced productivity.

In-Depth Studies

The in-depth study is a detailed study of a function or department directed at either the entire operation or a specific problem identified by the overview study or the productivity-quality reporting system. An in-depth study is warranted in the case of significant differences between existing and required staffing levels; significant quality control problems creating safety, health, or public relations problems; or ineffective interaction with other departments and functions that creates problems for those other departments.

In-depth studies are far more expensive than the overview study, often costing between 10 to 15 times that of the overview study. Therefore, the expected benefits must at least exceed this amount by a minimum of two or three times. One must be cautioned that some difference in staffing levels could be due to the scope of work and activities in the department, not improper staffing. The in-depth study accounts for these activities and establishes time standards for the work required to perform them.

The in-depth study is usually directed at a specific problem, such as organization, scheduling, employees, patients, information flow and handling, methods improvement, patient/materials movement, and layout and equipment. Many references are available on identification of problems and problem-solving approaches.[20,21] A few comments on each of these problems follow.

Organization

Organization studies are directed at achieving the correct balance between span of control and delegation of responsibility with related authority. Too large a span of control may result in poor supervision and, in turn, low productivity. Determining the appropriate number of persons to be supervised by each supervisor is further complicated by their location of work. In a hospital, staff members may work on different floors and in different departments; for example, housekeeping personnel. Conversely, too small a span of control may result in additional levels of hierarchy. Such levels may be established to provide opportunities for promotions within departments. In a nursing department, there may be several levels of supervision before one finds a nurse totally committed to patient care; these levels may include a nursing director, associate nursing director, assistant nursing director, nursing supervisor, head nurse, assistant head nurse, team leader, or nurse. Are they all necessary?

Scheduling

The installation of effective scheduling systems can yield a big payoff in terms of achieving cost containment and improvement in productivity. This very broad area involves patients, employees, and available facilities. Facilities is a limiting factor (that is, not enough rooms available), although an artificial one in many ways, if one thinks of 24-hour, 7-day-a-week operations.

Scheduling of patients may be difficult because of the random arrival of certain types of patients. However, statistically arrivals do follow certain patterns, and upon further analysis, one finds that a majority of inpatients and outpatients can be scheduled. The biggest fault in scheduling is the peak load

syndrome. In too many cases, patients are scheduled "en masse" for a block of time. Examples are 8:00 A.M. surgery, admissions from 1:00 P.M. to 3:00 P.M., and the noon meal from 11:00 A.M. to 12:00 P.M. When one realizes that the processing of 10 patients in 1 hour takes twice as many personnel as 5 patients per hour for 2 hours, the peak load scheduling problem should be obvious. The usual case is that the number of required employees is determined by the peak load, with the rest of their 8 hours being used with fill-in operations. Usually, reduction of the peak load requirements—spreading out the patient schedule—results in reduction of staff.

A larger inefficiency in scheduling employees is in the 7-day operations (nursing, dietary, housekeeping) that involve the majority of employees. Because most employees work only 5 days, coverage is required for the other 2. The actual requirement for a 7-day position is 1.4 full-time equivalents (FTEs). It is not uncommon to see scheduling of 3 employees for every 2 positions, which results in an excess of 0.2 FTEs for every 3.0 FTEs. In a 300-bed hospital with 450 nursing, 90 housekeeping, and 75 dietary personnel, this coverage represents over 40 extra personnel.

Scheduling work for hospital personnel is made difficult by the lack of repetition of tasks during an 8-hour shift. The key to effective scheduling of tasks is to ensure that personnel understand all tasks that must be performed, why they are necessary, when they must be done (not necessarily at which time, but by what time they must be completed), and what the priorities are. Peak load requirements must be smoothed as much as possible, and traditional hours (that is, 7:00 A.M. to 3:30 P.M., 8 A.M. to 5:00 P.M.) must be examined to determine whether they are the times appropriate to the necessary tasks. In past studies, the author has found that a midnight nursing shift (11:00

P.M. to 7:30 A.M.) was primarily staffed to provide personnel for the early morning activities for patients (6:00 A.M. to 7:30 A.M.).[22] A change in the daily shift hours resulted in reducing the midnight shift requirements by almost 50 percent. Scheduling studies and analyses really are just the application of common sense. Why must a task be performed, for whom, by what skill, by what time?

Information Flow

Information technology systems has profoundly influenced hospital information storage, retrieval, and flow. Information flow is not only concerned with how effectively information flows from one organization level to another, as well as from department to department, but just as importantly what information does not flow.

Management cannot function without a proper flow of information, both historical reporting and projecting for the future. Departments cannot effectively interact with and serve other departments without the timely receipt of adequate information indicating the others' needs. Some studies have suggested that up to 25 percent of all activities in a hospital are involved with information handling. Therefore, a reduction in this activity must lead to improved productivity. The major problem in achieving real cost containment is that most of the information handling effort is spread over all employees. Therefore, an improvement in information handling may decrease an employee's workload by 30 minutes, but he or she still has 7½ hours of work to do. To realize this 30-minute savings may require extensive reorganization of tasks.

Several improvements in information flow and handling result in cost-containment benefits. Improvement in recordkeeping in many hospitals has resulted in increased revenue and greater knowledge of resources expended. Planning ahead can enable services and supplies to be requested on a scheduled "batched" basis, eliminating "stat" requests and processing of single requests, rather than in a batched or bulk basis. However, a deterrent to achieving cost containment through the substitution of automated information processing equipment may be the increased cost of hardware and skilled computer programming staff.

Case management is yet another organizational development which utilizes information systems. With integrated health delivery systems, case management must coordinate an episode of illness in multiple settings with varied resource use. Both case management and disease management make economic and organizational sense.

Disease management spans the entire continuum of care from prevention to diagnosis and treatment including follow-up and ongoing maintenance. Informational flow allows both management techniques greater efficiency.

Methods Improvement

Methods improvement is the study of how work is performed, and its objective is to reduce human motion (walking, handling, reaching). In the global sense, everything mentioned in this section is methods improvement. There is always a better way to perform a task, and there is never a "best" way, only a "least worst" way. Improvement is always possible.

Patients and Materials Movement

Patients and materials movement studies apply methods improvement and information handling analysis. This is the key to effective interaction among departments. Too often one hears from a department manager that department members are doing the best they can but that they never have the patients or materials on time. It is rare to find a hospital staff that does not complain about its messenger service or its patient escort system; they are easy scapegoats for all problems. The important step in this analysis is the recognition that movement problems cannot be solved by individual departments because they involve all those departments that must interact with each other. It is difficult to project the potential cost savings from an effective patient and material movement system because there are usually new costs associated with the system. System benefits come from smoothing the workload in the individual departments.

A related activity is material management studies: the analysis of the purchase, storage, handling, movement, and use of supplies and other purchased materials. Greater benefits are being derived from these studies because of both the increased use of such items and the inflationary price spiral. Labor considerations become important when one analyzes handling and movement requirements.

Layout and Equipment

Layout and equipment studies should be geared to reduction of walking distances and total labor input. For existing operations, layout of equipment and workstations is usually limited by the space within existing walls and the cost of moving permanent fixtures. The management engineer is usually frustrated by this analysis because many mistakes could have been avoided by more effective facility planning. It is rare that significant labor savings can be achieved through layout changes. The major benefit is usually a more effective use of space that results in the availability of more space, which in most hospitals is a real benefit. One must recognize that this benefit is still limited by total existing space.

Labor savings are being achieved through automation, such as in the dietary department (automated dishwashing and tray preparation) and in housekeeping (floor washers). The clinical laboratory also benefits from highly automated processing of procedures, as does the radiology department. A major question is whether the labor replacement results in real cost reduction. In the clinical laboratory, if one is seeing an increased volume and number of procedures, is it clear that productivity is increasing? Is this increase proportionate to the capital investment in equipment? Even more serious is the question that medical professionals are asking: Is this increase in laboratory procedures really necessary?

When an analysis of the cost benefits of an equipment investment is made, the objectives of using the new equipment must be clearly understood. For example, is the objective of the investment to increase service, reduce labor, or both? If the objective is labor reduction, a labor savings must be realized; saving one hour per day for each of eight persons is not a cost reduction unless work can be reassigned to achieve a reduction in one staff position. Another weakness in equipment studies lies in the basis for comparison. Most comparisons are with the existing operations. Despite the many reports that have justified a large investment in automated material handling systems, one is hard pressed to justify such systems when looking at how the existing system can be improved without (or with very little) capital investment. In other words, justification for equipment should be made based on comparison with the most effective manual system.

Implementation of Productivity and Quality Control Programs

The development of recommendations and new systems is academic if it is not followed by implementation.

A variety of quality and productivity systems have been developed over the last 20 years and are in use today in various institutions. Key problems encountered with the implementation and use of these productivity and quality control programs have been:

- complexity and subsequent difficulty in implementation that have resulted in only partial use
- reports produced that are neither used at all nor integrated into the management process or review of managers' performance
- systems that have not been comprehensive or specific enough, resulting in the common and easy practice of blaming lack of productivity or quality on another department
- lack of attention paid to interactive effects among departments

The process of implementation requires that the responsible operating manager fully understand and concur with it. The manager must understand the basis for the recommendations, how the new systems and procedures are to work, and what the expected benefits are. Many times, all of the recommendations may not be acceptable to the manager. This situation may result in partial implementation, with further development by the analyst and the manager of the remaining recommendations.

The next step in implementation is to establish with the manager a timetable of activities and expected results. This should then be followed by an orientation of all employees involved in any changes. They in turn must be informed of the desired goals and the timetable of the implementation. If a change in procedures, methods, or use of equipment is proposed, instructions must be formalized and training must take place. If new sched-ules are developed, then assignment of tasks must be developed to be consistent with new schedules.

The actual change to new schedules and procedures necessitates close monitoring and continuous support in the form of directions and encouragement. As the new recommendations become more and more routine, this monitoring and support can be decreased. Included in the implementation plan must be a periodic review, such as monthly, to ensure that everything is going as expected.

In implementing changes, people are being asked to change their routine way of doing things. This is never easy!

Performance Reward Systems

Underlying the entire process of managing productivity gains is the realization that some reward should ultimately result from the improved performance. The nature and extent of the reward mechanism are certainly dependent upon the level of employee considered. The range, however, should encompass cost-reduction cash bonuses, incentives, perquisites, improved reimbursement formulas with third-party payers, alternative uses of funds, and compensatory time off. In no case can it be expected or warranted that improved results will be obtained without some form of recognition of an individual's contribution to these results.

Monitoring, Review, and Change

Cost containment for ongoing operations must be a continuous activity. Productivity and quality control reporting systems provide regular feedback that must be monitored on an exception basis; that is, to detect when productivity and quality deviate from an expected range, including both high and low deviations. When productivity or quality is below performance expectations, it should be investigated. Above-expected performance, which should be examined as well, may be due to the use of new procedures, services, or equipment. This would then require updating the productivity and quality control program.

This continuous reporting system has several by-products. Evaluation of new equipment purchases may be based on their effect on productivity. Personnel budgets can be developed based on existing utilization of personnel. The justification for new positions should have a very reliable basis. Performance objectives for management can target increased productivity or quality level goals that can be quantified. Performance reward systems must also be reviewed and updated. When a hospital has gone through the above cost-containment steps, it should be able to compare itself favorably with any well-managed business.

MANAGEMENT ENGINEERING FOR FUTURE OPERATIONS

Management engineering should be as useful in long-range planning as it is in ongoing operations. Many planning decisions have major effects on the cost of operating any facility. Initial decisions establishing demand projections are used to establish staffing budgets. Facility layout and design affect movement distances, and equipment decisions influence labor utilization.

The first step in long-range planning is to determine who the institution is serving with what services. Next, projected changes in service areas and services to be provided are made. Management engineering can provide mathematical forecasting models. Too often the effects of these changes are assumed without question. For example, if the projected service area is doubling in size, the planner assumes that a proportionate change

will take place in the institution. Likewise, the planner assumes that all new technology must be provided by the institution. It is rare to have the planner say, "Wait a minute, we can't be all things to all people!" This happens only after some sort of financial study is performed and infeasibility is indicated, which occurs usually after large amounts of time, dollars, and effort have already been expended.

Early in the planning stages, the resource implications of programmatic decisions must be assessed. The two major resources of a hospital are facilities and labor. The early question to be answered is: Who is going to pay for the new service? A part of any early long-range planning efforts must be a preliminary financial feasibility or debt load study to determine how much money is required. Another realistic concern is the availability of sophisticated skills to operate new services.

The technology of the management engineer must be utilized in the planning effort. Labor forecasting, itself a skill, should not be based on what is now done, but on what should be done and what can be done if the constraints of existing sites, buildings, and equipment are removed.

The projected volume of service workload will dictate the amount of space required. There is a direct relationship between workload, labor, and space. Most space programmers now determine space based on workstations, the major centers of activity within a department. These workstations either are a function of labor or dictate labor. Inaccurate or nonprecise projections of workload may have a negative effect on the utilization of manpower.

Facility design can affect labor utilization in at least two ways. Layouts of departments and workstations would be based on the function that is to be performed and should incorporate ways in which labor utilization can be reduced, such as reductions of walking distances, elimination of reaching at workstations, or provision of sufficient and easily accessible storage. It is rare that the management engineer and users are brought into the facility design process.

The other effect on labor utilization is lack of sufficient facilities. Seldom does a health facilities planner consider life-cycle costs, the total costs of acquiring and operating a facility over the life of the facility. Ongoing operating costs and initial capital costs are equated utilizing present value or present worth techniques.[23] Too often, the capital budget is exceeded and must be reduced, resulting in smaller spaces, less elevators, and less automation, all of which increase labor requirements. Because the operating costs of any health institution exceed the initial capital costs in two to four years, they should be the deciding factor in the establishment of the initial capital budget.

Most Certificate of Need regulations and investment bankers require financial feasibility studies and labor budgets. These studies establish a base for developing a productivity reporting system and illustrate the relationship between operating costs and capital investment costs. The author recently has been involved in two building programs ($20,000,000 plus and $60,000,000 plus) in which projected labor savings due to increased productivity provided the basis for pursuing the project. In one case, a one-year cost containment program reduced the payroll in excess of $4 million. The effect on the profit and loss and balance sheets was sufficient to handle the additional debt financing required for the project. In the second case, projected labor savings due to more efficient facility organization, layout, and equipment was accepted by planning authorities for the issuance of a Certificate of Need.

New facilities can be designed, planned, and operated in many ways to increase productivity and achieve cost-containment goals. One such way is to eliminate a centralized nursing station in nursing unit design. The "no-nursing station" concept decentralizes many nursing duties, transfers nonnursing administrative duties to nonnursing personnel, provides sophisticated communication and message handling systems, and enables storage of all supplies in the patient room. A study in one hospital, which was subsequently confirmed in several others, showed that although the number of nonnursing personnel increased, the same quality of patient care had been provided with a 14 percent reduction in total labor.[24]

Management Engineering in the Organized Delivery System

The tools of the management engineer are applicable to a department or a multiunit organized health care delivery system. The major differences are in one's perspective. The major need for an organized delivery system is to be price competitive in a highly competitive health care delivery environment. Price competitive implies that the organized delivery system can satisfy all the health care needs of its customers (constituents, covered lives) at a price that is equal to (with service differentiation) or less than a competitor. The major elements are keeping your customers healthy, identifying and containing costs, pricing strategies that differentiate both customer needs and services provided, and monitoring and reporting on the quality/service levels of its customers.

Keeping Your Customers Healthy

Disease management is the current term used to produce "healthy" customers. The development of a disease management program for any "at risk" population is the basic application of management engineering tools:

- measure existing system (how large is the population group, what are the outcome measures)
- identify improvements (decreased mortality, reduced hospitalization)
- provide design criteria (monitoring behavioral changes, therapeutic interventions)
- monitor implementation (compliance of constituents to plan)
- monitor output (goal achievement)

Identifying and Containing Costs

Most, if not all, organized delivery systems result from the consolidation of health care providers and in some cases payers. This consolidation, with the decrease in inpatient utilization of inpatient health care services, has resulted in significant excess capacity. Many authors have suggested that consolidation of health care providers has not resulted in decreased health care delivery costs. Some even imply increased costs. The author's perspective is that in most cases, this is true. However, this is not because the opportunity for reduced costs does not exist, but because the management engineering tools are not applied.

The key word in consolidation is *resize*. Resize to recognize the change in market demand (decreased inpatient, increased outpatient) and the duplication of services, be it diagnostic and treatment or administrative.

This resizing can be facility directed by:

- identifying the market demands
- allocating these to locations (both current and new)
- translating these workloads into manpower and space requirements
- resizing the existing facilities to accommodate the projections and/or sizing new locations
- establishing a resized management organization to implement and manage the resizing
- identifying the cost of the resized delivery system
- establishing management controls to contain the resized costs

Pricing Strategies

The resizing provides the first step in developing pricing strategies. The potential that costs are too high to be competitive still exists. The resizing step identifies costs of all programs. The next step will require the reduction, elimination, or outsourcing of certain services. The management engineer's analysis provides the basis for these decisions. The analysis also should provide a basis for "loss leader" pricing.

Quality and Service

The final application is to engineer a monitoring and reporting system that can be utilized to demonstrate to the customers/payers how the organized delivery system works. This requires a systemwide quality and productivity reporting system.

NOTES

1. G. Salvendy, *Handbook of Industrial Engineering* (New York: John Wiley & Sons, Inc., 1982).
2. Ibid.
3. Ibid.
4. H.E. Smalley and J.R. Freeman, *Hospital Management Engineering: A Guide to the Improvement of*

Hospital Management Systems (Englewood Cliffs, NJ: Prentice-Hall, Inc., 1982).

5. K.G. Bartscht et al., *Hospital Staffing Methodology Manuals* (Ann Arbor, MI: Community Systems Foundation, 1968).

6. N.H. Berg, "Medical Center Applies Financial Strategies to Renovation Project," *Hospitals* 53 (February 1979).

7. S.P. Gray and W. Steffy, *Hospital Cost Containment Through Productivity Management* (New York: Van Nostrand Reinhold Co., 1983).

8. American Hospital Association, *Management of Hospital Employee Productivity: An Introductory Handbook* (Chicago: American Hospital Association, 1973), 1.

9. Arthur Andersen & Co. and the American College of Hospital Administrators, *Health Care in the 1990s: Trends and Strategies* (Alexandria, VA: ACHA, 1984).

10. K.G. Bartscht, "Productivity Management: Integral Element in the Management Process," *Health Care Systems* 15 (May/June 1976): 3.

11. American Hospital Association, *Management Engineering for Hospitals* (Chicago: American Hospital Association, 1970), 13.

12. D.D. Rutstein, *Blueprint for Medical Care* (Cambridge: MIT Press, 1974).

13. L. Urdang, ed., *Random House Dictionary of the English Language, College Edition* (New York: Random House, 1968), 1080.

14. W.J. Gavett, *Production and Operations Management* (New York: Harcourt, Brace & World, Inc., 1968).

15. H. Weiner, *The Human Use of Human Beings* (Boston: Houghton Mifflin Co., 1950).

16. R.A. Johnson, F.E. Kast, and J.E. Rosenzweig, *Theory and Management of Systems* (New York: McGraw-Hill, 1963).

17. Chi Systems, Inc., *A Proposal To Develop and Implement an Innovative Quality-Productivity Management Program to Blue Cross of Greater Philadelphia, Pennsylvania for Graduate Hospital of The University of Pennsylvania, Philadelphia, Pennsylvania* (Ann Arbor, MI: Chi Systems, Inc., 1976), 11.

18. R.J. Coffey, Preadmission Testing of Hospitalized Patients and Its Relationship to Length of Stay (dissertation, University of Michigan, 1975).

19. D.M. Warner, Preliminary Analysis of Benefits of Preadmission Tested (PAT) Patients (Unpublished paper, University of Michigan, 1972).

20. E.L. Grant, and G.W. Ireson, *Principles of Engineering Economy*, 5th ed. (New York: The Ronald Press Co., 1970).

21. Comptroller General of the United States, *Study of Health Facilities Construction Cost, Report to Congress* (Washington, DC: U.S. Government Printing Office, November 20, 1972).

22. K.G. Bartscht, "An Analytic Approach to Nursing Scheduling," *Hospital Topics* (September 1963).

23. D.D. Rutstein, *Blueprint for Medical Care.*

24. Comptroller General of the United States, *Study of Health Facilities Construction Cost.*

KARL BARTSCHT, MSE, FAAHC, has planned, designed, and managed health systems since 1961. He is presently CEO of The Chi Group, Inc., and its affiliated companies: Chi Systems, Inc., Michigan Health Systems, and International Health Care Management, Inc.

At Chi Systems, Mr. Bartscht has directed the development of long-range strategic plans and implementation strategies for numerous health care institutions. His expertise includes strategies for minimizing institutional life-cycle costs through evaluation of the trade-offs between capital investment and reduced operating costs.

Mr. Bartscht also serves as CEO of Michigan Health Systems, Inc. (MHS), a for-profit organization formed by Chi Systems and a number of Michigan not-for-profit hospitals. MHS has developed networks for the sharing of services among cooperating institutions, distribution of MHS products, and establishment of competitive strategies to improve market position and revenue generation for network participants. International Health Care Management, Inc., is a management company for 18 nursing homes with 2,700 beds.

Consulting assistance has been provided by Mr. Bartscht for some of the nation's largest health care organizations, as well as for the U.S. and Canadian governments.

In addition, Mr. Bartscht has been extremely active in research and development efforts, including the development of computerized financial planning models; the design of planning/ marketing databases; development, design, construction, and operation of a prototype nursing station; design of burn care units; design of patient scheduling systems; development of hospital staffing methodologies; and development of methodologies for planning and evaluating departmental space requirements.

Mr. Bartscht is publisher of two monthly professional journals: *Health Care Strategic Management*, which deals with the full range of strategic planning issues facing today's health care organizations, and *Hospital Materials Management*, a journal of health care materials management.

Part II

The Hospital in an Organized Delivery System

This Part is devoted to matters that relate to the hospital or functions that occur at the hospital level, particularly those in an organized delivery system.

Chapter 14

History of Hospitals

Lawrence F. Wolper and Jesus J. Peña

MEDICINE AND HOSPITALS AS POLITICAL FACTORS

Traditionally, medical historians and educators often have overlooked the relationship of medicine, in general, and hospitals, in particular, to political and economic affairs, prevailing social attitudes, and discoveries related to medicine.

Medicine and surgery date back to the beginning of civilization because diseases preceded humans on earth. Early medical treatment was always identified with religious services and ceremonies. Priests were also physicians or medicine men, ministering to spirit, mind, and body; priest/doctors were part of the ruling class, with great political influence, and the temple/hospital was also a meeting place.

The role of the priest/doctor and later the role of the temples as houses of refuge for the sick and infirm and as training schools for doctors are closely associated with the civilization's level of political development. The sophistication of the health care system has often been used for political propaganda to demonstrate the superiority of civilization. The pagan Greek temples served a political role, as was evidenced when the Christian Emperor Constantine closed the Aesculapia. The same political motivation can be seen in the spread of Moslem hospitals under Islamic rule in the seventh century and the efforts of the Soviet bloc health care system to manipulate health statistics to prove its claims of success in Cuba. For example, in a careful analysis of Cuban demographic data, Kenneth Hill of the National Academy of Sciences found that "the consistency between the indirect and official incidence of infant mortality disappears. The indirect estimates indicate constant, or even rising child mortality, while the official figures show a continuous rapid decline."[1] This is a classic example of the use of the health care system for political purposes. The current movements toward health care reform in the United States, as well as in many European (Eastern and Western) countries and the former Soviet Union are further and current examples of the interrelationships among politics, economics, and societal values.

MESOPOTAMIA

Medicine as an organized entity first appeared 4,000 years ago in the ancient region of Southwest Asia known as Mesopotamia. Between the Tigris and Euphrates rivers, which have their origin in Asia Minor and merge to flow into the Persian Gulf, this fertile land has been called the cradle of civilization.

The first recorded doctor's prescription came from Sumer in ancient Babylon under the rule of the dynasty of Hammurabi (1728–1686 B.C.). Hammurabi's code of laws provides the first record of the regulation of doctors' practices, as well as the regulation of their fees. The Mesopotamian civilization made political, educational, and medical contributions to the later development of the Egyptian, Hebrew, Persian, and even Indian cultures.

GREEK HOSPITALS

For hundreds of years, the Greeks enjoyed the benefits of contact and cross-fertilization of ideas with numerous other ancient peoples, especially the Egyptians. Although patients were treated by magic rituals and cures were related to miracles and divine intervention, the Greeks recognized the natural causes of disease, and rational methods of healing were important. In addition, what was known of human anatomy and physiology was more of a rational than a superstitious or religious nature.

Hippocrates is usually considered the personification of the rational nonreligious approach to medicine, and in 480 B.C., he started to use auscultation, perform surgical operations, and provide historians with detailed records of his patients and descriptions of diseases ranging from tuberculosis to ulcers. The temples of Saturn, Hygeia, and Aesculapius, the Greek god of medicine, all served as both medical schools for practitioners and resting places for patients under observation or treatment.

INDIAN HOSPITALS

Historical records show that efficient hospitals were constructed in India by 600 B.C. During the splendid reign of King Asoka (273–232 B.C.), Indian hospitals started to look like modern hospitals: They followed principles of sanitation, and cesarean sections were performed with close attention to technique in order to save both mother and infant. Physicians were appointed—one for every 10 villages—to serve the health care needs of the population, and regional hospitals for the infirm and destitute were built by Buddha.

ROMAN HOSPITALS

The Roman talent for organization did not extend as readily to institutional care of the sick and injured. Although infirmaries for the sick slaves were established, it was only among the military legions that a system for hospitalization was developed. After the injured were cared for in field tents, the soldiers were moved to valetudinaries, a form of hospital erected in all garrisons along the frontiers. Apparently, those stone and wooden structures were carefully planned and were stocked with instruments, supplies, and medications.

The decree of Emperor Constantine in 335 A.D. closed the Aesculapia and stimulated the building of Christian hospitals. However, it was not until 369 A.D. that the wealthy Romans, converted to Christianity, started to build hospitals from Justinian to the benefactress, Fabiola, who built a hospital in 394 A.D.

ISLAMIC HOSPITALS

During the seventh century, the new evangelical religion of Islam began to preserve the classical learning still extant, which it later yielded to the European world.

The development of efficient hospitals was an outstanding contribution of Islamic civilization. The Roman military hospitals and the few Christian hospitals were no match for the number, organization, and excellence of the Arabic hospitals.

The Arabs' medical inspiration came largely from the Persian Hospital in Djoundisabour (sixth century, Turkey), at which many of them studied. Returning to their homes, they founded institutions that were remarkably well organized for the times. During the time of Mohammed, a real system of hospitals was developed. Asylums for the insane were founded 10 centuries before they first appeared in Europe. In addition, Islamic physicians were responsible for the establishment of pharmacy and chemistry as sciences.

Some of the best known of the great hospitals in the Middle Ages were in Baghdad, Damascus, and Cairo. In particular, the hospital and medical school of Damascus had elegant rooms, an extensive library, and a great reputation for its cuisine.

In the Arabic hospitals, separate wards were set aside for different diseases, such as fever, eye conditions, diarrhea, wounds, and gynecological disorders. Convalescing patients were separated from sicker patients, and provisions were made for ambulatory patients. Clinical reports of cases were collected and used for teaching.

THE MIDDLE AGES

From the early Middle Ages in the fourth century to the late Middle Ages in the fifteenth century, trade was almost totally suppressed, and many city dwellers returned to the land. Religious communities assumed responsibility for care of the sick. The rational nonreligious approach that characterized Greek medicine during the era of Hippocrates was lost, as hospitals became ecclesiastical, not medical, institutions. Only the hopeless and homeless found their way to these hospitals, in which the system of separation of patients by diseases was eliminated, three to five patients were accommodated in each bed, and principles of sanitation were ig-

nored. Surgery was avoided, with the exception of amputation, in order not to "disturb the body" and to avoid the shedding of blood per the church edict of 1163 that, in effect, forbade the clergy from performing operations. Religious orders emphasized nursing care; the first religious order devoted solely to nursing is considered to be the St. Augustine nuns, organized in approximately 1155.

Yet, hospital construction increased in Europe during the Middle Ages for two reasons. First, Pope Innocent III in 1198 urged wealthy Christians to build hospitals in every town, and second, increased revenues were available from the commerce with the Crusaders. The oldest hospitals still in existence are the Hotels-Dieu in Lyons and Paris, France. The term "Hotel-Dieu" indicates that it is a public hospital. The earliest mention of the Hotel-Dieu in Lyons is found in a manuscript of 580 A.D., in which its establishment by Childebert is recorded. The Hotel-Dieu of Paris was founded by Bishop Landry in 660, on the Ile de la Cite. In 1300, the hospital had an attending staff of physicians and surgeons caring for 800 to 900 patients, and its capacity was doubled in the fifteenth century. By the seventeenth century, it had been enlarged to two buildings, linked by the Pont au Double. In about 1880, these buildings were replaced on the island by the present Hotel-Dieu.

St. Bartholomew's Hospital, which was established in London in 1123, was attached to the Augustinian Priory of (Great) St. Bartholomew. Both church and hospital still exist, but the hospital was rebuilt between 1730–1759. The Hospital of Santo Spirito was built in Rome in 1204 by Pope Innocent III. By 1447, it housed 360 beds and utilized a system of stretcher-ambulances. The hospital survived on the same location until 1922, when it was destroyed by fire, but it was later rebuilt. The development of hospitals in Germany occurred largely in the thirteenth and fourteenth centuries through the activities of the Order of the Holy Ghost and the Order of the Lazarites. In Belgium, the still-active hospital of St. John in Bruges was established in the twelfth century.

In contrast, in Asia and Africa during the same period, construction of effective and efficient hospitals was spurred by Islamic rule and the Crusades. The two hospital systems enforced sanitary measures, performed surgery, and separated patients according to diseases: the Islamic hospitals because they were still following the Greek and early Roman traditions, and the hospitals created by the Crusaders because injuries sustained in combat necessitated surgery and the presence of pests and contagious diseases necessitated sanitary conditions and the strict separation of patients.

During the period of the Crusades (1096–1270), religious orders, which had as their chief duty the care of the sick, built a number of hospitals in the Mediterranean area. The most famous of these orders was the Knights of Saint John of Jerusalem. Because of the need to treat the casualties of combat, large hospitals with up to 2,000 beds were built. For years, those hospitals were the only active institutions following the advanced hospital practices other than the Islamic hospitals. For the first time, medical systems of the East and West vied for the supremacy of medical care.

HOSPITALS DURING THE RENAISSANCE

The Renaissance period lasted from the fourteenth to the sixteenth centuries. It received its name from the Italian "rinascita," meaning rebirth, because of a common belief that it embodied a return to the cultural priorities of ancient Rome and Greece. The healing arts were again characterized by a scientific, rational approach.

The academic world of northern Italy was tolerant of new cosmopolitan ideas. By the mid-fifteenth century, all major courts and cities of Europe sent their finest physicians to Italy for advanced training.

If the Middle Ages can be seen as the period of the great hospitals, the Renaissance was really the period of the great schools of medicine. Schools of medicine flourished in Germany and in central and eastern Europe. The scientific study of human anatomy as a science was facilitated by dissections of animals. In 1506, the Royal College of Surgeons was organized in England, followed by the organization of the Royal College of Physicians in 1528.

The major contribution of the Renaissance to the development of hospitals was in improved management of the hospital, the return to the segregation of patients by diseases, and the higher quality of medicine provided within the hospital. Clinical surgery took great strides during this period, not only in Italy but also in France, especially under Ambrose Pare, who reintroduced the ancient methods of stopping hemorrhage by using ligatures and abandoned the barbaric system of cauterizing irons. Epidemic chorea, sweating sickness, and leprosy had almost ceased to exist, although syphilis continued to be common.

In the English Reformation from 1536–1539, hospitals affiliated with the Catholic church were plundered by King Henry VIII and were ordered to convert to secular uses or be destroyed. Many hospitals in the countryside of England were forced to close their doors and remained closed for two centuries. Only the powerful hospitals in London survived when the citizens petitioned the King to endow St. Bartholomew, St. Thomas, and St.

Mary of Bethlehem hospitals. This was the first instance of secular support of hospitals.

HOSPITALS ON THE AMERICAN CONTINENT

The first hospitals of the New World were built in colonies of Spain, France, and England. Those built under the flags of Catholic Spain and France retained the ideals of the Jesuits, the Sisters of Charity, and the Augustinian Sisters and their hundreds of years of hospital knowledge. Hospitals built in the English colonies, however, reacted against English traditions.

The first hospital in the New World was constructed as part of a system for the occupation of overseas territories. Bartolome de las Casas, one of the priests who accompanied Columbus on his first voyage and a well-known historian, referred to the founding of the village of La Isabella in Hispaniola (today, Santo Domingo) in January of 1494: "Columbus made haste in constructing a house to keep supplies and the ammunition for the soldiers, a church and a hospital."[2] No further information survives to indicate whether the hospital was actually built. However, extant documents show that a hospital was built in St. Nicholas of Bari by mid-1494 and that, during the same year, it housed 40 Spaniards who were injured during an Indian revolt. Unfortunately, most of the hospital records were destroyed during the pillage of the city by Sir Francis Drake in 1586. The same hospital, in a different location, provided health care until 1883.

In Mexico, Hernan Cortes erected the Immaculate Conception Hospital in Mexico City in 1524, which is still an active hospital. In 1541, the Spanish crown passed a decree that required construction of a hospital in all Spanish and Indian towns of the New World.

In Quebec, Canada, in 1639, the French constructed the first hospital, the Hotel Dieu du Precieux Sanz, which was founded by the Duchess d'Aquilon. The Hotel Dieu de St. Joseph was founded in Montreal in 1644. In the English colonies, the oldest hospital was a small alms-house for the poor that was supported by a church in the city of New Amsterdam. This house and a tiny hospital established by the West Indian Company in 1658 eventually were combined and grew into the City Hospital of Bellevue in New York City.

The eighteenth-century American hospitals, except for the New Amsterdam Hospital and the one constructed in New Orleans by the Catholic church in 1720, departed from the charitable and religious spirit of the Old World hospitals. American institutions followed the model of the Pennsylvania Hospital, which was founded in 1751. According to an inscription on its wall, the institution intended to foster patients' self-respect and remove any stigma from a hospital visit by charging fees. Benjamin Franklin helped to design the hospital, which was built to provide a place for Philadelphia physicians to hospitalize their private patients. Franklin served as president from 1755 to 1757.

In another break with tradition, the New York Hospital was founded in 1771 by private citizens who formed the Society of the New York Hospital and obtained a grant to build it. The hospital was characterized by a spirit of learning and research. As with other hospitals founded before the era of large fortunes, the New York Hospital was built on the contributions of small merchants and farmers.

Another innovation was the first hospital conducted only by women. The New York Infirmary for Women and Children was opened in 1853 by the first woman to earn a medical degree in the United States, Elizabeth Blackwell, and her sister. Again, this is another example of a privately owned hospital that was founded to accommodate physicians' needs.

The earliest federal involvement in hospital care was mandated by the 1798 United States Marine Hospital Service Act, which provided hospital care for disabled seamen. This Act was, in reality, a compulsory insurance plan, because wages were deducted for health care. As a result of the Act, the first Marine hospital was built in Norfolk, Virginia, in 1802, and in the same year, another was built in Boston, Massachusetts. In the following year, another Marine hospital was built in Newport, Rhode Island, and by 1861, there were 30 Marine hospitals. After the Civil War, the Marine hospitals admitted Army and Navy personnel and became the forerunner of the Veterans Affairs Hospitals.

At the beginning of the twentieth century, nearly all of the U.S. hospitals were independent, either under voluntary or private auspices. However, after 1926, the number of tax-supported hospitals increased dramatically, and tax refunds were used to pay for many poor patients in voluntary hospitals.

The first psychiatric hospital in the United States was built in Williamsburg, Virginia, in 1773. This was the beginning of a large-scale construction of state psychiatric hospitals, which by 1950 reached a total of 557 hospitals with 628,300 beds. This movement came to a halt in 1955 with the discovery of psychotropic medication and the movement toward deinstitutionalization. In 1984, there were only 275 psychiatric hospitals, with 157,600 beds.

The European and Latin American tradition of charity hospitals, based on love of God and neighbors and the conviction that the government owed a responsibility to helpless citizens, was never part of U.S. hospital traditions. As a result, a more competitive system

of hospitals developed, with fewer subsidies and less involvement of religious organizations in total health care. Massive government involvements in health care began in 1926 with the return of veterans from World War I. The possible bias in the system is indicated best by the fee schedule of 1870, in which delirium tremens cases were charged twice the normal fee. Yet, the positive element of the early system was that those who paid and those who did not slept side by side, but nonpaying patients were assigned housekeeping or simple nursing duties.

HOSPITALS IN THE SEVENTEENTH, EIGHTEENTH, AND NINETEENTH CENTURIES

The seventeenth century was the age of the scientific revolution, a major turning point in the history of hospitals and medicine. The mood of the century was not to find out why things happened, but how they happened. No longer was speculation accepted, but experimentation was the common denominator of scientific work. William Harvey's (1578–1657) proof of the continuous circulation of the blood within a contained system was the seventeenth century's most significant achievement in physiology and medicine. Experimentation led to the wide use of thermometry in clinical practice.

One of the most important inventions in the development of medicine and general science was the microscope. The two giants of seventeenth-century microscopy were Marcello Malpighi (1628–1694) and Anthony van Leeuwenhoek (1632–1723).

In 1661, a book published in England, *Natural and Political Observations...Made Upon the Bill of Mortality* by John Gaunt, for the first time presented the idea that a large population was an asset to a country and that public health measures were a necessity. The book advocated measures to preserve and restore health, such as separate hospitals for plague victims, specialized maternity institutions, government concern for the health of occupational groups, and the establishment of a central health council to organize public health. However, these measures were too far advanced for the seventeenth-century thinking and were ignored.

In the seventeenth century, new hospitals were only constructed in the new lands colonized in the Americas. The old hospitals in Europe were either slumbering under the maternal care of the Church, as in Italy; were passing into the control of national or municipal governments, as in France and Germany; or new hospitals were being founded by an enlightened crown, as in Denmark, Germany, and Austria.

During the eighteenth century, there was a partial revival in the construction of hospitals in England. A movement was started to build a hospital in every parish by 1732. A total of 115 hospitals were already built by the parishioners, with the best known of them being St. Peters of Bristol. At the same time, philanthropists, such as Thomas Guy, founded hospitals for both charity and paying patients, including the Guy's Hospital in 1724, St. George's Hospital in 1733, and the Great London Hospital in 1740. The Quakers were very active in hospital construction as well, with William Tuke (1732–1822) founding the York Retreat for the Humane Care of the Mentally Ill.

The discovery of vaccination was the key medical achievement of the eighteenth century. Lady Mary Wortley Montagu (1689–1762) brought back to England the Asian technique of variolation, which she had observed in Turkey. In this procedure, serum extracted from the sore of a person with smallpox was injected into another person's skin to produce a resistance resulting from a mild case of the illness.

The eighteenth century was not merely a period of mass construction of new hospitals, but a period of consolidation and systematization. Physicians and hospitals, overwhelmed by the revolutionary discoveries of the previous century, struggled bravely to absorb and utilize the mass of new technology.

The nineteenth century is the keystone in the history of hospitals and is considered to be the beginning of modern medicine. Several events combined to produce the framework for the modern hospital.

The building of factories and the expansion of cities, with overcrowding of urban areas, occurred during the Industrial Revolution (1790–1825). The health of workers in the factories was important to their efficient functioning, and because the spread of epidemic disease was a danger to all segments of the population, the need for remedial measures was obvious. As a result, in every major city the construction of hospitals accelerated.

The assembling of large numbers of troops for the American Civil War (1861–1865) was accompanied by the inevitable outbreaks of communicable diseases. In the armies of both the North and South, little attention was paid to camp sanitation, and no provision was made for decent housing or food. Due to the lack of planning, the enormous numbers of casualties from the first few battles lay abandoned in the field for as long as two or three days.

Gradually, both armies evolved effective ambulance and hospital systems, procured adequate medical supplies, and developed well-trained surgeons. Yet, it was not until the battle of Gettysburg (July 1863) that the Union forces were able to remove their wounded from the field at the end of each day's fighting. It took two years of bloodshed to develop a good medical corps and an effective system of field hospitals. These advances in hospital management became part of the increasing development of the American hospital system and led to the creation of the Veterans Affairs hospitals.

The legacy of Florence Nightingale may be the greatest contribution of the nineteenth century to the evolution of hospitals. The introduction of professional nursing services, which provided kindly treatment and emphasized a clean environment, was a giant step forward in institutional treatment.

Miss Nightingale began nursing training in Germany in 1836 and almost immediately wrote about the lack of hygiene in the German hospitals. Upon returning to England, she started implementing her ideas and acquired a reputation as an innovator. In 1854, the English government called her to improve the conditions of the sick and wounded soldiers during the Crimean War. She organized laundry services, kitchens, and a central supply department, and in 10 days reduced the death rate from 38 percent to an acceptable 2 percent.

Her capacity for organization and administration was endless. After returning to England, Nightingale founded the first school of nursing in 1860. In 1863, the school graduated the first group of 15 nurses, who later devoted their efforts to the promotion of nursing schools. Nightingale's writings were largely responsible for the transformation of nursing from a low, unpopular, and almost casual endeavor into a highly respected, essential part of the healing art.

Another important event in the history of hospitals was the discovery of bacteria as the causes of disease. Before that discovery, the principal focus of preventive medicine and elimination of infections in hospitals was sanitation: The provision of potable waters and the dispersal of foul odors remedied problems that were considered to be the important factors in causing epidemics.

It was Ignaz Semmelweis (1818–1865), who, in keeping with the new statistical spirit of the nineteenth century, assembled and analyzed the clinical care data in the obstetrical wards of the Allgemines Krankenhaus Hospital in Vienna to prove the contagious nature of postpartum infections. The next step for Semmelweis was clear: to require physicians and students under his charge to scrub their hands with soap and water and soak them in a chlorinated lime solution before entering the clinic or ward and to repeat this after each examination. In 3 months, the obstetrical death rate declined from 18 to 1½ percent.

A few years later, Louis Pasteur (1822–1895) proved that bacteria were produced by reproduction and were not spontaneous, as previously believed. He is considered the father of bacteriology. Joseph Lister (1827–1912) continued Pasteur's work. Lister noticed that broken bones over which the skin was intact usually healed without complication; when they were exposed, however, fractures developed the same type of infection that grew in amputations and other operations. He suggested that this finding provided additional evidence that some element circulating in the body was responsible for the infections. By 1870, the hospitals in Germany were paying strong attention to Lister's theories and sprayed carbolic solution in the operating room, drenching both surgeons and patients. As a result, it was possible to perform major surgery without fear of infection.

The discovery of anesthesia and steam sterilization modernized the practice of surgery and enabled it to be performed frequently. By 1831, all three basic anesthetic agents—ether, nitrous oxide gas, and chloroform—had been discovered, but no medical applications of their pain-relieving properties had been performed. It is believed that Dr. Clariford W. Long (1815–1878) of Georgia was the first to perform minor operations using sulfuric ether in 1842. The introduction of steam sterilization in 1886 was the beginning of surgical asepsis, in contrast with earlier, less effective antisepsis measures.

The three discoveries—bacteria as the cause of diseases, anesthesia, and steam sterilization—enabled the development of the modern hospital. By 1895, the foundation of the modern hospital was completed with the discovery of the X-ray by Wilhelm Konrad Roentgen (1845–1923). Hospitals were no longer a place where the sick and homeless found refuge and care, but rather a special place where treatment and more exact diagnosis were aided by technology. At the same time, the cost of hospital care increased dramatically, and hospitals were placed in direct competition with the private practitioner, who usually was unable to afford the costly equipment.

The American Medical Association was founded in 1847 under the leadership of Dr. Nathan Smith Davis (1817–1907). In 1864, 16 nations signed a treaty establishing the International Red Cross and specifying regulations for the treatment of wounded soldiers, including the provision that all hospitals—military and civilian—were to be neutral territory. Another landmark in the history of hospitals occurred in the nineteenth century when women were finally accepted as full-fledged medical practitioners, after a long struggle.

The next logical step in the development of medicine was specialization. By the end of the nineteenth and the beginning of the twentieth centuries, specialties and subspecialties developed to the extent that no general branch of medicine or surgery was without its subdivision of specialization.

As a result of all the above-mentioned discoveries and events, a great number of hospitals were constructed in the United States in a short period of time: for example, in Chi-cago—Mercy Hospital, 1852; Cook County, 1863; St. Luke, 1864; Chicago Hospital for Women, 1865; and the Jewish Hospital, 1868; in New York City—Roosevelt Hospital, 1871; Presbyterian Hospital, 1872; Polyclinic, 1881; and Cancer Hospital, 1886; and in Baltimore, Johns Hopkins Hospital, 1889.

By the end of that century, there were 149 hospitals in the United States with a bed capacity of 35,500. Less than 10 percent of all these hospitals were under government control of any kind.

THE MODERN HOSPITAL AND HEALTH SYSTEMS

The ideal modern hospital is a place both where ailing people seek and receive care and where clinical education is provided to medical students, nurses, and virtually the whole spectrum of health professionals. It provides continuing education for the practicing physicians and increasingly serves the function of an institution of higher learning for entire neighborhoods, communities, and regions. In addition to its educational role, the modern hospital conducts investigation studies and research in medical sciences both from clinical records and from its patients, as well as basic research in science, physics, and chemistry.

The construction of the modern hospital is regulated or influenced by federal laws, state health department regulations, city ordinances, the standards of the Joint Commission on Accreditation of Healthcare Organizations, and national and local codes (building, fire protection, sanitation, etc.). These requirements safeguard patients' privacy and the safety and well-being of patients and staff, and control cross-infections. The popular ward concept of the mid-nineteenth century is no longer permissible, and today hospitals have mainly semiprivate and private rooms. Although permissible in most states, four-bed rooms are seldom planned.

The changing emphasis from inpatient to outpatient service and rapid advances in medical technology have focused recent facility planning activities on medical ancillary expansion and freestanding outpatient centers. Developing separate or freestanding buildings has allowed hospitals to minimize the financial impact of restrictive hospital building codes and regulations.

However, the rapid expansion of nonhospital-based and independent ambulatory care facilities slowed substantially beginning in the late 1980s as a result of changes in reimbursement, deteriorating rates of reimbursement, and an overall decline in the economy. Hospital failures increased, as did bed closings. In addition, there was an increase in federal and state antikickback and safe harbor regulations that dampened the enthusiasm for joint ventures for nonhospital-based facilities.

The early 1990s and beyond place the hospital in the position of being only one component in the evolution toward organized delivery systems and other provider networks. In fact, hospitals in the future may be the subordinate organization within the emerging organized delivery system, replaced by a corporate enterprise with responsibility for operating a large system. Currently, most of these systems may be developing to protect the interests of the hospital. In the future, and as a new generation of health care system executives replace the hospital executive, the role of the hospital may be narrowed to serve patients with extreme problems or those with no financial or insurance capability to be cared for at home or at nonhospital provider organizations.

Inpatient care will diminish with continued advances in medicine, and hospitals are likely to downsize. Simultaneously, ambulatory and doctors' office care will increase. The hospital, particularly compared with its earliest days, will play a very different role in the future as part of an integrated collection of providers and sites of care.

CLASSIFICATION OF HOSPITALS

The need has long been recognized for a system that would both integrate and differentiate terminology, definitions, and essential characteristics of health care institutions. The difficulties encountered in trying to relate and compare data obtained by different agencies using differing terminology and definitions have been apparent for many years. So also have been problems related to licensure, registration, accreditation, certification of institutions, and the financing of health care. The following discussion summarizes the most common systems of hospital classification now in use.

Public Access

One of the oldest and most useful systems of classification is used by the American Hospital Association (AHA) in its annual Hospital Statistics manual. That classification divides hospitals into community and noncommunity hospitals according to the degree of public access to the hospital.

Community hospitals include all nonfederal short-term general and other special hospitals, excluding hospital units of institutions, the facilities and services of which are available to the public. Noncommunity hospitals include federal hospitals; long-term hospitals; hospital units of institutions, such as prison hospitals or college infirmaries; psychiatric hospitals; hospitals for tuberculosis and other respiratory diseases; chronic disease hospitals; institutions for the mentally retarded; and alcoholism and chemical dependency hospitals.

Ownership

Another type of classification is by ownership or control of the policies and operation of the hospital. Institutions are divided into four groupings under this classification: (1) government, nonfederal; (2) nongovernment, not for profit; (3) investor-owned, for profit; and (4) government, federal.

Government, nonfederal, includes all hospitals that are owned or operated by states, counties, or cities and are supported by state, county, or city appropriations. Although these appropriations are decreasing and are being replaced by reimbursements from third-party private payers, the political subdivision still retains the legal responsibility to cover deficits and to control policies and operations. Even though the administration of government, nonfederal hospitals has changed over the past decade, with most of these hospitals now being run by some type of a board of trustees, the power of the trustees is limited. The board oversees the quality of care rendered, but does not assume the combination of quality assurance and fiduciary responsibilities held by the boards of nongovernment, not-for-profit hospitals.

The largest group of the government nonfederal hospitals—the state psychiatric hospitals—has considerably decreased in number since 1955 because of the policies of deinstitutionalization of mentally ill patients and the availability of psychotropic medication.

Nongovernment, not-for-profit hospitals or voluntary institutions are owned and maintained by the organization represented in their incorporation certificate, which has no connection with any government subdivision. Their operating expenses are covered from patient fees, including third-party payments, donations, endowments, or assessments of its donors. In some localities, a city or state may agree to subsidize a not-for-profit hospital to enable it to provide services to nonpaying patients or to offer special services, but this is considered a subsidy with no control attached. The nonprofit, nongovernment hospitals comprise the largest group of hospitals, and their percentage of total beds has increased in the last three decades with the decreasing number and size of the state and local psychiatric centers. Yet, a new force in the hospital industry, the for-profit hospital, is becoming an increasingly strong competitor.

Control and ultimate responsibilities over nonprofit, nongovernment hospitals are vested with a board of trustees. The hospital is tax-exempt because of its charitable nature, but it is not dependent on government appropriations. The largest group among the not-for-profit hospitals are the religious organization hospitals, which are usually incorporated under a church or under a separate charter.

Due to the increase in operating costs of the independent not-for-profit hospitals, a new entity has flourished during the last 20 years—the multihospital system. The for-profit sector has very successfully applied the principle of economy of scale in the ownership of several hospitals, and recently not-for-profit hospitals have joined together to enhance their ability to obtain capital, increase revenues through the greater number of beds, and generate purchasing savings through volume purchasing and management consolidation.

Actually, the multihospital concept originated in the year 1204, with the founding of the Hospital of Santo Spirito in Rome by the Pope. Hearing about the efficiency of the Hospital in Montpelier in France that was conducted by Guy de Montpelier, the Pope sent for him and entrusted him with the directorship of the Order of the Holy Ghost. Under Guy de Montpelier, the Order administered a tremendous number of hospitals throughout

Europe, either starting them as new institutions or taking over the management of previously established hospitals. Almost 2,000 hospitals were founded in Germany and a great number were established in France under this Order.

Investor-owned hospitals are owned and maintained by individuals or corporations for the purpose of generating profits. The for-profit hospital has no source of funds other than those produced by the institution. The hospital is operated in a businesslike fashion. As a rule, the policy-making functions are carried out by the owners, but in the case of large for-profit institutions, a board of directors may be elected among the stockholders. It is a common practice for physicians working in the for-profit hospital to be shareholders in it as well. The most exclusive of the for-profit hospitals cater to self-paying patients, with the great majority relying on reimbursements from patients' insurance.

Government, federal is a narrow classification that includes hospitals owned and controlled by the federal government and supported by federal funds. The largest group is the Veterans Affairs hospitals. The Veterans Affairs hospitals are controlled directly by the federal government. Their physicians work on a full-time basis at the hospitals, and admissions are limited to disabilities connected with war or military service.

In addition to the Veterans Affairs hospitals, a decreasing number of public health service hospitals serve the medical needs of merchant marines. There are now only six public health hospitals, which also care for federal employees and Native Americans living on reservations. In addition, the federal government owns and operates Army, Navy, and Air Force hospitals for each of the three branches of service. All these hospitals are federally funded and under the direct responsibility of the Surgeon General.

Length of Patient Stay

According to the average length of stay, hospitals are classified as either short- or long-term-stay hospitals. A short-term hospital stay is one that averages less than 30 days, with a national average under 7 days. A long-term institution has an average stay of over 30 days.

Number of Beds

Hospitals are also grouped by the number of beds: 6 to 24 beds, 25 to 49, 50 to 99, 100 to 199, 200 to 299, 300 to 399, 400 to 499, and 500 or more. This categorization is usually combined with other classifications, such as regional and teaching or nonteaching hospital, to provide an average cost per type of institution. For example, the cost per bed of operating a 50-bed nonteaching hospital in the Southwest is less than the cost per bed operation of a 400-bed teaching hospital in the Northeast.

Accreditation

Hospitals are also classified as accredited and nonaccredited, depending on whether they have been found to be in substantial compliance with the standards of the Joint Commission and/or the American Osteopathic Association. For over 60 years, the health care industry has participated in a voluntary accreditation process that is designed to improve the quality of services provided in hospitals and health-related facilities. The term "voluntary" is misleading, because accreditation for hospitals has become so closely tied to the receipt of third-party payments that without the ability to make this claim, financial jeopardy constantly looms. Although accreditation is vitally important to hospitals for financial reasons, it also is a mark of distinction for the quality of patient care provided by hospitals and for the many nonhospital programs that are also eligible for it.

Teaching

Teaching or nonteaching is also a common classification in the hospital field. Teaching hospitals participate in the education of physicians through a residency program. Depending upon the type and number of residency programs offered, a hospital is either a major teaching or minor teaching institution. To be a full teaching hospital, the hospital should offer, at minimum, the following residencies: medicine, surgery, obstetrics/gynecology, and pediatrics. Many full teaching hospitals offer residencies in every subspecialty of medicine and surgery, in addition to pathology, anesthesiology, family practice, and many other programs. A partial teaching hospital usually has only two or three programs: medicine, surgery, pediatrics, obstetrics/gynecology, or any combination amounting to less than four.

Depending on the involvement and the participation of a university in its teaching programs, teaching hospitals are university hospitals, university-affiliated, or freestanding. Teaching costs are reimbursed under a complicated formula, but this is a subject of great controversy, with many state legislators advocating for an end to what is considered a subsidy to medical education.

Vertical Integration

Finally, hospitals can be classified according to vertical integration or the concept of regionalization. Under this system, hospitals are divided into primary care, secondary care, and tertiary care centers. Primary care facilities, regardless of location or structure, offer services on a need/demand basis to the public. Those entities are designed, equipped, staffed, organized, and operated as an integral part of a comprehensive health care system and offer health services in an available, personalized, and continuous fashion on an outpatient basis. Secondary care facilities render care that requires a degree of sophistication and skills and that is usually associated with the confinement of the careseeker for a definite period of time. General acute hospitals or specialized outpatient facilities, such as ambulatory surgical centers, fall under this category. Tertiary care facilities render highly specialized services requiring highly technical resources. This type of care is usually offered by university medical centers or specialty hospitals, such as burn centers.

NOTES

1. K. Hill, *Wall Street Journal*, December 10, 1984.

2. B. de las Casas, *History of Hispaniola* (1495).

SUGGESTED READINGS

Adams, F.R. 1891. *The genuine works of Hippocrates.* Translated from Greek, with preliminary discourse and annotations. New York: William Wood.

Albutt, T. 1921. *Greek medicine in Rome.* London: Macmillan & Co.

Ali, S.A. 1977. Europe's debt to Muslim scholars of medicine and science. *Studies in the History of Medicine* 1:36–48.

Aristotle. 1910. *Aristotle's works.* Translated by D.W. Thompson. Oxford: Clarenden Press.

Ashhurst, A.P.C. 1927. The centenary of Lister (1827–1927): A tale of sepsis and antisepsis. *Annals of Medical History* 9:205.

Baas, J.H. 1971. *History of medicine.* Translated by H.E. Anderson. Huntington, NY: R.E. Krieger Publishing Co.

Barrow, M.V. 1972. Portraits of Hippocrates. *Medical History:* 16.

Bell, E.M. 1953. *Storming the citadel: The rise of the woman doctor.* London: Constable & Co.

Blake, J.B., ed. 1968. *Education in the history of medicine.* New York: Hafner Publishing Co.

Boland, F.K. 1950. *The first anesthetic: The story of Crawford Long.* Athens, GA: University of Georgia Press.

Bowers, J.Z., and E.F. Purcell, eds. 1976. *Advances in American medicine: Essays at the bicentennial.* New York: Josiah Macy, Jr., Foundation and National Library of Medicine.

Brim, C.J. 1936. *Medicine in the Bible.* New York: Froben Press.

Brock, A.J. 1929. *Greek medicine: Extracts of medical writers from Hippocrates to Galen.* London: J.M. Dent & Sons.

Brockington, C.F. 1975. The history of public health. In *The theory and practice of public health*, 4th ed., ed. W. Hobson. London: Oxford University Press.

Browne, E.G. 1921. *Arabian medicine.* Cambridge: Cambridge University Press.

Campbell, D. 1926. *Arabian medicine and its influence on the middle ages.* London: Kegan Paul, Trench, Trubner & Co.

Clarke, E.G. et al. 1876. *Century of American medicine, 1776–1876.* Philadelphia: H.C. Lea.

Corlett, W.T. 1977. *The medicine-man of the American Indian and his cultural background.* 1935 reprint. New York: AMS Press.

Duffy, J. 1971. *Epidemics in colonial America.* Baton Rouge, LA: Louisiana State University Press.

Ebbel, B. 1939. *The papyrus ebers: The greatest Egyptian medical document.* With translation. Copenhagen: Ejnar Munksgard.

Edwards, C. 1921. *The Hammurabi code.* London: Watts & Co.

Frazer, J.G. 1963. *The golden bough: A study in magic and religion.* Abr. ed. New York: Macmillan & Co.

Hamarneh, S.K. 1975. *The genius of Arab civilization, sources of Renaissance.* New York: New York University Press.

Hanlon, J.J. 1974. *Public health: Administration and practice*, 6th ed. St. Louis: C.V. Mosby Co.

Harley, G.W. 1941. *Native African medicine.* Cambridge, MA: Harvard University Press.

The historical relations of medicine and surgery to the end of the sixteenth century. 1905. London: Macmillan & Co.

Hospitals, medical care, and social policy in the French revolution. 1956. *Bulletin of the History of Medicine* 30:124–149.

Hurd-Mead, K.C. 1973. *A history of women in medicine.* 1938 reprint. Boston: Milford House.

India's contribution to medieval Arabic medical education and practice. 1977. *Studies in the History of Medicine* 1:5–35.

Jayne, W.A. 1925. *The healing gods of ancient civilizations.* New Haven: Yale University Press.

Kelly, E.C. 1905. *Medical classics.* Vol. 5. Baltimore: Williams & Wilkins Co.

Kump, W.L. 1973. Health care delivery system in ancient Greece and Rome. *Pharos:* 42–48.

A medical history of Persia and the Eastern Caliphate. 1951. Cambridge: Cambridge University Press.

Metchnikoff, E. 1971. *The founders of modern medicine: Pasteur-Koch-Lister.* 1939 reprint. Books for Libraries Press.

Moll, A.A. 1944. *Aesculapius in Latin America.* Philadelphia: W.B. Saunders Co.

Moodie, R.L. 1923. *The antiquity of disease.* Chicago: University of Chicago Press.

Moon, R.O. 1914. The influence of Pythagoras on Greek medicine. In *Proceedings of the seventeeth international congress of medicine, London.* London: H. Frowde.

Natural diseases and rational treatment in primitive medicine. 1946. *Bulletin of the History of Medicine:* 19.

Osler, W. 1921. *The evolution of modern medicine.* New Haven: Yale University Press.

Phillips, S.D. 1973. *Aspects of Greek medicine.* New York: St. Martin's Press.

Piggott, S., ed. 1967. *The dawn of civilization.* New York: McGraw-Hill.

Riesman, D. 1936. *The story of medicine in the Middle Ages.* New York: Paul B. Hoeber.

Rosen, G. 1974. *From medical police to social medicine: Essays on the history of health.* New York: Neale Watson Academic Publications.

Taton, R., ed. 1963. *Ancient and medieval science from the beginnings to 1450*. New York: Basic Books.

Taton, R., ed. 1964. *The beginnings of modern science from 1450 to 1800*. New York: Basic Books.

Thorndike, L. 1923. *A history of magic and experimental science*. New York: Macmillan & Co.

Toole, H. 1963. Asclepius in history and legend. *Surgery* 53:387–419.

Underwood, E.A., ed. 1953. *Science, medicine, and history: Essays on the evolution of scientific thought and medical practice written in honour of Charles Singer*. London: Oxford University Press.

Vallery-Radot, R. 1906. *The life of Pasteur*. New York: McClure, Phillips.

Walton, A. 1894. *The cult of Asclepios: Cornell Studies in Classical Philology*. Boston: Ginn & Co.

Werner, D. 1941. *History of the Red Cross*. London: Cassell & Co.

Withington, E.T. 1894. *Medical history from the earliest times*. London: Scientific Press.

Wong, K.C., and L.T. Wu. 1976. *History of Chinese medicine*. New York: Gordon Press Publications.

Wylie, W.G. 1877. *Hospitals: Their history, organization, and construction*. New York: D. Appleton & Co.

Wynder, E.L. 1975. A corner of history: John Gaunt, 1620–1674, the father of demography. *Preventive Medicine* 4:85–88.

JESUS J. PEÑA, MPA, JD, was a senior Vice President at Saint Michael's Medical Center, Newark, New Jersey. In this capacity, he was responsible for day-to-day operations and marketing. A member of the American Arbitration Association, he has studied hospital settlements that have affected the health industry and has served as a consultant to the World Health Organization in several Latin American countries. Mr. Peña worked with the Office of Technical Assistance of the United Nations to improve the health care system in Latin America through the application of new managerial techniques by those committed to serving large numbers of indigent patients.

Chapter 15

Hospital Organization and Management

I. Donald Snook, Jr.

THE HOSPITAL INDUSTRY

There are more than 5,000 community hospitals in the United States with a total capacity of 873,000 hospital beds. There has been an 8 percent decrease in the number of both hospitals and beds since 1981. The key index used to measure a hospital's size still remains the institution's number of inpatient beds, though this is changing. Inpatient care has been and remains the core product of the nation's hospitals. As a measure of the hospital industry's output, in 1996 and 1997, hospitals handled an estimated 30 million admissions and had close to 200 million inpatient days.[1] The hospital industry represents a mix of public and private sectors. Hospitals can be classified in several ways, among them community or noncommunity; and teaching or nonteaching, and general or specialty. Community hospitals include federal hospitals as well as certain specialty hospitals.

Community hospitals also may be classified as investor-owned (proprietary) or not-for-profit (voluntary) institutions. Hospitals most commonly register with the American Hospital Association (AHA) located in Chicago. Although the number of investor-owned hospitals continues to increase, they represent a minority of community hospitals. Those institutions referred to as general hospitals are able to handle a wide variety of medical problems. Specialty hospitals (e.g., a children's hospital or a psychiatric hospital) limit their care to specific illnesses or types of patients. Hospitals can also be classified by religious affiliation. In the United States, Catholic hospitals are represented by the Catholic Health Association and are a major segment of the religious hospitals.

SERVICES PROVIDED BY HOSPITALS

Although there has been a decline in the nation's hospital inpatient bed capacity over the past decade, at the same time hospitals provided increased services on an outpatient basis. The movement toward outpatient care is a result of extraordinary technological advancements, the trend to move away from high cost in patient care, and increased hospital efficiency in the delivery of patient care. In 1984, about 50 percent of the community hospitals provided outpatient care, whereas today almost all community hospitals (more than 86 percent) have outpatient departments. Many community hospitals (about 95 percent) also provide ambulatory surgery services. Nearly all community hospitals (93 percent) have 24-hour staffed emergency departments. There has been a decrease in the number of hospitals offering trauma care centers, largely because of the high operating costs of such units.[2]

Hospitals have shown rapid growth in both home health care and subacute care services. Contributing to this growth are several factors: (1) the drive to form integrated delivery networks or systems that can offer managed care organizations a continuum of services at lower costs, (2) technological advances, (3) the aging of America, (4) anticipated Medicare and Medicaid cuts, and (5) the fact that home health care remains one of the few Medicare services reimbursed on a retrospective basis. Subacute care, or care for patients who no longer require acute care services but still need highly skilled nursing care and access to technologically advanced therapies, is yet another diversified service that has grown dramatically in recent years. Patients requiring subacute care can include accident and stroke victims, ventilator-dependent patients, and acquired immune deficiency syndrome and cancer patients.

Increasingly, hospitals are working with community agencies including public health departments, social service agencies, business and government leaders, and other groups to assess and address the issues and problems of the community's health. Collaborations, formal assessments, and public education regarding the availability of health care were also common activities for hospitals.

CHANGE IN THE HOSPITAL INDUSTRY

During the past decade, hospitals have undergone unprecedented change. Some hospitals have closed, others have merged, and still others have been converted to nursing homes or providers of other health care services. There are fewer rural hospitals today than a decade ago. The average length of stay for hospital inpatients also has declined. For the most part, these decreases are a reflection of improvements in medical technology and the change in hospital reimbursement systems. Decreases in inpatient care are also the result of the need for hospitals to improve economies of scale through mergers and acquisitions.

Increasingly, community hospitals have adopted strategies to deal with the changing political and economic landscape, and especially are attempting to adjust to the growth of managed care. Many hospitals have adopted strategies such as hospital-to-hospital and hospital-to-physician collaborations in order to offer patients increased access to care across a continuum of services; through coordination, these strategies can also improve efficiency and lower costs.

THE MAJOR CHANGES AND THEIR IMPLICATIONS

The desire to merge has grown as a survival strategy. To remain competitive and reduce costs, hospitals view joining a network or system as a way to reap the benefits of sharing services such as information systems and selected clinical facilities. One of the most prevalent forms of industry consolidation is occurring between hospitals and hospital systems. Hospitals have formed alliances with each other to combine their resources and thereby eliminate duplicative services, reduce excess capacity, cut costs, and increase market share. They also hope to enhance the quality of care, improve access to capital and the ability to invest in information technology, and offer more cost-effective health care service delivery to their region.

As a result of the recent surge of merger and acquisition activity, a number of new integrated delivery networks also has been growing. These networks, which also are referred to as integrated delivery systems, consist of networks of providers and payers that combine health care financing and delivery under one umbrella.

WHAT IS AN ORGANIZATION?

An organization is a systematic arrangement of two or more people or entities who fulfill formal roles and share a common purpose. Aside from the hospital, a college or university is an example of an organization, as are fraternities, government agencies, churches, Microsoft, and the neighborhood pharmacy. They are all organizations because they all have three common characteristics.

First, every organization has a distinct *purpose* or mission. The purpose is typically expressed in terms of a goal or set of goals. Second, every organization is composed of *people*. Third, all organizations develop a *systematic structure* that defines formal roles and limits the behavior of its members. Development of a structure would include, for example, creating rules and regulations, defining terms, identifying formal leaders and giving them authority over other members, and writing up job descriptions so that members know what they are supposed to do. The term *organization* therefore refers to an entity that has a distinct purpose, includes people or members, and has a systematic structure.[3]

Most hospitals in the United States are organized traditionally; that is, they tend to follow the classical theory of organization. The traditional organization structure derives from the theory of bureaucracy described by the nineteenth century German sociologist Max Weber (1864–1920).[4] Hospitals mainly are structured as bureaucratic organizations and employ bureaucratic principles. A principle of bureaucratic organization that applies to hospitals is the grouping of individual positions and clusters of positions into a hierarchy or pyramid.

Another effective principle of hospital organization is the consistent system of rules. Hospital rules are guidelines or official boundaries for actions within the hospital. Examples of such rules include the set of personnel policies outlined in the employee handbook and written nursing procedures for the care of patients in each nursing unit.

Hospitals also use the principle of span of control very effectively. The concept of span of control dictates a limit to the number of persons a single manager can effectively supervise. In a hospital a span of control of between 5 and 10 people in a given functional area is normal to achieve operational effectiveness. This is especially true in the classical functional hospital areas such as housekeeping, dietary, and nursing. There is also a division and specialization of labor in hospitals. Specialization refers to the ways a hospital organizes to identify specific tasks and to assign a job description to each employee. For example, a nurse's aide has specific tasks to perform that are different from those of a physician, a registered nurse, or a medical technologist.

Notwithstanding the preceding, it is thought that the hospital of the future, perhaps as a member of an integrated network, will be required to be more flexible in its approach to organizational structuring and broaden the job descriptions and to have more multiple worker job descriptions.

THE STRUCTURE OF THE HOSPITAL ORGANIZATION

Although there can be a variety of organizational structures, the traditional freestanding hospital structure is a pyramid or hierarchical form of organization. This arrangement is common also within the different hospital functions and departments. Under this structure, individuals at the top of the pyramid (e.g., department heads) have a specified range of authority, and this authority is passed down to employees at the lower levels in the pyramid, in a chain-of-command fashion (Figure 15–1). In this way, hospital authority is dispersed throughout the organization. Hospitals encourage a pyramidal structure; for example, a department head may delegate to two supervisors and they in turn delegate to two or three subordinates, who in turn may even delegate farther down the pyramid. Such organizations tend to follow the principles of bureaucracy.

THE BUREAUCRATIC PRINCIPLES

Division of Labor

Hospitals have scores of specialty tasks that need to be accomplished and have found that division of work has made it easier to accomplish these tasks. Written job descriptions and task lists are mandatory tools for the modern-day hospital's director of human re-sources. There are so many tasks to be performed in a hospital that each worker must know his or her precise limits and sphere of influence if the hospital is going to operate efficiently.

Pyramid or Hierarchal Organization

Another key bureaucratic structure is a pyramid or hierarchical form of organization, in which the various employee positions within each hospital department are arranged in a hierarchical fashion. At the top of the pyramid is a department head, who has very clearly specified lines of authority. This authority is passed down to supervisors at lower levels in the hierarchy. These levels of authority create the principle of the chain of command.

A System of Rules

Hospitals operate according to a set of rules and regulations that outline the boundaries

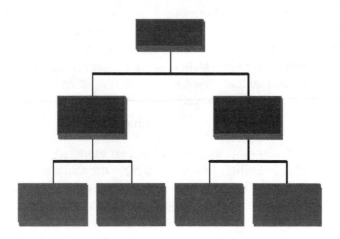

Figure 15–1 Chain of Command Within the Organization

for employee actions within the institution. A hospital's personnel policies are described in a handbook that is distributed to employees. Written nursing procedures that outline how to care for patients are an example of an effective and consistent system of hospital rules. The hospital support departments of housekeeping, dietary, and maintenance are also run according to rules. The modern-day hospital cannot operate efficiently without detailed organizational rules and regulations.

Unity of Command

Each employee in the hospital should be responsible to one person: his or her boss. Unfortunately, because hospitals have both business and clinical functions, an employee may have more than one boss. This situation can produce inefficient communication and decision making.

This traditional approach to having a single boss is part of the concept of the chain of command and authority. Violation of the unity of command principle by employees can lead to disciplinary action because it represents a violation of authority. The traditional concept of unity of command is being challenged by a more contemporary form of hospital organization called matrix or team organization, in which members from more than one department are organized into teams for the purpose of completing ad hoc projects that require a range of skills. In addition, very formal unity of command runs a risk of dampening employee motivation and creativity, increasing unionization risk, and otherwise engendering an attitude of inflexibility. Few of these are favorable paradigms for the future.

Span of Control

According to classical organization principles, each supervisor can direct only a lim-ited number of subordinates or functions. The exact number that a supervisor can properly supervise is debatable and may depend on the supervisor's or manager's level in the organization. The hospital's chief executive officer (CEO) has such broad responsibilities and functions that three, four, or five subordinates (referred to as span of control) reporting to this individual might be quite appropriate, whereas managers at lower levels in the organization might be assigned twice that number of functions. Classical organizational theories hold that the more efficient organizations have a smaller span of control.

Delegation

The classical theorists agree that it is best for an organization to have decisions made at the lowest level possible that is reasonable and consistent with good management. Therefore, decisions of a relatively routine nature should be made by subordinates, and, when appropriate, top management can and should assign decision-making power to lower levels in the organization. One of the complaints often heard from young, assertive managers seeking to grow in their position is, "My boss does not delegate." However, delegating authority to subordinates does not release department heads or managers from their responsibility for control over the activity that is delegated.

Line and Staff

Line authority denotes direct supervision over subordinates; for example, the head pharmacist is directly responsible for all the employees within the pharmacy under his or her supervision. In contrast, the staff function in the hospital generally is associated with advisory activities rather than direct supervision. The distinction between line and staff is seen dramatically within the hospital's nursing service department. In the nursing department, line authority is carried out by managers and supervisors who hold the positions of nurse managers, head nurses, or nursing supervisors. The staff functions in nursing are frequently the responsibility of the trainers or educators. They conduct training called inservice; they are usually advisory to the managers and their line employees.

Coordination

With so many activities, departments, and functions in today's hospital, it is essential that they be coordinated effectively. Coordination is making sure that the different work efforts within the institution are synchronized and that they work together in harmony in order to achieve the hospital's purpose or mission. Usually it is the hospital's middle management staff that is responsible for ensuring coordination among departments. Unfortunately, departmental activities are not always coordinated. One of the main barriers to effective coordination is poor communication. Generally when a hospital has mastered communication among departments, coordination is much easier to accomplish.

A TEAM OF THREE

One of the reasons that hospitals as organizations are so complex lies in the relationship among the three major sources of power within the institution: the governing body, the CEO and his or her administration, and the physicians and their formal medical staff organization. These relationships may be viewed as a tripartite hospital management concept. Just as the activities of the medical staff significantly affect the hospital administration and governance of the institution, so do the governing body's actions impinge on

the physicians as well as the employee staff. The main organizational units designed to enable the medical staff to relate formally to the governing board are two committees: (1) the medical staff's executive committee and (2) the governing board's joint conference committee. However, the more dynamic links between the board and the medical staff are in the informal day-to-day dealings between the groups, both within the hospital setting and socially and informally outside the institution. Also, many hospitals have found it beneficial to have physicians serve as voting members on the board. Thus, all of this adds up to a team approach to hospital organization.

As the hospital industry changes, the traditional tripartite relationship is being strained by the increasing pressure to provide high-quality, low-cost services that require a greater cohesiveness between the physicians and the hospital's administrative staff. More common goals and motivators must be sought as the industry moves toward the probability of fewer payees, bundled (hospital and physician) reimbursement, and capitation.

GOVERNANCE

The governing body of a voluntary (not-for-profit) hospital may be referred to as the board of trustees, board of directors, or board of governors. Regardless of the name, this is the organizational body with ultimate responsibility for all decisions in the hospital. The board functions as the hospital owners and is accountable to the community. The institution's governing body is at the head of the hospital's formal organization (Figure 15–2).

The governing body is responsible for both the medical staff's actions, and the hiring and evaluation of the hospital's CEO. Trustees undertake the ultimate responsibilities of managing the assets of the hospital and of set-

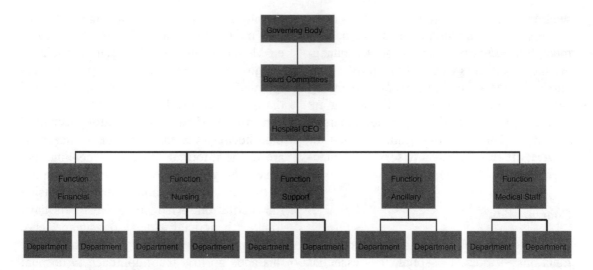

Figure 15–2 A Typical Hospital Organizational Chart

ting policy. In so doing they are holding the hospital's resources in trust and assume a fiduciary responsibility. The courts have found that the governing body has to be responsible for all activities within the hospital. Therefore, members who serve on the governing body have significant responsibility.

Trustees are usually private citizens whose motive to serve is clear—to help their neighbors and their community. One of the initial reasons for establishing private citizens as hospital trustees was to secure financial support for the institution. By appointing local citizens who had some influence and affluence, the hospital could guarantee a certain amount of contributions to underwrite the care of the poor and the hospital's overall operation. In years past, hospital boards were often appointed so that the hospitals could obtain monetary benefits from their members. Now hospital boards frequently appoint individuals who have particular skills that can help the hospital, for example, with legal advice, accounting assistance, or business and management support. Today's hospital

has a range of legal and accreditation requirements. It is the board of trustees that is required by law to watch over the hospital and its operations.

Hospital trustees generally serve without pay: They are prohibited from profiting financially from their membership on the board of trustees. The rewards for being a trustee are the satisfaction of having rendered a service to others in the community and the receipt of some measure of community status by being on the board. Because the trustees represent the ownership of the hospital, they have the ordinary liability of any owners of property. But they have the additional burden of protecting the patients from all foreseeable and preventable harm.

Selection and Evaluation of the CEO

To assist the board of trustees in managing the hospital, the trustees have an obligation to hire a competent CEO to oversee the day-to-day management of the hospital. One of the board's most important functions is the investigation, review, and selection of the CEO. Hospitals are big business, and trustees must seek executives who have strengths in planning, organizing, and controlling, as well as proven leadership skills. The board then delegates to the CEO the authority and responsibility to manage the day-to-day operations of the hospital while still retaining the ultimate responsibility for everything that happens in the hospital. Thus, the relationship between the CEO and the governing board is primarily that of employee-employer, but not in the usual sense of the term. Since the hospital is a very special type of organization, the relationship between the CEO and the governing board is similar to a partnership. Just as it is the responsibility of the governing board to hire the CEO, it also is its responsibility to evaluate the CEO's performance and discharge the CEO, if necessary.

Functions of the Board of Trustees

The basic function of the governing body is to guide, protect, and when appropriate, change the hospital's service mission in accordance with the institution's structure and the needs of the community. The board of trustees has an explicit or implicit obligation to act on behalf of the community's interest. This is referred to as a fiduciary responsibility to the community. This responsibility is founded upon trust and confidence. It involves: (1) the formal and legal responsibility for controlling the hospital and assuring the community that the hospital works properly, (2) the responsibility to see that the hospital gains support from its community, and (3) the responsibility of ensuring that the board of trustees is accountable to the citizens and the community it serves. Specifically, hospital trustees establish hospital policies. These policies are general written statements or understandings that guide or channel the think-

ing and action of the hospital's medical staff and administration in decision making.

THE TRUSTEE IN AN ORGANIZED DELIVERY SYSTEM

Since the trend is toward organized delivery systems and networks, it is necessary to note the role of the trustee in a hospital that is part of that type of structure. In spite of growing centralization of hospitals, hospital management usually includes some degree of dual reporting responsibility, first to the local board of trustees, then to the corporate staff of the organized delivery system. However, the local governing body often retains primary responsibility for key medical staff relationships. The assumption of a role as a trustee in an organized delivery system need not mean the loss of autonomy of the local hospital governing board.

How Does the Board Operate?

The board of trustees operates in accordance with the bylaws of the hospital and organized delivery system. The bylaws identify how the board is founded and how it operated to attain its objectives. Typical bylaws include a statement on the organization's purpose and the responsibilities of the board. They also contain a statement of authority for the board to appoint the administrator and the medical staff. In addition, the bylaws outline how board members are appointed and for what period of time. Most bylaws indicate an elaborate committee structure. It is through these committees that the governing board usually gets its work accomplished. The committee structure is frequently established along special functional lines. There is remarkable consistency throughout the nation's hospitals in board committee structure. Perhaps the reason for this consistency is the impetus toward the review of and recommendations for hospital bylaws from the Joint Commission on Accreditation of Healthcare Organizations (Joint Commission). The most common committee is the executive committee, which is found in most hospitals. Other examples include a finance committee, a planning committee, and perhaps a committee for the building, operations, and grounds. Generally, recommendations through the separate committees affect the governance, management, and administration, as well as the medical staff in the hospital.

It is the duty of the board to select the members of these board committees. The caliber of the recommendations that emerge from these committees and subsequently the caliber of the resulting board action is frequently a function of the quality of selection that went into the committee assignments. The CEO, through the application of leadership skills and management delegation and in close relationship with these board committees, frequently provides the ultimate key to success in all aspects of the hospital operation.

Hospital boards are operating more like publicly owned corporate boards. Corporate board members are accustomed to providing an independent voice. Clearly hospital trustees are respected for their independence and their overview of the hospital. This is the result of an increasing need to make hospitals more efficient and competitive.

THE CEO AND THE ADMINISTRATION

Years ago, many CEOs, also referred to as hospital administrators, often were chosen from the nursing department. In many church-related hospitals, it was common for the CEO to be selected from the ranks of the religious order or from among retired clergy. These administrators were hardworking and dedicated to patient care, but they inherently followed the physicians' wishes. On the other hand, some administrators worked their way up from the business office or the chief financial officer position to become the hospital's CEO. It also was common in some hospitals to have a retired businessperson or physician assume the CEO position.

Functions of the Hospital Administration

A debate continues among those who study and write about management on exactly how to categorize the administrator's role in the hospital or in an organized delivery system. This argument is by no means purely academic. There are different management classifications in today's hospital. These classifications may vary depending on the size and complexity of a particular hospital (Figure 15–3).

In the early part of the century, the French industrialist Henri Fayol wrote that all managers perform five functions: They plan, organize, command, coordinate, and control. Today, the use of *management functions* as a way to classify the hospital administrator's job is still appropriate. Now, however, they are usually condensed to four: planning, organizing, leading, and controlling.

Because hospitals, like other organizations, exist to achieve some mission or purpose, someone has to define that purpose and the means for its achievement. The CEO fulfills this role. The *planning* function encompasses defining an organization's goals, establishing an overall strategy for achieving those goals, and developing a comprehensive hierarchy of plans to integrate and coordinate activities. Managers in administration are responsible for designing an organization's structure. This function is called *organizing*. It includes the determination of what tasks are to be done, who is to do them, how the tasks are to be grouped, who reports to whom, and where in the organization decisions are to be made. Every hospital contains people, and it is the hospital administration's job to direct and coordinate those people. This is the *leading* function. When managers motivate employees, direct the activities of others, select the most effective communication channel, or resolve conflicts among members, they are engaging in leading. The final management function administrators perform is *controlling*. After the goals are set, the plans formulated, the structural arrangements delineated, and the people hired, trained, and motivated, something may still go wrong. To ensure that initiatives are proceeding as they should, management must monitor the organization's performance. Actual performance must be compared with the previously set goals. If there are any significant deviations, it is management's responsibility to resolve the causes. This process of monitoring, comparing, and correcting constitutes the controlling function.

Management Roles

In the late 1960s, Professor Henry Mintzberg of McGill University undertook a careful study of five chief executives at work.[5] On the basis of diaries kept by these executives and his own observations, Mintzberg concluded that managers perform 10 different but highly interrelated roles. The term *management roles* refers to specific categories of managerial behavior. Mintzberg's 10 roles can be grouped around three themes: interpersonal relationships, the transfer of information, and decision making.

Interpersonal Roles

All managers are required to perform duties that are ceremonial and symbolic in na-

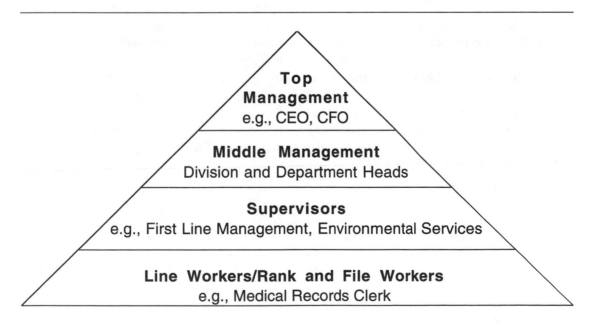

Top Management
e.g., CEO, CFO

Middle Management
Division and Department Heads

Supervisors
e.g., First Line Management, Environmental Services

Line Workers/Rank and File Workers
e.g., Medical Records Clerk

Figure 15–3 Management Classifications

ture. When the president of the hospital distributes diplomas at a nursing school commencement, or a nursing supervisor gives a group of high school students a tour of the hospital, he or she is acting in a figurehead role. All managers have a role as a *leader*. This role includes hiring, training, motivating, and disciplining employees. The third role within the interpersonal grouping is the *liaison role*. Mintzberg described this activity as contacting external sources who provide the manager with information.[6] These sources are individuals or groups outside the manager's unit, and they may be inside or outside the organization. The public relations director who obtains information from the human resources manager in his or her hospital has an internal liaison relationship. When the public relations director has contact with other marketing executives through a health care marketing trade association, he or she has an outside liaison relationship.

Informational Roles

All managers will, to some degree, receive and collect information from organizations and institutions outside their own. Typically, they do this by reading health care trade journals and talking with others to learn of changes in the physician's needs and what other hospitals may be planning. Mintzberg called this the *monitor* role.[7] Managers also act as a conduit to transmit information to organizational members. This is the *disseminator* role. When they represent the organization to outsiders, managers also perform a *spokesperson* role.

Decisional Roles

Finally Mintzberg identified four roles that revolve around the making of choices.[8] As *entrepreneurs*, managers initiate and oversee new programs that will improve their hospital's performance. As *disturbance handlers*, managers take corrective action in response to unforeseen problems. As *resource allocators*, managers are responsible for distributing human, physical, and monetary resources. Last, managers perform as *negotiators* when they, for example, discuss and bargain with health maintenance organizations (HMOs) to gain their own advantages.

CONCLUSION

The delivery of health care in the United States will continue to be transformed. Changes will continue with respect to controlling costs, evaluating and improving quality, and access to care issues. For years the hospital was the focal point of health care. Its nature and service will continue to change, but in its new form, it will continue to be a major part of the health care industry.

NOTES

1. American Hospital Association, *Hospital Statistics 1996–97* (Chicago: American Hospital Association, 1997).

2. Ibid.

3. Robbins, S.P., *Managing Today!* (Upper Saddle River, NJ: Prentice Hall, 1997).

4. Weber, M., and T. Parsons, *Theory of Social &* *Economic Organization* (New York: Free Press, 1947).

5. Mintzberg, H., *The Nature of Managerial Work* (New York: Harper & Row, 1973).

6. Ibid.

7. Ibid.

8. Ibid.

I. DONALD SNOOK, JR, PHD, is Senior Lecturer at Penn State Great Valley School of Graduate Professional Studies in Malvern, Pennsylvania. Prior to this position he was President and CEO of Presbyterian-University of Pennsylvania Medical Center in Philadelphia.

Dr. Snook has contributed numerous articles to health care management literature, has conducted seminars on conflict and leadership and health care marketing, and is the author of several books including *Hospitals: What They Are and How They Work*, *Building a Winning Medical Staff*, and *50 Effective Hospital Print Ads*. He is the originator of the "hotel-hospital" concept. He is the recipient of the American Healthcare Marketing Association's CEO Marketer of the Year Award.

Dr. Snook holds a BBA in Marketing from Wharton School of the University of Pennsylvania and an MBA in Hospital Administration from George Washington University. He earned his PhD from the University of Pennsylvania. He has also completed the Health Management Systems Program at the Harvard Business School.

Chapter 16

Patient Access Services (Admitting): Into, Through, and Out of the Health Care Process

John Woerly

Health care organizations have made a commitment to provide quality health care to the community they serve. Thus, health care organizations must be financially viable, cost effective, and sensitive to the needs of patients. Patient relations are influenced by employee attitudes, effective information gathering and processing systems, scheduling, and interdepartmental communications and coordination.

A health care admission/registration system (also referred to as patient access), like those of a hotel, university, or general business in its induction and intake procedures, is a system used to input information in an orderly manner to prevent overburdening the organization and its resources. The Patient Access Department plays an important part in developing and managing a planned strategy for patient flow. This patient flow, in many respects, dominates other admission/registration activities in that it regulates the frequency and speed with which all other health care services may be performed.

AREAS OF RESPONSIBILITIES

The Patient Access Department is responsible primarily for the timely, courteous, and accurate registration of patients. In this respect, the department supports quality assurance in the documentation of the patient's records. The registration function creates the patient records and the patient identification system for future record storage, and ensures the institution's data integrity as it relates to patient records. As such, the department creates the patient history for the Patient Accounts and Medical Records Departments. The patient information obtained in the registration process is entered into the institution's data system, either creating a new patient record or updating the current record. The Patient Access Department, in most cases, assigns the patient account number and/or medical record number that will be used by the institution for recordkeeping and billing purposes. As such, the department serves as the foundation for medical records and billing/collections. Incomplete and/or inaccurate collection of information and disposition of the patient will adversely affect other departments and individuals. The advent of electronic billing is but one example in which the importance of data integrity can be observed. The process of submitting claims electronically demands complete and accurate collection of information by the Patient Access Department, in order to ensure timely, accurate billing. The Medical Records Department also must depend upon the Patient Access Department to properly assign medical record numbers in order to prevent potential duplication of patient records. This is vital to the Medical Records Department, as it is called upon to retrieve records for medical review in the delivery of health care. Additionally, the Medical Records Department uses demographic and clerical information obtained during registration in the abstracting of the medical records. In most cases, this transfer of information has been automated. Incomplete and inaccurate information will delay various processes and result in manual intervention (rework) by the Patient Accounts and Medical Records Departments.

Basic data gathered at the time of registration include: demographic, financial/legal, social, clerical, and clinical information. Primary data components may include:

- demographic
  1. patient name
  2. patient address and phone number
  3. date of birth
  4. sex and race
  5. Social Security number
- financial/legal
  1. employer name, address, and phone number
  2. guarantor (person financially responsible for bill) name, address, and phone number
  3. guarantor's employer name, address, and phone number
  4. insurance name, address, phone number, policy number, preauthorization/precertification number, eligibility dates, injury information if liability or workmen's compensation case, subscriber information, billing priority if more than one insurance
  5. details of previous unpaid balances
  6. precertification and benefit information
  7. completion of insurance forms and other third-party payer information
  8. patient, guarantor, and/or responsible party signatures for release of information, consent for treatment, financial agreement/payment for services, release from liability, receipt of Medicare/Medicaid/CHAMPUS information, and receipt of advanced directives/living will information
- social
  1. contacts in case of emergency—names, addresses, and phone numbers
  2. permission to receive visitors or notify the newspapers
  3. religion and church preference
- clerical
  1. valuables taken for safekeeping
  2. registration date and time
  3. who provided and entered the information
  4. referral source, i.e., name of other hospital
  5. method of arrival, i.e., ambulance, walk-in, etc.
  6. room preference and assignment if an inpatient admission
  7. patient account number and/or medical record number
- clinical
  1. diagnosis or chief medical complaint
  2. treatment plans, i.e., surgery
  3. physicians' names, addresses, and phone numbers
  4. physician orders

Additionally, the admission/registration department may go beyond the traditional role of the admission process. Today's health care environment has led to further expansion of job responsibilities in the admission department to include:

- patient scheduling
- patient placement

- preadmission, outpatient, clinic, physician office, nursing home, and emergency department registration
- financial screening and counseling
- acceptance of patient deposits
- patient information
- birth and death certificate preparation
- processing of consent forms for treatment, release of information, treatment, and living wills
- precertification
- preparation of daily census and other special reports
- maintaining patient identification system
- guest relations/patient representatives
- telecommunications
- patient transportation
- diagnostic testing
- marketing/liaison with physicians' offices
- other related areas, such as patient accounts management, utilization management, managed care contracting, discharge planning, and risk management

With the need to maintain cost effectiveness, organizations are restructuring lines of authority and responsibility. As such, the traditional Patient Registration Department's focus on direct customer service has evolved to encompass utilization and financial management. It is evident that the department's role will expand even further.

Depending upon job responsibilities, the traditional admission department may be referred to as Patient Registration or Patient Access Services. The latter reflects a wider spectrum of job functions and will be used as the model for this chapter. As defined by the National Association of Healthcare Access Management (NAHAM), "Patient Access Services provides quality services in registration and all of its support processes to patients, providers and payors into, through and out of their healthcare experiences."[1]

Considering the frequency and nature of this interaction, the department must be structured to maximize its effectiveness and efficiency through excellent management. The basic policies relating to patient admission generally stem from the governing board, based upon the recommendations from the administrator and medical staff. The role and function of the department may vary from institution to institution. Some are narrow in focus, whereas others encompass a broad scope of duties.

When a patient enters a health care institution for treatments or testing, the patient must be registered. One of the staff's goals is to create a smooth, pleasant transition for the patient from home to personal contact. Patients often get their first impression of the health care institution when they first speak to the person registering them. These feelings often remain with the patient and affect their attitude toward the institution, the staff, and their medical care. Patient Access staff can ensure that the institution's first impression is positive, by providing efficient, personable, and compassionate care.

DEPARTMENTAL FUNCTIONS

Inpatient admission services, the first of which also relate to outpatient registration, are[2] (Figure 16–1):

- intake
  1. reservations/appointment process
  2. registration/interviewing process
- financial and utilization management
  1. verification of insurance eligibility and coverage
  2. precertification/authorization process
  3. early utilization management and discharge planning (i.e., social work,

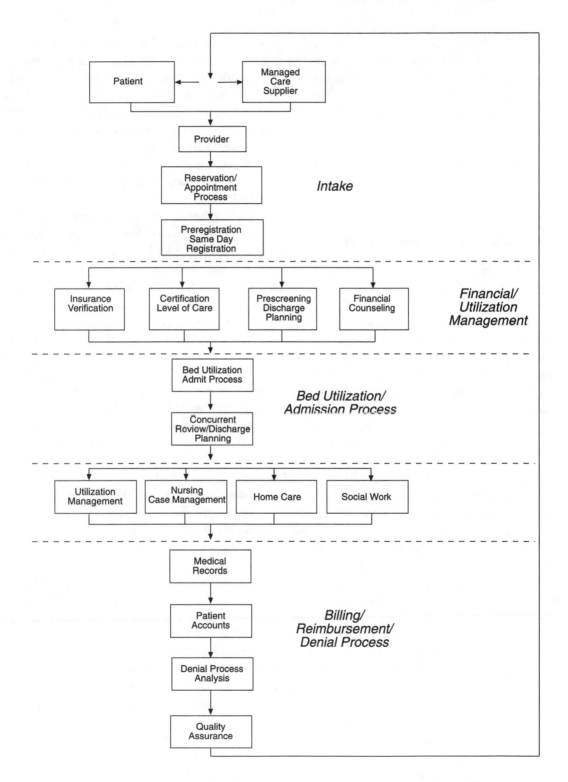

Figure 16–1 Critical Process Essential to the Patient Access Department (Macro Model)

home care, preadmission testing)
4. patient education regarding their insurance company's requirements, financial responsibility, and collection (i.e., deposits, payment contracts, etc.)
- bed utilization management
- billing/reimbursement/denial analysis

Intake

Reservations/Appointment Process

The reservations/appointment process is an orderly way to prevent overburdening the organization and its resources. The first activity of such a control system may be described as a mechanism to cushion the complex internal hospital services from becoming overloaded. Therefore, it is critical in order to ensure positive patient relations and ensure stable utilization of resources to take patients into a general hospital using a planned strategy for patient flow. This patient flow, in many respects, dominates other access system activities in that it regulates the frequency and speed with which all other activities must be performed. In this respect, the controlling of input into the health care institution is a first and key function of a patient access system.

The second activity of a control system is primarily concerned with getting patients to where they need to be. In this activity, two additional functions are required: efficient initiation of the information flow (record keeping) and patient contact. In addition to a patient's personal apprehensions, problems or delays in the information flow, record-keeping functions, or in the input control function could project disorganization as viewed by the public.

The patient access system has a direct effect on other systems within the hospital.

There is an immediate effect on staffing levels and resource utilization. One objective of a scheduling system is to optimize the available resources. There is a great need in the health care industry to balance capabilities and capacities with patient demand to ensure that the patient flow remains smooth.

Although still somewhat limited in its development, many health care providers are establishing a centralized patient scheduling system to better satisfy their customers. The primary objective of developing a centralized scheduling system is to provide an effective means for physicians and their staff to schedule patients for services by calling a centralized telephone number, instead of calling each diagnostic department. Additionally, the development of the scheduling system should allow the review and analysis of existing procedures to ensure that they are meeting the needs of our physicians, patients, and hospital staff in an effective manner.

Case Example: Workflow in Patient Scheduling. The sequence of events for the scheduling of an outpatient appointment (i.e., the initial step in the admission process) as developed at the Methodist Medical Center of Illinois exemplifies a typical centralized patient scheduling process. The following steps are utilized:

1. *Call made to schedule.* The physicians' office personnel wishing to schedule an appointment will call the Patient Scheduling Center.
2. *Scheduling personnel will check availability.* The scheduling personnel will check the department schedule for the day the physician desires the appointment to be scheduled. All times are scheduled on a first call, first served basis, with the exception of emergency situations.
3. *Scheduling personnel will schedule,*

enter data, and provide information. The scheduling personnel will schedule a time and record needed identification information into the department's computer system. To book an appointment, the user selects the appropriate "book" and types in information to accurately identify the department/test and patient. If the patient is in the database, a list of candidate names matching the search criteria will be displayed. If the patient is not in the database, the patient can be registered into the system by entering basic information such as the name, date of birth, and Social Security number. Other demographic and scheduling information is then entered, including: physician(s), principal diagnosis/chief complaint, and primary insurance coverage.

A search of appropriate times is then automatically generated by the system. Specific or general appointment criteria related to the desired appointment can then be selected. Available appointments can be retrieved by selecting any combination of the following search criteria:

- specific date
- appointment type
- appointment duration

After specifying the search criteria, the user can display available appointments. The appointment is reserved at the end of the browse mode, in order to make the appointment inaccessible to other users. The system prevents booking conflicts through conflict messaging. If any preparatory instructions are needed, the scheduling personnel will review the instructions with the calling party. If two or more tests are scheduled for the same day, the scheduling personnel will schedule the testing times as close to one another as possible, utilizing proper test sequencing techniques.

4. *Scheduling time confirmed.* Upon agreeing on an appointment time with the patient, the scheduling personnel will confirm the scheduled time with the physicians' office personnel.

5. *Physicians' office personnel complete required documentation.* The physicians' office personnel scheduling the test should complete the preprinted physicians' order form and the patient orders envelope and place the first two copies of the order form in the provided envelope. The remaining copy of the order form should be retained in the physicians' office for reference.

6. *Scheduling paper trail and reports.* Upon production of the patient flowsheet, the scheduling personnel will file the slip in chronological date order for future reference, preregistration, and patient check-in functions. The outpatient scheduling report will be distributed to the appropriate department(s) prior to the date of the patient's arrival.

Registration/Interviewing Process

Traditionally, preregistration is the means by which patients can be expedited through the intake process. When used to the maximum, preregistration also can be a good foundation on which to build a strong fiscal security. Additionally, interviewing patients at the time of admission or service can be difficult, because of their stress and anxiety. Thus, information may not be complete and/or accurate. The best time to verify the means of reimbursement is at the time the preregistration is completed. Pre-existing clauses, deductibles, and co-insurance coverage should be reviewed prior to the patient's service. Overall, preregistration is the building block that allows the patient and the institution to look at financial options prior to service to ensure complete and timely payment.

Financial and Utilization Management

The next step beyond preregistration is the concept of precertification and financial counseling. The act of registration places the health care giver at risk for the service delivered and the ensuing expenses. The two principal areas of financial risk are: the justification of the appropriateness of the service to assure that the third-party payer can be billed for the charges incurred by the patient, and compliance with third-party prior-approval programs.

Many employer groups and third-party payers have established prior approval programs for all elective admissions along with emergency admission reporting mechanisms. The policy benefits of the insured are usually keyed to the approval process. Typically, the patient is responsible for ensuring compliance. However, it usually reverts to the health care provider to follow up or risk financial loss. Patients who must meet or comply with these specific requirements prior to service must be identified. Thus, the ability to monitor both the employers and the insurance companies involved in these special requirements is essential.

A preregistration assessment of each patient scheduled for admission and outpatient testing will lower the financial risks of retrospective review prior to payment. A preregistration assessment program should include aspects of preregistration, utilization management, financial verification and counseling, discharge planning, and results reporting of preadmission tests.

The department also may be involved in other financial management processes, including managed care contracting, case mix analysis, billing and collections, charge entry functions, managing a patient transfer system, and managing the process for the Patient Self-Determination Act/Living Will. Managed care contracting may involve the review of the contractual agreement, establishing processes to ensure that the agreement provisions are followed, and providing basic utilization statistics.

The Congress of the United States has set a public policy into law, requiring under section 1867 of the Medicare Act that "all participating hospitals and their 'responsible physicians' provide a screening examination to any individual, regardless of ability to pay who comes into the emergency department . . . to determine if the individual has an 'emergency medical condition' or is in 'active labor.'" This public policy issue directly affects the Patient Access Department because the financial resources and payment ability of individuals who present to the Emergency Department and other entry points must be determined and documented by patient access staff. To further aid the health care provider, many institutions have developed a transfer center, which has the centralized authority to resolve clinical, financial, and political concerns in dealing with the acceptance of interhospital transfers. Although a transfer center can be viewed incorrectly as a "financial triage," it has an important mission of developing proper and timely referrals of medically appropriate transfers. Historical information including the name of the hospital(s), the number of like procedure(s) or diagnosis, the length(s) of stay, total charges, and funding source(s) must be analyzed for continued fiscal viability.[3]

The Patient Self-Determination Act also has had a major impact on hospitals and health care providers because it establishes guidelines that require the maintenance of written policies and procedures governing patients' rights to make health care decisions, and the obligation of health care providers to communicate this information as well as other related information to their adult patients. This includes the patient's right to accept or refuse medical or surgical treatment, as well as the patient's right to make advance directives. The law defines an advance directive as a written instruction, such as a Living Will or a Durable Power of Attorney for health care, recognized under state law, relating to the provision of health care when the patient is incapacitated. Providers will also be required to provide adult patients with written policies respecting their patient rights.[4]

Future state and federal regulations will continue to demand the expertise of the Patient Access Department. As the department serves as a central source for patient database entry and point-of-entry communication with the patient, it is likely that the department will continue to serve a vital role in the carrying out of state and federal health care regulations.

Bed Utilization Management

Maximizing bed occupancy, while balancing patient care needs, nursing acuity levels, and external/internal utilization management restrictions relative to length of stay and coverage payment, is a critical element in the daily operations of a Patient Access Department. Ensuring that beds are used effectively is not only a function of the creative deployment of beds as they become available, but also requires effective communication with the physicians who admit these patients to the hospital. Additionally, successful access management requires the development and maintenance of effective relationships with other departments, primarily the nursing de-

partment and environmental services, to ensure the timely notification of discharging patients and the proper assignment of beds to meet both the needs of the patient and the nursing personnel. The high degree of interaction between these areas must be achieved to fully optimize patient placement and to reach expected levels of customer satisfaction. Additionally, the very issue of patient placement can affect patient outcome and length of stay, as well as the optimal utilization of staffing, equipment, and other facilities. The Patient Access Department also may be responsible for census maintenance, which would include facility, bed, and nursing unit statistics and room charges.

Departmental Information Standards

The importance of having accurate, up-to-date demographic and insurance information is essential. Equally important is the need to make the collection of this information as burdenless as possible to the patient. Various models for collecting and updating patient registration information exist today, ranging from a totally centralized approach to a virtually decentralized method. These approaches also may vary in regard to overall management responsibility, as well as the location of the transaction.

In May 1993 NAHAM conducted a study to determine average waiting times, registration times, and approach to registration. It was found that 63 percent of the survey participants had a centralized registration approach. The average waiting time for an outpatient registration was 8 minutes, while the average waiting time for an inpatient admission was 7.5 minutes. The average interview time for outpatient registrations was 7.88 minutes and 10.57 minutes for inpatient admissions. On a daily basis, a registrar averages 37 outpatient registrations and 17 inpatient admission registrations. Although these numbers may vary from institution to institution due to departmental procedures, processes, and the amount of data collected, these numbers may serve as a benchmark for registration activities.

Admission department standards were proposed in April 1992 by NAHAM to ensure high quality performance in the field of admissions. The standards state:

- The Admission Department is provided with adequate direction, staffing, and facilities to perform required functions.
    1. The Admission Department services are directed by a qualified admission administrator or director who possesses the administrative skills necessary to provide effective leadership and management of admission information systems.
    2. When employment of an accredited individual (accredited access manager [AAM]) is impossible, the hospital secures the consultative assistance of a qualified accredited access management administrator.
    3. Verification checks for accuracy, consistency, and uniformity of data recorded and used in quality assessment and improvement activities are a regular part of the admission process.
- The admission record contains sufficient information to identify the patient.
    1. Although the format and forms in use in admissions will vary, all admission records contain the following:
        (a) identification data
        (b) evidence of appropriate consent
        (c) the patient's name, address, date of birth, and next of kin
        (d) the chief complaint
- The Admission Department is guided by written policies and procedures.
    1. There are written policies and procedures concerning the scope and conduct of admission services.
    2. The director of the Admission Department is responsible for ensuring that the development and implementation of the policies and procedures are carried out in collaboration with appropriate clinical and administrative representatives.
    3. The policies and procedures are consistent with hospital and medical staff rules and regulations relating to patient care and medical records, and with legal requirements.
- The Admission Department policies and procedures relate to at least the following:
    1. the confidentiality of information
    2. the relationship of the department to other hospital services
    3. the role of the department in advising patients of their rights and responsibilities
    4. the role of the department in addressing advance directives
- The role of Admission Personnel in the hospital's overall program for the assessment and improvement of quality and in committee functions is defined.
- The role of the Admission Department in the utilization review program is defined.
    1. delineation of the responsibilities and authority of those involved in the performance of utilization review activities
    2. confidentiality policy applicable to all utilization review activities, including any findings and recommendations
    3. description of the method(s) for identifying utilization-related problems, including the appropriateness and medical necessity of admissions

The Patient Access Department also should have quality standards and a defined quality assurance program. Measurement of departmental functions should be monitored with performance compared to preset, agreed-upon standards. The frequency of monitoring performance should be dependent upon the relative importance of the function to the total departmental or institutional functions, history of error rates, and improvement opportunities identified.

The Quality Assurance Goal as established at the Methodist Medical Center of Illinois states: "Achievement of excellence in patient processing for the delivery of high quality patient care to the public we serve." Process effectiveness, efficiency, and economy are measured through critical success factors: customer satisfaction, accuracy, completeness, customer wait time, customer interactions, and service costs. As established in the department's Quality Assurance Policy, all information processed by the department will be of the highest accuracy possible, with a goal of 100 percent accuracy. Information will be processed and services provided on a timely basis, with turnaround time established in keeping with priority assignment and good practice. The area's manager is responsible for the ongoing review of the standards and for overseeing of the process to include evaluation and follow-up procedures. As such, the manager is responsible for consultation in the determination of the standards and for conducting monitoring and training processes when appropriate. All employees are expected to participate in the process to the greatest extent possible to include conducting their own monitoring and problem identification processes where feasible.

The process includes the measurement of accuracy, completeness, timeliness, and cost effectiveness through the monitoring of performance based upon established standards.

Principles of total quality management (TQM) will be incorporated, when possible, to enhance the measurement, analysis, and action process. The frequency of monitoring will be dependent upon the relative importance of the function, history of errors, and themes/improvement opportunities identified.

Standards have been established for various performance indicators, including:

- data accuracy
- utilization management/productivity
- efficiency/service time
- safety
- customer satisfaction

As an example, efficiency/service time is one of the primary indicators for the centralized patient scheduling areas, and is measured by the area's call handling activities, including:

- percentage of calls answered directly, sequentially answered, and abandoned
- percentage of time that staff are available/unavailable for calls
- percentage of calls and average time that calls are placed on hold
- average service time (time that staff member is speaking with customer)
- average call volume per time of day and day of week
- average call volume per staff member

Utilization management/productivity may be measured by the volume and type of appointments made. This will be based upon historical time studies and observation, and will vary from institution to institution. An average employee at the Medical Center should handle 40–55 appointments each day. A scale is utilized to measure achieved performance. Another example used in the analysis of services offered by the centralized patient scheduling area compares monthly statistics reflecting the number of scheduling calls received compared to the number of actual appointments scheduled, and the number of patients scheduled for service compared to the number of outpatient registrations. A breakdown of program utilization by physician, the number of tests scheduled in multiple ancillary departments, and the number of appointments scheduled more than 24 hours in advance of the testing date are also recorded for review.

MANAGEMENT RESPONSIBILITIES

Patient Access Services has a high degree of visibility and interaction with patients, the medical staff, and other organizational departments. The impact of advanced technology, judiciary decisions, and budgetary restraints requires an understanding of management principles. Information systems and networks affect staff efficiency, and set the tone of the customers' perception of the institution. Additionally, the department is a multifunctional service department, operating 7 days a week, 24 hours a day, and 365 days a year.

The Patient Access Manager oversees the collection and coordination of necessary medical, financial, and demographic information needed for patient scheduling and registration to the institution. The manager affects the institution's financial stability through efficient registration and preadmission strategies, as well as through charge entry and test requisition input. As such, the manager must research, recommend, and implement improvements in the patient access systems, policies, and procedures to enhance services and optimize reimbursement. Additionally, the manager formulates the department's annual personnel, equipment, and supply budgets.

The manager should be business oriented, prioritizing departmental activities and those of the staff in terms of their relevance to achieving organizational goals. The manager must plan and cooperate with the medical team and the managers of other departments in meeting patient needs and information requirements. The manager also must ensure a systems orientation in the design and management of the department to best meet customer needs both in terms of quality service and financial savings to the patient, provider, and institution. Some specialized duties of the department manager include analyzing statistical data; planning, designing, and implementing new and upgraded information systems and networks; performing financial analyses on new and upgraded equipment; negotiating various types of contract and service arrangements with vendors; and analyzing business operations to identify applications for new technologies. The changing regulatory scene, whether the result of legislation or accrediting guidelines, requires that the manager keep abreast of the latest criteria that affect the department and the institution as a whole. Evaluation of the manager's performance includes consideration of (1) the department's credibility within the organization and with the medical staff, (2) the effectiveness of the manager's working relationships, and (3) the efficiency and quality of the department as demonstrated by time studies and accuracy feedback.

The position of manager requires the ability to comprehend and retain information that can be applied to work procedures. Excellent problem-solving skills are essential, as decisions and judgment utilized by the manager affect the operations and workflow of the institution and medical staff. Creativity and the ability to solve problems through fact finding, reasoning, intuition, and sound decision making are important attributes.

The position requires significant registration experience and/or advanced education in health care or business administration. The manager should have previous patient-related experience and a proven registration-related project track record. The attainment of the credentials of AAMs through NAHAM would be beneficial to this position. Continuing educational opportunities in Patient Access Services are available at local, regional, and national levels through NAHAM.

STAFF RESPONSIBILITIES

Department staff perform various clerical duties such as patient scheduling, patient transportation, preregistration and intake interviewing, patient placement, and insurance verification. Depending upon the complexity and organization of the institution, the staff member may be cross-trained in various job functions or, in the case of larger institutions, be more specialized. With the implementation of patient-focused care strategies, the traditional registrar may be cross-trained to perform clinical testing, as well as job functions beyond the traditional scope of registration.

The position's greatest challenges are ascertaining the informational, escort, and transport needs of the patients and visitors; ensuring timely registration/transportation service; accurately obtaining and processing patient registration and billing information; and promoting a pleasant and friendly environment for the great variety of persons coming to the institution. The staff member must have a thorough knowledge of various insurance documentation requirements, the institution's billing system, the proper registration type, and various data entry codes to ensure proper service documentation and billing of the patient's account from information obtained from the patient/family. Given the continual development of new programs, the staff member must assimilate new policies/procedures into their established work assignments.

Departmental personnel must be selected for their ability to handle a responsibility that requires thoroughness and accuracy, but also for specific personality traits. The registrar/interviewer must be patient, caring, and vivacious, asking the required questions as if they had never been asked before. Because of the sensitive information that may be gathered during the intake process, the staff members must follow strict patient confidentiality guidelines.

EMERGING TECHNOLOGIES AND TRENDS

New technologies and workflow designs will enhance the level of service delivered by the Patient Access Department. Automation, hand-held computers, bar-coding, and voice recognition systems are but a few of today's technologies that, if applied to Patient Access Services, could increase work productivity while enhancing customer satisfaction.

Today's health care delivery system is undergoing unparalleled change. Emerging health care reform, managed care, total quality improvement, the development of integrated health care delivery systems (alliances/networks/mergers), and organizational downsizing are but a few developments that are changing the delivery system on a macro and micro level. These efforts will have a drastic effect on patient access departments and their evolution. Although the services and functions offered by the department will remain fundamentally the same, the organizational structure may be modified. Opportunities to increase functional linkages to foster collaborative efforts among various health care disciplines will create uncertainty in the short term, but will as an outcome develop a fully orchestrated access delivery system.

These changes must be anticipated and greeted with enthusiasm. Ultimately, it should be noted that the health care delivery system must contain the four critical macro processes described earlier. They most certainly will vary on the micro level and may ultimately be organized differently. What remains, however, is the need to process intake information in a timely, accurate, and professional manner, while positively affecting the fiscal integrity of the health care provider.

CONCLUSION

The profession's future will not rely on past history, but on the future commitment to be leaders in the development of a seamless intake and processing system. The successful health care provider will view the department as multidimensional and fully utilize the department's expertise to contribute to institutional goals. Looking at the intake process globally will prevent functional limitations due to organizational structure, and should lead to greater customer satisfaction.

NOTES

1. National Association of Healthcare Access Management (NAHAM), 1101 Connecticut Avenue, N.W., Suite 700, Washington, DC 20036. 202–857–1125.
2. Based upon Access to Accounts Receivable Model. D. Graham, Access to Accounts Receivable, *The NAHAM Management Journal* 20, no. 1 (1993): 7.
3. A. Freeman, Don't Use the 'D' Word, *The NAHAM Management Journal* 17, no. 4 (1992): 20–22.
4. M. Taubin and the Law Offices of Nixon, Hargrave, Devans, and Doyle, The Patient Self-Determination Act (Washington, DC: NAHAM, 1991).

JOHN WOERLY, RRA, MSA, AAM, has been the Director of Patient Registration/Telecommunications at the Methodist Medical Center since 1980. Under his direction the department has implemented various patient amenity services, centralized scheduling, preadmission planning, physicians' answering service, and other customer-oriented programs. Mr. Woerly is a Board Member of the National Association of Healthcare Access Management, serving as the Chairman of Accreditation and Education, and a member of the Editorial Advisory Board for both *Healthcare Access Management* and *Benchmarking*. He is a past recipient of the NAHAM Literary Award and the President's Award.

Chapter 17

Ambulatory Care

Kevin W. Barr and Charles L. Breindel

Prompted by the reimbursement incentives of the 1980s, and facilitated by advances in medical technology, surgery, and anesthesia throughout the 1980s and 1990s, the delivery of health care is shifting from traditional hospital-based inpatient care to ambulatory and non–hospital-based settings. Some hospitals have experienced an erosion of their share of the ambulatory care market as physician, independent, corporate, and payer-sponsored facilities entered the marketplace in search of revenue diversification and/or cost management benefits. The migration from inpatient-based care to ambulatory care has been further fueled by increasing pressure from managed care organizations, national corporations, local businesses, and the federal government to curb the unbridled growth of health care expenditures.

Simply defined, ambulatory care includes those diagnostic and therapeutic procedures and treatments provided to patients in a setting that does not require an extended overnight stay in a hospital. Ambulatory care service settings include medical groups and group practice plans, home health programs, community health clinics, industrial clinics, ambulatory surgery centers (ASCs), outpatient diagnostic centers, urgent-care facilities, oncology centers, rehabilitation centers, and hospital-based ambulatory care facilities. Numerous managed care organizations and payers are beginning to define outpatient or ambulatory care as any treatment episode that does not exceed 24 hours in length regardless of whether the protocol includes an overnight stay in an inpatient or recovery care bed.

The most common hospital-based and non–hospital-based ambulatory care services include:

- urgent care or emergency care
- outpatient diagnostics (including diagnostic radiology, ultrasound, CT, mammography, electrocardiograms, endoscopy/colonoscopy/arthroscopy and MRI)
- home care
- outpatient surgery
- physician practice

Many of these services fall into the category of high-volume procedures that industry experts believe are most likely to be performed predominantly outside the traditional hospital-facility setting in the future. These services represent the core of most hospital-based outpatient revenues today. They also represent the core of services provided by organized delivery systems.

The range of ambulatory care services and providers in today's health care marketplace is large and entire texts have been dedicated to this topic. Accordingly, this chapter focuses on that portion of the service spectrum most closely aligned with traditional hospital-based and emerging freestanding ambulatory care services. This includes those outpatient treatments and/or procedures that do not require an overnight stay in an inpatient facility, and includes care provided by hospital–organized delivery systems and non–hospital-sponsored facilities alike. The chapter also includes a discussion on home care and the routine cognitive and diagnostic ambulatory care services provided by physicians in a traditional medical office setting.

AMBULATORY CARE SERVICES— PAST AND PRESENT

Providers in the 1980s and 1990s

The provision of ambulatory care services has evolved dramatically during the mid- to late 1980s and early 1990s. Traditionally, the vast majority of outpatient care (excluding cognitive and basic diagnostic care provided in physician offices) has been provided in hospital-based facilities and, in most cases, on the campuses of such hospitals. However, in recent years, there has been explosive growth in the type and ownership of facilities in which ambulatory care is offered, blurring the definitions of what historically has been defined as hospital-based outpatient care and other ambulatory care services (Exhibit 17–1).

Until the late 1980s, competition for ambulatory care services was limited to a few traditional health care providers, including hospitals, independent physician groups, and other community health providers. Hospitals, once the dominant players in the outpatient market, now face aggressive competitors with significant capital resources. In certain markets, the competition for ambulatory care has evolved to include a range of traditional and nontraditional providers and owners, including corporate employers, managed care orga-

Exhibit 17–1 Ambulatory Care Service Settings

Past	*Present*
• Hospital outpatient departments	• Chemotherapy and radiation therapy centers
• Physician offices	• Dialysis centers
• Home health agencies	• Diagnostic imaging centers
• Outpatient surgery centers	• Mobile imaging centers
• Hospital emergency rooms	• Fitness/wellness centers
	• Occupational health
	• Psychiatric outpatient/partial hospitalization
	• Rehabilitation centers
	• Freestanding ambulatory surgery centers
	• Sports medicine clinics
	• Urgent/primary care centers
	• Women's health clinics
	• Wound care centers

Exhibit 17–2 Ambulatory Care Providers/Owners

Past	Present
• Hospitals	• Corporate employers
• Independent physician practitioners	• Insurance companies/managed care organizations
• Community health providers/agencies	• Hospitals
• Home health agencies	• Independent physician practitioners
	• Independent corporate chains
	• National physician chains
	• Community health providers/agencies
	• Home health companies
	• National diversified health care companies

nizations (e.g., health maintenance organizations [HMOs] and other insurers), corporate physician chains, and national diversified health care corporations (see Exhibit 17–2). Such competition largely has occurred in areas of abundance where financial access to care, population base, and supply of clinical subspecialists facilitate provider entrance. Geographically, these areas of abundance have translated into urban–suburban markets populated by employer-insured residents and Medicare recipients. Conversely, in other areas of limited abundance (e.g., rural and inner-city markets) and for certain populations (e.g., the poor, uninsured, and elderly), access to ambulatory care and breadth of providers is still limited. Hospitals, once the dominant outpatient provider in areas of abundance, now face aggressive competitors with significant capital resources and agility. In rural areas, hospitals often still are the dominant providers of ambulatory care.

A 1992 survey of outpatient care providers ranked Kaiser Permanente, a staff model HMO, as the second largest provider of freestanding ambulatory care in terms of number of operational facilities in the United States. Independent physicians, national ambulatory care corporations, and HMOs represent a source of continued competition for the tradi-

tional hospital organization.[1] This is particularly true in those markets that may be characterized as areas of abundance. The ambulatory care market of the 1990s has evolved to include numerous owner organizations, for example:

- outpatient chains
- imaging companies
- managed care organizations
- health care systems
- physician chains/franchises
- diversified health care companies

Changing Clinical Technology and Reimbursement

The rapid growth of ambulatory services and movement to freestanding and independently owned facilities has been driven primarily by three factors:

1. payer pressure to check rising health care costs associated with inpatient care
2. increased availability of reimbursement for ambulatory care procedures and providers
3. technological advances in ambulatory care occurring at an unprecedented pace

An additional factor contributing to the rapid growth (in some states) is the deregulation of Certificate of Need (CON) legislation. CON laws have traditionally restricted the expansion of new health services and providers.

Dramatic breakthroughs in diagnostic imaging, pharmaceuticals, therapeutics, biotherapeutics, anesthesia, analgesics, and optical and laser surgical instrumentation have resulted in significant reductions in inpatient stays, sharp growth of same-day surgical procedures, and empty postsurgical beds. The development of new and advanced technologies and instrumentation, occurring at this historically unprecedented rate, will continue to affect the growth of ambulatory care beyond the turn of the century.

One example of this unprecedented change is the rapid acceptance of endoscopic surgical instrumentation. As reported by Biomedical Business International of Santa Ana, Califor-

nia, within two years after the introduction of the laparoscopic cholecystectomy procedure (by 1992), this surgical method accounted for nearly 20 percent of the gallbladder removals in the United States. Industry experts suggest that endoscopic surgery will account for 70 to 90 percent of the most common high-volume surgeries performed in hospitals, specifically cholecystectomies, kidney removals, appendectomies, hysterectomies, and hernia repairs. Others predict that 80 percent of all abdominal and thoracic surgery will be performed laparoscopically before the year 2000.[2]

Figure 17–1 illustrates the dramatic impact of technological advances and reimbursement pressures on hospital-based surgery. In 1993, slightly more than 55 percent of total community hospital surgical procedures were performed on an outpatient basis.

Such changes accent a myriad of management and medical staff challenges for health

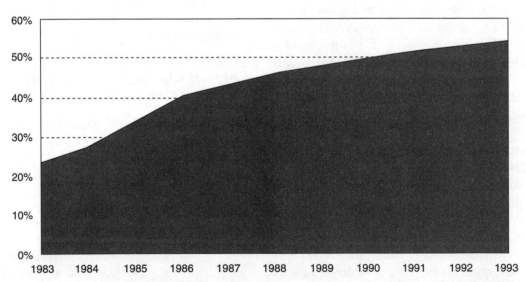

Figure 17–1 Percent of Surgeries Performed on Outpatient Basis, All Community Hospitals in the United States. Most current data available. *Source:* Adapted with permission from *1984 Hospital Statistics, 1985 Hospital Statistics*, and *1996/97 Hospital Statistics*, Healthcare InfoSource, Inc., a subsidiary of the American Hospital Association, © 1984, 1985, and 1996.

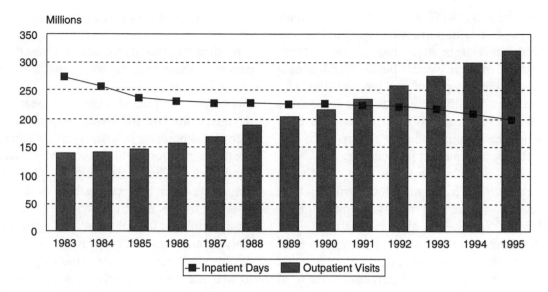

Figure 17–2 Shifting Trends in Hospital Utilization, All Community Hospitals in the United States (Outpatient Data Exclude Emergency Department Visits). *Source:* Adapted with permission from *1984 Hospital Statistics*, *1985 Hospital Statistics*, and *1996/97 Hospital Statistics*, Healthcare InfoSource, Inc., a subsidiary of the American Hospital Association, © 1984, 1985, and 1996.

care executives, including careful selection and acquisition of new technologies, physician privileging criteria for new procedures, training of surgical support staff, and continuing medical education for medical staff.

Hospital-Based Services

In recent years, hospital administrators have realized that establishing a firm position in the ambulatory care market is critical to the continued survival of their organizations. The Health Care Advisory Board (a national health care research and advisory group based in Washington, D.C.) has emphasized that "the shift to ambulatory care is not simply another trend in healthcare; it is the future of the hospital. Outpatient [care] is . . . the only part of the hospital business that is booming."[3]

Between 1990 and 1995, community hospital outpatient visits in the United States increased at an annual growth rate of 8.3 percent, growing from 214.6 million visits in 1990 to 319.6 million visits by 1995. During this same five-year period, community hospital inpatient days dropped approximately 2.4 percent. Figure 17–2 shows the shifting trend in hospital-based outpatient visits and inpatient days.[4]

As the percentage of community hospital gross revenue generated by ambulatory care services advances to 50 percent by the year 2000, hospitals are expected to evolve into high-acuity service sites with significant ambulatory care components rather than the full-continuum inpatient facilities of the late 1980s and early 1990s. This transformation will produce new challenges for health care executives in the way they structure, organize, manage, staff, and market their organizations. It is important that hospital executives view ambulatory care as an essential portion of their overall health care business rather than a supplemental product-line of an inpatient facility. This change in the culture of management thinking comes at a time when the hospital industry's share of the ambulatory care market is declining.

Prior to 1985, outpatient care constituted less than 15 percent of total gross patient revenue for all community hospitals in the United States. The shift in treatments and procedures to the outpatient setting has been dramatic, with a typical community hospital capturing 30 or more percent of its total gross patient revenue from outpatient care by 1995. Most industry planners believe that by the year 2000, ambulatory care will account for 50 percent or more of the total gross patient revenue of a community hospital (Figure 17–3).

Hospital-Based Medicare Payments

Medicare payments for hospital-based outpatient services have grown dramatically between 1984 and 1994 (Table 17–1). During this period, the rate of increase in Medicare payments for hospital-based outpatient services (13.3 percent) was nearly double that of hospital inpatient and outpatient services combined. Medicare payments for hospital-based outpatient services include diagnostic tests and therapeutic treatments (e.g., laboratory, radiology, and physical therapy), renal dialysis, and ambulatory surgery. The growth of outpatient payments for services provided to Medicare beneficiaries has been influenced by several significant developments:

- introduction of Medicare's inpatient prospective payment system (PPS)
- growth of managed care plan enrollment and market penetration

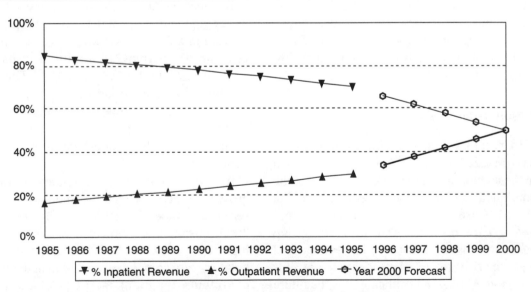

Figure 17–3 Percent Inpatient and Outpatient Gross Revenue, All Community Hospitals in the United States. Most current data available. *Source:* Data from *Hospital Statistics*, 1984/85–1996/97 editions, American Hospital Association.

Table 17–1 Growth in Total Medicare Payments, Hospital Payments, and Home Health Agency Payments (Most Current Data Available)

Calendar Year	Total Payments Medicare Services	Medicare Payments for Hospital-Based Services				Medicare Payments for Home Health Agency Services	
		All Hospital Payments	Outpatient Services Only			Home Health Agency Payments	% Total Medicare Payments
			Outpatient Payments	% Total Medicare Payments	% Total Hospital Payments		
1984	$59,146	$41,887	$3,387	5.7	8.1	$1,666	2.8
1985	$63,694	$44,282	$4,082	6.4	9.2	$1,773	2.8
1986	$88,883	NA	NA	NA	NA	$1,796	2.0
1987	$75,816	$49,688	$5,600	7.4	11.3	$1,792	2.4
1988	$81,403	$53,251	$6,372	7.8	12.0	$1,948	2.4
1989	$93,844	$59,783	$7,161	7.6	12.0	$2,432	2.6
1990	$101,419	$64,888	$8,172	8.1	12.6	$3,714	3.7
1991	$110,887	NA	NA	NA	NA	$5,389	4.8
1992	$120,710	$74,917	$9,941	8.2	13.3	$7,397	6.1
1993	$129,388	$78,378	$10,939	8.5	14.0	$9,726	7.5
1994	$146,549	$82,437	$11,814	8.1	14.3	$12,661	8.6
Change 1984–1994							
> $ Amount (Millions)	$87,403	$40,550	$8,427	—	—	$10,995	—
> Average Annual Growth	9.5%	7.0%	13.3%	—	—	22.5%	—

Note: All $ amounts shown in millions.

Source: Reprinted from *Health Care Financing Review: Medicare and Medicaid Statistical Supplement,* 1996, Office of Research and Demonstration, Health Care Financing Administration.

- technological innovations in outpatient surgery and diagnostic testing

The introduction of diagnosis-related groups (DRGs) encouraged hospitals to find lower-cost treatment options, leading to the transfer of diagnostic testing and therapeutic treatments from the inpatient environment to outpatient service departments and freestanding outpatient facilities. This result was further enhanced by similar reimbursement control incentives introduced by commercial managed care organizations focused on physician behavior. As managed care organizations worked to influence physician behavior favoring more aggressive referral to outpatient care environments, Medicare utilization of outpatient services has been likewise affected.

The rapid growth in Medicare outpatient service payments to hospitals has proven to be a significant force in regulatory mandates to develop prospectively based reimbursement methodologies for ambulatory surgery, home care, and general outpatient service areas. Such prospectively based payment methodologies are examined later in this chapter.

Freestanding Ambulatory Care Services

Freestanding ambulatory care centers can provide a variety of diagnostic and therapeutic services, including rehabilitation, diagnostic radiology, mammography, radiation therapy, chemotherapy, urgent care, and outpatient surgery. The most common types of freestanding centers are:

- diagnostic imaging centers
- urgent-care centers
- outpatient surgery centers

Diagnostic imaging centers typically have capabilities such as basic radiographic and fluoroscopic radiology, ultrasound, mammography, and often computed tomography (CT). Highly competitive and mature markets tend to have other types of freestanding ambulatory care services complementary to these conventional facilities, including women's imaging centers, women's health centers, mobile imaging units, rehabilitation centers, and sports medicine centers. Similar services often are available in independent physician and medical group practices as well, particularly obstetric/gynecologic physician groups likely to offer mammography and ultrasound testing.

Forces influencing the evolution of ambulatory care services from traditional hospital-based settings to freestanding facilities include:

- tightened reimbursement, particularly for high-volume Medicare procedures (e.g., cataracts and cardiac catheterization)
- emerging technology supportive of freestanding facilities
- dramatic growth of proceduralists and the lucrative reimbursement thereof for outpatient procedures
- easing of CON laws
- physician interest in increasing efficiency resultant from one-stop location

The growth of independently owned and freestanding ambulatory care centers is forcing hospitals to become more responsive to customers' needs and preferences, including factors such as convenience, easy access, and limited waiting time. Freestanding ambulatory care centers are consuming an ever-larger portion of the market for outpatient procedures. In the 1980s, hospital emergency departments were challenged competitively by a significant growth in minor emergency and urgent care centers, which focused on the minor injury and simple urgent care needs of the population. These facilities successfully skimmed off higher margin business from the traditional hospital emergency department and filled a void for consumers without an established family physician relationship.

Another example, the freestanding ASC market, is heavily dominated by independents and physicians. The most active specialty group to enter the freestanding ASC market was ophthalmology. As Medicare pushed for more cataract operations to be performed on an outpatient basis, and implemented its ASC Payment Groups, a dramatic increase in physician interest and ownership of freestanding surgical facilities occurred. Other specialties that became involved in building independent surgery centers include orthopedics and urology. The list of procedures routinely performed on an outpatient basis has grown steadily, to include cataract surgery, breast biopsies, arthroscopic knee surgery, hernia repair, removal of lesions, and gynecological procedures such as dila-

tion and curettage. During the five-year period 1988 to 1992, the number of freestanding surgery centers increased in excess of 75 percent from 964 facilities to 1,696 facilities (see Figure 17–4).

Four factors account for the rapid success of freestanding surgery centers:

1. rising consumer demand for same-day surgery
2. market penetration of managed-care plans and pressure from third-party payers to control costs
3. additions to the Medicare-approved list of ambulatory procedures covered for outpatient reimbursement
4. technological advances in surgical techniques

The federal government is expected to continue to expand its list of surgical procedures approved for Medicare reimbursement in freestanding and hospital-based ambulatory surgery centers. Managed care plans will follow suit and continue to be an important in-

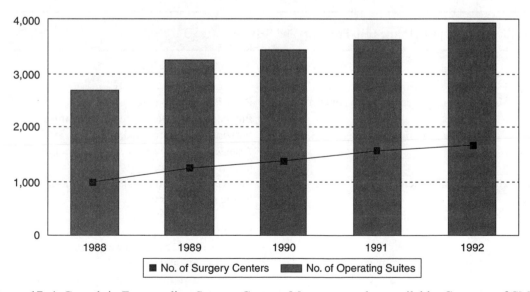

Figure 17–4 Growth in Freestanding Surgery Centers. Most current data available. Courtesy of SMG Marketing Group, Chicago, Illinois.

gredient in the growth of freestanding surgery centers, particularly as their market penetration increases.

Although the transition of inpatient procedures to the outpatient setting is certain to continue as medical technology advances, certain new technologies will be dependent on access to advanced hospital-based services in cases where inpatient back-up or conversion may be required. This will buffer somewhat the erosion of the hospital industry's share of the ambulatory surgery market. However, innovative freestanding center executives already are beginning to adjust by establishing accommodations for overnight or extended stays. This is taking the form of extended recovery capabilities, including 23 recovery care and nurse-attended overnight stay facilities.[5]

Home Care Services

Broadly defined, home care service providers include certified and noncertified skilled nursing agencies, private duty nursing agencies, home infusion therapy companies, home respiratory therapy providers, and durable medical equipment (DME) suppliers. Most providers have a dominant core service complemented by ancillary service offerings rather than a full spectrum of home care services/products. Consequently, home care providers have generally followed a market niche strategy with many agencies maintaining a very narrow service offering (Exhibit 17–3).

The market opportunities for niche players is changing, however, as more hospitals develop integrated full-service home care organizations and home care reimbursement tightens.

Proprietary home care agencies dominate the industry, accounting for nearly 45 percent of the Medicare-certified home care providers in the United States. Hospital-based organizations follow, claiming more than 25 percent of the industry. Visiting nursing associations (VNAs), which used to hold 20 to 35 percent of the home care industry in the 1970s and early 1980s, represent less than 10 percent of all Medicare-certified providers.

Exhibit 17–3 Typical Home Care Providers and Services Offered

Provider Types	Core Services
• Skilled nursing (certified and noncertified)	• RN/LPN nursing care
	• Physical/occupational/speech therapies
• Private duty nursing	• Personal care (homemakers/aides)
	• Assisted living activities (housekeeping/shopping/transportation)
• Home infusion therapy	• Intravenous pharmaceuticals/antibiotics
	• Home chemotherapy
• Home respiratory therapy	• Respiratory treatments/education
	• Oxygen
	• Rental/sale of respiratory equipment
• Durable medical equipment	• Sale of medical supplies
	• Rental/sale of medical equipment (e.g., hospital beds, wheelchairs, IV pumps)

Between 1985 and 1995, the total number of Medicare-certified providers increased approximately 52 percent from 5,983 certified agencies to 9,120 agencies (Figure 17-5).

The most common home care service is skilled nursing care. Historically, hospital-based agencies have focused primarily on skilled nursing care while proprietary agencies have been more aggressive in developing home infusion, chemotherapy, and assisted living services and DME products. Home infusion and nutrition therapies are becoming more prevalent offerings as a result of pharmacological breakthroughs, home chemotherapy treatment, and a growing trend for home-based rather than institutional treatment approaches for these care needs. Skilled nursing care and physical therapy services continue to grow, fulfilling a critical role in the postsurgical care for ambulatory and inpatient surgical patients.

Home care services have been one of the fastest-growing segments of the ambulatory care marketplace for the past decade due to clinical and treatment advances, emphasis on noninstitutional approaches to care, aging of the population, and advanced life span for Americans. Accordingly, home care agencies continue to see increases in the number of patients suffering from Alzheimer's disease, other forms of dementia, AIDS, and other types of chronic illnesses.

Formation of hospital-based organized delivery systems in the late 1990s prompted hospital systems to develop large home care organizations with full-service offerings from skilled nursing care, DME, and infusion therapy to hourly home health aide and homemaker services. With pressure to reduce inpatient lengths of stay, many patients are discharged to home care for continued rehabilitative care, including chronic medical and postsurgical care needs. The growth of Medicare patients discharged to home care is expected to increase further as Medicare HMOs successfully penetrate the population.

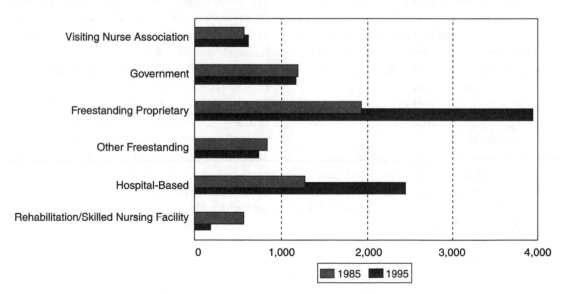

Figure 17–5 Number of Medicare Certified Home Care Agencies. Most current data available. *Source:* Reproduced by permission of the National Association for Home Care, 1996. Not for further reproduction.

Medicare Payments for Home Care Services

Medicare payments for home health agency services have increased even more dramatically than hospital-based outpatient services. Prior to 1984, home health agency payments were less than one half of Medicare expenditures for hospital-based outpatient services. By 1994, however, home health agency payments had grown so dramatically that Medicare expenditures for home health services exceeded the aggregate dollar amount and percentage of total Medicare program payments made for hospital-based outpatient services (see Table 17–1).

Growth in Medicare home health agency expenditures has been influenced by several significant developments beginning in 1989. These developments include:

- revision of Medicare coverage guidelines in the Medicare Health Insurance Manual (HIM-11)
- rapid growth of Medicare-certified home health agencies
- increased home health agency utilization in terms of visits per member served
- introduction of Medicare's inpatient prospective payment system
- growth in the over-65 population (the largest single consumer group of home care services)

Home health coverage for Medicare eligibles was significantly affected by revision of the HIM-11, effective July 1, 1989. A key objective of the revised HIM-11 was to clarify coverage policies governing Medicare home health benefits. HIM-11 specified that certain services requiring skilled nursing judgement and technical skill should be considered skilled services (for Medicare eligibility and coverage purposes), and that beneficiaries who require such skilled services should be eligible for all Medicare-covered home health benefits (e.g., home health aide service visits). As a result, Medicare home health aide eligibility and coverage provisions were significantly expanded and skilled nursing and home health aide visits increased. Figures 17–6 and 17–7 illustrate the related parallel trends in average number of visits per person served and average charge per visit by ownership type.

Hospice

Hospices offer a special approach for delivering care to individuals who are terminally ill. This care is organized around a core interdisciplinary team of skilled professionals—physicians, nurses, medical social workers, therapists, counselors, and volunteers. Unlike the traditional medical model of health care, hospices provide palliative care, as opposed to curative care (the custom in acute care settings), emphasizing pain and symptom control measures. Hospices may be freestanding, home health agency–based, skilled nursing facility–based, or hospital-based (Figure 17–8).

Freestanding hospices are independent, mostly nonprofit organizations. Home health agency–based hospices are owned by nonprofit and proprietary home care agencies, typically as an ancillary service offering to a Medicare-certified home health agency. Hospital-based hospices are operating units or departments of nonprofit or proprietary hospitals. Skilled nursing facility–based hospices are operating units or departments of skilled nursing home facilities. Since 1990, the number of Medicare-certified hospices has grown rapidly at an average annual growth rate of approximately 19 percent. Freestanding hospices represent the fastest growing type of hospice provider.[6]

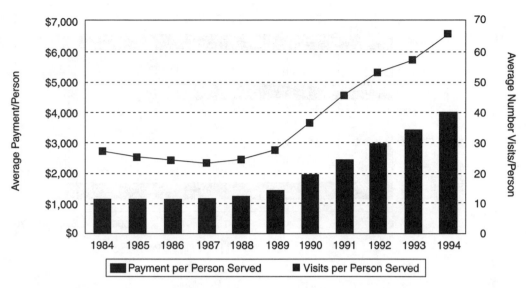

Figure 17–6 Medicare Program Utilization of Home Health Agency Services. Most current data available. *Source:* Reprinted from *Health Care Financing Review: Medicare and Medicaid Statistical Supplement*, 1996, Office of Research and Demonstration, Health Care Financing Administration.

Care is primarily provided in the patient's home in order to maintain the peace, comfort, and dignity of the patient and support family participation. The underlying principle of

hospice care is to afford to terminally ill patients and their families the right to participate fully in the end-of-life (or as many hospices prefer to reference "preparing for the

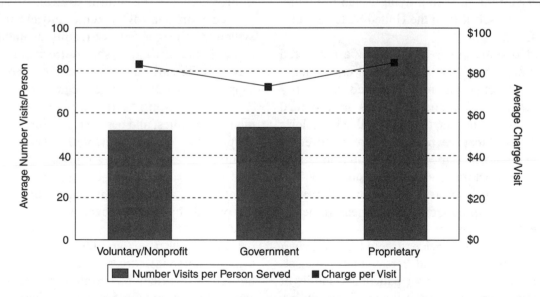

Figure 17–7 Medicare Program Utilization of Home Health Agency Services. Most current data available. *Source:* Reprinted from *Health Care Financing Review: Medicare and Medicaid Statistical Supplement*, 1996, Office of Research and Demonstration, Health Care Financing Administration.

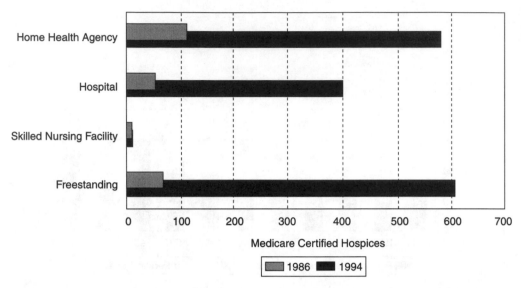

Figure 17–8 Number of Medicare Certified Hospices. Most current data available. *Source:* Reproduced by permission of the Hospice Association of America, 1995. Not for further reproduction.

next life") experience. While the U.S. hospice movement, as defined formally, began in the 1960s, some religiously sponsored groups serving the poor and dying began providing hospice services in the United States decades earlier.

Nursing care is provided by a registered nurse or by a licensed practical nurse (under the supervision of a licensed registered nurse). Medical social services are provided by social workers, typically with a bachelor's degree. Hospice programs are required to have a hospice medical director who is a licensed doctor of medicine or osteopathy. The medical director assumes the overall responsibility for the medical component of the patient care program.

Counseling services (including caregiver support, dietary, and bereavement counseling) are provided to the patient and family or other caregivers in the home. Typically bereavement counseling is provided to the family for up to one year after the patient's death.

Short-term inpatient care may be provided in a participating hospice inpatient unit, hospital, or skilled nursing facility. Inpatient care is provided for the administration of advanced pain control or acute and chronic symptom management not readily available in the home setting. A short-term inpatient stay (respite care) also may be provided to support the family or primary caregiver.

DME (including "self-help" appliances), medical supplies, and personal comfort items for palliation or management of the patient's terminal illness typically are offered to hospice patients. Drugs and biologicals for the relief of pain and symptom control are key to the overall quality of hospice service provided.

Home health aides and homemakers may provide personal care services or perform household services to maintain a safe and sanitary environment. Services include bed changes, light cleaning, and laundering essential to the comfort and cleanliness of the patient, and they are provided under the general supervision of a registered nurse.

Rehabilitation services (e.g., physical and occupational therapies and speech language pathology) are used for symptom control or to enable the patient to maintain basic activities of daily living and functional skills.

Volunteers fulfill a significant role for most hospices and are trained to perform specific patient support functions. Volunteers provide to patients and families an extra measure of support not often available from salaried staff. Typically volunteers participate in administrative (e.g., correspondence with families, particularly after death), patient visitation, and community awareness/education activities.

For acute care and home care organizations, a quality assessment committee oversees the quality of care delivery, staff skills, program policies, and patient treatment considerations. The committee includes the medical director, the chief administrative officer (e.g., vice president or director), and representatives from each professional and support service area. Committee responsibilities can include

- a review of hospice program performance and quality indicators
- an evaluation of the appropriateness of the scope of services offered
- an evaluation of staffing policies, including personnel qualifications, position descriptions, education policies
- an evaluation of admission, discharge, and complaint handling policies
- a review and evaluation of the medical record and treatment plans for a sample of active and discharged patients

Figure 17–9 shows a typical hospice organizational chart for a hospital-based hospice program.

Physician-Based Services

Independent and group medical practices account for a significant portion of ambulatory care treatment activity in the United States. Per capita physician office utilization has remained relatively steady over the last decade. The National Ambulatory Medical Care Survey reported an average of 2.7 physician visits per person per year in the United States in 1995, as shown in Table 17–2.

Faced with a trend toward tightened hospital and physician reimbursement throughout the 1980s and 1990s and growth of outpatient care alternatives, a significant number of entrepreneurial physicians and for-profit corporate chains have evolved within the ambulatory care market. These new entrants have focused on the more profitable business segments thereof. Physicians represent perhaps the most aggressive source of competition, one that essentially controls all outpatient referrals. In many communities, physicians represent a significant challenge to hospital executives, as they have established independent outpatient service capabilities.

In the face of declining reimbursement, physicians have found diversification into conventional hospital-based outpatient service areas to be an enticing and lucrative source of additional revenue and income. Factors accelerating this progression and its financial attractiveness include:

- introduction of Medicare's Physician Payment Reform and payer conversion to resource-based relative value scale (RBRVS) payment methodologies, causing compression of physician revenues
- inflation of medical practice overhead expenses, resulting in increased attention on future practice profitability
- growth of large group practices creating sizable patient bases, an immediate

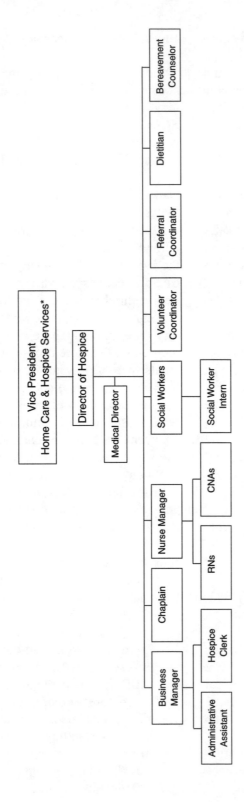

*For a typical hospital-based hospice program, the vice president also may be responsible for home care services.

Figure 17–9 Typical Hospice Organizational Chart

Table 17–2 Physician Office Visits* in United States, 1990–1995 (Most Current Data Available)

	1990	*1991*	*1992*	*1993*	*1994*	*1995*
Number of Office Visits						
(in Thousands)	704,604	669,689	762,045	717,191	681,457	697,082
Visits per 100 Persons per Year	286.3	269.3	303.1	282.0	262.5	266.2
Visits per Capita per Year	2.9	2.7	3.0	2.8	2.6	2.7

*Represents office visits made to nonfederally employed, office-based physicians in United States.

Source: Data from *National Ambulatory Medical Care Survey: 1990 Summary, 1991 Summary, 1992 Summary, 1993 Summary, 1994 Summary, and 1995 Summary*, U.S. Department of Health and Human Services, Centers for Disease Control and Prevention, National Center for Health Statistics.

source of referrals for outpatient services
- growth of national medical practice franchises (organizations with significant capital and management resources) making physician-only ventures increasingly feasible, for example PhyCor, Pacific Physician Services, and Caremark International
- decreasing price of technologies, making equipment more affordable

Nontraditional Ambulatory Care Services

During the late 1980s, some hospitals followed a path of diversification into nontraditional ambulatory care services as a means to expand beyond traditional hospital-based services and augment current sources of revenue. Hospitals following this strategy largely were in pursuit of new sources of revenue to offset declining inpatient volume and income. Examples of some of the more frequently developed programs and services include:

- medical malls
- wellness and fitness centers
- weight management programs
- urgent care centers

- occupational health and industrial medicine programs

Such service diversifications were successful for some hospitals, but many did not capture the financial returns sought. In retrospect, some of these "early adopters" recognized the shifting delivery of health care from traditional inpatient settings to new and ambulatory service settings.

ORGANIZATION AND MANAGEMENT OF AMBULATORY CARE SERVICES

Types of Ownership

Before discussing the various organizational and management structures for ambulatory care service providers, it is useful to briefly define several common classifications of ambulatory facility ownership, specifically, hospital-based, hospital-owned, joint venture, and freestanding.

Hospital-based ambulatory care facilities are solely owned by and are a central part of the physical plant of a hospital organization, whether the hospital organization is a taxable or not-for-profit corporation. Hospital-owned ambulatory care facilities are owned (in full or jointly) by the hospital organization, but usually are not part of the core physical plant of the hospital. A hospital-owned facility may be located on the hospital's campus or off-campus, whether wholly or jointly owned. Joint venture ownership is defined as a legal entity controlled by two or more parties organized under a contract or lease agreement, corporation, general partnership, or limited partnership. Freestanding ambulatory care facilities are not owned by a hospital. Common freestanding facility owners include independent physicians, physician partnerships, for-profit corporations, and insurance companies.

Organization and Management

Various organizational and management structures are found within the ownership arrangements identified above. Hospital-based ambulatory care services are usually organized under a traditional pyramid-style management design with various portions of the overall ambulatory care services reporting to multiple managers or administrators on the hospital's management team. The distinguishing characteristics of this form of organizational structure are the lack of a separate manager with distinct line authority for all outpatient services and the resulting hierarchical process for decision making (Figure 17–10). Under the hospital-based organizational structure, the provision of ambulatory services is typically fragmented and viewed as an ancillary component to the more dominant inpatient service lines. Some hospital systems have established more progressive management structures for ambulatory care, organizing all outpatient functions (including patient registration) into an integrated business line under a single member of the hospital's senior management team.

Joint venture and freestanding ambulatory care facilities frequently have more streamlined organizational and management structures. These facilities are commonly organized under the direction of a policy board or management committee with a senior manager or administrator responsible for day-to-day operations and management. Representation on the policy board or management committee is determined by the degree of ownership and status of the shareholder corporation(s), or the general and/or limited partners.

The vast majority of hospital-based ambulatory services are located on-campus and

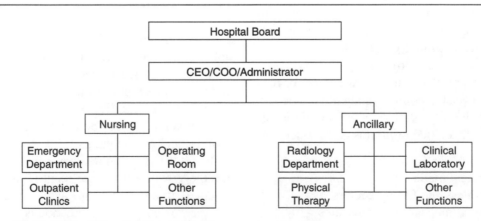

Figure 17–10 Typical Hospital-Based Structure

thereby are affected by the constraints of the site, inpatient-oriented units, and other physical limitations of the hospital plant. Typically, this contributes to a lack of convenience and accessibility to the patient—service deficiencies of significant importance to routine, frequently performed outpatient procedures such as radiology, ultrasound, rehabilitation, and oncology. Frequently performed low-end procedures are those where convenience and accessibility are critical to customer satisfaction. Such attributes of service quality are less serious, yet not inconsequential, to the more intermittent ambulatory procedures and tests, for example, magnetic resonance imaging (MRI), ambulatory surgery, and cardiac catheterization.

While the percentage of hospital revenue attributable to ambulatory care continues to expand, a recent American Hospital Association survey of hospital CEOs revealed that only 21 percent of U.S. hospitals have a separate manager with distinct line authority for total outpatient activity and that this structure has changed little compared to preceding years.[7]

Physician Practice Structures

Physician practices can be organized under various designs and structures, including independent practice, group practice (single specialty and multispecialty), hospital-based, hospital-affiliated, faculty practice plan, or group and staff model HMO practices. Common physician ownership configurations include sole proprietor, professional corporation, and partnership arrangements.

Hospital-affiliated physician practices include solo and group medical practices linked to a hospital (or hospital system) contractually through a management services organization (MSO) or employment by the hospital or a subsidiary hospital corporation

or physician organization. A faculty practice plan is a multispecialty physician group practice based at a medical teaching university. This type of physician practice, while typically independent of university or medical school ownership, is an integral part of its medical education and residency programs. Group model HMO practices are prepaid group practices, commonly multispecialty groups, under contract to provide health care to members enrolled in the HMO plan. Group model physicians are not employees of the HMO. Staff model physician groups fulfill a similar function but are employed by the HMO plan.

There is a distinct trend for physicians to seek out group practice opportunities as they face growing economic and efficiency challenges. The growth of managed care and flattening reimbursement are the two single greatest forces prompting physicians to seek out group practice opportunities. Thirty percent of all nonfederal physicians were organized under a group practice arrangement in 1988.[8] A panel of physicians who participated in a 1991 Delphi study conducted by Arthur Andersen and the American College of Healthcare Executives concluded that the percentage of physicians organized under a group practice would reach 40 percent by 1996.[9] Many physicians have found the group practice setting to be a more secure environment providing additional leverage in negotiating with managed care plans as well as an alluring method for controlling practice overhead expenses and realizing economies of scale benefits.

The consolidation of physicians into group practice organizations is taking shape under several approaches, including:

- mergers of individual physicians and groups into single-specialty and multispecialty groups

- formation of group practices without walls (a hybrid group practice model whereby independent office locations and some autonomy are maintained)
- growth of national medical practice franchises
- formation of hospital-affiliated group practices

Other less formal group networking initiatives include physician contracting networks and physician–hospital organizations (PHOs). These initiatives typically take the form of an alliance or coalition of independent practitioners joined with a hospital for direct contracting with self-insured employers and other payer groups.

Evolution of Hospital-Affiliated Medical Groups

The benefits driving physicians and hospitals to physician–hospital networks include the opportunity to:

- facilitate managed care and self-insured employer contracts
- enhance contract negotiating leverage
- offset increased administrative overhead
- share skilled expertise and staff required to handle the increased business complexity of medical practice
- improve recruitment and retention of physicians

In recent years, a definite trend for hospital organizations to acquire physicians' practices has emerged. This has been motivated by hospital executives' desire to protect market share, preserve historical referral sources, enhance payer contract negotiating leverage, and support the formation of vertically integrated delivery systems. The most popular acquisition target is primary care. Specialty practice acquisitions are occurring at a relatively infrequent pace. Rather, hospital-based

and specialty physician relationships are forming around affiliations and alliances versus ownership.

The growth of hospital-affiliated and hospital-owned medical practices is demonstrative of a transformation in the way many health care executives are thinking about and approaching the marketing strategies for their organizations. In the 1980s, promotional-based marketing (specifically, consumer-focused advertising) dominated the marketing strategies of most hospitals. This approach, while still effective for very focused objectives and target audiences, is now outdated. A new direction, marketing distribution channel strategies, has already begun to emerge as the dominant strategy for the 1990s and is the foundation of many of today's successful integrated health care systems. This will continue through the turn of the century.

The development of hospital-affiliated group practices—whether they be through ownership, organizational affiliation, merger, or new corporate entities like a PHO—is representative of this shift and a means for hospitals to protect their position in the ambulatory care market. Ironically, most hospitals may have introduced hospital-owned and affiliated medical group actions as an inpatient strategy rather than an outpatient approach. Two other compelling, yet often less recognized, factors driving the formation of hospital-affiliated medical groups are the need to improve the efficiency in the delivery of care and to support the transition to bundled and capitated payment methodologies, a near-future reality for hospitals nationwide.

REIMBURSEMENT

Reimbursement for ambulatory care varies by the ownership structure of the facility providing the service, the nature of the service provided, and the payer responsible for payment. With the exception of Medicare, most payers reimburse providers of outpatient services on a percent-of-charge basis for general diagnostic and therapeutic services. Some HMO/PPO payers have carved out certain high-cost procedures such as cardiac catheterization and MRI with payment for such services prospectively set at a fixed fee per procedure.

With outpatient services consuming a larger portion of the Medicare budget, legislation to control payments for outpatient services has been introduced through the Omnibus Budget Reconciliation Acts of 1986, 1987, and 1990. The result of this legislation has been to convert the payment of outpatient services (specifically laboratory, radiology, and outpatient surgery services) from full-cost reimbursement to various prospectively set payment methodologies. Further, with hospitals aggressively developing outpatient services and shifting costs as a means to offset declining inpatient income, other payers are focusing on the conversion from percent-of-charge-based reimbursement to fixed-fee payments.

Outpatient Service Reimbursement under Medicare

Prior to 1986, Medicare reimbursed hospitals for outpatient services on a "reasonable-cost" basis, paying the lower of reasonable cost or customary charges. The Omnibus Budget Reconciliation Act of 1986 (OBRA 86) instituted several fundamental changes in the payment methodology for outpatient services provided by hospitals and freestanding ambulatory surgery centers (ASCs). The most significant of these changes include:

- a Congressional mandate for the Health Care Financing Administration (HCFA) to develop a prospective payment system (PPS) for outpatient services by 1991

- the qualification of hospital-based ASCs for Medicare reimbursement according to a prospectively set schedule of fixed, per-procedure payment rates
- a "blended" payment methodology for hospital-based ASC surgical procedures based upon a combination of the traditional reasonable-cost approach and the prospective rates for ASCs
- a limit on hospital-based radiology service payments as determined by the lesser of the traditional reasonable-cost approach or a blended payment based upon a combination of reasonable cost and the Medicare prevailing charge.

The Omnibus Budget Reconciliation Act of 1990 (OBRA 90) required that Medicare expenditures for outpatient service be reduced by 5.8 percent between fiscal years 1991 and 1995. Current Medicare payment methodologies for hospital-based and freestanding providers are discussed below. To receive reimbursement from Medicare for the provision of services to Medicare recipients, ambulatory service providers must be a Medicare-certified facility.

Freestanding Ambulatory Surgery Centers

Payment for services provided in freestanding ASCs is based upon a prospectively set schedule of rates as determined by the HCFA. Freestanding ASCs did not qualify for Medicare reimbursement prior to September 1982 when the ASC benefit was first implemented. Since that time, the number of covered procedures has expanded from 54 to over 2,400. Surgical procedures eligible for Medicare reimbursement in ASCs are classified into eight ASC-approved procedure groups. Each of the eight groups has a corresponding prospective payment rate, which is updated annually, to cover the "facility fee" portion of the ambulatory surgical procedure.

The Group 6 and Group 8 rates correlate to ophthalmic surgical procedures, which currently include a $150 add-on allowance to cover the cost of an intraocular lens prosthesis (IOL). The facility fee rates are intended to cover the standard overhead expenses incurred in providing ambulatory surgical services, including nursing services, supplies, equipment, and use of the ASC facility. Physician professional fees are reimbursed independent of the ASC methodology directly to the physician.

ASC facility fee payments include two components—a labor-related portion and nonlabor-related portion. This provision allows for the variation in worker compensation across geographic markets. The labor-related portion represents 34.45 percent of the total ASC payment amount and is determined according to regional wage indices as established by HCFA (HCFA Wage Index) published annually in the *Federal Register*. Table 17–3 shows the calculation of the payment rates (ophthalmic and nonophthalmic) for a freestanding ASC located in Richmond, Virginia.

In cases where multiple ambulatory surgical procedures are performed concurrently, the ASC receives 100 percent of the payment for the procedure falling into the highest payment group and 50 percent of the applicable payment for all other procedures performed.

Hospital-Based Ambulatory Surgery

Medicare's reimbursement methodology for hospital-based ambulatory surgery specifies that hospital providers be paid the lesser of the hospital-specific reasonable cost or actual charge; or a 42/58 percent blended payment based upon the hospital-specific cost or charge and the ASC payment rate.

For the period October 1987 to October 1988, the blended payment was based upon a ratio of 75 percent hospital-specific cost and 25 percent of the ASC payment rate. Similarly, for the period October 1988 to October 1989, the blended payment was based upon a ratio of 50 percent hospital-specific cost and 50 percent of the ASC payment rate. The 42/58 percent blend became effective January 1991. Blended payments for services rendered after January 1, 1991, are based upon the following formula:

$$\text{(Lower of Hospital Cost or Charge} \times .42) + \text{(ASC Payment Rate} \times .58)$$

The blended payment applies only to those surgical procedures identified by Medicare as ASC-approved procedures. For those outpatient surgical procedures not classified as Medicare-approved ASC procedures, hospitals are reimbursed on a reasonable-cost basis. Section 1833(I)(2)(C) of the Social Security Act (as amended by the Social Security Act Amendments of 1994, Public Law 103-432) requires that ASC payment rates be reviewed and updated annually, and that the list of ASC-approved procedures be reviewed and updated every two years by the Secretary of the Department of Health and Human Services. Updates to the Medicare ASC payment rates are based on surveys of actual audited costs incurred by ASCs (conducted not more than every five years) or an automatic inflation adjustment during years when payment amounts are not updated based on actual cost survey data. Such automatic inflation adjustments are based on the percentage increase in the consumer price index for urban consumers (CPI-U) for the related year.

Hospital-Based Radiology Services

Under OBRA 86, payment for hospital-based diagnostic and therapeutic radiology services is based upon the lesser of the pro-

Table 17–3 Example Calculation—ASC Payment Rates (Richmond, Virginia)

	Group 4 Procedure	Group 8 Procedure
Step 1: *Wage-Adjusted Labor Component*		
ASC payment rate	$591	$773
multiplied by		
Labor-related percent	.3445	.3445
multiplied by		
Wage Index Value*	.9194	.9194
equals		
Wage-adjusted labor component	$187.19	$244.83
Step 2: *Nonlabor Component*		
ASC payment rate	$591	$773
multiplied by		
Nonlabor-related percent	.6555	.6555
equals		
Non-labor component	$387.40	$506.70
Step 3: *Adjusted ASC Payment Rate*		
Wage-adjusted labor component	$187.19	$244.83
plus		
Nonlabor component	387.40	506.70
equals		
Adjusted ASC payment rate	$574.59	$751.53
Step 4: *Composite Adjusted ASC Payment Rate***		
Adjusted ASC payment rate		$751.53
plus		
IOL allowance		$150.00
equals		
Composite adjusted payment rate		$901.53

*Wage index for Richmond-Petersburg, Virginia, Metropolitan Statistical Area (MSA). Each MSA or non-MSA is assigned an index to reflect differing wage levels of the specific locality or area. Wage indices are established by HCFA and published annually in the *Federal Register*.

**Since the IOL allowance is not subject to the labor adjustment, the $200 allowance must be subtracted from the standard ASC payment rate before the wage index adjustment is applied.

Source: Data from Medicare Program: Revision of Ambulatory Surgical Center Payment Rate Methodology, *Federal Register*, February 8, 1990; and Medicare Programs: Update of Ambulatory Surgical Center Payment Rates Effective for Services on or After October 1, 1996, *Federal Register*, October 1, 1996.

vider's reasonable cost or actual charge; or a blended payment of the lower of the provider's cost or actual charge times the Medicare prevailing charge for the specific procedure performed.

Blended payments for services rendered after January 1, 1991, are based upon the following calculation:

(Lower of Hospital Cost or Charge × .42)
+ (Medicare Prevailing × .80 × .62 × .58)

The prevailing charge is the amount paid to nonhospital providers for similar radiology procedures performed in physician offices as specified by the Medicare prevailing charge (i.e., fee schedule) for radiology services. Reimbursement under the above methodology applies to diagnostic and therapeutic radiology, nuclear medicine, ultrasound, MRI, and CT procedures.

Commercial/HMO/PPO Reimbursement

Commercial and managed care payers traditionally have paid for outpatient services on a percent-of-charge basis, discounting a provider's actual charge by 15 to 30 percent (or more) depending on the aggressiveness of the provider's pricing. In an effort to control rapidly rising outpatient expenditures, such payers have begun instituting prospectively set and fixed-fee payment methodologies for ambulatory surgery and other high-cost and high-volume outpatient testing (e.g., cardiac catheterization, CT, and MRI).

Payment of ambulatory surgery based upon Medicare's ASC payment groups or a single fixed rate for all procedures (i.e., a single average payment rate) is replacing discount from charge methodologies as commercial and managed care payers renegotiate provider contracts. Some payer contracts have taken further measures to control outpatient surgical costs by combining the facility fee and professional fee components into prospectively set global payment rates. This payment approach is facilitated by physician ownership of ASC facilities where the physician collects both the facility and professional fee components.

Similar prospective and global payment methodologies are evolving for other outpatient services mentioned, including payment schedules based upon relative value systems (e.g., the McGraw-Hill relative value system for radiology procedures).

Home Care Reimbursement

Reimbursement for home health agency services varies by the ownership structure of the agency providing the service and the payer responsible for payment. Agencies are reimbursed by Medicare primarily on a cost-per-visit basis. Medicaid reimbursement is similarly based on a fee-per-visit arrangement. Other payer reimbursement methodologies are based upon either a per-visit-fee schedule or a percentage of the provider's actual charge. Medicare is by far the largest payer for home health services, representing upward of 75 percent of the total volume of a typical hospital-based home health agency (Figure 17–11). Accordingly, Medicare reimbursement is the focus of this section.

The Medicare program reimburses home health agencies at the lesser of per visit cost limits (as established by HCFA); per visit charges (actual provider charges); or per visit actual costs (actual aggregate costs incurred by a provider).

Since most, if not all, agencies price their charges above the Medicare cost limits in order to avoid lost reimbursement, charges rarely determine the level of reimbursement received from the Medicare program. Consequently, reimbursement from Medicare is based on either actual costs or cost limits (commonly referred to as "caps").

Standard per Visit Cost Limits

As provided for in the Social Security Act, Section 1861(v)(1)(A), HCFA is authorized to establish limits on allowable costs incurred by home health providers for payment of services rendered to Medicare recipients. Such

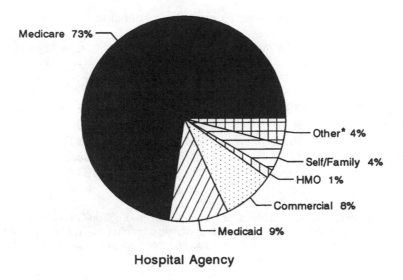

Hospital Agency

*"Other" includes charity, Veterans Affairs, and workers' compensation cases.

Figure 17–11 Payer Mix Profile. Courtesy of SMG Marketing Group, Chicago, Illinois.

limits on home health agency per visit costs have been maintained by HCFA since 1979 and are organized by six care modalities:

1. skilled nursing care
2. physical therapy
3. speech pathology
4. occupational therapy
5. medical social services
6. home health aide

These per visit limits are published annually in the *Federal Register*. The limits are applied to direct and indirect costs of the agency, including the cost of medical supplies routinely furnished in conjunction with patient care. Durable medical equipment, orthotics, prosthetics, and other medical supplies directly identifiable to an individual patient are excluded from the per visit costs and are paid on a cost basis without regard to the established limits. A cost report must be filed

by each home health agency in order to receive Medicare reimbursement. Table 17–4 illustrates the standard per visit limits for freestanding home health agencies.

Wage-Adjusted Cost Limits

In order to normalize for differences in wage levels across different geographic markets, the Medicare program provides for adjustment of the standard limits using regional wage indices applicable to the locality of the provider agency. Table 17–5 shows the calculation of the cost limit for skilled nursing care adjusted by the appropriate wage index for Richmond, Virginia.

Adjustment for Reporting Year

In addition to adjusting the standard per visit limits for market-specific wage differ-

Table 17–4 Standard per Visit Limits for Home Health Agencies

Type of Visit	MSA (NECMA) Locations		Non-MSA Locations	
	Labor Portion	Nonlabor Portion	Labor Portion	Nonlabor Portion
Skilled nursing care	$79.01	$22.28	$92.35	$20.72
Physical therapy	86.51	24.30	100.66	22.72
Speech pathology	86.96	24.64	109.22	24.97
Occupational therapy	85.97	24.55	108.26	24.96
Medical social services	114.01	32.38	154.33	35.24
Home health aide	38.34	10.88	40.63	9.00

Note: MSA denotes Metropolitan Statistical Area. NECMA denotes New England County Metropolitan Area. Per visit limits shown above are effective for cost reporting periods beginning on or after July 1, 1997. Nonlabor portion limits for home health agencies located in Alaska, Hawaii, Puerto Rico, and the Virgin Islands are increased by additional cost of living adjustment factors. See *Federal Register*.

Source: Medicare Program: Schedule of Limits on Home Health Agency Costs per Visit for Cost Reporting Periods Beginning on or After July 1, 1997, *Federal Register*, July 1, 1997.

ences, the adjusted per visit limits are subject to an additional modification to account for a provider's individual Medicare cost reporting year. The standard per visit limits set by HCFA are based upon a common cost reporting year beginning July 1 and ending June 30. If a home health agency has a cost reporting period beginning on or after August 1, an adjustment factor corresponding to the month and year in which the provider's cost reporting period begins is applied.

The factor represents the compounded rate of monthly increase derived from the projected annual increase in the market basket index (as determined by HCFA). The purpose of this adjustment is to account for the inflation in a provider's costs that occurs after the effective date of the common cost reporting period. As with the other provisions of Medicare reimbursement for home health agencies, the cost reporting year adjustment factor is updated annually and reported in the *Federal Register*.

Add-on Payment for Hospital-Based Agencies

Historically, hospital-based home health agencies received an "add-on" payment equal to approximately 11 to 12 percent of the standard per visit limits for freestanding agencies. This hospital-based provider adjustment was suspended for all hospital-based agencies for cost reporting periods beginning after October 1, 1993. Consequently, hospital-based and freestanding home health agencies are subject to the same Medicare cost limits prospectively.

Year-End Settlement

Interim payments made to a home health agency throughout the year are based on the prior year's cost report settlement amount for the agency, adjusted for anticipated inflation. At year-end, the agency prepares and files (with the local Medicare intermediary) a cost report in order to reconcile actual reimbursement due to the agency. This process is commonly referred to as the year-end settlement.

The cost report is based upon aggregate actual costs versus aggregate per visit cost limits. As indicated above, Medicare will reimburse the agency for the lesser of the per visit cost limits or the actual costs. This is determined on an aggregate basis for all types of visits rather than each individual care modality. As an example, if actual costs are above the cost limits in one visit modality—skilled

nursing, for instance—the agency would still be reimbursed the actual aggregate cost. This would occur only if the cost levels for other visit modalities are less than their respective limits by a sufficient amount to offset the skilled nursing care coverage. Table 17–6 shows an illustration of this year-end settlement process.

In this example, the agency receives cost reimbursement of $924,160, even though the actual costs for skilled nursing care exceed the aggregate per visit limit by $40,600. The

Table 17–5 Example Calculation, Adjusted per Visit Cost Limits (Richmond, Virginia)

		Skilled Nursing Care	Home Health Aide	Physical Therapy
Step 1:	*Adjusted Labor Component*			
	Labor portion multiplied by	$79.01	$38.34	$86.51
	Wage Index Value* equals	.9194	.9194	.9194
	Wage-adjusted labor component multiplied by	$72.64	$35.25	$79.54
	Special adjustment for budget neutrality** equals	1.078	1.078	1.078
	Adjusted labor component	$78.30	$38.00	$85.74
Step 2:	*Nonlabor Component*	$24.30	$10.88	$24.30
Step 3:	*Adjusted Cost Limit*			
	Adjusted labor component plus	$78.30	$38.00	$85.74
	Nonlabor component equals	$24.30	$10.88	$24.30
	Adjusted per-visit limit	$102.60	$48.88	$110.04
	Cost reporting year adjustment factor	1.00509	1.00509	1.00509
	Revised per-visit limit	$103.12	$49.13	$110.60

*Wage index for Richmond-Petersburg, Virginia MSA. Each MSA or non-MSA is assigned an index to reflect differing wage levels of the specific locality or area. Wage indices are established by HCFA and published annually in the *Federal Register*.

**Special adjustment to account for transition of the base year of the wage index applied to home health agency cost limits. For additional explanation, see *Federal Register*.

Source: Medicare Program: Schedule of Limits on Home Health Agency Costs per Visit for Cost Reporting Periods Beginning on or After July 1, 1997, *Federal Register*, July 1, 1997.

Table 17–6 Example Year-End Settlement (Richmond, Virginia)

Type of Visit	# of Visits	Adjusted Limit	Aggregate Limit	Aggregate Actual Cost
Skilled nursing care	5,000	$102.60	$513,000	$553,600
Physical therapy	2,000	$111.32	$222,640	$206,160
Home health aide	4,000	$49.10	$196,400	$164,400
Total	11,000		$932,040	$924,160

agency is reimbursed the $924,160, as this is the lesser of the aggregate cost limit and actual cost amounts.

Medicare Home Health Payment Reform

The Balanced Budget Act of 1997 (BBA-97) introduced dramatic changes to the reimbursement for Medicare home health care services. These reimbursement changes, effective for all home health agencies (hospital-based and freestanding) for cost reporting periods beginning on or after October 1, 1997, were driven by the goal of balancing the federal budget by the year 2002. As a result of BBA-97, Medicare program expenditures were reduced by $115 billion over the five-year period 1997–2002, with home health care services accounting for 14 percent or $16.2 billion of these reductions. This legislation mandated the most substantial changes in home care reimbursement since establishment of the per visit cost limits reimbursement program in place since 1979. The payment reform provisions include an interim payment system for home health agencies and development of a PPS to replace the interim payment system for cost reporting periods beginning on or after October 1999.[10]

Interim Payment System

The interim payment system maintains the traditional cost-based elements but includes provisions for reduced limits that affect per visit cost limits and aggregate payments to home health agencies. Under the interim payment system, home health agencies are paid the lowest of actual, reasonable cost; aggregate cost limits; or aggregate per beneficiary annual limits.

Cost Limits

Home health agency cost limits under the interim payment system are calculated at 105 percent of the median per visit costs applicable to freestanding home health agencies (compared to 112 percent of the mean per visit costs for freestanding home health agencies prior to the introduction of BBA-97). Interim payment system cost limits apply to the six standard care modalities: skilled nursing care, physical therapy, speech pathology, occupational therapy, medical social services, and home health aides. According to various estimates, the net effect of the interim payment system was a reduction in cost limits for the six individual modalities ranging between 14 percent and 22 percent, with an average reduction of approximately 15 percent (compared to pre–interim payment system standard cost limits).

Aggregate per Beneficiary Limit

The interim payment system introduced a new payment provision—the annual per beneficiary limit. The annual per beneficiary limit places a restriction on the aggregate reimbursement available to the home health agencies based upon the agencies' average per beneficiary limit multiplied by the unduplicated Medicare census. The unduplicated Medicare census is the number of individual Medicare beneficiaries served during the year, regardless of the number of times the patient was admitted (discharged) and the number of care visits made by the home health agency. The aggregate per beneficiary limit does not place a restriction on the number or frequency of visits to individual patients. It caps the total beneficiary payments a home health agency may receive within the 12 months fiscal year. As noted earlier in this chapter, the number of home health visits to Medicare beneficiaries has increased dramatically in recent years. The annual per beneficiary limit is expected to prevent further increases in the average utilization per patient.

The per beneficiary limit is based upon a 75/25 percent blend consisting of the home health agencies' actual reasonable cost per patient (75 percent), and the home health agencies' applicable census division average reasonable cost per patient (25 percent). These reasonable cost amounts are adjusted to 98 percent of the actual amounts for the baseline cost report year.

Per beneficiary limit = ((home health agency reasonable cost per patient × .75) + (applicable census division average reasonable cost per patient × .25)) × .98

These calculations do not apply to newer home health agencies without adequate historical baseline cost report information established in years prior to the introduction of BBA-97. Special provisions for reimbursement under the interim payment system (as set forth in BBA-97) apply to such home health agencies.

Prospective Payment System

BBA-97 mandated that a PPS be established and implemented for cost reporting periods beginning on or after October 1999. The methodology for implementing PPS is not yet finalized; however, BBA-97 has established that the Secretary of Health and Human Services consider the following:

- an appropriate home care unit of service for determining payment (UOS-P)
- the number, type, and duration of visits within the selected UOS-P
- annual market basket inflation and area wage adjustments
- adjustment provisions for clinical outliers and case mix variances
- potential changes in the mix of services provided within the selected UOS-P and the respective costs related thereto
- provisions to preserve continued access to quality services

BBA-97 mandates that PPS cost limit and per beneficiary limit payment amounts yield a 15 percent reduction in Medicare home health expenditures. If PPS is not fully designed for implementation on October 1, 1999, the Secretary of Health and Human Services is required to reduce interim payment system cost limits and per beneficiary limits by 15 percent.

Effect of Home Health Payment Reform

The effect of home health payment reform is likely to be significant and far-reaching, particularly for hospital-based Medicare-certified home health agencies dependent upon the historically cost-based reimbursement structure. Interim payment system and PPS payment reductions will challenge most, if not all, home health agencies (freestanding and hospital-based) to implement strategies to control and/or reduce per visit costs and the frequency of patient visits. This is particularly important to the home health agencies' ability to remain within the annual per beneficiary limit for Medicare patients. Strategies will be focused on the:

- number and mix of staff visits across the entire multi-disciplinary team (e.g., skilled nursing, home health aides, and therapists)
- provision and consumption rate of medical supplies
- service area limits and staff travel distances (affecting staff productivity in visits per day)
- geographic team assignments (affecting staff productivity)

- use of clinical, computer, and communications technology

As evident in other health care delivery settings, payment reform will prompt the implementation of advanced clinical and computer technology. Such advances will manifest in the form of home monitoring and telecommunication applications for evaluating and communicating patient vital signs and condition. Such technology will determine the need for and frequency rate of follow-up visits. Another likely outcome is an increased expectation of self-care and caregiver participation in the care delivery process. Finally, reductions in administrative overhead staff (assumed to be excessive because of the historical cost reimbursement structure) will occur.

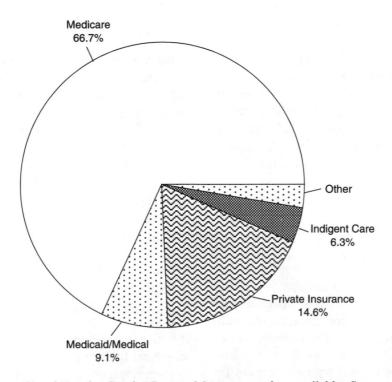

Figure 17–12 Profile of Hospice Service Payers. Most current data available. *Source:* Reproduced by permission of the Hospice Association of America, 1995. Not for further reproduction.

Table 17–7 Medicare Payments for Hospice Services (United States)

Year	Medicare Program Payments (000's)	Total Days of Care	Average No. of Days per Beneficiary	Average Payment per Day	Average Payment per Beneficiary
1994 (1)	$1,582,769	15,637,368	60	$101.22	$6,087
1995 (2)	$1,855,739	17,990,578	59	$103.15	$6,078

Source: Data from *Health Care Financing Review: Medicare and Medicaid Statistical Supplement, 1996 and 1997,* Health Care Financing Administration.

Hospice Reimbursement

Detailed data are available on hospice expenditures and utilization for Medicare beneficiaries from HCFA. Less definitive information is available on hospice expenditures by state Medicaid programs and other payers. Medicare represents the largest payer for hospice services with additional payments from Medicaid, private insurance companies, community donation, and grants. Figure 17–12 provides a profile of representative payer sources for hospice care.

The Tax Equity and Fiscal Responsibility Act of 1982 (TEFRA-82) authorized hospice care benefits under the Medicare program. Hospice benefits are paid on a per diem basis. Medicare per diem rates vary by state of residence, with the average ranging from approximately $100 to $103. Hospice providers receive the per diem payment for as long as the patient is enrolled under the Medicare hospice benefit. Medicaid reimbursement for hospice typically parallels that provided under the Medicare program. Table 17–7 shows total Medicare payments, average number of days of care per beneficiary, and average payment per beneficiary for Medicare-certified hospice programs in the United States.

Medicare Part A beneficiaries are eligible for hospice care if (1) their physician certifies that the beneficiary is terminally ill, and (2) the beneficiary elects the hospice benefit option. "Terminally ill" is defined as having a life expectancy of six months or less when allowing the illness to run its normal course. The patient's attending physician and the hospice program medical director must certify life expectancy. In electing the hospice benefit option, the beneficiary chooses to receive care from a Medicare-certified hospice instead of the standard Medicare benefit. There are no deductibles under the hospice benefit; however, the beneficiary is responsible for modest co-insurance amounts for outpatient drugs and inpatient respite care.

The Medicare hospice benefit[11] is divided into four benefit periods: an initial 90-day period, a subsequent 90-day period, a subsequent 30-day period, and a fourth and final extension period of indefinite duration. To receive Medicare benefits, the beneficiary must be certified (or re-certified) as terminally ill at the beginning of each period. The Medicare hospice benefit covers:

- skilled nursing care
- medical social worker services
- physician care
- counselor (including dietary and pastoral care) services
- home health aide/homemaker services
- short-term inpatient care (for procedures to control pain and acute/chronic system

management and respite care)
- medical devices and supplies
- drugs and biologicals
- physical and occupational therapies
- speech pathology services

Bereavement support services for family of the beneficiary are provided for up to 13 months from date of death. While postdeath bereavement counseling is a required hospice service under the Medicare program, it is not reimbursable.

Ambulatory Patient Groupings

In response to the significant growth of Medicare outpatient service payments during the past decade, HCFA was mandated to develop a prospective payment methodology for other hospital-based outpatient services. This methodology, while not yet finalized by HCFA, is known as the ambulatory patient groupings (APGs) PPS. The two main components of the APG methodology include a patient classification system and a prospectively set payment schedule similar to that established by the diagnosis-related group (DRG) methodology initiated for Medicare reimbursement in 1984. The APG methodology applies to payment for facility fees only, not professional fees.

The objectives of the APG payment system include:

- Eliminate cost-based reimbursement for hospital-based outpatient services.
- Encourage provider efficiency in care delivery.
- Make equitable payments to providers for like outpatient services.
- Reduce unnecessary outpatient testing and ancillary procedures.

There are three major types of APG classifications: significant procedures and thera-

pies, medical visits, and ancillary services only.

Significant procedure APGs are those involving a significant diagnostic or therapeutic procedure such as ambulatory surgery or endoscopy. Medical visit APGs are related to ambulatory visits to a clinician that do not involve a significant procedure. Ancillary service APGs include minor treatments (e.g., immunizations) or diagnostic tests (e.g., laboratory, radiology, or pathology).

The APG methodology requires that each hospital-based outpatient service visit be classified into one of 290 APG categories according to similar clinical characteristics and the associated clinical and administrative resources required to provide the care. There are 139 significant procedure/therapy APGs, 83 medical visit APGs, and 58 ancillary service APGs.[12]

A patient can be assigned to multiple APGs depending on the care setting (e.g., emergency department versus outpatient surgery) and the reason for the provision of the service (e.g., trauma versus well-care).

The basic unit of payment for the APG is an outpatient visit rather than the historical approach based upon each individual procedure or test performed. This variation provides an incentive for providers to control the cost of each visit through management of the services rendered and choice of the most effective clinical procedures and tests. As such, the APG payment rates include a portion to cover all routine services associated with the specific outpatient diagnosis, which determines the APG to which the patient visit is assigned.

If a patient is assigned to more than one APG or receives multiple ancillary tests during a single visit, payment would be based upon one of the prevailing discounted payment or procedure consolidation rules. Discounting or procedure consolidation would occur under one of the following conditions:

- significant-related-procedure consolidation
- ancillary service packaging
- multiple unrelated-significant-procedure consolidation and ancillary service discounting

Significant related procedure consolidation would result in situations where a patient undergoes multiple related procedures during a single visit if the additional procedure(s) involves minimal incremental time and resources. Ancillary service packaging relates to the inclusion of routine ancillary tests in the base APG payment. This would include ancillary tests, which are relatively low-cost services and typically performed in conjunction with a wide range of outpatient procedures and visits.

Multiple unrelated significant procedure consolidation and ancillary service discounting would result in situations where the patient undergoes multiple procedures or ancillary tests unrelated to the primary APG to which the patient is assigned. In these situations, payment for the additional procedures and ancillary tests would be based upon a discounted percentage of the standard APG payment rate under the theory that the cost of performing the multiple procedures concurrently is less than that of providing them under separate visits.

The APG system has not yet been proposed as legislation to Congress. The degree to which hospital providers will be affected by the APG payment methodology is dependent upon:

- the percentage of the hospital's net revenue captured from outpatient services
- Medicare patient revenues as a percentage of total outpatient patient revenue
- efficiency of outpatient department operations
- capabilities of the hospital's existing information systems to capture outpatient data in visit episodes

FUTURE CONSIDERATIONS

The future prospects for ambulatory care are limitless. Some elements of the future are clear; others are less clear and some have yet to be imagined. What is clear is that the future of ambulatory care will be significantly affected by clinical trends, regulation, and reimbursement.

Clinical Trends

Advances in technology will continue to affect ambulatory care through the turn of the century and beyond. Industry experts predict that genetic medicine and drug therapy may eradicate various major diseases over the next 20 to 40 years, the result of emerging technologies such as gene transplants, antisense viruses and vaccines, advanced drug therapy, and genetically engineered vaccines tailor-made for the patient requiring the treatment.

Continued advances in diagnostic and surgical instrumentation and treatment techniques will provide opportunities to increase the range of treatments furnished on an outpatient basis. These advances will include improved laser technology, bloodless surgery, programmable home infusion pumps, equipment miniaturization, advanced computerization of test results and transmission via ISPN telephone networks, and advances in fiber optics. These new technologies and treatment approaches will shift the focus of hospital-based ambulatory providers off-campus and into the home. As patients are discharged from inpatient treatment settings earlier and more are directed to ambulatory surgery, managers and clinicians will need to enhance their educational programming and home care services to ensure that patients get proper, thorough, and timely education and follow-up.

Regulation

Many physicians fear that the enactment of stricter restrictions on physician ownership in ambulatory centers is inevitable. Countless new regulations already have been considered and proposed. Passage of safe harbor legislation will have a significant impact on physician ownership of ASCs because most prevailing ASCs employ some form of physician ownership. There is a shifting mindset among physicians about the long-term viability of ambulatory facility ownership. Physician actions to divest or alter existing ownership positions in ambulatory care centers will affect hospital strategies and relations with medical staffs. This already is seen in mature markets where physician ownership has been transferred to national nonhospital ambulatory care chains.

Reimbursement

Hospital-based and freestanding ambulatory care providers will face challenges associated with changing reimbursement, including Medicare's APG methodology. The introduction of APGs will create significant management and information systems challenges for hospital-based providers, as hospital outpatient statistics have not evolved to the extent that their inpatient counterparts have, and are often fragmented through individual department collection efforts. Further, the volume of data transactions is significantly greater.

Management Considerations

Future prospects for ambulatory care raise numerous management and medical staff challenges for health care executives, including careful selection and acquisition of new technologies, physician privileging criteria for new procedures, training of surgical support staff, and continuing medical education for medical staff. A thorough understanding of ambulatory care trends is critical to maintaining a strong position in this segment of the health care market. For many hospitals, developing a focused approach to ambulatory services has been handicapped by:

- fragmented measures of volume and costs
- a long-standing perspective of such services as supplementary to their inpatient counterpart
- an inability to focus planning efforts due to the diverse nature of outpatient care

In developing strategies for ambulatory care, health care executives must pursue new relationships with physicians, nontraditional management structures, and heightened attention to standards for and measurement of service quality. Many health care organizations are applying continuous quality improvement (CQI) principles to outpatient service areas with the goal of improving customer satisfaction and service quality. As a result, some organizations have seen dramatic results in improving key process variables such as patient registration time, reducing the overall patient waiting and registration time from 25 or more minutes to less than 10 minutes.

Organizing outpatient service areas as a separate operational division, or developing discrete ambulatory care centers, is another example of a fundamental change in the management culture. The characteristics of the effective ambulatory care manager will include superior service and customer-oriented qualities with solid marketing skills, an acute attention to customer satisfaction, and a passion for superior service quality.

Reimbursement and health care reform changes visible on the horizon are prompting hospitals to develop new relationships with physicians and other institutional providers in order to expand care delivery vehicles and develop a comprehensive ambulatory care network. Greater integration in the provision of care will require new treatment and service protocols, systems to measure outcomes, quality report cards, and investment in hospital information systems.

Service Excellence

With outpatient services making up an increasingly more significant portion of the health care industry, providing quality, customer-oriented service is a paramount concern. Most health care managers have tested the total quality management (TQM) waters of the 1980s; some presumably found TQM to be calming and others more faddish. TQM essentially involves attention to process, commitment to customer, involvement of employees, and benchmarking of best practices.[13]

The two primary customer groups for outpatient services are the referring physician and the patient. Key service quality indicators important to the physician as customer include:

- convenient location
- timeliness of service, specifically the speed in processing tests and/or treatments and reporting results
- rapid scheduling, specifically the ability to schedule a procedure or test within days (versus weeks) of identifying a need

Speed and timeliness of service are the most important criteria to this customer group. Universally, physicians characterize a superior outpatient provider as one with early appointment dates, coordinated registration of multiple tests, and minimal turnaround time for results reporting.

Key service quality indicators important to patients as customers include:

- convenient location and easy access
- speedy service, specifically registration and waiting time
- low anxiety atmosphere

As with physicians, patients rate outpatient service providers according to the speed and timeliness of service, characterizing a superior provider as one with minimal waiting time, smooth registration procedures, and limited interdepartment transfers. Nearby parking and a pleasant atmosphere where outpatients are not co-mingled with sicker inpatients are also important attributes.

With the exception of ambulatory surgery, service sites should be located such that patient convenience and access are maximized. Ambulatory surgery facilities should be placed in a location that surgeons find convenient and easy to use. For the hospital-based provider, this may mean the provision of services proximal to each other yet separate from inpatient areas that an outpatient may find unpleasant.

For many hospital-based providers, a focus on outpatient customer preferences and satisfaction has not been an acute priority. Until recent years outpatients typically have been treated as second-class citizens in a setting dominated by inpatients, a setting that favors the more acutely ill patient, who receives more immediate attention and treatment. In short, the "well" outpatient with lower acuity received lower priority. Further, most inpatient service facilities and support systems (modified to handle outpatients) were not designed to meet the specific service needs of the ambulatory patient. As a result, many hospital-based providers have aggressively worked to improve service quality for outpatients through implementation of numerous customer-friendly programs, such as valet parking, controlled-access outpatient parking, escort service, rapid results, express testing protocols, and electronic transmission of results reporting to physician offices. The overriding goal of these efforts has been to win customers by providing unparalleled convenience.

CONCLUSION

The framework with which a health care organization defines itself in the future will be dependent upon how it envisions its role in the provision of ambulatory care. Many industry experts have argued that hospital-based providers have been slow to respond to the changing consumer and payer demands for different care delivery options. Further yet, these experts argue that the very foundation of a hospital-based provider in the way it operates, manages itself, and is embodied through its physical plant are barriers to superior success in the ambulatory care market. All of these premises are true to some degree. More important, however, to the future of health care providers in the ambulatory care market is the organization's ability to recognize the changes in the industry and conceive the possibilities (i.e., vision) of providing health care outside of the typical inpatient setting and treatment protocols.

NOTES

1. "Outpatient-Care Providers Notch Another Year of Robust Growth; Rehab, Dialysis among Top Gainers," *Modern Healthcare* May 24 (1993): 76, 78, 80.

2. "New Surgical Technologies Reshape Hospital Strategies," *Hospitals* May 5 (1992).

3. *Maximizing Outpatient Revenues—Existing Hospital Strategies and Tactics* (Washington, DC: Healthcare Advisory Board [The Advisory Board Company], 1991), xv.

4. *Hospital Statistics, 1984/85 –1996/97 Editions* (Chicago: American Hospital Association).

5. J. Henderson, "Hospitals Seek Bigger Cut of Outpatient Surgeries," *Modern Healthcare* June 28 (1993): 82–85.

6. Hospice Association of America, *Hospice Facts & Statistics* (Washington, DC: Hospice Association of America, 1995), 1.

7. "CEOs Outline Outpatient Management Strategies," *Hospitals* March 20 (1992): 1.

8. P.L. Havlicek, *Medical Groups in the U.S.: A Survey of Practice Characteristics* (Chicago: American Medical Association, Division of Survey and Data Resources, Department of Professional Activities, 1990).

9. Arthur Andersen & Co. and American College of Healthcare Executives, *The Future of Health Care: Physician and Hospital Relations* (Chicago: American College of Healthcare Executives, 1991).

10. National Association For Home Care, *Transition to PPS: The Interim Payment System For Medicare Home Health Services* (Washington, D.C., National Association For Home Care, 1997).

11. Hospice Association of America, *Hospice Facts & Statistics*.

12. Health Care Financing Administration, Office of Research and Demonstrations. *Health Care Financing Review, Medicare and Medicaid Statistical Supplement, 1996* (Baltimore, MD: Health Care Financing Administration, 1996), 118, 119.

13. "TQM—More Than a Dying Fad?," *Fortune* October 18 (1993): 66–72.

Kevin W. Barr, MBA, is a member of the senior management team of Bon Secours Richmond Health System located in Richmond, Virginia, where he serves as the executive vice president of Bon Secours-Virginia HealthSource, Inc., the corporation's subsidiary organization for hospital-affiliated physician activities, home care and hospice services, managed care contracting, and various community and diagnostic service centers. Prior to joining Bon Secours Richmond Health System in July 1991, Mr. Barr worked with the Northeast Healthcare Consulting Practice of Ernst & Young serving hospital and physician clients.

His career experience includes financial feasibility studies, strategic planning, certificate of need, assessment of health care service needs, valuation of medical practices, medical practice management, physician–hospital networks, managed care, and integrated delivery systems. He has contributed various articles to health care management literature and is a senior lecturer to the faculty for the Department of Health Services Administration at the Medical College of Virginia.

Mr. Barr holds a BS in health care management/administration from the Medical College of Virginia and an MBA from Virginia Commonwealth University. In addition, he has an AAS degree in Radiologic Technology and worked in hospitals in a clinical capacity for several years.

Charles L. Breindel, PhD, is in seminary and is studying theology at Catholic University of America in Washington, D.C. Previously Dr. Breindel was Professor and Director of the Graduate Program in Health Services Administration at the Medical College of Virginia campus of Virginia Commonwealth University, Richmond, Virginia, and Director of International Development at Virginia Commonwealth University. Prior to joining the University, he was a Senior Manager in the Mid-Atlantic Healthcare Consulting Practice of Arthur Young & Company (later Ernst & Young), where he directed strategic planning services.

Dr. Breindel has extensive experience in assisting public and private organizations in strategic, program, and market planning for health and hospital services. He has published numerous articles, book chapters, and monographs and done consulting in the United States and internationally for hospitals, governments, and private organizations with health care interests.

In addition to his doctorate from the Pennsylvania State University in health planning and administration, he holds three degrees in areas of mathematics. He has been a professor of health planning and marketing, and has held executive positions in hospital, nursing home, and health systems management.

Chapter 18

Physician Practice and Organization

Michael J. Kelley

Traditionally, the curricula of health administration programs, as well as medical schools, contained little emphasis on the business and financial aspects of physician practice. Yet, over 20 percent of the national health care budget is spent on direct physician's services. While significantly less than the portion of the budget devoted to hospital expenses, the size and impact of physician practices on the health care industry are even greater than its number would indicate. It is estimated that an additional 50 to 60 percent of health care costs are directed by physicians.[1] Indeed, physicians are responsible not only for the provision of services, but also for the ordering of hospital services and admissions and the prescription of drugs and various ancillary and home health care services.

While the physician and physician group sectors of the industry always have been considered highly fragmented and vertically isolated in nature, they are undergoing radical changes consistent with, and often in concert with, other sectors of the industry. In this chapter, the role physicians play in traditional and alternative health care delivery models and the outlook for the physician segment of the health care industry will be covered.

FORMS OF PHYSICIAN PRACTICE

There are four major forms of physician practice: individual or solo physician practice, single-specialty group practice consisting of two or more physicians, multispecialty group practice, and the emerging form of physicians' practice management companies (PPMCs). Any of the forms may be either hospital-based or independent. According to the American Medical Association (AMA), 33 percent of the U.S. total of 492,711 nonfederally-employed active physicians practice in a group setting of three or more physicians. In 1997, 50 percent of all nonfederal physicians in noninstitutional settings were in practices of more than three physicians.[2] The number of physicians who practice in group settings is higher than the numbers indicate in that the AMA defines group practice as three or more physicians. An additional 32 percent of physicians provide patient care in a setting other than group, solo, or two-physician practice. Included in this category are physicians employed by health maintenance organizations (HMOs), hospitals, medical schools, and state governments, among others. Only 34 percent of physicians identify themselves as being in a solo or two-physician practice.[3]

Solo Practice

Solo practice is the choice of few individuals currently embarking on a medical career. Only 5.5 percent of physicians under the age of 35 years are reported to be in solo or two-physician practices.[4] Physicians in solo practices often cite the freedom and self-determination made possible by independence as one of the major benefits. With no other physicians involved in the practice, a solo practitioner can practice medicine without the need to consult associates. The practice is able to directly meet the personal needs of the practitioner in terms of scheduling, working style, and professional interests.

The autonomy and flexibility of solo practice is not without costs: financial, professional, and personal. Solo practitioners have lower average earnings than members of a group practice. It also can be difficult for a solo practitioner to develop areas of special interest or competence within the field of medicine due to the time constraints of constantly being available to patients and referring physicians. Also, the lack of collegial exchange of opinion and information can lead to a certain professional stagnation. Of increasing importance, solo practitioners, particularly those who do not have a highly specialized area of practice, have difficulty obtaining and retaining managed care contracts unless affiliated with an external contracting organization such as an independent practice association (IPA) or preferred provider organization (PPO).

The autonomy of solo practice also creates a corresponding responsibility for all aspects of the practice. Delegation of areas of responsibility among other physicians is impossible, and decisions need to be made without the benefit of alterative opinions and group decision making. A solo practitioner may function as a self-employed individual or as an employee of the corporation that the physician wholly owns, whether a subchapter S or subchapter C corporation. Selection of the specific form of practice should be determined in conjunction with legal and tax planning advice. Each form has its own specific tax planning issues, including the deductibility of certain expenses, retirement plan options, and taxation of fringe benefits. In addition, there are legal consequences, including, among other things, the degree to which the practitioner's estate is protected from certain liabilities.

Single-Specialty Group Practice

Single-specialty group practices are a common form of practice, with approximately half of physicians' group members affiliating in this manner.[5] In a single-specialty group practice, all the physicians practice in the same field of medicine. This does not mean, however, that the practices need to be identical. For example, an ophthalmic single-specialty group might incorporate subspecialties of the eye, such as retina, cornea, oculoplastic, and anterior segment subspecialists.

Physicians in group practice can enjoy a number of benefits. Historically, compensation for group practicing physicians, whether single or multispecialty, is higher than that of solo practitioners. This difference in compensation level amounts to over $29,000 for the average physician.[6]

While often cited as a reason for group success, there is little evidence that economies of scale are created in a group. In fact, group physicians have a higher expense ratio than do nongroup physicians. Group practices, however, often are able to make larger capital investments. Additionally, these practices often are able to employ more highly trained support staffs. This may help explain both the higher expense ratios and higher incomes of physicians in group practice, a setting in which physicians generally see more patients per week while working a comparable number of hours.[7] The physician in group practice also can achieve lifestyle benefits from delegated responsibility, reduced call schedules, and cross coverage during times of vacation, illness, or disability.

Offsetting these advantages is a real need to develop consensus among physicians regarding practice philosophies and administrative policies. The difficulty of this task, combined with the inherent interpersonal relationships, causes a large number of group practices to end in dissolution. This often can be traced to failures in the recruiting process. During the recruiting process, physicians often spend insufficient time gaining an understanding of each other as individuals, determining the compatibility of personality traits, leadership styles, and expectations. More often, an inordinate amount of time is focused on the medical experiences and scholastic achievements of the candidate. The costs, both personal and financial, associated with the need to disassociate can be extremely high. When investigating group practice opportunities, physicians would be unwise to overlook the personal and business relationships entailed in group practice. Group practices are, in a social and economic sense, group marriages. Individuals need to reconcile decisions about financial matters, social and personal behaviors, personality, and ethics.

The recruitment or affiliation process should start with the basic requirements. These include licensure and clinical competence acceptable to all parties. Thereafter, the process should be driven by the factors that will influence professional and group success. How will the candidate "fit in" in terms of life goals? Is there a compatibility of styles, approaches, and decision making? The goal of all parties is to achieve a viable, pleasant, long-term relationship, and the decision process needs to be driven with this in mind.

Group practices also can be formed under different legal entities. A partnership is an unincorporated form of practice that can be established as a vehicle for group practice. Group members own and distribute practice income based upon the partnership agreement. There are clear disadvantages to partnerships with regard to liability issues. Each partner may be held individually responsible for the acts of any other partner related to the operation of the partnership. In some states, limited liability partnerships (LLPs) afford some protection from creditors that is unavailable to general partnerships.

Group practices are more often incorporated as either subchapter S or C corporations, with the same advantages and disadvantages as previously discussed. The group physicians act as employees of the corporation. The governance of the group is carried out under the articles of incorporation and bylaws of the corporation. Not all group physicians need be shareholders and officers of the corporation. Indeed, it is common for physicians new to the group to work for some period of time before they are offered the opportunity to purchase stock in the corporation.

Increasingly, physicians are not being offered ownership in the group. Rather, they are compensated through incentives that recognize the role they play as individuals in the achievement of the corporate mission. This can include phantom stock plans, bonuses based upon productivity, incentives for proper utilization, as well as other rewards for other tangible and intangible achievements.

Multispecialty Group Practice

A multispecialty group practice shares many of the characteristics of single-specialty group practice, but will cross lines of specialization. Such groups might include primary, secondary, and tertiary care. Often these types of groups exist in a managed care or academic organization. Many advantages can be cited for this model of practice. Multispecialty group practices tend to be, by their nature, larger than single-specialty groups. Many patients will have more than one significant medical problem, thereby creating opportunities for cross referral to physicians within the group practice. The size of the enterprise also can produce opportunities whereby each practitioner can benefit from the professionally developed corporate administrative systems and cross-marketing plans. Multispecialty group practices often can posture themselves as regional centers, drawing both self- and physician-referred patients from a larger geographic area than they would otherwise enjoy.

Offsetting these cited advantages are a number of problems associated with running a large enterprise. The number of physicians in a multispecialty group can make governance a difficult issue. In the typical single-specialty group practice, each physician may play a role in the joint governance of the enterprise. In the typical multispecialty environment, governance is accomplished through an executive committee with a chief medical and administrative officer. Income and resource allocation often is a difficult subject. Primary care and surgical specialties are often at odds because of financial and professional conflicts. Primary care physicians often seek to be subsidized by the higher revenue-producing specialists and subspecialists for whom primary care generates referrals and patient volume.

Notwithstanding the negative issues associated with group practice, many physicians believe the support services generated by the group and the presence of ancillary services, as well as the freedom from administrative and managerial tasks, can offset the disadvantages. Group practice, whether subspecialty or multispecialty, is a growing force in the health care industry. Mergers and affiliations are becoming more common given the changes in the health care marketplace. Many health care experts predict the trend toward group practice medicine will accelerate and become an increasingly attractive choice for physicians beginning medical careers, as well as an alternative to be considered by solo and small group members. The trend to consolidation often is viewed as a natural economic result of increased competition within the larger health care market.

Physician Practice Management Companies

An emerging form of practice is the PPMC. PPMCs are organizations that exist, primarily, to perform nonclinical services that support the delivery of health care services. Several factors have led to their existence. Entrepreneurs, including hospital organizations, health care professionals, venture capitalists, and Wall Street, have realized that health care represents a huge segment of the economy, and therefore, cash flow. While previously citing that physician expenses account for approximately 20 percent of health care costs, there also was the realization that physicians controlled, through hospital admissions, pharmaceutical prescription, and referrals to other entities, a far greater percentage of health care spending than was self-evident. Physicians also were increasingly aware of both their role in the delivery system and the threat posed by the evolution taking place in the nonphysician segments of the industry.

The consolidation of hospital systems; the emergence of large, powerful, and restrictive health plans; and the diminishing role of indemnity insurance gave rise to new concerns, business imperatives, and strategic choices. Physicians, for the first time, experienced external threats that could seriously impact the style, method, and income potential traditionally associated with their profession. Large multispecialty groups were now positioned to negotiate for exclusive contracting relationships with large insurers. These new arrangements had the potential to affect revenue not only to the physicians, but also to a web of interdependent organizations (Figure 18–1).

Another driving force that led to the expanding PPMC industry was the exponential growth in the complexity associated with operating the nonclinical activities of the physician practice. Authorization processing, contracting with managed care organizations (MCOs), and compliance with federal guidelines all created new administrative burdens that some physician practices were and are ill-prepared to perform. Theoretically, business practices used in other industries, such as consolidation and specialization of activities, could significantly impact both the effectiveness and efficiency of the operation leading to increased revenues and profits. Also significant was the need for capital to invest in data processing, to implement capitation systems, and to build new cost-effective business and administrative systems.

PPMCs also offer the potential, but not certainty, of financial gain through stock appreciation. The overwhelming majority of PPMCs have significant equity positions held by affiliated physicians who hope to achieve not only business objectives but also long-term equity appreciation.

PPMC Structure

There are a variety of PPMC structures. Equity model PPMCs purchase the assets of the physician practice and manage, through supervisory oversight, the nonclinical activities of the practice including employment of all nonphysician personnel, supplies contracting, and, frequently, centralized accounts receivable and payable management. At the time the PPMC purchases the physician practice, an exchange of cash, notes, and equity in the PPMC occurs at a negotiated value. This value is derived from an estimate of the value of the cash flow that the PPMC will derive through a contract that entitles it to a percentage of profits, frequently between 10 percent and 30 percent. The management contract is typically for a period of 15 to 40 years and is noncancelable.

Service model PPMCs are emerging to provide management services to physicians without acquiring the practice. These often take the form of management service organizations (MSOs). MSOs provide, under a fee basis, selected management services. This could include managing contracting activity for the practice or a group of practices that are affiliated with an IPA or other network. The service model PPMC may provide centralized billing and collection activity, centralized group purchasing systems, and also discounted consulting services. Frequently, these organizations are capitalized by the physicians themselves as a way to build aggregate negotiating power. The differences between the models is that the practice remains in the ownership of the physicians.

PPMCs may provide services to a variety of organizations. Single-specialty PPMCs have emerged in ophthalmology, oncology,

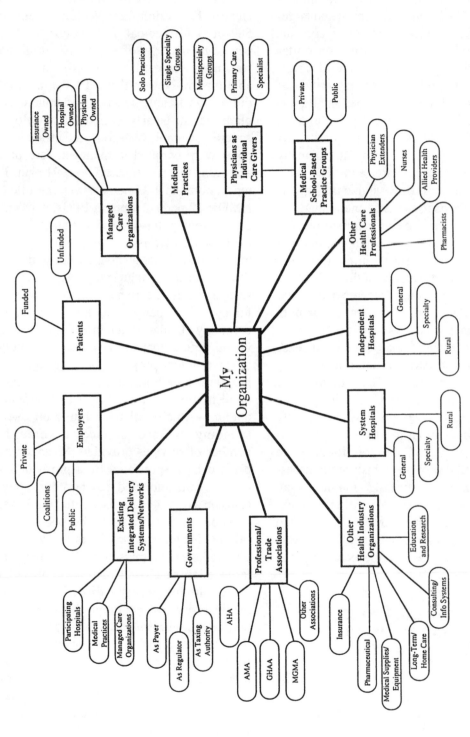

Figure 18–1 Health Care Stakeholders. *Source:* Reprinted with permission from the Center for Research in Ambulatory Health Care Administration, 104 Inverness Terrace East, Englewood, Colorado 80112-5306, 303-779-1111, Copyright © 1995.

neurology, and emergency care, to name a few. Some PPMCs only concentrate on larger multispecialty practices with significant market penetration. Large, multibillion dollar PPMCs such as PhyCor, FPA, and Medpartners have emerged with the assistance of public capital. Hundreds of other smaller organizations, both public and private, have been formed to address this new market dynamic. Some have been successful, and many others, among them the largest PPMCs, have achieved dismal failure and bankruptcy. Concerns have risen in the financial markets, however, that the pace of acquisitions and high prices paid for physician groups will lead to a lack of effective integration and poor financial performance of the PPMC.

The ultimate question is whether this new form of practice will create value for both physicians and investors. The potential for value exists. PPMCs may develop disease management and care pathways that are effective and more efficient. This will give their organizations pricing advantages in the pursuit of managed care contracts. Frequently cited contraindications to success and the reason for major PPMC failures include the costs associated with the infrastructure necessary to accomplish their tasks, and the social, economic, and professional conflicts that exist between the service provider (PPMC) and the service purchaser (MCO), with both seeking to maximize profits at the expense of the other.

MANAGED CARE DELIVERY SYSTEMS AND FORMS OF PHYSICIAN ORGANIZATION

Faced with the high cost of or the inability to obtain traditional medical insurance, organizations began to experiment with alternative delivery systems and insurance mechanisms in the 1920s and 1930s.[8,9] In 1965, a survey conducted by the Department of Health, Education, and Welfare identified 582 prepaid medical plans.[10] For the overwhelming majority of Americans, traditional fee-for-service medicine was the only available option. Not until the 1970s and 1980s did a significant growth in managed care plans begin. Nearly half of all employees covered by employer-sponsored group health plans were enrolled in managed care plans, according to a report based on 1991 data. The report noted that 25 percent were enrolled in HMOs; 22 percent were in PPOs, and 5 percent were in point-of-service plans.[11]

Managed care is a widely touted phrase, but one that is not necessarily easily defined. Strictly speaking, managed care could be defined as medical care being directed and paid for by a third party, generally an insurance company. Under strict interpretation, this would define virtually any insurance policy or government program as a managed care program. Few policies or programs contain no restrictions on the services an insured can obtain. Virtually all have limits on overall spending, types of services covered, and number of services provided. Managed care plans can be sponsored by a profit or nonprofit organization and may reimburse physicians on a capitated or discounted fee-for-service basis. Services can be provided by salaried health care providers or by contract with independent physicians. They may have large open or closed panels of providers. They can function by directly providing medical services or through the indemnification or reimbursement of incurred costs. On the basis of just these 5 characteristics, 32 permutations are theoretically possible. On a more general basis, though, managed care is defined as care that offers comprehensive benefits delivered by selected providers and financial incentives for members to use providers who are members of the plan.

Health Maintenance Organizations

HMOs are medical care organizations that are responsible "for the provision and delivery of a predetermined set of comprehensive health maintenance and treatment services to a voluntarily enrolled group for prenegotiated and fixed periodic capitation payment."[12] Cowan defines five common characteristics shared by such plans:

1. a defined population of enrolled members
2. payment by the members determined in advance for a specific period of time and made periodically
3. medical services provided on a direct service basis rather than on an indemnity basis
4. services provided to patients by HMO physicians for essentially all medical needs with referrals to outside physicians being controlled by HMO physicians
5. voluntary enrollment by each family or member[13]

In an HMO, a primary care physician is responsible for determining what services are necessary and who will provide the services for enrolled patients. In the event the patient seeks care on a nonemergency basis from any health care provider not authorized by the HMO physician, payment is denied for the services. The effect of this health care delivery model is that it limits the services received by the patient to those deemed medically necessary by the primary care provider and attempts to eliminate duplicative or unnecessary costs. A frequently cited problem of traditional fee-for-service medicine is that the provider receives a direct financial benefit from ordering additional tests and procedures. Under the HMO model, the provider receives no financial benefit from the tests and referrals initiated. In fact, in the event that utilization targets are exceeded, the primary care physician may be penalized for health care costs incurred by the patients for whom he has accepted responsibility.

There are three models for organizing physicians in an HMO: the staff model, group model, and IPA model.

Staff Model HMO

In the staff model HMO, physicians are salaried employees of the HMO. They furnish care exclusively to members of the HMO, with the HMO responsible for all nonclinical management. In some cases, these physicians are given incentives to control costs through bonus mechanisms that reward the physician for controlling costs.

Group Model HMO

In a group model HMO, the physicians are organized as a multispecialty group. These groups often have their own separate legal entity and contract with the HMO to provide services to its members. The group receives a direct capitation payment from the HMO, which has been predetermined by negotiation, and may be entitled to supplemental payments based on the profitability of the HMO. The group then compensates individual physicians based on either a salary, productivity, or utilization basis or a combination of all three methods.

The group model HMO can result in significant risk shifting to the group practice. Inasmuch as the physicians often are owners of the group practice, their net income can be directly affected by services provided to HMO members. Incentives to hold down overall health costs can take two forms. First, there may be prenegotiated accruals, or withholds, payable in the event costs are under budget. Second, higher profits can be generated internally within the group through the lower costs associated with the provision of fewer services. The physician group often provides services to patients independent of the HMO and may operate a component of the group practice on a traditional fee-for-service basis.

IPA Model HMO

An IPA is a legal entity composed of physicians and physician groups, each of which functions as a separate and independent practice. Under an IPA model HMO, large panels of physicians contract with the HMO to provide health services within a defined geographic area. Traditionally, physicians have been paid on a fee-for-service basis, but at a rate that discounts their customary charges. In many cases, the fee schedule is set by a discount to or multiple of the Medicare fee schedule. A portion of the discounts, referred to as withholds, may be paid to physicians if a surplus exists after payment of hospital, external, and administrative costs.

Faced with the desire of insurers to decrease their claims risk, some IPAs are developing capitated payment agreements. Under such an agreement, the IPA contracts to provide specified services at a fixed cost per beneficiary per month. The IPA then controls utilization issues within its organization and compensates individual practitioners for care on either a discounted fee for service or a capitated basis.

IPA physicians often derive a large percentage of their practice income from traditional fee-for-services patients. One of the cost control weaknesses of this model is that the overwhelming majority of the physician income is still generated on a fee-for-service basis with the smaller remainder being dependent upon the IPA's cost behavior. Physicians continue to receive the bulk of their in-come from the number of examinations, procedures, and tests they perform.

Preferred Provider Organizations

PPOs are similar to IPAs in that physicians function on a fee-for-service basis. Unlike the HMO model, in which there usually is a primary-care gatekeeper who controls the services provided to enrollees, PPO-enrolled patients are free to make their own choice of member providers. PPO physicians enter into an arrangement with the sponsoring organization, often an insurance company or hospital affiliated organization, and agree to a discounted fee for service. By offering the discount and thereby maintaining access to patients converting from traditional indemnity plans, the physicians hope to stabilize or increase the size of the patient population they service.

Subscribers typically are free to seek the care of physicians outside of the PPO panel, but are penalized by receiving a lower rate of reimbursement, resulting in higher cost to the beneficiary. PPOs often incorporate low copayments and limited or nonexistent in-network deductibles in order to create an incentive for patients to obtain discounted care and remain within the PPO panel. The patients may opt out of the panel and seek care elsewhere if they feel value is generated equal to the higher cost. PPO physicians typically do not share in any withhold pool and receive no direct incentive to hold costs down. The physician practices medicine on a discounted fee-for-service basis; income is directly related to the value and volume of services rendered.

All of these managed care models share a common goal: the reduction of health care costs. They vary substantially in the method and degree of control they exert on the individual practitioners. Not surprisingly, the lowest physician costs are typically found where control upon physician activity is highest. Indemnity insurance, the traditional insurance program in which patients are free to choose any physician for any health care problem, has the highest costs. PPOs, which are the least restrictive on physician behavior of the managed care models, are also the most expensive managed care product. HMOs, with the highest levels of physician control, are generally the lowest cost model.

Provider Sponsored Organizations

The Balanced Budget Act of 1997 created a new form of organization to provide services to Medicare beneficiaries, provider sponsored organizations (PSOs). PSOs can be formed, generally, by any licensed health care practitioner that can provide a large majority of services through affiliated providers and has the ability to provide all other items and services under contract. Thus, a multispecialty medical group directly affiliated with a hospital could offer its services to Medicare beneficiaries and bypass the MCOs (usually an HMO) with which beneficiaries currently contract.

If the growth in PSOs is significant, the competition between them and HMOs is expected to be fierce, as providers now seek to expand their role into that of the insurer.

OPERATIONAL ASPECTS OF PHYSICIAN PRACTICE

The operations of a traditional physician practice can be divided into a few key functional areas.

Resource Management

Operations management in a physician setting is similar to that of any other organiza-tion. The goal is to maximize net revenue through the efficient utilization of resources. Resources include plant and equipment, physicians, ancillary staff, and time. A number of resource costs are fixed, including rent and many other occupancy expenses. Other expenses, such as supplies, are variable in that they rise and fall in direct relation to the volume of procedures. Some expenses, such as staffing costs, are semivariable in that they can only be changed in incremental fashion, with a minimum level of cost that is essentially fixed. For example, a receptionist is necessary whether the physician sees two or five patients per hour.

Operations management seeks to provide services at the lowest possible cost. Inasmuch as the physician is usually the highest cost resource, effective utilization of this resource requires that the physician's activity be concentrated in areas where he or she is uniquely qualified: the practice of medicine.

Principles of Staffing

Physician activity can be optimized by delegating some aspects of patient care. For example, there are scientific measurement aspects of medicine such as the range of motion of a joint or the weight and height of an individual. As a general rule, measurement activities can be provided at a lower cost by well-trained clinical assistants or physician extenders. Measurement activities take time, and time is a scarce resource for many physicians. When an activity is performed by physician extenders, the physician may increase the number of patients served as a result of the time savings. The "art" of medicine, a function that can only be performed by a qualified provider, is the cognitive function, the evaluation of quantitative and subjective data, followed by the definition of a management plan. Practices that utilize staff for measurement activities and physicians for the cognitive functions tend to operate far more efficiently.

Appointment Scheduling

It is for this reason that the appointment scheduling process is one of the key variables in physician productivity. The goal of the process is to have the physician rendering medical care as continuously as possible during scheduled hours.

There are two basic types of appointment scheduling: standard segment and wave. Under a standard segment system, the number of patients the physician sees per hour is divided into 60 minutes and scheduled in equal segments. If a physician sees 6 patients per hour on average, an appointment is scheduled every 10 minutes. The problem with this scheduling system is that patients require varying amounts of time per visit. If it is assumed in this example that visits actually range from 5 to 15 minutes, the physician can encounter substantial periods of time when no patient is available to be seen.

Wave scheduling attempts to correct this natural variability by establishing a queue of patients. Under the same assumptions as above, a wave schedule would have three patients scheduled at the top of the hour and three scheduled at the half-past-the-hour time slot. Thus, if the first patient takes five minutes to be seen, the physician can move to the next patient who is already available to be seen. A hybrid solution, called the modified wave, combines aspects of segment and wave scheduling. If a physician sees six patients per hour and the minimum visit is five minutes, appointments would be scheduled from the top of the hour in five-minute intervals until half past the hour. This assures that the physician is always busy, but can lead to longer patient wait time.

Another alternative scheduling method is based on time units. Typically, the 5-minute exam has distinct characteristics from the 15-minute exam. The 5-minute exam might be a routine postoperative exam and represent 1 unit of time, while the 15-minute exam would be an initial new patient visit using 3 units of time. By determining the type of exam, the number of units of time it will take can be determined. This can help to minimize patient wait times, which are stressful on both physician and patient, while reducing or eliminating periods of physician inactivity.

Physician Billing

CPT Coding

In order for both physicians and their patients to be properly reimbursed for services by insurers, the identification of the procedure or procedures performed must occur. Medicare, as well as most insurance companies, utilizes the American Medical Association's *Physicians' Current Procedural Terminology*[14] (CPT) to describe the services provided to the patient. This process of reviewing the service and categorizing it is referred to as coding. The CPT book (updated every year) contains some basic coding information, as well as thousands of defined services or procedures. Each of the described procedures is defined by a specific five-digit code.

Under some circumstances, a code must be reported with one or more additional two-digit modifiers that identify relevant additional information needed to determine the amount or type of service performed. For example, modifier 50 identifies that a bilateral procedure was performed during the same operative session. Modifier 54 identifies that the surgical care was provided by the billing physician and that another physician provided the preoperative and postoperative components of the surgical procedure. There are 25 surgical modifiers commonly used for surgical procedures and an additional 6 that refer to the evaluation and management sections of the CPT code.

Some physician activities require the use of Health Care Financing Administration (HCFA) Common Procedural Coding System descriptors, HCPCS (pronounced "hic-pics"). Level 2 codes are a series of national codes that describe supplies, injectable drugs, and physician and other health care provider services not described in the CPT (HCPCS Level 1), as well as dental services.[15] A third level of descriptors, HCPCS Level 3, are local codes used by the Medicare carrier to describe services and activities for which national coverage has not been determined. The number of local codes is decreasing as Medicare and other private and governmental insurers move toward a uniform national payment policy.

Care must be taken when coding, not only to ensure that the service was provided as described, but also to avoid the unbundling of charges. Unbundling occurs when a procedure is broken down into discrete components rather than being identified by the procedure code that defines the entire service. The reason that unbundling represents an incorrect coding method relates to the way in which the value of procedures is determined. The value of the work performed by improperly componentizing the procedure would be significantly greater than the work value that would derive from the global or bundled procedure. In other words, the sum is greater than the whole.

As an example, during the repair of a retinal detachment, a physician may inject medication, use a laser to seal the tear, and drain subretinal fluid. Each of those three procedures has its own discrete CPT code. When taken as a whole, they are regarded as components of CPT code 67105; repair of retinal detachment (Exhibit 18–1). The amount paid if the procedure were broken down by components would be significantly greater than that billed under the "global" code.

Evaluation and Management Coding

CPT coding also includes physician evaluation and management services. Evaluation and management services is the term applied to what most people would consider "a visit with the doctor." This can take place in a variety of settings, such as the physician's office, a hospital room, a nursing home, or the patient's house. The level of intensity of the visits also can vary from a blood pressure check by a nurse to a comprehensive examination of a life-threatening disease.

HCFA, working in conjunction with the AMA and other industry groups, has expended significant effort in an evolving process to measure the complexity and intensity of these widely variable activities. Major revisions to the process occur every several years, as the trend is to make the evaluation and management coding system less subjective and easier to interpret and audit.

The purpose of the coding structure is to accurately evaluate the relative value units (RVUs) associated with the activity. The site of service (e.g., hospital or office) has an impact on costs associated with the provision of service. The premise in this instance is that it is less expensive for the physician to provide services in a physical location that is paid for, maintained, and staffed by another organization, such as the hospital.

Documentation Guidelines for Evaluation of Management Services

Seven components are recognized in defining the level of evaluation and management services. These are:

1. history
2. examination
3. medical decision making
4. counseling
5. coordination of care
6. nature of the presenting problem
7. time

History, examination, and medical decision making are the key differentiating components in the overwhelming majority of evaluation and management services. The other components are only important when the majority of the time is spent counseling and coordinating care.

There are four types of patient history that can be selected for proper coding: problem-focused, expanded problem found, detailed, and comprehensive. Each type, at varying levels of detail, encompasses the following categories from HCFA:

- *Chief complaint:* A concise statement that describes the symptoms, problems, conditions, diagnoses, physician recommendations for return visit, or other factors.
- *History of present illness:* A chronologic description of the development of the patient's current illness from the first sign or symptom (or from the last visit) through the present time. This description should include the location, quality, severity, duration, timing, context, modifying factors, and associated signs and symptoms of the illness.
- *Review of symptoms:* An inventory of body systems obtained through questions intended to identify the patient's current or previous signs or symptoms. The recognized systems are constitutional symptoms, eyes, ears, nose, mouth, throat, cardiovascular, respiratory, gastrointestinal, genitourinary, musculoskeletal, integumentary, neurologic, psychiatric, endo-

Exhibit 18–1 Example of Bundled Codes

BILLED CODE

67105—Repair of retinal detachment, one or more sessions; photocoagulation (laser or xenon arc) with or without drainage of subretinal fluid

BUNDLED CODES

67015—Aspiration or release of vitreous, subretinal, or choroidal fluid, pars plana approach (posterior sclerotomy)

67101—Repair of retinal detachment, one or more sessions; cryotherapy or diathermy, drainage of subretinal fluid

67141—Prophylaxis of retinal detachment with or without (e.g., retinal break) drainage, one or more sessions; cryotherapy, diathermy

67145—Prophylaxis of retinal detachment (e.g., lattice degeneration) with or without drainage, one or more sessions; photocoagulation

67208—Destruction of localized lesion of retina one or more sessions; cryotherapy, diathermy (e.g., small tumors)

67210—Destruction of localized lesion of retina; photocoagulation (laser or xenon arc)

67227—Destruction of extensive or progressive retinopathy, one or more sessions, cryotherapy, diathermy (e.g., diabetic retinopathy)

67228—Destruction of extensive or progressive retinopathy, one or more sessions; photocoagulation

67500—Retrobulbar injection; medication (separate procedure—does not include supply of medication)

92504—Binocular microscopy (separate diagnostic procedure)

Source: CPT codes only © 1997 American Medical Association. All rights reserved.

---

crine, hematologic/lymphatic, allergic/immunologic.

- *Past, family, and/or social history:* The patient's previous experiences with illnesses, operations, injuries, and treatments; a review of medical events in the patient's family, including hereditary diseases and risk factors; and a review of previous and current social activities.

Diagnosis Coding

The International Classification of Disease (ICD) is used to specifically code a diagnosis or diagnoses applicable to the service rendered. Published by the World Health Organization, the current version is the ICD9 Manual. The U.S. Public Health Service and the HCFA mandate the use of the ICD9 Manual for its programs. Approximately 1300 pages in length, the manual lists thousands of diagnoses. Each diagnosis is given a unique 3-digit code, which can be further subclassified with an additional 2 digits, if necessary. The ICD9 coding of disorders resulting from impaired renal function, 588, is shown in Exhibit 18–2.[16]

Methods of Physician Reimbursement
Usual, Customary, and Reasonable

Many indemnity insurers use what is referred to as a usual, customary, and reasonable (UCR) methodology, or a close variant thereof. Under this method, the insurer collects a database of charges for each service submitted by all similar physicians in a geographic area. The insurer then sorts these from the lowest charge to the highest and limits payment to a determined percentile. Some commercial carriers will pay at the 50th percentile of the charge array, while some others may pay as much as the 90th percentile charge. This is referred to as the "customary charge." The fee that the physician normally charges for the procedure is the "usual

Exhibit 18–2 ICD9 Codes for Disorders Resulting from Impaired Renal Function

588 Disorders resulting from impaired renal function
588.0 Renal osteodystrophy
 Azotemic osteodystrophy
 Phosphate-losing tubular disorders
 Renal:
  dwarfism
  infantilism
  rickets
588.1 Nephrogenic diabetes insipidus
Excludes: diabetes insipidus NOS (253.5)
588.8 Other specified disorders resulting from impaired renal function
 Hypokalemic nephropathy
 Secondary hyperparathyroidism (of renal origin)
Excludes: secondary hypertension (405.0–405.9)
588.9 Unspecified disorder resulting from impaired renal function

Source: Reprinted with permission from ICD-9-CM, Practice Management Information Corporation.

charge." The third fee that the insurer considers is a "reasonable fee." This fee allowance can vary based upon documented special circumstances of the case. The insurer will pay the lower of the usual or customary charge, unless a reasonable-fee adjustment is warranted. An example of a UCR system is shown in Exhibit 18–3.

Relative Value Systems and Resource-Based Relative Value Systems

As early as the mid-1950s, payers began investigating a relative value based method

Exhibit 18–3 Determination of Allowable Fee under UCR Method

Table of Historical Charge Data		Examples—Insurer pays 90th percentile
Physician	*$*	• Dr. Smith submits charge for $75. Insurer allows $60. Charge exceeds 90th percentile UCR.
Dr. Smith	75	
Dr. Gomez	60 ← 90th Percentile	
Dr. Casper	55	• Dr. Felix submits charge for $50. Insurer allows $50, the usual fee for Dr. Felix.
Dr. Felix	50	
Dr. Felix	50 ← 50th Percentile	
Dr. Singer	47	• Dr. Alex submits charge for $75. Insurer allows $45 based upon his historical charges.
Dr. Alex	45	
Dr. Alex	45	
Dr. Jones	40	

of physician payment. Under relative value payment methodologies, the economic cost of providing a service is the basis under which it is reimbursed. Physician time, training, and the intensity of the service, as well as practice and malpractice expense components, are all factors in the economic costs of providing a service. Rather than a reimbursement system based upon historic charges, a relative value system quantifies the resources necessary to perform a service.

Relative value systems, when properly constructed, will have increasing value as a management tool. They offer the opportunity for an organization to measure the resources necessary to deliver services and to compare them to an independently derived value. An organizational efficiency measurement can then be derived. Services can be measured in terms of both cost and revenue on an individual basis.

Relative value systems also provide organizations with a method to quantify the number of units of service provided. This method provides a common denominator that is unaffected by changing case mix and fee schedules. Many practices track, as part of their financial management systems, the number of

patient encounters. Relative value system-based management recognizes that some encounters and services are worth more than others. For example, Medicare has established that a comprehensive consultation with a physician expends 4.86 units of resources, whereas a comprehensive established patient visit expends 2.37 units.

Relative value systems also are useful in the measurement of the costs involved in providing care under capitated systems. The organization can track the number of units of service it provides and the capitated payment to compute the reimbursement per unit of service. By comparing the payer's reimbursement per unit of service to the organization's cost to provide a unit of service, management can make informed decisions about the profitability of managed care contracts.

The most significant relative value system in terms of impact on the industry was adopted in 1992 by Medicare, the Resource Based Relative Value Scales (RBRVS). The RBRVS system came into effect because of the belief that the historical Medicare payment structure favored subspecialty and surgical procedures rather than primary care and cognitive medical activities. Many felt there was a serious inequity when primary care physicians such as family practitioners were earning significantly less than subspecialty surgeons. For example, the median compensation of family practitioners in group practices was $112,585 in 1992. During that same year, the median compensation for orthopedic surgeons in group practices was $289,323.[17] Significant disparities continue to exist.

Determination of Relative Values

A team of Harvard researchers commonly referred to as the Hsiao Team, named after its principal researcher, surveyed a cross section of physicians in multiple specialties to determine the amount of physician work involved in a number of described encounters. Physician work took into account the amount of time, intensity of effort, and technical skill required to provide the service. The physicians evaluated the work components relative to other defined encounters, indicating their perception of the amount of work involved in the task. These work values were then cross linked against all of the procedures surveyed. The intent of the study was to have a uniform scale under which all physician activities could be evaluated. HCFA then adapted and expanded upon the work done by Hsiao to develop a schedule of work values for all covered Medicare procedures.

Beginning January 1, 1992, the Medicare approved fee for any service could be defined by calculating the following formula:

$$PAYMENT = (WORK + PRACTICE\ EXPENSE + MALPRACTICE) \times CF$$

$$[(RVUw_s \times GPCIw_a) + (RVUpe_s \times GPCIpe_a) + (RVUm_s \times GPCIm_a)] \times CF$$

where:

$RVUw_s$ = Physician work relative value units for the service

$RVUpe_s$ = Practice expense relative value units for the service

$RVUm_s$ = Malpractice expense relative value units for the service

$GPCIw_a$ = GPCI value reflecting one-fourth of geographic variation in physician work applicable in the fee schedule area

$GPCIpe_a$ = GPCI value for practice expense applicable in the fee schedule area

$GPCIm_a$ = GPCI value for malpractice expense applicable in the fee schedule area

CF = Conversion factor (dollar denominated)

Once the work components had been valued, two additional values had to be determined: practice expense and malpractice expense. The practice expense component reflects the overhead costs associated with providing the service. Practice expense and malpractice expense components were calculated by reviewing their historical costs. These costs were based on specialty-specific overhead ratios. The practice and malpractice expense ratios for a particular service were calculated to reflect a weighted average based upon all the specialties performing the services. During the consideration on the OBRA-89 legislation, debate arose over the need for adjustments to the fee schedule to account for variations and geographic costs. Geographic practice cost indices (GPCIs: pronounced "gypsies") were developed to make geographic adjustments against each of the fee schedule components. The practice-expense GPCI is intended to account for variations of office rents, employee wages, and other operating expenses. The malpractice GPCI was used to adjust the malpractice component of the cost in order to reflect the varying costs of malpractice liability insurance in different localities. The third factor, the physician–work–component GPCI, was the most controversial. Rural physicians complained that it was unfair to reward urban physicians with higher incomes simply because they practiced in areas with higher costs. They persuasively argued that physician cost of living was directly linked to the attractiveness of the location. Compromise was reached where only one-quarter of the geographic variations of physician GPCI would be used to adjust the payments.

Once the work, practice expense, and malpractice components are determined, after adjustment for geographic costs, the sum is multiplied by the conversion factor. The conversion factor is a monetary multiplier and is used nationally to compute the reimbursement level. The conversion factors can be adjusted annually to meet the budgetary goals of the Congress.

Transition to the Full RBRVS Schedule

As part of the change in the Medicare reimbursement method, a phase-in period was incorporated into the law. Beginning January 1, 1992, and ending on January 1, 1996, under a series of formulas enacted in 1989 and modified in 1993, the impact of downward revisions in the fee schedule was buffered by an annual limitation on the amount of adjustment. The intent was to create breathing room for the practices, primarily surgical, that were most negatively affected by the changing reimbursement formula to adapt their practices to the changing economics.

An additional "down payment" by surgical specialties was implemented during 1997 to reduce overall Medicare spending. Reform of the payment system and refinement of the relative value system occur continuously, as the government seeks to control health care costs, and various special interests seek more favorable treatment.

The Billing and Collection Process

Once the task of defining the service and linking it to its appropriate diagnosis is completed, the billing and collection phase of the physician reimbursement process is actuated. Each physician or group needs to create a billing and collection policy, a written set of procedures under which patients are expected to pay for the services they receive. A number of factors need to be considered when determining the payment policy. Does the group expect payment at the time of service (PATOS)? The advantages of this payment system, one of which is a rapid payment cycle with a low level of accounts receivable outstanding at any point in time, have to be weighed against the potential loss of patients who resent the unwillingness of the provider to bill the insurance companies for their appropriate balances. Patients may choose to obtain their services at competitors who offer more liberal collection policies. The group or physician also needs to decide whether it will become a Medicare-participating provider. Under this reimbursement option, the physician agrees to undertake the responsibility of collecting 80 percent of the approved charge directly from the Medicare carrier, making the patient responsible only for the 20 percent copayment and deductibles. Again, the socioeconomic characteristics of the target market shall be considered.

Insurance Submission

After the CPT and ICD9 codes have been selected for the encounter, claims are submitted to insurance companies for payment. Claims can be submitted on paper, often on universal billing forms, or electronically if the practice is automated. Each year, greater numbers of practices utilize automated billing, as payment often is made more quickly and important management information can be produced. The payer applies its own rules when processing the claim. It may reject a charge based on inappropriate use, such as billing a follow-up visit as a new patient encounter. The insurer also may apply a fee screen (an automated edit of information). The fee screen will approve payment only for charges with specific diagnoses related to the services rendered. The rationale behind these fee screens is that tests and procedures are only valid for a limited range of diagnoses and appropriate patient types. For example, Medicare will not pay for a fundus photograph (a photograph of the retina) when the diagnosis is cataract (cloudiness of the lens).

Insurance companies also often will reject unbundled codes. Unbundled charges represent multiple components of a global service. The insurance companies often adopt their own proprietary screens. These screens also may incorporate frequency-of-use limitations. This trend has continued to accelerate in both the private and governmental insurer field as software is developed to enforce compliance with the insurers' disease management criteria.

The Accounting Process

In order to evaluate the efficiency of the billing process, the physician should establish an accounting system that collects all the pertinent information. One of the commonly used systems is the chart of accounts developed by the Center for Research in Ambulatory Health Care Administration (CRAHCA).[18]

Gross charges are defined as the full value of medical services provided before any ad-justment. Gross charges are then reduced by the following items:

- charity adjustments
- contractually agreed-upon reimbursement discounts (i.e., the difference between the charge and what the insurer allows on an assigned claim)
- courtesy adjustments (such as for other physicians)
- employee discounts

The result is the adjusted (net) gross charges or the maximum amount of payment that could be collected if all payers (insurers and patients paying co-insurance and deductibles) met their obligations. Net gross charges then become the collection goal of a physician practice. The next step in the collection process is to record all cash payments collected from patients or the amount paid on their behalf by insurance companies and other payers. Noncash adjustments are referred to as payment allowances. These noncash adjustments are comprised of bad debts, settlements, and provision for bad debts. Any remaining balance after the deduction of these items would represent a change in the accounts receivable.

The importance of timely and careful evaluation of the collection process cannot be overemphasized. Disruptions of cash flow have major negative impacts. First, if fees are not collected in an efficient manner, the practice could suffer a liquidity crisis and be unable to meet its ongoing obligations. Second, and perhaps more important, the older a receivable is, the less likely it is to be collected. As the time period between the rendering of the service and demand for payment increases, patients will rationalize reasons why the fee was too high or they didn't receive what was expected. There is a greater perceived value to the service at the time the service is rendered.

Billing and Collection Systems

A physician practice has a number of options, manual and computerized, under which it can manage the collection process. There are effective manual accounting systems, adequate for smaller practices, that operate under a payment-at-time-of-service collection policy. The two common manual accounting systems used are the double entry system and the pegboard system.

A double entry system uses a charge and payment journal and individual records for each patient that list the individual's charges and payments, referred to as a ledger card. When a charge is incurred, a charge is entered into the charge and payment journal, as well as the ledger card. Thus, there is a double entry for each account activity.

The pegboard system improves upon the double entry system by relying on a single entry system. The ledger card is aligned in such a way that activity recorded in it also is recorded on a day sheet (listing all the day's transactions) by the use of carbon or duplicating paper. It also simultaneously creates the bill. Such systems, however, rely heavily on manual clerical functions for the billing and aging of receivables. Both of these approaches are rudimentary and do not create important management information.

The trend in collection systems is toward computerized systems for a number of reasons. Most computerized collection systems are able to generate standard health claim policies efficiently, a process that is very inefficient for manual systems, requiring work that duplicates efforts performed in the charge posting activities. The overwhelming majority are capable of electronically transmitting these claims to Medicare carriers and other insurance companies. Many systems can post payments electronically as well. The net result is faster and more accurate turnaround of claims payments. Computer systems also can be programmed to generate bills efficiently to patients without interrupting normal office procedures. In addition, most of these systems include automated patient scheduling capability.

More sophisticated computer systems are able to pre-edit insurance submissions as well. By applying diagnosis and procedure linkages, submission errors due to miscoding or inappropriate coding can be prevented or corrected prior to submission. This helps to control the costs associated with the processing of denials, manual refilings, and telephone hearings with the insurer. It also flags inappropriate practice patterns, reduces the inflation of gross charges that can occur through inappropriate and uncollectible activities, and speeds the collection of patient co-payments, as well as payments made by insurers.

Of particular importance is the ability to generate an aged accounts receivable and other analyses. This report categorizes the age of a receivable. The age is calculated by number of days since the service was rendered. This is an extremely important benchmark to monitor because of the previously described loss of collectibility over time. Such a system also can be set up to force the write-off or placement with collection agencies of uncollected debts.

Computerized collection systems also help reduce labor costs associated with manual systems. Submission of insurance claims on behalf of Medicare patients, now required by law, requires the repetitive entry of demographic and policy information. Many individuals also will expect the practice to generate commercial insurance claim forms as well. This activity helps to expedite the payment of physician services to the patient. Basic computer and software packages capable of handling small practices are available for under $5,000, although systems for large groups can exceed $250,000.

The need for information about the practice also makes computerization valuable, particularly in a managed care environment. The data entered in the course of recording account activity can give important insights into the demographics, case mix, and referral patterns in the practice. The ability to identify changes and extrapolate trends allows the physician to react proactively.

Computerized collections systems need not be owned by the practice. The practice can contract with an independent billing organization referred to as a service bureau. A service bureau functions solely to collect payments owed to physicians and other health care providers. By providing a collection function for a number of physicians, economies of scale and attention to the collection process can be achieved that may not occur within the physician's practice. Service bureaus typically are paid on a percentage-of-collection basis, and this motivates them to collect efficiently and promptly. This is not to disparage in any way the ability of a physician's own employees to effectively collect patient accounts. Many can and do achieve results comparable to or significantly better than those provided by service bureaus. Management oversight, training, and system design always are the key to a successful collection procedure, whether the activity takes place within the physician's office or through a service bureau. The efficiency of the collection function can be compared to collection data compiled by independent sources. A number of organizations, such as the Medical Group Management Association (MGMA), collect median data indicating gross and adjusted collection rates, as well as accounts receivable aging data.[19]

Evaluation of Managed Care Contracts and Opportunities

Few physician practices can afford to ignore opportunities presented by managed care contracting. Some specialties, such as cosmetic plastic surgery, are unaffected by insurance requirements as there is generally no coverage. Yet, even these practitioners would limit their access to the patient marketplace to those seeking reconstructive surgery following an accident. Physician groups that enjoy a monopoly in their marketplace can remain relatively resistant to the fee controls that can be a part of managed care contracting, but may suffer a diminishment in patient demand due to higher out-of-pocket costs.

The majority of managed care contracting continues to take the form of negotiated discounts. These may be a percentage reduction in the charge. Most frequently, prices are set at a premium or discount to the Medicare fee schedule or other relative value system. Patients pay a co-payment amount, which may be fixed or a percentage of the amount allowed for the services.

It is important to understand the current or projected market share of the prospective MCOs. The reimbursement that a physician accepts under the contract is often heavily dependent on the projected volume of services that the practice will gain, retain, or forfeit through nonparticipation. Careful intelligence and networking, along with requests for information from the MCO, should include:

- a general plan description
- the number of covered lives in the marketplace
- affiliated insurance companies

- sample provider contract
- financial status of the plan
- payment terms and co-payments
- withhold amounts
- authorization processes and guidelines

Inasmuch as any arrangement with an MCO requires substantial administrative time and expense, the practice should focus its MCO contracting efforts on those plans that offer the best reimbursement terms and meaningful populations of patients.

Management of the patient mix between private pay, discounted, and capitated patient population is essential. A useful analogy is often made between a physician practice and an airline. Each day planes/physicians roll out to start a schedule. To be maximally efficient, the plane/schedule has to be full. To maximize revenue, the plane/physician wants to provide as many first class seats/full fee patients as possible, followed by business class seats/discounted fee for senior patients, filling the remainder of the plane/schedule with discounted advanced booking/capitation seats. If the plane/physician books too many advance booking/capitation patients, revenue suffers as first class seats/full fee patients and business class seats/discounted fee for service patients cannot be accommodated. The mix of filled seats/office appointments is critical to maximize profit. Portfolio analysis can be used to manage this mix.

Authorization Process

The overwhelming majority of managed care contracts require some level of authorization before providing services to the insured. These may be quite limited, as in general indemnity policies where authorization may only be necessary prior to a nonemergency hospital admission. Other tightly controlled plans, such as HMOs, may require preauthorization for any visit to other than a primary care physician, restrictions on approved hospitals and home health services, as well as authorization for diagnostic testing and office-based surgical treatments. It is important for the physician services organization to set up a system that provides the pertinent information to the appropriate personnel in a timely fashion; that is, before the services are rendered. Health plans vary in their willingness to authorize even necessary and emergent care after the fact, when authorization could have been obtained. The practice can incur significant losses through poor authorization control, and every member of the staff needs to be attuned to strong authorization compliances.

Capitation is another method by which MCOs contract with physicians for services. Under capitation, physicians agree to provide a designated list of services to patients for a fixed payment, per member per month (PMPM). Risks are then transferred from the insurer to the physician to control costs associated with the listed procedures. In essence, the physician becomes the insurance company for risk associated with the amount and level of care provided.

In order to set capitation rates, the physician practice, utilizing the data derived from actuaries, attempts to project the amount and cost of service the population will require to be adequately served. The age, sex, and employment status of the population can have important cost implications. The cost of providing eye care escalates dramatically in senior populations, whereas the cost of obstetric care is very low in older individuals. Specialty-specific analysis is necessary to fully understand the population subject to be bid. Frequently, stop-loss provisions are included to protect the physician from extraordinary costs, such as those associated with organ transplants or complications that can require extremely intensive therapies.

Financial Benchmarking

Financial benchmarking, often referred to as ratio analysis, is an important management tool necessary for sound practice management. Benchmarks are numerical indexes, used regularly and systematically, measuring overall performance or the performance of a specific target process. While a numeric index, the data reviewed may consist of either quantitative or qualitative measures. Two levels of benchmark comparison are possible. First, the organization compares its performance against past or projected performance in order to evaluate trends. Secondarily, the organization may compare and contrast its performance with external data compiled by organizations such as the Medical Group Management Association (MGMA) covering larger populations of self-reporting organizations. Benchmarks are useful in that they

- summarize complex information
- allow early detection of financial problems
- help in the management of payables and receivables
- provide a framework for revenue and expense budgeting
- allow the monitoring of re-engineered processes

For analysis to be appropriate and sensitive, the design of the benchmarking system needs to consider the comparability, consistency, predictability, and relevance of the measure.

When comparing ratios, particularly to externally derived benchmarks, it is important to understand the characteristics of the external measure. Is the group in the same specialty? Are there geographic biases? Is the data set composed of high performing practices rather than "average" organizations?

Consistency refers to measurement of the item being reported. Are expenses carefully and uniformly classified by the reporting sites? Predictability is another important feature of good indexing. Does the measure offer insight into future organizational or financial performance? And is that insight relevant or meaningful?

There are four types of practice ratios:

1. liquidity—the ability to meet payment obligations
2. profitability—the difference between the organization's expenses and revenues
3. capitalization—ratios that compare the relationships between debt and equity
4. activity—the relationship between input and output

Examples of each of the ratio types appear in Exhibit 18–4. All are powerful tools that require skilled and knowledgeable use. It is important to understand that average does not denote the "best," and what can be perceived as a negative variance can reflect relative excellence in performance due to structural or environmental peculiarities by which the practice is affected. As an example, a higher than average overhead structure can reflect a strategic decision to offer exceptional service in order to attract and retain a higher payment patient mix, resulting in better than average physician compensation. Notwithstanding these weaknesses, it is important to benchmark in order to carefully measure the impact of internal change, as well as performance against the peer group. Benchmarking and ra-

Exhibit 18–4 Examples of Ratio Types

Liquidity Ratios

$$\text{Common Ratio} = \frac{\text{Current Assets}}{\text{Current Liabilities}}$$

$$\text{Quick Ratio} = \frac{\text{Cash} + \text{Marketable Securities} + \text{Accounts Receivable}}{\text{Current Liabilities}}$$

$$\text{Receivable Days} = \frac{\text{Accounts Receivable}}{\text{Net Collections} / 365}$$

Profitability Ratios

$$\text{Write-Off Ratio} = \frac{\text{Charge Adjustments and Allowances}}{\text{Gross Charges}}$$

$$\text{Adjusted Collection Percentage} = \frac{\text{Gross Charges} - \text{Allowances and Adjustments}}{\text{Net Collections}}$$

Capitalization Ratios

$$\text{Fixed Asset Ratio} = \frac{\text{Total Operating Revenue}}{\text{Fixed Assets}}$$

Activity Ratios

$$\text{Surgery Yield (Specific type of) or Laser Yield} = \frac{\text{Total Patient Visits}}{\text{Surgeries (or Lasers)}}$$

$$\text{New Patient Ratio} = \frac{\text{Total Patients}}{\text{New Patients}}$$

---

tio analysis are powerful tools that take data and turn it into information.

THE FUTURE

Physician practice is undergoing a period of rapid evolution. Cost pressures applied by payers, as well as increasingly competitive markets, are causing the creation of new organizational structures and affiliations. The physician will continue to play a key role in the health delivery system. The nature of that role will be defined by the political process, by economic forces, and by how much capital physicians are willing to invest into repositioning themselves for the future.

NOTES

1. D. Coddington, et al., *The Crisis in Healthcare* (San Francisco, CA: Jossey-Bass, Inc., 1990), 38.

2. American Medical Association, *Physician Marketplace Statistics 1997/98* (Chicago: American Medical Association, 1998).

3. P. Havlicek and M. Eiler, eds., *Physicians in Medical Groups: A Comparative Analysis* (Chicago: American Medical Association, 1993), 5–17.

4. Ibid., 7.

5. Ibid., 28.

6. Ibid., 16.

7. Ibid., 14.

8. H. Hyman, *Health Planning: A Systematic Approach* (Gaithersburg, MD: Aspen Publishers, Inc., 1975), 10–13.

9. Health Insurance Association of America, *Source Book of Health Insurance Data* (Washington, DC: 1992), 2, 116–117.

10. Hyman, *Health Planning: A Systematic Approach*, 13.

11. Health Insurance Association of America, *Source Book of Health Insurance Data*, 17.

12. R. Shouldice and K. Shouldice, *Medical Group Practice and Health Maintenance Organizations* (Washington, DC: Information Resources Press, 1978), 10.

13. D. Cowan, *Preferred Provider Organizations: Planning, Structure and Operation* (Gaithersburg, MD: Aspen Publishers, Inc., 1984), 5.

14. American Medical Association, *Physicians' Current Procedural Terminology* (Chicago: American Medical Association, 1993).

15. J. Brittenhom, ed., *1991 HCFA Common Procedure Coding System* (Los Angeles: Practice Management Information Corporation, 1991), 1.

16. *ICD.9.CM* (Los Angeles: Practice Management Information Corporation, 1993), 270.

17. *Physician Compensation and Production Survey: 1993 Report Based on 1992 Data* (Englewood, CO: Medical Group Management Association, 1993), 33.

18. E. Schafer et al., eds., *Management Accounting for Fee-for-Service/Prepaid Medical Groups* (Englewood, CO: Center for Research in Ambulatory Health Care Administration, 1989).

19. *Physician Compensation and Production Survey*, 33.

MICHAEL J. KELLEY, MBA, CMPE, is the Executive Director of Retina Consultants of Southwest Florida, a tertiary care ophthalmic group practice offering comprehensive medical, surgical, and rehabilitation services, with locations throughout Southwest Florida. Mr. Kelley began his health care career in 1980 as an administrator of an ophthalmic primary care group practice. He has participated as a lecturer in numerous professional educational programs, with a focus on financial management and employee motivation. Currently, he serves on the executive committee of the Ophthalmology Assembly, Medical Group Management Association, and serves on the American Academy of Ophthalmology's committee that guides the development of administrator skill levels. He received a BS in biology as a Faculty Scholar at Florida Atlantic University and an MBA with an emphasis in marketing and management.

Chapter 19

Inpatient Hospital Reimbursement

Michael J. Dalton

Most hospitals receive a substantial amount of their revenues from regulated payers such as Medicare, state Medicaid programs, and, in some areas of the United States, the Blue Cross and Blue Shield programs. Many of these payers use the reimbursement regulations that are published by the Medicare program. In addition, with the aging of the U.S. population, and the expanded coverage to people who are under 65 and disabled, over 50 percent of a hospital's revenue very often is received from the Medicare program. Therefore, this chapter will focus on Medicare reimbursement, both past and present, which should give the reader an understanding of the methods by which hospitals receive payment for rendering services to their patients, and of the major functions of the finance department.

Since the inception of the Medicare program in 1966 and the Medicaid program in 1967, most inpatient hospital care was paid based on the cost per day to treat all patients, and outpatient care was paid on the average cost per outpatient visit. This payment system was based on the general principles of cost finding and, even though the Medicare inpatient system changed effective October 1, 1983, and the Medicare outpatient system changed effective 1986, the principles of cost finding are still used by hospitals to report information to the various regulated payers.

COST FINDING

Cost finding is the apportionment or allocation of the costs of the nonrevenue-producing cost centers to each other, and to the revenue-producing centers based on statistical data that measure the amount of service rendered by each center to other centers. The purpose of general cost finding is to determine the full costs of operating the revenue-producing centers of the hospital. Generally, centers that provide the greatest amount of service to the greatest number of other centers, and receive the least in services from others, are apportioned in the first stages of the cost finding procedure; centers that provide service to fewer centers are apportioned in the later stages.

Cost finding, therefore, is the process of recasting or reclassifying the costs accumulated in the routine accounts maintained by the hospital for responsibility reporting purposes. The recasting produces information as to the full costs of operating the various revenue-producing organizational units or departments of the hospital. Cost finding is a procedure that is done apart from, but supplemental to, the regular accounting system. The results produced by cost finding are not recorded in the hospital's accounts or usual income statement. Instead, the results of cost finding are presented in a special cost-finding report.

The cost finding process was designed so that at the end of each fiscal year, a hospital would allocate the costs attributable to Medicare, Medicaid, and other cost-based payers. This method is referred to as step-down cost finding. The first step in this process is listing all costs of a provider in a trial balance format. Indirect costs—those not associated with direct care—are attributed to such cost centers as administration and general, depreciation, utilities, housekeeping, and dietary, among others. Direct costs include radiology, laboratory, operating rooms, emergency departments, room and board, and routine care. Once this list is prepared, costs are further divided into salary and other expenses. An example of this trial balance format is shown in Table 19–1.

Adjustments to cost then are made according to numerous government regulations, in an attempt to arrive at patient-care-related costs. For example, cafeteria sales offset dietary costs because sales of meals in a cafeteria to visitors and/or staff are not considered allowable or necessary to patient care.

The next step is taking the adjusted trial balance and allocating indirect costs to direct costs using certain statistics. An example of this step-down process is shown in Table 19–2.

Other costs that are not included in Table 19–2, but would also be allocated, are listed below, with the most commonly used unit of measure to determine the appropriate allocation:

- laundry: pounds of laundry utilized
- nursing: hours spent in units
- house staff: time spent in units

Table 19–1 Example of a Trial Balance Format

Description	Salaries	Other	Total	Adjustments	Adjusted Cost
Depreciation	—	100,000	100,000	20,000*	120,000
Administration and General	400,000	100,000	500,000	—	500,000
Utilities	—	150,000	150,000	—	150,000
Housekeeping	200,000	50,000	250,000	—	250,000
Dietary	100,000	75,000	175,000	(15,000)**	160,000
Radiology	500,000	50,000	550,000	—	550,000
Labs	300,000	200,000	500,000	—	500,000
Operating Room	150,000	200,000	350,000	—	350,000
Emergency Department	75,000	75,000	150,000	—	150,000
Routine Care	700,000	300,000	1,000,000	—	1,000,000
Total	$2,425,000	$1,300,000	$3,725,000	$5,000	$3,730,000

*Adding accelerated depreciation to straight-line depreciation.
**Offsetting cafeteria costs because they would be recorded in dietary and are not allowable.

Table 19–2 Step-Down Cost Finding

Description	Transfer from Trial Balance (Dollars)	Depreciation (Square Feet)	Administration and General (Total Costs)	Utilities (Metered Use)	Housekeeping (Square Feet)	Dietary (Meals Served)	Stepped-Down Costs (Dollars)
Depreciation	120,000	120,000					
Administration and General	500,000	10,000	510,000				
Utilities	150,000	5,000	24,500	179,500			
Housekeeping	250,000	5,000	40,800	10,000	305,800		
Dietary	160,000	7,500	26,500	30,000	24,000	248,000	
Radiology	550,000	6,000	88,000	25,000	18,000		687,000
Labs	500,000	6,000	80,000	12,000	18,000		616,000
Operating Room	350,000	3,000	55,900	12,000	9,000		429,900
Emergency Department	150,000	3,000	24,300	5,000	9,000		191,300
Routine Care	1,000,000	74,500	170,000	85,500	227,800	248,000	1,805,800
Total	$3,730,000	$120,000	$510,000	$179,500	$305,800	$248,000	$3,730,000

- telephones: number of lines or usage
- data processing: usage of central processing unit
- patient accounting: volume of charges by department

After allocating (or stepping down) indirect costs to direct costs, the next step is allocating direct costs between inpatient and outpatient costs, most often on the basis of charges. The next step is to allocate program or Medicare costs based on charges, except for routine care, which is allocated based on days. This process is outlined in Table 19–3.

Charges also are the basis of the allocation of outpatient costs to Medicare, and the system works similarly with Blue Cross and Medicaid.

While the cost finding process has remained virtually unchanged since it was first developed, the hospital reimbursement system under the Medicare program underwent major changes during the 1980s with the implementation of the prospective payment system (PPS).

MEDICARE PROSPECTIVE PAYMENT SYSTEM

The Medicare PPS currently applies only to inpatient acute care services. The following types of hospitals, hospital units, and other types of providers are specifically excluded from system coverage:

- psychiatric hospitals
- rehabilitation hospitals
- distinct part psychiatric and rehabilitation units of acute care hospitals
- children's hospitals
- Christian Science sanitoria
- risk basis health maintenance organizations and competitive medical plans
- Veterans Affairs hospitals

- hospitals in states that have a waiver from the PPS program

For most covered hospitals, the PPS became effective for their fiscal years beginning on or after October 1, 1983. Payment under PPS was based on a "blended" rate during a five-year transition period to national rates. One component of that blended rate was based on the Tax Equity and Fiscal Responsibility Act (TEFRA) target rate concept, using a hospital's base year cost-per-discharge, updated for inflation. This component represented the "hospital-specific" rate. The other component of the blended rate, the "federal" rate, was based on a combination of regional and national prices established by the Health Care Financing Administration (HCFA). These two payment components—the federal rate and the hospital-specific rate—were used in combination throughout the transition period to determine the payment rates for specific categories of illnesses or diagnosis-related groups (DRGs). Since the transition period ended, DRG payment rates are determined solely by the federal rate.

The DRG payment rates represent full payment to a hospital for all inpatient hospital costs, including the costs of inpatient routine care, ancillary services, and special care units, with the exception of the following cost components:

- capital-related costs
- direct medical education costs

Hospitals may not bill Medicare patients for differences between PPS payments and actual charges. As in the past, those patients may be billed for the Medicare co-insurance and deductible amounts.

Costs that are excluded from the DRG payment rates are known as "pass through" costs. Pass through costs are reimbursed under the

Table 19-3 Cost Allocation to Program

	a	b	c	d	e	f	g	h
	Allocated Costs	Inpatient Charges	Outpatient Charges	Inpatient (%)	Inpatient Costs (d x a)	Medicare Inpatient Charges	Medicare Inpatient (%) (f ÷ b)	Medicare Costs (g x e)
Radiology	687,000	450,000	250,000	64	440,000	150,000	33.3	147,000
Labs	616,000	450,000	250,000	64	394,000	150,000	33.3	131,000
Operating Room	429,900	300,000	150,000	67	288,000	100,000	33.3	96,000
Emergency Department	191,300	60,000	200,000	23	44,000	20,000	33.3	15,000
Total Allocated Medicare Ancillary Costs								389,000

Total Routine Costs 1,805,800
Total Routine Patient Days 60,000
Average Per Diem 30.1
Medicare Routine Days 20,000

Medicare Routine Costs (days x per diem)   602,000
Total Medicare Reimbursable Inpatient Costs $991,000

pre-PPS retrospective cost-based system, subject to certain limitations and reductions. Hospitals must file Medicare cost reports annually to be reimbursed for those costs. In addition, incremental payments are made under PPS for outlier cases and indirect medical education costs. Outliers are defined as cases involving atypical lengths of stay or atypical costs. Special payment provisions also apply when patients are transferred from one hospital to another as well as in other defined transfer situations.

Diagnosis-Related Groups

DRGs are the basis for payment to hospitals under the Medicare PPS. Originally developed at Yale University, DRGs, as adapted for use by Medicare, are intended to represent groups of hospital inpatients that are clinically similar to one another and relatively homogeneous with respect to use of resources.

HCFA has established specific payment rates for each DRG. The formula for calculating payment for a specific DRG is based on the PPS payment rate multiplied by the cost weight or relative weight of the DRG to which the case is assigned. Each DRG cost weight is intended to represent the average resources required to care for a case in that particular DRG, relative to the national average of resources consumed per case. For example, a case assigned to a DRG with a weight of 2.0 would, on average, require twice the amount of resources as the average case (i.e., a weight of 1.0). Periodic adjustments in DRG classifications and weighting factors are made by HCFA to reflect changes in resource consumption, treatment patterns, technology, and other factors that may affect the relative use of hospital resources. Generally, updates to the list of DRGs and cost weights are issued by HCFA in September of each year.

Each Medicare discharge is assigned to only one DRG regardless of the number of services furnished or the number of days of care provided. First, the physician records the patient's principal diagnosis, any additional diagnoses, and procedures performed. The hospital expresses this information on the patient's bill using classifications and terminology consistent with the *International Classification of Diseases, 9th Revision, Clinical Modification (ICD-9-CM)*. The principal diagnosis, up to four secondary diagnoses, the principal procedure, and additional procedures are reported along with the patient's age, sex, and discharge status to the hospital's fiscal intermediary with the hospital's request for payment.

The fiscal intermediary enters this information into its claims system and subjects the data to a series of automated screens called the Medicare code editor (MCE). These screens identify cases that require further review before being classified into a DRG. Cases are then classified by a computer program (grouper) into the appropriate DRG. DRGs are organized into 25 major diagnostic categories (MDCs). The principle diagnosis (the medical condition ultimately determined to have caused the hospitalization) determines the MDC assignment. Patients in each MDC are subsequently assigned to a specific DRG, depending on certain variables. Within most MDCs, cases are divided into surgical DRGs (based on a hierarchy that orders individual procedures or groups of procedures by resource intensity) and medical DRGs. The medical DRGs generally are differentiated on the basis of the principal diagnosis. Both medical and surgical cases may be further differentiated based on age, sex, and the presence or absence of complications or comorbidities. With some exceptions, the grouper does not consider other procedures, such as nonsurgical procedures or minor procedures that generally do not require the use of an operating room. The typical DRG assignment process is shown in Figure 19-1.

Hospitals that are dissatisfied with the intermediary's decision regarding DRG as-

signment must request a review within 60 days after the date a claim is paid. The hospital may submit additional information as part of its request. The fiscal intermediary or the peer review organization (PRO) then reviews

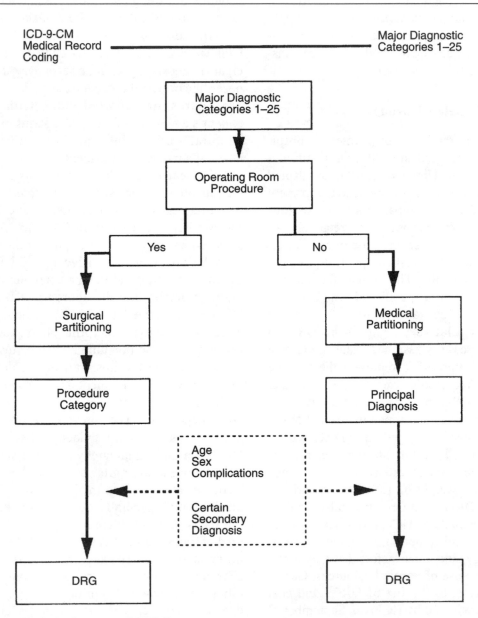

Figure 19–1 Assignment of a DRG

the case, and, if appropriate, changes the DRG classification.

Because of its extensive use of averages, a major shortcoming of the DRG payment mechanism is its failure to take into account the severity of a patient's illness. Current payment policies for both cost and day outliers do not adequately address the severity of illness issue.

Congress has directed HCFA to evaluate a variety of patient classification systems to address this shortcoming of the current system and to assist HCFA in measuring and monitoring the quality of care. According to HCFA, the process of evaluating various severity of illness methodologies, as well as refining DRG classifications, is still underway. Currently, there is no deadline by which HCFA must select or recommend a particular severity of illness methodology.

Hospital Payment under PPS

The Medicare PPS generally applies to hospital fiscal years beginning on or after October 1, 1983. On the surface, the program initially appeared to simplify the process of reimbursing hospitals because it provided predetermined, fixed-price payments. However, PPS has proven to be much more complicated than was anticipated initially because of the lack of predictability of the payment rates, ongoing capital cost payment uncertainties, continued modifications to medical education payments, and a range of other regulatory actions motivated by federal deficit reduction initiatives.

When Congress approved the PPS, it initially established a three-year phase-in period to ease the transition from cost-based reimbursement to the fixed-price PPS. The phase-in period, which was subsequently extended to five years, is shown in the transition schedule in Table 19–4. During the phase-in period, Medicare payments were based on a blend of hospital-specific rates and regional and national DRG rates (federal rates). The base period for PPS was each hospital's fiscal year ended during the period from September 30, 1982, through September 29, 1983. The hospital-specific rate was established based on each hospital's allowable cost-per-case during the base period, trended forward for inflation. As shown in Tables 19–4 and 19–5,

Table 19–4 Transition Schedule for Hospital-Specific and Federal Percentages

Cost Reporting Period Beginning on or After	Hospital-Specific Percentage	Federal Percentage*
October 1, 1983	75%	25%
October 1, 1984	50%	50%
October 1, 1985		
–The first seven months of the cost reporting period	50%	50%
–The remaining five months of the cost reporting period	45%	55%
October 1, 1986	25%	75%
October 1, 1987		
–The first 51 days of the cost reporting period	25%	75%
–The remaining days of the cost reporting period	0%	100%
October 1, 1988, and thereafter	0%	100%

*The regional and national components of the federal rate are shown in Table 19–5.

Table 19–5 Regional and National Percentages Comprising the Federal Rate

Federal Fiscal Year Beginning	Regional Percentage	National Percentage
October 1, 1983	100%	0%
October 1, 1984	75%	25%
October 1, 1985	75%	25%
October 1, 1986	50%	50%
October 1, 1987		
–October 1, 1987 through November 20, 1987	50%	50%
–November 21, 1987, and subsequent periods	0%	100%

the federal rate was comprised of regional and national components during the transition period. Also, note that the hospital-specific portion of the blended rate changes was based on the cost reporting period of the hospital while, in general, the federal rate changes were based on the federal fiscal year.

The DRG payment rates are the essence of the PPS. They represent fixed payment amounts for each Medicare patient, regardless of the patient's length of stay or use of resources (with the exception of incremental payments for outliers). These fixed prices vary depending on whether the hospital's location is urban or rural and are adjusted for differences in area wage levels.

During the transition period, the wage-adjusted federal rates were blended with the hospital-specific rate in accordance with the transition schedule (see Table 19–4) and multiplied by the relative weight factor for the particular DRG to which the patient had been assigned to determine the specific amount the hospital would be paid for that patient. Now that the transition to the federal rate is complete, only the federal rate is used in the calculation. Co-insurance and deductibles due from the patient are subtracted from this amount to arrive at the amount of Medicare payment to the hospital.

The federal rates are updated annually. Typically, preliminary federal payment rate schedules are published in June and final federal rates are published in early September of each year. In recent years, congressional tinkering and deficit reduction initiatives have delayed the annual determination of final federal rates to as late as November or December. Specific urban and rural federal payment rates are established for each of the nine census regions (regional rates) in addition to the national urban and rural payment rates. The federal rate is a blend of the regional and national rates during the transition period as shown in Table 19–5.

Calculating PPS Payment Rates

Described below is the method for calculating the adjusted federal payment rate for a PPS hospital:

1. Determine the appropriate regional and national payment rates, based on the hospital's geographic location.
2. Multiply the labor-related component of the payment rate(s) by the appropriate area wage index. Applicable area wage indexes are published by HCFA in the *Federal Register*.
3. Add the respective labor-adjusted component to the nonlabor component for the applicable rate(s).

Exhibit 19–1 illustrates how a blended PPS payment rate is calculated.

The federal portion of the DRG base rates is supposed to be adjusted for inflation on an annual basis. Initially, the annual update factor was defined as the Hospital Market Basket Index plus one percent. Because of federal deficit reduction initiatives and allegations of excess hospital profits on Medicare business, the annual updating process has become highly political.

Patient Transfers

PPS payments are made on a per-discharge basis. Under PPS, a discharge is defined as occurring when a patient is formally released from the hospital, dies in the hospital, or is transferred to another hospital or unit that is excluded from participation in PPS. Accordingly, if the patient is transferred to another hospital that participates in PPS, a discharge, as defined under PPS, has not occurred. Because the prospective payment rates are designed to compensate hospitals for a patient's complete treatment, payment is adjusted when a hospital releases a patient without meeting the patient discharge requirements. Adjustments to PPS payments for transfer situations are handled as described below.

If a patient is transferred to another hospital that participates in PPS, the hospital transferring the patient is paid on a per diem rate basis, not to exceed that hospital's DRG-specific payment rate. The per diem rate is that hospital's DRG-specific rate, divided by the mean length of stay for the specific DRG to which the patient is assigned. The hospital from which the patient is ultimately discharged receives the full prospective payment rate. Exhibit 19–2 gives examples that illustrate how to calculate payments to hospitals in transfer situations.

Outlier Payments

Under the PPS, additional payments are made for outlier cases; current legislation limits these payments to approximately 5 percent of total federal PPS payments. Since the inception of PPS, this target percentage has ranged from 6 percent in the initial year of the program to the current 5 percent level that has prevailed since fiscal year 1985. The criteria discussed below are used to identify outliers. If a case qualifies as both a day and a cost outlier, the claim is paid at the higher of the two amounts.

A discharge is considered to be a day outlier if the patient's length of stay (excluding days not covered by Medicare Part A) exceeds the geometric mean length of stay for discharges in that DRG by the lesser of 28 days or 3.0 standard deviations from the mean length of stay (day threshold). Final regulations for fiscal year 1991 increased the day outlier thresholds to the lesser of 29 days or 3.0 standard deviations. Hospitals receive an additional per diem payment for each covered day of care exceeding the day threshold. This amount is equal to 60 percent (marginal cost factor) of the average federal per diem rate for the applicable DRG. Burn cases are also paid based on a 60 percent marginal cost factor. The average per diem payment is derived by dividing the wage-adjusted federal payment rate for the DRG by its geometric mean length of stay.

The following example illustrates how the additional payment was determined for a day outlier in federal fiscal year 1990.

> Hospital X is a teaching hospital located in Nashville, Tennessee. Hospital X has a ratio of interns and residents to beds of .1 and is eligible for a disproportionate share adjustment factor of 5 percent. Mrs. Smith was admitted to Hospital X on July

Exhibit 19–1 Sample Calculation: PPS Payment Rate, Excluding Indirect Medical Education and Disproportionate Share Adjustments

Assumptions:
Patient discharged on April 30, 1990
DRG assigned: Simple Pneumonia and Pleurisy (DRG 89)
Hospital location: Nashville, Tennessee
Hospital fiscal year: June 30, 1990
Regional and national rates from *Federal Register*, April 20, 1990
Area wage index factor from Table 4a of *Federal Register*, September 1, 1989
Transition percentages from Table 19–5

Step 1 *Regional Portion*

	Regional Rate	Area Wage Factor	Adjusted Rate	
Labor	$2,385.26	.8893	$2,121.21	
Nonlabor	722.37	N/A	722.37	
Regional Portion of Federal Payment Rate			$2,843.58	(A)

Step 2 *National Portion*

	Regional Rate	Area Wage Factor	Adjusted Rate	
Labor	$2,467.88	.8893	$2,194.69	
Nonlabor	874.11	N/A	874.11	
National Portion of Federal Payment Rate			$3,068.80	(B)

Step 3 *Federal Portion Blending of Regional and National Rates*

	Blend Percentage from Table 19–5	Amount	
Regional Portion (A)	$2,843.58	0%	$0.00
National Portion (B)	3,068.80	100%	3,068.80
Federal Payment Rate			$3,068.80

Step 4 *Calculation of DRG Payment*

	Transition Percentage from Table 19–5	Amount	
Federal Payment Rate (Calculated Above)	$3,068.80	100%	$3,068.80
Blended Base DRG Payment Rate			3,068.80
DRG Cost Weight (DRG 89)			x 1.2059
Blended DRG Payment Rate—DRG 89			$3,700.67

Exhibit 19–2 Sample Calculation: Payments to Hospitals in Transfer Situations, Excluding Indirect Medical Education and Disproportionate Share Adjustments

Example A:
Hospital A (transferring hospital)—LOS 2 days, DRG Y
(Blended payment rate is $6,000.)
Hospital B (receiving and discharging hospital)—DRG Y
(Blended payment rate is $8,000.)
(Mean length of stay for DRG Y equals 10 days.)
Payment:

Hospital A—2 days   x $\dfrac{\$6,000}{10 \text{ days}}$ = $1,200

Hospital B—$8,000 when discharging   = $8,000
Total Medicare payment for patient   = $9,200

Example B:
Hospital A (transferring hospital)—LOS 4 days, DRG X
(Blended payment rate is $16,000 and the mean length of stay is 8 days.)
Hospital B (both receiving and subsequently transferring)—LOS 4 days, DRG Y
(Blended payment rate is $10,000; the mean length of stay is 10 days.)
Hospital C (receiving and discharging)—DRG Y
(Blended payment rate is $15,000.)
Payment:

Hospital A—4 days   x $\dfrac{\$16,000}{8 \text{ days}}$ = $8,000

Hospital B—4 days   x $\dfrac{\$10,000}{10 \text{ days}}$ = $4,000

Hospital C—$15,000 when discharging   = $15,000
Total Medicare payment for patient   = $27,000

3, 1990, and was discharged on August 31, 1990.

Mrs. Smith's stay was classified in DRG 89. Because Mrs. Smith's 59-day stay exceeds the 35-day length-of-stay outlier threshold for DRG 89, Hospital X is eligible for payment for 24 outlier days in addition to the otherwise applicable prospective payment. The amount of Hospital X's total DRG payment for this case, including the outlier payment, is calculated as illustrated in Exhibit 19–3.

Prior to October 1, 1997, a discharge that qualified as a day outlier may have also qualified as a high-cost outlier, if the cost of covered services exceeded the cost threshold established by HCFA. The hospital was paid the greater of the day outlier payment amount or the cost outlier payment amount. For federal fiscal year 1991 (October 1, 1990, through September 30, 1991), the cost threshold was the greater of two times the federal rate for the

Exhibit 19–3 Sample Calculation: Day Outlier Patient

Step 1

Computation of Federal Rate (Excludes
Payment for Capital, Indirect Medical
Education Costs, and Disproportionate
Share Hospital Adjustments)
National Other Urban Standardized*

Amounts:

Blended Base DRG Payment Rate (from Exhibit 19–1)	$3,068.80
DRG Cost Weight	x 1.2059
Blended DRG Payment Rate (DRG 89)	$3,700.67

Step 2

Computation of Day Outlier
Payments

Outlier days	59 – 35 = 24
DRG 89 geometric mean length of stay	7.2 days
Marginal cost factor	60%

Outlier payment (excludes
adjustments for disproportionate
share and indirect medical
education costs) = Number of
outlier days x (Total federal
prospective payment ÷ Geometric
mean length of stay for DRG) x
Marginal cost factor = (24) x
($3,700.67 ÷ 7.2) x (.60) =
$7,401.34

Total Day Outlier Payments =	$7,401.34

Step 3

Computation of Federal DRG
Revenue

Regular federal payment	$3,700.67
Day outlier payment	7,401.34
Total federal DRG revenue	$11,102.01

Step 4

Computation of Indirect Medical Education
Adjustment

Intern and resident/bed ratio = .1
Indirect medical education adjustment factor
$1.89[(1 + .1)^{.405}–1] = .0744$ or 7.44%
Indirect medical education adjustment = Total
federal DRG revenue x Indirect medical
education adjustment factor = ($11,102.01)
x (.0744) = $825.99

Step 5

Computation of Disproportionate Share
Payment

Disproportionate share adjustment factor =
5% or .05
Disproportionate share payment = Total
federal DRG revenue x Disproportionate
share adjustment factor = ($11,102.01) x
(.05) = $555.10

Step 6

Computation of Total Federal DRG Payments

Total federal DRG revenue (including outlier payments)	$11,102.01
Indirect medical education adjustment	825.99
Disproportionate share payment	555.10
Total federal DRG payment	$12,483.10

*Region is not subject to the regional payment floor.

DRG or $35,000, both adjusted for area wage differences. For high-cost outliers, hospitals received an additional payment (marginal cost factor) equal to 75 percent (90 percent for burn cases) of the difference between the hospital's adjusted cost for the discharge and the cost threshold.

In 1997 Congress passed the Balanced Budget Act, which included changes to the Medicare reimbursement regulations. Among the changes was the elimination of additional reimbursement for day outlier. As a result, as of October 1, 1997, only cost outlier cases will receive additional reimbursement from the Medicare program.

Pass Through Costs

The Medicare PPS DRG payment rates represent payment for all hospital inpatient costs except for those defined as pass through costs. Pass through costs are not subject to PPS, but continue to be reimbursed on a reasonable cost basis, subject to specific limits. Pass through costs include capital costs and graduate medical education costs.

In addition, teaching hospitals receive an additional payment to defray the indirect costs of medical education. In a health reform environment, and to dissuade the education of specialists, these payments are threatened.

The data included in Table 19–6 illustrate the significance of pass through costs to PPS hospitals.

Capital Costs

When PPS was signed into law in April 1983, capital and related costs were to be excluded from it until October 1, 1986. On June 3, 1986, proposed rules to implement prospective payment for capital and related costs were published. However, on July 2, 1986,

the Urgent Supplemental Appropriations Act for fiscal year 1987 postponed the implementation of prospective payment for capital and related costs until October 1, 1987. The Omnibus Budget Reconciliation Act of 1987 further postponed prospective payment for capital and related costs until October 1, 1991. Until that time, capital and related costs continued to be paid on a reasonable cost basis, subject to certain payment reduction amounts discussed herein.

Since the inception of PPS, various prospective capital payment methodologies have been proposed by the administration, the Prospective Payment Assessment Commission (ProPAC), Congress, and hospital industry groups. Determining whether capital costs can or should be included in DRG rates and establishing the appropriate amounts have been highly controversial issues. The federal government is likely to continue to take actions to minimize capital payments to hospitals as a means to reduce Medicare outlays.

Prospective capital payment rates will have diverse effects on hospitals depending on:

- the age or condition of the facility
- the level and cost of debt financing
- the amount of new technology previously acquired or needed in the future
- the hospital's Medicare and non-Medicare utilization levels

The variation of capital costs among hospital groups is illustrated in Table 19–7.

Medicare capital cost reimbursement principles have remained largely unchanged since the beginning of the Medicare program in 1966. Under the reasonable cost principles established at that time, providers are reimbursed for the Medicare portion of their capital-related costs.

Medicare regulations define capital costs to include:

Table 19–6 Medicare Pass Through Payments as a Percentage of Total Medicare Inpatient Hospital Payments in the Fifth Year of PPS, by Hospital Group

Hospital Group	Capital Payments	Direct Medical Education Payments	Combined Total
All hospitals	10.1%	2.9%	13.0%
Urban	10.0	3.3	13.2
Rural	11.0	0.4	11.4
Large urban	9.8	4.2	14.0
Other urban	10.1	2.2	12.2
Rural referral	10.7	1.0	11.7
Sole community	11.0	0.2	11.2
Other rural	11.2	0.1	11.2
Major teaching	7.4	9.3	16.7
Other teaching	9.3	3.8	13.1
Nonteaching	11.5	0.2	11.7
Disproportionate share:			
Large urban	9.2	6.1	15.3
Other urban	9.9	2.4	12.3
Rural	11.0	0.8	11.8
Nondisproportionate share	10.4	2.0	12.4
Urban <100 beds	11.3	0.3	11.6
Urban 100–249 beds	11.7	1.1	12.8
Urban 250–404 beds	10.0	2.8	12.7
Urban 405–684 beds	8.9	4.7	13.6
Urban 685+ beds	8.0	7.5	15.5
Rural <50 beds	10.3	0.1	10.4
Rural 50–99 beds	11.6	0.1	11.7
Rural 100–169 beds	11.4	0.2	11.6
Rural 170+ beds	10.5	1.1	11.6
Voluntary	9.8	3.2	13.0
Proprietary	13.4	0.5	13.9
Urban government	8.4	3.8	12.2
Rural government	10.4	0.5	10.8

Note: Total pass through payments also include organ acquisition payments and other Medicare inpatient hospital payments not paid under PPS. Only capital and direct medical education payments are included in this table. Excludes hospitals in Maryland and New Jersey.

Source: ProPAC analysis of Medicare Cost Report data from the Health Care Financing Administration.

- net depreciation expense, adjusted by gains and losses from the disposal of depreciable assets
- leases and rentals
- taxes on land and depreciable assets
- costs of betterments or improvements
- net capital interest expense, offset by a prorated amount of investment income on investments of unrestricted and borrowed funds

- costs of minor equipment, if depreciated over three years
- insurance on depreciable assets
- capital costs of related supplier organizations, subject to reasonableness
- capital costs of unrelated suppliers, only if:
  1. Capital equipment is leased or rented by the provider.

2. The equipment is on the provider's premises.
3. The charge for capital equipment is separately stated.
- return on equity for investor-owned providers (phased out)

The regulations define betterments and improvements as those that extend the estimated

Table 19–7 Average 50-Year PPS Capital Costs, by Hospital Group

Hospital Group	Average Medicare Inpatient Capital Costs per Case	Average Capital/ Operating Costs Ratio
All hospitals	$517	.123
Urban	565	.123
Rural	356	.123
Large urban	609	.121
Other urban	518	.126
Rural referral	425	.131
Sole community	353	.117
Other rural	324	.119
Major teaching	676	.102
Other teaching	542	.118
Nonteaching	480	.134
Disproportionate share:		
Large urban	649	.117
Other urban	528	.125
Rural	337	.123
Nondisproportionate share	495	.125
Urban <100 beds	506	.132
Urban 100–249 beds	583	.141
Urban 250–404 beds	548	.121
Urban 405–684 beds	565	.114
Urban 685+ beds	628	.109
Rural <50 beds	283	.107
Rural 50–99 beds	337	.121
Rural 100–169 beds	385	.131
Rural 170+ beds	403	.126
Voluntary	521	.122
Proprietary	596	.162
Urban government	492	.097
Rural government	318	.111

Source: ProPAC analysis of Medicare Cost Report Data from the Health Care Financing Administration.

useful life of an asset at least two years beyond its original estimated useful life, or that significantly improve an asset's productivity. Betterments and improvements are depreciated over the remaining useful life of an asset.

The following costs are specifically excluded from capital costs:

- repair or maintenance expenses, including service agreements involving lease or rental arrangements
- interest expense on working capital loans
- general liability insurance
- taxes not assessed against property
- minor equipment expense

It is in a hospital's best interest to capitalize equipment or other property that can legitimately be considered as capital items as defined in the regulations. In addition, because capital costs are, under present law, to be folded into the prospective DRG rates, it is advisable to depreciate assets as rapidly as possible within existing Medicare guidelines.

Significant changes in capital cost reimbursement occurred as part of the Congressional budget balancing efforts of 1986 and 1987. The Omnibus Budget Reconciliation Act (OBRA) of 1986 began a process of defined reductions in Medicare's payment for capital costs until such time as a prospective payment system for capital could be implemented. Since this act, virtually all budget reconciliation amendments have included a continuation of the capital payment reductions. A summary of such reductions is shown in Table 19–8.

On August 30, 1991, HCFA released final rules for implementing a PPS for hospital inpatient capital costs. The final rule, effective for hospital cost reporting periods beginning on or after October 1, 1991, established a payment system that replaced the reasonable cost-based payment methodology with prospective payment for capital-related costs.

When fully implemented, the new capital payment system will provide hospitals with a fixed payment amount (adjusted for each hospital's case mix) for each Medicare admission.

At inception, the PPS capital payment regulations utilized a standard federal rate for all capital-related inpatient hospital costs based on the estimated fiscal year 1992 national average Medicare cost per discharge for hospitals paid under PPS. The federal rate is updated each year based on HCFA's projected increase in capital costs, and is adjusted to account for each hospital's case mix, number of patient transfers, extraordinarily costly or lengthy cases (outliers), geographic location, and higher costs experienced by certain hospitals that treat a disproportionately high number of indigent cases or that have teaching programs. A hospital-specific capital payment rate was determined using the hospital's cost report covering the most recent 12-month cost reporting period that ended prior to December 31, 1990.

Under the PPS capital payment methodology, a hospital is paid using the following two methodologies:

1. If the hospital-specific rate is below the federal rate, then the hospital is paid under the fully prospective payment rate methodology.
2. If the hospital-specific rate is above the federal rate, then the hospital is paid under the "hold-harmless" rate payment methodology.

A hospital paid under the fully prospective payment rate methodology receives a payment based on a blend of its hospital-specific rate and the federal rate based on the transition schedule shown in Table 19–9. (Under this option, the fiscal year 1994 rate would be based on a blend of 70 percent of the hospital-specific rate and 30 percent of the federal

Table 19–8 OBRA Reductions in Capital Cost Reimbursement

Period Covered	Hospitals Subject to PPS	
	Inpatient Services	*Outpatient Services*
Historical Information:		
October 1, 1987–November 20, 1987	3.50%	—
November 21, 1987–December 31, 1987	7.00%*	—
January 1, 1988–March 31, 1988	12.00%*	—
April 1, 1988–September 30, 1988	12.00%	—
October 1, 1988–September 30, 1989	15.00%	—
October 1, 1989–October 15, 1989	—	15.000%**
October 16, 1989–December 31, 1989		
OBRA Reduction Factor	—	15.000%
Plus Gramm-Rudman Reduction	2.092%	2.092%
Effective Capital Reduction Rate	2.092%	17.092%
January 1, 1990–September 30, 1990	15.00%	See below
January 1, 1990–March 31, 1990		
OBRA Reduction Factor		15.000%
Plus Gramm-Rudman Reduction		2.092%
Effective Capital Reduction Rate		17.092%
April 1, 1990–September 30, 1990		
OBRA Reduction Factor		15.000%
Plus Gramm-Rudman Reduction		1.400%
Effective Capital Reduction Rate		16.400%
October 1, 1990–September 30, 1991	15.00%	15.000%

*Further increased by 2.324 Gramm-Rudman reduction factor
**Because of a drafting error in the budget legislation, capital costs applicable to outpatient services were reduced to 85% of actual costs retroactively to October 1, 1989.

rate. Over the next 7 years, the federal portion of the payment will increase by 10 percentage points per year, while the hospital-specific rate will decrease by the same percentage. In the seventh year, hospitals will be paid 100 percent of the federal rate.) This transition schedule applies only to those hospitals that will receive higher payments under the fully prospective payment rate.

A hospital paid under the hold-harmless rate payment methodology receives a payment per discharge based on *the higher of:*

1. Eighty-five percent (90 percent in the proposed rule) of the reasonable costs associated with "old" capital (a hold-harmless payment) plus a payment for new capital based on the proportion of the new Medicare inpatient capital costs to total Medicare inpatient capital costs multiplied by the newly created federal rate. (Note: hold-harmless payments for old capital will be made at the rate of 100 percent for sole community hospitals.)

2. One-hundred percent of the federal rate.

The PPS capital rules provide a hospital with the opportunity to recalculate its hospital-

Table 19–9 Fully Prospective Payment Rate Methodology Transition Schedule

Cost Reporting Period Beginning In	Hospital-Specific Blend Percentage	Federal Blend Percentage
Fiscal Year 1994	70.00%	30.00%
Fiscal Year 1995	60.00%	40.00%
Fiscal Year 1996	50.00%	50.00%
Fiscal Year 1997	40.00%	60.00%
Fiscal Year 1998	30.00%	70.00%
Fiscal Year 1999	20.00%	80.00%
Fiscal Year 2000	10.00%	90.00%
Fiscal Year 2001	0.00%	100.00%

specific rate in subsequent years to reflect changes in old capital costs as determined in a cost reporting period subsequent to the base year. "New" capital costs are excluded from the redetermination of the hospital-specific rate. Such requests for redeterminations may be made for any cost reporting period subsequent to the base period but no later than the later of the hospital's cost reporting period beginning in fiscal year 1994 or the cost reporting period beginning after obligated capital that is recognized as old capital is put in use.

Because of the significant decrease in the federal rate included in the final rule for fiscal year 1994, HCFA has been directed to redetermine every hospital's payment methodology using their cost report for the cost reporting period beginning during fiscal year 1994.

"Old" capital costs are defined as allowable interest and depreciation expense related to capital assets that were put in use by December 31, 1990, or that were legally obligated through a contractual agreement entered into on or before December 31, 1990, and put in use for patient care before October 1, 1994. The regulations also include a number of other specific circumstances where assets may be treated as if they had been legally obligated at December 31, 1990, and accordingly recognized as old capital.

New capital costs are defined as allowable capital-related costs that are related to assets that were first put into use for patient care after December 31, 1990, and those allowable capital-related costs related to assets in use prior to December 31, 1990, that are excluded from the definition of old capital costs.

Graduate Medical Education Costs

The Medicare PPS provides for the reimbursement of defined medical education costs in addition to the prospective DRG payment rates. Medical education costs are excluded from the prospective DRG rates and have been addressed separately in order to recognize the direct and indirect costs associated with approved medical education programs. Reimbursement for medical education is segregated into direct and indirect medical education.

On September 29, 1989, HCFA issued the long-awaited final regulations pertaining to Medicare's reimbursement of graduate medical education (GME) costs. These final regulations implement the direct medical education provisions of the Consolidated Omnibus Budget Reconciliation Act of 1985 and the Omnibus Budget Reconciliation Act of 1986. Prior to those acts, direct costs of GME programs were reimbursed on a reasonable cost basis under the initial PPS regulations. The final GME regulations provide for Medicare payment based on the following method:

1. Determine a fixed, base-year amount per intern/resident.
2. Update the base-year amount for inflation.
3. Multiply the updated amount by the number of allowable intern and resident full-time equivalents (FTEs) for the cost reporting period.
4. Determine Medicare's portion of allowable graduate medical education costs based on the ratio of Medicare patient days to total patient days multiplied by the product of step three above.
5. Allocate Medicare's portion of allowable graduate medical education costs derived in step four to Part A and Part B based on the ratio of Medicare's share of reasonable costs excluding GME attributable to Parts A and B.

Implementation of the final GME regulations has been applied retroactively to hospital cost reporting periods beginning on or after July 1, 1985. The implementation of these final regulations is expected to result in retroactive recoupment of approximately $400 million from teaching institutions.

The new reimbursement methodology determines a hospital-specific base year per intern/resident amount by dividing a hospital's allowable costs of direct GME by the number of its interns and residents. The base year is the cost reporting period beginning on or after October 1, 1983, and before October 1, 1984 (federal fiscal year 1984). In establishing the base year per intern/resident amount, HCFA instructed Medicare intermediaries to reexamine or reaudit FY 1984 GME costs for nonallowable and misclassified costs. This

was to occur even if the base year is beyond the normal three-year period for reopening a cost report.

In its audit instructions to intermediaries, HCFA identified certain costs that were to be considered nonallowable GME costs. Those costs include GME costs allocated to the nursery, research activities, and other nonreimbursable cost centers. Some examples of misclassifications of operating costs as GME costs would be unrelated physicians' costs, administrative and general service costs, meal costs, travel costs, and medical library costs. GME costs incurred in distinct-part units or other PPS excluded units that participate in Medicare are included in allowable GME costs. Because the payment methodology sets future payments utilizing the FY 1984 base year as the initial starting point, it was critical that all allowable GME costs be identified. During the audit process, the hospital had an opportunity to present documentation of any factors that should be taken into account in the final determination of the base year per intern/resident amounts.

If during the audit process the intermediary determined that certain operating costs were inappropriately classified as GME in the 1984 base year, the intermediary proposed an adjustment to have them treated as normal operating costs and excluded from allowable GME costs. In this situation, the hospital could have requested its intermediary to reopen all PPS transition years and recalculate the hospital-specific portion of the PPS rates for those years. Hospitals not subject to PPS also could have requested to have their target rate recomputed to reflect adjustments for misclassified costs. This request needed to be received no later than 180 days after the date of the notice by the intermediary of the hospital's average per intern/resident amount, and it needed to include sufficient documentation to demonstrate that the adjustment was warranted. If the hospital's PPS or TEFRA base-period cost report was not subject to reopening, the hospital's reopening request must have explicitly stated that the review was limited to the one issue, i.e., misclassified GME costs or misclassified operating costs that affect its average per intern/resident amount.

Intermediaries were instructed not to increase 1984 base year GME costs for costs that were initially misclassified by the hospital as operating costs in the 1984 base period unless the hospital could demonstrate that the same misclassification occurred in its PPS/Tax Equity and Fiscal Responsibility Act (TEFRA) base period. Hospitals were to be notified by the Medicare intermediary as to their base year GME costs per intern/resident. From the date of notification, hospitals had 180 days to appeal the base year determinations, as well as to request an adjustment to the hospital-specific or TEFRA rate.

Base year GME costs are only one component of the formula in computing the base year per intern/resident amount; the other component is the base year number of interns/residents. The number of residents in the base year is generally equal to the total number of interns/residents working in the hospital complex; this includes hospital-based providers and subproviders. No matter how many hours an intern or resident works, he or she cannot be counted as more than one FTE. Interns/residents assigned to the nursery, to research activities, and to other nonallowable cost centers are to be included in the count. However, costs attributable to interns/residents in these areas will not be included in base year costs. This mismatching of costs and counts reduces the per intern/resident amount and likely will be challenged during the appeal process. Hospitals are required to document the number of interns/residents in the base year. The best documentation consists of time sheets or

scheduled assignments. If auditable documentation is not available, the intermediaries have been instructed to contact HCFA for further instructions.

In addition to prospective DRG payments for inpatient hospital services, teaching hospitals receive a payment adjustment for the indirect costs of medical education, which is intended to compensate for the incremental, but not separately identified, patient care costs associated with approved intern and resident programs. Those costs may reflect factors such as an increase in the number of tests and procedures ordered by interns and residents relative to the number ordered by more experienced physicians or the need of hospitals with teaching programs to maintain more detailed medical records. In establishing the additional payment for indirect medical education costs, Congress emphasized its view that these teaching expenses are not to be subject to the same standards of efficiency implied under PPS, but rather that they are legitimate expenses involved in the postgraduate medical education of physicians that the Medicare program has historically recognized as worthy of support under the reimbursement system.

Because the indirect costs of medical education are defined in terms of increased operating costs, they are not separately identifiable on the cost report or in other financial or accounting records. Instead, these incremental costs have been statistically estimated as a function of teaching intensity. A proxy measure—the hospital's ratio of the number of interns and residents to the number of beds—has been used to measure teaching intensity. The coefficient describing this statistical relationship has been expressed as a percentage and applied as the indirect medical education factor.

To determine the payment estimated for indirect medical education, the formulas given

Exhibit 19–4 Formulas for Computing Indirect Medical Education Adjustment Factors

---

Formula Effective for Discharges through April 30, 1986

$$.1159 \ \times \ \left(\frac{\text{Number of FTE Interns \& Residents}}{\text{Number of Beds}} \div .1 \right) \ =$$

Formula Effective for Discharges from May 1, 1986 through September 30, 1988

$$2 \ \times \ \left[\left(1 - \frac{\text{Number of FTE Interns \& Residents}}{\text{Number of Beds}} \right)^{.405} -1 \right] \ =$$

Formula Effective for Discharges from October 1, 1988 through September 30, 1995

$$1.89 \ \times \ \left[\left(1 - \frac{\text{Number of FTE Interns \& Residents}}{\text{Number of Beds}} \right)^{.405} -1 \right] \ =$$

---

in Exhibit 19–4 are applied to the federal component of PPS payments (including outliers but excluding disproportionate share payments). The formulas were not applied to the hospital-specific component of PPS rates during the transition years because indirect medical education costs were included in the base-year costs that were used to establish that component.

CONCLUSION

The rapid changes in the industry and the assumed evolution to negotiated rates of payment motivated by managed care might appear to diminish the importance of the current methodologies for reimbursement. Whether capitated methods replace the current methodologies and their regulatory underpinnings may be moot because the PPS/DRGs are more than a reimbursement system.

This chapter and Chapter 20 describe not only reimbursement methods, but approaches by which the consumption of hospital resources (human, equipment, etc.) can be measured and accounted for. This is even more true of the Medicare resource-based relative value scales for physician reimbursement. In a more competitive, revenue-restrained environment, the need for measures of resource use seems apparent. It may take years for the industry to evolve, but there also is a strong likelihood that PPS/DRGs will remain well into the future—perhaps, in the end, as an important means of financial and resource management rather than reimbursement.

MICHAEL J. DALTON has been a Consulting Partner in Health Care and Life Sciences at KPMG Peat Marwick. He is also Practicing Director of Reimbursement and Financial Planning for the New York tri-state region. Mr. Dalton was also employed for 14 years as Vice President of the Provider Audit and Reimbursement Department at Empire Blue Cross Blue Shield. He received his bachelor's degree in Business Administration from St. John's University and is a member of AICPA, NYSSCPA, and HFMA.

Chapter 20

Outpatient Hospital Reimbursement

Michael J. Dalton

Historically, a hospital's main purpose was to provide treatment in an inpatient setting that was usually accompanied by care in an outpatient clinic. During the past decade, however, the trend has been toward health care delivery in the outpatient setting, which has included not only emergency departments and clinics, but private referred ambulatory services and ambulatory surgery. As a result, hospital outpatient services have increased steadily and currently account for approximately 30 percent of a hospital's total revenue.

Most health insurers provide coverage for services delivered in both the outpatient and inpatient settings. While most commercial insurance companies and the Blue Cross and Blue Shield plans reimburse hospitals for their care based on hospital charges, the Medicare program has developed its own methodology for reimbursement of outpatient hospital care. This chapter describes this payment methodology, as Medicare continues to be a growing source of revenue for hospitals.

The Omnibus Budget Reconciliation Acts of 1986 (OBRA 86) and 1987 contain a number of provisions that affect Medicare payments for outpatient services. The legislation required that, beginning July 1, 1987, hospitals report claims for outpatient services using the HCFA's Common Procedure Coding System and that, by 1991, the Secretary of Health and Human Services develop designs and models for a prospective payment system for other hospital outpatient services.

Specifically, the acts required "bundling" of outpatient services rendered on or after July 1, 1987, outlined a new payment system for certain outpatient ambulatory surgical procedures performed by hospitals, and placed a cap on cost-based reimbursement for hospital outpatient radiology procedures equal to the prevailing charges for similar services provided in physician offices.

The Budget Reconciliation Act for fiscal year 1991 made several changes that affect payment for outpatient services. These changes included a 15 percent reduction of capital payments applicable to outpatient services for payments attributable to portions of cost reporting periods occurring during federal fiscal year 1991; reduction of capital payments by 10 percent for payments attributable to portions of cost reporting periods occurring during federal fiscal year 1992,

1993, 1994, or 1995; and a 5.8 percent payment reduction for outpatient hospital services that were reimbursed on a cost-related basis, for portions of cost reporting periods occurring during fiscal years 1991, 1992, 1993, 1994, or 1995. This 5.8 percent payment reduction also applies to the cost portions of blended payment limits for ambulatory surgery and radiology services.

BUNDLING OF OUTPATIENT SERVICES

Effective with services furnished on or after July 1, 1987, all hospitals must agree to furnish, directly or under arrangement, all items and nonphysician services received by Medicare patients that can be covered as hospital outpatient services when these services are furnished during an encounter with a patient registered by the hospital as an outpatient, or diagnostic procedures or tests (e.g., magnetic resonance imaging [MRI] procedures) furnished outside the hospital but ordered during or as a result of an encounter with an outpatient, if the results of the procedure or test must be returned to the hospital for evaluation.

Bundling is required not only for diagnostic and therapeutic services furnished during such an encounter, but also for prosthetic devices (e.g., intraocular lenses implanted or fitted during an encounter in the hospital). Ambulance service to or from a patient's residence is not subject to the bundling requirement. However, bundling is required for transportation of patients by ambulance or other vehicle regularly used between the hospital and diagnostic testing site for a test that is bundled.

The application of the above requirements requires considerable interpretation. Guidelines issued by Medicare to date have been limited. The following guidelines may assist in evaluating the impact of bundling:

1. *Definition of an encounter:* An encounter is defined as a direct personal exchange in a hospital between a patient and a physician or other practitioner operating within hospital staff bylaws and state licensure law, for the purpose of seeking care and rendering health care services.

2. *Services provided under arrangement:* All services ordered during any patient/physician encounter that occurs in a hospital must be provided by the hospital either directly or under arrangement with another provider. The term "under arrangement" simply means that the hospital is purchasing the service from an outside provider, and that it assumes responsibility for those services. Under the bundling provisions, all services provided to hospital patients must be provided either directly or under arrangement. Thus, any service ordered during an encounter will be handled by Medicare as though it was provided under arrangement, whether or not the hospital in which the encounter occurred and the provider of the service actually have entered into a formal agreement. A hospital must have agreements with all providers of services ordered during an encounter occurring in the hospital; the fact that a hospital may not have an agreement with a particular provider does not change the responsibility of the hospital to purchase the services ordered on behalf of the patient.

3. *Definition of a bundle:* All services ordered during an encounter will be part of the bundle, whether provided by the hospital or a provider other than the

hospital. If, however, the patient is referred to a second physician, only those services ordered during the encounter between the patient and the first or referring physician must be bundled by the hospital. The encounter between the patient and the second physician forms a second bundle. Presumably, follow-up visits between a patient and a physician will each form a separate bundle together with the services ordered during each follow-up visit.

4. *When bundling is required:* Bundling affects only services provided to hospital patients. Physicians are not required to bundle their services in a hospital that are not otherwise bundled under Medicare physician billing guidelines. Nor is a hospital required to bundle individual services provided to patients referred to it by physicians or providers other than hospitals. Individual services provided to patients on referral from nonhospital providers form their own bundles. However, the general language does require the bundling of services ordered during an encounter between a member of a hospital's medical staff and a patient if that encounter occurs in a hospital outpatient clinic, emergency department, ambulatory surgical center, or other outpatient treatment area, and if the results of the tests for service are returned to the hospital.

5. *Definition of hospital patients:* The requirements are based on a specific, but somewhat peculiar, definition of a hospital patient. When an encounter between a patient and a physician occurs in a hospital setting, the patient becomes the hospital's patient in the sense that the hospital is financially and otherwise responsible for the ser-

vices ordered by the patient's physician.

6. *Billing requirements:* Hospitals are affected by the bundling requirements in two ways: as a purchaser of services from other hospitals or providers and as a provider or vendor of services to other hospitals.

7. *Purchaser role:* When a hospital provides services to a patient that were ordered during an encounter occurring outside of a hospital setting, the hospital will bill Medicare directly and collect required co-payments from Medicare beneficiaries. It is not necessary to bill the physician or provider making the referral.

8. *Vendor role:* When a hospital provides services to a patient of another hospital (i.e., provides services that were ordered during an encounter between a patient and a physician that occurred in another hospital), the hospital is expected to bill the hospital in which the original encounter between the patient and physician occurred. The hospital in which the original encounter between the patient and physician occurred will pay the hospital providing the ordered service, include the charges for the service on its bill to Medicare, and collect required co-payments from the Medicare beneficiary as though it had provided the service directly.

9. *Payment determination:* Payments to vending hospitals will be determined according to billing and payment arrangements negotiated between them and the hospitals to whom they vend services. Payments to "purchasing" hospitals will be determined under current Medicare payment rules. These rules include a combination of Medicare defined costs and fixed fees.

NON–COST-BASED OUTPATIENT REIMBURSEMENT

Several outpatient services—namely, outpatient surgery and ambulatory surgical procedures, outpatient laboratory services, and outpatient radiology procedures—are no longer subject to full cost reimbursement and are instead reimbursed under the following payment mechanisms.

Outpatient Surgery and Ambulatory Surgical Procedures

As part of the Omnibus Budget Reconciliation Act of 1980, the Medicare program instituted payment for ambulatory surgical procedures performed in approved ambulatory surgical centers (ASCs). Approximately six years later, OBRA 86 extended the ASC payment methodology to hospitals. Effective for cost reporting periods beginning on or after October 1, 1987, payment for covered outpatient ambulatory surgical procedures performed in a hospital is based, in part, on what the Medicare program pays for the same surgical procedures in an approved ASC.

The stated purpose of the new payment methodology for outpatient hospital ambulatory surgical procedures is to align Medicare payments for covered ASC surgical procedures performed in a hospital with payments to freestanding ASCs. HCFA believes that ASCs have lower fixed costs than hospitals, and is attempting to impose greater cost efficiencies on hospitals for outpatient ambulatory surgical procedures. To remain competitive, their charges must be similar to those of freestanding ASCs.

The Secretary of Health and Human Services determines which surgical procedures performed on an inpatient basis in a hospital also can be performed safely in an ASC or hospital outpatient department. The identification of covered and noncovered ASC surgical procedures is based on the following criteria:

- Procedures commonly performed on an inpatient basis but that may also, consistent with accepted medical practice, be safely performed in an ambulatory surgical facility should be included.
- Procedures included should be limited to those requiring a dedicated operating room and not requiring an overnight stay.
- Procedures commonly performed, or that may be safely performed, in physicians' offices should be excluded.
- Procedures not covered by Medicare should be excluded.

Generally, the two elements of the total charge for a surgical procedure are the physician's professional component and the facility services component. The ASC payment rates are for the facility services component only. Physicians continue to bill for their professional components separately and directly.

The ASC facility services component includes the following types of services: nursing, technician, and related services; use of ASC property and equipment; drugs, biologicals, and supplies directly related to the provision of surgical procedures; diagnostic or therapeutic services directly related to the provision of surgical procedures; administrative costs; materials for anesthesia; and blood.

The following items are excluded from the definitions of ASC facility services, and are separately billable under other Medicare provisions: laboratory, radiological, and diagnostic procedures other than those directly related to the performance of a surgical procedure; prosthetic devices, excluding intraocular lenses (IOLs); and durable medical equipment.

Payments to ASCs for facility services are based on prospectively set rates known as standard overhead amounts. All covered ASC surgical procedures are classified into one of eight standard overhead payment groups, each of which is associated with a prospective payment amount. ASC payment rates were originally set forth by Medicare in August 1982. These prospective payment rates, developed from 1979 and 1980 cost and charge information, were intended to reflect costs incurred by ASCs. HCFA classified procedures into groups using a charge-based index that is similar to the weighting process used for PPS. The published labor rates must be adjusted for area wage differences. The labor component of ASC prospective rates is established by HCFA as 34.45 percent of the published prospective rate. OBRA 86 mandated that, effective July 1, 1987, and annually thereafter, the Secretary must review and update ASC payment rates. Table 20–1 shows the calculation of an ASC payment rate.

Consistent with payments to freestanding ASCs, if more than one covered ambulatory surgical procedure is performed at a time, the ASC receives 100 percent payment for the procedure classified in the highest payment group, and 50 percent of the applicable group for each of the other procedures. Covered surgical procedures performed by a hospital on

Table 20–1 Sample Calculation: ASC Payment Rate

Assumption:
Facility Location: Tampa, Florida
Date of Service: July 10, 1990

	Payment Group 1	Payment Group 8
Step 1		
Labor portion of rate:		
Aggregate Payment Rate for Group	$271.00	$871.00
Less IOL Allowance	—	–200.00
Aggregate Payment Rate (Net of IOL)	271.00	671.00
Labor Component of Rate	x0.3445	0.3445
HCFA Wage Index (Tampa, FL)	x0.8996	0.8996
Adjusted Labor Component of Rate	= 83.99	207.95
Step 2		
Nonlabor portion of rate:		
Aggregate Payment Rate (Net of IOL)	$271.00	$671.00
Nonlabor Component of Rate	x0.6555	0.6555
Adjusted Nonlabor Component of Rate	=177.64	439.84
Step 3		
Labor-adjusted payment rate:		
Adjusted Labor Component of Rate	$ 83.99	$207.95
Nonlabor Component of Rate	+177.64	439.84
IOL Allowance	+ —	200.00
Labor-adjusted Payment Rate	$261.63	$847.79

Table 20–2 ASC Transition Schedule

Cost Reporting Period Beginning on or After	Hospital-Specific Amount	ASC Payment Amount
October 1, 1987	75%	25%
October 1, 1988	50%	50%
Portion of cost reporting for periods occurring on or after January 1, 1991	42%	58%

an outpatient basis that are not included in the current listing of ASC surgical procedures are reimbursed under other payment methodologies (i.e., reasonable cost, fee schedule, etc.).

The enactment of the OBRA 86 made significant changes in Medicare payment for ambulatory surgical procedures performed in hospital outpatient departments. The legislation mandated the development and implementation of a fully prospective payment system for outpatient hospital ambulatory surgical procedures effective for hospital fiscal years beginning on or after October 1, 1989. As of this date, a full transition to the ASC prospective payment methodology still has not been implemented by HCFA. The historical cost reimbursement method for these services was being phased out commencing with hospital cost reporting periods beginning on or after October 1, 1987. Payment for outpatient hospital facility services relating to ambulatory surgical procedures in the aggregate is now the lesser of:

1. The amount that would be paid for the services under the traditional lower of cost or charges reimbursement methodology, reduced by deductibles and coinsurance (the hospital-specific amount)
2. A blended amount based on the hospital-specific amount as defined above and on the amount that would be paid

to a freestanding ASC for the same procedure within the same geographic area, which is equal to 80 percent of the standard overhead amount net of deductibles (the ASC payment amount).

The blended amount is based on the transition schedule shown in Table 20–2.

For cost reporting periods beginning on or after October 1, 1987, but before October 1, 1988, the blended amount was determined by using 75 percent of the hospital-specific amount and 25 percent of the ASC payment amount attributable to the procedure. For cost reporting periods beginning on or after October 1, 1988, but before January 1, 1991, the blended amount is determined by using 50 percent of the hospital-specific amount and 50 percent of the ASC payment amount. For portions of cost reporting periods beginning on or after January 1, 1991, the blended amount is determined by using 42 percent of the hospital-specific amount and 58 percent of the ASC payment amount. The regulations have not specified when the transition to the full ASC payment amount will take effect.

OBRA 86 required a further disaggregation of costs and charges for cost reporting periods beginning on or after October 1, 1987. To implement the new payment methodology, all costs and charges related to ambulatory surgical procedures must be aggregated and treated separately from all other outpatient costs and charges. This allows for a separate lower of cost or charge calculation for covered ASC services. Reimbursement to providers (other than comprehensive outpatient rehabilitation facilities and hospices) for Medicare Part B services is subject to the lower of reasonable cost of services or customary charges for those services. Thus, if actual charges for Part B services are less than the related costs of those services, reimbursement is limited to actual Part B charges.

IOLs used in cataract surgery are subject to the outpatient bundling requirements and must be furnished directly by a hospital or under arrangements. Prior to March 12, 1990, an IOL furnished in connection with a covered ASC procedure was not considered to be a facility service and was instead reimbursed based on actual cost. Regulations issued in February 1990 eliminated the separate payment for IOLs and required that, as of March 12, 1990, payment for IOLs furnished in ASCs must be included in the facility fee in an amount that is reasonable and related to the cost of acquiring the class of lens involved. All ASC procedures that involve the use of IOLs are grouped into payment group numbers six or eight. These two groups include an "add-on" amount of $200, which is intended to cover the cost of the IOLs. This provision is effective for both freestanding ASCs and hospital-based outpatient department programs. The IOL payment rate was frozen at the $200 level through December 31, 1992.

Outpatient Laboratory Services

Substantially all clinical diagnostic laboratory tests are paid based upon area-wide fee schedules. Because Medicare payment is based on the lesser amount of the actual charge or Medicare's fee schedule, hospitals must ensure that actual charges for clinical laboratory services exceed fee schedule amounts in order to obtain full Medicare payment for clinical laboratory services. In addition, laboratory drawing services associated with clinical laboratory testing are billable separate from the clinical test itself.

Outpatient Radiology Procedures

As part of the Omnibus Budget Reconciliation Act of 1987 (OBRA 87), outpatient radiology services provided by hospitals on or after October 1, 1988, became subject to a blended payment limitation. This limit applies to aggregate payments for hospital outpatient radiology services, including diagnostic and therapeutic radiology, nuclear medicine, magnetic resonance imaging, ultrasound, and computed tomography (CT) procedures.

Under the provisions of OBRA 87, the amount of payments made for all or part of a cost reporting period beginning on or after October 1, 1988, will be the lesser of the hospital's reasonable cost or charges (the lesser amount of the two) or a blended amount. Formulas for calculating the blended amount are shown in Exhibit 20–1.

For other outpatient departments, such as the emergency department and clinics, reimbursement is based on the cost of providing these services, which was more fully described in the previous chapter. However, Medicare is currently studying different methods of reimbursement, such as those described above, in order to avoid the continuation of cost reimbursement to hospitals. As in the past, this will typically result in less payment to hospitals for services rendered to the Medicare population.

THE FUTURE

Prior to the move toward managed care, other outpatient reimbursement methods were being developed. Ambulatory practice-related groupings (APGs), not dissimilar in

Exhibit 20–1 Formulas for Calculating Blended Payment Amount

**Services Provided
from October 1, 1988, through September 30, 1989**

Blended Payment Amount =
(.65 x lesser of cost or charges for outpatient radiology procedures) +
(.35 x .62 x .80 Medicare prevailing charges)

**Services Provided
from October 1, 1989, through December 31, 1990**

Blended Payment Amount =
(.50 x lesser of cost or charges for outpatient radiology procedures) +
(.50 x .62 x .80 Medicare prevailing charges)

**Services Provided
on or after January 1, 1991**

Blended Payment Amount =
(.42 x lesser of cost or charges for outpatient radiology procedures) +
(.58 x .62 x .80 Medicare prevailing charges)

---

intent from DRGs, were being considered as an outpatient reimbursement method. APGs, or similar methods, may have a place as common units of measure. The health care industry generally has lacked common units of measure. As such, even if they lose their use as reimbursement methods, DRGs, APGs, and resource-based relative value scales may retain their usefulness as a means to measure services.

The Balanced Budget Act of 1997, which was signed into law in August 1997, mandates certain changes in the way Medicare pays for hospital-based outpatient services. Among the changes will be the implementation of a prospective payment system for most outpatient services. This change will become effective in January 1999. Medicare has indicated that this outpatient prospective payment system probably will incorporate the above-mentioned APGs, which will represent a single price (excluding physician services) for hospital outpatient service delivery.

MICHAEL J. DALTON has been a Consulting Partner in Health Care and Life Sciences at KPMG Peat Marwick. He is also Practicing Director of Reimbursement and Financial Planning for the New York tri-state region. Mr. Dalton was also employed for 14 years as Vice President of the Provider Audit and Reimbursement Department at Empire Blue Cross Blue Shield. He received his Bachelor's degree in Business Administration from St. John's University and is a member of AICPA, NYSSCPA, and HFMA.

Chapter 21

Managed Health Care

Peter R. Kongstvedt

INTRODUCTION

What is managed health care? Any simple answer would miss the very real forces at work in the health care industry today that have led to the evolution of managed health care and would likewise miss the substantial positive contributions managed health care has made to the American health care system as we struggle to balance the three key elements of access, cost, and quality.

There are many who believe that unrestrained fee-for-service medicine has led to inappropriately high utilization and is, therefore, the root cause of our health care cost crisis. While there is merit in the argument, it is simplistic. Health care costs have escalated in the past decades at an alarming rate because of many causes, not just one single reimbursement model. Even with the current increased presence of managed care, costs continue to increase and managed care organizations are beginning to experience premium increases. These other causes include rapidly developing (and usually expensive) technology, cost shifting by providers to pay for care rendered to patients who either cannot pay or who are covered by systems that do not pay the full cost of care, shifting demographics as our population ages, appropriately high expectations for a long and healthy

life, the current legal environment leading to defensive medicine, administrative costs related to the care that is delivered, wide variations in efficiencies and quality of care rendered by all types of providers (professional and institutional), serious inequities and variations in incomes between all types of providers (regardless of efficiency or quality), and a myriad of other reasons. There are no easy answers to these problems, but neither are the problems insurmountable. While health care costs recently have slowed, there is no guarantee that they will remain under control since these forces continue today. Many of these forces, which are new to managed care companies, have been experienced by indemnity insurers for decades. The historical growth of managed care is undeniable and is a one-way phenomenon, as illustrated in Figure 21–1.

A few years earlier, there were several attempts at massive health care reform at the federal level. While those attempts failed, the final result was a federal reform of certain aspects such as portability of coverage and limitations on certain underwriting practices. Of far greater significance is the amount of health care reform taking place at the state level. Various forms of laws constraining certain aspects of managed care (e.g., mandatory length of stay for obstetrics or the require-

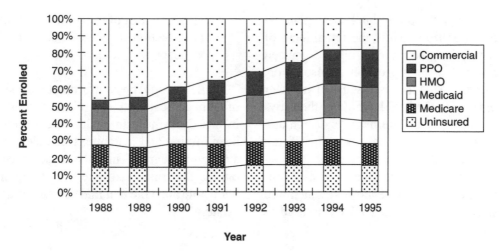

Figure 21–1 Changes in U.S. Health Plan Type. *Source:* Data from AAHP, Interstudy, Department of Commerce, and Hoechst Marion Roussel, 1996.

ment for health plans to cover mandated benefits). These changes continue and will do so for as long as we can see.

A few definitions will assist in the reading of this chapter. The term "member" applies to an individual who is insured. The term member may be used interchangeably with the term "patient" (although clearly, one may be a member and receive no medical services and thus not be the patient of any provider, a concept important to actuaries when they calculate risk). A subscriber is the individual who actually has the insurance contract, while that subscriber's dependents receive insurance by virtue of that same contract; both the subscribers and their dependents are considered members. The term "provider" applies to any person or institution that provides medical care. Provider most often refers to a professional (e.g., a physician), but may be used more broadly. Lastly, the term "plan" refers to the managed care organization that provides the insurance coverage and manages the delivery system.

DEFINITION OF MANAGED HEALTH CARE

Managed health care, or managed care, is an approach to managing both the quality and the cost of medical care. Having said that, in the current environment there really is no single definition of managed health care; it is a term applied to a variety of methodologies. In general, there are at least two elements common to managed health care systems: an authorization system and some level of restriction imposed on a member's choice of providers. The authorization system may be minimal, such a simple hospital precertification requirement; or it may be comprehensive, such as a primary care physician (PCP) gatekeeper model. The restriction on choice of provider may be minimal, such as a minor increase in co-insurance to see an out-of-network provider in a preferred provider organization (PPO); or it may be strict, such as in a highly restrictive health maintenance organization (HMO). This chapter focuses on managed care as defined through benefit plan design and operations. Thus, the actual locus of the activity may be resident in an organized delivery system, in a provider sponsored organization (PSO; this is discussed in other chapters), or in the health plan; but the activity still takes place. The benefits design and operations remain the basis for classifying managed care plans.

Managed care may be thought of as a continuum of models. These models, which will be discussed later, are generally classified as follows:

- indemnity with precertification, mandatory second opinion, and large case management
- service plan with precertification, mandatory second opinion, and large case management
- PPO
- point-of-service (POS)
- "open access" HMO
- traditional HMO
  1. open panel
     –individual practice association (IPA)
     –direct contract
  2. network model
  3. closed panel HMO
     –group model
     –staff model

As models move down the continuum, certain changes occur. These changes include:

- Elements of control over health care delivery become tighter.
- New elements of control are added.
- More direct interaction with providers occurs.
- Overhead cost and complexity increase in the health plan.

- Greater control of utilization is made.
- Net reduction in rate of rise of medical costs occurs.

While it would be comforting to classify all of managed care into one of these categories, in fact the American health care system has been mixing and matching these elements to a dizzying degree. Thus, the reader must recognize that managed care is nothing if not malleable and take that into account as appropriate.

TYPES OF HEALTH PLANS

Government Programs

In the United States, much of health care is actually provided or financed by the federal and state governments. These programs include Medicare for the elderly and disabled, Medicaid for the poor, military programs (both direct care by military providers as well as the Civilian Health and Medical Program of the Uniformed Services [CHAMPUS]), the Federal Employee Health Benefits Program (FEHBP), the Veterans Administration, the U.S. Public Health Service, and some other programs. These programs may incorporate few to all managed care features, but are not the topic of this chapter.

The exception to this is the PSO. This type of organization, enabled under federal legislation, is able to contract directly with the Health Care Financing Administration (HCFA) to receive prepaid revenue for medical services to a defined population of Medicare eligible members who voluntarily enroll in the PSO. In a PSO, the providers must own at least 51 percent of the contracting entity; a substantial percentage of care is delivered by the PSO providers, and the PSO must meet many other standards including access and quality.

Self-Funded Plans

Many large corporations actually do not insure their employees at all in the sense that they do not purchase insurance from an insurance company. Insurance is a financial vehicle that protects the purchaser of the insurance from unexpected costs for which the insurer provides coverage at a premium rate calculated to cover those costs on average. Insurance, however, comes with a lot of other baggage. First, insurance is taxed by each state via a premium tax. Second, most states have passed mandated benefits laws that require insurance policies to provide coverage for defined diseases, providers, procedures, and so forth. Last, the cost of insurance is affected by the costs of everyone in the coverage pool. In other words, if one group has high medical costs, the costs for all of the others goes up as well (the degree of that effect is determined by the type of policy, whether it is community rated, experience rated, and so forth. A discussion of rating and underwriting is beyond the scope of this chapter).

Large employers are able to escape these burdens through self-funding as allowed by the Employee Retirement Income Security Act (ERISA). ERISA allows large employers to assume the risk of medical costs themselves, and thus not be subject to premium tax or mandated benefits, and their cost is determined solely by the costs of their own group. It is most common for the large employer to contract with a third-party administrator (TPA) to perform the management activities. Often the TPA is actually a large insurance company or Blue Cross Blue Shield plan, thus confusing in the minds of both members and providers who the insurer actually is. These large carriers not only provide administrative functions, but also provide substantial discounts to the employers when the carrier has such discounts with providers. Self-funded plans may mimic any type of insurance coverage as described below.

Traditional Insurance

Traditional insurance is basically made up of two types: indemnity insurance and service plans.

Indemnity Insurance

Indemnity insurance indemnifies the insured against financial losses from medical expenses. The only restriction is in the schedule of benefits. There are generally no restrictions on licensed providers. The insurance company reimburses the subscriber directly, or may pay the provider directly but has no actual obligation other than to pay the subscriber. Professional reimbursement (i.e., payment to physicians and other professional providers) is subject to usual, customary, or reasonable (UCR) fee screens or discounts on generally accepted fee schedules such as the Medicare schedule of allowances, while institutional reimbursement generally is based on charges.

Benefits generally are subject to deductibles (a flat dollar amount paid by the subscriber before any benefit is paid by the insurance company) and co-insurance (a percentage of the covered charge that is paid by the subscriber, for example, 20 percent). Any charges by the provider that are not paid by the insurance company are strictly the responsibility of the subscriber.

Most indemnity plans require precertification of elective hospital admissions and may apply a financial penalty to the subscriber for failure to precertify. The plan may also perform some additional utilization management on hospital cases, but generally this is done over the telephone by plan-employed nurses located elsewhere. Large case management may also be used to help control the cost of catastrophic cases. Mandatory second opinion programs may also be present for certain elective procedures (e.g., cardiac bypass surgery).

Historically, costs for this type of health care coverage have been escalating faster than for any other type of health plan.

Service Plan

This term applies primarily, though not exclusively, to Blue Cross and Blue Shield plans. In service plans, there are generally few restrictions on licensed providers who agree to sign a contract with the plan. That provider contract contains certain key elements: the plan agrees to reimburse the provider directly (eliminating collection problems with patients); the provider agrees to accept the plan's fee schedule as payment in full and not bill the subscriber for any payment not made by the plan (other than the normal deductible or co-insurance), and the provider agrees to allow the plan to audit the provider's records. Precertification, large case management, and mandatory second opinion may be present and operate as they do for indemnity insurance.

The principal advantage of a service plan over indemnity insurance is the presence of the provider contracts and the reimbursement models that the contracts support. Professional fees are paid under a schedule of allowances that may in effect provide a discount to the plan. More importantly, the plan usually has significant discounts at hospitals that give it a competitive advantage. The hospitals grant these discounts for a variety of reasons, including a large volume of business, rapid payment, ease of collection, and occasionally, advance deposits. The actual reimbursement to the hospital may be based on charges, per diems, diagnosis-related groups (DRGs), "cost plus," or some variation; these reimbursement methods are discussed later in this chapter.

Preferred Provider Organization

PPOs are similar to service plans with some important differences. The total panel of providers is reduced to some degree, often substantially (e.g., only 20 percent of the total available providers). While the PPO may limit the number of providers in the network, there are two broad approaches: "any willing provider" versus criteria-based selection. In the former, any provider who wishes to participate and who agrees to the terms and conditions of the PPO's contract must be offered a contract, at least until the PPO feels it has adequate numbers of providers. In the latter category, the PPO uses some objective criteria (e.g., credentials, practice pattern analysis, and so forth) that a provider must meet before a contract will be offered.

While reimbursement mechanisms to providers may fall along the lines mentioned under service plans, in general, the discounts are greater. It should be noted that many service plans require providers to give them "favored nation" pricing; in other words, a provider may not provide a better discount to a competitor than it does to the service plan. Favored nation pricing has been challenged in the courts; as a rule, PPOs do not place the providers at risk for medical costs. The concept of risk-sharing with providers is discussed later in this chapter.

Precertification, large case management, and possibly mandatory second opinion are almost always present. The main difference is that failure to comply with these programs results in a financial penalty to the provider, not the subscriber. As under service plans, a contracting provider may not "balance bill" the subscriber for any payment not made by the PPO, except for normal deductibles and co-insurance. Balance billing is the practice of a provider billing a patient for all charges not paid by the insurance plan. In the event a subscriber chooses to seek care from a non-participating provider, the responsibility then falls on the subscriber, and the subscriber is at risk for any financial penalties or charges not paid by the PPO.

A hallmark of PPOs is a benefits differential if a member sees a provider who is not in the PPO network. A common benefits differential is 20 percent. For example, if a member sees a network provider, coverage is provided at 90 percent of allowed charges; if a member sees a provider not in the network, the coverage may be at the 70 percent level.

A distinction between two types of PPOs is worthwhile: that of risk bearing versus non-risk bearing. A risk-bearing PPO combines both the insurance, or payment function, with the management of the network of providers. A non–risk-bearing PPO refers solely to the network and not to the insurance function. For example, a commercial insurer may build a network and sell coverage to clients; this would be an example of a risk-bearing PPO. Alternatively, a group of providers may come together as a legal entity, establish fee allowances, credentialing criteria, utilization review, and so forth, and contract with independent insurers to provide medical services to those insurers' customers; this would be an example of a non–risk-bearing PPO.

Health Maintenance Organization

HMOs are fundamentally different from the health plans described above. Although there are a few exceptions, known as "open access" HMOs, which are similar in benefits design to PPOs, the vast majority of HMOs operate in such a manner as to further manage utilization and quality. It should be noted that HMOs often form the in-network portion of a point-of-service plan, which is described later. Benefits to members in an HMO are restricted (with some exceptions) to those provided by HMO providers and in compliance with the HMO authorization procedures. Benefits obtained through the HMO tend to be significantly richer than those found in traditional insurance or in PPOs. Except for true emergencies or unless specifically authorized, services received from non–HMO providers are the responsibility of the subscriber, not the HMO. Services rendered by contracting providers who fail to obtain proper authorization are the responsibility of the provider, who may not balance bill the member.

Traditional HMOs currently fall into two broad categories: open panel and closed panel. A third category, the true network model, is not common except in certain parts of the country, but is likely to become more common in the future. Some HMOs mix model types in the same market. Open access HMOs will be described briefly, and then traditional HMOs will be described in further detail.

Open Access HMOs

Open access HMOs are more like PPOs than traditional HMOs. In the open access HMO model, members may access any provider in the HMO without going through a PCP. The PCP model is a hallmark of the traditional HMO and is described below. In the open access model, members may see any PCP or specialist in the network on a self-referral basis. While this looks much like the PPO as described earlier, in the open access HMO, the physicians share at least some level of risk for costs. Therefore, if professional costs exceed budget, the physicians accept lower fees, lose their withholds (physician contingency reserves), or incur some other penalty. It is theoretically possible to capitate specialists in this model, but it is extremely hard in practice because there is no reliable base to use for the capitation (in other words, members are not required to select specific PCPs or specialists, so the actuaries cannot decide who should receive the capitation payment).

Open access plans were popular in the late 1970s and early 1980s, especially with plans that were sponsored by organized medical societies. Unfortunately, with a few exceptions, these plans failed and suffered substantial losses due to high medical costs. There has been a recent revival of interest in open access plans because of strong consumer demand and because many HMOs have been successful in reducing costs for specialist care. HMOs that are currently adopting these plan designs also are doing so based on the assumption that since so few referral authorizations are denied, it is not worth the cost and may even raise the cost to add an unnecessary PCP visit. This line of reasoning ignores the value in asking a PCP to make a judgment about the need for a referral rather than relying on a patient to make that judgment; in other words, it is assumed that all (or most) patient-generated requests for referral will either be appropriate or will not be diverted by visiting a PCP. The PCP model assumes that the PCP has the requisite training and knowledge in the subspecialties to know when or how quickly a patient needs to see a specialist. While open access HMOs failed miserably in past years, it remains an unknown whether they will fare better now that physicians and hospitals are functioning more efficiently than in the past.

Open Panel Plans

Open panel HMOs contract with private physicians and other professional providers to see members in the providers' own offices. The provider is an independent contractor and may contract with more than one competing health plan (and usually does), as well as having fee-for-service patients. The provider may be reimbursed through a variety of mechanisms (discussed later). The total number of providers in an open panel plan is larger than in a closed panel plan, but usually fewer than in a PPO. Members must choose a single provider to be their PCP, sometimes referred to as a gatekeeper, who must authorize any other services (discussed later). A member may change PCPs at designated times if necessary.

Open panel plans fall into two broad categories: independent practice associations (IPAs) and direct contract models. While the terms often are used synonymously, they are technically distinct. In an IPA, the HMO contracts with a legal entity known as an IPA and pays the IPA a negotiated capitation amount (discussed later). The IPA in turn contracts with private physicians. The IPA may reimburse the physicians through capitation or may use another mechanism such as fee for service. The providers can be at risk under this model in that, if medical costs exceed the capitation amount, the IPA receives no additional funds from the HMO and must accordingly adjust the reimbursement to the providers.

In direct contract models, the HMO contracts directly with the providers; there is no intervening entity of an IPA. The HMO reimburses the providers directly and performs all related management tasks. Direct contract models are currently the most common form of HMO.

Closed Panel Plans

Closed panel plans differ from open panel plans in that the closed panel plan uses physicians whose practices are confined to the

HMO. These physicians practice from facilities that are likewise dedicated to the HMO. The total number of providers in the plan is by far the smallest of any model type. Members usually do not have to choose a single PCP, but may see any PCP in the HMO (although they may be asked to choose a primary facility in order to provide continuity). Closed panel plans fall into two broad categories: group model and staff model.

In group model plans, the HMO contracts with a medical group to provide services to members. The HMO pays the group a negotiated capitation, and the group in turn reimburses the physicians through a combination of salary and risk/reward incentives. The group is responsible for its own governance, and physicians are either partners in the group or associates. The group or the HMO may provide the dedicated practice facilities and support staff, but most commonly this is the HMO's responsibility. The group is at risk in that if the costs of the group exceed the capitation amount, the reimbursement to the providers is lowered, although the HMO generally provides stop-loss insurance coverage to the group to protect the group from catastrophic cost overruns. Some groups exist primarily on paper and actually operate strictly as cost pass-through vehicles for the HMO, thus resembling staff model plans.

In staff model plans, the HMO contracts with the providers directly, and the providers are employees of the HMO. Physicians are reimbursed by salary, with an incentive plan of some sort. The HMO has full responsibility for management of all activities.

Network Model

The last major category of HMO usually is referred to as a network model. The term network model is occasionally used to refer to an open panel plan, but this section will discuss only the "true" network model. In this model, the HMO contracts with several large multispecialty medical groups for medical services. The groups are paid under capitation, and they, in turn, reimburse the physicians under a plethora of mechanisms. The groups operate relatively independently. The HMO contracts with more than one group, but the number is usually limited.

Mixed Model

Many HMOs have adopted several model types, even in the same market, in order to capture additional market share. The most common form of mixed model involves grafting a direct contract model to either a closed panel or a network model. The HMO also may need to expand its medical service area and may choose to contract with private physicians rather than make the expenditures required to maintain a facility. In mixed model plans, the models often operate independently of each other.

Point of Service

POS plans combine features of HMOs and traditional insurance. An older but still technically valid use of the term refers to a simple PPO arrangement. In a POS plan, the member may choose which system to use at the point the service is obtained. For example, if the member uses the PCP and otherwise complies with the HMO authorization system, the benefits for services may be quite rich and require the member to pay only a minor co-payment; if the member chooses to self-refer or otherwise not use the HMO system to receive services, the plan still provides insurance coverage, but at a much lower level, such as requiring a deductible and co-insurance. The difference between in-network and out-of-network coverage for services generally ranges from 20 percent to 40 percent.

POS plans have been developed to meet the conflicting issues of cost control and total freedom of choice of providers. By bringing the issue of cost differential directly to the members at the point they seek medical services, the members become more active participants in the process.

PROVIDER REIMBURSEMENT

The topic of reimbursement is as varied and intricate as anything one can imagine. In fact, a common problem in managed care is that managers create new methods of reimbursement that are designed to yield a positive result, only to find that the health plan has no systems capability to support it. Even worse, the cost of programming to support the new reimbursement methodology may far outweigh any advantage it had in the first place.

Before describing the more common forms of reimbursement, it is worthwhile to spend a few minutes discussing how a health plan might calculate the level of fees, capitation, or case rates. Capitation is a set amount of money paid regardless of the services delivered. A case rate is a reimbursement model used by hospitals and/or physicians to establish a flat rate per admission. The hospital sets rates based on an assumed average length of stay per admission, and the HMO is charged this rate for each member admitted. There are several approaches to reimbursement, and a health plan may use one or more of these methods. In the first instance, the plan looks primarily to the market to see what level of premiums the market will bear, and that sets the total amount of money available per member (the same is done for Medicare Risk or Medicaid Risk, except that in this case, there is no elasticity—rates are what they are, with no real negotiation). Starting with this base, the plan then calculates or esti-

mates what percentage of those dollars will go into the broad categories of care (e.g., hospital, primary care, specialty care, pharmacy, ancillary services, and so forth). The plan then either calculates the capitation rate based on that or uses prior and expected utilization patterns to determine what level of fee or case rate is sustainable.

Another method is to build up the fees using a prior fee schedule and extrapolate from that, depending on how the plan wants to handle different types of services. For example, it may choose to increase fees to primary care physicians, but lower them for certain specialty procedures. Lastly, the plan may be in a position to increase fees only if utilization is lowered and periodic across-the-board fee adjustments are made depending on overall medical costs.

Hospital Reimbursement

As illustrated in Exhibit 21–1, there are a variety of methods for reimbursing hospitals in managed care. Figure 21–2 provides the

---

Exhibit 21–1 Models for Reimbursing Hospitals

- charges
- discounts
- per diems
- sliding scales for discounts and per diems
- differential by day in hospital
- DRGs
- differential by service type
- case rates or package pricing
  –institutional only
  –bundled
- bed leasing
- capitation or percent of revenue
- penalties and withholds
- outpatient care

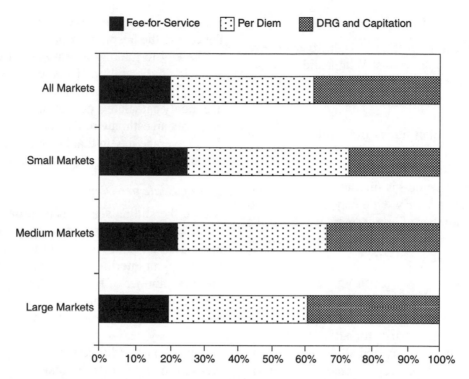

Figure 21–2 Hospital Reimbursement in Managed Care. *Source:* Data from Interstudy, 1995.

relative distribution of the most popular methods of reimbursement. A very brief description of these methodologies follows.

Straight Charges

As with any other payment mechanism in health care, the easiest method is straight charges. It is also the most expensive and the least desirable for the insurer after the option of no contract at all. In the past, some plans would agree to this simply to have a hospital in the network.

Straight Discount on Charges

A common arrangement is a straight percentage discount on charges. In this case, the hospital submits its claim in full, and the plan pays an amount discounted by the agreed-to percentage. The hospital accepts this payment as payment in full and does not balance bill the member for the difference, except for allowed deductibles and co-insurance as appropriate.

The presence of co-insurance in the setting of a discount has led to a serious dispute in a number of plans. The issue is to what does the co-insurance apply: the full charges or the discounted amount? Unless the benefits contract clearly states that co-insurance is to be applied to full charges, regardless of what the plan ultimately pays, an argument can be made that the co-insurance should only apply to the discounted payment, since co-insurance is a percentage of the total payment.

Sliding Scale Discount on Charges

More common than straight discount are sliding scale discounts. With a sliding scale, the percentage discount is reflective of total volume of admissions and outpatient procedures.

How the plan tracks the level of discount needs to be established. Some may wish to vary the discount on a month-to-month basis, but more common is quarterly or semiannually, or even yearly. One may track total bed days or number of admissions. Whatever the final agreement, it must be a clearly defined and measurable objective.

Straight per Diem Charges

Unlike straight charges, a negotiated per diem is a single charge for a day in the hospital, regardless of any actual charges or costs incurred. In this very common type of arrangement, the plan negotiates a per diem rate with the hospital and pays that rate without adjustments.

Hospital administrators are sometimes reluctant to add days in the intensive care unit or obstetrics to the arrangement unless there is sufficient volume of regular medical–surgical cases to make the ultimate cost predictable. In a small plan or in one that is not limiting the number of participating hospitals, the hospital administrators are concerned that their hospital will be used for expensive cases at a low per diem, while their competitors will be used for less costly cases. In such cases, one approach is to negotiate multiple sets of per diem charges based on service type (e.g., medical–surgical, obstetrics, intensive care unit, neonatal intensive care, rehabilitation, etc.) or a combination of per diem and flat case rate for obstetrics. A related topic is the occasional high cost medical device that becomes widely available after the per diem has been established; in such cases, it is possible to negotiate an outlier payment that equates to the cost to the hospital for that new device.

The key to making a negotiated per diem work is predictability. If you can accurately predict the number and mix of cases, you can accurately calculate a per diem. The per diem is simply an estimate of the charges (or costs) for an average day in that hospital, minus the amount of discount to which the parties agree.

Sliding Scale per Diem

Like the sliding scale discount on charges discussed above, the sliding scale per diem is also based on total volume. In this case, one negotiates an interim per diem; depending on the total number of bed days in the year, the plan either pays a lump sum settlement at the end of the year or withholds an amount from the final payment to the hospital for the year to adjust for an additional reduction in the per diem from an increase in total bed days. Adjustments are made on a quarterly or semiannual basis so as to reduce any disparities caused by unexpected changes in utilization patterns.

Differential by Day in Hospital

This simply refers to the fact that most hospitalizations are more expensive on the first day. For example, the first day for surgical cases includes operating suite costs, the operating surgical team costs (nurses, recovery, etc.), and so forth. This type of reimbursement method is generally combined with a per diem approach, but the first day is paid at a higher rate. This is not common, primarily because it is complicated, difficult to support on most claims systems, and should not be necessary if standard per diems have been calculated properly.

Diagnosis-Related Groups

Similar to Medicare, plans may use DRGs to pay for inpatient care. There are publications of DRG categories, criteria, outliers, and trim points (i.e., the cost or length of stay that causes the DRG payment to be supplemented or supplanted by another payment mechanism) to enable parties to negotiate a payment mechanism for DRGs based on either Medicare rates or, in some cases, state-regulated rates. DRGs are perhaps better suited to plans with loose controls rather than plans that tightly manage utilization, since DRGs put the risk and reward solely on the hospital, rather than the health plan.

Service-Related Case Rates

Similar to DRGs, service-related case rates are more crude. In this reimbursement mechanism, various service types are defined (e.g., medical, surgical, intensive care, neonatal intensive care, psychiatry, obstetrics, etc.), and the hospital receives a flat per-admission reimbursement for whatever type of service the patient receives. If services are mixed, a prorated payment may be made (e.g., 50 percent of surgical and 50 percent of intensive care).

Case Rates or Package Pricing

Whatever mechanism is used for hospital reimbursement, a plan frequently finds it necessary to address certain categories of procedures and negotiate special rates. The most common of these is obstetrics. It is common to negotiate a flat rate for a normal vaginal delivery and one for a cesarean section, or a blended rate for both.

Another area in which plans commonly wish to negotiate flat rates is specialty procedures at tertiary care hospitals, for example, negotiating a flat rate for coronary artery bypass surgery or for heart transplants. These procedures, while relatively infrequent, are costly.

A broader but increasingly common and important variation is package pricing, which refers to an all-inclusive rate paid for both institutional and professional services. The plan negotiates a flat rate for a procedure (e.g., bypass surgery), and that rate is used to pay all parties who provide services connected with that procedure. Bundled case rates require a certain measure of cooperation and trust between a hospital and its medical staff.

Bed Leasing

A very uncommon reimbursement mechanism is bed leasing. This refers to a plan actually leasing beds from an institution, regardless of whether those beds are used or not. This ensures revenue flow to the hospital, ensures access to beds for the plan, and is budgetable. It is perhaps best used in those situations where a plan is ensured of a steady number of bed days, with little or no seasonality. The problem with bed leasing is that there is no real savings from reducing utilization unless contract terms allow the plan to lease the beds back to the hospital if they are not being used.

Capitation or Percentage of Revenue

Capitation refers to reimbursing the hospital on a fixed per member per month (PMPM) basis to cover all institutional costs for a defined population of members. The payment may be varied by age and sex, but does not fluctuate with premium revenue. Percentage of revenue refers to a fixed percentage of premium revenue (i.e., a percentage of the collected premium rate) being paid to the hospital, again to cover all institutional services. The difference between percentage of revenue and capitation is that percentage of revenue may vary with the premium rate charged and the actual revenue yield. In both cases, the hospital absorbs the entire risk for institutional services for the defined membership base; if the hospital cannot provide the services itself, the cost for such care is deducted from the capitation payment.

In order for this type of arrangement to work, a hospital must know that it will serve a clearly defined segment of a plan's enrollment and that it can provide most or all of the necessary services to those members. In these cases, the primary care physician is clearly associated with just one hospital or group of hospitals.

Hospitals and physicians, through physician hospital organizations (PHOs) or other forms of organized delivery systems, may come together to accept a full capitation contract with a managed care plan. While that may be attractive to a plan (assuming the PHO did not actually form simply to be a union and thus drive costs up), the PHO must be careful to understand how the proceeds of the capitation will be distributed among the hospital, physician, and other providers. It is common for each of the two parties in a PHO to feel that the other party deserves less of the capitation than it is receiving and for disputes to arise.

POS plans with an out-of-network benefit make capitation methods difficult to use, since capitation in POS may mean having to pay twice for a service: once under capitation and again if the member seeks service outside of the network. In areas where there are no real alternatives to a certain hospital (e.g., a rural area or an area where a hospital enjoys a monopoly) this problem may not be material, but that is the exception. Capitation tied to the percentage of admissions to that hospital may also attenuate this problem.

The other issue in this arrangement is that some state insurance departments may consider full-risk capitation excessive. It may be reasoned that, if the health plan is not actually assuming the risk for services, then it is not really a health plan at all, but only a marketing organization. In such a case, there may be a question as to who should hold the Certificate of Authority or license to operate the health plan.

Penalties and Withholds

As with physician services, penalties or withholds occasionally are used in hospital reimbursement methods. Goals are set for average length of stay and average admission rate; part of the payment to the hospital may be withheld, or conversely, the plan may set aside a bonus pool. In any event, if the goals are met or exceeded, the hospital receives its withhold or bonus, and vice versa. One complication with this is the possibility that a hospital can make its statistics look good by simply sending patients to other hospitals, similar to problems encountered with physician capitation. If a service area is clearly defined or the hospital is capitated, then it may be easier to apply a risk or reward program.

Outpatient Procedures

The shift from inpatient to outpatient care has not gone unnoticed by hospital administrators. As care has shifted, so have charges. In some cases, outpatient charges exceed inpatient charges. Most managed care plans will require this to be negotiated so as not to lead to an unexpected increase in costs as utilization shifts to outpatient care. The most common reimbursement methods are discounts, flat charges, case rates, and capitation. Ambulatory groupings are a newer form of outpatient reimbursement.

Professional Reimbursement

While there are fewer basic ways of reimbursing physicians and other professionals when compared to hospital reimbursement, there are numerous hybrids. The ability of a health plan to support new and unusual reim-

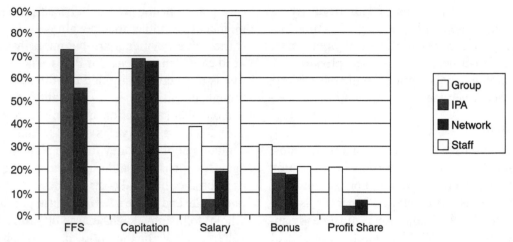

Figure 21–3 Compensation of Primary Care Physicians in Managed Care

bursement methods is even more acute when dealing with professionals since there are so many more of them. These professionals have a broad range of specialty training and experience, and their costs to provide services vary. The three basic methods of paying physicians are salary, capitation, and fee for service. Withholds, penalties, and incentive compensation may be applied to any method. Figures 21–3 and 21–4 illustrate the predominance of the most popular of these forms of reimbursement at this time.

Salary

Salary is the predominant method of reimbursement in closed panel plans, as well as in

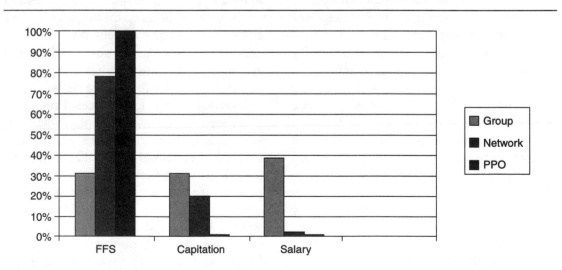

Figure 21–4 Compensation of Specialty Physicians in Managed Care. *Source:* Reprinted from Physician Payment Review Commission, 1994.

some group practices or situations where physicians are employees (e.g., full-time faculty, government-employed physicians, or some full-time hospital-based physicians). Withholds may be applied to the base salary, and incentive plans are common.

Capitation

Although fee for service remains the most common form of reimbursement, capitation continues to be a popular option for managed care. The use of capitation generally is confined to HMOs. Capitation is most easily applied to PCPs in HMOs (well over half of open panel HMOs capitate PCPs), but may be used for high volume specialties as well.

Capitation payments are fixed payments made on a per member per month (PMPM) basis, regardless of the use of services. Payments are most often adjusted based on the age and sex of the member group and on the actuarial incidence of disease, since there is some correlation between those factors and utilization. Rarely, capitation may be adjusted based on other factors such as geographic location.

The key to capitation is the denominator: the number (and demographics) of the members for whom the provider is receiving capitation. That is why PCPs may be easily capitated in a model where the member must select a single PCP to provide and coordinate care. For specialists, there must be some mechanism to ensure that all of the members for whom capitation is being paid will not seek or receive services from a noncapitated provider (except under special circumstances).

Capitation paid directly to providers may be subject to a withhold. A withhold is a portion of the payment (e.g., 20 percent) held back by the plan to pay for any excessive utilization. Withholds are somewhat less common than they once were, as many managed care plans opt for programs based primarily on incentives rather than penalties.

Incentive payments are common in managed care plans, at least for PCPs. The incentive is most commonly tied to utilization, although incentives based on quality, access, and member satisfaction are being seen more often. The incentive is usually tied to a capitated pool of money that the plan applies against expenses in a defined category, such as referral or hospital costs. Money left in the pool at the end of the year is paid (in part or in whole) to the physicians, based on utilization patterns, either of the entire panel of physicians or each individual physician. The variations on this approach are legion and beyond the scope of this chapter.

Fee for Service

Fee for service remains a significant form of reimbursement in HMOs and nearly the only form of reimbursement in PPOs, service plans, and indemnity plans. While somewhat less conducive to managed care than is capitation, fee for service is not grossly antithetical to managed care. Even in HMOs that capitate PCPs, referral specialists are usually fee for service. In those managed care plans in which POS is heavily represented, capitation presents problems as noted earlier, thus leading many of those HMOs to reimburse even PCPs on a fee-for-service basis.

Nevertheless, fee for service, if not managed properly or if used in a plan where the provider's first priority is to make money, can lead to increased costs when compared to capitation. Therefore, it is common for HMOs that use fee for service to place fees at some form of risk. A withhold on a percentage of the fee is the most common mechanism. If utilization exceeds budget, the withhold is used to cover the overage; if utilization is below budget, the withhold is paid out.

Another form of risk is reductions in fees if utilization gets too high. Some plans have experimented with global fees (to avoid upcoding and unbundling) with some success. Other plans have tried adjusting each physician's fees on an individual basis according to that physician's utilization pattern.

UTILIZATION MANAGEMENT

Total health care costs may be thought of simplistically as the result of only two variables: price times volume. The preceding section briefly described issues germane to price; this section briefly will discuss volume, i.e., utilization. The management of utilization may be divided broadly into three categories: prospective, or before the event occurs; concurrent, or while the event is occurring; and retrospective, or after the event has occurred.

Prospective

Prospective management of utilization applies to several major categories: health risk appraisals, demand management, referral services, and institutional services.

Health Risk Appraisals

Health risk appraisals (HRAs) are not new to most physicians, especially PCPs. HRAs traditionally have been used to perform an overall assessment of a new patient's medical condition and risk factors. In managed care, the same activity takes place, but the instruments also are designed to elicit information on member issues in which the plan needs to intervene in order to preserve health and lower overall costs. These appraisals also may be focused on specific lines of business such as commercial members, Medicare members, and Medicaid members.

Many advanced Medicare HMOs go well beyond the data-gathering forms and history and physical exams and actually send a nurse or home aide into the home of the new Medicare member. On that visit, the nurse may do a nutritional assessment, check for compliance with prescribed medications, and so forth. This assessment also may look at simple interventions that can save problems later, such as providing an inexpensive bath mat to prevent the senior member from slipping in the tub and breaking a hip.

Demand Management

Demand management refers to managing the demand for medical services before such services are incurred. The most common methods of doing this include providing home care manuals, access to preventive services, and convenient hours of operation by providers. Recently, a more aggressive approach has shown considerable promise: the provision of 24-hour-per-day nurse advice lines. These advice lines provide access to a trained nurse on a 24-hour-per-day, 7-day-per-week basis on a toll-free number. These advice lines often are provided via contracting with companies that specialize in such services and rely heavily on clinical protocols. Many plans that use this service find that use of the emergency department is reduced.

Referral Services

Management of referral services is principally confined to HMOs and to those HMOs that use a PCP to coordinate care (the gatekeeper model as discussed above). In this model, all care from any professional other than that rendered by the PCP must be authorized by the member's PCP. The only physician the member may see without authorization is the PCP, although many plans make exceptions for obstetrics and gynecology for women and occasionally for mental health and substance abuse services. This authorization requirement allows the PCP to determine if the problem may be treated by the PCP, and if a referral is required, the PCP utilizes a specialist under contract to the plan. The authorization is rarely open-ended, but rather for a limited number of visits (e.g., one to three) except in defined circumstances (e.g., chemotherapy may be fully authorized for all visits).

It is exceedingly rare for the plan to become involved in this process other than to capture the authorization data in order to process the claim properly. The PCP is expected to exercise proper clinical judgment without the plan's intervention. The plan should provide periodic reports to the PCP with data regarding referral rates and costs and reports regarding the PCP's capitation pool or withhold if that is appropriate.

Institutional Services

Prospective management of institutional services, both inpatient and outpatient, is a staple of managed care in all types of plans. The procedure is simple: someone calls the plan to request authorization for an elective admission or outpatient procedure; the plan checks it against clinical criteria and authorizes (or denies, though that is unusual) the procedure and a set amount of inpatient days, as appropriate.

Who calls the plan depends on the type of plan. For indemnity plans or the out-of-network benefits in PPOs and POS, the member must call or face an economic penalty. For HMOs and the in-network benefits in PPOs and POS, the responsibility is on the provider, who must bear the economic penalty for failure to comply.

Clinical criteria for authorization are commercially available, or the plan may have developed its own. Likewise, maximum allowable length of stay guidelines are commercially available, or the plan may modify those guidelines to suit the local area. Most managed care plans are now using computerized programs to provide this information quickly and to capture pertinent data.

Concurrent Review

This topic applies almost solely to inpatient care and large case management.

Inpatient Care and Continued Stay Review

This refers to the plan monitoring an active inpatient case. Some plans such as indemnity or service plans or PPOs perform this activity from a remote site via telephone. The plan's utilization management (UM) nurse calls the hospital to ascertain the status of the case. If the case is on track, no further action is taken. If the case is going to exceed the previously authorized days in the hospital, the UM nurse collects clinical data and either authorizes continued days or denies them. Many HMOs send their UM nurses on-site to the hospital. This allows the nurse to obtain more detailed and timely information and to more actively help manage the case.

In the event that there is any ambiguity or disagreement during this process, the UM nurse refers the case to a physician working with or for the health plan (either the medical director or a physician advisor). This physician may call the attending physician to discuss the case and may then make a determination regarding authorization for further payments.

Large Case Management

This area has some of the greatest cost savings potential of any activity in managed care. Large case management refers to those catastrophic or chronic cases that exceed routine costs by several orders of magnitude and in which active intervention by trained nurses at the plan can have a significant effect. Examples of such cases include acquired immune deficiency syndrome (AIDS), transplants, serious trauma, brittle diabetes, and so forth. The nurses at the plan are able to coordinate many aspects of care such as rehabilitation, home care, and health education, in order to better manage the case.

Disease Management

Disease management refers to a special form of large case management. In this instance, the plan focuses on a handful of selected clinical conditions and works very proactively with the patient to control the course of the disease. This provides for greater continuity and better outcomes. Common examples of clinical conditions that receive attention include AIDS, insulin-dependent diabetes mellitus, childhood asthma, and congestive heart failure. The hallmark of these programs is the combined activities of numerous professionals, not just physicians. For example, a clinical pharmacist may be more active in childhood asthma than the pediatrician (e.g., teaching the child how to use inhaled steroids). Disease management differs from many preventive care activities in that the diagnosis is clear, and cost savings occur concomitantly with improved outcomes (as opposed to, say cholesterol screening, where improved outcomes come at an enormous increase in cost).

Retrospective

Retrospective management refers to managing utilization after the utilization has actu-

ally occurred. It falls into two broad categories: case review and pattern analysis.

Case Review

In this type of management, individual cases are reviewed to look for appropriateness of care, billing errors, or other problems associated with an individual case. In some cases, a plan may place a provider on regular review if there is some suspicion of regular improprieties.

Pattern Analysis

Pattern analysis refers to amassing significant amounts of utilization data in order to determine if patterns exist. These patterns may be provider specific, such as over- or underutilization, or they may be planwide, such as an unanticipated increase in cardiac testing costs. After the pattern has been found, the reasons for it must be investigated so that action may be taken.

Managed care plans now are attempting to provide greater retrospective data to the providers in the network to allow the providers to compare themselves to their peers and modify their own practice as appropriate. This form of feedback promises to be a powerful adjunct in helping to control health care costs.

QUALITY MANAGEMENT

Managed care plans vary by model type in their approach to medical quality management. Indemnity and service plans, and even PPOs, generally are somewhat less aggressive in managing quality than are HMOs, although, like all generalizations, there are notable exceptions. As in utilization management, as model types progress through the continuum, greater attention is paid to the subject, and more resources are expended in managing quality. Almost all plans begin the quality management process through credentialing of the participating providers. In addition to credentialing, two general approaches to quality management exist, often in conjunction with each other: classic quality management and "new" approaches such as total quality management or continuous quality improvement.

Credentialing

Credentialing refers to the activity of collating and reviewing the professional credentials of the participating providers. For hospitals and institutions, this generally is confined to accepting the accreditation of the Joint Commission on Accreditation of Health Care Organizations. For professionals, the plan does its own credentialing. Exhibit 21–2 provides an example of data elements that an HMO may require. HMOs, like hospitals, also query the National Practitioner Data Bank.

Plans usually recredential every two years; basic data are reconfirmed; copies of current licenses and insurance face sheets are obtained, and changes are updated. Plans also may add data regarding member satisfaction,

Exhibit 21–2 Basic Elements of Credentialing

- training (copy of certificates)
  - location of training
  - type of training
- specialty board eligibility or certification (copy of certificate)
- current state medical license (copy of certificate)
  - restrictions
  - history of loss of license in any state
- Drug Enforcement Agency (DEA) number (copy of certificate)
- hospital privileges
  - name of hospitals
  - scope of practice privileges
- malpractice insurance
  - carrier name
  - currency of coverage (copy of face sheet)
  - scope of coverage (financial limits and procedures covered)
- malpractice history
  - pending claims
  - successful claims against the physician, either judged or settled
- National Practitioner Data Bank status
- Medicare, Medicaid, and federal tax ID numbers
- Social Security number
- location and telephone numbers of all offices
- hours of operation
- yes/no questions regarding:
  - limitations or suspensions of privileges
  - suspension from government programs
  - suspension or restriction of DEA license
  - malpractice cancellation
  - felony conviction
  - drug or alcohol abuse
  - chronic or debilitating illnesses
- provisions for emergency care and backup
- use of non-physician (i.e., midlevel) practitioners
- in-office surgery capabilities
- in-office testing capabilities
- areas of special medical interest
- record of continuing medical education

quality management, and administrative activities to the credentialing database.

Classic Quality Management

The classic approach to managing quality is based on the three key elements of structure, process, and outcome.

Structure

Structure looks at the infrastructure of the plan as it relates to quality. Examples include the makeup of the medical record (e.g., presence of a drug allergies list, laboratory notes, etc.), immunization records, access to care (e.g., how long it takes to get routine and urgent appointments), waiting times in the office, and telephone responsiveness. Structure studies usually are done through on-site review by the plan's quality management nurses. A special form of structure study relates to the effect of the utilization system on access to care, where the plan performs studies to ensure that utilization is not inappropriately low and that the authorization system is not forming a barrier to necessary care.

Process

Process refers to how care actually is rendered. One common method of management is through medical care evaluations (MCEs), in which plan nurses review a sample of outpatient medical records against practice parameters established by the quality management committee; these practice parameters often are specific to a particular disease or procedure. Degrees of compliance are measured and reported to the providers as well as to the plan. Similar reviews of inpatient care also are common.

Outcome

Outcome refers to the result of the care that is rendered. Plans generally look at outcome from two perspectives: planwide and adverse events. Adverse events refer to negative outcomes that could have been prevented, such as a hospital-acquired infection. Planwide outcomes refer to whether or not the medical care is beneficial; for example, successful treatment of designated conditions in outpatient care (e.g., control of hypertension without preventable side effects) and good outcomes from hospitalized cases. A special form of outcome is member satisfaction; the plan regularly surveys members and analyzes complaints to determine overall satisfaction levels and to act on identified problems.

OTHER OPERATIONAL ASPECTS OF MANAGED CARE

Managed care plans are fully operating companies that combine the operational activities of medical management with those of an insurance company. Exhibit 21–3 provides a listing of key operational activities, and Exhibit 21–4 provides a listing of common management positions in a managed care plan.

THE NUMBERS

Although the primary business of managed care is the financing and delivery of health care services, managed care plans cannot escape a reliance on statistics, similar to any business. Numbers and ratios are used to calculate premium rates, to track expenses, to track medical utilization, and generally to manage the business of the plan. The insurance industry, and the managed care industry in particular, uses certain formats to track

Exhibit 21–3 Other Operational Activities of a Managed Care Plan

1. claims
   - efficiency
   - throughput
   - accuracy
   - timeliness
   - link to authorization system
   - review process for pended claims
   - explanation of benefits statements
2. management information systems—computer and data support
   - hardware
   - software
   - report generation
     –medical utilization
     –operational
     –ad hoc versus routine
   - support for reimbursement and utilization policies
3. membership and billing
   - enrollment and disenrollment processing
   - eligibility checking
   - evidence of coverage
   - timely and accurate billing and reconciliations
4. finance
5. underwriting and pricing
6. marketing
7. general administration
   - coordination of all activities
   - regulatory relations
   - member services
   - negotiations
   - strategic planning
   - office management
   - public relations

both cost and utilization in addition to the more common methods such as net income and return on investment. A few of those formats are described as follows.

Per Member per Month

PMPM is an exceedingly common unit of measurement. It refers to the number of "units" per applicable enrolled member (subscriber and dependents) per month. The "units" may be dollars or units of utilization such as visits (although other measures of utilization are more common). Cost PMPM is the most common use of the format. For example, if the plan has 50,000 members and is spending $600,000 per month on primary care services, then the cost is $12.00 PMPM.

While cost is generally applied over all enrolled members, plans may restrict the measurement to only members to whom the measure applies. As an example, general medical costs for primary care services would apply to all members in the plan, while pharmacy services may only apply to 75% of enrolled members. In that case, the plan would report

---

Exhibit 21–4 Key Management Positions

- chief executive officer, executive director, or plan manager
- chief financial officer
- medical director
- other management positions critical for success
  –claims manager
  –customer services manager
  –utilization management manager
  –quality management manager
  –data and systems manager
  –provider relations manager
- other management positions required depending on plan configuration
  –marketing director
  –legal support
  –facilities manager
  –manager of medical support staff

PMPM pharmacy costs using only those members who had the benefits, otherwise a misleadingly low PMPM cost would be reported.

Per Member per Year

Similar in concept to PMPM, per member per year (PMPY) simply is calculated for a full 12 months rather than a single month. This measure is used not only for dollar costs, but also is often used for measuring utilization as well. For example, pharmacy costs may be reported as averaging 5.2 prescriptions PMPY, at a cost of $9.04 PMPM; simple arithmetic also yields two other common measures: $108.24 PMPY and $20.81 per prescription.

Per Thousand Members per Year

This unit of measurement applies almost solely to utilization. It is used to track units of utilization on an annualized basis. The most common example is bed days per thousand per members per year, usually referred to simply as bed days per thousand. This is the total number of days as hospital inpatients used by an average one thousand members in a year. For example, a typical HMO might report 300 bed days per thousand, meaning that for every one thousand members in the HMO, 300 inpatient days will be incurred. Since most plans calculate this number every month, a formula must be applied to take one month's data and annualize it, both for the single month and for the month to date.

Related to bed days per thousand are admissions per thousand. For example, a typical HMO might incur 78 admissions per thousand. If that same plan also reports 300 bed days per thousand, that means the average length of stay is 3.8 days. Other examples of this format include outpatient visits per thou-

sand, surgical procedures per thousand, and so forth.

Other Measurements

Financial measurements not only track utilization costs as described, as well as direct costs such as the cost of administration, but also must track costs for which no complete record yet exists. The reason for this is that a risk-bearing plan must accrue a liability each month for medical costs even when the claims have not yet been submitted. These costs are referred to as incurred but not reported (IBNR) costs. If a plan fails to accrue such expenses, it will seriously underestimate the true cost of health care and not have enough money to pay claims. The inability to monitor IBNR costs has led to significant financial problems for many HMOs.

Premium Rate Development and Budgeting

Premium rate development and budgeting is a requirement of any risk-bearing health plan. Using combinations of historical trends, actual prior experience, and management estimates of future costs, the plan must create premium rates to apply to its products. The variety of mechanisms to calculate rates, as well as different types of rates (e.g., community rates, adjusted community rates, rate banding, experience rates, minimum premium rates, and administrative services only rates) are extensive.

CONCLUSION

Managed care remains in a rapidly evolving state, as does the entire health care system in the United States. Managed care, as broadly described in this chapter, is subject to the economic, regulatory, and creative forces that led to its creation. However, above all else, it is possible, through the intelligent application of management, for managed care to provide good access to and high quality health care at an acceptable cost.

PETER R. KONGSTVEDT, MD, FACP, is a partner in the international accounting and consulting firm of Ernst & Young LLP. Based in the firm's Washington, D.C., office, Dr. Kongstvedt both leads and assists consulting engagements for the firm's larger clients. He is the Practice Leader for the Managed Care Strategy and Medical Management section of the firm's Managed Care Group, where he also serves as one of the key leaders of the practice. Dr. Kongstvedt is a member of the firm's national health care consulting operating committee.

In addition to his management and consulting experience, Dr. Kongstvedt is also an experienced author and educator. *The Managed Health Care Handbook*, 3rd Edition, was published in July of 1996 and is widely considered the leading reference text in the country, as well as globally. Dr. Kongstvedt also has developed a course in the fundamentals of managed health care, and his textbook, *The Essentials of Managed Health Care*, 2nd Edition, Aspen Publishers, is used in over 90 university programs. His most recent book, *Best Practices in Medical Management* (co-edited with Dr. David W. Plocher) was published in September 1998 by Aspen Publishers.

Chapter 22

Quality Assurance and Improvement

Mary Reich Cooper

Quality control, quality assurance, continuous quality improvement, total quality management, clinical guidelines, re-engineering, process redesign—this plethora of terms reflects the multiple approaches used to ensure that a health care institution is providing high-quality care to its patients. What, however, is high-quality care? More important, are the patients the only customers that require high-quality services? The health services industry has grappled with these questions for the past 25 years. As health care is a service industry that must address very specific issues, the evolution of the quality movement in health care has differed from that of the quality movement in industry.

CONTRIBUTORS

Many individuals have contributed to the quality process in health care since its inception. Some names, however, are heard repeatedly. Recognition of those names and the ideas that stemmed from those individuals is necessary to understanding the foundation of quality and its progress.

Ernest Codman

A surgeon trained at Harvard Medical School and Massachusetts General Hospital, Ernest Codman practiced at Massachusetts General Hospital for 15 years until his ideas led to such dissonance within the Boston medical community that he resigned from his post. Although he resigned from his hospital position, he did not retreat from his ideas, which he summed up as "merely the common-sense notion that every hospital should follow *every* patient it treats, long enough to determine whether or not the treatment has been successful, and then to inquire 'if not, why not?' with a view to preventing a similar failure in the future."[1] Codman was following both the process and the outcomes of the clinical care given by the physician and the hospital. Like those who adhere to the current quality assurance model of quality assessment, he was looking at indicators (1) to determine if the problems were patient-related, system-related, or clinician-dependent; (2) to assess the frequency with which each indicator occurred; and (3) to evaluate and correct the variables so that preventable problems would not recur.

Others outside the Boston medical community embraced Codman's ideas. His colleague Franklin Martin brought Codman's "end result system" to the fledgling American College of Surgeons (ACS), and it served as the basis for the minimum standards for hospitals that the ACS developed. Thirty-eight years later, the ACS, the American College of Physicians, the American Hospital Association, the American Medical Association, and the Canadian Medical Association banded together to form the Joint Commission on Accreditation of Hospitals (JCAH), a not-for-profit organization to evaluate the quality of hospitals' care.[2]

W. Edwards Deming

Unlike Codman, W. Edwards Deming's work was not in health care. His teachings have had a profound effect on the development of quality practices in the health care industry in the United States even so. Frequently called a founder of the quality movement, Deming was a statistician who was asked by Japanese industrialists to help them change the work process in Japan after World War II. Their goal was to develop quality merchandise and change the perception of Japan as a purveyor of inferior and cheap products. Deming developed a system of management that encouraged worker participation and input, relied on data and training, and analyzed system performance and problems to recommend change. His recommendations were codified in his 14 points, which he used as the basis of his teachings and philosophy. The 14 points include directives such as the following:

- Create a constancy of purpose toward improvement of product and service.

- Improve constantly and forever the system of production and service.
- Drive out fear.
- Substitute leadership for management by objective.[3]

Deming had throngs of converts to his methods of quality control and organizational behavior, and many of the subsequent processes for quality improvement incorporated his philosophy. All experts in the quality field in health care acknowledge the perspective gained from Deming's work in quality assurance in the manufacturing industry. Although Deming died in 1993, his adherents are still teaching his ideas.[4,5]

Joseph M. Juran

Another founder of the quality movement, Joseph M. Juran, also worked in the industrial rather than the health care arena. Juran expanded quality control and statistical techniques into a more comprehensive process of total quality management. Like Deming, his training in process and data analysis (through his education as an engineer and a lawyer) was the foundation for the management techniques that he advocated. Juran has had a long career as a consultant, educator, author, and director of the Juran Institute until 1987. He retired from all but writing in 1994.[6]

Juran wrote the first edition of the *Quality Control Handbook* in 1951, and now in its fourth edition, it continues to be a tool for quality managers today.[7] His next seminal book was *Managerial Breakthrough*, originally published in 1964 and revised in 1995.[8] Many quality management concepts are discussed in the two books. For example, Juran developed the Pareto principle, postulating that the "vital few" are responsible for most of the (choose one) cost, errors, customer needs, process features, and so on. By identifying those vital few, a quality improvement group can direct resources to an area where they can have the greatest impact.[9]

Juran also advocated the Juran trilogy of quality planning, quality control, and quality improvement. Quality planning involves the identification of customers and their needs, as well as the organization's response. Quality control is a feedback loop that entails the evaluation of performance and the comparison of performance to goals. Quality improvement from Juran's perspective is a universal sequence of events that include the identification of a problem, ownership, diagnosis of the cause(s), development of the remedies, and change at the operational level.[10]

Many of the principles either formulated or popularized by Juran remain part of health care institutions' quality improvement efforts today. Statistical charts, cause-and-effect diagrams, quality circles, Pareto analysis, control charts, and step-by-step planning are all described in Juran's *Quality Control Handbook*,[11] and all are referred to in the handbooks published by the Joint Commission on Accreditation of Healthcare Organizations (Joint Commission), the largest accreditation organization for the health care industry. Juran's methods have served the health care industry well by focusing on analytical, valid, and reliable methods of assessing processes.

Avedis Donabedian

A professor in the School of Public Health at the University of Michigan, Avedis Donabedian was one of the first to concentrate on quality issues as they pertained to the health care industry. Like Juran, Donabedian has focused on total quality management, but Donabedian's primary method has been to divide health care quality into structure, process, and outcome. Structure, according to Don-

abedian, includes material and human resources, and the organization of the institution. Process is the actual activity of the patient and the practitioner to ensure the delivery of care. Outcome is the improvement, or lack thereof, in the patient's health status after the treatment is or should have been delivered.[12,13]

One of the striking differences in Donabedian's approach originates in the fact that he is a clinician. As a result, his quality improvement processes take into account the difficulty of standardizing care caused by variances not only in the populations of patients, but also in the populations of health care providers. Unlike the manufacture of widgets or automobiles, the provision of care to a patient has inherent variations. Donabedian has espoused criteria, or best practices, to minimize the effect that those variations have on the process and outcome of care. He has recognized that different clinical efforts can achieve the same outcome and that the role of the quality analyst in health care is to find the most efficacious, acceptable, and legitimate processes to arrive at the greatest benefit for the patient with the least cost to that patient.[14] Although Donabedian does not delineate specific practices to utilize his structure–process–outcome model, his understanding of the delivery of care in health care institutions has made him very popular in the health care quality field.

Donald Berwick

Another clinician who has had a parallel career in quality improvement in the health care industry is Donald Berwick. Trained as a pediatrician and on the staff at Harvard Medical School and the Harvard School of Public Health for a number of years, Berwick is currently the president and chief executive officer of The Institute for Healthcare Improvement. He was a principal investigator for the National Demonstration Project on Quality Improvement in Health Care and currently serves on the Advisory Commission on Consumer Protection and Quality in the Health Care Industry.[15,16]

Berwick, like Donabedian, has focused on the application of known quality improvement methods to the health care industry. One of his interests has been in organizational solutions to quality improvement in health care. He sees The Institute for Healthcare Improvement's "mission [as] accelerating improvement in healthcare systems."[17] He has suggested that institutions set clear goals, measure their progress, and utilize multiple resources to define best practices.[18]

As one of the founders of the National Demonstration Project, Berwick has worked with a number of health care institutions to effectuate the implementation of various quality experiments. As a result of those efforts, he noted that quality efforts are more easily transplanted to the business and organizational components of health care institutions than to the clinical side.[19] Many quality managers and clinicians in health care share this impression. Berwick's other interest in quality assessment is a focus on the patient/consumer response to the quality improvement efforts undertaken by health care organizations, a focus that presently is driving quality assessment at many institutions.

John Wennberg

Although John Wennberg's work has not been as comprehensive in scope as that of some of the other individuals mentioned, the impact of his work has been profound within the quality movement. Wennberg specializes in small area analysis, a statistical method of determining patterns of practice and utilization by evaluating activities in small geo-graphic areas. When the patient populations are controlled for some variables, comparisons of activities in small areas can reveal utilization and delivery differences that are not attributable to patient differences.[20] The postulated cause of the differences then becomes physician or hospital characteristics. In fact, many researchers have used small area analysis to show that style and type of clinician practice account for the majority of practice variations and utilization differences.[21] This same theory has been the foundation for the use of clinical pathways and practice guidelines.

Others

Many other individuals have contributed to the quality movement in health care. Robert Brook, at the RAND Corporation; Dennis O'Leary, at the Joint Commission; Paul Cleary, with his work on patient satisfaction; and hundreds of other individuals have spent careers researching and clarifying the quality improvement process. As a result of their efforts, quality in health care has engendered significant popular and financial support.

ORGANIZATIONS

Accreditation

Joint Commission on Accreditation of Healthcare Organizations

The Joint Commission is a not-for-profit organization founded in 1951 to assess compliance with standards designed to ensure quality care to patients. Because of a regulation in the Medicare Act of 1965, hospitals accredited by the Joint Commission are eligible for Medicare and Medicaid payments from the federal and state governments. Joint Commission accreditation is also necessary for Graduate Medical Education (residency) reimbursement. Thus, accreditation is necessary for a hospital to survive financially. Hospitals are surveyed every 3 years, as are psychiatric facilities, long-term care organizations, alcohol and substance abuse programs, community mental health centers, home care associations, ambulatory health care centers, and laboratories.[22]

For many in health care, the words *Joint Commission* are synonymous with quality. In fact, many health care practitioners do not realize that the measurement or evaluation of quality exists outside the umbrella of the Joint Commission. The efforts expended by many institutions to prepare for their Joint Commission surveys may be responsible for that perception. Institutions may spend thousands to millions of dollars in preparation for the periodic accreditation evaluations, which often indicates a lack of understanding of the quality movement in industry and health care. Quality assessments should be integrated into the everyday culture of a health care organization; they should not be made events that require special training and education. Recognizing that problem, the Joint Commission added random, unannounced surveys to its 3-year accreditation cycle in 1993.

The Joint Commission has attempted many projects to alter this perception of quality evaluation as an event for which to prepare rather than as behavior that an organization continually demonstrates, but history is difficult to alter. The earliest standards reflected minimal levels of care that hospitals needed to achieve; later, these standards became goals of optimal quality to which hospitals should strive. Punitive measures, such as probationary status or withdrawal of accreditation, went into effect for health care providers that failed to meet the standards. The early undertakings of the peer review organizations had similar results.

A different venture for the Joint Commission began in the late 1980s with the develop-

ment of the indicator measurement system. The indicators were the beginnings of a focus on the outcomes of clinical care rather than an emphasis on standards of the departmental structure and process of a hospital. The evolution has been slow, however. Not until 1998 did the Joint Commission require hospitals to submit intrahospital outcome measures, such as the rates of mortality or postoperative wound infections. These submissions have been controversial among members of the health care community.

ORYX, as this outcome measurement system is called, requires the quarterly submission of data to an intermediary organization. The intermediary decides how to measure the outcome, collects the data, compares the data to those collected from other institutions associated with the intermediary organization, and submits the data to the Joint Commission. The problems that occur in any mass submission of data, such as hospital stratification, severity adjusting, and inconsistent definitions for various parameters, are also evident in the ORYX efforts. For example, mortality may be defined as death within 24 hours, death within 48 hours, death within 72 hours, death within 7 days, or death within 30 days, depending on the intermediary. Because the intermediary organization sets the definitions, large comparisons among health care institutions are inherently flawed. Despite the difficulties, many clinicians agree with the use of outcome measurements for quality assessments.

Along with the move toward outcome measurement, there has been a move from quality assurance to performance improvement. The primary difference in these techniques is that one, quality assurance, involves retrospectively reviewing indicators for compliance with standards, while the other, performance improvement, involves continually reevaluating processes to enhance quality prospectively. The Joint Commission began moving toward an emphasis on performance improvement in the early 1990s and, to enhance that effort, changed the standards to reflect functional rather than structural programs.[23]

As noted earlier, the Joint Commission surveys and accredits many health care organizations. Accreditation for home care organizations is the largest program in volume for the Joint Commission at this time, and as in hospitals, accreditation means Medicare reimbursement.[24] There are other certifying groups for some of the organizations surveyed, however—departments of health in the various states, the Clinical Laboratory Improvement Amendments of 1988 (CLIA), and for managed care entities, the National Committee on Quality Assurance.

National Committee on Quality Assurance

Like the Joint Commission, the National Committee on Quality Assurance (NCQA) is a not-for-profit organization that provides accreditation, but its focus has been other groups of care providers, such as the managed care providers. Accreditation surveys began in 1991. Although quality indicator measurement is the most publicized component of the surveys, the NCQA also measures physician credentials, member rights and responsibilities, utilization, and medical record documentation. The accreditation information is available to employers to help them choose health care plans for their employees and to consumers to help them evaluate the plans to which they belong. Currently, the NCQA evaluates more than 300 managed care plans covering more than 37 million insured lives.[25]

Like the recent efforts of the Joint Commission, the impetus of the NCQA has been to provide performance measurements that reflect standards of care delivery and outcomes to be achieved. These are published as the Health Plan Employer Data and Information Set, or HEDIS. Version 3.0, released in early 1998, has 71 performance measures covering areas such as the use of preventive health services, (e.g., Pap smears for cervical cancer screening, eye examinations for patients with diabetes); effectiveness measures, (e.g., the use of recommended medications to decrease the complication rate for persons following a heart attack, the frequency of counseling for smoking cessation); access measures (e.g., the time required to schedule a visit with a primary care physician, the ability to obtain specialty group referral); and organizational information, such as the financial stability of the plan or disenrollment of members.[26]

Although the NCQA covers approximately three quarters of individuals enrolled in managed care plans, penetration of these plans has not yet exceeded 20 percent of all insured lives in many parts of the United States. The NCQA's efforts, while commendable, are limited in scope. Because managed care participation often is available only to those families in which at least one person is employed, a reasonably large section of the population has had no outpatient performance measures. The NCQA recently has submitted report cards for participants in Medicaid managed care, apart from the other HEDIS data, but these are limited in number. Other agencies and organizations provide oversight and regulation, however, even if they do not call their activities accreditation.

Regulation

Health Care Financing Administration

An agency of the Department of Health and Human Services, the Health Care Financing

Administration (HCFA) administers the Medicare and Medicaid programs and regulates all nonresearch laboratory testing on humans in the United States.[27] As noted earlier, health care organizations must be accredited to be a HCFA-reimbursed provider. HCFA controls the monetary reimbursement for a large proportion of patients in the United States (up to 90 to 100 percent of inpatients in some hospitals), so the quality of care provided, the access to that care, and the cost of the care are matters of great concern to the agency. Because Medicaid is jointly administered and funded by the federal government and each state, much of the monitoring occurs in Medicare patients, whose care is wholly funded by the federal government.

Peer review organizations (PROs), groups of health care providers in each region who have contracted with HCFA to monitor the utilization and the quality of care, assess some aspects of care. Their activities have changed significantly since their original establishment as professional standards review organizations in the 1970s. To make them more effective and efficient, a federal act in 1982 revamped these organizations to perform as PROs. At this juncture, the PROs also received increased authority to enforce the regulations that they were overseeing.

Although the initial focus of the PROs was on hospital care, the Omnibus Budget Reconciliation Act of 1986 required an extension of that review process to ambulatory care services, long-term care, and home health care agencies. The PROs used sampling criteria to assess the appropriateness, timeliness, and necessity of care in retrospective chart reviews. If health care organizations were found to be noncompliant, sanctions such as increased review, denial of payments, or civil monetary penalties could occur.[28] A report in 1990 initiated changes in the PRO process and resulted in the 1993 implementation of the Health Care Quality Improvement Program.[29] The underlying premise for this program is that PROs can be more effective in the long run by encouraging "best practices," or evidence-based medicine, rather than by punishing those who provide substandard care.[30] The method again is to provide performance measurement data to the providers, comparing the performance of health care providers with national standards of care. This is the same method encouraged by the NCQA and, on a more global basis, the Joint Commission.

Measurements of access to care are not so extensive as are measurements of utilization and quality of care, but there are severe penalties for restricting access in federally funded hospitals. Part of the Hill–Burton Act, first enacted in 1946, required that states provide adequate health care services to all their residents, including those unable to pay. After the Medicare Act was passed in 1965, the Secretary of the Department of Health and Human Services explicitly stated that Medicare and Medicaid recipients were not to be included in that category of persons unable to pay according to the Hill–Burton Act, because the hospitals were receiving compensation for those patients. When the American Hospital Association challenged the Secretary's decision, the federal courts upheld it, noting that the act contemplated that a hospital would have to devote some of its own finances to charitable care. Severe civil penalties can be imposed if a federally financed hospital (i.e., one receiving Medicare funds for patient payments or federal financing for construction) restricts access because of an inability to pay.[31]

Another federal act, the Emergency Medical Treatment and Active Labor Act, can lead to severe civil penalties if a hospital receiving federal funds "dumps" patients (i.e., refuses to provide care for certain patients, usually indigent, and transfers them to another institution), thus restricting their access to the hospital that they initially chose. The law applies both to indigent and to nonindigent patients; the receipt of federal funds by the hospital is the key factor in determining whether HCFA and the Department of Justice can intervene. The law applies only in cases in which an individual requires emergent stabilization or a woman is in active labor, however. Once the patient's condition is stable, a transfer to another institution can occur.[32]

Of course, federal laws that prohibit discrimination can also be used to prevent restrictions on access to care. These include the antidiscrimination regulations found in Title VII of the Civil Rights Act[33] and the regulations within the Americans with Disabilities Acts.[34] The applicability of either of these two acts does not depend on the receipt of Medicare funds, and therefore, any potential case requires evaluation to see if the provisions of either act apply. For example, cases involving the Americans with Disabilities Act and private practitioner offices are constantly evolving, and rulings may vary in different parts of the United States.

The cost of care is another segment of quality that HCFA evaluates. HCFA provides billions of dollars to pay patient care. With that much money at stake, HCFA is committed to ensuring that the care provided is reasonable and efficient. Hospitals receive the majority of those payments, and to improve efficiency, HCFA implemented in the mid-1980s prospective payment systems based on diagnosis-related groups (DRGs) for hospital reimbursement. Currently, HCFA does not use DRGs to reimburse providers for home health care or for ambulatory care, but this is expected to change within the next few years. The agency does monitor the cost of home and ambulatory care, however. A certain number of visits within each group are audited for cost and utilization purposes, usually by one of the PROs with which HCFA has contracted. Payment may be denied and civil penalties imposed if misuse of HCFA funds occurs. If the misuse is intentional (e.g., false billing, bribes or kickbacks, or misrepresentation of compliance with the conditions of the act), a hospital, practitioner, or other health care provider may face charges of fraud and abuse, with the accompanying civil and criminal penalties.[35]

National Practitioner Data Bank

Although the National Practitioner Data Bank (Data Bank) is not truly a regulatory organization, it functions to control the movement of errant practitioners from state to state. This central registry is the result of a provision in the National Health Care Quality Improvement Act of 1986.[36] Although the major focus of the act is to limit liability for the quality assurance process within health care organizations, a second section of the act requires that various entities report malpractice and adverse actions to this central registry.[37] Actions that must be reported include adverse licensure actions, certain adverse clinical privilege actions (e.g., mandatory revocation or reduction of privileges, as well as voluntary reductions that occur to avoid an investigation), professional society actions against dentists and physicians, and medical malpractice payments for all clinical practitioners.[38]

In addition to collecting information, the Data Bank responds to requests for information from health care organizations. Queries may be mandatory or voluntary. Hospitals must query the Data Bank when a practitioner applies for or updates his or her staff privileges and at least every 2 years that the practitioner is on staff. Voluntary queries include queries for credentialing by other health care organizations (i.e., home care agencies or managed care organizations); self-queries by a practitioner; queries by state licensing boards; and in very limited cases, queries by attorneys.[39] Patients and the general public may not ask for information.

The Data Bank has been very successful in some facets, less so in others. As a resource to hospitals for new malpractice or adverse event information, the Data Bank appears to be helpful. Studies by the Office of the Inspector General at the Department of Health and Human Services showed a significant decline in the amount of new information that hospitals received in response to their queries when data from the period 1990 to 1992 were compared with data from the period 1992 to 1994.[40] This decline suggests that practitioners applying for privileges are now less likely to withhold information on their staff applications. The receipt of "disclosure notices" makes less of an impact, however. These reports of a malpractice payment rarely engender further review, and Oshel and associates postulated that the reason for the lesser reaction is that competence is not assumed to be in question when the legal system rather than the quality assurance process initiates the complaint.[41]

Of some concern is the fact that state licensing boards have no mandate to query the Data Bank. Not all physicians and dentists are on staff at a hospital. Were state licensing boards required to query the Data Bank, perhaps fewer incidents of incompetent practice would occur. Additionally, other health care practitioners do not have to be reported; thus, chiropractors, podiatrists, and midlevel practitioners, such as physician's assistants and nurse-practitioners, are reported only if a malpractice payment is made. The regulations could be made much tighter.

State Licensing Boards

As noted earlier, state licensing boards may have some responsibility to query the Data Bank, but they also have other functions in ensuring quality of care. In addition to ensuring that academic, training, and testing requirements have been met before they grant a license, the state licensing boards also are responsible for limiting or revoking licenses in their states. Many states license an individual who has practiced elsewhere, whereas others require the individual to be tested again before granting a license. All states require significant amounts of supporting data before granting a license, however.

Once a license has been granted, states vary in the frequency at which the licenses must be renewed and the amount of continuing education required for renewal. The licensing boards also vary in the conditions under which a license may be terminated. Because the Fifth and Fourteenth Amendments of the U.S. Constitution guarantee due process to an individual, states must have a procedure and process in place that allow hearings and appeals if a license is to be terminated. The courts have been very reluctant to overturn state licensing board recommendations and, in most cases, rule in favor of the state board. Thus, if a state licensing board reduces or revokes an individual's privilege to practice in that state, the practitioner loses his or her ability to earn an income in that profession for some period of time.

There are many reasons to limit or revoke health care practitioners' licenses:

- Medicare or Medicaid fraud
- patterns of unacceptable behavior, such as the sexual abuse of patients
- felonies committed that are unrelated to the practice of the profession, such as the murder of a spouse

- egregious incidents of inappropriate patient care, such as gross negligence (e.g., removal of the wrong limb)
- compromised ability to practice, such as impairment due to substance abuse (alcohol or drugs)

The trend since the early 1980s has been to recognize alcoholism and substance abuse as diseases. Because health care providers are at such risk for substance abuse, many states now offer programs that treat and supervise compromised health care providers as long as they voluntarily enter the program; in this way they can avoid the loss of licensure as long as they remain free of any alcohol or controlled substance. The hope has been that providers will seek help rather than risking loss of licensure.

Many health care organizations are reluctant to report practitioners to the state licensing board because of the potentially severe repercussions to the practitioner. Organizational liability due to such reports used to be an issue, but the National Health Care Quality Improvement Act of 1986 has reduced this concern if all the procedures of the health care organization follow due process. The primary constraint on reporting is the awareness of individuals that a practitioner may lose his or her livelihood, one that in many cases required 7 to 10 years of education and training. Mandated event reporting has eliminated some of this reluctance at the local level, but a patient complaint or an anonymous (except to the state) tip still initiates more investigations than does a report from an institution. Few practitioners are officially disciplined each year, although the frequency of significant variations from the standards of care is much greater.

Departments of Health

Each state and many counties and municipalities have departments of health that may be involved in monitoring the quality of care given to patients within their jurisdictions. The extent of regulation and quality assessment varies tremendously from region to region. Most health departments were formed as venues for public health initiatives, such as control of infection (e.g., tuberculosis); immunization against preventable disease; (e.g., polio, hepatitis); health screenings to detect disease in its early, most treatable forms (e.g., diabetes, high blood pressure); and charitable care for the indigent.[42] In some states and municipalities, however, the department of health surveys hospitals to ensure their compliance with state or local regulations that may be much more narrowly prescribed than those at the federal level. In others, the department of health requires health care organizations to submit data for publication so that consumers have a comparative basis for assessing hospital results and outcomes. The topics and content of those data submissions vary significantly from state to state.[43] In many states, surveys by the Joint Commission have replaced separate surveys by the state, and Joint Commission accreditation is deemed to suffice for state accreditation.

Food and Drug Administration

The responsibilities of the Food and Drug Administration (FDA) include oversight of all medications and medical devices; thus its purview places the FDA squarely in the scope of quality of health care. The agency has rigorous regulations just to get a product to the human testing phase, probably the most rigorous in the world. Moreover, companies must perform several levels of human testing before the FDA approves the product, a process that can take up to 10 years. The FDA also has the power to recall batches of a product; to control the labeling, advertising, and information handouts on all medical products; to withdraw a product from the market if it is found to cause adverse outcomes in any proportion of the population (the more adverse the outcome, the smaller the proportion required for withdrawal); to regulate all medical devices; and to provide for both civil and criminal penalties to ensure compliance with all regulations.[44] The FDA requires health care organizations to report adverse drug reactions and problems with medical devices (e.g., pacemakers that malfunction or pieces of equipment that break off).

Occupational Safety and Health Administration

Although hospitals generally consider patient and visitor safety within the reach of quality improvement, they less often address worker safety as a quality issue. The Occupational Safety and Health Administration (OSHA) has published several pamphlets addressing worker safety in health care organizations. Protections against the transmission of blood-borne pathogens for worker safety in acute care facilities, long-term care facilities, and dental offices are not unexpected topics of health care quality assurance. OSHA did surprise many health care organizations with its *Guide to Reducing Workplace Violence Toward Health Care and Social Workers*, however, a topic chosen because the incidence of workplace violence in health care organizations is one of the highest in all sites measured. This violence results from altercations with patients and their families rather than interactions with other employees or within employees' families.

OSHA is responsible for the material safety data sheets that OSHA and the Joint Commission require to be readily available to health care workers. A material safety data sheet must list all toxic substances to which a worker may be exposed. In health care organizations, this list may include chemotherapeutic agents, bacteriocides or other anti-infectious agents, and cleaning solvents. OSHA has no jurisdiction over patient or visitor safety.[45]

Nuclear Regulatory Commission

Quality in a health care organization is a very minor part of the role of the Nuclear Regulatory Commission (NRC). Health care organizations that use any radioactive material must account for it to the NRC, however. Diagnostic tests frequently involve radioactive material, and records covering its purchase, storage, dosage, and disposal must be available for review. The NRC is also responsible for ensuring that health care workers are exposed to a minimal amount of radiation, that badges are worn by all health care workers who work with radiation, and that the badges are monitored monthly. It is the responsibility of the employing organization to ensure that no worker is exposed to higher levels of radiation than those approved by the NRC, to maintain a radiation safety committee, to monitor and control patient exposure, and to provide lead shielding to protect all vulnerable body parts.[46]

METHODS

Quality Control

Usually, quality control refers to the monitoring of a particular procedure and the recording of any variations from the expected process. The roots of a significant portion of the quality movement lie in quality control, and quality control still exists in the monitoring of equipment and processes. For example, a patient may use a blood glucose–monitoring device called a glucometer two or three times daily, or a nurse in a nursing home may use a glucometer two or three times daily on each of 25 patients. If either device is not calibrated frequently through an external mechanism, the blood sugar (glucose) levels indicated by the device may vary significantly from the true values and lead to incorrect treatments. Monitoring the external validation of such a device is an example of quality control. Measuring of radioactive exposure and ensuring that the institution does not use expired or recalled medications are other examples. Quality control requirements include keeping records of the testing or monitoring, and these records frequently must be made available to an external regulatory or accreditation agency.

Quality Assurance

An extension of quality control, quality assurance frequently was the underpinning of the quality movement in health care until the early 1990s. Quality assurance focuses on the identification and monitoring of indicators that reflect standards of care. The institution sets goals of compliance before monitoring begins and attempts to reach those goals. The emphasis of the quality assurance process is on the achievement of those goals rather than on an understanding of what prevents the goals from being achieved.

Tracking and Trending

Quality assurance remains an appropriate method of ensuring quality by employing a parallel technique called "tracking and trending." This technique begins with the identification of the event to be monitored. Examples are the incidence of postoperative wound infections or the time required to answer a telephone call in an ambulatory care clinic. The next step is to search the literature or to survey other practitioners to find a benchmark, which is the optimal goal or best practice associated with that event. Once that goal has been determined, the event is measured on a

routine and periodic basis, and the outcome of that measurement is compared to the established goal.

Three scenarios may occur. First, the measurement may fall short of the goal; the traditional response to this situation has been to continue to measure or, occasionally, to lower the goal. Second, the measurement may exceed the goal, and the organization frequently rests on its laurels. Some organizations raise the bar in response to this situation, acknowledging that the goal may have been set too low. Third, the measurement and the goal may be the same, but this rarely happens in a repeated fashion.

Tracking and trending is a method by which indicators are followed over time and compared to the expected goals. It takes into account the inherent variation in a process. The difficulty is that tracking and trending frequently require extensive data collection by individuals familiar with the processes being measured.

To use tracking and trending for wound infections, for example, it is first necessary to have some system of tracking surgical cases both in and out of the operating rooms. As many surgical procedures now take place in ambulatory surgery or procedure rooms (e.g., cardiac catheterizations, endoscopy), tracking the incidence of these procedures has become more difficult.

Next, the procedures must be classified according to the type of wound involved. An infection in a wound that is "contaminated" prior to the surgical procedure (e.g., contamination from a gunshot wound to the abdomen that opens up bowel contents to the peritoneum) indicates less about the quality of care provided than does an infection in a "clean contaminated" wound (e.g., contamination from spillage of gall bladder contents during a cholecystectomy). In turn, infection is less significant in a clean contaminated procedure than in a clean operation, one in which the expectation is that no contamination has occurred, such as open heart surgery. Of course, classifying these procedures by type of wound requires some expertise in infection control and/or the type of surgery being assessed.

Personnel who collect the data then identify the in-hospital outcomes of the procedure. The data collection usually involves a person reviewing the chart and marking down the location and extent of the infection in a separate location. Most hospitals do not place any quality assurance information in the medical record because there is no privilege accorded to medical records. In other words, if a malpractice claim were to be entered against the hospital and records of all wound infections were kept in non–quality assurance databases, that summary information would be accessible to the attorney suing the hospital. Therefore, the staff must obtain the information and transfer the results to another manual or electronic database.

Another problem has arisen over the past few years. Because hospital stays have decreased so markedly, many wound infections do not appear until the patient already has been discharged. In most communities, unless the patient is readmitted to the same hospital, the outcome is never recorded for quality assurance. Following up on posthospital outcomes such as wound infection is a significant reason to move to an organized delivery system.

Electronic databases have removed some of the obstacles to data collection and assessment. Mortality review, for example, can be performed to a significant degree with qualifiers in an electronic database. All hospitals and many other health care organizations (e.g., ambulatory care practices, nursing homes) now collect medical record and charge data in electronic databases. To be used for mortality review, the database must have a field for disposition upon discharge. The proportion of patients who are discharged as "expired" is determined and that number is compared to the total number of patients discharged. The purpose of mortality review is to search for preventable deaths, however, and the volume data cannot show the degree to which a death was preventable. Qualifiers such as reason for admission, date of any intervention, and severity of illness derived from the International Classification of Diseases, Ninth Revision (ICD-9) codes used for billing diagnoses and procedures can reveal with reasonable accuracy whether the death was expected or unexpected. Although an electronic search for these qualifiers is not 100 percent reliable, it can highlight most unexpected deaths for further chart review. This eliminates the need for 100 percent manual chart review to determine whether deaths were predictable and is especially effective when the staff generally reports any untoward events or unexpected deaths. In this era of staff reductions in support functions such as quality assurance, electronic databases can be a useful adjunct.

Benchmarking

The process of comparing an organization or a process to other organizations or processes in an industry, called benchmarking, allows for external comparisons in addition to internal or sequential comparisons. Benchmarking is frequently used with the term *best practice*, denoting that one, or a few, organizations or processes are considered the ideal to which others should aspire. Like many practices in the evaluation of health care quality, benchmarking grew out of an industry practice. The Xerox Corporation popularized it after results from an internal process started by Xerox in 1979 showed tremendous operational benefits.[47] Xerox adopted benchmarking, along with employee involvement in the quality process, in order to understand customer requirements and to implement the best practices to fulfill those requirements.[48] By the end of the decade, benchmarking had become a way by which any function or cost center could identify management processes, practices, and methods, from any industry, to motivate change within an organization.[49]

In general, the health care industry has had a much more constrained definition of benchmarking, with comparisons made primarily within the industry rather than throughout the service and manufacturing world. For example, health care organizations have been much slower to embrace information technology as a path to more efficient delivery of results and data. Bar coding, used throughout many industries for materials management, is not as prevalent in health care organizations, despite the large numbers of supplies that move through a hospital or other health care organization at any given time. In health care, benchmarking typically has been applied to clinical practices and outcomes rather than to business activities.

The use of external databases to compare clinical information (e.g., mortality, complications, utilization, cost) among institutions with some similar factor, such as patients on Medicare (MedPar database), or hospitals in New York State (SPARCS database), or hospitals with an academic affiliation (University Healthcare Consortium [UHC] database) has been increasing. Many of these databases are in the public domain. It is possible to purchase the data already stratified by a vendor and analyzed for best practices among the member organizations. Health care organizations use this information to pinpoint opportunities to improve quality or to reduce utilization. Vendors such as HBOC, HCIA, or Healthshare Technologies sell these database analyses or sell user-friendly platforms to manipulate the databases.

Despite its popularity in benchmarking an organization's clinical practices, there are several drawbacks to database analysis. Primary are the questions of data validity (i.e., the accuracy of the data) and data reliability (i.e., the accuracy of the representation). In the medical record coding of pneumonia, for example, 100 percent validity means that 100 percent of the patients who had pneumonia coded actually had pneumonia; 100 percent reliability means that the coder noted the pneumonia in all cases in which pneumonia was present and did not code for pneumonia in any cases in which pneumonia was not present. Reliability implies that another coder would code the cases in exactly the same way. Data reliability and validity are issues in many of these external databases because organizations have different incentives for making the data accurate. Most data are entered for billing purposes, and a hospital that wants to maximize its revenue may code more complications to increase the "weight," or severity, of the diagnosis. Alternatively, if the databases publish results in the local press, the incentive to undercode may be more pressing than the extra revenue derived from accurate coding, especially if the hospital revenue derives mostly from predefined contracts with third-party payers. In only a few instances are the databases checked frequently for reliability and validity of data; Pennsylvania, for example, checks the state database by means of the Mediqual program from Medisgroup.

Another drawback to the use of external databases is the variability among participating institutions. Large and small, urban and rural, or coastal and midwestern health care institutions frequently are grouped together despite the inherent differences in the institutions. Similarly, many of the databases do not account for differences in severity of illness, although they are more likely to do so now that vendors are stratifying the data for purchase. Even when there is an adjustment for severity of illness, however, the vendor generally uses a single method for stratification rather than adjusting for severity of illness within different diagnosis groupings. Recent research has questioned the use of severity of illness stratification that cuts across a wide swath of patients, as it appears that severity of illness as a basis for benchmarking requires a system especially applicable to a certain subset of patients, (e.g., the APACHE system for surgical intensive care patients).[50]

Finally, there is a lack of reliability among databases. The same information purchased from different vendors is unlikely to show the same results. It may be that the vendors manipulate their data with internal sorts and rankings, thus causing the outcomes of any one hospital to vary when databases are compared. Perhaps the process ensures that a health care organization will use the same vendor repeatedly. Practically speaking, health care organizations often buy data from several vendors, using each database for different purposes. Despite the drawbacks in the external databases, they are presently the only way to compare hospitals' outcomes.

Continuous Quality Improvement

Following quality assurance both in time and in logic, continuous quality improvement (CQI) assumes that monitoring is not adequate to ensure adherence to standards and attainment of quality. Organizations that use CQI techniques rely on an ongoing prospective assessment of processes, constant evaluation to see if the processes are resulting in the desired outcomes, and a feedback loop to the persons involved in the process so that they can make any necessary upgrades. Many health care organizations may state that they are using CQI—or performance improvement, an analogous term used by the Joint Commission to describe the activities being performed to assess quality—but there are key indicators in a true CQI program.

Key Indicators of CQI

Constant Process. Responding only to decreasing revenue or market share, to complaints from clinicians or patients, or to specific incidents involving patient care is not CQI. This approach is not about putting out fires. Health care organizations frequently respond to problems in the same way that clinicians respond to illness. They want a treatment that will resolve the problem—for clinicians, a medication to treat the illness; for health care executives, a Band-Aid to provide relief. CQI results from ongoing evaluation, a continual search for opportunities to improve the systems and processes of health care delivery. CQI entails identifying the problem and the customer, recruiting senior management to lead the process, evaluating the problem, suggesting solutions to the identified problem, implementing those solutions, and evaluating the implementation. Subsequently, when a different problem arises within the same organization, the process continues. CQI occurs over years, not months or weeks, and requires constant reappraisal of the goals of improvement.

Leadership. Unlike quality assurance, which can take place at many levels, inherent in CQI is the supposition that senior management is leading the improvement effort. Leadership may lie within a division or a function, but because of the interdisciplinary nature of most health care organizational problems, it may be difficult to effect solutions without the support of key individuals at the top level of management. Furthermore, without the participation of senior management, resources for evaluation and implementation may be scarce.

The commitment by senior management usually requires substantial buy-in, because CQI frequently does not produce short-term results; without buy-in, management may lose interest. Showing the results in monetary terms can obtain that buy-in by senior management, but rarely does the implementation of a quality program save dollars in the short run. Thus, a detailed analysis showing how those dollars eventually will be saved and the other benefits that arise from implementing the program may help maintain interest by senior management.

Change in the Culture of the Organization. For a CQI program to be effective, it is critical to integrate quality awareness into the day-to-day activities and the job descriptions of all the employees of the organization. For example, employees of a health care organization must constantly be on the outlook for opportunities to improve the delivery of care, regardless of whether those opportunities are incremental or require large changes in the organization's operations. To increase employee awareness, the organization should involve as many people as possible in the quality process, empower employees to suggest changes and make accommodations at a much lower level than the hierarchical nature of health care organizations has permitted in the past, and convert to a systems evaluation process rather than a punitive response to errors. Quality circles have been used by many organizations to effectuate change within a division or function, but they may not have an interdisciplinary membership or have senior management buy-in. Perhaps because the issues frequently require multidisciplinary input, quality circles have not been widely used in health care organizations to address problems.

CQI Scenario

To illustrate, a CQI program can be helpful in solving a difficulty that arises in many health care organizations: getting a patient admitted to a bed. The first stage of analysis may identify many components in this problem: a late discharge of the prior occupant; a delay in relaying the information that the previous occupant has departed; a cleaning crew that is otherwise occupied; a lack of linens or other supplies; perhaps a roommate that wants to move into that bed; a delay in informing the admissions department that the bed has been cleaned; a discussion about who has the responsibility for allocating that bed and the type of patient to be placed in the bed; levels of approval that may be required to make that decision; an outdated insurance card that makes it impossible to obtain billing information and precertification; a computer glitch that prevents the entry or exchange of information; a staff member who is at lunch, with no other personnel able to gather the information on the incoming patient; an emergency on the floor that diverts everyone's attention to another patient; the lack of an escort service to transport the patient to the bed; the disappearance of the patient, who became so frustrated with the process that she and her family members went to the cafeteria for their first food since their arrival at the hospital hours before. The second stage of analysis requires the identification of the customer. The patient is easily identified, but there are other customers in this scenario: the family, the staff awaiting the patient on the floor, the physician waiting to admit the patient and write orders, the admissions personnel subject to the ire of the patient and her family.

Perhaps not all the components occur with each patient, or perhaps one of the components occurs with every patient. Using the CQI process to break down each component in the process, the staff can analyze what is happening, how frequently, and why. Solutions can be offered by the people who are directly affected by the problem and who can see the benefits and risks of the various solutions. Data can be collected and evaluated to see if the variations are statistically significant or if isolated horror stories have resulted in changes to the process that benefit only a few entities. Requirements for training and education can be formalized. Past conclusions can be analyzed. Interdisciplinary solutions can be formulated and funded with senior management buy-in.

Organizations have responded to the problem in this scenario in a variety of ways. They have decentralized admissions and put the admissions people on the floor; empowered admissions and floor personnel; removed admissions personnel from the process and put all the decision making at the floor level; implemented clinical service lines or product lines so that all decision making is interdisciplinary at any given time; written protocols and guidelines to direct the processes. Each organization must decide what is the best solution, and each solution has to be individualized not only for the floor, but also for the patient. Most important, it is essential to re-evaluate the solution periodically to see if it is still the appropriate solution.

Customer Satisfaction

Identification of the proper customer is difficult at times; nothing ever affects just one person. Health care organizations are spending significant amounts of money to survey patients, their families, and, less frequently, physicians and staff members to evaluate the quality of the health care that the organizations are providing. An industry has grown up to gather that information and provide it to health care executives. All the accreditation organizations currently assess patient satisfaction measurements, and advertisements publicize high satisfaction measures. Patient satisfaction is important. People return to a hospital if they are satisfied with its care, and they presumably refer others to that same institution. A few precautions exist, however.

There is tremendous variability among instruments, and many organizations rely on home-grown instruments that may be skewing the responses obtained. Not only is it important to have an instrument that is valid, but also it is necessary to have an instrument that does not eliminate a portion of the respondents because of one of its own characteristics. Surveying nonresponders to determine if they mirror the responder patient population is a very important step in ensuring the survey's reliability. Literacy and languages may be problems, so a health care organization should be aware of the number of patients who do not respond because they cannot read or understand the survey instrument. Most social science surveys are written at a fifth- to sixth-grade reading level so as to include as many responders as possible. Questions must be nonbiased so that no judgment is implied if a respondent answers a question in a particular way. A scale should be used so that answers can be aggregated and compared.

Response rates are easy to calculate and do not require the distribution of an inordinate number of surveys. The first step is to sample the population randomly, again with care not to introduce bias by over- or undersampling certain populations. After the names and number of persons to be surveyed have been obtained, the survey instrument is administered. This can be done in several ways. The survey can be given to the patient at the time of service, completed by means of a telephone call to the patient, mailed to the patient, or any combination of the three. The response rate is the number of returned surveys divided by the number distributed. Again, this is an area where bias may occur. If the survey is sent only to the first 50 people of a sample of 500 people, the names must be checked to ensure that those people were not selected by last name, by payer class, or by discharge date, for example. If the only instrument sent out is in English, the Hispanic population will likely be undersampled. If the population is transient, a mailed survey will undersample. If the population is impoverished, a telephone survey will undersample. A response rate of 35 to 45 percent is average, and greater than 45 percent shows a recognition of the systems by which a particular patient population responds.

Two companies, Picker and Press-Ganey, seem to be the most popular among patient satisfaction survey vendors. Health care organizations consider their instruments and survey methods reliable and valid. Each benchmarks an institution against like institutions, as well as against the aggregate data. There are other organizations, and they should be evaluated on a case-by-case basis.

Family surveys, physician surveys, and staff surveys are rarely standardized and even less rarely evaluated for validity and reliability. The information provided may offer a starting point for CQI activities or for communication with the group being surveyed, however. The literature, especially the literature in nursing, offers some staff surveys, but their use requires caution because of the possibility that the respondents may have other agendas.

Measurement of Severity of Illness and Functional Status

One of the difficulties with data comparisons in health care organizations is the significant amount of variation among patients. Even those patients admitted for the same procedure or with the same diagnosis can vary with regard to the clinical co-morbidities or clinical outcomes of their condition. Although stratifying demographic data is relatively easy, stratifying these clinical parameters is more difficult. Two major methods have been employed to control for clinical parameters; one relies on the severity of illness, which ultimately is based on the clinician's assessment, and the other relies on the patient's perception of illness and function.

Severity of illness is a compilation of clinical information that is used to control for risk factors that affect the response to a treatment.[51] The difficulty with using severity of illness for risk adjustment, however, is in determining which risks are related to which outcomes.[52] A second issue with risk adjustment is the cost of clinical abstracting by trained reviewers so that the risk adjustment is valid and reliable. Instead of actually abstracting each chart for risk adjustment, many organizations rely on databases with data elements resulting from ICD-9 codes, demographic data, hospital outcomes such as discharge disposition, and the analysis indigenous to each database. Recent research has shown, however, that severity analyses based on computerized data elements are not particularly effective at assessing quality of care.[53]

Risk adjustment avoids penalizing organizations and providers who care for high-risk patients.[54] Without risk adjustment, there would be more report cards published with results like that of HCFA's first report card of hospital mortality, in which one hospital was identified as having an 87 percent mortality rating as opposed to its 23 percent adjusted expected mortality rate—but the hospital was a hospice for the terminally ill.[55] The conclusion is that risk adjustment remains potentially beneficial, with the caveat that it must be clinically relevant.

Few dispute the clinical relevance and benefit of functional assessment of a patient from his or her own perspective. The only dispute is the cost that such an assessment entails. Multiple survey tools exist for assessing functional status, and many are validated and reliable. They may be designed specifically for certain groups of patients (e.g., cancer patients), or they may have a more global intent in their design.[56]

Disease Management and Clinical Service Lines

Health care assessment has changed to include the care given outside the four walls of a hospital and to reflect the evolution toward interdisciplinary teams of caregivers treating diseases. Disease management is the process of optimizing the diagnosis, treatment, and care of a patient with a chronic condition so that the patient objectively and perceptively has minimal symptoms and requirements for intervention.

The difficulty with performing any type of quality monitoring across such a continuum of care stems not only from the size and the volume of the patient visits, but also from the lack of geographic proximity and, more often than not, the inability to track data rigorously across multiple sites and providers. Several groups have been successful, however, by using electronic alerts, protocols, electronic data capture, and specific parameters for measurement. The benefits to using an organized health care delivery system for quality monitoring are that expected and unexpected outcomes can be observed more easily because they are not confined to a hospital stay; data on co-morbidities and pre-existing conditions can be captured at the primary care provider site; preventive maintenance compliance, such as immunizations and screening examinations, can be monitored from various locations of input; and a cohesive approach to quality assessment can be devised for all medical conditions and all types of patients.

At a different level, the delivery of care is being organized through clinical service lines or product lines. When successfully implemented, clinical service lines cut across the traditional departmental structures and rise above the turf battles often seen in health care organizations. Cardiac services, for example, may incorporate medical cardiology, interventional cardiology, cardiothoracic surgery, cardiac anesthesiology, ambulatory care clinics, and cardiac rehabilitation services. Clinical service lines allow physicians to take the lead in strategic planning for market growth, medical cost management, and improvement of quality standards.[57] The benefit from the quality perspective is similar to that benefit from using organized delivery systems. Care is not fragmented, and neither is the collection of data.

Evidence-Based Protocols, Electronic Reminders, and Practice Guidelines

A more recent effort to deliver quality care has been to develop standards of care to ensure that the care delivered is based on recommendations in the literature or consensus opinions from medical organizations or health care assessment groups. The Agency for Health Care Policy and Research (AHCPR) has published 19 different guidelines that are available in both a clinician's and a consumer's version.[58,59] Organizations such as the American College of Surgery, the American College of Physicians, the American Academy of Pediatrics, the American Academy of Ophthalmology, and the National Heart, Lung, and Blood Institute have issued guidelines in their specialty areas that practitioners often use as starting points for the development of clinical pathways with specific parameters in the delivery of health care. Data collection takes place on an ongoing basis in order to determine if the reason for any variation from the clinical pathways is attributable to patient, clinician, system, or community.

Electronic alerts and reminders are evolving as the newest way to enhance health care delivery. Frequently, they arise from internal protocols or logic within a computer program that is tied to a pharmaceutical, radiology, or laboratory ordering system. When a clinician orders a contraindicated medication or test, a reminder pops up to give the clinician an opportunity to change the order. The use of similar logic may prevent doses of medications that are toxic or to which a patient is allergic, suggest alternative tests that may be more appropriate for a diagnosis, or report results that require the immediate attention of a practitioner. Because systems or unintentional human errors are responsible for most hospital errors, fail-safe systems must be designed, and electronic methods are most likely to be effective in such systems.

TOOLS

Quality can be measured and reported via a number of graphic and textual devices. Included in this section are not only many of the more popular tools for evaluating quality, but also descriptions of situations in which these tools may be most effective.

Fishbone Diagram

Scenario 1: Physicians and administrators at a local hospital were disturbed by the decline in the number of surgical procedures being performed in the operating rooms. The possible reasons for the decline in the number of surgical procedures are listed on a fishbone diagram.

Also known as Ishikawa or cause-and-effect diagrams,[60] fishbone diagrams delineate and organize the possible causes of an event noted by the organization. The event is placed at the end of an arrow; the possible causes, grouped by similarity, are spines coming out of the arrow.

The performance improvement team at this hospital brainstormed about possible causes of the decline in the number of surgical procedures (Figure 22–1). They attributed one source of the decline to delays in performing the procedures. Perioperative services, the group in charge of the operating rooms, postulated that many surgical procedures were delayed because of the lack of operating rooms. The surgeons complained that missing equipment from the central supply organization often forced them to cancel surgery or to postpone their start times. The perioperative nursing staff requested an increase in nursing staff, indicating that the extra nurses could facilitate flow and, thus, decrease the number of delays. The quality management organization analyzed operating room delays for the month of May.

Pareto Analysis

The Pareto principle is defined as the separation of the "vital few" issues that contribute to a problem from the less important issues.[61] To measure the impact of these "vital few," a chart that illustrates the frequency of the problems is often helpful. For example, to assess the reasons for operating room delays in the month of May, a first step may be to formulate a Pareto chart listing the reasons and the measured frequencies for each reason (Table 22–1).

This does not, however, show the entire picture. More valuable may be the number of days delayed in addition to the reason for the delay (Table 22–2).

The assumptions drawn from the first Pareto analysis in Table 22–1 differ from

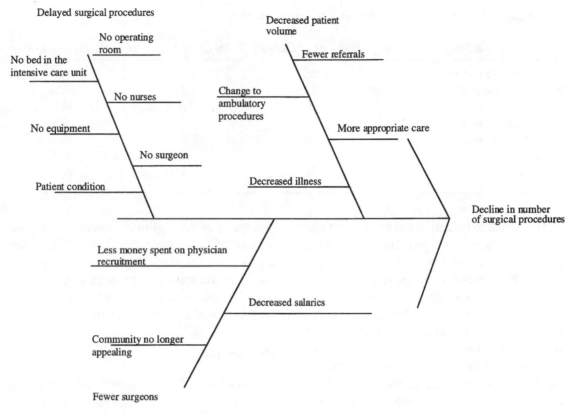

Figure 22–1 Fishbone Diagram

those drawn from Table 22–2, but in each, the principal causes for delay are the lack of operating rooms and the lack of intensive care beds. The lack of equipment, although vociferously noted by the physicians, results in minimal disruption to the operating room schedule, and the lack of nurses ranks only fourth out of the six reasons examined. Interestingly, the lack of a surgeon, never mentioned by those who used the operating rooms

Table 22–1 Reasons for Operating Room Delays in May

Reason	Number of Cases	Percent of Delay
No operating room	15	31%
No bed in the intensive care unit	12	25%
No nursing staff	5	10%
Patient condition	7	15%
Surgeon not available	3	6%
Equipment not available	6	13%
TOTAL	48	100%

Table 22–2 Reasons for Operating Room Delays in May

Reason	Number of Cases	Total Days Delayed	Percent of Delay
No operating room	15	20	21%
No bed in the intensive care unit	12	27	28%
No nursing staff	5	15	16%
Patient condition	7	9	9%
Surgeon not available	3	18	19%
Equipment not available	6	6	6%
TOTAL	48	95	100%

and assumed to be a minimal cause even after the initial Pareto analysis, accounted for 19 percent of the number of days that surgery was delayed; this percentage ranked it a close third in importance. In this scenario, the lack of intensive care beds accounted for almost one-third of the operating room delays. If the frequencies measured for a 3- to 6-month period mirrored those frequencies found during the month of May, the hospital may benefit from enlarging the intensive care unit. Further analysis shows that enlarging the intensive care unit may not be necessary, however.

A third Pareto chart shows the usage of the intensive care unit by days of the week (Table 22–3). Changing the way in which the operating rooms are utilized may solve the problem of intensive care bed utilization. That same change in utilization may benefit the second highest cause of operating room delays, the lack of an operating room. Pareto analysis is useful to separate fact from assumption. By actually measuring frequencies, the important causes of a problem can be quantified.

Histograms

Scenario 2: A practice guideline with recommendations for the treatment of patients who had hip replacements was put into place at a regional health care system. Several hospitals had participated in the development of the guideline and were expected to follow the recommendations. When the guideline was

Table 22–3 Usage of the Intensive Care Unit (ICU)

Day of Week	Operations	ICU Beds Available	ICU Beds Needed	Overutilization	Percentage Problem
Sunday	0	10	0	0	0
Monday	35	10	10	0	0
Tuesday	50	8	15	7	41
Wednesday	52	6	15	9	53
Thursday	23	8	9	1	6
Friday	18	10	1	0	0
Saturday	3	10	0	0	0

evaluated 6 months later, the following results had been measured.

- Prehospitalization evaluation and rehabilitation training
- Use of perioperative antibiotics
- Postoperative rehabilitation beginning within 24 hours
- Discharge in 5 or fewer days

The results were then compared among hospitals. Histograms were used to illustrate the comparison (Figure 22–2).

A histogram is a graphic representation of frequency and/or distribution. Histograms can show patterns of reproducibility, distribution of events in periods of time or locations, or frequency of occurrences at different points in time or location. The data from histograms provide another way to capture the vital few contributing causes to a result.

The histogram clearly may show that initiating rehabilitation within 24 hours is corre-

lated with a short length of stay. Any correlations, of course, would require further testing before any firm conclusion could be drawn.

Scenario 3: Clinical users of a laboratory complain about the length of time needed to get laboratory results returned. The measured distribution is shown in Figure 22–3 in a scatter chart, a type of histogram that represents discrete events plotted against results and time.

The same data can be shown with a traditional bar chart histogram (Figure 22–4), but the impression is different. The user gains more information from a display of the discrete points than from a bar chart.

Control Chart

Scenario 3, continued: After the data were measured and the variability of time to results was shown,

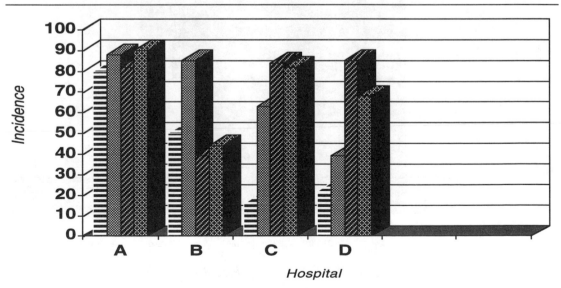

Figure 22–2 Histogram

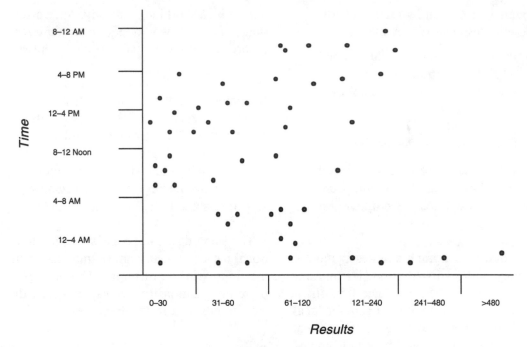

Figure 22–3 Scatter Chart

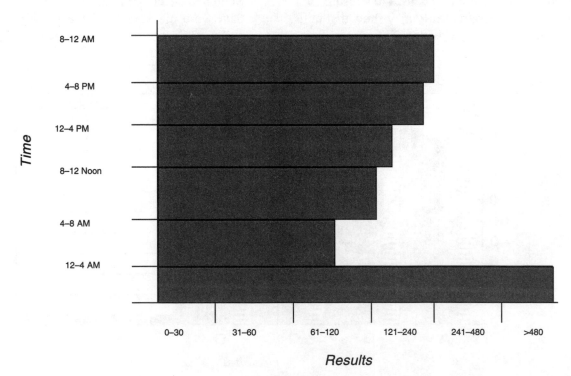

Figure 22–4 Bar Chart

the laboratory decided to set parameters for results turnaround time that did not vary by the hour of the day. The parameters that were set were 15 minutes for the minimum and 45 minutes for the maximum. After a month, the results were evaluated with the help of a control chart.

A control chart is a graphic representation of deviation and statistical significance when measuring a process. Realizing that inherent deviation occurs, the designers of a process must set goals to delineate when deviation is acceptable and when it is not. A control chart captures that deviation pictorially.

The control chart in Figure 22–5 shows that for the laboratory results reported during that time, only 3 of 14 fell outside the parameters set by the laboratory, and one of those was faster than the times allowed.

Flowchart

Scenario 4: An ambulatory care clinic determined that patients were waiting for up to 2 hours before seeing a physician. In order to determine where the delay was occurring, the clinic personnel developed a flowchart of the process of registration.

A flowchart is a representation of the steps in a process. Ovals represent beginnings and endings; diamonds represent decision points. Rectangles indicate the other events. The persons mapping the process can make the flowchart as detailed as they choose.

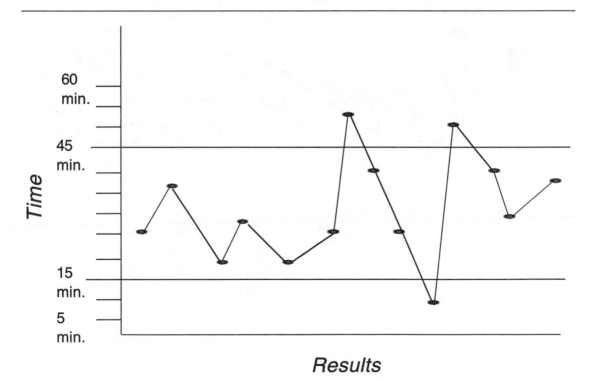

Figure 22–5 Control Chart

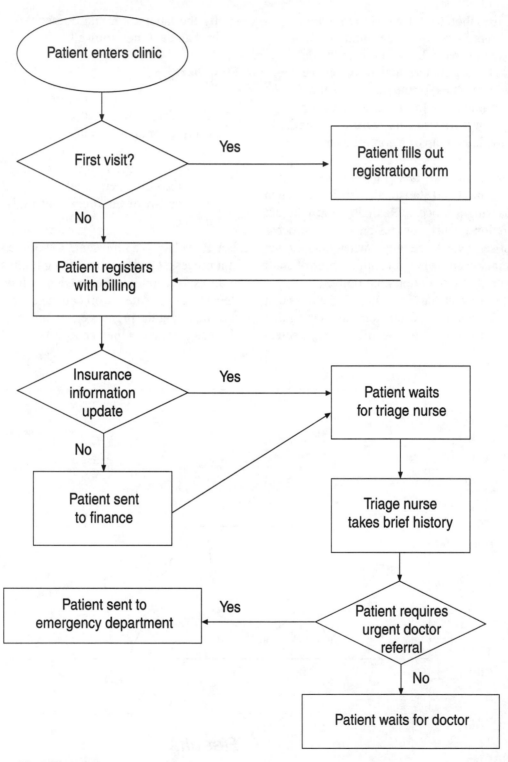

Figure 22–6 Flowchart

Evaluating the registration process as shown in Figure 22–6, it is evident that a group of patients are being registered, and thus consuming the registrar's time, who are seen in the clinic but instead are being referred to the emergency department. Thus, the clinic personnel need to devise a new process so that those individuals who need urgent care are triaged to the emergency department much earlier in the process.

Incident Reports

Many facilities use incident reports to manage risk, but these reports are also valuable quality tools. Not only do they highlight where a system has broken down, but "tracked and trended," they can indicate areas where there is an opportunity for improvement. Control charts are an effective adjunct to show patterns of incidents.

CONCLUSION

The difficulty for most organizations, when defining quality, is where to begin. Not only is it important to define the type of quality that an organization or a group within the organization is trying to achieve, but also it is important to enumerate the specific goals. Service quality, for example, may be stratified into internal and external customers; the goals for each vary tremendously. Clinical quality may be divided at the points along the continuum of care; the goals to achieve in outpatient vs. inpatient care, or short-term vs. long-term care, are quite different. What defines quality, however, is that continual effort to improve the most recent results—to set the bar higher each time it is achieved, to encompass a wider circle each time the net is cast, and to delve deeper each time a process is analyzed.

NOTES

1. A. Donabedian, "The End Results of Health Care: Ernest Codman's Contribution to Quality Assessment and Beyond," *The Milbank Quarterly* 67 (1989): 233–256 (quoting E.A. Codman, *A Study in Hospital Efficiency: As Demonstrated by the Case Report of the First Five Years of a Private Hospital* [Boston: Thomas Todd, 1916]).

2. History of the Joint Commission is found at http://www.jcaho.org/about_jc/mh_hist.htm, the Web site for the Joint Commission on Accreditation of Healthcare Organizations.

3. W.E. Deming, *Out of the Crisis* (Cambridge, MA: Massachusetts Institute of Technology, Center for Advanced Engineering Study, 1986).

4. Information about W.E. Deming can be found at http//www-caes.mit.edu.html and http//www.lii.net/deming.html

5. Deming, *Out of the Crisis.*

6. J. Butman and J. Roessner, Foreword to the second edition to J.M. Juran, *Managerial Breakthrough* (New York: McGraw-Hill, 1988).

7. J.M. Juran and F.M. Gryna, eds., *Juran's Quality Control Handbook*, 4th ed. (New York: McGraw-Hill, 1988).

8. J.M. Juran, *Managerial Breakthrough*, 2d ed. (New York: McGraw-Hill, 1995).

9. Ibid., 47–48.

10. Juran and Gryna, *Juran's Quality Control Handbook.*

11. Ibid.

12. A. Donabedian, "The Quality of Medical Care," *Science* 200 (1978): 856–864.

13. A. Donabedian, "The Quality of Care: How Can It Be Assessed" *Journal of the American Medical Association* 260 (1988): 1743–1748.

14. A. Donabedian, "The Seven Pillars of Quality," *Archives of Pathology and Laboratory Medicine* 114 (1990): 1115–1118.

15. D.M. Berwick et al., *Curing Health Care* (San Francisco: Jossey-Bass, 1990).

16. http://www.hcqualitycommission.gov.html; http://www.acponline.org.html

17. D. Berwick, *Return on Quality Report* (New Rochelle, NY: Corporate Research Group, Inc., 1998).

18. Ibid.

19. Berwick et al., *Curing Health Care*, 24–25.

20. J. Wennberg and A. Gittelsohn, "Small Area Variations in Health Care," *Science* 182 (1973): 1102–1108.

21. See, for example, N.P. Roos, "Hysterectomy: Variations in Rates Across Small Areas and Across Physician Practices," *American Journal of Public Health* 74, no. 4 (1984): 327–335; B.A. Barnes et al., "Report on Variation in Rates of Utilization of Surgical Services in the Commonwealth of Massachusetts," *Journal of the American Medical Association* 254, no. 3 (1985): 371–375; M.R. Chassin et al., "Variations in the Use of Medical and Surgical Services by the Medicare Population," *New England Journal of Medicine* 314 (1986): 285–290.

22. http://www.jcaho.org/*.htm

23. The Joint Commission's *Accreditation Manual for Hospitals* and its Web site are important references for anyone wishing to understand more about the accreditation process.

24. http://www.jcaho.org/about_jc/mh_hist.htm

25. http://www.ncqa.org/*.htm

26. Ibid.

27. http://www.hcfa.gov

28. B.R. Furrow et al., *Health Law*, 2d ed. (St. Paul, MN: West Publishing Co., 1991), 767 (quoting T. Jost, "Administrative Law Issues Involving the Medicare Utilization and Quality Control Peer Review Organization (PRO) Program: Analysis and Recommendations," 50 *Ohio St. L.J.* 1 [1989]).

29. http://www.hcfa.gov

30. D.L. Frankenfield et al., "Quality Improvement Activity Directed at the National Level: Examples from the Health Care Financing Administration," *Quality Management in Health Care* 5, no. 4 (1977): 12–18.

31. Furrow, *Health Law*, 2d ed., 628-629.

32. 42 U.S.C. § 1395dd.

33. 42 U.S.C. §§ 2000 et seq.

34. 42 U.S.C. 12131 et seq.; 42 U.S.C. 12181 et seq.

35. 42 U.S.C. § 1320a-7b.

36. 42 U.S.C. §§ 11101 et seq.

37. R.E. Oshel et al. "Use of National Practitioner Data Bank Disclosure Information for Decision Making," *Quality Management in Health Care* 5, no. 4 (1997): 34–42.

38. Ibid., 35.

39. Ibid.

40. Ibid., 42.

41. Ibid., 41.

42. T.A. Hatzell et al., "Improvement Strategy for Local Health Departments," *Quality Management in Health Care* 4, no. 3 (1996):79–86.

43. For example, Pennsylvania analyzes all hospital discharges using Medisgroup evaluations and publishes periodic comparisons of specific diagnoses or procedures. New York collects cardiac surgery data at the state level and publishes outcomes and complications of specific cardiac surgical procedures. Massachusetts collected data for a period of time, but no longer requires hospitals to submit data because of the cost issues.

44. 21 U.S.C. § 301 et seq.

45. The Occupational Safety and Health Administration maintains a Web site at http://www.osha.gov where all of these documents can be ordered.

46. The Web site for the Nuclear Regulatory Commission can be found at http://www.nrc.gov. Information about environmental safety can also be found in the *Accreditation Manual for Hospitals* published annually by the Joint Commission on Accreditation of Healthcare Organizations.

47. R.C. Camp, *Benchmarking: The Search for Industry Best Practices That Lead to Superior Performance* (Milwaukee, WI: Quality Press, 1989), 6–7.

48. Ibid.

49. Ibid.

50. L.I. Iezzoni, "The Risks of Risk Adjustment," *Journal of the American Medical Association* 278 (1997): 1600–1607.

51. Ibid., 1600.

52. Ibid.

53. Ibid., 1605.

54. Ibid., 1606.

55. Ibid., 1602.

56. I. McDowell and C. Newell, *Measuring Health*, 2d ed. (London: Oxford University Press, 1996).

57. D.L. Carmichael, "Developing a Joint Office Strategic Planning Between a Medical School and Teaching Hospital," American Association of Medical Colleges presentation, April 1997.

58. AHCPR was formed in 1989 as a part of the Department of Health and Human Services to improve access to care and quality of care, and to reduce costs.

The focus of the agency is to encourage research that supports these endeavors.

59. http://www.ahcpr.gov.html

60. Juran and Gryna, *Juran's Quality Control Handbook*, 4th ed., 22.38.

61. Ibid., 6.20.

MARY REICH COOPER, MD, JD, has been in the field of quality management since 1990. She has been at The New York Hospital for the past 3 years and was named the Vice President for Patient Care Evaluation, encompassing quality, utilization, and risk management, when New York–Cornell merged with Columbia–Presbyterian Hospital in January 1998. After graduating from Temple University School of Medicine and practicing Internal Medicine for 9 years in Philadelphia, she completed a degree in health law at Pace University.

Chapter 23

The Management of Nursing Services

Marjorie Beyers

The purpose of nursing administration is to design, manage, and facilitate patient care. Nurses in leadership positions work collaboratively with all types of health professionals to provide patient care. The professional base for their work is the clinical practice of nursing devoted to patient assessment, care planning and implementation, and evaluation of care for individuals, groups of patients, and communities. Nurses in executive practice create the environment and develop the resources necessary for quality patient care, partly by contributing to executive decision making and innovations in care delivery. Nurses provide a unique clinical perspective to policy and strategic planning in health care organizations, represent the clinical services provided by the organization in the community served, and connect the local nursing practice with the broader nursing community to keep the nursing practice up to date with developments in the field.

Roles and functions of nurses in executive practice are complex. Having originated in hospital organizations, the science of nursing administration evolved in response to the need to manage the nursing resource and to develop coordinated care delivery processes. An applied science, nursing administration includes components of clinical nursing care

delivery, collaborative practices, and management theories and concepts. The nursing clinical care components are grounded in a strong philosophy and value system of caring and compassion, critical thinking, and coordination of care. Nurses provide the "intangibles" in patient care, those aspects of their function that are difficult to define and measure in terms of resources, cost, and outcomes, but are notable in the quality in health care delivery. Nurses in executive practice interpret nursing care, providing a structure and parameters for nursing care and for the resources needed to meet patient requirements for care.

THE EVOLVING PRACTICE OF NURSE-EXECUTIVES

Just as health care delivery is changing, nursing administration practice is changing. Evidence of the change is found in the new titles and new roles of nurse-executives. Although the term *nursing service administration* remains in use in academia and in the literature, the titles used in practice settings are changing. Corporate titles, such as vice president for nursing or patient services, or clinical titles, such as chief nurse, are more commonly used in today's practice. Titles for nurse-managers are also changing. Managers are now directors of nursing, or directors of patient care services, or clinical coordinators. Even though the titles are changing, nurses in executive practice continue to manage clinical services. For clarity, the term *nurse in executive practice* is used to refer to nurse leaders in management and clinical leadership positions. The term *patient care delivery* is used to refer to the nursing role and function in management.

Over time, nursing administration has become synonymous with hospitals, a reasonable association because, until recently, hospitals have employed two-thirds of the nation's nurses. The roots of nursing practice lie in the work of Florence Nightingale, who established the elegance of systematic organization for patient care, with attention to the physical and emotional environment and to data-based decision making. The science of nursing administration as known today is grounded in a study conducted by Herman Finer and supported by the Kellogg Foundation to find ways to improve nursing services in hospitals.[1] The findings indicated a need for nursing administration in the complex hospital environment and led to demonstration projects with the continued support of the Kellogg Foundation. These projects identified the theories, concepts, and principles of nursing administration practice and established the graduate curricula to prepare nurses for this specialized practice.

These demonstration projects in the development and application of nursing administration provided the field with models and information to structure nursing services. The models included key aspects of the practice that continue today:

- creating the environment for practice
- establishing and ensuring the standards of nursing care delivery

- coordinating patient care with inputs from all types of health professionals
- selecting and developing the nursing workforce
- evaluating and planning the work of nursing to meet patient requirements for care
- staffing
- evaluating and developing relationships within and external to the hospital services

Influenced by the management theories of the time, nursing services became well organized, and the nursing care unit became the focus for care delivery. In the course of time, clinical support services, including nursing staff development and quality management, were developed. The practice was stabilized, with fairly homogeneous definitions and applications of nurse administration practice in hospital settings.

Twenty years later, the growth of nursing professionalism is evident in the Magnet Hospital Study, conducted under the auspices of the American Academy of Nursing.[2] In this study, magnet hospitals were found to have common characteristics that drew and retained staff nurses. These characteristics included the visibility and accessibility of nurse leaders at every level, open communications on matters that affect patient care and the quality of work life, participatory management, qualified nurse-managers, leaders who could be respected by staff, emphasis on quality patient care, and administrative support. In the 20-year period between studies, nursing practice clearly has developed new dimensions that emphasize administrative leadership in enduring resources and support for professional nursing practice. The growth of nursing professionalism can be attributed to the maturing of the profession; the increasing numbers of nurses educated in baccalaureate, master's, and doctoral programs; and the development of the science of nursing through research and scholarly activities.

Some significant developments in nursing services that have withstood the passage of time and change are shared governance models designed to facilitate nurse participation in improving patient care, the development of quality assurance methods to engage nurses in the evaluation of patient care quality, and research-based practice. Collaboration among health care professionals also increased in this period of time, particularly on the psychiatry, cardiology, rehabilitation, and oncology services. In these collaborative models, the development and implementation of joint care planning and evaluation methods benefited patients through the combined and coordinated inputs of the broad-based expertise that the interdisciplinary teams provided. Nurses continued to be the coordinators of care, the 24-hour service providers, and the evaluators of the effectiveness of the patient care experience. Another significant development commensurate with the development of specialties was the design of the clinical specialist function in nursing. Prepared in master's programs, clinical specialists added a new depth of expertise to the clinical care delivery. Serving as direct care providers, as innovators and developers of new care delivery methods, and as clinical support and mentors for staff nurses, these nurses provided knowledge and experience that supported the continued professional development of staff nurses.

In both the Finer and the Magnet Hospital studies, staff nurses reported fairly consistent values. They considered important the role of the top nurse-executive; decentralization of decision making for patient care; opportunities to participate in professional activities and development through committees, task forces, and collaborative initiatives; and a positive relationship with nursing schools and professional nursing groups. Staffing, salaries, benefits, and the quality of work life were important, but less so than quality patient care. These nurses identified strongly with the hospitals in which they practiced and valued the reputation of the hospital for quality patient care as part of their own professional identity. The Magnet Hospital Study findings included reports that other departments in the hospital had "mixed feelings" about nursing, related to perceptions that nurses received considerable attention within the organization. These feelings reflect behaviors within the hierarchical structure of hospitals at the time, as well as the essential contribution of nursing to patient care.

Another study that provides a "snapshot" view of the evolution of nursing's executive practice is the VHA, Inc., study of the impact of organizational redesign, conducted in 1993, 10 years after the Magnet Hospital Study.[3] During the intervening time, management practices had been changing, and the seeds of redesign and restructuring had been growing not only in health care organizations, but also in business and industry worldwide. The VHA study of redesign was conducted first in 1993 and repeated in 1995. Findings indicated that in 1993, the redesign was being contemplated and discussed. In 1995, redesign and restructuring were being implemented. As stated in the 1995 study, organizational change had become a real movement, with the expansion of the operational role of nurse-executives and the introduction of restructuring initiatives in 85 percent of the reporting hospitals. Core features of redesign reported in the survey were, in order of highest frequency: integration across the department; use of critical pathways, multiskilled workers; managing the restructuring; initiating patient-focused care, case management; combining units; and, in slightly more than

25 percent of the respondents, physical changes in the patient care settings.

Concurrent with the VHA studies, another national effort was under way, an effort that significantly changed perceptions about hospital nursing and patient care. Strengthening Hospital Nursing: A Program To Improve Patient Care, funded by the Robert Wood Johnson Foundation and the Pew Charitable Trusts, engaged 20 grantees in a 5-year project to demonstrate change.[4] Prior to 1990, major changes in nursing services took place through careful planning, pilot testing, and extensive preparation of the staff. Health care professionals, including nurses, were being plummeted at this time into rapid and significant change with the onset of health care reform, threats of declines in the already scarce resources for patient care, and significant changes in the utilization of hospitals. This situation provided a fertile field for the project to stimulate change. In the first round of grant selection, 80 planning grants were approved. Of these 80, 20 were selected for the long-term demonstration. Even though the remaining 60 were not selected, many of these planning initiatives were fully implemented. The Strengthening Hospital Nursing project was atypical in many respects. First, the grantees had developed insights about the need to change as a result of the crush of health care reform. Second, the program incorporated broad-based education on change for interdisciplinary leadership teams from the participating health care entities, which included hospitals and health care systems.

One of the most significant discoveries from this grant program was that real and long-standing change commensurate with the social and political environment and the rapidly developing health care technology required systems thinking. In addition, because nurses in executive practice were leaders of substantial change in health care delivery, the determination was made to change the focus of the program from nursing to patient care services. The change was helpful in beginning to address the mixed feelings of hospital employees about nurses. Changing mindsets from a focus on departments and specialized functions to the unified patient focus on care was key in this change.

The bureaucracy and notions of power and control continue to be conflictual. For example, the world tends to view and measure change in the role and functions of nurse-executives by titles, that is, how many have become chief executive officers or chief operations officers and how many are on the board of directors. The fact is, the focus on patient care transcends this traditional view of hierarchy to a vision of health care that involves patients and families in a seamless continuity of care that promotes health. The redesign effort focused on open communication and decision making.

Information and experiences shared during the project revealed the diversity in health care delivery. The geographic and community variations were clear. The commonly shared themes of providing patient-focused care; breaking down traditional organizational barriers, both internal and external, in hospitals; and developing new mindsets about care delivery were also clear. One of the significant impacts of this grant program was the broadening of the field of change. Systems thinking affected not only nurses, but also others in the health care environment. Using Senge's concept of leverage, the systems thinking moved the action from the "symptom" to the "system" analysis.[5] What had been considered a major change in nursing proved, in some cases, to be treating the symptom rather than the system. Changing the title of nurse-executives to patient care executives is evidence of this shift in thinking. The nurse-executive is responsible for the structure of the patient care delivery, which includes care provided by nurses and care provided by interdisciplinary teams and co-workers from all departments. Improvements in the way that health care professionals work together for patient care requires the leverage of the system. Actions are different when teams are aware of the way in which all the parts fit and work together. Redundancies and gaps become evident. Systems thinking allows the analysis of work processes and relationships with the goal of simplifying and streamlining the work across departments and beyond traditional boundaries to improve patient care.

Systems theory has been only one of the change engines in health care. Another prominent change engine has been total quality management, the methodologies of which provided substance for the work of interdisciplinary teams. Both systems and total quality management theories emphasize breaking down barriers and separations between and among departments and practice areas in health care. Both focus on identifying the desired future and working on plans to achieve the future, and both engage people from all aspects of health care delivery to develop a new culture of interactive participation for the greater good of the patient. Systems thinking provides a perspective of organizational behavior and relationships. Total quality management provides the tools, resources, and methods for interactions. It can be safely posited that the change is a work in progress.

Some scholars believe that the current changes in nursing and health care are not new, but rather a return to the "natural order" of patient care delivery. From a nursing perspective, the key relationships in health care delivery are the nurse–patient and nurse–physician relationships, and the collaboration among patients, physicians, and nurses in patient care.[6]

Thirty-five years ago, people were admitted to the hospital to receive all necessary services. In 1999 and beyond, maturing technology and educated patients allow mobilization of care services to settings more convenient to the patients. The next phases in the evolution of nursing executive practice exemplify this perspective of patient care. Early in this century, nurses were practicing in public health, in communities, in schools, churches, and businesses. They worked with patients and families in their homes. As patients began to utilize hospitals, nurses gravitated to the hospital setting. Now nurses are gravitating to new sites in the community because that is where the patients are. The infrastructure for nursing administration has shifted away from the hospital.

Nursing administration practice embodies the variations and complexity of diverse health care organizations and management. Health care organizations have absorbed management practices and theories from every decade in this century to create unique approaches. In addition, many of the current nursing management structures reflect some aspects of reorganization, restructuring, revamping and reconfiguration of health care. A continuum might be drawn from the most self-contained nursing department to the most organized patient care function.[7] Examples of practice at any point on this continuum are reality in different health care settings throughout the United States.

In summary, the science of nursing administration is now a study of change. Grounded in the traditional hospital structure, the science incorporates service and resource design, development, and use of resources for patient care delivery to create an environment for quality patient care and quality management. The changes taking place in nursing services are not well documented, however. Little attention has been given to nursing's infrastructure for several decades. Most of the studies on nursing have focused on the numbers of nurses, their educational preparation, participation in the workforce, turnover and vacancy rates, and on career mobility. Issues of resource evaluation and management have concentrated on patient classification systems, workload measurement, quality assurance, and efforts to match scarce resources to patient requirements for care. This emphasis is evident in the numbers of studies on nursing that relate to the cost and outcomes of nursing care; the configuration of the nursing workforce; and satisfaction studies of nurses, physicians, and patients. Few, if any, of these studies have related what happens in nursing care delivery to the nursing leadership. The best source of information about the changes in nursing service is found in the documentation of the previously described Strengthening Hospital Nursing program.

ORGANIZATION OF NURSING/ PATIENT CARE SERVICES

Every health care organization has a unique blend of traditional, new, and evolving nursing practices. Even though each organization is unique in its application of nursing models and practices, all share a common goal to improve relationships, work flow, and systems for care delivery on the pathways toward creating health care for healthy communities.

The Nursing Department/Division

Nursing may be structured as a nursing department, division, or service within the organization. In this model, it relates at a departmental level for coordination of resources, planning, and policy making. The nursing staff provides services through patient care delivery units, such as the inpatient nursing units, ambulatory care, outpatient, or emer-gency services. A unit nurse-manager (traditionally, the head nurse) is accountable for care delivery. Staff nurses are assigned to a unit or service, where they are assigned to patients. In ambulatory care settings, they may function as case managers. Their role includes assessing patients, developing care plans with inputs from other health care professionals (e.g., physicians, pharmacists), and planning continuity of care with others. Policies, procedures, rules, and job descriptions facilitate care coordination. Nurses, with 24-hour accountability, coordinate the care, making sure that all care is provided according to plan. Nurses provide patient counseling and education, help patients cope with their disease or illness, and prepare them for self-care following discharge. Preparation for patient discharge involves ensuring that the patient has the appropriate information, referrals, equipment, and supplies for care.

In this structure, the nurse-executive represents nursing in almost every executive and management arena—administration, physicians, and community leaders. At the unit level, nurse-managers and staff nurses relate mainly with physicians, working with the diagnosis and treatment plan, and others who provide care on the unit. Relationships with other care entities take place primarily on paper through written discharge plans and referrals. The staff nurses are supported in their functions by the nursing department resources, including clinical education (orientation, in-service, and staff development). Departmentwide support leaders, working with the unit manager and staff nurses, manage care quality. In some settings, clinical specialists or case managers with advanced training assist with care planning and implementation, collaborate with physicians in patient care, and mentor staff nurses. These nurses also assist with quality management and improvement initiatives.

The management structure includes the chief nurse and clinical support services, such as staff development, recruitment, financial services, quality assurance, and project development. The nursing management includes leaders who manage one or more patient care units, which are designated by the type of care generally provided there, such as intensive care, critical care, medical–surgical, pediatric, obstetric, or psychiatric. Hospitals with a sufficient volume of patients who need a particular type of care may have specialized units, for example, neurology, oncology, cardiac/respiratory, and orthopedics. Emergency services, clinics, operating room services, and outpatient services are part of the nursing department. Smaller hospitals may group patients with similar needs across the specialization. One of the issues in downsizing is categorizing patient care to place patients with similar care needs together to facilitate effective resource organization and utilization.

The Patient Care Department/Division

The patient care organization may be a department/division, or it may be designated as a functional area in the organization.[8] Patient care executives in such an area are responsible for the patient care, including clinical resources and the quality of nursing care. They manage clinical negotiations, business plans and relationships, and in some cases, the hotel-type services. Usually, the patient care model involves elimination of departments, downsizing of the management staff (often with reductions in an entire layer of management), and decentralization of decision making to the patient care level. With fewer departments and fewer executives and managers, members of the patient care staff, including the nursing staff, are empowered to make decisions, and to design and coordinate

patient care services at all levels in the organization. The patient care executive has a global perspective of patient care delivery and uses collaborative practice teams, integrated management councils and structures, and coordinated, participative planning for patient care improvements across areas of expertise. The management models and structures, such as patient classification, and the nursing components of care in this model are usually the same or very similar to the nursing care structures in the nursing department models. Likewise, the executives and managers relate to community leaders and either manage or align services with patient services provided in the home, in long-term care facilities, and in the community.

Nurses in the patient care models have new functions. The changes are not strictly "additive," but incorporate accountability for the quality of patient care, management of the reimbursement and financial aspects of different services (e.g., pharmacy, social work, laboratory), as well as the design and implementation of innovations and adaptations in care. In smaller hospitals or care services, the quality management programs often require outreach to develop peer clinical groups. For example, there may be only one or two social workers, who depend on peers from other settings to participate in practice review and evaluation. The trend toward integration in patient care departments tends to move negotiation for collaboration and coordination from the level of department head to the level of interdisciplinary teams. The executives work on the vision, the strategies, and the resources to facilitate the patient care. In effective patient care models, the nurse-executive is not simply managing more departments, but is integrating the care delivery processes around the patient requirements for care (Figure 23–1). A comparison of nursing department and patient care focus for selected nurs-

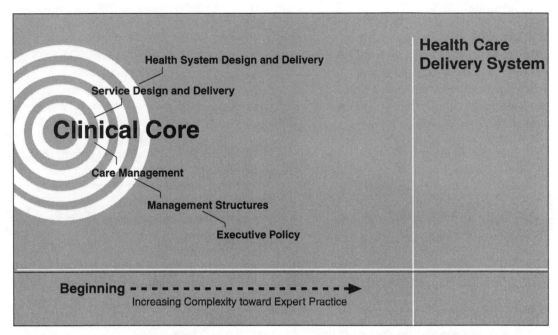

Figure 23–1 Role of Nurses in Executive Practice. Courtesy of American Organization of Nurse Executives, Chicago, Illinois.

ing executive functions illustrates the changed focus of the nurse-executive's role and functions (Exhibit 23–1).

CHANGING HEALTH CARE DELIVERY METHODS

Change to adapt these basic frameworks for patient care delivery to new care delivery methods is a work in progress. Decreased dependency on facilities and on bureaucratic structures allows thinking about care processes in new ways. Initial stages of change are associated with innovations that are unique and sometimes simultaneous in the field. Eventually, there will again be order—a new order. Anecdotes and word of mouth tend to spread news of change in excess of actual occurrences, however. A recent study completed in New Jersey revealed that although there were perceptions of grand

change throughout the state, the majority of respondents had not made significant changes in their nursing departments.[9] The study disproved the widespread belief that change was not only eminent, but accomplished.

Interviews with selected nurse-executives throughout the United States who had been in their positions for 5 to 8 years were replete with stories of accepting expanded accountability and increasingly complex relationships within and external to the hospitals, meeting challenges to leadership to help staff adapt to new ways of work, and learning about new rules, regulations, and the intimate details of the various clinical practices among health care professionals vicariously.[10] These interviews confirmed the VHA study finding that nurses are natural leaders of change in organizations because many of the participative nursing management methods, such as shared governance, are compatible with the

Exhibit 23–1 Comparison of Nursing Department and Patient Care Focus for Selected Nurse Executive Functions

Traditional Nursing Department	Emerging Patient Care Focus
• Participate in executive management	• Participate in executive management
• Manage the nursing department/service	• Manage patient care services
• Develop and implement nurse staffing	• Develop and implement patient care staffing
• Manage nursing care quality	• Continuously improve patient care quality
• Create the environment for nursing care	• Create the environment for patient care
• Manage nursing resources	• Manage patient care resources
• Relate to external groups for discharge planning	• Participate in continuous care planning
• Develop and implement the nursing budget	• Develop and implement patient services budget
• Monitor and manage staffing	• Monitor and manage care resources
• Lead nurse-managers of care units	• Lead collaborative practice groups
• Introduce change incrementally	• Lead immediate and lasting change
• Facilitate staff nurse development	• Facilitate patient care staff development

Courtesy of American Organization of Nurse Executives, Chicago, Illinois.

new approaches. These models are just as attractive and useful for interdisciplinary teams as they are for nurses. Health care professionals share a desire to be engaged in decisions affecting patient care. It is also clear that the nursing expertise in the coordination of care facilitates the important work of improving patient care, of redesigning work processes, and in making the transition from "nursing care" to "patient care" meaningful in hospitals and health care systems. Collaboration is gained, efficiency is gained, but vigilance and attention to the quality parameters in pracice must be developed in concert with the collaborative practice.

The following models illustrate the continued and gradual evolution of patient care delivery from the facility-dependent organizational structure in which nursing departments are self-contained to the more virtual, integrated models for patient care delivery in which staff work in responsive, integrated

decision-making groups to provide care in a structure that supports staff with information systems; analysis and quality improvement support; and long-range, visionary planning and development. These changes fit well into nursing's framework of nursing leadership, clinical support services, and focus on patients.

Service Line Models

The introduction of service line models significantly changes the structure and the interaction within health care organizations. Typical of service line models is the formation of interdisciplinary teams that plan and implement patient care. Service lines are structured around the patient care experience, organized around patient care requirements for all phases of the illness or disease. Usually, service lines include acute, outpatient, and ambulatory care services. Many organizations have established a matrix structure to support service lines. In the matrix structure, the departments such as pharmacy, nursing, laboratory, and physical therapy, and clinical information that serve the mainstream functions cut across all service lines. In some settings, designated staff provide support services for specific service lines; in other settings, all staff provide services across all lines. Services such as operating room, emergency, and clinic services support all the service lines. Nurse leaders and staff function within a service line, reporting to the nursing chief in matters of quality, professional standards, and professional development. In some service lines, the management of nursing units is traditional, but nurses and other health care professionals usually report to both the service line manager and the chief of nursing.

Positive aspects of the service line model include attention to the requirements of patients in selected population groups, usually according to clinical categories. The patient care sequences and planning in the service line are designed to meet the special needs of these patient populations throughout the continuum of care, across settings. Resource allocation is aligned with the patient populations served. Service lines may have a planned progression for patient care, as in step-down patient care units to move patients from critical care to less intensive care. Typically, the staff includes advanced practice nurses and/or clinical nurse specialists who provide direct patient care, support staff development, and conduct special projects.

Service line models have many features in common with other models, but differ in the organization of staff around services. Despite the great many variations in service line structures, the chief nurse's staff accountabilities for nursing practice generally include standards and policies for overall staffing, recruitment, staff development and

quality management, counseling, and coaching. The service line leaders are usually responsible for the business plan, budget, standards of care, and staffing. Service lines that incorporate the inpatient unit, the outpatient services, and home care in the service configuration may be considered precursors of integrated clinical care delivery.

Patient-Focused Care

The guiding principles for the patient-focused care model have been and are being applied in diverse ways. In this patient care–driven model, services are structured and shaped according to patient need. Categories of patients are defined and patients with similar needs identified to capitalize on the operating efficiencies of tailoring services for them. Some of the redesign initiatives associated with patient-focused care are "cross-training" staff to perform tasks so that one person can provide more comprehensive care for patients, thus decreasing the number of staff–patient interactions required. In later versions of the patient-focused care models, services are tailored for patient population groups across the continuum of care.[11] For example, a given patient may use oncology services throughout the diagnosis, treatment, and care toward recovery or palliative care. Both inpatients and outpatients may use the resources of a specialized unit during varying phases of illness and over time. Information about work flow patterns and about the educational level and training required for patient care drive the development of the model. The most frequently performed activities for a given patient population form the work focus for the staff. Interdisciplinary teams, trained for specified tasks, make the work more efficient. Locating equipment and supplies close to or in the unit facilitates economies of time.

Self-contained patient-focused care units may include the admitting, discharge, accounting, and patient follow-up functions. The patient-focused care unit is often structured as a small business, with its own budget and accounting service. Nursing services are usually decentralized, with one nurse caring for patients in a geographic designation. Patient charts are kept in or near the patient rooms, and many sites have information systems for communicating with physicians in their offices, entering orders, completing charts, and communicating with other departments. The patient care unit is the central location of services not only for nursing, but also for the most frequently performed laboratory, x-ray, and other services located on the unit. Patients must leave the unit only for more complex diagnostic and treatment services in the "regular" departments. Staffing the patient care unit resembles both the typical nursing care unit and the interdisciplinary team with a different mix to fulfill the functions of the business unit.

Total patient care models are a blend of primary nursing care models and the patient focused care models. Many of the concepts and methods of the two overlap. Current applications of total patient care models emphasize comprehensive patient care. Total patient care is compatible with the integration of care.

Organized Delivery Systems

More advanced, systemwide "global" restructuring with elements drawn from each of the existing model frameworks results in the clinical integration model. The term *organized delivery* is commonly used to define structural, business, financial, and physician integration. From the nursing perspective, clinical integration is the way to achieve the desired continuum of care. Integrating care

processes so that they are seamless and serve patient care requirements throughout the life cycle is the goal of clinical integration models. In these models, a person has a lifetime connection with the caregivers and participates in activities and initiatives for wellness, staying healthy, managing short- and long-term illnesses and diseases, and coping with life phase changes and planned and unplanned life events. The integrated care approach is holistic. In many respects, clinical integration is an advanced form of primary nursing care, which was somewhat limited by location in the hospital setting and boundaries. Emerging integrated care models give patients and caregivers access to health care resources of all types to improve the continuity of care.

Clinical Integration of Care

The primary nursing care model paved the way to integrated patient care by formalizing the concepts and tools now employed in integrated care. Not only did the primary nursing care model empower staff nurses, but also it helped shift the nurse-executive role toward strategic and long-range planning foci. Some of the tools of integrated care are (1) clinical pathways or care maps, which are advanced forms of the nursing care plan; (2) case management techniques, with the typical electronic communication supports; and (3) extended interdisciplinary relationships. The effectiveness of these tools depends on the cooperation and coordination of interdisciplinary teams, as well as the involvement of the patient, family, and significant others in the care decisions and practices. It is not unusual to find models in which patients are active initiators of care. It is also not unusual to find staff nurses who, as case managers, coordinate and manage care across settings.[12]

Clinical integration for lifetime care can rest on some of the same principles. Tools and resources once thought to be "hospital"-based have proved useful in all types of care settings. Furthermore, they are not limited by the time and space dimensions of lifelong care. For example, there are clinical pathways that begin with the physician's diagnosis and end with full recovery from a long-term illness. Eventually, pro forma computer-based planning tools will replace these tools. The groundwork for the electronic communication already under development is in the pathways. The principle is to develop tools to facilitate communication and organization of the patient's diagnostic and treatment care. Finally, integrated patient care is not dependent on a facility or a location. Figure 23–2 illustrates the shift in thinking from the hospital as a location and center of patient care to the integrated focus that is not site-dependent.[13]

Integrated care does not yet meet the expectations of those who advocate clinical integration. In the business interpretations of integrated care, connections between and among the components of the delivery system—namely, acute, long-term, home, hospice, ambulatory, and alternative care—made up the integration. There has been some controversy about whether owning all components is preferable to forming agreements and affiliations to create the organized delivery system. The decreased utilization of acute care services, together with the shifts to home and ambulatory care, have partly answered the question. Two half-full hospitals in geographic proximity may as well merge—and they do. The outpatient and ambulatory care services that hospitals are now establishing throughout communities provide care convenient to patients. Hospitals have been devel-

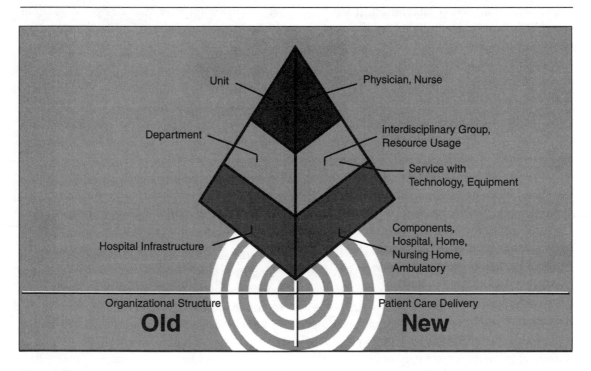

Figure 23–2 Organizational Fucus. Courtesy of American Organization of Nurse Executives, Chicago, Illinois.

oping long-term and home care services, in addition to ambulatory care services. The result is "full service" capability.

The shift of patients from hospitals to alternate sites of care occurred to some extent because of technology; as treatment became less invasive, hospitalization was no longer necessary. Part of the shift, however, is due to the relocation of patients. Only the most acutely ill patients require hospitalization. Various institutions such as nursing homes and subacute care centers can provide care during the recovery and recuperation phases of illnesses. Home care is now an option for more and more patients, as evidenced by the increase in intravenous therapy business. The renewed interest in using hospital facilities for the components of integrated care is similar to putting Humpty Dumpty back together again.

Although clinical integration can occur independent of financial integration, it has potential for improving the quality of care and reducing cost. Institution-dependent reimbursement rules and policies warrant examination for relevance. From a business perspective, outdated and underutilized facilities are expensive. Changing the care delivery is more feasible when the entire industry undergoes change. Changes in financial and facility organization have, in fact, affected nurse-executive roles by influencing the evolving patterns of executive management, just as clinical integration will continue to affect the provision of patient care services.

Horizontal and Vertical Integration

When either horizontal integration (i.e., integration of organizations of the same type) or vertical integration (i.e., integration of organizations of different types) takes place, patient care management may continue at the organizational level through one of the previously described models of hospital care. In some cases, there is a nurse-executive for two or more organizations, and the nursing structure within the organization remains similar to those described. In other cases, there is a "corporate" nurse-executive with staff responsibilities for the standards and quality of nursing care; for consultation, oversight, and development; and for evaluation of care provided in all care settings within the organized delivery system. Factors influencing the models are the geographic location, size, and scope of services in each of the organized delivery system entities; the patient populations; and the complexity of care provided.

Nurse-executives are positioned in several different places within the organized delivery system. At the broadest level, the nurse-executive functions at the infrastructure level, participating as a member of the executive management team to deal with facilities, the environment, financing issues, systems to integrate the enterprise, and design of services throughout the system. Quality management and improvement are central to all of these management functions. In some systems, the nurse-executive functions at a health system (corporate) level, where the focus of the role continues to be managing quality and improvement, designing care delivery for patient populations, and providing the economies of scope and scale inherent in systems. Some of these economies involve the development of systemwide staff education and clinical support services, processes for care, and communication tools. Nurses in executive practice also function at a service level, designing and managing care for patients from an aggregate perspective. The role closest to the patient is the care management role, in which the nurse manages care for designated groups of patients, working with physicians and interdisciplinary care teams.

The nursing role is expanding in its scope and in the settings where nursing care is delivered. Those models of nursing care most popular from 1960 to 1990 are still in use today, but they are changing to accommodate the integration of services. Developing themes in nursing and patient care are the management of care for designated patient populations; the integration of services for the continuum of care; and the more conceptual work of developing corporate services for clinical care service design, education, and development of health care professional staff and devising methods for quality improvement and total quality management. In organized health care delivery systems, the roles for nurses in executive practice include shaping a new health care culture, defining new terms to relate care processes to business processes, and developing interdisciplinary care practices and new care systems for managed care populations.

EMERGING MODELS FOR NURSING CARE DELIVERY

In addition to the various models for the organizational design of patient care, nurses are engaged in developing alternative care models to provide wellness, health promotion, and chronic care services. These models are not necessarily defined by type of setting and by scope of services, but by the type of patient population served. Although the literature and reported experience of nurses in executive practice is primarily hospital-based, nurses have been functioning and continue to function in public health settings, in nursing homes, in homes, and in other care settings. The structure in these alternative settings differs from that in hospitals in many ways. In nursing homes, for example, the care provided is along the lines of "functional care." Nursing homes now serve patients who need subacute care during their recovery from illness or surgery, as well as those who

require intensive care owing to disability or frailness. The management infrastructure also differs. In nursing homes, there is typically a director of nursing, and the ratio of registered nurses to licensed practical nurses and support staff has increased recently. Home care has more regulations than infrastructure, and the variety of services influences staffing. Home care services range from assisted living to intensive clinical care, with interdisciplinary care teams providing care.[14] The staffing matrix includes clinical nurse specialists who assess and manage patient care, staff nurses, and support staff to provide ongoing care.

Parish nursing, one of the oldest types of nursing, provides patients with health care services in their church or church-related settings. The role of the parish nurse includes health education, counseling, referrals to health care services, and support of patients and families in times of stress or trouble.[15] As a liaison with other community agencies and health care services, the parish nurse is often instrumental in obtaining new or improved services to meet patient needs. The dimension of spirituality makes parish nursing unique. The parish nurse embodies the holistic approach to patient care, with integration of mind, body, and spirit. Resources within the church community are also available to provide support and help for people in need.

Many of the concepts and practices of parish nurses are used and further developed in community-based nursing centers. In some settings, the parish nursing programs have become full-fledged nursing centers. Currently, there is a movement to define standards for parish nursing, to develop more universally similar models of parish nursing, and to establish peer review for parish nurses. Educational requirements for parish nurses have increased with the scope of services. In a recent study, it was reported that educational levels have steadily increased over the past 20 years.[16] There is an International Parish Nurse Resource Center that offers educational programs for parish nurses and a few universities have a master's concentration in parish nursing. An emerging management role exemplifies the increasing use of parish pursing in the mainstream of health care services.

Community-based nursing centers are a 1990s innovation that originated in two streams of development: (1) outreach initiatives to serve the poor and uninsured, and (2) the development of faculty practice in graduate nursing education programs. Community centers have proliferated in a variety of settings, mainly in underserved areas, such as institutions that provide care for the elderly, school health centers, and emerging nursing practices that serve designated populations. Nurse-practitioners, prepared at the graduate level and fully certified, are now functioning in direct patient care roles, with emphasis on health promotion, wellness, and provision of services for the chronically ill and the elderly. Generally, a nurse-practitioner is supported by a physician practice and is liaisoned with hospital and other care settings to provide referral sources and to ensure continuity of care. Nurse-practitioners in every state have prescriptive authority for selected medications.

NEW COMPETENCIES FOR NURSES IN EXECUTIVE PRACTICE

Recent changes in care delivery models include the movement toward stronger patient participation in care; increasingly complex care for acutely ill persons who are hospitalized; increased assessment and planning for the continuum of care, such as making the transition from acute to subacute care; and assurance that patients have the resources and access to information, emotional support, and

emergency or urgent care as they assume more responsibility for their own care following many types of outpatient procedures. The roles and functions of nurse-executives have changed concurrently and involve developing new cultures and new staffing configurations for the more "progressive" patient care, ensuring effective relationships between and among patient and caregivers within the continuum of care, reconciling outdated and often restrictive financing and regulation, and establishing patient-focused services that involve the family and others important to the patients. Each achievement toward the continuum of care creates new issues, problems, and requisites for development, which keeps the nurse-executive role in an ever-changing state.

The general definition of what nurses in executive practice do is design, facilitate, and manage patient care. Some aspects of the role are integral with the organization, but there are common elements in the role in place in every setting. The common elements in the nurse-executive role relate to direct patient care, including the following[17]:

- defining parameters and methods for care quality
- establishing the environment for care delivery
- designing the models for patient care
- establishing nurse–physician relationships around care processes and outcomes
- defining the parameters and methods for care quality
- managing the resources needed for care
- organizing and coordinating systems for care delivery
- recruiting, retaining, and developing staff
- managing the fiscal components of care resources

- establishing intra- and extraorganizational relationships for clinical and management functions
- measuring and improving the care delivery and systems that support care

Depending on the mission, the scope of services, and the placement of the patient care services, the nurse-executive role increasingly includes

- designing systems and processes for integrated care delivery
- designing systems for managed care, including care/case management
- participating in executive staff functions such as strategic planning
- developing and implementing business plans for care services
- establishing performance parameters for patient care services
- creating new cultures within care delivery environments
- working with communities for assessment and prioritization of services

Functions related to the organization inherent in the nurse-executive role include

- participating in decision making on policy and planning
- demonstrating leadership in the organization
- serving as champion for patient care resources and services
- participating in the establishment of new organizational cultures
- participating in leading and implementing change
- developing new business parameters for care services
- defining and establishing broader clinical roles for nurses
- exploring and implementing innovations to improve patient care

- evaluating and improving intraorganizational processes and work flow

These lists are not inclusive, but they contain the most prominent of the nurse-executive functions. These are the competencies necessary to meet the challenges of the day.

CHALLENGES FOR NURSES IN EXECUTIVE PRACTICE

Managing the Nursing Resource

Nurse-executives need to redefine the management measurement tools for nursing practice. Although tools such as patient classification systems that were developed decades ago have been continuously updated, they do not fit today's practice. A number of initiatives are under way to identify priorities and establish a new terminology to describe actual practice.[18] The measurement of patient care services has moved away from the specific cost accounting approaches popular 10 years ago to the analysis of data from relational databases. At the patient care and caregiver level, variance from predicted, expected, or best practices provides needed data. At the service and system level, data that provide insights into cause and effect, and systems interactions are more useful for improving care. At the organized delivery system level, data on the extent to which the processes and management methods influence the quality of practice is an important question.

The traditional methods of measuring patient requirements for care and for staffing are also less useful in today's practice. For example, when patients were hospitalized for the extensive period of time needed for recovery in the past, the nursing staff cared for patients in different phases of illness and disease. Patient classification systems differentiated patient requirements for care. In today's settings, only patients who need intensive and acute care are hospitalized. Patient classification systems based on long patient stays do not always account for the patient with the 23-hour admission, the patient who uses hospital services for treatment as an outpatient, or the patient who remains only briefly on the hospital unit. Measuring the workload for nurses who care for patients across settings and those who work with interdisciplinary teams is yet another challenge. Staffing so that qualified nurses are with patients at the right time for the right care is a continued challenge in both traditional and emerging health care delivery systems.

With the development of new approaches to patient care, new parameters are needed with commensurate methodology to measure the resources required for that care. One of the age-old issues is the nurse–physician relationship. The preferred perspective on the nurse–physician relationship is that the relationship is complementary. The practices are very different, and collaboration makes it possible to extend clinical resources to serve greater numbers of patients. Adversarial relationships between nurses and physicians inhibit the benefits. There are some gray areas in which nurses are functioning more like physicians and physicians are functioning more like nurses. Most of these are setting-specific and have not become the national norm. Best practices evaluated on patient care outcomes for quality and cost will drive this development.

Managing the Effects of Redesign on the Staff

Changes that have resulted from redesign are only the tip of the "change iceberg." Events such as consolidation of services, downsizing, mergers, or other initiatives that have resulted in realignment of staff have been met with varying responses. Staff now need renewal, reenergizing, and respect. The realignment of the staff has been both positive and negative, with gains and losses for staff. Added to this turmoil of change and reactions to change is the fact that there are fewer managers and fewer departments. The previously dedicated "unit manager" now manages several patient care units, oversees ambulatory care services, and participates in business planning and development of new services inside and outside the hospital. An effect of all of this change is that staff members are more vulnerable than ever, but there are fewer people providing leadership and support. This situation is a challenge for nurses in executive practice.

Managing Quality

Almost every report of the expansion of nurse-executive roles and functions mentions managing quality. Nurses understand patient care processes and outcomes management. They work well with interdisciplinary care teams. Nurses are accustomed to developing and using process, and to helping other health care professionals understand and use techniques such as utilization review and risk management, as well as advanced tools such as critical pathways and clinical algorithms. Staff development experts have been a valuable resource for quality initiatives. In institutions with downsized education departments, the advanced practice nurses provide some of the needed expertise, as do leaders in nursing services.

New methods for measuring quality are also being designed. Some of the total quality management techniques and some new techniques that fit the new interdisciplinary collaboration around patient populations are the basis for these new methods. At the baseline, financial and clinical outcome data indicate what is happening in patient care. In the past, nurses had become expert in the implementation and evaluation of incremental change. Now, however, executive teams, interdisciplinary teams, patient groups, and others are all involved in changing or revising some aspect of care. Keeping track of what works, what does not work, and what needs to be improved is increasingly difficult. Measurement of patient satisfaction is so far the best indicator of the organization's health.

Keeping Nursing Aligned with the Health Care System

At the same time that health care systems are changing, nursing itself is undergoing significant changes. The nursing profession is in the midst of a transformation that is having profound effects in the delivery of nursing care. The driving force for this transformation is the focus on patients in a managed care environment. The critical mass of nurses taking care of patients in hospitals is moving into community, home, and long-term care settings that require new ways of working within nursing and with others. The nursing transformation is characterized by a renewed emphasis on the values and practice of nursing, intensive interdisciplinary care collaboration, and expansion of the role of nurse leaders into territory that is new to them, such as business and financial arenas, community education, and facilitation of patients' involvement in their own care.

One of the effects of the transformation, or revamping, of the nursing resource is a renewed attention to nursing's administrative infrastructure. The most recent extensive national study of the influence of nursing's leadership is the Magnet Hospital Study published almost 20 years ago.[19] Clearly, nursing administration practice has been changing

without the benefit of scientific studies or systematic study of the changes. Information gleaned from anecdotes and trends indicates that nurse-executives are concentrating on innovation to make the resources stretch to meet patient care requirements, to incorporate emerging practices associated with new and advanced technology, and to find ways to support patients in the continuum of care across settings and issues. The demand for nursing leadership has not lessened, but has increased in what many term a chaotic situation within the health care industry.

Creating Learning Environments

The changing models of health care delivery partially define the gradual changes in the way that health care professionals work together. Because change is ongoing and inevitable, one way to manage change is to learn from experience. Creating a learning organization that values improvement initiatives is essential to continuous quality improvement. The learning organization is grounded on concepts of patient care, rather than on the unit or the service structure, and on respect for the talents and contributions of the various health care professionals who work together to provide patient care. Although this patient-focused care provides the constancy of purpose for the interdisciplinary teams, learning organizations require more. Learning to understand processes, to analyze and interpret data, and to trust intuition are all behaviors to be developed by leaders in the learning organizations. All staff, including housekeeping and dietary, maintenance and environmental services, pharmacists and therapists, physicians and nurses, should participate in learning. Nurses in executive practice, along with other leaders, are continuously challenged to learn from mistakes, events, and successes; to identify ways to promote improvement; and to keep the philosophy and spirit of service alive.

The question for executives is how to maintain and nurture the collaboration gained from change in which all types of staff members from all levels learned teamwork and bonded around patient care. For example, people have learned to cover the walls with flowcharts, to share experiences about what must be done to create improvements, to chart their pathways for improvement toward action, and to tolerate change. The challenge for nurse-executives and others is to determine the next step, to continue to open new vistas for the staff, and to develop different types of care models that are consistent with the spirit and intent of health care reform.

Increasing Nursing's Capacity To Provide Care

For nurse-executives, a significant challenge is the systematic development of nursing's capacity to provide patient care. Nursing is surrounded by superlatives in the health care industry. Nurses comprise the largest single group of health care professionals. Nursing care is the most intangible and least understood component of patient care. Nursing has the most entry routes to practice, the highest number of professional organizations, and the best articulated educational mobility programs of any of the vocational and technical health care workers. Nurses work in all types of health care settings, on all shifts. The management of this complex and valuable patient care resource is a study of change, of innovation, of chaos, and of values. Dichotomies abound, structure is diffuse, and roles are as varied as the situations of patient care. Breakthroughs in developing a more unified approach to planning and utilizing the nursing workforce are essential if nursing's full capacity for care is to be realized.

The obvious benefits of having a "full-service" profession in today's pluralistic health care industry has brought new insights into long-standing issues. Emphasis on clinical expertise, on outcomes, and on efficiency has demonstrated the importance of staff qualifications in new ways. Now, differentiated practice is not an ideal; it is a necessity to use the nursing staff appropriately. The requirements and expertise needed in clinical nursing care become more visible in the shift from hospital care to ambulatory care and home care. The emerging emphasis on patient education, counseling, and teaching in managed care has put the spotlight on the decision-making and assessment skills of nurses.

The nursing workforce will need to address such issues as the aging of patients and the increased life expectancy. The number of persons who require assisted living support to maintain themselves at home is expected to increase. It seems likely that there will be a need for more nurses at every level to meet patient care requirements. Furthermore, nurses at different levels may need different competencies. New staffing configurations that match nursing resources with patient need are being demonstrated in hospitals and home care, in managed care, and in alternative care settings. The challenge to the nurse-executive is to have the right nurses caring for the right patients at the right time and in the right place. The highest demand for nurses in today's practice is for advanced practice nurses, who have the appropriate graduate education and certification in critical care, emergency care, and special care.

Updating and preparing nurses in practice for change is another major challenge. The nursing profession is just catching up with the new requirements for patient care.[20] In practice settings, nurse-executives have initiated staff nurse education on the changes in health care delivery, new expectations for nursing care, and new ways to participate in the organizational change and redesign of patient care. Competency-based orientation and evaluation have also become increasingly essential to ensure staff qualifications for care. There are trends to establish credentialing and systems privileges for nurses in advanced practice roles.

Maximizing Scarce Resources for Patient Care

Nurses in executive practice continue to act as patient care advocates in whatever type of position they hold. In recent years, the complexity of patient care organization and the application of clinical and business concepts and expertise to patient care design have expanded this role. Organized delivery systems raise new issues as a result of their single management structure. Initiatives to reduce redundancy through partnerships among accrediting and certifying bodies have been a step toward not only simplifying the processes of regulation, but also aligning the expectations for performance with the actual processes and outcomes of patient care. As the variations in regulations and expectation are brought forward and resolved, the resources are more likely to be used effectively for developing the continuum of care. This process of unfolding and resolution is an executive challenge.

Designing competitive services to meet productivity and profitability targets in the health care market is another challenge, especially in view of the return to basic values and fundamental belief systems in patient care. The ethical issues associated with choices in health care and allocations of scarce resources are major and multidisciplinary. Emerging care models challenge nurses to produce useful services and to develop the connections and competencies essential to complex organizations. Even as new clinical and management imperatives for nursing services have been explored, the purpose and mission of nursing have not changed. To continue the process of integrating nursing into the health care system, the following research and development agenda is recommended:

- interdisciplinary relationships
- consolidation/mergers
- outcomes
- population management
- chronic care/elder care
- customized care
- knowledge management
- consumer involvement

Changing the Culture

Changes in health care have strong cultural implications. Hofstede described power distance in the workplace.[21] There are the superiors and the subordinates; the hierarchy of types of education and status; the differences in salary and decision-making responsibilities, reporting relationships, and status. The goal of new health care delivery systems is to treat all as equals in the enterprise. Patients have a role, as do their families and significant others. Each person who contributes to the care, whether from the housekeeping, engineering, dietary, or medical staff, is interdependent in achieving the desired quality process and outcome of the care. In this culture, patient satisfaction is the measure of how well the whole is working for the patient.

To some extent, the utilization of new information systems facilitates culture changes. Health care systems of the future will use electronic communication for business and care activities. Breakthroughs in nursing have begun with telemedicine, the electronic exchange of information for individuals and groups across oceans, and in staff communications. Coping with e-mail and developing work patterns that use it efficiently are important aspects of the new roles. On the very positive side is the hoped for breakthrough allowed by electronic communications for transmittal of patient data.[22] Knowledge of the patient's history, the development of the current condition, and the previous care and treatment has been essential in care management.

THE FUTURE OF NURSE-EXECUTIVE PRACTICE

If trends continue with downsizing, empowerment of staff nurses, and increased ratios of advanced practice nurses functioning close to patients, the nurse-executive of the future will be very different from the nurse-executive of today. Leadership development and modeling will continue to be important. Mentoring and development of the cadre of experienced and qualified nurses will be needed. Continuing work to keep the credentialing and educational processes up to date will be essential. Nurse-executives will continue to design, facilitate, and manage patient care; they will continue to build relationships not only among interdisciplinary teams,[23] but also between and among the varying organizations that deliver patient care, such as hospice, community health care centers, outreach clinics, industrial and school health services, and increasingly, alternative health care services.

In the future, the management component of practice may be more fully integrated in the role of advanced practice nurses and others who are the nursing profession's knowledge workers. These knowledge workers may be less involved in operations, as the infrastructure for health care continues to be dismantled in favor of clinical practice with telemedicine, virtual organizations, and patient-driven care systems.[24] The knowledge workers can use their drawing boards and conceptual ability to develop the new systems and the new approaches to patient care, however.

The unique contribution of a nurse-executive in a health care organization will continue to center on the organization and delivery of quality patient care.

NOTES

1. H. Finer, *Administration and the Nursing Services* (New York: Macmillan, 1961).

2. M. McClure, *Magnet Hospital Study.* Kansas City, MO: American Academy of Nursing, 1983.

3. VHA, Inc., *The Impact of Organizational Redesign on Nurse Executive Leadership: II* (Irving, TX: VHA, Inc., 1995).

4. W. Schmeling, *Facing Change in Health Care: Learning Faster in Tough Times* (Chicago: American Hospital Publishing, 1996).

5. P.M. Senge, *The Fifth Discipline: The Art and Practice of the Learning Organization* (New York: Doubleday Currency, 1990).

6. S.S. Blancett and D.L. Flarey, *Reengineering Nurs-*

 ing and Health Care (Gaithersburg, MD: Aspen Publishers, 1995).

7. *Nursing Staff in Hospitals and Nursing Homes: Is It Adequate?* (Washington, DC: Institute of Medicine National Academy Press, 1996).

8. American Organization of Nurse Executives, *Refining the Art and Science of Nurse Executive Practice* (Chicago: American Organization of Nurse Executives, 1998).

9. New Jersey Hospital Association Quality Patient Care Advisory Committee, *Chief Nurse Executive Title and Patient Care Restructure Survey Report* (Princeton, NJ: Department of Hospital Operations, 1997).

10. American Organization of Nurse Executives, *Refining the Art and Science of Nurse Executive Practice.*

11. J.P. Lathrop, *Restructuring Health Care: The Patient Focused Paradigm* (San Francisco: Jossey-Bass, 1993).

12. Ibid.

13. American Organization of Nurse Executives, *Quality Monograph* (Chicago: American Organization of Nurse Executives, 1996).

14. P. Pritchett et al., *After the Merger: The Authoritative Guide for Integration Success* (New York: McGraw-Hill, 1997).

15. M.A. McDermott et al., "Promoting Quality Education for the Parish Nurse and Parish Nurse Coordinator," *Nursing and Health Care Perspectives* 19, no. 1 (1998): 4–6.

16. Ibid.

17. American Organization of Nurse Executives, *The Business of Nursing* (Chicago: AHPI, 1997).

18. D. Huber and C. Delaney, *The Minimum Nursing Management Data Set* [monograph] (Chicago: American Organization of Nurse Executives, 1997).

19. McClure, *Magnet Hospital Study.*

20. American Association of Colleges of Nursing, *Essentials of the Baccalaureate Curriculum* (Washington, DC: American Association of Colleges of Nursing, 1998).

21. G. Hofstede, *Cultures and Organizations: Software of the Mind: Intercultural Cooperation and Its Importance for Survival* (New York: McGraw-Hill, 1997).

22. C. Martin, *The Digital Estate: Strategies for Competing, Surviving and Thriving in an Internetworked World* (New York: McGraw-Hill, 1997).

23. G. Kushel, *Reaching the Peak Performance Zone* (New York: American Management Association, 1994).

24. E.M. Marshall, *Transforming the Way We Work: The Power of the Collaborative Workplace* (New York: American Management Association, 1996).

MARJORIE BEYERS, RN, PhD, FAAN, is Executive Director for the American Organization of Nurse Executives, an association of nurses in executive practice that provides leadership and direction for nurses in executive practice. Previously, she was the Vice President for Nursing and Allied Health in Mercy Health Systems. Dr. Beyers is a member of the Catholic Health Initiatives Board and several editorial boards. Her numerous publications cover clinical nursing and quality and nursing management.

Chapter 24

Laboratories

Paul J. Brzozowski and Ellen A. Moloney

Clinical laboratories are one of the most dynamic environments in health care today. The medical community is exerting pressure on laboratories to expand their scope of service and improve quality at a time when changes in reimbursement regulations, the advent of organized delivery systems, and competition are forcing laboratories to become even more efficient and operate under increasing fiscal constraints. Those responsible for laboratories must look beyond traditional management styles and marketing strategies to keep their laboratories viable, while at the same time remaining technologically up to date.

Patient testing has expanded well beyond the traditional acute care and reference testing settings. Today's laboratory environment ranges from reference laboratories where low-volume esoteric testing takes place to physician offices where phlebotomy and basic laboratory analyses are routine. Quality and cost-effective laboratory services have become a major requirement of integrated networks that cover the continuum of care and whose sites include wellness centers, home care, physician's offices, acute care settings, and long-term care operations. The testing requirements at each of these sites vary significantly.

No one laboratory can provide all the testing services required of today's health care delivery system. Therefore, efforts to integrate testing from all provider sites in a well-designed, organized system are important. Because the laboratory's product is information, much of the change in technology is related to the information systems needed to register patient demographics, track specimens, and report patient results for testing performed in a variety of settings across the continuum of care.

Change related to analytical equipment is twofold. First, the development of point of care testing (POCT) equipment enables providers of varying skills and training to perform basic laboratory analyses in the same location and at the same time that other services are provided. This reduces the amount of testing that needs to be referred to larger regional centers, improving services and decreasing their cost. Second, the development of robotics to process specimens, combined with the expansion of test menus and throughput on larger analytical systems, has allowed for the growth of large, low-cost regional centers that serve many providers in today's integrated networks.

In response to these changes in technology and service demands, laboratory professionals are redefining their roles to serve patients effectively in all types of settings. This redefinition of roles is a major issue as health care continues to evolve beyond traditional boundaries with new tools and technology. Managed care initiatives for increased efficiency, reduced utilization, and expansion of test menus have accelerated the process of change in a manner that will make it impossible for laboratories to remain in existence if they do not remain flexible in their approach to staffing, skill mix, and technology.

To provide a better understanding of the laboratory operation and the changes in organization, roles, and technology necessary to manage the limited resources available to clinical laboratories, the following characteristics of clinical laboratories are discussed:

- service levels
- organization
- staffing
- information systems
- physical plant and equipment
- laboratory regulation
- strategic planning

Issues such as skill mix, workstation configuration, workload, workflow, and customer service are examined in the context of these operational characteristics.

SERVICE LEVELS

The variety of tests offered; the turnaround time associated with that testing; and other services, such as technical/clinical consultation, access to information systems, and/or phlebotomy and courier services, determine a laboratory's service level. Properly defined service levels provide the basis for effective laboratory management, because they drive decisions on staffing, skill mix, information systems design, equipment configuration, fa-

cility design, and strategic planning. Factors to consider in developing the range of testing performed by a laboratory fall into one of these four categories:

1. medical needs
2. legal or professional requirements
3. technical and personnel capabilities
4. administrative/financial considerations

Questions pertaining to the factors in each category were incorporated into a questionnaire/worksheet format that has been used as a formal decision-making tool to help answer two questions, Should we offer this service? What is the appropriate site? Originally developed by Boutweil and Stewart at the Centers for Disease Control,[1] the criteria have been updated and the format modified by Hager and Brzozowski.[2]

Defining 75 percent of a laboratory test menu is not difficult. It is the remaining 25 percent that presents a significant challenge. Condensing information into a well-defined, easy-to-use, structured format enables a laboratory to use a multidisciplinary approach to define the remaining 25 percent of its service. Administrative, fiscal, clinical, and laboratory professionals are all encouraged to offer input into a final decision on whether a procedure will be performed in the laboratory or sent elsewhere in the network. Once the service level has been determined, a laboratory can evaluate the other operational characteristics necessary to support the organization's mission.

With more of the laboratory business coming from the outpatient population, laboratories have had to adjust their service level definition in order to remain competitive. Service level changes include more frequent courier pickups, on-site phlebotomy services and drawing stations, expanded POCT, longer hours of operation, access to the laboratory information system, and use of telecommunication technology for technical and clinical consultation.

ORGANIZATION

Laboratories are usually divided into two major divisions: anatomic pathology and clinical pathology. Anatomic pathology relates to the processing of surgical and gynecological specimens (e.g., Pap smears). Its subsections usually include surgical pathology, histology, and cytology. Occasionally, in reference laboratories or teaching centers, electron microscopy and similar specialties may be assigned to the anatomic division.

Clinical pathology is the division that processes the test requests more familiar to the general public, such as blood cell counts, coagulation studies, urinalyses, blood glucose level determinations, and throat cultures. Its subsections include chemistry, hematology, microbiology, urinalysis (microscopy), and blood bank. Recently, laboratories have begun to combine some of these sections into more efficient larger units, such as an automation section that incorporates hematology and chemistry. Other subsections may include endocrinology, toxicology, serology, tissue typing, molecular biology, and cytogenetics. The number of formally designated subsections reflects the previously defined service levels. Appendix 24–A contains a representative list of tests performed in these sections.

Laboratory Configuration

In order to deliver these services in a quality, cost-effective manner, an organized delivery system needs several types of laboratory configurations:

- a large regional laboratory
- rapid response laboratories located at acute care facilities, ambulatory surgery centers, and large clinics
- drawing stations at various locations throughout the network
- POCT capabilities

Figure 24–1 illustrates the organized delivery system structure and the flow of specimens throughout the system.

Large regional laboratories function as hubs for the organized health care delivery system's laboratory service. Technology at this site includes the central information system, robotics for pre-analytical specimen processing, and highly automated large-capacity testing equipment. The regional laboratory is likely to operate 24 hours per day, with the busiest times and bulk of the testing performed during the early evening and late night hours to accommodate the testing needs of the physician's offices, late admissions into hospitals, and home health care providers. Other services often located at this site include marketing, client support, and courier functions.

The services offered at regional laboratories include the full range of clinical laboratory testing, with the exception of transfusion services and the anatomic pathology services that require the presence of a physician. It is becoming more common for the regional laboratory to process surgical specimens, however. A regional center may be one of a system's larger laboratories located at a large teaching center, an acute care hospital, a commercial reference laboratory, or a separate freestanding operation centrally located within the network's service area. Location is a key operational characteristic of the regional laboratory.

There are two major types of rapid response laboratories: one in the acute care setting and another in the outpatient clinic or physician's office. The rapid response labo-

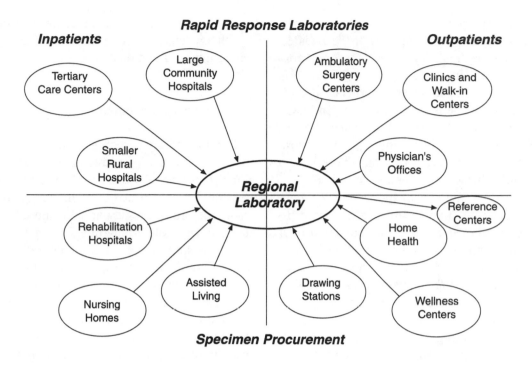

Figure 24–1 Organized Delivery System Structure

ratory in the acute care setting has a broader test menu than that in the outpatient settings, and it provides transfusion and anatomic pathology services. Furthermore, it remains open 24 hours per day. In the outpatient setting, the rapid response laboratory's hours of operation reflect the hours that the clinic or office is open for patient appointments. In both settings, the goal is to refer as much testing as possible to the regional laboratory, where the technology available and the economies of scale make the cost of performing laboratory analyses significantly less.

Drawing stations fill an important role in the organized health care delivery system. They can be located almost anywhere, but are most frequently found in clinics, physician's offices, and locations convenient to patients

(e.g., drugstores, major shopping areas). They allow patients to have their laboratory work drawn with minimal interruption in their daily routines. In today's competitive marketplace, customer service must be a goal of any organization. Drawing stations also provide a drop-off point for home care professionals, enabling them to initiate their patient testing in a timely and efficient manner.

POCT is one of the most controversial topics in laboratory medicine. The controversy is due to the high cost of the testing, the competency of individuals who perform the testing, and the correlation with similar testing performed at other sites in the system. POCT allows providers of a variety of skills, (e.g., physicians, nurses, respiratory therapists, technicians) to perform testing. It takes place in the physician's examination room, emergency department, home, or at the bedside. This approach is very convenient for all concerned and, in some cases, very important clinically, such as in an emergency department when time is critical. The cost of POCT may be five to ten times higher than the cost of the same test in a rapid response or regional laboratory, however. Therefore, it should be used only when indicated.

Given the number of individuals, devices, and locations involved in POCT, it is difficult to control quality and ensure proper documentation of results and billing. A laboratory professional should have responsibility for the POCT program and monitor compliance through rigorous training, proficiency testing, and quality control programs.

Re-engineering efforts in many organizations have significantly affected laboratories. One of the major changes is the consolidation of services along functional rather than clinical characteristics. For example, many laboratories now have a section referred to as the automation laboratory that contains high-speed analyzers used for both chemistry and hematology tests, eliminating the need for separate chemistry and hematology sections. This type of change has a significant impact on physical plant layout, staffing, skill mix, and cross training. The amount of space required is less and the layout is more open. In the past, there were walls between the various sections even though an open design is more conducive to an efficient workflow. There are fewer workstations, requiring less staff. In larger laboratories a more cost effective skill mix, with an increased use of technicians, is possible, since they are easier to supervise in an open laboratory with well-defined workstations.

Entire functions have also been re-engineered out of the laboratory. Some examples include phlebotomy, data entry, and POCT.

Staff in hospitals, walk-in centers, home health agencies, and long-term care facilities perform these functions.

Laboratory Management

The goal of any system should be to minimize the bureaucracy and to have clearly defined reporting relationships. While re-engineering has had a positive impact on this issue, the problems may arise in the laboratory manager role. Many times, this person's loyalty is split between the medical director and an administrator, such as the chief operating officer or vice president. Divided loyalties are particularly common when an individual is managing several sites or departments, usually in an acute care setting or large regional center. Ideally, the medical director should assume overall responsibility for the operation of the laboratory, and the laboratory manager should be a key support person. Access to senior management and a high degree of autonomy are crucial to the success of both the laboratory manager and the medical director, however.

Through formal and informal feedback from the medical staff and other providers, the medical director determines the appropriate service levels, including the variety of testing to be available at each site, the turnaround times associated with that testing, and the tolerance limits (e.g., quality control, utilization) for services rendered. On receiving this information the laboratory manager can identify the resources necessary to carry out these services. Issues such as the physical plant, staffing/skill mix, information systems, and equipment needs must be resolved within the financial and administrative constraints placed on the operation by the board and senior management and must reflect the hospital mission statement.

The medical director also provides feedback to direct care providers. He or she must take an active role in effecting changes in physician practice patterns (e.g., ordering of microscopic urines, routine differentials, and general utilization of laboratory services). To be successful, the medical director needs a reliable database of physician utilization of laboratory services and a thorough understanding of viable alternatives and constraints that the laboratory operation presents. These factors have clinical laboratories paying more attention to administrative duties, expectations, and compensation for these services in their contractual arrangements. Appendix 24–B contains a sample job description of a clinical laboratory medical director.

As a result of the time required to prepare for and perform these duties, the medical director needs a strong laboratory management team to keep him or her informed and to deal with the day-to-day operation. In addition to the operational issues mentioned, the responsibilities of the management team include

- development of strategies that improve staff productivity
- cost reduction
- development and interpretation of management reports

The laboratory management team must be responsive to budget performance, maintenance of service levels, and personnel administration—recruitment, retention, and individual performance—and should have direct access to the people and information necessary to carry out this role. The medical director and the management team need a strong clinical and supervisory team not only to address the day-to-day technical issues, but also to support them in the financial performance of the laboratory operation.

Bureaucracy grows when an organization tries to reward employees with new, impressive titles and roles in lieu of proper recognition through promotions, pay raises, or similar incentives. In the long run, an organization will suffer if reporting relationships become confused and territorial issues arise and cause a deterioration in the quality of relationships. A key lesson learned from re-engineering is that appropriate incentives must be in place both to motivate staff and to support the mission of the organization.

In summary, organizational structures should be as flat as possible, with a minimal number of titles; they should be based on the size and scope of the operation and the number of people employed.

STAFFING

Proper laboratory staffing is possibly one of the greatest challenges facing laboratory management today. To staff their operations, laboratories employ a blend of medical, technical, and support staff. The number, titles, and job descriptions vary according to the size of the organization and the scope of services provided.

Personnel Requirements

Most regional and rapid response laboratories employ personnel in the following positions:

- pathologists
- laboratory scientists
- section supervisors
- technologists
- technicians
- phlebotomists
- clerks/medical secretaries
- couriers
- marketing/account representatives

With the exception of the physician's office laboratory, all laboratories, from large regional centers and reference laboratories to small rural hospital laboratories and drawing stations, have pathologists associated with them. Usually, one pathologist serves as the director. Large teaching and research facilities may appoint one pathologist the director of anatomic pathology and another pathologist the director of clinical pathology. The pathologist is a physician who generally is board-certified in anatomic and/or clinical pathology. Laboratory scientists may be employed to assist pathologists in directing the laboratory. These are individuals with advanced degrees, usually doctorates, in areas such as biochemistry, microbiology, or virology. They are usually found in large teaching centers, specialty hospitals, or regional laboratories. They may also serve as laboratory directors, depending on the scope of the services provided in the laboratories where they work.

The majority of revenue associated with pathologist compensation is derived from interpreting surgical and cytology specimens. Other income is derived from administrative services provided to laboratories. In some cases, pathologists are employees of the laboratory, but this is not usually the case. They generally provide their services through contractual arrangements with laboratories. Thus, pathologist contractual arrangements and negotiations are important issues for laboratories.

Laboratory managers, administrative technologists, and laboratory coordinators are normally medical technologists with administrative skills acquired through experience and/or formal education, such as completion of a master's program in business administration. In very large organizations, they may have only a business background and no clinical experience. If this is the case, a second individual, a chief technologist, may be responsible for the technical aspects of managing the laboratory operation (e.g., quality control, instrument maintenance), or the section and site supervisors may assume responsibility for technical supervision and report directly to the business manager. This alternative may present some organizational problems if section supervisors report to a business manager for administrative activities and a medical director for clinical activities. Such a dual reporting relationship slows down the decision-making process, particularly when decisions affect both administrative and clinical aspects of the department. Such is the case with equipment acquisition, for example.

Section and site supervisors are usually assigned to one section of a large laboratory operation, such as the chemistry or hematology section of a regional laboratory. Their time is usually split between bench work (performing test analysis) and supervision. In small laboratories, such as a rapid response laboratory, one supervisor may oversee work in several disciplines. In larger laboratories, where one section may employ from 30 to 40 staff technologists, section supervisors do very little, if any, bench work. The size and scope of the operation determine their roles.

Senior technologists may assist supervisors in major subsections of a department. For example, in the chemistry department of a large laboratory, senior technologists may be assigned to subsections, such as those that deal with immunoassays, toxicology, or automation. Senior technologists may also have functional rather than line management roles, such as responsibility for POCT, quality control, or preventive maintenance. Technologists usually possess a bachelor of science degree in medical technology and have passed a registry examination given by one of several accrediting bodies, such as the American Society of Clinical Pathologists. Certain states, such as Rhode Island, California, and Florida, require licensure. These individuals perform all types of laboratory analyses and function independently.

Technicians possess less formal education, such as associate degrees. They require more supervision and function less independently. Generally, they make up a major portion of the technical staffing at laboratories. Along with technologists, they provide the core of the laboratory staffing.

The primary job of phlebotomists is to procure blood specimens, and they usually receive their training on the job. Clerks/secretaries process the information in the laboratory, sort patient reports, register outpatients, do general typing, and handle departmental mail. With more formal training than clerks, secretaries transcribe pathology reports and perform duties such as giving verbal reports, cross-indexing reports and slides, and assisting with tumor registry. Often, smaller laboratories combine clerk/phlebotomist duties and secretary/receptionist functions. Large operations with formal medical technology training programs, complex service levels, and sophisticated data-processing systems may have education coordinators, quality control supervisors, or information systems supervisors.

New roles for the laboratory include marketing specialists and POCT quality control coordinators. These roles reflect the changed mission of the laboratory. In smaller institutions, several roles can be combined. For example, the information system supervisor may also be the account representative. Those in the chemistry section may be responsible for POCT since much of this testing involves chemistry (e.g., glucometers).

Workload and Staff Utilization

The workload at a clinical laboratory can be divided into two major categories: technical and nontechnical. The technical workload can be defined as the number of analyses (tests) requested of the laboratory. The hours needed to complete these analyses are linked primarily to the methodology employed and secondarily to the turnaround time required and the staff proficiency. In the past, the College of American Pathologists (CAP) used time and motion studies to determine the amount of labor necessary to perform individual analyses,[3] and the results have provided the basis for many of today's staff measurement tools. Standards were expressed in terms of CAP units, with one CAP unit equal to one minute of supervisory, technical, clerical, and aide time necessary to perform an analysis. These time studies paid particular attention to the degree of automation, often establishing unique labor standards for different manufacturers' analyzers. Applying these standards to both patient and nonpatient (quality control) test volumes determines the number of minutes required to perform the technical portion of the workload. The technical workload usually consumes 60 to 70 percent of paid hours.

The nontechnical workload consists of activities such as the ordering of supplies, continuing education, human resource functions, and equipment evaluations. The time required for these activities is more difficult to assess. Laboratory organization, mission statement, size, support systems, and physical facilities vary too much from institution to institution to permit industrywide standards for nontechnical laboratory activities. Allowances also are necessary for downtime, personal time, fatigue, delay, and standby, such as on the night shift in acute care settings. Together, nontechnical workload and downtime consume 15 to 25 percent of paid hours. The remaining 10 to 15 percent of paid hours are consumed by benefit hours (i.e., vacation, sick, holiday). Actual payroll registers can be used to determine benefit hours.

These ratios vary, depending on the type of laboratory and support services offered. A rapid response laboratory will have a larger percentage of downtime and nontechnical work than a regional laboratory. The provision of a great many support services, such as couriers and phlebotomists, will also add to the nontechnical workload.

To properly assess the time requirements associated with workload, some basic quantitative analyses are needed. Work sampling, frequency distributions, or time ladders (self-logging techniques) can all be useful. An organization's management engineering department, consultant, or professional society can be used to assist laboratory personnel in completing these studies. Not only should the studies be comprehensive, but also they should include technical activities. Much of the information in the literature, as well as that available for purchase, is based on averages. Thus, batch size and skill mix have influenced the data, and they may not be applicable in a laboratory with operational characteristics that do not reflect industry averages (usually the case with both very large and very small laboratories). A detailed quantitative analysis will determine if the staffing ratios or relative value units (RVUs) assigned to various laboratory activities are appropriate for a particular laboratory; at the same time, it will identify the technical activities, the nontechnical activities, and the downtime characteristics. Often, this complete approach results in work simplification and streamlining of the operation through better integration of all activities and skills. Internal studies should be combined with benchmarking, available through various third parties (e.g., professional societies and consulting firms) and can be conducted as part of other studies.

Cost accounting is one approach to quantifying chargeable tests and associating them with a cost. The cost of laboratory testing varies dramatically, based on the size, type, and location of the laboratory. Total direct costs generally range from $7.50 to $12.50 for most laboratories. In smaller laboratories and specialty laboratories, costs may run higher; in larger regional laboratories, lower. Although labor remains the largest single cost (approximately 50 percent in most laboratories), costs associated with the blood bank and the cost of blood products are significant in laboratories that are in acute care settings. Because of automation and large volumes, chemistry and hematology have the lowest cost per test, approximately $3.00 to $4.00 per test. Blood bank, microbiology, and histology have higher costs per test because they involve less automation, the volumes of chargeable tests are lower, and they are labor-intensive.

In June 1993, the CAP ceased using its workload recording method. Instead, it is supporting the Laboratory Management Index Program (LMIP), a series of productivity modules that will use specific input data to allow the assessment of individual laboratory sections. The input data will provide a central core of information to calculate productivity, utilization, and cost-effectiveness ratios. Peer group analyses will be structured into billable groups and complexity groups, and will take into account the variability between sections in laboratories.

Once these analyses are completed, workload can be compared to staffing levels to determine staff productivity. Staff utilization should not be confused with productivity. Someone can be busy without being productive (e.g., turn out one test result per hour in a very inefficient laboratory). In the laboratory, productivity is the number of patient test results reported per unit of time.

Monitoring two ratios—paid hours per chargeable test and chargeable tests per patient encounter—helps avoid the confusion between staff utilization and productivity. These ratios also are useful in assessing batch size, number of urgent requests, single test draws, number of nonpatient tests, and impact of equipment in terms of degree of automation. For example, a small laboratory with minimal automation and small batches will require more time per chargeable test than a large operation with large batches and highly automated procedures. An institution with a low number of urgent requests and few single test draws will have a higher number of chargeable tests per encounter, a desirable trait.

The manner in which tests are counted will affect these ratios. Basically, if a laboratory counts groups of tests as outlined in CPT-4 coding guidelines—a complete blood cell count chemistry profile as one chargeable test—a traditional hospital laboratory can expect to see 0.27 to 0.33 paid hours per chargeable test and two to four chargeable tests per venipuncture. If that hospital has a significant number of tests from the outreach market, the labor requirements will drop to 0.20 to 0.24 paid hours per test.

Large regional laboratories and reference centers will have even lower labor requirements. Regional laboratories can process tests with 25 to 50 percent less labor and lower supply costs than even the best traditional laboratories. This is one of the driving forces behind regional networks.

Workstation Configuration

The basic functional unit in the laboratory is the workstation. Tests performed at a particular workstation usually require the same skill level, the same equipment, and the same general resources; often, they provide the same type of clinical information. For example, most laboratories have a coagulation workstation. Two common procedures performed at this workstation are the determinations of prothrombin time and activated partial thromboplastin time, which aid the physician in assessing the ability of a patient's blood to clot. Depending on volume, these procedures are either semiautomated or automated.

A workstation may not be staffed for an entire shift. Properly configured workstations offer the manager the most flexibility in moving people from workstation to workstation as the day progresses to obtain maximum staff utilization and peak productivity. For example, after completing the morning batch of testing at the coagulation workstation, the person assigned to that workstation usually moves to a different workstation in the laboratory. This flexibility leads to the best possible service at the lowest possible cost.

Certain criteria should be reached before a staff member is reassigned from one workstation to another. Usually, workload would need to decrease to the point at which two consecutive hours of personnel time can be identified before an individual is reassigned workstations. This decrease could reflect as much as 30 percent of the workload at a given workstation. Two hours is approximately the amount of time needed to set up and operate a second workstation. If less time is available, reassignment usually increases downtime, leading to lower productivity and higher costs. An alternative to reassigning staff is to increase the amount of testing performed at a workstation that is operating at less than capacity, for example, by locating similar workstations adjacent to each other and having staff cross-cover additional workstations in times of low demand. These adjustments eliminate the two-hour requirement of time.

Large laboratories may have two or three people assigned to one workstation, each doing a very limited number of similar procedures. Smaller laboratories may assign one individual to several workstations throughout the shift. Such work assignments present challenges to managers and strategic planners, because they affect skill mix and cross-training, two operational characteristics linked directly to cost.

Skill Mix and Cross-Training

To understand skill mix, three ratios should be studied:

1. percentage of staff made up of support personnel (clerical/aide)
2. percentage of medical technologists that are registered
3. full-time to part-time staff ratio

A low percentage of support staff in a laboratory usually indicates that technicians are performing clerical functions, certain clerical activities are automated, or some clerical activities are going undone. A high percentage of registered medical technologists usually increases labor costs. Having too few part-time staff members reduces flexibility in terms of staff scheduling, and can lead to increased downtime by having personnel on the premises when they are not needed.

Small laboratories tend to have a higher percentage of registered medical technologists and a lower percentage of support staff or medical technicians than do large laboratories. The staff technologists in small laboratories function more independently, exercise more judgment, do more of their own troubleshooting, are more extensively cross-trained, and often use less automation. These individuals may function as phlebotomists, clerks, and technicians when necessary to meet the workload fluctuations of the department. Although a clerk cannot perform testing, a technologist can fill downtime with clerical activities. The skill level of a technologist makes his or her time more expensive, however, and is one major reason why smaller laboratories have higher unit costs.

Skill mix and cross-training are closely related, particularly in the technical areas. A great opportunity exists for cross-training among phlebotomy and clerical/computer operator personnel. Staff who are cross-trained in these areas could support a central specimen-processing area. To facilitate this process, many laboratories have introduced a laboratory assistant job classification. Employees in this category would have four levels through which they could be trained: clerical, phlebotomy, specimen processing, and basic testing, such as planting of cultures. This strategy would have several benefits:

- increased flexibility
- provision of relief to the technical staff
- reduced turnover
- combined clerk and phlebotomist positions
- opportunity for promotion

Cross-training may become more prevalent as the organizational structure and design of hospitals and ambulatory care centers turn toward patient-focused care. The phlebotomy responsibility, function, and related staffing may be assigned to the patient unit, not the laboratory. This function also could be part of nursing's responsibilities, particularly in critical care areas (e.g., the emergency department, intensive care unit) and remote sites (e.g., clinics, ambulatory surgery facilities).

INFORMATION SYSTEMS

The laboratory's product is information. The primary objective of any laboratory information system is to present data in the most orderly, legible, and timely manner possible. Clinical laboratory information systems have become highly automated and sophisticated data-handling systems. A well-designed network laboratory information system has the benefit of integrating inpatient and outpatient laboratory data. In an organized health care delivery system, all testing centers—reference laboratories, regional laboratories, rapid response laboratories, and POCT facilities—should be encompassed by this information system.

In the late 1960s and early 1970s, when most laboratory services were provided at a hospital site, and only a limited number of software systems were available in the marketplace, the in-house development of information systems was a popular decision. In the mid-1970s and mid-1980s, stand-alone turn-key systems became popular because of problems in the integration of the laboratory information system with the hospital's mainframe. The more recent trends of the 1990s have used the integrated system approach. There have been major improvements in the ease and cost of interfacing stand-alone systems with network system mainframes and file servers. Also, several major laboratory vendors have developed systemwide clinical information systems. This integration provides many benefits from both a system administration and cost perspective. The level of integration includes off-site locations such as satellite laboratories, drawing stations, nursing homes, and physicians' offices. A recent integration trend is the bidirectional interfacing between the network laboratories and those not part of the system, such as commercial reference laboratories. These bidirectional interfaces eliminate time-consuming manual entry of requisitions and automate the result entry process for tests performed out of the network.

Vendor-supplied clinical information systems have become well established as a regular part of the laboratory and are critical to its mission and management. Not only do these systems organize the work, accumulate data on specimens, generate clinical reports, maintain a longitudinal patient record, and post bills, but also they keep audit trails, monitor quality, log workload, and keep department policies and procedures on-line. Laboratory clients, such as physicians' offices, nursing homes, and home health care agencies, can have access to patient results via their personal computers (PCs), terminals, and scheduled reports to printers. Most laboratory information systems use PCs that are part of the network's information system. Improved communications and easy access to databases have been the key factors behind the numerous gains in productivity.[4]

The benefits to the laboratory of information technology are in the more orderly and timely presentation of laboratory data and the utilization of these data beyond traditional uses, such as effecting changes in physicians' ordering patterns, performing laboratory–pharmacy reviews, monitoring changes in antibiotic susceptibility patterns more completely, and conducting product line and diagnosis-related group (DRG) costing studies. Exhibit 24–1 presents a side-by-side comparison of the operational differences of an automated versus a manual information system, and Exhibit 24–2 shows the benefits of automation.

Among the leading information systems, the key features include

- bar coding
- hand-held devices (particularly useful for the phlebotomy team or POCT)
- image scanning and storage
- limited voice recognition
- optical disk storage

Exhibit 24–1 Workflow: Manual Versus Automated Information System

Manual System	*Automated System*
Requisitioning	
• Laboratory test ordered by MD on physician order sheet	• Interaction of MD with information system
• Requisition prepared by nursing personnel	• Order entry via hospital information system
• Requisition transported to lab	• Activity eliminated
Specimen Procurement	
• Requisition time stamped when received	• Activity automated
• Specimen drawn by phlebotomist	• Same (using computer bar-coded label)
• Tube labeled	• Same (using computer bar-coded label)
• Time of collection stamped or written	• Function automated, improved quality by forcing user response
Specimen Preparation	
• Pour-off tubes and sample cups labeled	• Use of preprinted bar-coded aliquot labels and primary tubes
• Specimen logged in	• Activity automated
• Accession numbers assigned	• Activity automated
• Requests entered on worksheets	• Activity automated
Analysis and Data Handling	
• Analysis performed	• Less technologist involvement due to bar-codes and robotics
• Results recorded on worksheet	• No change for manual test, automated tests run on-line
• Results recorded on logs	• Reference laboratory interfaced
• Data review by supervisor	• Activity automated and process made easier by on-line delta checks
Reporting	
• Forms separated	• Activity eliminated
• Forms sorted by ordering station	• Activity eliminated
• File/distribution	• Activity eliminated
• Results written or taped on summary sheets	• Activity eliminated
• Multiple documents charted	• Process simplified by handling only one document
Financial Data	
• Charge tickets sorted	• Activity eliminated
• Entry of charges into information system	• Activity eliminated (charges captured at time of order entry or by direct interface)
Management Reporting	
• Statistics compiled	• Activity eliminated and capabilities expanded

Exhibit 24–2 System Improvement Because of Automation of Laboratory Information Systems

Benefits	*Reason*
Reduced errors in reporting results	• On-line delta checks • On-line instrument interfaces • Better presentation of data for supervisory review
Shorter turnaround time of patient results	• CRT inquiry as opposed to manual file searchers • On-line instrument interfaces with automatic send result features • More organized cumulative report format
Increased productivity	• Less transcription • Reduced filing • Less time spent charting, with telephone inquiries, and finding results • Automated statistics gathering
New features available with no increase in personnel	• Ability to update procedure manuals online • DRG/case mix analysis
Reduced paper costs	• Use of stock computer paper rather than expensive multipart forms • Use of optical disk
Improved legibility	• Reports printed, not handwritten, and prepared in more orderly fashion
Automated statistics gathering	• Statistics computerized

• improvements in remote communication
• improvements in graphics
• limited electronic patient medical record

Bar coding is standard at most institutions, and the major laboratory analyzers have the capability to interpret bar code labels on the primary sampling tubes. Bar coding provides several advantages, including improved turnaround time, better specimen tracking and accountability, and fewer specimen identification errors.

The improvements in remote communication have allowed laboratories to market their services to physicians' offices, with one of the key components being access to a pa-

tient's test results throughout the continuum of care by means of terminals or printers located in the physician's office or home. Many physicians have access both to the laboratory test results and to other pertinent clinical information through their personal PCs.

In response to what was perceived as neglect (i.e., improper monitoring, maintenance, and repair protocols), inspection has become part of the laboratory information system operation. Voluntary accrediting agencies (e.g., CAP, American Association of Blood Banks [AABB]) and federal regulatory agencies (e.g., Food and Drug Administration [FDA], Health Care Financing Administration [HCFA]) have begun focusing attention on laboratory information systems to ensure that they are properly tested and monitored.

The CAP has included questions about laboratory information systems on its accreditation checklist for many years. In 1989, the AABB updated its guidelines to include more stringent documentation, testing, and standard operating procedures for blood bank computer systems. Since 1987, the FDA has made the inspection of the computer system a routine part of every blood bank inspection. HCFA, through its Clinical Laboratories Improvement Act (CLIA) regulations, has announced its intention to include laboratory information systems in its regular laboratory inspections.[5] Clearly, these agencies are requiring proof of validation of information systems used in clinical laboratories.

The laboratory manager, or the pathologist acting as a manager, oversees both bench technologists and the computer support group as they generate, process, store, and transmit information. In the past, these supervisory responsibilities consisted primarily of selecting, purchasing, and deploying laboratory information systems, analytical instruments, and test methods. In the future, the laboratory manager will work more closely with the daily information management component of the laboratory and the health care delivery system. Some of the elements of this collaboration are listed in the following[6]:

- As major capital expenditures, the laboratory information system and other components of the information architecture are carefully scrutinized at higher organizational levels in hospitals for gains in quality and efficiency.
- The success of the laboratory increasingly will be measured in terms of the value added to the laboratory database.
- Competition is increasing within hospi-

tals for control of the laboratory and other clinical databases, adding a political dimension to information management that requires the close attention of laboratory managers.
- Decisions involving information management tend to have a horizontal effect on all laboratories and are frequently mission-critical, thus requiring macro-management expertise.
- Information systems increasingly generate so-called information by-products, such as test turnaround times, that enhance the efficiency and quality of all laboratory operations.

PHYSICAL PLANT

After human resources, the physical facility is the most important element in providing laboratory services. Service levels and workload dictate staffing and equipment configuration, which, in turn, dictate the amount of space required. Workflow influences layout, and the size and type of institution determine the location(s) of the laboratory within the facility. In general, laboratory equipment is becoming smaller, more self-contained, and more efficient to operate. As a result, less space is necessary for both equipment and staff, and fewer safety issues, such as toxic waste and noxious fumes, arise. More tests are being performed in the patient care areas, and this trend is likely to continue. These features make design of the laboratory easier.

A very good source of specific guidelines for determining actual space requirements is the CAP *Manual for Laboratory Planning and Design*.[7] The manual's appendix lists such indicators as net square feet or linear feet of bench space per bed, test, or full-time employee (FTE), which can be used to calculate the size of a laboratory. All of these figures and ratios are meant to be used as guidelines and starting points, not absolute standards. In general, wide-open rooms with movable cabinetry are preferable to small sectioned areas. Open space allows flexibility in altering the layout in this dynamic environment and enhances productivity and staff utilization through improved workflow and people movement.

An open floor plan for the laboratory provides the greatest opportunity for staff and operational efficiencies and effectiveness. Today, many laboratories are breaking down the walls that have traditionally separated the clinical areas into chemistry, hematology, microbiology, and blood bank sections. Laboratories of the late 1990s are establishing work circles by arranging the equipment according to function rather than clinical definition. For example, a workcircle may include coagulation, drug testing, fertility, and endocrine testing. Traditionally, these workstations would have been separated between the hematology and chemistry sections. With an open floor plan, workcircles, and cross-trained technologists, a laboratory is able to configure itself based on its customers' needs and maximize the efficiency and productivity of its staff.

Work areas such as virology, histology, or microbiology laboratories that perform testing for tuberculosis and other contagious diseases should be excluded from the open-space approach. Because these sections handle virulent pathogens and toxic chemicals, they should be in more isolated areas. When possible, these areas should be located near outside walls to facilitate installation of exhaust hoods and to meet more stringently controlled HVAC requirements.

The functional relationship between the laboratory and direct care providers also influences the appropriate location for the laboratory. In acute care settings, the rapid response laboratories should be near the intensive care unit, emergency department, operating rooms, and clinic areas. This approach minimizes the need for satellite laboratories and, thus, avoids any inefficiencies and expense that they may bring to an operation through smaller batch sizes, minimal staffing levels and corresponding downtime, and duplication of equipment. For some acute care settings, usually larger tertiary care facilities and health care networks, satellite laboratories may be necessary to reduce test turnaround time for patients in critical care and outpatient areas located great distances from the rapid response laboratory. The use of pneumatic tube systems has made the location of the laboratory a less critical issue, as they allow the movement of laboratory specimens between locations in a fast and efficient manner. Some of these systems have carriers large enough to transport blood products through the system. This eliminates trips to the blood bank.

The use of satellite ancillary services is a major concern in today's reimbursement environment. Decentralization makes monitoring and controlling utilization more difficult. Not only are systems and equipment duplicated, but also the output itself may be different. Requisitions, reporting procedures, and charting policies may vary significantly from those in the central laboratory, causing confusion for clinicians.

LABORATORY REGULATION/ COMPLIANCE

At one time, federal regulations for clinical laboratories applied only to those that participated in the Medicare and Medicaid programs or engaged in interstate commerce. All of this changed significantly in October 1988. After conducting extensive hearings on the quality of laboratories in the United States, Congress passed the Clinical Laboratories

Improvement Act of 1988. This act superseded other regulations and brought under its regulation all U.S. laboratories that conduct testing on human specimens for health assessment or for the diagnosis, prevention, or treatment of disease; only three types of testing are excluded from regulation by CLIA:

1. testing for forensic purposes
2. research testing for which patient-specific results are not reported
3. drug testing performed by laboratories certified by the National Institute on Drug Abuse (NIDA)

Published on February 28, 1992, the final regulations set minimum standards for laboratory practice and quality, and specify requirements for proficiency testing, quality control, patient test management, personnel, quality assurance, certification, and inspections. The same regulations apply to all testing sites, including physician's office laboratories.

The regulations are based on technical complexity in the testing process and risk of harm in reporting erroneous results.

CLIA has established four categories of testing based on the complexity of the test methodology:

1. waived tests
2. physician-performed microscopy (PPM)
3. tests of moderate complexity
4. tests of high complexity

For waived tests, the regulations do not specify quality control, quality assurance, personnel, or proficiency testing. Laboratories that have a certificate of waiver and carry out PPM are not subject to routine inspections. Laboratories that perform moderate- or high-complexity testing, or both, must meet requirements for proficiency testing, patient test management, quality control, quality assurance, and personnel. The regulations for moderate-and high-complexity testing differ mainly in the standards for quality control and personnel.

All laboratories that are subject to regulations under CLIA must obtain appropriate certification documents. Initially, laboratories must obtain either a certificate of waiver or, if performing nonwaived testing, a registration certificate from HCFA. A certificate of waiver is valid for a maximum of 2 years. A registration certificate is valid for 2 years or until an inspection to determine compliance can be conducted, whichever is shorter. A laboratory that meets the requirements of inspection receives either a certificate (for laboratories complying with the Department of Health and Human Services [DHHS] program) or a certificate of accreditation (for laboratories complying with DHHS-approved private, nonprofit accreditation programs). A laboratory may acquire a state license in lieu of either certificate if it is a state with a federally approved licensure program. Laboratories that obtain state licenses must comply with state rules and are exempt from the CLIA program.

With these regulations come cost. There is cost associated with participation in a proficiency testing program and with the implementation of a system to ensure the integrity and identification of patient specimens throughout the testing process, as well as the accuracy of results. For some laboratories, particularly in remote areas, there is cost associated with the personnel standards. For all laboratories, there is the cost of inspections in order to maintain certification. Laboratories that perform unsatisfactorily on two consecutive or two of three proficiency testing events risk sanctions for that specialty, subspecialty, or test. Sanctions may include suspension of the laboratory's certificate or cancellation of its Medicare approval.

Concern about the quality of cytology testing services, particularly Pap smears, was one of the issues that prompted Congress to pass CLIA. Although the act does not contain standards for the other laboratory subspecialties, the law contains specific requirements for cytology proficiency testing, quality control, and personnel. The cytology standards became effective in March 1990, in advance of the other components of CLIA. One of the most significant requirements for the cytology section is that the technical supervisor must establish and monitor the workload of each person who evaluates slides by a non-automated microscopic technique. Personnel can examine no more than 100 slides in no less than 8 hours, but no more than 24 hours, regardless of location. Personnel who have other duties or who work part-time must have their workload limit prorated by the number of hours spent examining slides. There are also specific requirements for the review of slides and the correlation with histopathology results. These regulations make an information system with these tracking abilities almost a necessity.

In addition to CLIA, laboratory management must deal with other regulatory agencies (e.g., CAP, the Joint Commission on Accreditation of Healthcare Organizations) and their requirements. Many states also have enacted regulations for clinical laboratories. The FDA regulates and inspects (unannounced) several thousand blood banks and facilities that manufacture or produce blood products. NIDA operates an inspection and approval program for laboratories that test blood and urine specimens obtained from federal employees for the presence of drugs of abuse. NIDA has comprehensive standards for its inspection program, which is separate from those under the direction of HCFA.

Laboratories are subject to regulation regarding safety and infection control, and they need stringent hazardous chemicals and universal precautions programs in order to meet the regulations and ensure a safe working environment for their employees. The major agency involved in this area is the Occupational Safety and Health Administration (OSHA). For occupational exposure to hazardous chemicals in laboratories, OSHA's final rule outlines specific requirements for

- written hazard communication programs
- labels and other forms of warning
- material safety data sheets (MSDSs)
- employee information and training
- exposure monitoring

OSHA published its final rule for Occupational Exposure to Bloodborne Pathogens on December 6, 1991. The regulation requires an exposure control program with the following components:

1. exposure determination for employee infection control
2. control methods including:
   - universal precautions
   - engineering controls
   - work practices controls
   - personal protective equipment
3. hepatitis B virus vaccination
4. postexposure evaluation and follow-up
5. regulated waste disposal
6. labels and bags
7. housekeeping practices
8. laundry practices
9. training and education of employees
10. record keeping

Additional requirements of the Nuclear Regulatory Commission and the Department of Transportation may also apply, depending on the scope of services offered or the need to transport specimens across state lines.

In recent years, the Office of the Inspector General (OIG) of the DHHS has established a zero tolerance policy for fraud and abuse of federally funded health care programs and has created anti-abuse programs directed at investigating fraudulent activities associated with laboratory testing. Therefore, in 1997, the OIG published a Model Compliance Plan for Clinical Laboratories. This was revised in August 1998. The model is a guide to help laboratories establish a compliance program that will identify, minimize, and/or eliminate fraudulent actions associated with federally funded health care programs. The government is recommending that laboratories voluntarily establish such programs, although those laboratories previously found in violation of Medicare's rules have been required to implement such programs as part of their penalty negotiations. Elements of a true program include the following:

- documented standards of conduct for employees
- development and distribution of policies that promote the laboratory's commitment to compliance and address specific areas of potential fraud (e.g., billing, marketing, claims processing)
- designation of a chief compliance officer
- compliance education and training programs that are offered to employees
- use of audits to demonstrate compliance
- policies that specify the disciplinary action to be taken against employees who violate the compliance plan
- investigation and remediation of identified systemic and/or personnel problems
- evidence in the performance evaluations of supervisors and managers that adherence to compliance plan is a performance criterion for them
- policy to address the dismissal or retention of sanctioned individuals
- hotline mechanisms to receive complaints anonymously

- policies regarding record creation and retention

Laboratory regulation is becoming an increasingly important area that requires laboratory management and staff time as well as coordination with other hospital departments.

STRATEGIC PLANNING

Extensive regulation and competition among clinical laboratories have forced them to expand their service areas and develop networks in order to remain viable. These changes began with the design and implementation of ventures that allowed hospital laboratories to enter new markets. Often, they used a two-tiered approach. Hospitals initially marketed their services within the hospital community and then transferred the benefit of their efforts to external users. The traditional issues of price and service gain importance in this phase of marketing. Entering new markets resulted in volume increases that reduced unit costs and enabled the expansion of service levels in-house to include procedures that were not economically viable without this additional volume.

Current government cost-containment efforts include experimentation with managed care and risk sharing. This type of pressure is not new in laboratories. In the late 1970s, the lowest charge reimbursement regulations had a similar cost-containment objective; in the early 1990s it was regional competitive billing. Some specific alternatives that hospital laboratories are considering to respond to these pressures include

- entering into joint ventures with other hospitals to form regional laboratories
- sharing resources with other hospitals through cooperative ventures in which

certain nonemergent procedures are performed in only one of the participating hospitals (e.g., microbiology studies at Hospital A and chemistry profiling at Hospital B)

- marketing excess capacity to both traditional users, physicians' offices and group practices, and nontraditional users, such as other hospitals, industry, and veterinarians

The major goal of any of these ventures is to reduce unit costs, increase profitability, and generate additional revenue while improving or, at a minimum, maintaining quality and service. In the recent past, marketing the excess capacity was deemed the most desirable. Findings reported in the literature, however, indicate that joint ventures consisting of four hospitals in a geographic area with a total of 750 beds could reduce their workforce by 25 to 33 percent while reducing overhead and equipment needs and gaining more sophisticated data-processing systems.[8]

A critical mass of 1.5 to 2 million tests is necessary to make such a joint venture feasible. It appears that 40 to 60 percent of hospital laboratory chemistry and hematology testing can be sent off-site to a regional or reference center. Nearly all the microbiology, histology, and cytology testing can go offsite. Significant political issues (involving medical staff, particularly pathologists; infectious disease physicians; hematology/oncology physicians; and collective bargaining units) and operational issues (involving information systems, equipment configuration, and test menus) must be resolved prior to implementing such a venture.

The pressure to reduce costs remains intense. In 6 years, from 1992 through 1997, the hospital share of the laboratory marketplace has decreased from 50 to 35 percent.[9] Therefore, finding new ways to remain competitive will continue to be high on the agenda of clinical laboratories. Other alternatives have some savings associated with their strategies, but are less attractive than a joint venture regional laboratory.

In evaluating these alternatives, laboratories have developed more sophisticated management information systems than have other clinical services. The previously mentioned CAP workload reporting system was one of the first attempts to apply management engineering concepts in the laboratory workplace in order to identify various components of cost, specifically labor, the largest component. The incorporation of these concepts into costing systems makes it possible to determine unit costs. Costing systems are crucial in determining if an institution is competitive and what the parameters should be in developing fee schedules and managed care contracts.

Product line costing has become an important topic in health care. Many laboratories have been developing costing systems to determine marginal and incremental costs as a way to evaluate a variety of issues, ranging from equipment purchases to joint ventures. Those hospital laboratories that have not kept pace are finding that their laboratory services may be in jeopardy. Commercial laboratories and other hospitals are taking over in-house operations with the support of government regulations and policies that seem to foster this type of marketplace behavior.

CONCLUSION

The location and type of laboratory (i.e., regional, rapid response, or reference) in an organized health care delivery system will determine the service levels that a clinical laboratory will provide. The operational characteristics of a well-designed laboratory will reflect these service levels. Furthermore, they provide the basis for determining what goals and objectives the planning process must develop and implement to keep a laboratory system viable in today's health care environment.

NOTES

1. J.H. Boutweil and C.E. Stewart, Jr., "Service Levels in a Hospital Laboratory," *Laboratory Management* (November 1971).

2. R.E. Hager and P.J. Brzozowski, Determination of Service Level Feasibility: Should We Buy and Staff This New Gizmo? (Paper presented at the Center for Hospital Management Engineering Forum, Boston, MA, June 13–14, 1983).

3. College of American Pathologists, *Manual for Laboratory Workload Recording* (Skokie, IL: CAP Workload Recording Committee, 1984).

4. T.L. Lincoln and D. Essin, "Information Technology, Health Care, and the Future: What Are the Implications for the Clinical Laboratory?" *Clinical Laboratory Management Review* 6, no. 1 (1992): 95.

5. R.D. Aller, "The Laboratory Information System As a Medical Device: Inspection and Accreditation Issues," *Clinical Laboratory Management Review* 6, no. 1 (1992): 59.

6. B.A. Friedman and W.R. Dito, "Managing the Information Product of Clinical Laboratories," *Clinical Laboratory Management Review* 6, no. 1 (1992): 6.

7. College of American Pathologists, *Manual for Laboratory Planning and Design* (Danville, IL: CAP Subcommittee on Laboratory Resources, 1977).

8. G.A. Fattal et al., Operational and Financial Outcomes of Shared Laboratory Services in a Consolidated Hospital System, *Journal of the American Medical Association* 253, no. 14 (1985): 2076–2079.

9. J.W. Steiner, "The Virtual Laboratory: Regional Clinical Diagnostics for Integrated Delivery Systems," *Healthcare Financial Management* (November 1997).

PAUL J. BRZOZOWSKI, MT(ASCP), MPA, is a partner with Applied Management Systems, Inc. (AMS), a health care consulting firm in Burlington, Massachusetts. He is responsible for the clinical and general consulting services of AMS. He is also experienced in mergers and consolidations. Prior to joining AMS, Mr. Brzozowski was the Executive Vice President of Addison Gilbert Hospital in Gloucester, Massachusetts. As Chief Operating Officer, he was responsible for the daily operation of the hospital. Prior to joining Addison Gilbert Hospital, he was a health care consultant for Peat, Marwick, and Mitchell, and the Massachusetts Hospital Association, with a primary focus on clinical laboratory operation.

Mr. Brzozowski has participated in many seminars, client in-service programs, educational programs, and special lecture series, such as those sponsored by E.I. DuPont. He has over 25 years of health care experience.

He received a BS in medical technology from SUNY Upstate Medical Center, Syracuse, New York, and an MPA from Pennsylvania State University.

ELLEN A. MOLONEY, MT(ASCP), MBA, is the Director of Laboratory and Imaging Services at Newton–Wellesley Hospital in Newton, Massachusetts. Ms. Moloney is responsible for the operations of the laboratory and radiology departments. Prior to joining Newton–Wellesley Hospital, Ms. Moloney was a Senior Manager with Applied Management Systems, Inc. (AMS), a health care consulting firm in Burlington, Massachusetts. At AMS, she was involved primarily in laboratory-related engagements, including operational audits and support, needs assessment and acquisition of laboratory information systems, outreach marketing, and management support/training. Prior to joining AMS, Ms. Moloney was the Laboratory Operations Coordinator at Salem Hospital.

She received an MBA from Bentley College, Waltham, Massachusetts; a Certificate from Salem Hospital School of Medical Technology, Salem, Massachusetts; and a BS from Rivier College, Nashua, New Hampshire.

Appendix 24–A

Sample of Test Type by Section

- Anatomic pathology
  1. Gross and microscopic examination of surgical specimens
  2. Histochemical special stains (e.g., immunoperoxidase)
  3. Cell blocks
  4. Decalcification
- Cytology
  1. Papanicolaou smears
  2. Fine needle aspirates
  3. Body fluid (e.g., bronchial washings, pleural fluids) examinations
- Chemistry
  1. Electrolytes (e.g., sodium, potassium chloride, CO_2 measurement
  2. Blood glucose levels
  3. Drug levels
  4. Enzymes (SGOT, CPK, LDH)
  5. Electrophoresis studies (serum protein, hemoglobin)

- Hematology
  1. Complete blood cell count (CBC)
  2. White cell differential
  3. Coagulation studies (e.g., prothrombin time, factor assays)
- Microbiology
  1. Cultures (throat, sputum, wound—from any body source)
  2. Gram stains
  3. Sensitivities (studies used to determine most effective antibiotic therapy)
- Microscopy
  1. Urinalysis
  2. Examination of other body fluids (e.g., synovial, or joint, fluid; spinal fluid) for cells, crystals, etc.
  3. Semen analysis
- Blood bank
  1. Crossmatch (compatibility) testing
  2. ABO and Rh typing

Appendix 24–B

Job Analysis Checklist: Medical Director

Listed below are the specific duties and responsibilities associated with the general categories of activity included in most descriptions of a medical director position.

1. *Clinical Service*
   a. The medical director must review annually, or as changes occur, manuals (or their equivalent) for requesting laboratory services, specimen collection, patient preparation, reference values, and other pertinent information for utilizing laboratory services. This is to ensure that the manuals are available, that they are up to date, and that their testing parameters are acceptable to users.
   *b. Test methodologies and procedure manuals must meet the approval of accrediting agencies.
   *c. The quality control program must be directed so that it is acceptable to accrediting agencies and the medical staff.
   d. A pathologist, qualified physician, or, when appropriate, a qualified doctoral scientist must be available to provide consulting services that include
   • frozen section diagnosis in the surgical suite on both an emergency and scheduled basis

   • requests by staff physicians for help in selecting and interpreting laboratory tests
   e. Frozen section diagnosis must be ready in a timely fashion and recorded on the patient's chart while the patient is in the operating room.
   f. Reports of laboratory findings and analyses must be completed and in the patient's chart in a timely fashion.
   *g. Appropriate outcome criteria must be established, monitored, and reported to the hospital quality assurance committee.
   h. Slides, reports, and other appropriate materials must be sent to pathology specialists when so requested by the attending physician, or deemed necessary by the medical director.
   i. Work with the medical and surgical staff and transfusion committee must determine the adequacy of the inventory and utilization of blood products.
   *j. All departments must meet the standards of the Joint Commission on Accreditation of Healthcare Organizations, Food and Drug Administration, College of American Pathologists, and other agencies (e.g., American Association of Blood Banks) when accreditation is requested by the hospital.

---

*Function often delegated to section chief

*k. The laboratory must conform to hospital standards for data and systems control, forms control, computer applications, and results delivery.

 l. Records must be maintained in accordance with hospital, government, and accrediting agency requirements.

*m. New procedures must be introduced as appropriate for physicians, nursing service, laboratory staff, and patient needs.

*n. Assistance must be provided to other clinicians when necessary to obtain specimens for analysis. Such assistance includes bone marrow aspirates and fine needle biopsies.

2. *Human Resource Management*
   *a. The continuing education program must meet standards of accrediting agencies and the organization. A minimum continuing education requirement must be established for each category of employees.

   b. Appropriate meetings of the laboratory department must be held for announcements and education. A record of such meetings will be included in monthly and annual laboratory reports.

   *c. Input must be provided as to the type of reference material to be maintained so as to meet standards of the hospital medical library. Appropriate technical books and manuals must be available at the workbenches.

   *d. There must be participation in clinical department meetings.

   e. The continuing education requirements of the American Medical Association, College of American Pathologists, or equivalent must be met.

   *f. Appropriate CEU credits must be maintained.

   *g. There must be participation in the development of staff performance criteria and staff performance evaluations when appropriate. The medical director should provide input into the laboratory manager evaluation, and section chiefs should review the section supervisor evaluations as they pertain to technical ability.

3. *Administrative Responsibilities*
   a. Goals and objectives put forth by laboratory management and approved by the medical director must be compatible with those of the hospital as judged by the senior management of the organization.

   b. Policies, rules, and regulations must be appropriate, understandable, and complete as judged by the senior management of the hospital. They must conform to those of the organization and not violate those of any government, accrediting, or regulatory agency.

   c. Physical plant and departments must be organized to provide maximum efficiency.

   *d. Services must be scheduled with full consideration of need, cost, and regulatory priorities to the satisfaction of clinicians and administrator.

   e. It is essential to determine feasibility and maintain fiscal responsibility in introducing changes; therefore, requests for space, equipment, services, and personnel must be reasonable and justified with data. Purchases should be evaluated in light of cost-effectiveness, quality, and service.

   f. There must be participation in the strategic planning process.

   g. Budgets (capital and operating) must be submitted on time and adhered to unless deviations are adequately justified and approved.

Chapter 25

Material/Resource Management

William L. Scheyer and Barbara B. Friedman

It is commonly estimated that 30 to 50 percent of a hospital or organized delivery system's budget is related to material, equipment, and purchased services. Approximately half of this amount derives from the direct cost of acquiring materials and services; the other half, from the cost of managing them after acquisition. Labor expenses make up the largest portion of this second component.

Prior to 1970, the management of material was often haphazard, which was one of the contributing factors to the escalation of the cost of hospital care. In the 1970s, as these costs reached increasingly unacceptable levels, the concept of centralized materials management began to gain favor. As a result, methods of controlling expenses that had been used for many years in other industries began to be routinely applied in the health care industry. During the 1980s, greater emphasis was placed on group purchasing programs, centralized management of total inventories, and increased reliance on suppliers to provide additional services, such as consignment buying, supplier management of in-house inventories, and "just-in-time" shipments. In fact, this shift to the practice of using the supplier to provide hospital support services has continued into the 1990s to such an extent that some people have difficulty defining the rightful place of a material/resource manager in the hospital.

As the national debate over health care cost control intensifies, so does the search for ways to reduce the total cost of acquiring and managing materials and services. Regardless of how the job of material/resource manager is structured, the function of reducing cost will continue to be essential. Because not every hospital or organized delivery system has an effective materials management system in place, administrators must take a serious and critical look at the performance of this function in their organizations. The shift to organized health care delivery systems creates an ideal opportunity to consolidate the function of material/resource management and to achieve exemplary economies of scale for all entities in a system.

The authors thank Mr. Marty Edelman, Director of Material Management at New York University Medical Center, New York, for assistance in reviewing the material contained in this chapter.

The classic definition of materials management in hospitals is "the management and control of goods, services, and equipment from acquisition to disposition."[1] The essence of this definition is that there should be centralization of the purchasing, receiving, supply, storage, and distribution functions within the hospital. In addition, there should be centralized reprocessing of sterile, reusable supply items. The three most critical elements in a materials management program are (1) a corporate strategy for ensuring that materials (i.e., goods, services, and equipment) are purchased at the lowest total cost, (2) a related strategy to ensure that inventories and their associated carrying costs are aggressively monitored and controlled, and (3) availability of all required materials.

SUPPLY CHAIN

The flow of materials can best be visualized as a closed loop. This supply chain is shown in Figure 25–1. Opportunities for significant cost reductions exist at each point along the chain.

Originating Department

The actual decision to acquire supplies and equipment almost always takes place in individual departments throughout the hospital or organized delivery system. The material/resource manager can assist the head of the originating department in a number of ways, however, such as helping forecast needs for the coming year, providing information on sources of supply and prevailing market conditions, conducting negotiations with suppliers, and designating effective systems for storing and maintaining materials until they are consumed.

Generally, hospital managers have been trained either in specific clinical disciplines or in general administration, but rarely have they been trained in the techniques of materials management. As a result, the material/resource manager is a valuable resource for

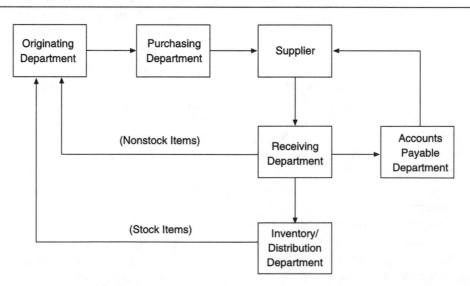

Figure 25–1 Supply Chain

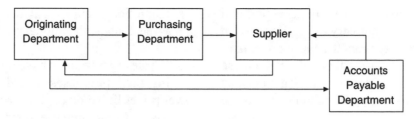

Figure 25–2 Supply Chain (Alternate 1)

ensuring that supplies, equipment, and purchased services are used in a cost-effective manner throughout the organization. The material/resource manager normally has direct responsibility for managing the functions of centralized purchasing, receiving, storage/distribution, and central sterile reprocessing. He or she normally has no direct relationship with the accounts payable department. It is vital that there be open lines of communication between the accounts payable, purchasing, and receiving departments, however. These departments must work together effectively to process the high volume of purchase/receipt/payment transactions that occur every day.

Because there usually is no direct relationship between the materials management department and other departments within the hospital, there should be a corporate level statement of policy concerning the execution of materials management functions. It is important that the material/resource manager

establish a consultative relationship with all of the departments within the hospital in order to ensure that appropriate materials management practices are followed.

As hospitals utilize more special services from suppliers, the originating departments have come to play a more critical role in ensuring proper management of their supplies. For example, suppliers may deliver orders directly to the originating department (Figure 25–2). Another variation is for the supplier to conduct PAR-level inspections in the originating department and then deliver the needed materials directly to the department (Figure 25–3).

In both of these cases, the receiving department may not control the actual receipt of the materials. It is important, therefore, for the originating department head to make sure that the goods are actually received in the right quantities and reported correctly to the accounts payable department. There is a risk that the originating department personnel will

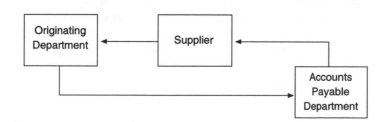

Figure 25–3 Supply Chain (Alternate 2)

not exercise sufficient care in accepting and documenting the delivery or, particularly in the PAR-level situation, that the supplier may overstock the department in order to increase sales. The material/resource manager must be involved in setting up and monitoring these special supplier services so that the interests of the hospital and/or organized delivery system are protected.

Purchasing Department

The primary contribution of the purchasing department is to lower the price of goods and services. The two main tools to be used in accomplishing this objective are competitive bidding and direct negotiation. By consolidating control of the purchasing function under the direction of the material/resource manager, it is possible to ensure that the use of these tools is consistent and effective throughout the organization. In addition to negotiating lower prices, the purchasing department can obtain favorable terms and conditions, which managers outside the purchasing department often neglect to request at the time the transaction is conducted. Payment of freight charges, extended warranties, and other special services can frequently be obtained.

Sometimes it is possible to obtain lower prices and additional services through participation in formal group purchasing arrangements. Such groups have continued to gain in power and importance within the health care industry. They range from groups organized by local hospital associations to huge national groups with hundreds of participating organizations. Some of the advantages are

- extensive legal review of contracts
- purchasing staff freed from routine bidding of products

- promotion of standardization
- agreements with national product leaders

All these organizations have the same goal: pooling their purchases in order to obtain lower prices based on the high volume of the purchases. As the pressure to cut bottom line operating costs continues to intensify, the importance of joining the most effective purchasing groups increases. In the 1990s, mergers of hospitals effectively made groups out of systems or networks of hospitals, which essentially attempted to negotiate their own deals from major manufacturers and distributors.

As the new millennium approaches, groups will merge, create long-term agreements up to 7 years, and further enhance their contracts with value-added services such as risk-sharing market share incentives within the group.

The Supplier

Although suppliers are not under the direct control of the material/resource manager and their contributions to cost reduction are essentially extensions of the efforts of the purchasing agents, suppliers have it within their power to provide the hospital and/or organized delivery system with many cost reduction opportunities, such as lower prices, favorable payment terms, local warehousing, consulting assistance, special usage reports, and in-service training. The material/resource manager should become skilled at establishing relationships with suppliers that result in the hospital's receiving as broad a range of benefits as possible. The hospital invests its business in the relationship with the supplier, and the supplier invests benefits and services that go beyond the normal selling price. It is important that both participants receive an adequate return on their investment.

Consistent with the trend of shifting the functions of materials management to suppliers, many hospitals or organized delivery systems rely on a just-in-time approach to the delivery of supplies. Accurate forecasting of department needs is required, along with accurate interaction between the computer systems of both hospital and supplier. In essence, the supplier makes more frequent deliveries of smaller quantities in order to ensure that the hospital department has the needed items just in time for use. This reduces on-hand inventories within the hospital, thus freeing the funds related to maintaining inventories.

Some professionals in the industry feel so strongly about this approach that they believe organized delivery systems and hospitals should not even be in the materials management business. Suppliers would not provide these services, however, if the services did not add to their own profits. Administrators and material/resource managers should keep in mind that the basic work must be done; the question is whether it is more efficient and less costly for the supplier or the hospital/network to do the basic work. Issues such as cost of labor, economies of scale, and access to technology must be weighed. Another circumstance to be considered is that the organization that controls the details of the work usually controls the outcome of the process. Thus, if the hospital relinquishes too much control over the work to the supplier, it risks losing control over the final cost of the program.

Special supplier services are definitely of value, particularly when the supplier is willing to be creative and work with the hospital or organized delivery system to customize programs that meet the special needs of the organization. Such programs are an increasingly common component of the management armamentarium of the modern hospital

or organized delivery system. As in any area of management, however, measurement and monitoring are the keys to success.

Receiving Department

It is the responsibility of the receiving department to ensure that the correct items, in proper condition, are officially received into the organization. Savings result from detection of supplier shipping errors, identification and correction of damaged goods, and timely notification of receipt to the accounting department in order to obtain all available discounts. This department's contribution to the hospital or organized delivery system's bottom line rests largely on two key functions: (1) matching invoices and (2) adjusting the timing of payments to suppliers. It is essential that the supplier's invoice be accurately matched to the documents verifying receipt of the goods in the hospital. If this is not done consistently and accurately, there is a high risk of paying for goods not actually received.

When goods bypass the receiving dock and go directly to the originating department, the challenge to the receiving supervisor is to make sure that the goods are properly inspected and recorded into the inventory and payment records of the hospital. In many hospitals, inspection of the inner contents of packages remains with the ordering department. Typically, they just have to communicate mistakes prior to the payment of the invoice.

In general, payments should be held for as long as possible—up to the point that a discount will be lost. Excessive delays in making payments damage the business reputation of a hospital or an organized delivery system and weaken its future negotiating power. Excessive speed in making payments unnecessarily gives away the use of the hospital's money, however. In fact, two principles are inherent in getting excellent prices: (1) provide a decent size order, usually a minimum of $100.00, and (2) pay on time, preferably within 30 days. Above all, in order to maintain an effective schedule of correct payments, there must be a smooth flow of communication between the purchasing, receiving, and accounts payable departments.

Inventory and Distribution Departments

In recent years, a great deal of attention has been paid to managing inventories within hospitals or organized delivery systems. Benefits that result from reducing inventory levels include the release of money to be used for other purposes; the release of space to be used for other purposes; avoidance of the need to construct new space; lower expense as a result of reduced obsolescence, damage, and theft; and somewhat less labor needed to handle the reduced level of supplies. In other words, the opportunity cost of utilizing monies for a more beneficial cause.

Most hospitals and organized delivery systems still spend the major part of their efforts on controlling official inventories, usually found in the central storeroom, but the more aggressive hospitals are starting to concentrate on the unofficial inventories. Some have adopted the special supplier–services approach to the extent that they have eliminated their central inventories. Unofficial inventories are stocks of supplies that have already been entered as an expense in the accounting records. They should be considered inventories in that they are in storage and awaiting consumption. There is a particularly significant cost reduction potential in supply-intensive departments, such as operating rooms and catheter laboratories.

The selection of methods for distributing materials throughout the organization also can have an impact on the total cost of operations, particularly in organized health care delivery systems. In general, the most effective systems are those that replenish supplies to predetermined levels on a scheduled basis, without the end user having to initiate the request. Such automatic replenishment systems reduce the amount of time spent by relatively well paid, clinically trained employees in ordering and handling supplies. In addition, such systems more accurately link the issuance of supplies to actual patterns of consumption, for example, through bar coding. As a result, they tend to reduce overall inventory levels, with associated savings. The maintenance of such systems provides another opportunity to monitor and promote product standardization, which further enhances the efficiency of the inventory system.

Computer Support

In the past, most materials management information systems were integrated with a hospital's financial information systems. As a result, enhancements to the materials management system often received lower priority. The proliferation of mini- and microcomputers has made it possible to acquire specialized hardware/software packages to support materials management functions at a relatively low cost. These programs are far more flexible and effective than in the past; moreover, they can be operated as standalone systems or can be linked to the accounts payable system via specially written programs.

In order to maximize the benefits of a centralized materials management program, it is vital to have accurate and detailed information about the multitude of transactions that take place within the system every day. Larger hospitals and organized delivery systems almost have to computerize the materials management function in order to handle the large volume of transactional data generated each day. If the basic materials management functions are well designed, the advantages of computerized information support far outweigh the costs of the computer system.

MANAGING THE CORE FUNCTIONS

Purchasing

An effective purchasing department is the cornerstone of a successful materials management program. The keys to success in this area lie in (1) setting up well designed systems for routinely processing large amounts of information both effectively and efficiently and (2) establishing operational priorities that focus the most attention on those items that have the greatest impact on the organization. The three purposes of the purchasing department are to

1. Assist all departments in obtaining products and services of appropriate quality from reputable and reliable suppliers at the lowest total cost to the organization.
2. Ensure that appropriate and ethical business practices are applied throughout the organization.
3. Serve as a source of information for the rest of the organization concerning available products, sources of supply, current and anticipated market conditions, and application of effective purchasing techniques.

The first step in establishing a strong purchasing program is to obtain a written statement of support from the organization's chief executive officer (CEO). Circulating this statement to all entities and departments, along with a description of the way that the purchasing system will work, will make it clear to everyone that all purchasing transactions must be carried out by means of the centralized purchasing process. The best method for enforcing this requirement is to establish a numbered purchase order system and to refuse delivery of any item not covered by a hospital purchase order number. In the 1990s, some organizations began to use procurement cards.

The physical layout, procedures, and filing systems of the purchasing department can be organized in any number of ways as long as adequate provision is made for the following elements:

- use of a legally acceptable purchase order form that ensures terms and conditions favorable to the organization
- a method for determining who is authorized to make purchases for the organization
- a file of approved signatures for use in ensuring that purchases are made only by authorized people
- a clearly defined requisitioning process
- a list of approved suppliers from whom purchases can be made
- clearly defined procedures for obtaining competitive bids from suppliers
- a method for tracking and expediting open purchase orders
- a method for ensuring that proper credit is received for goods returned to the supplier
- a method for monitoring and documenting supplier performance
- a method for monitoring the timeliness and effectiveness of the performance of the purchasing department

The purchasing manager should develop and adhere to a strategic plan that focuses attention primarily on those items that have the greatest financial impact. Application of a technique known as ABC analysis is helpful in developing this strategic plan. This technique is most frequently used in the area of inventory control, but it can also be used in analyzing purchases. First, all expenditures are classified into major categories. Then, the individual items within each category are rank-ordered according to dollar value. Approximately 80 percent of the dollars expended will come from approximately 20 percent of the items acquired. Some items, such as X-ray film, certain classes of pharmaceuticals, and capital items, represent a major portion of the budget, and their purchases warrant particular attention. Specific strategies for handling capital acquisitions, supplies, and purchased services should be developed. As more individual hospitals become members of larger corporate organizations or organized delivery systems, purchasing groups will play an increasingly important role.

Competitive Bids

Ideally, competition for the hospital's and/or system's business will be sought in every case. Competitive bids can be obtained by

- requesting formal, sealed bids to be opened publicly
- requesting written quotations to be evaluated in the purchasing department
- seeking comparative prices over the telephone
- negotiating fixed contract prices for items or groups of items
- joining a purchasing group that provides access to negotiated, competitive prices

The method used to obtain competitive prices depends on the nature of the items being purchased. Major capital items may require sealed public bids, whereas smaller routine items may require only telephone price checking. Items that are purchased repeatedly lend themselves to fixed contract pricing. No matter what method is used, it is good practice to document routinely the percentage of purchases made using competitive bidding of any sort. Sample bidding instructions are shown in Appendixes 25–A and 25–B.[2]

The first step in the competitive bidding process is to issue a request for proposal (RFP) or request for bid (RFB) to potential suppliers. The request should very clearly specify the goods or services sought and should have sufficient detail to ensure a fair evaluation of competing proposals or bids. If additional negotiation will take place after the bids have been received, the initial request should include a statement to this effect.[3]

All qualified suppliers should have the opportunity to compete, and the purchasing agent should not divulge the details of one supplier's proposal to another. Once all have been received, the proposals should be evaluated not only on the basis of price, but also on total cost to the hospital. Such elements as price protection, warranties, freight charges, installation, operating costs, and repair costs should be considered part of the total cost. When the final selection has been made, sufficient time should be taken in preparing the purchase order so that all of the benefits obtained through the competitive process are protected in writing. Finally, all of the unsuccessful bidders should be notified of the selection. The hospital and/or organized delivery system should maintain a reputation for considerate and professional treatment of its suppliers in order to ensure active competition for future transactions.

Capital Equipment Purchasing

The process of acquiring capital equipment provides some of the greatest opportunities for cost savings. Whereas an entire supply inventory may account for $500,000, a single piece of high-technology clinical equipment can cost that much or more. As a result, reducing the cost of such items by even a few percentage points can lead to significant savings.

The initial step in managing capital acquisitions is the establishment of a program for financial justification. Ultimate approval of major requests must come from the CEO and the finance committee of the board of directors, but the process begins with the head of the originating department. In order to promote uniform practice throughout the hospital or organized delivery system and to enable the final decision makers to evaluate competing requests rationally, a standard system for developing financial justifications should be used. A worksheet for this purpose is shown in Exhibit 25–1.

Once a project has been approved, the purchasing manager should assist the requesting department head in the development of functional specifications. These should be written in terms of expected performance, and every effort should be made to make the specifications generic. Requesting department heads, as well as physicians involved in using the equipment, sometimes resist making the specifications generic. Traditionally, suppliers have focused their marketing efforts on the end users, who may be persuaded to write the requirements so that only one supplier's equipment is able to meet the specifications. Such specific requirements diminish, if they do not eliminate, the opportunity for competition, however, and the hospital pays a higher than necessary price for the item.

The standards of performance should be given to the competing suppliers so that all bids are submitted in an acceptable format for evaluation. In addition, once the equipment has been purchased and installed, these written standards should serve as the basis for ensuring that the equipment meets all safety and regulatory requirements. The assistance of in-house technical support staff or, if necessary, outside consultants should be obtained to verify that the equipment is fully acceptable. Any deviations or problems should be identified and resolved quickly in order to ensure that the hospital receives full value for its money.

As in all purchases, capital acquisitions require that

- A clear set of generic specifications be developed to serve as the basis for decision making.
- As many reputable and reliable suppliers as possible be allowed to submit bids for the order.
- All quotations be fairly evaluated.
- Negotiations be coordinated through the purchasing department.
- Upon installation, all equipment be tested according to written standards and by qualified technical personnel to ensure that all requirements are satisfactorily met.

Purchasing Techniques

Group Purchasing. Because larger purchases generally result in lower prices, groups of buyers who pool their buying power can usually gain lower prices than any of the individuals acting alone. There are costs involved in belonging to a purchasing group, however. These include the direct cost of membership, commonly expressed as an annual fee, and a certain loss of control in product selection. The members of the group must meet periodically to evaluate supplier proposals, products, and performance and to monitor the performance of the group itself. There are also costs associated with participating in these meetings, such as the costs of conference calls and electronic mail exchanges.

Exhibit 25–1 Worksheet To Evaluate Purchasing Requests

I. Costs

A. Estimated cost of equipment (including shipping) $ _____   _____
Dept. Manager
Purchasing

B. Estimated cost of installation, building modifications (please attach details) $ _____   _____
Dept. Manager
Maintenance

C. Depreciable life of project   _____   _____
yrs.   Dept. Manager
Accounting

D. Equipment to be replaced:

1. Description _____
_____
_____

2. Fixed asset number   _____

3. Present age   _____

4. Assigned useful life   _____

5. Current book value $ _____   _____
Dept. Manager
Accounting

6. Current market value $ _____   _____
Dept. Manager
Purchasing

E. Associated increase in expenses

	Year 1	Year 2	Year 3	Year 4	Year 5	Year 6	Year 7	Year 8	Year 9	Year 10
Training										
Labor										
Utilities										
Supplies										
Other										
Total increase in expenses										

II. Revenue and Decrease of Expenses

	Year 1	Year 2	Year 3	Year 4	Year 5	Year 6	Year 7	Year 8	Year 9	Year 10
A. Increases in revenue 1. Revenue increases from additional inpatients a. Medicare										
b. Medicaid										
c. Others										

continues

Exhibit 25–1 continued

2. Revenue increases from additional list of current inpatients											
a. Medicare											
b. Medicaid											
c. Others											
3. Revenue increases from additional outpatient testing											
a. Medicare											
b. Medicaid											
c. Others											
B. Decreases in revenue											
1. Revenue decrease from reduced length of stay											
a. Medicare											
b. Medicaid											
c. Others											
2. Revenue decrease from reduced number of inpatients											
a. Medicare											
b. Medicaid											
c. Others											
C. Net increase or decrease in revenue											
D. Decrease of expenses											
1. Reduction in expenses from reduced length of stay											
a. labor											
b. supplies											
c. utilities											
d. other											
2. Reduction in expenses from reduced number of inpatients											
a. labor											
b. supplies											
c. utilities											
d. other											
3. Reduction in expenses from new technology											
a. labor											
b. supplies											
c. utilities											
d. other											
4. Total reduction in expenses											

Source: Departmental document, reprinted with permission of St. Francis–St. George Hospital, Inc., Cincinnati, Ohio.

The question of whether a hospital or an organized health care delivery system should either join or maintain its membership in a group is purely an economic one. Will membership reduce total costs? If so, membership is worthwhile. Before committing to a particular group, however, the organization should consider some additional issues involving the group itself:

- How well do group goals and objectives correlate with those of the system or institution?
- Is the group program well focused and mature, or does the group still have to get its program fully organized?
- What are the administrative costs of the group? How efficiently does the group operate?
- How skilled is the group at negotiation? Is the group going to negotiate major contracts? Is the system or institution satisfied that the group can do that job well?
- How does the group handle product evaluation and standardization? Since product standardization is an essential element of group purchasing, is the system or institution sure it can participate effectively in that process?
- How does the group track record overall compare with that of other groups—or with what the system or institution can do on its own?

As for the suppliers who hold agreements with the group, are the products, quality, and service they offer generally acceptable to the organization? As for the others in the group,

- Are they larger or smaller than the system or hospital? Generally, smaller hospitals benefit most from being in groups with larger ones.
- What is the level of commitment of the member systems or hospitals? More committed groups generally produce lower prices.
- How well managed are the others in the group? Are they institutions with which the organization will be comfortable working closely?
- Has thought been given to the competitive position of the organization vis-à-vis others in the group?

Other hospitals, including members, should be asked about the group. Those questioned should include other hospitals that might have belonged to the group, but do not (Why not?) and hospitals that once belonged to the group, but left (Why did they leave?)[4]

Almost every system or hospital now belongs to at least one purchasing group, and many belong to more than one. This presents a dilemma in that a group's effectiveness depends in part on its ability to deliver agreed upon blocks of purchases to its suppliers. If members participate in more than one group and each group provides contracts for the same items, which group's contract will the members utilize? For a hospital, the answer is usually to use the contract that provides the lowest price or that provides a preferred brand at a satisfactory price. In terms of being an honest and effective participant in the groups, however, the purchasing manager needs to think through the hospital's policy position on the issue of membership in multiple groups.

The keys to maximizing the benefits of group purchasing include

- carefully selecting strong and effective groups to join
- establishing control over product standardization and support of the group within the system or hospital
- establishing a leadership position or, at

least, a position of strength within the group

- consistently using the group contracts
- continually monitoring the price performance of the group to ensure that the system or hospital is getting best value
- gaining hospital staff support at department head levels

Prime Suppliers. Another approach to obtaining lower prices and better service is to establish a relationship with a single supplier for a major portion of the system's purchases. In return, the supplier is expected to provide

- lower prices
- extended price protection
- minimal back orders
- lower in-house inventory levels
- simplified paperwork in purchasing, receiving, and paying for items
- other special services

Potential disadvantages of using a prime supplier include the following:

- Economic competition may be reduced over a period of time.
- Quality may be inconsistent across the supplier's complete line of products.
- The hospital may become overly dependent on the supplier, so that the change in suppliers would be disruptive to hospital routines.
- Prices may creep upward if inadequate controls are placed on the relationship.

Overall, a prime supplier relationship can provide significant economic and operational advantages to the hospital if it is well thought out, effectively negotiated, designed with adequate controls to protect the hospital or system, and carefully monitored. The absence of any of these elements can have a negative effect on the hospital or organized delivery system.

Buying on Consignment. In consignment buying, the hospital or organized delivery system takes physical possession of items, but does not pay for them until they are actually consumed. Obviously, this method provides a cash flow advantage to the hospital. It also should cause the supplier to work more aggressively with the hospital to reduce inventory levels, because higher inventories mean more supplies for which payment has not yet been received.

As in any special arrangement, however, there are potential disadvantages, including the following:

- Proper inventory control practices are necessary to avoid payment for lost or damaged goods.
- Prices may rise more than a normal amount to cover the supplier's additional costs.
- The supplier may place too little stock in inventory.
- The supplier may place too much stock in inventory in order to obtain free warehouse space.
- If the supplier "buys out" existing supplies, it becomes difficult to terminate the relationship because a major one-time expense will be required to reestablish the hospital's inventory.

Consignment buying traditionally has been used most often for expensive, specialized items that are not needed every day, but to which the hospital must have immediate access when they are needed. Examples include orthopedic hardware, intraocular lenses, and special types of sutures. However, a number of companies are now providing consignment programs for broad categories of medical/surgical supplies, including pacemakers and leads.

Stockless Purchasing. In some cases, certain categories of supplies are removed from the hospital's or organized delivery system's inventory and are kept in the supplier's warehouse. Departments send requisitions for supplies directly to the supplier instead of to the storeroom. The supplier then prepares the orders for shipment directly to the individual departments.

The purchasing staff does not review orders, nor does the receiving department staff check them in. Staff in the accounts payable department review consolidated invoices only to verify that they are generally reasonable in size. The risk, of course, is that payment will be made for items that were not actually received. The control on these purchases must reside in the ordering departments, as their staff both check in orders when they are received and reconcile charges against their department budgets at the end of the month.

This purchasing technique improves the cash flow of the hospital or organized delivery system because of reduced inventories and leads to operating savings because of the simplified paperwork and reduced workload in the purchasing, receiving, and, to some extent, accounts payable departments. It also allows the hospital or system to make use of the large-volume buying power of the supplier. For example, items that may be important, but of low volume to the hospital, would normally have a relatively high price. The supplier, because it buys for multiple accounts, usually can obtain a lower price. Part of this price reduction should be passed on to the hospital or organized delivery system as a benefit of the program.

One disadvantage is that there is no emergency stock in a central on-site inventory, which makes accurate forecasting and ordering by the individual departments even more important. Building a small reserve in the basic supply level of the ordering department can mitigate this problem, but this should be done carefully in order not to diminish the inventory reduction savings. As in consignment buying, the removal of supplies from the hospital's inventory has the effect of tying the hospital closely to the particular supplier. As a result, it can be difficult to terminate the relationship.

Stockless purchasing can afford the hospital or organized delivery system significant savings. It is vital, however, that the supplier be carefully selected and that performance, in terms of prices, order fill rate, and stock picking/billing accuracy, be closely monitored. In addition, the hospital or system should identify a list of critical items that it must have available at all times. The contract should include this list and bind the suppliers always to have these items on hand. Finally, the hospital or system should always have final authority over product selection; this should never be relinquished to the supplier.

Receiving

As noted earlier, the goal of the receiving department is to make sure that all ordered items are correctly counted, received into the organization's accounting records, and then delivered to the ordering departments. Every effort should be made to have receiving documents or computer images awaiting the arrival of shipments. These should be a duplicate of the purchase order, but without the expected quantities listed. This serves as a control to ensure that the receiving clerks actually count the items when they are being received.

Once the initial counting and paperwork are completed, the receiving documents should be reviewed by a receiving control clerk. This person compares the receiving documents to the log of open purchase orders and reconciles any problems involving overshipments, undershipments, unit of measure errors, or counting errors.

Separate areas within the receiving department should be designated for counting and completion of paperwork, holding items that are awaiting delivery, and holding items that are awaiting return to the supplier. Physical separation of shipments so that they do not become intermingled is important.

Many of the special supplier programs involve shipments directly to the ordering departments. Whenever possible, it is still best to bring the shipments physically through the receiving department. A special challenge for the receiving supervisor will be to make sure these shipments are processed not only accurately, but also rapidly. When shipments must go directly to the ordering department, it is worthwhile to assign a receiving clerk to work with the ordering department personnel to verify accurate receipt and posting. Even under new programs, it is worth the effort to follow tried and true materials management practices.

Inventory Control

The goal of inventory control is to hold the least possible number of supplies, while not running out of critical items. Usually, inventory has been considered to be only that material stored in the official storeroom and carried as an asset in the accounting records. It is more appropriate, however, also to classify as inventory those supplies stored in the various operating departments, even though they have been charged out as an expense to the department accounts. These so-called unofficial inventories can be worth up to three times the value of the official inventory.[5] Obviously, they provide a significant opportunity for total cost reduction.

The first step in reducing inventories is to conduct a physical count in each department. Most areas do not use a perpetual inventory system, that is, one that keeps a running record of the inventory's value as supplies are added to and deducted from storage. It is harder to determine the value of the inventory in these areas, because in addition to finding and counting each item, it is necessary to look up the most recent price of the items and calculate the total value for each storage location. Then the figures should be compared to the value of supplies charged to the departments during the past year. A turnover rate can then be determined using the following formula[6]:

$$\text{Turnover} = \frac{\text{Annual dollar value of issues}}{\text{Average inventory value}}$$

Some department inventories turn over slowly; some, more quickly because of their special nature. On the average, the goal should be inventory turnover approximately 12 times per year.

Once the initial inventory values and turnover rates have been determined, targets can be established for each department. The department head and the materials manager should work together to determine the goals and the strategies for achieving those goals. After the strategic plans have been established, periodic follow-up physical inventories should be taken to monitor progress.

The strategic plan should address (1) the identification of obsolete, expired, or slow-moving items and ways to dispose of them, and (2) the identification of excess supplies of normally moving items and ways to bring the inventory levels back into line and keep them there. Obsolete and slow-moving supplies may be disposed of through the following means:

- returning to the supplier for credit (a restocking charge may be applied)
- finding a user elsewhere in the organization
- selling or trading to other organizations

- selling to a salvage dealer
- donating to charity

Normally moving items that have become grossly overstocked can be reduced by returning the excess to the central inventory, finding a user elsewhere in the organization, or returning the excess to the supplier for credit. The last option should be used only if there is a significant excess that will not be consumed for a long period of time and if there is little or no restocking charge. Otherwise, these items can be brought into line simply by not reordering until a calculated reorder point has been reached. A formal reorder point (ROP) can be calculated using the following formula[7]:

$$\text{ROP} = \text{Usage per day} \times \text{Lead time} \\ \text{(in days)} + \text{Safety factor}$$

Once reorder points have been established for items, it is necessary to calculate how much to order. A standard method for determining order quantity in most other industries is to use the economic order quantity (EOQ) formula, which mathematically balances ordering cost and holding cost to determine the quantity that results in the lowest total cost.[8]

$$\text{Economic Order Quantity} = \sqrt{\frac{\text{Annual usage} \times 2 \times \text{Order cost}}{\text{Unit cost} \times \text{Holding cost (\%/100)}}}$$

The key elements of this formula include:

- Ordering cost: generally considered the cost to place an order, which includes labor, supplies, and overhead in the purchasing, receiving, and accounts payable departments
- Holding cost: generally considered the cost to handle and maintain the items once they are in the system's possession, which includes opportunity cost, labor, supplies, and overhead in the inventory departments
- Unit cost: generally considered the cost of a single unit of the item for which the EOQ is being calculated

The EOQ formula sometimes results in quantities that are impractical because the necessary storage space is unavailable; in those cases, the actual order quantity can be adjusted. Many hospitals do not use it, because the calculation is cumbersome unless it can be computer-generated. Again, however, the EOQ formula is helpful to understand and to use as a check system in setting final quantities.

In another approach the inventory manager may determine order quantity by (1) deciding how many days of inventory to keep on hand or, alternatively, the turnover rate desired; (2) adding the required safety stock; and then (3) calculating the required order quantity based on the lead time of the particular supplier.

A sound strategy for reducing and effectively managing inventories, then, includes the following steps:

- Conduct physical inventories of each storage location.
- Calculate turnover rates for each location.
- Establish target turnover rates for each item and each location.
- Calculate reorder points and EOQs for each item.
- Conduct periodic follow-up physical inventories to assess progress toward the goals.
- Adjust goals, reorder points, and EOQs as appropriate, based on changes within the system.

Distribution

The selection and design of systems for distributing materials throughout an organization and for replenishing stocks of supplies in user departments are key variables in the effective management of inventory levels.

Types of Distribution Systems

There are four basic options for distributing material: (1) requisitions, (2) PAR-level systems, (3) point-of-use replenishment systems, and (4) exchange carts. The application of computer software programs, which can more accurately and more quickly handle the large volume of data generated by the multitude of daily transactions, can enhance any of these systems, but computerization does not change the basic systems themselves.

Requisitions. The most traditional distribution system and generally the least effective is requisitioning. In this system, the personnel of individual departments control the process of deciding when and how much to order. It is common to find this function either performed by highly paid, clinically trained employees or delegated to lower paid employees without an inventory control background. In either case, it is often a low priority and does not receive adequate attention. As a result, the quality of the ordering process is inconsistent and random, which can lead both to unnecessarily high inventory levels and, at other times, to unacceptably low inventory levels. This system also can have the effect of inflating the inventory in the central storeroom, as the storeroom supervisor builds an extra cushion to prepare for random large orders. A final result of this system is that it generates many extra requisitions and telephone requests for additional supplies; these are time-consuming and ex-

pensive for both the ordering department and the central storeroom.

The only advantages to this system are that it is simple, is easy to understand (if not to do well), and requires minimal capital investment.

PAR-Level Systems. When an organization uses a PAR-level system a person from the central storeroom visits each ordering department on a scheduled basis, counts the supplies, writes an order to bring quantities up to par levels, obtains the supplies, returns them to the department, and replenishes the supplies up to a standard or PAR level. In a variation of this system, personnel use computer support to analyze data about past consumption and calculate a predicted order, and the storeroom employee delivers this order to the unit. Additional supplies that may be required are delivered on a later trip. In either case, this is a relatively labor-intensive system, and it provides somewhat weaker control over the productivity of the employees who deliver the orders.

The advantages of this type of system are that it more effectively links the disbursement of supplies to actual usage. It places the distribution function in the hands of employees who are lower paid than clinical employees and for whom the function is a high priority. Finally, it requires a relatively low capital investment.

Point-of-Use Replenishment. A variation of the PAR-level system is point-of-use replenishment. In this system, the use of a supply item triggers a request for replenishment. This is usually supported by automatic computer generation of an order, as the total number of transactions makes order generation by hand cumbersome and prone to errors of omission.

Replenishment orders can be filled from central inventory or directly from the supplier's warehouse. In either case, the orders for single units of an item can be held for a period of time and consolidated into a reasonably sized order to make more efficient use of the delivery system.

The materials management staff should consult with the ordering departments to set appropriate supply levels and delivery time requirements, and to verify stock levels and fill rates periodically. These systems also can be used to support cost accounting systems. When properly designed and managed, such systems can provide information on the total cost of supply usage for a patient with a particular diagnosis, or for particular procedures. This helps top management in making strategic marketing and operational decisions. The trend will continue to be more toward the installation of point-of-use systems, whenever possible, although the capital cost of the point-of-use installation will be a deterrent for some organizations.

Exchange Carts. Another variation on the PAR-level system involves the use of an exchange cart. In this case, all or most of the supplies for a department are placed on a movable cart. The standard quantities can be adjusted dynamically through the application of a computer program, if desired. A second, identical cart is also prepared. On a scheduled basis, the first cart, which has been depleted, is taken from the user department, and the second cart, filled, is exchanged with it.

The primary advantage of this system lies in the greater control possible over the productivity and performance quality of the employees who fill the carts. By having all carts replenished in a central area, the storeroom supervisor is better able to monitor performance. In addition, compared to the PAR-level system, this system reduces travel time by replacing multiple trips between the ordering department and the storeroom with a single trip to exchange the carts. The disad-

vantages are that a large capital investment in carts is required, and space is needed for holding carts in both the user department and the storeroom.

A variation of this system for use in the surgery department is the surgical case cart system in which carts are not exchanged, but are set up especially for each surgical case and then delivered to the surgery department when needed. The disadvantages of high capital investment and space intensity are also present here. Space formerly set aside in the surgery suite, a particularly expensive location, can be released for more productive purposes, however. The carts can be prepared and stored in a separate, less expensive location.

In addition, the cart can be used as a back table during the surgical procedure and can then be used to transport all used or soiled supplies and instruments back to the central processing area. This is helpful from an infection control standpoint.

Selection of a Distribution System

Several factors are important in the selection of a distribution system:

- design of existing systems and how well they are working
- number of individual departments and storage locations
- quantity and mixture of supplies in each area
- existing storage and handling equipment
- available space
- physical relationship between departments
- traffic routes
- labor costs for each area
- cash flow considerations

Kowalski, a materials management consultant, has developed a 15-step planning model for selecting, designing, and implementing distribution systems.[9]

1. Determine on-hand inventory levels in each affected department. This calculation will become the basis for identifying appropriateness and costs of the current inventory level, as well as for establishing target inventory levels and turnover rates.

2. Identify supply/demand/usage for each user department for a 24-hour period. The need/demand can be determined by sampling actual consumption for a period of time; usually 31 days is an adequate time period. High, low, and average daily demand figures for that sample should be noted. Numerical averages create a smoothing effect so the peak demands should be planned for. Finally, input should be obtained from the users by having them evaluate the data gathered. They often can identify a peak period that is unrepresentative of routine activity and can help establish more appropriate levels of inventory.

3. Draft a list of all products to be used for each department. This list should include such information as (1) item number, (2) source, (3) description, (4) units of issue, (5) unit cost, (6) optimum inventory level, and (7) charge versus noncharge status. It can be prepared before taking physical counts and can serve as a master catalogue/worksheet.

4. Determine the frequency of supply replacement, which depends on the type of system selected and the targets for on-hand inventory levels and turnover rates.

5. Identify the functional requirements and specifications required for all exchange carts, if that system is used.

Different-sized carts may be required for different areas, depending on the volume of products being maintained on the cart, as well as the frequency of restocking.

6. Determine the appropriate location for supplies at the user area. This should include a configuration for those supplies to facilitate reordering and restocking, as well as on-demand item location. It is important to include user department input in this vital process. Standardization layouts should be established as much as possible in order to enhance the productivity in the ordering, restocking, and retrieval-for-use processes.

7. Determine the timing for inventory review, ordering, and restocking. Essential variables for making this decision include times of peak supply demand, corridor and elevator congestion, and staff availability.

8. Identify and determine the preferred methodology: individual order processing or batch or zone processing.

9. Establish the appropriate paperwork/record-keeping systems. This step includes designing forms, setting up automated data systems communications, and so on.

10. Adjust layout, configuration, and inventory levels at the supply source in order to accommodate the new system.

11. Conduct in-service education programs for all personnel involved and affected by the system.

12. Establish a mechanism for tracking nonroutine/random demand for supplies that occur outside the basic system to determine the continuing effectiveness of the system and the appropriateness of the product mix and inventory levels.

13. Establish a policy and procedure for making changes as appropriate. It is essential to ensure that inventory levels will be adjusted routinely to match changing demand.
14. Begin implementation on either a pilot project basis, batch or zone basis, or systemwide. Either way can be equally successful, depending on the degree of complexity and sophistication of the method selected and the extent of the impact of the change.
15. Schedule meetings for reviewing progress and making any necessary modifications.

Central Sterile Reprocessing

The essence of materials management is to be found in the processes of purchasing, receiving, storing, and distributing materials. A number of other functions that involve these processes have come to be associated with the materials management program, however. The most common of these is the central sterile reprocessing (CSR) department, which is responsible for the decontamination, inspection, packaging, and sterilization of reusable materials. In some hospitals and organized health care delivery systems, this department's responsibilities also include the collection and disposal of trash and the collection and decontamination of dishes and utensils for the food service department. In any case, the CSR department should be responsible for the reprocessing of all reusable materials for the medical and surgical departments.

This department has three primary objectives. The first is to ensure that a well-designed and documented program is in place to assess and adjust the quality of reprocessing functions throughout the organization. Such a program involves (1) establishing

policies and procedures, (2) monitoring compliance with the policies and procedures, and (3) correcting deviations from the policies and improving inadequate performance of the procedures. The program should include elements such as the following:

- assignment of responsibility for the collection of soiled items
- definition of methods for containing soiled items during transport to the decontamination area
- procedures for decontamination
- procedures for inspecting items before repackaging
- definition of what constitutes acceptable packaging material
- procedures for properly setting up, packaging, and labeling reusable items
- procedures for operating and ensuring proper performance of sterilization equipment
- procedures for storing, distributing, and handling sterile items throughout the facility
- procedures for operating and ensuring proper performance of equipment used in decontamination

The second major objective is to ensure that all items leaving the CSR department have undergone a properly defined and executed sterilization process. The majority of items are sterilized—that is, made free of all living microorganisms—in a large-volume steam sterilizer. These are simply pressure vessels into which items to be sterilized are placed. All air is removed from the chamber, and then it is filled with saturated steam. The removal of all air is critical, because air acts as a buffer between the surface to be sterilized and the steam, which is the sterilizing agent. The steam must be of a defined temperature, and the contact with the steam must be maintained for a defined period of time. In order to state with confidence that sterilization has been achieved, it must be shown that the following steps have been taken:

- Items were properly packaged.
- Items were properly placed into the sterilizing chamber.
- All air was evacuated from the sterilizing chamber.
- The chamber was filled with saturated steam of the required temperature.
- The temperature and contact with the steam were maintained for the required period of time.

The only way to prove that an item is sterile is to open the package and perform a laboratory analysis of the item. Obviously, this is not feasible, because it destroys the item before it can be used. The most rigorous method available for testing the efficacy of the sterilization procedures and equipment is the use of bacteriological monitors. In this method, a package of live spores—the most difficult microorganisms to kill—of known strength is placed into the sterilizer. Upon completion of the sterilization process, the spores are analyzed in the clinical laboratory. If the spores are shown to have been killed, the assumption is that all other microorganisms in the sterilizer were also killed.

Because bacteriological monitoring is relatively expensive, it is not commonly used in every sterilization cycle. At most, it is performed daily and in many cases on a weekly basis. A program that includes (1) well defined policies and procedures; (2) tests to ensure proper air evacuation, time, and temperature for every cycle; and (3) periodic use of bacteriological monitors should provide sufficient confidence that sterilization is being properly performed.

The third major objective of the CSR department is to perform the second most common type of sterilization in hospitals, which involves the use of ethylene oxide (EtO) as a sterilant. A toxic chemical, EtO can be hazardous to employee health, but it is an extremely effective agent for sterilizing items that cannot withstand the rigors of steam sterilization. As a result, it must be used, but in a carefully controlled manner.

The Occupational Safety and Health Administration has established strict rules for the use of EtO. The current standard sets a limit for personal exposure of one part EtO per one million parts of air.[10] In order to ensure that this standard is met, a clearly defined safety program must be established; it should include

- policies and procedures for the use of EtO equipment
- proper design of the room containing EtO equipment
- proper ventilation of the room
- routine preventive maintenance and testing of the equipment and ventilation
- routine scheduled exposure testing of the work environment and the individual employees who operate the EtO equipment

Documentation must be maintained to prove compliance with all of these elements.

Other Related Functions

The material/resource manager almost always has direct management responsibility for the purchasing, receiving, central, inventory, distribution, and CSR departments. In addition, this person is often given responsibility for other departments that are involved with the production and distribution of material. The most common of these are (1) transportation services, including patient escort services; (2) mail services; (3) print shop; and (4) laundry. In some cases, the pharmacy may be attached to the material management division as well.

No matter what organizational arrangement is used, the most important fact is that materials make up a major portion of the operating budget of the modern hospital and health care system. Effective management of these materials is crucial to the survival of any facility in the increasingly competitive environment of today's health care industry.

MATERIALS MANAGEMENT IN ALTERNATE SITE LOCATIONS

The health care industry continues to experience rapid change. More patient activity takes place in alternate settings outside a hospital, such as in physicians' offices and ambulatory care centers. In many cases, hospitals provide ownership and/or management support for these off-site locations. Because the need for cost reduction is intense throughout the industry, effective materials management practices are vital in these alternate locations as well.

Basic techniques are valid no matter where they are used. The challenge in offices, clinics, and outpatient centers is to apply the principles of materials management with smaller staff, smaller space arrangements, and usually, smaller volumes of material. The key is to stay focused on the basic principles and find ways to adapt them to the nonhospital settings. Hospital material/resource managers, as well as suppliers, can be used as a resource in developing the nonhospital materials management control system. Administrators should commit themselves to ensuring good materials management practice in all operating settings under their control.

FUTURE TRENDS IN MATERIALS MANAGEMENT AND PURCHASING

Group Purchasing Future Trends

A survey of group purchasing executives conducted in March 1998 indicated that the primary goal of purchasing organizations rests on the promise to deliver a specific purchasing volume to suppliers.[11] The group purchasing executives described their perception of success as contract compliance. The key observations were that group purchasing organizations are endeavoring to fulfill their promise to deliver market share to suppliers, that for-profit hospital chains will obtain lower pricing than group purchasing organizations, and that these chains will obtain lower pricing than the committed volume programs of group purchasing organizations. In addition, they noted that more manufacturers will sell directly to organized health care delivery systems, and five national super groups will dominate the market by the year 2001.

Efficient Health Care Consumer Response

In the 1997 semiannual economic forecast conducted by the National Association of Purchasing Management, the top economic concerns for the years ahead identified by purchasing executives were labor benefits, the economy, inflation, strength of the dollar, rising interest rates, material shortages, environmental and regulatory costs, shortage of skilled employees, material costs, and import/export restraints.[12] The National Association of Purchasing Management survey also identified the top desired supply chain improvements: consolidation of volume with fewer suppliers; longer term agreements with partnering; cost reduction, analysis, and management; software development or improvement; electronic data interchange; improved inventory practice; improved communications with suppliers; improved supplier performance; lead time reduction; and more emphasis on quality.[13]

In the future, the health care materials manufacturers and distributors will clearly distinguish themselves by the value that they bring to the supply process, rather than simply the products and services that they can provide. A value-oriented rather than a supply-oriented environment will be created for a seamless flow of products by integrated information and financial flows.

As the new millennium approaches, it is clear that the health care industry is in transition. Some of the challenges ahead are mergers and acquisitions, managed care, vertical integration, competition (both in the United States and around the world), cost control, government regulation (local and national), an aging population with high expectations of quality and service, and inadequate systems integration, both within and between entities.

NOTES

1. C.E. Housely, *Hospital Material Management* (Gaithersburg, MD: Aspen Publishers, 1978), 2.

2. J.A. Dattilo and G. Meredith, "Capital Equipment Purchasing," in *Handbook of Health Care Material Management*, ed. W.L. Scheyer (Gaithersburg, MD: Aspen Publishers, 1985), 156–164.

3. R.E. Rourke, "Streamlining the Purchasing Process," in *Handbook of Health Care Material Management*, ed. W.L. Scheyer (Gaithersburg, MD: Aspen Publishers, 1985), 73.

4. Ibid., 101.

5. J.C. Kowalski, "Supply Distribution Options—A New Perspective," in *Handbook of Health Care Material Management*, ed. W.L. Scheyer (Gaithersburg, MD: Aspen Publishers, 1985).

6. J.W. Rayburn, "Inventory Control," in *Handbook of Health Care Material Management*, ed. W.L. Scheyer (Gaithersburg, MD: Aspen Publishers, 1985), 202.

7. Ibid., 190.

8. Ibid., 190.

9. J.C. Kowalski, "Supply Distribution Options," 229–230.

10. R.L. Corn, "Designing a Safety Program for EtO," in *Handbook of Health Care Material Management*, ed. W.L. Scheyer (Gaithersburg, MD: Aspen Publishers, 1985), 260.

11. "Survey of Group Purchasing Executives," *Healthcare Purchasing News* 22, no. 3 (1988): 11, 16.

12. Ibid.

13. Ibid.

WILLIAM L. SCHEYER, CPHM, currently serves as City Administrator for the City of Erlanger, Kentucky, and is active in local government affairs in the northern Kentucky area. His 20-year career in the hospital industry culminated in his role as Assistant Vice President for Materials Management at Bethesda Hospital, Inc., in Cincinnati, Ohio. Bethesda, a multisite organization combining two acute care, two long-term care, and numerous ancillary facilities, is a leader in health care management. Mr. Scheyer is the editor of the *Handbook of Health Care Material Management*, taught this subject at the University of Cincinnati, and has served as President of the Greater Cincinnati Health Care Materials Management Association.

BARBARA B. FRIEDMAN, MA, MPA, FASHMM, CPHM, is currently the Director of Material Management at Kingsbrook Jewish Medical Center in Brooklyn, New York, and serves as President of Greater New York Chapter of the American Society of Healthcare Material Management, which won the 1997 and 1998 chapter of the year awards. Her career spans more than 20 years as a health care administrator in both the public and private sectors specializing in purchasing and material management. Ms. Friedman has been an instructor at two colleges, lectured at numerous national conferences, is the author of many articles, and has served as an active participant on national professional committees.

Appendix 25–A

Bidding Instructions (Simple Format)

ITEMS BELOW APPLY TO AND BE-
COME A PART OF TERMS AND CONDI-
TIONS OF BID. ANY EXCEPTIONS
THERETO MUST BE IN WRITING.

1. Bidding Requirements:

   a. Late bids properly identified will be returned to bidder unopened. Late bids
   will not be considered under any circumstances.

   b. Bid prices must be firm for acceptance
   for thirty (30) days from bid opening
   date. Cash discount will not be considered in determining the low bid. All
   cash discounts offered will be taken if
   earned.

   c. Bids must give full firm name and address of bidder. Failure to manually
   sign bid should show title or authority
   to bind his firm in a contract. Firm
   name should appear on each page of a
   bid, in the space provided in the upper
   right-hand corner.

   d. Bid cannot be altered or amended after
   opening time. Any alterations made before opening time must be initiated by
   bidder or authorized agent. No bid can

be withdrawn after opening time without approval by the Hospital, based on
an acceptable written reason.

   e. Telegraphic response to any bid invitation must show: price bid, requisition
   number, opening date, description
   (brand, model, etc.) of product offered,
   and delivery promise. Confirmation on
   bid form should be postmarked on or
   before opening day and/or received
   within forty-eight (48) hours after
   opening day. Show regular information
   on envelope and add the word: "Confirmation." Telephone bids are not acceptable when in response to this invitation to bid.

   f. Engineering checklist must be completed and returned with this bid.

2. Specifications:

   a. All items bid shall be new, in first-class
   condition, including containers suitable for shipment and storage, unless
   otherwise indicated in invitation. Verbal agreements to the contract will not
   be recognized.

   b. Samples, when requested, must be fur-

Source: Departmental document, reprinted with permission of St. Francis–St. George Hospital, Cincinnati, Ohio.

nished free of expense. If not destroyed in examination, they will be returned to the bidder, on request, at his expense. Each sample should be marked with bidder's name, address, and requisition number. Do not enclose or attach bid to sample.

c. All quotations must be accompanied by descriptive literature giving full description of details as to type of material and equipment that is to be furnished under this contract. Samples, where required, shall be delivered to the purchasing department before the opening of quotations, unless otherwise stated in the specifications; failure of the bidder to either submit literature or supply samples may be considered sufficient reason for rejection of the quote. All deliveries under the contract shall conform in all respects with samples, catalog cuts, etc., as submitted and accepted as the basis for the award.

d. In addition to the requirements of paragraph c, all deviations from the specifications must be noted in detail by the bidder in writing at the time of submittal of the quote. The absence of a written list of specification deviations at the time of submittal of the quote will hold the bidders strictly accountable to the Hospital to the specifications as written. Any deviation from the specifications as written not previously submitted, as required by the above, will be grounds for rejection of the material and/or equipment when delivered.

3. Award:

Award of bid will be based on the information provided by the bidder. The award will be made consistent with PRUDENT BUYER POLICY of the Hospital. Considerations to this award will be:

1. Price
2. Quality
3. Service
4. Delivery
5. Design

(Not necessarily listed according to priority)

a. Cash discounts will not be taken into consideration in determining an award.

b. With regard to differences between unit prices and extensions, unit prices will govern and extensions will be modified accordingly.

c. Freight charges may be a determining factor only when all price, quality, and service specifications are equal.

4. Delivery:

a. Failure to state delivery time obligates bidder to complete delivery in fourteen (14) calendar days. A five- (5)-day difference in delivery promise may break a tie bid. Unrealistically short or long delivery promises may cause bid to be disregarded. Consistent failure to meet delivery promises without valid reason may cause removal from bid list.

b. No substitutions or cancellations will be permitted without written approval of the Hospital.

c. Delivery shall be made during normal working hours only, 8:30 A.M. to 4 P.M., unless prior approval for late delivery has been obtained from Agency.

d. Any freight charges applicable to this quotation must appear on the quotation. All freight agreed to by the Hospital must be prepaid and added to the Hospital's invoice.

e. In all cases, seller will be responsible for filing damaged freight claims with the transporter of the merchandise.

5. Patents and Copyrights:

The contractor agrees to protect the Hospital from claims involving infringement of patents or copyrights.

TEFRA STATEMENT

Section 1861(v)(1) of the Social Security Act (42 U.S.C. § 1395x) as amended, requires us, as Medicare providers, to obtain the agreement of persons who contract with us for services with a value or cost of $10,000 or more in any twelve-month period, that the books, documents, and records of such contractors must remain available for verification of cost by the Comptroller General for a period of four years following completion of the contract. Seller acknowledges and expressly agrees to this requirement, on its behalf and on behalf of any subcontractor who shall perform any part or all of this contract for Seller having a value or cost of $10,000 or more.

OSHA STATEMENT

Seller represents and warrants that all articles and services covered by this purchase order meet or exceed the safety standards established and promulgated under the Federal Occupational Safety and Health Law (Public Law 91-596) and its regulations in effect or proposed as of the date of this order. Seller will submit OSHA Form 20, material safety data sheet, upon request.

SUBMITTAL OR QUOTE CONSTITUTES ACKNOWLEDGMENT AND ACCEPTANCE OF THE TERMS AND CONDITIONS AS OUTLINED ABOVE.

INQUIRIES PERTAINING TO BID INVITATIONS MUST BE DIRECTED TO DEPARTMENT MANAGER, PURCHASING.

_____

Authorized Signature

Appendix 25–B

Bidding Instructions (Complex Format)

A. INSTRUCTIONS TO BIDDERS

In accordance with the contract documents set forth herein, proposals will be received by Hospital through _____(date)_____, at the (describe location).

1. *PROJECT SCHEDULE*

   Schedule installation to be completed by _____(date)_____.

2. *PREPARATION OF PROPOSALS*

   a. The bidder shall submit his proposal on the attached proposal forms and specification sheets. No other forms will be accepted. A unit price and extended price shall be stated on the specification sheets for each item either typed or written in ink.
   b. Each bidder is to bid on all items that he manufactures or supplies.

3. *SUBMISSION OF PROPOSALS*

   a. All bidders shall submit __ proposals enclosed in a sealed envelope marked "Bid Document Equipment" on or before ___(date)___.
   b. The proposals with all literature and the Bond shall be delivered to: (address and designate)
   c. Where proposals are sent by mail, the bidders shall be responsible for their delivery before the date set for the receipt of proposals. Late proposals will not be considered and will be returned unopened.

4. *WITHDRAWAL OF BIDS*

   a. Bids may be withdrawn on written request received from bidders prior to date fixed for opening bids.
   b. Negligence on the part of the bidder in preparing the bid confers no right for the withdrawal of the bid after it has been opened.

Source: Departmental document, reprinted with permission of St. Francis–St. George Hosp., Inc., Cincinnati, Ohio.

5. *COMPETENCY OF BIDDER*

   a. A contract will not be awarded to any person, firm, or corporation that has failed to perform faithfully any previous contract with the Hospital.

6. *CONSIDERATION OF PROPOSALS*

   a. The Hospital reserves the right to reject any or all quotations or to waive any informalities or technicalities in any quotations in the interest of the Hospital.

7. *BID GUARANTEE*

   a. Each proposal shall be accompanied by a bid guarantee for five percent (5%) of the amount of the total bid. Bid guarantees shall be a Bond made on the Proposal Bond Form or a cashier's check.

   b. The Proposal Bond shall guarantee that the bidder will not withdraw, cancel or modify his bid for a period of sixty (60) days after the scheduled closing date for receipt of bids. The Proposal Bond shall further guarantee that, if his bid is accepted, the bidder will enter into a formal contract in accordance with the method of contracting hereinafter specified.

   c. In the event the bidder withdraws his bid within the sixty (60)-day period or fails to enter into a contract if his bid is accepted, he shall be liable to the Hospital for the full amount of the bid guarantee.

   d. The Proposal Bond shall be returned to all unsuccessful bidders after the successful bidder has executed the Performance Bond and the bid has been accepted by the Hospital.

   e. The Proposal Bond must be endorsed by surety or sureties, and names of endorsers must be typed immediately below signature.

8. *METHOD OF CONTRACTING*

   a. Award of contracts will be in the form of a Purchase Order made by the Hospital on the basis of the best bid from a qualified contractor.

   b. The successful bidder shall deliver to the Hospital a Performance Bond with sureties satisfactory to the Hospital in the amount of one hundred percent (100%) of the total accepted bid.

   c. The agent of the surety bonding company must be able to furnish on demand:
     a) Credentials showing power of attorney.
     b) Certificate showing the legal right of the company to do business in the state of the Hospital.

9. *INTERPRETATION OF CONTRACT DOCUMENTS*

   a. Discrepancies, omissions, or doubts as to the meaning of the specifications should be communicated in writing to the Hospital for interpretation. Bidders should act promptly and allow sufficient time for a reply to reach them before the submission of bids. Any interpretation made will be in the form of an addendum to the specifications, which will be forwarded to all bidders and its receipt by the bidder must be acknowledged on the Form of Proposal.

10. *RESPONSIBILITY OF THE BIDDERS*

    a. Bidders shall visit the site and note local pertinent field conditions such as availability of loading docks, elevators, and all other receiving and inspecting facilities.

    b. Bidders are responsible for the installation and start-up of their equipment including the following:

    c. Bidders are to include with this quotation complete information on the local service center including:

    d. Bidders are to include with this quotation all warranty information concerning the system components outlined in Bidder's Proposal.

    e. Bidders shall provide an annual price for manufacturer's recommended preventive maintenance program to be provided by factory-trained and qualified personnel, after the warranty period.

11. *SALES TAX*

    a. The Hospital is a tax-exempt institution.

    b. Copies of the exemption certificate will be furnished upon request.

12. *METHOD OF PAYMENT*

    a. Requests for payments (invoices) must include the following information for processing:

        1) Purchase order number
        2) Manufacturer name and catalog item number
        3) Dollar amount.

    b. Payment for equipment shall be made according to the following schedule:

        1) Ten percent (10%) of contract price as down payment shall be made within ten (10) days of acknowledgment of order.

        2) Eighty percent (80%) of contract price shall be due and payable within ten (10) days of delivery, installation (to include field assembly, interconnection, equipment calibration to manufacturer's specification, and checkout), and acceptance by the Hospital of all system components as outlined in Bidder's Proposal.

        3) Ten percent (10%) shall be payable six (6) days after acceptance by the Hospital.

    c. The Hospital reserves the right to refuse payment on an invoice due to damaged item(s), quantity variance, model variance, or any failure to comply with the contract documents.

B. FORM OF PROPOSAL

Submitted by: Date:

_____   _____

TO: HOSPITAL

We, the undersigned, have familiarized ourselves with the local conditions affecting the cost of the work, and with all contract documents for this work, including:

INSTRUCTIONS TO BIDDERS   PROPOSAL BOND

PROPOSAL FORM   BID SPECIFICATIONS

And also have received and incorporated into the makeup of the specifications the following addenda:

Addendum No. _____ Dated _____ Addendum No. _____ Dated _____

Hereby propose to furnish all labor, equipment, and transportation to delivery and install all materials, and to perform and supervise all work as required.

TIME OF COMPLETION: Installation must be complete by _____ (date) _____.

EXECUTION OF CONTRACT: If written notice of acceptance of this bid is mailed, telegraphed, or delivered to the undersigned within sixty (60) days after date required for the receipt of the bid, or any time thereafter before this bid is withdrawn, the undersigned will, within ten (10) days after date of such notice, execute and deliver a Performance Bond.

NOTE A: Bids submitted by virtue of the proposal hereby acknowledged by the Hospital to be made under the assumption that the successful bidder will not be prevented, on account of strikes or other disruptions affecting sources of supply or affecting normal progress of the work, from obtaining the materials necessary to carry out this contract to complete the work covered thereby.

NOTE B: It is understood and agreed by the undersigned that the Hospital reserves the right to reject any or all bids, or to accept the bid that embraces such combination of proposal that will promote the best interest of the Hospital.

NOTE C: It is agreed that this proposal shall be irrevocable for a period of sixty (60) days after the date set for the receipt of proposals.

NOTE D: It is understood and agreed by the undersigned that they will cooperate and coordinate their work with the contractor who will be in the final stage of work at the Hospital.

The undersigned hereby designates the office to which such notice may be mailed, telegraphed, or delivered:

_____

_____

_____

Enter here the service information requested in 10-D of "INSTRUCTIONS TO BIDDERS":

_____

_____

SIGNATURE OF BIDDER

SEAL (if a corporation)   Date _____

                                         Name of Firm _____

                                                   By _____

                                                Title _____

                                    Business Address_____

                                                      _____

                                                      _____

                                     Telephone Number _____

                                  State of Incorporation _____

NOTE 1:   If bidder is a corporation, write state of incorporation, and if a partnership, give full
          name of all partners.

NOTE 2:   Any deviation from the specifications must be specifically stated. Include also an
          explanation where the bidder's project exceeds the above specifications.

NOTE 3:   Alternatives, where presented in addition to the base bid, will be considered but must
          follow the instructions above, listing deviations to the specifications, and include
          complete descriptions and literature.

C. PROPOSAL BOND

KNOW ALL MEN BY THESE PRESENTS, THAT WE, _____,
_____ (hereinafter called the Principal), as principal, and
_____, (hereinafter called the Surety), as surety, are
firmly bound unto the Hospital in the amount of _____
(amount not less than five percent (5%) of the accompanying bid plus the sum of all additive
alternates) in lawful money of the United States for payment of which said Principal and
Surety bind themselves, their heirs, executors, successors, administrators, and assigns,
jointly and severally.

WHEREAS, said Principal has submitted to the Hospital a written proposal for certain work
in connection with the (describe project), a copy of which is hereto attached.

NOW THEREFORE, the condition of this obligation is such that if said Proposal be accepted, the Principal shall, within ten (10) days of written notice thereof, enter into proper
contract for the work covered by the Proposal, and shall furnish a Performance Bond satisfactory to said Hospital. If there is a difference between the amount of the Proposal and the
amount accepted then, this obligation shall be reduced to five percent (5%) of the value of
the Proposal accepted. This Proposal Bond shall be valid for a period of sixty (60) days from
the date set for the receipt of the Proposal attached thereto.

Signed and sealed this _____ day of _____, _____

Witness: _____ (SEAL)

_____, _____

_____ Principal

Countersigned at _____(SEAL)

By _____

D. SPECIFICATIONS

PART 1—GENERAL

1. *RELATED DOCUMENTS*

   a. Contract Documents, including General and Supplementary conditions and General Requirement, and contract drawings for the Hospital, apply to the work specified in this section.

2. *DESCRIPTION OF WORK*

   a. Successful bidder shall furnish, delivery F.O.B. jobsite, and install, all equipment specified herein, including all necessary attachment devices and all incidentals and accessories required for a complete and operable installation. Any omissions of the details in specifications does not relieve the bidder from furnishing a complete functioning installation of highest quality for all purposes intended.

   b. The work shall be coordinated with the mechanical and electrical trades where services and connections are required for proper installation and operation of equipment.

   c. It shall be noted that all interconnecting cabling throughout the installation shall be furnished by the bidder at no additional cost to the Hospital.

   d. The Bidder is required to clean up, remove, and dispose of all debris resulting from work hereunder.

3. *QUALITY ASSURANCE*

   a. Manufacturer's Qualifications:

      1) Only manufacturers having a minimum of five (5) years experience in the manufacture and installation of the quality and type of the respective items of equipment specified herein shall be considered qualified.

      2) Manufacturer shall be able to demonstrate to the Hospital's satisfaction, proximity of spare parts and availability of experienced, competent maintenance service.

      3) Should the manufacturer find at any time during the progress of the work that, in his opinion, existing design or conditions require a modification of any particular part or assembly, he shall promptly report in writing such matter to the Hospital.

b. Substitutions:

1) The following specifications are to establish a standard of quality and performance and are not intended to exclude any manufacturer or company from bidding quality equipment that can be proven to meet functional standards as set forth. The equipment to be furnished must meet the highest standards of the profession.

4. *CODE COMPLIANCE*

a. All equipment furnished and installed under this section shall comply with all requirements of local, state, and federal building, health, sanitary, and NFPA Codes.

5. *STANDARDS*

a. In addition to the above, the following standard shall apply to the extent referenced herein:

1) Underwriters Laboratories, Incorporated (UL): Listings and approvals as required.
2) Electrical components and wiring: Furnish and wire electrical components of equipment in this section to conform to NFPA 70 (National Fire Protection Association).
3) All new equipment must be HHS certified.

6. *SUBMITTALS*

a. Roughing-In Drawings:

1) The Bidder will provide rough-in drawings and will coordinate and verify the dimensions and required service with the architect.
2) Roughing-in drawings must be supplied within two weeks after receiving notice of the award, to provide information to other contractors performing the roughing-in.

b. Shop Drawings:

1) Submit shop drawings and catalog cuts of standard manufactured items. Indicate in detail the methods of installation, connections, and all pertinent data relating to each item of equipment.
2) Catalog cuts shall indicate the specified model and characteristics of the item being furnished.

c. Operating and Maintenance Instructions:

1) The Bidder shall furnish the Hospital with four (4) bound copies of written instructions, giving detailed information as to how the equipment is to be operated and maintained. Maintenance manuals shall include appropriate parts list and the name of the service representative.
2) In addition, a representative from the equipment manufacturer shall visit the project and instruct the Hospital personnel on the proper operation and mainte-

nance of the equipment. The instruction period consists of not less than two (2) separate sessions, to be scheduled by the Hospital after occupancy.

d. Guarantee and Preventive Maintenance:

1) Upon completion, and as a condition for acceptance of the work, the Bidder shall submit written guarantee(s) covering each item included in this section for a period one (1) year from date of beneficial use. The guarantee shall cover all workmanship and materials and the Bidder agrees to repair or replace all faulty work and defective materials and equipment, including labor.

2) The Bidder shall be responsible for maintenance of the equipment for the first six (6) months, with all costs for parts, labor, and trips to and from the hospital covered by the warranty.

Chapter 26

Pharmacy

Andrew L. Wilson

INTRODUCTION

Pharmacy services in hospitals and organized delivery systems have changed greatly in recent years. Modifications in pharmacy practice reflect the transformation that has occurred in health care delivery as a whole. The evolution of health care at the millennium encompasses a renewed emphasis on outpatient and ambulatory care and an increased focus on patient care outcomes and treatment costs. Because pharmacists have traditionally provided services in both the ambulatory and inpatient environment, the pharmacy profession has adapted well to the movement of care delivery to the outpatient setting.

Pharmacists have a renewed practice mission that incorporates an emphasis on direct patient care and interaction. As a result, they are increasingly involved in team care provided at the inpatient bedside and in the ambulatory care clinic. The goal of pharmacy education is to give practitioners well-rounded patient care delivery skills in order to support this growth and change in emphasis. While not all pharmacies in organized delivery systems have adjusted to these changes, direct patient care activities are the core of pharmacy's new mission in care delivery. Effective pharmacies in organized delivery systems must take responsibility for medication therapy through direct care activities to ensure appropriate and effective use of pharmacy resources.

Biotechnology has grown rapidly as a means to identify disease pathology and to develop effective drugs to treat a specific disease process. Biotechnology has created treatment successes and positive outcomes for diseases that were previously untreatable or incurable. The short development cycle for "biotech" drugs leads to rapid availability of new therapies and often to "instant" patient demand. Private and government payers do not have an opportunity to gear up to cover new treatments and can place the financial risk for treatment on unwary providers. Pharmacy is at the center of these concerns and therefore must work to support a balance between patient needs and the interests of the health care system.

Pharmacies and pharmacists have made adjustments to secure biotech drug therapies and to deliver them in a timely and cost-effective manner. Proper patient screening, correct drug handling, appropriate preparation, and fastidious patient monitoring are key components of the ability to treat a patient with a growth factor, protein, enzyme, or antibody developed through biotechnology. Innovative therapies are arriving at an increasingly rapid pace and are ever more expensive. A number of newly discovered drug treatments that are now available cost well into six figures for a full year of treatment. It is not unusual for drug expenses alone to exceed $10,000 for a single course of treatment in oncology and acquired immune deficiency syndrome (AIDS) treatment.

The documented efficacy of these new therapies, combined with their sensational cost, places pharmacists and drug therapy at center stage in cost and outcome debates. Organized delivery systems and payers have struggled to incorporate new therapies into patient treatment while working to manage costs. Drug costs for some diseases and patient care programs have grown dramatically as increasingly effective therapies have been marketed at stratospheric prices. Patient demand often forecloses the option of limiting or denying care, even when modest improvements in effectiveness do not support the dramatically increased cost. Pharmaceuticals continue to be cost effective in the treatment of disease and to represent only a small portion of overall health care expenditures. However, the growth in the cost of drugs has far outpaced inflation and cost increases in many other areas of health care.

The pharmacy profession has changed to meet the new demands of society. Pharmacists have accepted direct patient care responsibilities, supported by information systems, automation, robotics, and enhanced roles for pharmacy technicians. Pharmacy education has become more sophisticated, and a doctoral-level will soon be the entry-level professional degree. Advanced pharmacy residencies and fellowship education and training supported by specialty board certification have created a new group of skilled pharmacist medication therapy managers. Pharmacy's core medication control and drug delivery roles remain key to providing ser-

vice, but the predominant focus of pharmacists and pharmacy practice is now the assessment and management of drug therapy in the patient care setting.

PHARMACY PRACTICE

Current pharmacy practice is based on the concept of pharmaceutical care. Hepler and Strand proposed the seminal definition of this concept in 1990. "Pharmaceutical care is the responsible provision of drug therapy for the purpose of achieving definite outcomes that improve a patient's quality of life. These outcomes are (1) cure of a disease, (2) elimination or reduction of a patient's symptomatology, (3) arresting or slowing of a disease process, or (4) preventing a disease or symptomatology."[1] The authors define pharmaceutical care as a core service, similar to medical care or dental care, and emphasize the responsibility of pharmacists in all care delivery models.

Pharmacists delivering pharmaceutical care have the task of integrating multiple drug therapies to achieve the best outcome for each disease or condition. Pharmacists working in this practice model have an overview of all medication therapies and treatment goals and practice as generalists with specific expertise in and attention to drug therapy. They initiate or recommend treatment and order laboratory tests and other assessment tools. They consult with nurses, physicians, other caregivers, and the patient to direct drug therapy and optimize treatment outcomes. The basic model for pharmaceutical care was developed in the acute care setting, but it easily translates to ambulatory care clinics, home care, and newer or nontraditional settings. The pharmaceutical care model is particularly suited to pharmacy practice in organized delivery systems, as it focuses on continuity of care and supports the transitions between acute care, ambulatory care, and chronic care.

The total patient management focus of the pharmaceutical care model also makes it particularly effective in an organized delivery system. Contracting, aggressive discounts, prospective payment, and capitation are used by payers to manage and control treatment costs in today's competitive health care marketplace. An organized delivery system can compete and be successful only if it controls costs, ensures the appropriate utilization of resources, demonstrates positive treatment outcomes, and delivers patient services and customer satisfaction. Control and management of pharmacy costs have been generally focused on the minimization of upfront drug costs. The pharmaceutical care model focuses on drug therapy decisions that accord with the overall goals of therapy and are carried out within a time frame that ensures effective evaluation and assessment.

The general way to manage and limit drug use is through the creation of a formulary. A health system formulary is a continually revised compilation of pharmaceuticals that reflects the current clinical judgment of the medical staff. It reflects current clinical practice and the specific needs of the patients served by the organization. The formulary is generally developed by the organization's pharmacy and therapeutics committee, with the primary goal of ensuring high-quality care and controlling cost. A tightly managed formulary with a complete drug purchase contract portfolio has been assumed to deliver the most cost-effective drug therapy outcomes. The selection of a drug at the formulary level is only a portion of the necessary support for appropriate and effective treatment outcomes. In addition to acquisition cost, the assessment of the total cost of therapy must take into account:

- drug administration schedules and dosing frequency
- complexity of dosing and the need to change dose as patient condition changes
- storage and preparation costs
- cost of ancillary devices, such as infusion pumps, and monitoring devices, such as blood glucose monitors
- nursing time associated with drug administration and monitoring
- costs and likelihood of side effects and adverse reactions
- costs of medical monitoring, including clinic visits and laboratory tests
- costs and likelihood of treatment failure
- costs of drug interactions

The task of selecting the most appropriate drug therapy can be complex, particularly in patients with multiple diseases or conditions. The consumption of resources, the effects of drug therapy on length of hospital stay, clinic visit frequency, and monitoring costs must be included in the assessment. Recent studies on the costs associated with a tightly controlled formulary have demonstrated that a narrow focus on drug costs can lead to cost growth in other areas, resulting from readmissions, emergency department visits, and outright treatment failures.[2] A focus on reducing the number of drugs or aggressive restrictions placed on new drugs or therapies may provide short-term cost reduction for an episode of care but lead to greater overall costs over the course of the disease.

The strategy of managing the entire spectrum of patient drug therapy based on treatment outcomes is consistent with the current health care business environment. The global assessment of treatment costs and outcomes ensures the optimal use of resources and focuses on a more robust model of cost-effectiveness. Older models were more concerned with upfront drug costs, and developed little information and fewer results based on the effectiveness of a treatment. Formularies, medication use review, technology assessment, the integration of new therapies, and the development of guidelines and support resources for drug use are appropriately evaluated under this model. Pharmacy information systems support the rapid and accurate identification of treatment strategies and patient responses, ensuring both cost-effectiveness and optimal treatment outcomes.

The pharmaceutical care practice model also uses data from the published medical and pharmaceutical literature, combined with internally generated patient care and cost data to determine appropriate medication therapy. This "evidence-based" approach ensures that the treatment decisions are based on current empirical evidence within the context of larger treatment issues. Selecting the therapy most likely to produce the best treatment outcome at the lowest cost includes a critical assessment of the likelihood of treatment failure and the frequency and impact of adverse reactions, drug interactions, and side effects. Effective treatment selection and management also encompasses the assessment of individual patient characteristics, including compliance with treatment protocols. It further incorporates the cost of the medication itself and medication preparation and administration costs. Models that fail to include these aspects of pharmaceutical care often minimize drug acquisition costs at the expense of larger overall costs outside the traditional pharmacy budget silo.

PHARMACY MANAGEMENT AND LEADERSHIP

An effective pharmacy in an organized health care delivery system must be led by a trained pharmacist leader with high-level management skills. The pharmacy director must be able to synthesize clinical pharmacy services with drug distribution and with general management principles and objectives under the pharmaceutical care model. He or she must create measures of the effectiveness of pharmaceutical care and ensure that systems, products, and services meet the objectives of the organization, the objectives of the medical staff, and the care needs of patients.

The pharmacy director must utilize an integrated information system that collects and organizes real-time patient care data to support drug therapy decision-making in the clinic and at the bedside. The pharmacy information system must collect and categorize summary data about drug therapies for use in determining the global effectiveness and cost of each therapy and supporting management decisions. Examples include nonformulary drugs used, drug costs and drug use by therapeutic category, and details about specific drugs used for each plan physician. Additionally, data describing drug costs and use by diagnosis and detailed drug utilization by disease state can be of use in determining trends in prescribing. These summary statistics offer rapid insight into prescribing trends and changes in patient mix and drug use. These data can also be combined with demographics, laboratory results, and other patient data to provide information about the success or failure of therapies. The competent pharmacy of today also utilizes patient care automation and robotics to ensure timely, accurate, consistent, and cost-effective medication handling.

The pharmacy director leads a staff composed of trained specialist pharmacist clinicians who manage specific therapy programs and services; a larger number of generalist clinical pharmacist practitioners who are trained in patient care service delivery; and pharmacists and pharmacy technicians who are responsible for the logistics of drug procurement, preparation, delivery, and management. The pharmacy of today continues to deliver the right drug at the right time to the right patient, but it is further involved in the drug selection and prescribing process at the patient level. It works effectively with systems that support physicians and nurses in their portions of the selection, administration, monitoring, and management of drug therapies. It develops and provides pharmacy-based medication monitoring and management and develops and implements policies to support the goals of the larger delivery system or network. These goals are based on continuing assessment of the effectiveness and outcomes of medication therapies. Control of drug costs revolves around the effective utilization of medications. It requires effective information systems and a sophisticated pharmacy director who understands the data and creates management systems to implement pharmaceutical care services based on them.

The pharmacy service should be organized in a manner that ensures an integrated approach to patient care and promotes the concept of pharmaceutical care. The structure of the pharmacy should mirror that of the overall health care organization, with specific pharmacists and pharmacy service teams assigned to each patient care service or unit. Each pharmacist should be responsible for determining that portion of the overall agenda that applies to his or her service or patient care unit. This ensures that overall pharmacy goals are achieved in a manner that maximizes synergy with the patient care goals set in each service area. Although it is tempting to create a centralized, functionally organized pharmacy, this approach can focus the pharmacy service agenda internally, creating conflict with larger organizational goals.

The pharmacy should be organized in a fashion that meets laws and regulations pro-

mulgated by the state and federal government, and by standard-setting agencies such as the Joint Commission on Accreditation of Healthcare Organizations (Joint Commission) and the American Society of Health-System Pharmacists (ASHP). Pharmacy services and drug products are among the most regulated parts of the health care delivery system. Pharmacy directors should review compliance and changes in regulations on an annual basis to ensure continued compliance. Many standards and agencies overlap in jurisdiction, so a careful reading and thoughtful review are required. Table 26–1 contains a partial list of agencies and jurisdictions that may review the pharmacy practice or drug use and records of a health system.

The pharmacy should be organized to provide the full spectrum of clinical, patient care, drug information, drug preparation, storage and distribution, purchasing, quality review, and medication use evaluations. The exact characteristics of the pharmacy will depend upon the size of the health system and a number of other factors, including

- patient care programs and services offered at each site
- patient populations served (e.g., geriatric, pediatric, general, or specialty)
- scope of services provided by the corporate pharmacy leadership
- drug distribution system(s)
- level of computerization and automation
- participation in pharmaceutical research activities
- clinical experience programs, including medical, pharmacy, and nursing student and resident programs
- level of pharmacy staff experience, education, and training

The organization of the pharmacy should support the mission of the health system.

Table 26–1 Pharmacy Standard-Setting and Regulatory Agencies

Agency	Type	Review Functions	Frequency of Review
State board of pharmacy	Regulatory	Pharmacy Practice Act, pharmacy records, facilities, personnel, computer systems, automation, policies and procedures	Annual site inspection and document review
State narcotic control board	Regulatory	State controlled substance act, narcotic dispensing records, practitioner records, facilities, security procedures	Annual site inspection and document review or upon report of loss or complaint
U.S. Drug Enforcement Administration (DEA)	Regulatory	Federal controlled substance act, practitioner record review, records of dispensing	Upon report of loss or diversion or based on complaint
U.S. Food and Drug Administration (FDA)	Regulatory	Federal Food Drug and Cosmetic Act, drug recall records, drug storage	No scheduled visits to providers or pharmacies
State medical board	Regulatory	Practitioner records	Upon report of diversion or based on complaint
Joint Commission on Accreditation of Healthcare Organizations	Professional standards, accreditation	Facilities, policies and procedures, training, competency, formulary	Every three to five years, random inspections, and upon complaint or sentinel event
National Committee on Quality Assurance (NCQA)	Professional standards, accreditation	Facilities, policies and procedures, training, competency, formulary, patient satisfaction	Every 3 to 5 years, random inspections, and on complaint
American Society of Health-System Pharmacists (ASHP)	Professional standards, accreditation	Facilities, policies and procedures, training, education, and competency	Inspect training sites every 6 years
American Council on Pharmaceutical Education (ACPE)	Professional standards, accreditation	Education and training	Inspect training sites as a part of college degree program accreditation
United States Pharmacopoeia (USP)	Professional standards	Drug product composition and equivalence, drug storage and potency	No inspections

Pharmacy departments generally report though the pharmacy administrator to an assistant or associate administrator for ancillary services or to a chief operating officer. Because of the significant impact of drug therapies in the clinical environment, reporting relationships with the chief medical officer, medical director, and pharmacy and therapeutics committee are also important. The pharmacy director and administrator should be comfortable meeting the competing priorities of their reporting relationships. Contemporary human resources management techniques and philosophies are key to ensuring that the pharmacy personnel work well together to meet their portion of the larger health system agenda. The pharmacy service team usually is composed of pharmacists, pharmacy technicians, and clerical support staff.

PHARMACIST TRAINING AND EDUCATION

At a minimum, all pharmacists must have completed a five-year baccalaureate program in pharmacy accredited by the American Council on Pharmaceutical Education (ACPE) and be licensed by the state in which they practice. Since the mid-1990s, most pharmacists have received the Doctor of Pharmacy, or PharmD, degree. The PharmD is conferred after six years of study. It provides substantial additional clinical and didactic information and a much more intense clinical experience component. All pharmacists will receive the PharmD degree after the year 2000. Clinical pharmacy programs in progressive pharmacy departments generally utilize PharmD-trained practitioners for clinical service delivery. Some practice standards and programs require the PharmD credential, including education, residency training, and research programs.

Pharmacists may continue their education through residencies and fellowships in pharmacy practice and in clinical specialties. A pharmacy residency is an organized postgraduate program that focuses on developing applied knowledge and skills in the practice environment under the mentorship of an experienced practitioner. Fellowships are directed individual programs designed to develop an independent researcher. Fellowships and residencies are accredited by ASHP. Pharmacists who possess a bachelor's degree may pursue the PharmD degree in programs designed for active practitioners. Pharmacists may also advance their knowledge through Master of Science in Pharmacy, Master of Business Administration, and Master of Public Health programs.

Pharmacy has developed a number of board-level certifications to document the acquirement of specific knowledge base and clinical skill sets. Experienced PharmD-trained practitioners may sit for board examinations in pharmacotherapy, nutrition support, oncology, psychiatry, and nuclear pharmacy practice. Specialty certified pharmacists generally practice in higher level clinical environments as researchers and teachers. They often support specialty clinical practice within an organized delivery system. Pharmacist-run clinics in anticoagulation, psychopharmacy, home IV therapy, congestive heart failure, hypertension, and other specialties have achieved great success. Pharmacotherapy referral clinics run by pharmacists can be used to optimize medication use and decrease both drug cost and adverse drug events in organized delivery systems.

Pharmacy practice education also continues after the receipt of a pharmacist license. Virtually all states require that 10 to 15 hours of approved continuing education be completed each year for license renewal. Much of this education is targeted toward the development of knowledge about new drugs. Continuing education also may serve as a means to develop new practice skills.

PHARMACY TECHNICIAN TRAINING AND EDUCATION

Many of the drug preparation and distribution tasks of pharmacists have been delegated to trained pharmacy technicians. Pharmacy technicians work under the direct supervision of a pharmacist. All pharmacy technicians have completed high school, and most have completed one or two years of college. In the past, technicians were trained in hospitals and health systems "on the job." As skill requirements and delegated tasks increased, pharmacy technician training programs were developed to provide basic skills and experience. Most such programs are found in local technical schools or community colleges.

Pharmacy technicians are trained to work in a variety of care delivery areas, including inpatient care, home care, and ambulatory care. Many states register or license pharmacy technicians and require applicants to pass an examination and complete continuing education to maintain registration. A growing number of pharmacy technicians seek certification on a national level to document skills and facilitate registration. The Pharmacy Technician Certification Board is a coalition of pharmacy organizations that supports testing of applicants for basic skills and pharmacy practice knowledge. Applicants who pass the test are awarded the designation Certified Pharmacy Technician (CPhT).

Certified technicians are able to provide valuable support for the pharmacist and pharmacy service. While certification is not required to perform most technician duties, the education and experience allow most CPhT holders to perform at a higher level than the typical on-the-job–trained technician. Certi-

fied technicians are also required to receive continuing education to retain certified status.

PHARMACY INFORMATION SYSTEMS

An effective pharmacy information system is necessary to support an integrated approach to delivering and managing pharmaceutical care in an organized delivery system. It is vital in both the inpatient and outpatient pharmacy service areas. Whenever possible, it should be part of the larger clinical and management information system of the organized delivery system to ensure that pharmaceutical care and drug therapy are evaluated with the same level of scrutiny as other treatments and services. Integration also provides a high level of coordination in care delivery by assembling information from all disciplines and ensuring consistency of patient care in all clinical practice areas.

Exhibit 26–1 lists the support functions provided by pharmacy information systems. These systems provide a means to support the operations of the inpatient and outpatient pharmacy services. They further enhance the ability of pharmacies to meet patient care needs and respond to growth in demand using only limited additional resources. They assist in identifying medication costs and in billing third parties or internal accounts for medications. Pharmacy information systems support clinical pathways and practice guidelines. They also ensure compliance with a formulary by providing cost and therapeutic information to prescribers and pharmacists for consideration in prescribing.

An integrated information system supports delivery and administration of medications to inpatients by nursing staff and ensures limited waits and complete prescription records for outpatient prescriptions. A well-run pharmacy computer can also provide cost data to

Exhibit 26–1 Pharmacy Information System Functions

Drug distribution
- Patient medication profiles
- Outpatient prescription records
- Drug use data
- Point-of-care automation
- Robotics
- Decrease in order entry errors
- Purchasing and inventory control
- Printing of labels, fill lists, reports
- Work planning and staffing

Clinical pharmacy service
- Drug/lab interaction detection
- Drug-drug interaction detection
- Drug-nutrient interaction detection
- Drug treatment protocol support
- Clinical intervention tracking
- Medication use evaluation
- Drug use trend identification

Business support functions
- ADT
- Medication billing
- Cost review reports

- Outpatient Rx adjudication
- Decentralized services support
- Standardized data collection
- Workload and productivity analysis

Health care team
- Physician order sets
- Remote physician order entry
- Decrease in medication order errors
- Medication administration records (MAR)
- Physician (prescriber) profiling
- Patient medication profiles

Clinical support and development
- Critical path support
- Decision support protocols
- Drug therapy outcome review
- Clinical benchmarking
- Formulary decision support
- Medication error and adverse drug reaction (ADR) review
- Ad hoc query of clinical and financial data

prescribers and determine the clinical and financial status of patients at the time and point of service. Determinations of benefit eligibility for outpatients and of clinical need for inpatients can be made through an effective pharmacy information system. Interfaces with physician office–based systems can also support appropriate prescribing and allow remote entry of medication orders by physicians for more effective service.

The chief medical officer, chief financial officer, medical staff committees, and pharmacy directors can use retrospective data generated by pharmacy information systems to identify trends in drug use, support formulary and inventory management decisions, and determine compliance with guidelines or protocols. Medication use evaluation, ad-verse drug reaction (ADR) review, and other clinical and regulatory requirements can also be met through a pharmacy information system. These include the requirements of the state board of pharmacy, the Drug Enforcement Administration (DEA), the Joint Commission, the Health Care Financing Administration (HCFA), and private and government payers. Pharmacy information systems can also help meet the research and patient care needs of medical and surgical specialties with high drug use profiles, such as oncology and anesthesiology. They can synthesize information to develop treatment methods and guidelines that support the appropriate selection of drug therapies and to determine algorithms and provide guidance for patient treatment.

Pharmacy information systems also provide data to support formulary decisions, select proper treatments, and improve financial results for a hospital, health system, or organized delivery network. Pharmacists and pharmacy technicians use these systems to manage and monitor the delivery and the results of care after treatment decisions have been made. Information systems can also support business decisions, including the decision to bid for managed care business, and can help ensure that medication budget projections are met.

INPATIENT PHARMACY SERVICES

Inpatient pharmacy services focus on providing clinical support for the correct utilization of drugs. Typically, pharmacy services, to support this objective, are provided in the patient care area by pharmacists assigned to a specific medical or surgical service or to a care team. The pharmacist who works in each area must be accountable for the level and quality of pharmaceutical care and should participate in the development of resources and plans to support improvements in care quality and the efficiency of care delivery. Patient care area pharmacists have responsibility for the full spectrum of pharmaceutical care, as described earlier. They organize other professionals who participate in drug therapy selection, administration, and monitoring and ensure that reliable, consistent, effective therapy is delivered. Following prescribing, they coordinate the delivery of the medication therapy. Pharmacists assigned to patient care areas support the execution of the medication therapy by evaluating the therapy to maximize the efficacy of drug delivery and administration.

The pharmaceutical care practice model creates efficiency and positive outcomes by ensuring timely, correct decision making, by managing therapy to make certain that it achieves the desired goal, and by directing the medication selection process. Inefficiencies, therapeutic failures, and higher costs are associated with insufficient monitoring, selection of less than the best alternatives, and micromanagement of therapies (e.g., frequent changes based on individual clinical findings rather than on clinical evidence).

Support resources, particularly information systems, can be used to identify patients for whom targeted interventions by pharmacists can benefit both patient care and the health care providers. The assignment of pharmacists to patient care teams also allows direct interaction with prescribers and the provision of feedback on the clinical and economic impact of drug therapy decisions. The pharmacists can identify drug-related issues across the continuum of care, including drug therapy–related admissions and readmissions. They can further facilitate the pharmaceutical transition from acute inpatient care to skilled care, home care, or an ambulatory environment. Skilled pharmacists responsible for a program or service can further participate in reviewing physician practice patterns related to drug therapy and suggesting alternatives to achieve the clinical and financial goals of the organization.

Inpatient clinical pharmacy services should be developed and targeted to meet the needs of the patients, the medical staff, and the organized delivery system or hospital. Hospital-specific plans should be made to ensure that necessary services are provided and that patient care quality and cost needs are met. Clinical pharmacy services vary with the nature of the patient care delivered by an organization. They also are driven by patient acuity and length of stay. The pharmaceutical care needs of an acutely ill heart attack patient differ from those of a psychiatric patient or a geriatric patient admitted for a prosthetic hip. Patients discharged to self-care require different types of support than those who move to skilled care facilities or to assisted living. Targeting services to meet the needs of the patients treated in a given organized delivery system ensures both positive outcomes and cost-effective service delivery.

Although clinical pharmacy services must be tailored, there is one group of core services typically accepted as a component of appropriate pharmacy services. These services generally are required or encouraged by standard-setting agencies such as the Joint Commission or ASHP. They may also be addressed in state health department, hospital, or pharmacy practice regulations. Increasingly, they are among the baseline services expected by payers. Basic inpatient clinical pharmacy services provided by a health system pharmacy should include

- ADR review
- antibiotic use review
- serum drug concentration (SDC) review
- renal and pharmacokinetic dosing of drugs
- management of drug therapies under approved protocols
- medication profile review
- general dosing review and support
- drug interaction screening
- medication histories and patient discharge teaching
- discharge planning
- medication use evaluation
- critical pathway support and development
- drug information services
- nutrition support
- IV to oral medication therapy conversion

The effectiveness of clinical pharmacy programs is best evaluated with a program that tracks the patient-specific clinical interventions of pharmacists assigned to each team or patient care area.[3] A number of manual and automated methods for tracking interventions have been developed. An intervention tracking program should identify every direct patient care activity of pharmacists. Several authors and ASHP have developed methods to assess the impact and desirable outcomes of interventions. A well-run intervention program identifies the nature of the clinical activities of pharmacists and ascribes them to specific pharmacists, patients, patient care programs, and physicians. It further develops an index of the costs and benefits associated with each intervention and with all interventions. Outcomes for an organization can be determined based on the quality and impact of patient care and on the avoidance of drug and other treatment costs, such as those associated with laboratory tests or increased length of inpatient stay. Pharmacy clinical intervention tracking programs should also develop methods to pass detailed intervention information to other providers. They can be of further use in the evaluation of pharmacist work performance and physician practice patterns.

The clinical activities of pharmacists should be recorded in the paper or electronic medical record. Recommendations and outcomes should be visible to all patient care disciplines to ensure the inclusion of drug therapy recommendations in care planning and monitoring. Electronic recording of interventions allows routine tracking and analysis. Most current pharmacy information systems support recording, tracking, and communication of pharmacist clinical interventions. Several stand-alone computer programs have been developed to facilitate recording and analysis of pharmacist interventions when these are not supported by the pharmacy information system.

INPATIENT DRUG DISTRIBUTION AND MANAGEMENT

The primary method for drug distribution in the inpatient setting is the unit dose method. The unit dose medication distribution system was developed over 30 years ago to provide a safe and effective means to distribute medications. It has been endorsed by a number of standard-setting and accrediting organizations, including the Joint Commission and ASHP. Pharmacy regulations and rules in most states now require some variation of the unit dose system for drug delivery. The unit dose system allows detailed tracking of medication use, and it avoids many opportunities for medication error by ensuring that a limited number of medications are available for administration. Further, the medications are sorted and organized to facilitate correct administration. The unit dose system minimizes drug costs by limiting waste, loss, spoilage, and diversion of medications in patient care areas.

The unit dose system is defined as a system in which medications are dispensed in labeled single-unit packages in ready-to-administer form. In most acute care settings, a 24-hour supply or less is available for use in the patient care area.[4,5,6] Pharmacists review direct copies of the physician's orders prior to medications' being dispensed or made available. Pharmacists enter medication orders into the pharmacy information system, where checks of appropriateness, dose, drug interactions, and appropriate inventory quantities and items to dispense are identified. In health systems where physicians enter medications directly into a computer, orders are reviewed by a pharmacist before they are made fully active for medication dispensing and administration.

The hub of the drug distribution system is a complete pharmacy computer information system. Pharmacy information systems are designed to support numerous functions, but a primary purpose is to support accurate, timely, cost-effective medication distribution. In the acute care environment, patient conditions, therapeutic needs, and medication orders change rapidly. A computerized information system provides the most accurate current description of each patient's medication needs. It also supports correct entry of medication orders and checking for errors in prescribing and dosing and for drug interactions. Pharmacy information systems support both manual and automated unit dose distribution systems.

In a unit dose system, active current medications are available on the patient care unit in sufficient quantities at all times. However, when a new order is placed, a supply of medication must be sent to cover the period until the next regular supply is delivered. The "first-dose turnaround time" can be a significant issue if transportation systems and pharmacy location preclude rapid delivery of newly ordered medications to the patient care area.

In a manual unit dose system, a medication supply for each patient is prepared by the pharmacy for each 24-hour period. The specific medications and quantities are based on the current medication order profile maintained in the information system for each patient. A sufficient quantity of each medication is placed in a bin specifically designated for that patient. Individual bins are combined in cassettes and delivered to each patient care area. Medication cassettes are placed in a secure area or in a locked cart on each unit. A duplicate set of patient medication bins and cassettes is kept in the pharmacy, where it is refilled for daily exchange. Most pharmacies exchange medication cassettes once daily at a predetermined time.

Although the unit dose system confers many safeguards and advantages in delivering medications, as a manual system it is highly labor intensive, so automation has been developed to support the patient care advantages of the system at a decreased cost. Two methods are used to improve unit dose drug distribution. The first method automates the bin filling process in the pharmacy using robotics. The second places automated medication dispensing units on the patient care unit at the point of care (POC).

Direct automation of the manual processes described above using a pharmacy information system, bar codes, and a robot is the most straightforward approach. Vendors have developed robots that fill unit dose bins for the next 24-hour period based on the patients' computerized medication profiles. When an order is entered in the pharmacy information system, it is translated into information that tells the robot to select an appropriate number of the correct unit dose medication and place it in the patient's medication bin as it moves along a conveyor. The use of bar codes ensures accuracy and allows detailed information, including lot numbers, expiration dates, and even unique dose identifiers, to be retained. Pharmacies using this type of automation generally continue to use a single daily cart exchange and operate the robot to fill the unit dose bins and cassette once each day.

First doses of drugs resulting from new medication orders can be set up by the robot, ensuring the accuracy and consistency that automation confers. However, each new medication still must be delivered from the robot's location to the patient care area. Advantages of the robotic cart-filling method include improved accuracy in medication dispensing and accounting. Disadvantages include high startup costs (partly resulting from needed facility renovations), high continuing support costs, large space needs, and limited robot capacity. Most general hospitals have 2,500 to 3,500 medications on their formulary; robots capable of handling so many medications are costly. Many medications require special storage and handling precluding their being dispensed by a robot. These medications must continue to be dispensed manually. Some state pharmacy regulations limit multi-site robot use and decrease the benefits by requiring manual checks of robot-dispensed doses by pharmacists.

Capital expense or lease costs for robotic technology are high, limiting use to larger hospitals. The decision to purchase and implement an automated bin fill system should be based on a keen and insightful analysis of the financial benefit, return on investment, and potential for demonstrated improvements in service quality and patient care. Although the cost of a robot continues to decrease, information systems and other support costs will remain high enough to make the decision to purchase or lease a robot hard to justify in many cases.

The second strategy for automating unit dose distribution is POC automation. POC automation places supplies of medications on the patient care unit in computer-controlled dispensing cabinets that function in a manner similar to the familiar automated teller machines used by the banking industry. Nurses or other authorized patient care staff are provided with personal identification codes and passwords that confer access to medications. Users, by responding to prompts given on a screen, select the appropriate medications for particular patients. Although a bin and cassette system is not used, dispensing cabinets are stocked with individually packaged and labeled drugs, a key component of the unit dose method. The available medication supplies are specific to each patient and are controlled by the pharmacy information system. Users can only access those medications that are currently ordered for a specific patient. A current medication order, reviewed and approved by a pharmacist, enables access to a specific drug for that patient. Although a 24-hour supply is not dispensed for each patient, access is directed by the electronic medication profile in the POC unit. This ensures tracking of drug use and also provides support to ensure that ordered medications are given in a timely fashion. Emergency medications are available through an override function that allows access to specific medications without a physician's order.

Patient data are transferred to the POC system through the admissions (ADT) module of the information system. Patient census, transfers, billing, and pharmacy medication profile data must be supplied to the unit on a real-time basis. Pharmacy data, including medication orders and substantial drug product details, must pass to the POC system instantaneously. Billing data, drug withdrawal, and medication administration information must be passed from the unit to the pharmacy and patient care information system. POC device users, including nurses, physicians, and pharmacy staff, must be credentialed and maintain access privileges to ensure both the security of medication supplies and the effective use of the POC system. A complete record of medication-related information for each transaction must move between the pharmacy, patient billing, and other information systems and the POC device or its computer server.

POC devices can eliminate up to 90 percent of the manual bin fill process if properly sized and configured. Substantial customization of the hardware devices and the software that drives each device is possible at each site. Medication inventories can be managed to follow trends in utilization to minimize cost and maximize resource use.

POC systems eliminate delays in medication delivery to the unit for the 90 percent of medications supplied on the unit. POC systems suffer from several of the same shortcomings mentioned for robotics above. For example, medications that require special storage and handling cannot be delivered through POC automation and must be dispensed manually. Although 90 percent of medications are available on the patient care unit in a well-run POC system, the 10 percent that are unavailable can consume substantial staff time and cause considerable delays in therapy due to delivery logistics and system reconfiguration and loading. Pharmacy regulations in some states limit POC functions and decrease the realizable cost benefits by requiring pharmacist checks.

Advantages of POC devices include the increased accuracy and accountability for dispensing of medications seen with robotic systems. POC systems extend the accountability to medication administration and other medication-related functions occurring in the patient care area. Nurses or other authorized staff are given access to necessary and appropriate medications based on current real-time medication profiles. Medications that are discontinued are immediately removed from access and cannot be administered. Unauthorized access to medications is prohibited, and controlled substance accountability is high. Disadvantages of POC systems include support costs, space needs on patient care units, and a requirement for high levels of accuracy and timeliness of medication order entry and review on the part of the pharmacy staff.

POC devices have an advantage over both robotic and manual systems in anesthesia care, operating rooms and postanesthesia recovery areas, and emergency departments. In these areas POC devices use ADT information and user data to support a very high level of accountability for stock medications. Although the system is not strictly "unit dose" in nature, the detailed accountability and rich transaction data allow for ready access to drugs in emergent situations with a high level of accountability for drug use and inventory. The POC supports similar stock medication procedures on the patient care unit. POC devices allow emergency access to selected medications that are not part of the patient's current medication profile. This access is generally limited to defined patient care needs and is supported by policies developed by the pharmacy and therapeutics committee of the hospital or organized delivery system.

The task of selecting a manual, robotic, or POC system is not simple. Substantial resources are consumed in setting up any of these systems. Vendor and pharmacy department expertise are required to accomplish the projected efficiencies and cost decreases. Table 26–2 compares features of the three methods and their advantages and disadvantages. Some general principles do apply when trying to determine the best method, but all three systems have been successfully used in all sizes and types of organized delivery systems. Some health care systems have implemented combinations of robotics and POC devices to gain the advantages of each across diverse sites and care needs.

Patient care bedside devices can be used to support further automation of pharmaceutical care delivery. These "handheld" devices can accomplish more than medication administration documentation, but they interface with both robotic and POC pharmacy systems. Advantages of bedside charting devices include enhanced accountability and data management for medications, along with convenience and accuracy in charting medications and other aspects of care.

STERILE PRODUCTS PREPARATION

In the acute care and home IV therapy environment, substantial pharmacy effort is de-voted to the preparation of sterile products for intravenous and other parenteral administration. Intravenous admixtures consist of drugs added to IV solutions. These encompass secondary IV medications, such as antibiotics, cytotoxic cancer chemotherapy agents, vasoactive and critical care IV drips, and total parenteral nutrition (TPN) solutions.

Drugs added to IV solutions suffer degradation caused by the diluting solution and the effects of light, heat, and the storage environment. Drugs mixed in an IV solution also can interact with each other, leading to decreased effectiveness or to toxicity. The IV admixture itself may be contaminated through manipulation, leading to bacterial growth and transmission of bacteria to the patient. Some new biotechnology-derived drugs have very short periods of stability and may require special techniques to achieve dilution and dispersion. Accuracy in preparation supports delivery of the labeled amount and ensures consistency from dose to dose and from patient to patient. For these reasons as well as technique and quality assurance issues, Joint Commission standards and most state pharmacy regulations now require pharmacy preparation of IV solutions. In the past, IVs were prepared by nurses on the patient care units, but this is no longer recommended.

The ASHP provides a number of standards and recommendations for facilities, procedures, training and qualifications for sterile products preparation.[7,8] An appropriate dedicated space for IV preparation, with written policies and procedures that meet practice standards, is also required. Pharmacies should meet these standards and institute process controls and staff training to foster appropriate preparation of medications. ASHP documents offer sound recommendations on quality assurance, staff education and evaluation, policies and procedures, facilities and equipment, and quality improvement.

Table 26–2 Comparison of Unit Dose Distribution Systems

	Manual Unit Dose System	*Robotic Unit Dose System*	*Point-of-Care Drug Delivery System*
Capital cost or lease cost	Low	High	High
Personnel cost	High; high pharmacist time requirements	Lowest; limits both pharmacist and pharmacy technician time	Low; limits pharmacist time, shifts work functions to pharmacy technicians
Computer support required	Basic	Substantial	Highest
Dispensing and billing accuracy	Low	High	High
Drug administration accountability	Limited	Medium	Very high
Stock medication capability	Open stock on patient care unit; manual accountability	Open stock on patient care unit; manual accountability	Limited user-specific access; high accountability
First dose delivery delays	Substantial and frequent	Lower, but still substantial	Lowest; none for 90% of medications
Medication error prevention	Lowest	Medium	Highest
Medication capacity	95–100% of all medications	80–90% of all medications	90% of all medications
Refill frequency	Daily 24-hour supply	Daily 24-hour supply	Daily restock of about 10% of items in POC device
Controlled substance applications	Limited; locked stock on patient care unit; manual accountability	Limited; locked stock on patient care unit; manual accountability	Best; locked, with patient- and user-specific controlled access
"Best fit" application type	Small hospitals with low "medication intensity" and hospitals that include long-term and skilled care	Large hospitals with high "medication intensity"	Medium to large hospitals at all medication use levels

The availability of suitable facilities is of paramount importance for ensuring the integrity of the final product. Federal standards exist for airborne particulate matter. Current pharmacy practice standards group pharmacy-prepared sterile products into three categories based on their potential for patient risk. Clean rooms are classified based on the number of particles of 0.5 μm or greater allowed per cubic foot of air. A class 10,000 environment allows up to 10,000 particles of 0.5 μm or greater per cubic foot of air. Low-risk products may be prepared in a class 100 laminar air flow clean bench. Higher risk products must be prepared in cleaner environments.

Practice standards include the maintenance of daily process records for both products and staff performance. Practice standards are particularly important in the home care environment, where caregiver training and storage conditions typically fall below the high levels associated with inpatient care. Although IV preparation standards do not change rapidly, an annual assessment of compliance with practice standards and state regulations should be performed. A sterile products preparation system utilizing trained pharmacy technician staff under the supervision of pharmacists has been demonstrated to provide appropriate, cost-effective service.

New methods and equipment are being made available for IV preparation. Computer-controlled compounding pumps are available to prepare intravenous nutrition (TPN) solutions. Software programs exist that perform calculations for preparations, provide product preparation worksheets, and support label preparation and quality assurance efforts. Pumps and devices that provide controlled delivery of drugs for treatment of pain, such as patient-controlled analgesia (PCA), and for epidural administration of drugs offer therapeutic benefits. Syringe pumps can provide medications in higher concentrations or with lower fluid volumes. A pharmacy with a well-run sterile products program can adapt to these changes easily, as the same techniques and procedures are used for calculations and preparation.

Cytotoxic agents used in the treatment of cancer create specific preparation problems.[9] Safe handling procedures should be a part of the training of all pharmacy staff who handle these agents. The pharmacy staff should participate in an active, vigorous program to train others who work with these agents, including nurses, physicians, and housekeeping personnel who handle waste, trash, and spills.

PHARMACY SERVICE LOCATION

Pharmacy services such as drug preparation, sterile products compounding, and unit dose distribution are typically housed in a main pharmacy area. This area may be far removed from the patient care areas, limiting interactions between physicians, nurses, and pharmacists regarding drug therapy. Of necessity, a number of pharmacy staff must work in the main drug preparation area to perform activities that require special facilities or conditions. This is also true of outpatient pharmacy services, where preparation, compounding, and distribution continue to occur in a pharmacy behind a counter or closed doors.

To achieve the goals of pharmaceutical care described above, however, pharmacists must be housed and work in areas where patients and professionals meet to assess, plan, and deliver care. Achieving this goal can be complicated by the distance, physical layout, and transportation systems available in a given facility. Several alternatives have been developed to accomplish the goal of clinical pharmacy service delivery in harmony with pharmacy's traditional distribution and medication control functions. Many hospitals and organized delivery systems utilize substantial information systems development and either type of automation described above to support these alternatives. The models described below are not mutually exclusive, and most organized delivery systems use a combination of systems to achieve patient care quality and efficiency goals.

Creating satellite pharmacies in patient care areas and remote clinics is one method used for placing pharmacists closer to patient care. Immediate medication needs, drug information, patient monitoring, and consultation services are delivered from the satellite pharmacies. The central pharmacy continues to be responsible for daily unit dose bin fill, sterile products preparation, and support services. In an inpatient decentralized system that uses satellite pharmacies, the bulk of pharmacy staff practice in the satellite pharmacy locations, while a core group remain in the main pharmacy. Advantages of this method include rapid delivery of first doses and ready availability of pharmacy staff for consultation and care planning. Disadvantages include space requirements in patient care areas, inventory growth, and staffing requirements to keep the satellites open.

A second approach involves placing pharmacy staff in patient care areas without creating satellites to provide distribution services. The pharmacists provide information and participate in care planning, patient education, and other services but do not use a satellite location to dispense. This practice model can be supported by distribution and drug preparation services located in a central pharmacy. Doses can also be delivered by automated devices. In ambulatory care environments, mail order and remote site filling of prescriptions also serve this model.

This alternative allows for the pharmacy services to be delivered in patient care areas and ensures a high level of support for appropriate prescribing and correct medication administration. Decentralized pharmacists can identify and resolve medication problems and misadventures, including drug interactions, adverse drug reactions, and medication errors. This model is frequently supported by POC device–based drug distribution. Information systems must support access to the pharmacy profile and pharmacy clinical and order entry systems throughout the patient care areas. Advantages of this model include the high level of participation of pharmacists in patient care, staffing flexibility, and the absence of space needs. Disadvantages are few, but the requirement for access to pharmacy information systems in the care area is nearly absolute.

Table 26–3 compares the three types of pharmacy service delivery systems. No particular system is best across all organization types. In many hospitals and organized delivery systems, a combination of two or all three of the service models is used. Some regional systems have accomplished centralization of parts of the distribution model across a city or service area. Major changes in the application and effectiveness of both centralized and decentralized models will most likely be driven by automation and information systems in the future.

AMBULATORY CARE AND OUTPATIENT PHARMACY SYSTEMS

Organized delivery systems have expanded their scope far beyond the traditional inpatient stay. Many systems include physician practices, short-stay surgery centers, urgent care centers, hospices, home care agencies, skilled nursing and long-term care facilities, rehabilitation centers, and retail pharmacies. In some larger systems, mail or-

Table 26–3 Comparison of Pharmacy Staffing Models

	Centralized Pharmacy Services	Satellite Based Pharmacy Services	Decentralized Pharmacy Services
Space requirements	Main pharmacy only	High; in proximity to patient care units	Least
Capital issues	None	Inventory growth; drug preparation equipment duplicated in satellite(s)	None
Computer support required	Basic to advanced	Basic to advanced; satellites must have access	Basic to advanced, but pharmacy information system must be accessible on care units
"Best fit" unit dose model(s) supported	Manual, robotic, and point-of-care	Manual, robotic	Robotic, point-of-care
Sterile products preparation model	Centralized preparation and distribution	First dose from satellite, then centralized	Centralized preparation and distribution
First dose delivery delays	Longest	Minimal	Intermediate
Medication transportation needs	Highest	Lowest	Intermediate
"Best fit" application type	Smaller hospitals; hospitals with good transportation systems; hospitals with homogeneous patient population	Hospitals with large physical plants or distant patient care areas; hospitals with diverse or dissimilar patient populations (e.g., pediatric unit in general hospital)	All hospital types with advanced information systems; POC devices add significant value

der prescriptions and pharmacy benefits management also have become included in the services provided. These two functions are generally added by systems when they move into providing and managing health maintenance organization (HMO) and insurance products. Many systems have created executive-level pharmacy director positions to tie these services together and to ensure regulatory compliance and consistency across organizational components. If the scope and size of ambulatory services warrant it, they may report to a pharmacy manager whose sole responsibility is to manage an ambulatory care pharmacy.

In many cases, some or all of these pharmacy services may be contracted to outside vendors under the oversight of a system pharmacy director. Services should be contracted outside the system whenever the pharmacy is too small to possess the necessary professional and management staff expertise. It may also be advisable when the unique drugs purchased to support a program do not allow contracts for the lowest available cost. "Alternate site delivery program" contracts are a part of most group purchasing portfolios. However, because of the diversity of "alternate site" definitions by groups, organized delivery systems, and vendors, these contracts are usually sparse and not as advantageous as inpatient contracts, where trade definitions are more uniform. In the case of larger functions, such as mail order prescriptions and pharmacy benefit management services, the size of the patient population required for development of a viable program may be beyond the scope of most systems.

Principles for managing the daily operation of pharmacy services for each of these units are generally similar to those described for an inpatient pharmacy. However, the application can vary greatly based on the population served and the pharmaceutical care needs of the patients. Physician office practices, urgent care centers, and short-stay surgery centers generally do not require daily on-site pharmacist staff, unless they are quite large. Pharmaceutical purchasing and drug policy can be coordinated from a central pharmacy, and global pharmacy and therapeutics and other policies can be modified to apply to each of these areas. Purchasing and inventory control generally are held separate from a system's hospitals, both because products used are somewhat dissimilar and to prevent contract problems. A business manager, nurse, or other technician in the practice or surgery center can order drug supplies and manage inventory under the supervision of a central pharmacy buyer or manager. This ensures that drug purchasing and disposition

meet appropriate regulations and that storage, recordkeeping, and other regulatory and practice standards are met. In some states, specific regulations apply to pharmacy practice in surgery centers. Particular attention should be paid to controlled substance regulations in all areas.

Hospice and home care pharmacies bridge the gap between traditional inpatient care and ambulatory care. They typically draw on the expertise of inpatient trained staff for the knowledge and mechanics of clinical care. They do, however, place a high premium on customer service, as in the ambulatory care model, so they also capitalize on the patient care skills of retail pharmacy. Home care and hospice pharmacies may be combined, particularly in a system that emphasizes oncology, where the patient populations served and the physicians involved in care management may overlap significantly. An emphasis on collaborative efforts and dedicated staff in these areas ensures that pharmacy service agendas are consistent with global system agendas. Home care and hospice pharmacies can operate independently, but many make use of the system's hospital pharmacy professional staff to cover emergencies and night or other off hours. Patient access problems and delivery requirements generally make home care pharmacies that are separate from inpatient facilities more advantageous. Because of limited downtime for equipment, and the amount of time staff spend in inpatient sterile products labs, there is little opportunity to capture unused hospital facility and staff time to deliver home care services.

Skilled nursing facilities (SNFs) and long-term care facilities have long been served by centralized pharmacies. These services typically grew out of retail pharmacies in the private sector, and they can probably best be supplied in this fashion in an organized delivery system. Drug use and acuity levels match those of an outpatient pharmacy most closely. Specific, detailed regulations exist for SNF and nursing home pharmacies. There are requirements for independent professional review of the need for continuing medication and for drug use evaluation. Communication with physicians regarding these requirements must be documented, and routine scheduled reviews must be performed to ensure both regulatory compliance and payment. System pharmacy directors should have methods to ensure continuing compliance in place.

Retail pharmacy services constitute a growth area for systems. Opportunities generally start with system employee prescription benefits coverage and expand as systems develop insurance and HMO products. Retail pharmacies must purchase independently of other parts of a system by law and regulation. In many cases, the ability to capture prescriptions from discharged patients and their families, along with support for physician practices, make retail pharmacies an excellent supplement to ambulatory care services. Each retail pharmacy can operate autonomously, but all pharmacies should fall under the oversight of the system's pharmacy and therapeutics committee, general pharmacy policies, and a system pharmacy executive.

Many unique systems and applications have been developed in ambulatory care environments. Outpatient pharmacy services also have become a growth area for organized delivery systems, particularly where sophisticated or unique drug therapies are delivered, such as in home intravenous therapy, or where the continuation of inpatient care provides efficiencies and better treatment outcomes. Centralization of resources, drug inventories, and distribution services work well when decentralized pharmacy staff are placed in clinics and in the field. Business plans and customer service issues drive ambulatory

care pharmacy service planning. An effective information system and automation can support high-level, cost-effective services in the outpatient environment as well. Physician office and patient usable automation devices are available to support the same sophistication in delivery as on the inpatient care side of pharmaceutical care.

PATIENT CARE COMMITTEES

Because the relationship between pharmacists and physicians is so close in the setting and implementation of drug policy, the pharmacy director and the representative clinical and management staff of the pharmacy should participate in hospital, ambulatory care, and medical staff committees at the local business unit and systemwide level to ensure adequate policy development and implementation support. The quality of medication use is directly related to the sharing of information in the multidisciplinary review of medication use, medication misadventures, and pharmacy business records. Pharmacists typically participate in the pharmacy and therapeutics, quality improvement, infection control, safety, risk management, institutional review board (human subjects research), and intensive care committees. They may also serve on other committees that address patient care, quality, or cost issues.

The most important committee relationship for the pharmacy is the pharmacy and therapeutics committee. This is usually a standing committee of the organization's medical staff. It advises the medical staff on drug use through the development of a formulary and policies and procedures to support appropriate and optimal use of medications by physicians, nurses, pharmacists, and patients. The committee is the direct link between the medical staff and the pharmacy service. It also supports staff and patient education, reviews drug use, and investigates drug-related problems and issues. The composition of the committee varies between organizations. Usually included are several physicians, one or more nurses, the director of pharmacy, at least one administrator, and other practitioners who prescribe or administer medications.

Pharmacy and therapeutics committees and the formulary system date back a number of years. Although the emphasis of formulary management has changed, the primary goal of a formulary is to create a usable listing of the most effective medications and to foster their proper and appropriate use through policies, procedures, and support systems. Due to the nature of medication use, pharmacy and therapeutics committees typically meet on a monthly or bimonthly basis.

Some organized delivery systems delegate some or all pharmacy and therapeutic committee functions to local operating units. The distributed approach makes a great deal of sense, particularly if geography or diversity of services or patients offer opportunities for closer monitoring of clinical practice and prescribers locally. Most organized delivery systems have centralized some committee functions to achieve economies of scale and to ensure that decisions that affect the financial health of the system are made at an appropriate level. These generally include drug quality and purchasing specifications, clinical pathways, service and pharmaceutical contracts, Joint Commission and regulatory compliance, and quality assurance. System pharmacy and therapeutics committees are generally composed of senior managers in nursing, pharmacy, and administration and of medical directors or medical staff leaders within the system.

The functions of these committees have been described by ASHP as follows:[10,11]

1. advising medical staff and administrators on all matters pertaining to the use of drugs (including investigational drug use)
2. developing a formulary of drugs accepted for use in the health system and providing for its annual revision (selections should be based on objective evaluation of therapeutic merit and economic impact)
3. establishing programs and procedures that help ensure cost-effective, safe drug therapy
4. establishing suitable educational programs for the system's professional staff on matters related to drug use
5. participating in quality assurance activities related to prescribing, preparation, distribution, and use of medications
6. reviewing adverse drug events, medication errors, and other medication misadventures occurring in the health system
7. initiating and directing medication use evaluation activities
8. advising the pharmacy service on the implementation of effective drug distribution and clinical pharmacy services

FINANCIAL MANAGEMENT

Expenditures for drugs vary widely in organized delivery systems. Most systems still devote less than 20 percent of their total expenditures to drug therapies, but many organizations with large specialty treatment populations, such as AIDS or oncology patients, may experience higher expenses. All organizations are experiencing growth in expenditures related to new drugs and therapies and to a lesser extent increased patient demand.

Pharmacies generate revenue that covers only a small portion of drug expenses. Reimbursement for inpatient drug expenses is bundled with overall patient costs and contracts. Organized delivery systems also are often "at risk" for outpatient drug expenses in newer delivery models. In general, selection of the most effective and least costly alternative is the prudent course of action. Involvement of the pharmacy and therapeutics committee and front-line clinical pharmacists will lead to better patient care and financial outcomes. Balancing effectiveness and cost is perhaps the most challenging part of pharmaceutical care today.

COST AND PRODUCTIVITY MANAGEMENT

Pharmacy departments are most often charged with the responsibility for managing drug and delivery system costs. Systems should be developed to utilize drug and delivery resources in a cost-effective fashion. Daily, weekly, monthly, and quarterly assessments of drug costs and salary costs should be done. Performance targets for both categories can be developed based on activity levels, such as admissions, visits, or prescriptions filled. Financial management systems in contemporary pharmacies should provide methods to quantify costs, monitor financial performance, and relate clinical information and service data to costs. Drug budgeting by therapeutic category and routine reporting of cost by service and by therapeutic category can support continued success in meeting financial targets. Adding detail to general reports also allows rapid evaluation of trends and changes in drug purchasing and utilization.

The pharmacy management team should focus on developing effective strategies to maximize leverage of drug and human resource costs. These include automation of distribution tasks and the use of technicians and other support personnel when warranted. Attention should also be paid to the level of experience and qualification of the pharmacist engaged in a particular activity. A mix of specialists, generalists, and support system pharmacists should be developed to meet the organization's needs. Specialist-trained clinical pharmacists are paid premium wages, so their use in drug distribution should be limited. Staff pharmacists can be appropriately deployed to maximize the productivity of professional resources.

To achieve these goals, the pharmacy management team can utilize a number of tools to assist in analyzing labor and supply parameters. The traditional comparison of actual and budgeted expenses does not give the pharmacy manager enough information to promote the most cost-effective use of supplies and services throughout the institution.

In a cost-critical environment, staff utilization requires ongoing monitoring. Staffing depends on the mix of clinical pharmacists, pharmacists, technicians, and other support staff and on the ability of each team to meet its care responsibilities effectively. A premium should be placed on the interaction between the pharmacy service and the other members of the care delivery team. Staffing ratios and the functions of each staff type should be evaluated at least yearly. Staffing systems should be reviewed and revised with an eye toward promoting productivity and staff morale as well as creating savings. Program changes, market competition, and therapy changes can dramatically affect the volume and distribution of the pharmacy workload within an organized delivery system.

Productivity measures should be established through a work measurement system, using standards established for different product and service categories (e.g., drug doses dispensed per adjusted discharge or clinical pharmacy service units per discharge). There are a number of benchmarks for staffing, drug cost, and worked hours. Systems can create internal systems for benchmarking, but most subscribe to services such as Mecon PEERx (Mecon Inc., San Ramon, California) that provide a range of benchmarks, including indicators for pharmacy expense and drug use. Published data sources include *Hospital Pharmacy Data Quarterly* (Aspen Publishers, Gaithersburg, Maryland) and pharmaceutical industry–sponsored digests, such as the *Managed Care Digest* (published by Hoechst Marion Roussel) and the *Novartis Pharmacy Benefit Report* (obtainable through company representatives).

Comparisons to published benchmarks generally work on a micro level and when looking at pharmacies within an organized system whose costs and definitions of service volume and patient type are consistent. Comparisons between systems may be problematic, as definitions for work are not standard and patient and drug product mix can vary. Global comparisons should serve as a starting point, but most benchmarks, even in the case of similar systems, bear substantial scrutiny before serious use.

By comparing a pharmacy department to those in other systems, areas of opportunity can be identified. Comparisons often relate a specific indicator or ratio that applies to both organizations; the indicator or ratio is then applied to industrywide ratios (e.g., costs, hours worked, and prescription volumes divided by patient days, discharges, or ambulatory care visits for some determined period). Common indicators are doses dispensed, patient care units earned (earned hours), full-time employees, IV doses prepared, prescriptions filled, drug costs, total supply costs, salary costs, and total costs. The functional strengths and weaknesses among the comparison organizations can be evaluated. It is important not to focus on a single indicator of cost or quality, as it may reflect differences in measurement or underlying differences outside the pharmacy. A constellation of indicators that map a function or service allows a more accurate and critical analysis of services. The areas that provide highest value to the pharmacy manager can be explored further. The best in an area can be ascertained. By networking with other institutions, it is possible to identify excellent practices and low-cost providers.

Since labor input does not always conform to volume changes, productivity should be monitored frequently. Significant volume increases may signal the need for additional staffing in a given area. On the other hand, volume decreases may lead the pharmacy manager to consider not replacing employees who resign or replacing pharmacists with technicians for the more traditional distributive functions. The use of overtime may be appropriate instead of hiring additional staff. However, overtime expenses can be limited by the use of part-time employees and per diem staff. Overtime is best used to cover peak work demands and to augment temporary increases in work volume. Automation can also smooth productivity variances between high- and low-volume periods.

Understanding the impact of changes in the type of services performed (e.g., pharmacokinetic dosing versus order clarification) and in the products dispensed (e.g., oral dosage forms prepared versus parenteral chemotherapy doses prepared) will also help to determine staffing requirements. Productivity variances are related to volume shifts and to the use of products that are more labor intensive versus ingredient cost intensive. A variance may be caused by the type of patients being treated, although the cause may not always be readily apparent. Analyses of cost per patient unit and changes in the drug volume per patient day on different units may help to assess the impact throughout the health care system. Similar variances may be seen in outpatient prescription drug costs and drug utilization. These can also be related to patient characteristics such as age and chronic disease prevalence, and to benefit design and the structure of physician incentives and risk in drug prescribing. Careful data analysis should be performed prior to taking action, particularly in the case of outpatient drug use, where patient choice and physician behavior play a greater role.

MANAGING DRUG COSTS

Two types of strategies can be applied to manage drug costs: administrative control and clinical review. Administrative control is implemented through reductions in drug acquisition costs, inventory management, use of appropriate drug distribution systems, and computerization.

The goal of reducing drug acquisition costs is to provide quality drugs at the lowest possible price. There are many chemically identical drug entities, known as generic equivalents, that are manufactured and distributed by many drug companies. The Food and Drug Administration requires that generic equivalents all act the same in the human body. Therefore, pharmacies can control drug acquisition costs by selecting the least expensive equivalent, whether through internal bidding, group purchasing, or negotiation with acceptable vendors. When a drug goes "off patent," many equivalent versions appear in the marketplace, and the cost per unit de-

creases. Pharmacy managers should stay abreast of patent changes. Group purchasing organizations generally focus on this aspect of the marketplace and provide a reliable source for current cost-effective contracts.

Drugs that are patented generally consume the largest portion of the drug budget. These agents are least amenable to switching, as many are unique or possess properties that make changing therapies less desirable. Pharmacies and pharmacy and therapeutics committees should not avoid the therapeutic controversies that can arise from evaluating these agents. Much of the supposed difference between these agents does not stand up to objective scrutiny. Although there may be limited opportunities for savings, they should be pursued, as the cost impact of ignoring them is high. Pharmaceutical companies have begun to engage in serious direct-to-consumer marketing to involve the patient in drug selection decisions, in some cases, to great effect. A sound basic formulary strategy provides the best opportunity to manage costs and achieve the best outcome in this portion of the drug marketplace.

A more critical emerging category of drugs that permit the pharmacist and the physician to select cheaper alternatives consists of "therapeutic equivalents." While not chemically identical, these drugs have similar therapeutic outcomes. Examples include two or more antibiotics that are effective in treating an infection or several drugs that reduce the action of stomach acid. Because this type of interchange is more advanced, implementation of a therapeutic interchange program requires medical staff commitment. The pharmacy and therapeutics committee should develop the programs, set policies and procedures, and manage and monitor the program. Therapeutic equivalents can also be candidates for group purchasing, internal bidding, or negotiation but only after the pharmacy and therapeutics committee has approved the drug candidates as therapeutic equivalents.

Bidding and contracting for pharmaceuticals has become more complex because organized delivery systems have blurred the differences between inpatient acute care and outpatient or ambulatory care. The pharmaceutical industry has traditionally provided "own-use" contracts to hospitals under a clause in the Robinson-Patman Act. This clause offers very favorable pricing for inpatients and the employees of a health system. The prices are not available for use in traditional retail or nonacute areas. This restriction even applies to non-inpatient programs owned by organized delivery systems. Contracts for these classes of trade are generally less favorable, and many drugs are substantially more expensive. These classes include home care, ambulatory care, mail order, and retail pharmacy services. Organized delivery systems are moving into these areas of pharmacy practice and must adjust accordingly.

Administrators and pharmacy managers must make certain that contracts are correctly applied to ensure legality. In some cases it may be desirable or necessary to completely separate drugs purchased under different contracts to prevent the mixing of drugs purchased for a specific use with those for another use. Drug cost projections should only be made using a contract portfolio that applies to the patient types being served. Organized delivery systems can and should apply pressure on purchasing groups and pharmaceutical manufacturers to provide favorable pricing for alternative sites and services to protect their cost positions.

Inventory management is another important management tool that can be used by the pharmacist to control costs. Avoiding redundant inventory increases working capital that can be used more productively in other areas of the system. Improving inventory turnover

can be partially achieved by implementation of both generic and therapeutic equivalence policies. Numerous other inventory control techniques, such as ABC and economic order quantity (EOQ) analysis, should be incorporated into the management system. Most drug wholesale vendors supply computer programs and services that allow for the detailed accounting of drug purchases using these techniques. These products and services are generally included in an overall agreement negotiated by a purchasing group or health system.

ABC analysis is a method for ascertaining the volume of products by expense (i.e., dollars) and by utilization (i.e., units). Whether sorting by a single criterion or by multiple criteria, the manager is able to analyze product use for various scenarios. This type of analysis can be useful as a snapshot of product movement for a given period of time as well as for identifying product shifts and utilization.

EOQ analysis is a mathematical method for determining the optimum product quantity to order. Its objective is to minimize the inventory costs associated with the product. The basic EOQ model takes into account the total costs associated with inventory (e.g., carrying costs and ordering costs). Carrying costs increase and ordering costs decline with higher inventories. The EOQ is defined as the level at which the total inventory cost is the lowest. This is at the point on an EOQ model line graph where the carrying cost and ordering lines intersect—the point where carrying costs and ordering costs are equal. Pharmacy directors should strive to meet a calculated EOQ and inventory level to minimize costs and ensure the reliable availability of drugs.

The type of drug distribution system used within the hospital can affect costs significantly. Most hospitals today use some variant of the unit dose system of drug distribution.

This system generally provides a 24-hour supply of drugs in ready-to-administer form in containers designated for individual patients. Computerization is necessary to provide important data for decision making in many areas of pharmacy management, including cost control.

Clinical strategies for reducing drug costs offer opportunities for affecting patient outcome positively while reducing institutional costs. Some of these strategies include formulary management, medication use review, and clinical (or therapeutic) intervention at the time the physician is writing the drug order. Other clinical strategies include

- developing guidelines for prescribing agents or classes of drugs
- creating educational programs for prescribers
- "academic detailing" by clinical pharmacists representing the health system
- setting selective restrictions on specific drug use
- requiring specialist approval for specific drugs
- using stop orders and expiration dates for medications

A formulary is a list of drugs approved by the pharmacy and therapeutics committee that the pharmacy will routinely stock and always have available for patient care. Although the formulary is primarily a clinically oriented tool, it should also have a major impact on costs by reducing the number of drug entities that the pharmacy carries in its inventory. The reduction is ideally achieved by continually reviewing opportunities to reduce the number of therapeutic and generic equivalents.

Drug use can be measured against treatment guidelines developed by standard-setting organizations and government regula-tors, including the FDA. Basic criteria for drug use originate with package insert recommendations and develop further as medical practice and published research move forward. Prescription records provide data on aspects of the prescribing process, patient compliance, and therapeutic outcomes. A treatment guideline strategy is most often supported by the pharmacy and therapeutics committee of the health system.

The ready availability of prescribing and utilization data has provided an opportunity to manage drug costs and led to the creation of a new entity in the health care industry, the pharmacy benefits management (PBM) company. PBMs offer opportunities to control the costs of drug therapy based on collection and analysis of clinical and financial information from an organized delivery system's or payer's database. PBMs typically focus on ambulatory drug use and work on behalf of insurers or payers.

PBMs use demographic and patient care data to direct drug use. They typically develop a drug formulary and use prescription data to profile patients, physicians, and the use of specific drugs and treatment modalities and to identify disease outcomes. In turn, they use these data to determine changes that would foster the prescription of more effective or less costly agents. Networks, hospitals, and organized delivery systems can use similar data generated by their own pharmacy information systems to understand current practice and allocate resources to direct both pharmacy services and pharmaceutical care.

PBMs also develop provider networks that offer outpatient prescription services, typically a mix of retail and chain drugstores. These networks often extend beyond traditional service boundaries. PBMs adjudicate drug claims and ensure that providers meet the cost and service requirements of the organized delivery system.

PBMs have also utilized outcomes management and disease management. Service quality is measured not only by service consumption but also by substituted services, including emergency department visits and other nonpharmacy costs. Disease management strategies apply to medication-intensive diseases, where effective medical management can prevent both long-term complications and decrease the cost and utilization of specific services. Disease management programs generally focus on the selection of appropriate therapies, aggressive monitoring of drug efficacy and side effects, and improving patient compliance. These programs have achieved impressive clinical and financial success in the case of patients with diabetes mellitus, asthma, congestive heart failure, and other diagnoses. Organized delivery systems with comprehensive pharmacy information systems can develop the data and methods to support this type of program through their pharmacy and therapeutics committee and pharmacy department.

CONCLUSION

Pharmacy departments and pharmacy services have become more important than ever for organized delivery system success in the changing health care environment. Biotechnology is providing expensive new agents that can achieve improved patient care outcomes—but at a high cost. Well-managed pharmacy services can ensure the appropriate, cost-effective delivery of care and maximize patient benefits while minimizing costs. Drug purchase costs are only one component of an organized delivery system's overall costs. The implementation of a pharmaceutical care practice model can ensure the appropriate deployment of professional resources to manage the costs and benefits of medication therapy. Pharmacy should be viewed as a clinical department with substantial business interests and impact within the health system. A well-run pharmacy can effectively bridge the gap between the clinical and financial aspects of drug therapy.

NOTES

1. C.D. Hepler and L.M. Strand, "Opportunities and Responsibilities in Pharmaceutical Care," *American Journal of Hospital Pharmacy* 47 (1990): 533–543.

2. S.D. Horn et al., "Intended and Unintended Consequences of HMO Cost Containment Strategies: Results from the Managed Care Outcomes Project, *American Journal of Managed Care* 2 (1996): 253–264.

3. R.M. Guerrero et al., "Documenting the Provision of Pharmaceutical Care," *Topics in Hospital Pharmacy Management*, 11, no. 4 (1992): 16–29.

4. "ASHP Statement on Drug Unit Dose Distribution," *Practice Standards of the American Society of Health-System Pharmacists 1997–1998* (Bethesda, MD: American Society of Health-System Pharmacists, 1998), 10.

5. "ASHP Technical Assistance Bulletin on Hospital Drug Distribution and Control," *Practice Standards of the American Society of Health-System Pharmacists 1997–1998*, 102–110.

6. "ASHP Technical Assistance Bulletin on Single Unit and Unit Dose Packages of Drugs," *Practice Standards of the American Society of Health-System Pharmacists 1997–1998*, 111–112.

7. Ibid.

8. "ASHP Technical Assistance Bulletin on Quality Assurance for Pharmacy Prepared Sterile Products," *Practice Standards of the American Society of Health-System Pharmacists 1997–1998*, 171–181.

9. "ASHP Technical Assistance Bulletin on Handling Cytotoxic and Hazardous Drugs," *Practice Standards of the American Society of Health-System Pharmacists 1997–1998*, 136–152.

10. "ASHP Statement on the Pharmacy and Therapeu-

tics Committee," *Practice Standards of the American Society of Health-System Pharmacists 1997–1998*, 3–4.

11. "ASHP Guidelines on Formulary System Management," *Practice Standards of the American Society of Health-System Pharmacists 1997–1998*, 62–65.

ANDREW L. WILSON, PHARMD, FASHP, is Director of Pharmacy Services at the Medical College of Virginia Hospitals in Richmond, Virginia. He also serves as an associate professor and as Associate Dean for Institutional Program Development at the School of Pharmacy of Virginia Commonwealth University. He has worked as a hospital pharmacy manager and director in academic health care for over 20 years. He has served as editor of *Pharmacy Practice Management Quarterly* since 1987. Dr. Wilson's areas of practice interest include productivity assessment, formulary management, and pharmacoeconomics. He holds a Bachelor of Science in Pharmacy from the University of Connecticut and a Doctor of Pharmacy degree from Wayne State University. Dr. Wilson has authored over 50 articles in the pharmacy literature.

Index

G

H